Political Neoliberalism

Political Neoliberalism

Political Neoliberalism

Order and Rupture

CHRISTIAN JOPPKE

OXFORD
UNIVERSITY PRESS

Oxford University Press is a department of the University of Oxford.
It furthers the University's objective of excellence in research, scholarship,
and education by publishing worldwide. Oxford is a registered trade mark of
Oxford University Press in the UK and in certain other countries.

Published in the United States of America by Oxford University Press
198 Madison Avenue, New York, NY 10016, United States of America.

© Oxford University Press 2025

All rights reserved. No part of this publication may be reproduced, stored in a retrieval system, transmitted, used for text and data mining, or used for training artificial intelligence, in any form or by any means, without the prior permission in writing of Oxford University Press, or as expressly permitted by law, by license or under terms agreed with the appropriate reprographics rights organization. Inquiries concerning reproduction outside the scope of the above should be sent to the Rights Department, Oxford University Press, at the address above.

You must not circulate this work in any other form
and you must impose this same condition on any acquirer

CIP data is on file at the Library of Congress

ISBN 9780197801925
ISBN 9780197801918 (hbk.)

DOI: 10.1093/oso/9780197801918.001.0001

Paperback printed by Marquis, Canada

Hardback printed by Bridgeport National Bindery, Inc., United States of America

The manufacturer's authorised representative in the EU for product safety is Oxford University Press España S.A. of El Parque Empresarial San Fernando de Henares, Avenida de Castilla, 2 – 28830 Madrid (www.oup.es/en or product.safety@oup.com). OUP España S.A. also acts as importer into Spain of products made by the manufacturer.

For Catherine

"The fact that the 'free world' had an alternative made it an alternative itself . . . (W)hen freedom is the only reality, you are no longer free."

Amit Chaudhuri, *Sojourn*, New York Review Books 2022, p. 61

Contents

Preface	viii
Introduction	1
1. Liberalism versus Neoliberalism	13

I. ORDER

2. End of the Liberal-Democratic Synthesis: An Inventory	55
3. From Right to Left, and Back? A Genealogy	110

II. RUPTURE

4. The Populist Right: Illiberal Democracy and the Economics–Culture Conundrum	149
5. The Identity Left: Antiracism and Transgender	190

III. OUTLOOK

6. End of Neoliberalism? The COVID-19 Pandemic, and After	247
Endnotes	312
Bibliography	340
Index	375

Preface

This book makes the case for neoliberalism as a useful lens for understanding a broad range of political phenomena, those pertaining to the political order and the governing of advanced Western societies, but also others that signal rupture and conflict at the extreme right and left ends of the political spectrum, often referred to as identity politics. I arrive at this topic through a long-standing interest in immigration and citizenship policies and surrounding ethnic and multiculturalism struggles, which I had initially looked at from the vantage point of advancing liberalism.[i] However, neoliberalism does not equal liberalism. To clearly demarcate and set the two apart, head-on,[ii] and without denying their common roots and shared features, is the main purpose of this book.

The notion of neoliberalism is rejected by many as shrill and overspent. A proper use of it needs to avoid both: a narrow understanding as a political economy category, but also an overly broad understanding as an "encompassing constructivist framework," as Patrick Le Galès (2016, 154) criticized a line of thinking pioneered by French philosopher Michel Foucault, in which *everything* from states to subjectivities is, well, "neoliberal," and thus *nothing* is. A celebrated account by the Foucault-inspired geographer, Jamie Peck (2010, xiii, 8), for instance, follows from its "adaptive, mutating, and contradictory" ways of operating, that neoliberalism "will not be fixed." Against this, I concur with a recent review that there *is* a "minimum common core" to neoliberalism, which is to "subordinate the state and all social domains to the market . . . thereby undermining democracy" (Laruffa 2023, 1). The formulation may not be elegant, but it is concise. It also suggests that between the narrow and broad alternatives, a proper understanding of neoliberalism *must* tilt toward the broader end because it is simply in the nature of neoliberalism to subject, if not all, at least much of society to market principles.

While not just a tension with but hostility to democracy is perhaps *the* defining principle of neoliberalism, I state up front that this book will be of little help to resolve what a non-deficient form of democracy in an advanced society could mean or be. This is for the normative theorist, which I am not, or rather, for ordinary citizens, to decide. By the same token, readers who expect to find in this book the hint of an alternative to neoliberalism, or an idea when and how it could end, will also be disappointed. The vexing thing about neoliberalism, noticed by some of its best chroniclers and critics (such as Beckert 2020 or Gerstle 2022), is that it is not at all clear what the alternative could be, and an end to it is not in sight.

An open society, which the (neo)liberal society is, may require the thinning of solidarities, the "self-responsibilizing," and the hyper-individualism that have become the signature of our time. These ethical dispositions and policy tenets are at the same time "breezing common sense" (Mounk 2017, 1), *and* what neoliberalism pushes to the fore. But the price to pay is to impair equality and freedom, and thus the two foundational principles of liberalism. Equality, not in a formal-legal but socioeconomic sense, has been neoliberalism's victim in its first forty years. I agree with *Financial Times* editorialist Martin Wolf's (2023, ch. 3) *cri de coeur* that "democratic capitalism," this marriage of "complementary opposites," has become "dangerously unbalanced over the past four decades," expressed in exorbitant wealth increases at the top and "economic disappointment" for the rest. Escalating inequality is, indeed, as Wolf suspects, "one of the chief explanations for the rise of left- and right-wing populism in high-income countries" (ibid., ch. 1). However, freedom, and thus liberalism's first principle and the one that neoliberalism originally had set out to rescue, is also at risk. This, at least, is my reading of the authoritarian management of the COVID-19 pandemic and of the enforced digitalization of everything that has followed from it, which receive detailed treatment toward the end of this book.

I am grateful to Liav Orgad, who assembled a stellar group of friends and scholars to discuss the draft chapters of this book at the Wissenschaftszentrum Berlin (WZB), on December 19, 2023, in sometimes heated and not always amical atmosphere—commensurate with some of the claims raised in this book. I am humbled that Yossi Harpaz, Udo Knapp, Dimitry Kochenov, Gideon Sapir, Yuli Tamir, John Torpey, Roman Zinigrad, and, of course, Liav himself, all took time out for it. I also wish to thank the two reviewers of this manuscript for the press, one of whom, Rogers Brubaker, lifted his anonymity.

Bern, October 2024

---

[i] See Joppke 1999, 2005, 2010, and 2017.

[ii] My most recent book (Joppke 2021a) was a first exercise of tackling the neoliberalism versus liberalism question, with a focus on immigration and citizenship policies.

Introduction

A leading critic of neoliberalism rejects the idea of a basic "citizen's" income in surprising terms: "At its most robust as a claim, citizenship is a system of rights and responsibilities, entitlement to its privileges coming in exchange for the contributions we make to our society" (Crouch 2019, 97). By removing the contribution factor, thus "making entitlement mere existence," Colin Crouch fears, the basic income would "obscure this tough, resilient core" to claims for citizenship rights (ibid.). This reasoning by someone who had influentially indicted as "post-democracy" neoliberalism's destructive political impact (Crouch 2004) surprises not only for rejecting a warhorse of the left.[1] More interesting is the fact that Crouch's rejection of a basic income is couched in the neoliberal logic that he denounces, in this case, a contractual understanding of citizenship as a quid pro quo.

In the liberal tradition, John Stuart Mill was the first to argue that "society is not founded on a contract" (2003 [1859], 147). Mill pointed to the fact that the "cultivation of individuality" (ibid., 132), liberalism's beating heart, could not be the precondition but had to be the result of society, which provides the necessary means for the individual to grow. A century later, T. H. Marshall (1950) put flesh on Mill's social liberalism when canonizing liberal citizenship as "basic human equality associated with the concept of full membership of a community" (ibid., 8), which is precisely *not* dependent on one's contribution. Marshall added that even modern citizenship's costliest and most recent achievement, "social rights," were an "absolute right to a certain standard of civilization,"[2] which did "not depend on the economic value of the individual claimant" (ibid., 43). Social rights, as he put it memorably, implied an "invasion of contract by status" (ibid., 68).

One way of understanding neoliberalism is as an invasion of "status by contract," thus reinstating the original order of Maine's famous notion, in domains where a market logic had previously been absent, such as citizenship. Of course, this is where the liberal in neo*liberal* shines. Had not the liberal tradition, with Hobbes before the word, started with the assumption of the civic condition as resting on a "covenant" that saves people from the "force and fraud" of the state of nature (Hobbes 1998 [1651], 84)? Thus Crouch, a Fabian liberal socialist, may be forgiven for slipping from liberal

---

Political Neoliberalism. Christian Joppke, Oxford University Press. © Oxford University Press (2025).
DOI: 10.1093/oso/9780197801918.003.0001

2 POLITICAL NEOLIBERALISM

to neoliberal logic in his understanding of citizenship. But a slippage it is, nevertheless. It suggests a larger point to be made in this book: the reach of neoliberalism is pervasive, leaving few, if anyone or anything, untouched so that even a nominal critic like Crouch explicitly concedes that "we are all (partly) neoliberals now" (2013, ch. 2).

The least to say is that neoliberalism is not just what it originally was: an economic doctrine or policy to protect or liberate the market, and to insulate it from democratic interference. Reviewing the state of "social power" in the age of globalization, Michael Mann found neoliberalism in this narrow sense dominant only in Anglo societies and "faltering" by the early millennium (2013, 178). Against such a narrow understanding, I follow Wendy Brown's (2015, 176) view of neoliberalism as pervasive "governing rationality" of contemporary Western societies, thoroughly transforming the social fabric from the individual upward, and one that is still evolving and enduringly without alternative. Indeed, Margaret Thatcher's famous diction that "there is no alternative" remains as true today as when she pronounced it at the onset of the neoliberal age—the political management of the COVID-19 pandemic, as I shall argue at the end of this book, attests to this. Brown builds her case on the late Michel Foucault, in his Collège de France lectures on the "Birth of Biopolitics," held in 1978/1979. There Foucault defined the "radical" nucleus of neoliberal reasoning as "generalizing (the economic form of the market) throughout the social body" (Foucault 2008, 243).

But a broad understanding of neoliberalism, one that finds it at its most poisonous when operating *outside* its home ground of political economy, is risky. Educated folk tend to reject the term for its inherent negativity, or they use it in scare quotes only. It is true: Like its polemical Other, populism, neoliberalism denotes a position one does not like. A confessing neoliberal is hard to find, while the position from which someone or something is denounced as neoliberal remains strangely unmarked—liberal, progressive, socialist, nationalist? One does not know.

Commenting on the uses of neoliberalism in contemporary anthropology, where next to human geography, cultural studies, and other domains the concept circulates prodigiously, Stephen Collier (2012) distinguishes between two different approaches. In one, "neoliberalism is associated with a specified set of elements (thinkers, institutions, policy programs) that have to be teased out from a tangle of other things." In the other, "the concept is expanded and the entire ensemble of elements is identified with neoliberalism" (ibid., 189). Collier's formulation tells where his preference lies. Who would want to give up on nuance and precision?[3] Foucault (2008), as noted, was the first to provide a diagnosis of the totality of society under the sway of *homo oeconomicus*. Under his influence, there has been a wordy and often arcane genre that detects neoliberalism everywhere, while denying that there are "other things" (Collier 2012) and logics around.

However, it is incontrovertible that "liberal" has been the name for an "entire ensemble of elements," to reiterate Collier's (2012, 189) words for the conception of "neoliberal" that he dislikes. "Liberal" denotes nothing less than the domestic and international order of Western societies after World War II, particularly when there was still a non-liberal alternative around. By that logic, "neoliberal" would need to be of the same broad scope. This raises the knotty problem of how to demarcate liberalism and neoliberalism. A first provocative answer is that a broad understanding is required *even more* for neoliberalism than for liberalism. This is because liberalism is, as Michael Walzer put it concisely (1984, 315), the "art of separation" that is congenial to a functionally differentiated society. It guarantees that each sub-system functions autonomously—the exemplary case being the democratic polity operating without undue interference by the capitalist economy. By contrast, it is the precise mark of neoliberalism to tear down the liberal separations. The result is, to stay with the pivotal polity-economy distinction, that "governmental mechanisms developed in the private sphere (are put) to work within the state itself . . . The question of what should be public and what private becomes blurred" (Ferguson 2010, 173). In this spirit, an apt metaphor for neoliberalism is "market fundamentalism" (Block and Somers 2014). It suggests a necessarily "expanded" usage of the concept, pace Collier.

Order

This is a book about the political forms of neoliberalism, or, in short, "political neoliberalism." I take "political" in two different senses, institutional and non- or even counter-institutional; that is, as "order" and as "rupture." On the part of order, neoliberalism is not, as many think, the retreat but a refashioning of the state and of the political at large. The state's staying power, even its proactive role in the process, is not fully captured in the notion of "market fundamentalism," even though its content (not the word) is attributed to Karl Polanyi (Block and Somers 2014). And Polanyi knew that "markets

4   POLITICAL NEOLIBERALISM

and regulation ... grew up together" (1944, 68). From this follows that even de-regulation is still a form of regulation, requiring the state.

The most fundamental development on the side of order is the disso-ciation between liberalism and democracy, putting to an end the liberal-democratic synthesis, cynically speaking, "(c)apitalism's shotgun-marriage with democracy" (Streeck 2016, 2) that had provided unprecedented pros-perity to the working- and middle-classes throughout the West in the second half of the twentieth century. This dissociation has found expression in a variety of institutional forms, whose common denominator is a tension with, if not hostility to, democracy.

First and foremost, because most obviously the opposite of democracy, there is *authoritarianism*. The Weimar social democratic jurist Hermann Heller (2015 [1933]) coined the notion of "authoritarian liberalism" for the dramatic last phase of the Weimar Republic. More mundanely, from the German "ordoliberals" on, the "strong state," a state that is "de-pluralized" and standing "above the interested parties," has been a fixture in the the-ory and practice of neoliberalism (Biebricher 2020). Some see it revived in the European Union-imposed austerity policies after the 2008 financial crisis. Unquestionably, public health authoritarianism, partially taking its clues from China, has been the pan-Western response to the COVID-19 pandemic.

Secondly, and diametrically opposed to authoritarianism, there is *gover-nance*. This is perhaps the most important neoliberal innovation in the polit-ical realm. It flags non-state-centric, non-hierarchical, network-type forms of rule that involve society's "stakeholders"—another favorite of neoliberal speak. While governance is meant to bring back-in democracy, and thus is primarily advocated by the neoliberal left, it demotes citizens to consumers and thus confirms rather than alleviates the notorious democracy deficit in a neoliberal order.

Thirdly, governance comes with the pretension that, not interest medi-ation and conflict resolution, but rational problem-solving is the stuff of politics. This moves to the fore a third political form of neoliberalism on the side of order, which is *technocracy*. The idea of knowledge-led rule has a long tradition, going back to Greek antiquity. The novelty in neoliberal times is technocracy's ideological association with democracy. This association is to be scrutinized and, as I suggest, rejected.

Fourthly and fifthly are *federation* and *constitutionalism*. I cover them jointly because they are exemplarily combined in the European Union, which I shall look at more closely as the purest case of a neoliberal polity. Federation is the idea (going back to the early Hayek [1939]) and the reality (from the European Union to the World Trade Organization) of neutralizing democratic rule through a transnational market regime (see Slobodian 2018). It is intimately related to a certain (not the only possible) understanding of constitutionalism, as locking-in market rules and property rights through democratically unassailable agencies like high courts and central banks. We thus return to neoliberalism's first political form, authoritarianism—a major recent work, plausibly in my view, considers the European Union tout court an instance of "authoritarian liberalism" (Wilkinson 2021), which is constitutionally "other" to democracy.

Finally, there is *meritocracy*. I cover it at the end of the list because it is less a political form than a legitimation of the social structure that neoliberalism seeks to build. It suggests (falsely, I shall argue) that positions of privilege are based on individual merit and achievement, not on class transmission. In this respect, there is a disjunction between neoliberal theory and practice. At the theoretical plane, Hayek rejected the principle of merit, because he deemed market outcomes to be chance outcomes that defy justice. In neoliberal practice, by contrast, meritocracy is perhaps the central legitimation of a "just" neoliberal society.

Evidently, these six concepts—authoritarianism, governance, technocracy, federation, constitutionalism, and meritocracy—are not all of the same cloth and are situated at different levels of abstraction. Most of them do denote elements of political order, but it is not always apparent that it should be the same. Meritocracy stands apart from the other concepts in being more a legitimation of neoliberal social structure than a political form of neoliberalism. My simple point is to show that these concepts are widely in use to understand the neoliberal beast from the point of view of rule, but that their mutual implications, compatibility as well as tensions, have rarely been brought to light. The challenge is to explore and calibrate their relationship, and their combined impact on the state and the political at large.

Next to providing an *inventory* of the political forms of neoliberalism, this book also provides a *genealogy* of the neoliberal order as it emerged from the late 1970s on and continues to evolve today. The most significant change has been that a movement initially associated with the political right was quickly embraced by the political left, the so-called Third Way. This was the moment for neoliberalism to gestate from doctrine or movement into "political order," as I argue with Gary Gerstle's (2022) seminal history of the "rise and fall" of neoliberalism in America. While the Third-Way transformation of the left has been well-studied (e.g., Mudge 2018; Piketty 2020), it is mostly with a focus on economic policy. But there are, in addition, social policies and multiculturalism policies to look at. Overall, the Third Way's implications for our understanding of political neoliberalism are "still underdeveloped" in the literature, as a recent study of "progressive neoliberalism" in Italy put it (Fifi 2024, 1436). Thus, the leftist turn of neoliberalism is worthy to be more fully charted.

Rupture

Political neoliberalism is not only order, but also rupture. The line between both is not obvious to draw, and some have argued that neoliberalism per se operates by way of rupture (most fulminant, Naomi Klein [2007]). I nevertheless suggest distinguishing the two. I concur with William Callison and Zachary Manfredi (2029, 3) that there is a need for "understanding the relationship between neoliberalism and contemporary political ruptures." However, I differ from them, and from many other authors, including Brown (2019), in arguing that neoliberal "ruptures" have occurred not only at the far *right*, but also at the far *left* end of the political spectrum.

In most Western democracies, the political center forces are shrinking, while radical forces at the edges expand. With regard to the centrist forces, Richard Katz and Peter Mair (1995) diagnosed the rise of colluding "cartel parties" that are disconnected from society and its interests and cleavages, and have become self-serving agents of the state. In a political arena "without alternatives," to repeat the core neoliberal mantra that is also acidly descriptive of the reality shaped by it, new forces arise at the extreme right *and* left ends of the political spectrum. They dwell in the idiom of identity, whether that of long discriminated minorities or of newly aggrieved majorities. Both claim to be authentic articulations of democracy, and thus they seem to recover the main casualty of neoliberalism. But they show contempt for key liberal precepts, in particular, for the rights of minorities on the right end, and for rights of free speech and the value of robust debate on the left end of the political spectrum. Democratic illiberalism is the joint mark of right *and* left identity politics. They thus widen the rift between liberalism and democracy, which is the iron hold of the neoliberal condition.

Why are the forces of rupture *identity* politics, concerned more with "recognition" than with "redistribution," to use Nancy Fraser's (1995) influential binary? There are several elements to a plausible answer. With respect to the right, the key feature of political neoliberalism is the bracketing of the demotic and the territorial, and hence of the national dimension of political life. Wolfgang Streeck (2013) captured this in his evocative distinction between rooted "state people" and footloose "market people," arguing that the latter run the shots in the neoliberal austerity state that offers socialism to the rich but forces competition on the rest. On that account, the revolt of the sedentary against the mobile must be identity-oriented, as, in fact, the nationalist and xenophobic discourse of populist radical right parties proves.

Yet the micro-dynamics of identity politics are more complicated. The first mover has not been the right but the left, for whom, in fact, the concept of identity politics was initially coined (Fraser 1995). One of the first accounts of "extreme right parties," by Piero Ignazi (1992), depicts these parties as a "silent counter-revolution" to the rise of "post-materialist values" on the political left. To the feminists' right to abortion, say, family-value rightists respond with the right to life (a root cause of America's "culture wars"); and to the minorities' right to be different, the majority answers that it wants to be different too, yet alone on its territory, in a kind of exclusion-minded majority multiculturalism (that the French *Nouvelle Droite* championed in the late 1980s). Because immigrant minorities and their multicultural defense forces within the elites are the persistent target of populist radical right mobilization, the left-to-right causal path of identity politics is eminently plausible. By the same token, this dynamic proves that the left has achieved discursive hegemony in the neoliberal order (this is the joint claim by Braunstein [2022], Rufo [2023], and Hanania [2023]).

However, the causal path of identity politics is not one-directional. Particularly in the United States (in Europe much less), the recently radicalized antiracist movement, which in many respects is a surprise rehearsal of 1960s' Black Power nationalism, is fired by a perception that "white supremacy" is not only the nostalgic phantasy of the extreme right but plain reality, epitomized by the first Trump presidency (2017–2020) and, more enduringly, the Republican party that Trump helped transform into the equivalent of a populist right party. As the American notion of "culture wars" suggests, there is a feedback loop from left to right *and back*, from right to left, one whipping up the other, which leads to ever more radical forms of identity politics (Gusterson 2017, 212).

8 POLITICAL NEOLIBERALISM

While the right–left identity politics pincer is certainly a political rupture, I suggest that both parts of it are better seen as opposition *within* rather than *to* neoliberalism because neither can credibly claim to recover the neoliberal order's biggest casualty, which is democracy, the indispensable tool to reign-in The Market. At first sight, one might think that the populist right is opposition *to* neoliberalism because it advocates nationalist "closure" against the globalist-cum-multiculturalist great "opening" (dubbed "apertistic liberalism" by German sociologist Andreas Reckwitz [2021, ch. 5). Brown (2019) trail-blazed a rather different reading of the populist right, as complicit *with* neoliberalism, in a furious indictment of "neoliberal rationality prepar(ing) the ground for ferocious antidemocratic forces" (ibid., 7). Alas, she complacently locates these "antidemocratic" forces exclusively on the right—the "new right" as neoliberalism's unintended "Frankenstein creation" (ibid., 10). In Brown's dystopian lens, the "aggression and viciousness" of the underdog, ingeniously while deceptively incorporated by Donald Trump, "is fed by (the) neoliberal valorization of libertarian freedom," among other sources (ibid., 170). While the causality is questionable, Brown is right that "wounded angry white maleness" hardly qualifies as opposition to neoliberalism. In Europe also, one looks in vain on the populist right for a viable alternative to neoliberalism, except unconstitutional calls for welfare chauvinism in its western half, and the rather more serious building of "illiberal states" in the east (in particular, Hungary; see Chapter 4).

But on the left as well, which Brown (2019, 178) romanticizes as "the vulnerable (LGBT, women, minorities)" in a fight for "democracy," there is no real opposition to neoliberalism.[4] The enemies have other names: "transphobes" for the T-part of the LGBT movement, "racists" for the antiracists, to name only the two most vocal expressions of left identity politics that I shall look at in this book. Moreover, as in the case of the populist right, there is a Frankenstein element in the identity left, being unwittingly formatted by the neoliberal order despite its oppositionist posture. A shared element with the populist right is the identity left's undermining of the liberal public versus private distinction, as a result of which society fragments into competing groups, at least on the political plane.[5] The right does so by stipulating a popular unity that defies liberal distinctions and constraints; the left questions the very possibility of a neutral public sphere inhabited by citizens, denouncing this as camouflaged ethnic or heteronormative majority power.

INTRODUCTION 9

Overview

Chapter 1, "*Liberalism versus Neoliberalism*," addresses the central question of how to demarcate neoliberalism from liberalism, both understood less as philosophical doctrines than as political ordering principles. One influential, Foucault-inspired definition of political neoliberalism, as "governing at a distance" (Rose and Miller 1992), which operates through the individual's "freedom to choose," slights the difference between liberal and neoliberal because this freedom surely applies to both. Mirroring Foucault's own difficulties in this regard, such definition of political neoliberalism is indistinguishable from the "game of liberalism," which is "letting things take their course" (Foucault 2007, 41). A concise demarcation requires going to the sources, most importantly the work of Friedrich Hayek. Following Hayek, a key (although not only) difference is neoliberalism's exorcising of the "social justice" component from liberalism, which has been central to John Rawls's (1971) canonical twentieth century reconstruction, but which has deeper historical roots. Because social justice claims have been imported into the modern polity through the door of democracy, one could simplify that neoliberalism is liberalism minus democracy. This raises yet another knotty issue, that of the relationship between liberalism and democracy, which this chapter must address.

Chapter 2, "*End of the Liberal-Democratic Synthesis: An Inventory*," discusses the political forms of neoliberalism on the side of order, and its ideational underpinnings: authoritarianism, governance, technocracy, federation, constitutionalism, and meritocracy. Each one of them, subtly or less subtly, sidelines democracy, which is the common denominator of all forms of political neoliberalism. Despite its random appearance, there is method in both this list and in this particular sequence. *Authoritarianism* was the first institutional form of neoliberalism and it has been a persistent presence in a neoliberal order. *Governance* is authoritarianism's direct opposite, often propagated by a neoliberal left that likes to see itself as re-injecting democracy into neoliberal rule—a futile attempt, I shall argue. *Technocracy* is much of the content of governance, which is in the mode of problem-solving rather than of conflict resolution. *Federation* was the earliest blueprint of political neoliberalism (Hayek 1939), and much of the European Union is anticipated in it. It is intrinsically connected with *constitutionalism*, understood as the locking-in of market freedoms with the help of non-democratic precepts and agencies, for what, again, the European Union will serve as prime

10 POLITICAL NEOLIBERALISM

example. Finally, *meritocracy* is less an institutional form than the legitimation of status and privilege in a neoliberal society, camouflaging its class structure.

Chapter 3, "*From Right to Left, and Back? A Genealogy*," traces the development of the neoliberal order, which has entailed an important and still understudied change from an initial association with the political right and with nationalism in the early 1980s to being embraced by the Third Way political left in the 1990s and onward. The joining of the left was the moment for neoliberalism to graduate from political "movement" into political "order" (Gerstle 2022). I will examine a new conception of welfare policies as social investment, and the rise of neoliberal multiculturalism, which pursues an agenda of antidiscrimination and diversity. What Fraser (2017a) calls "progressive neoliberalism" is the dominant face of political neoliberalism today, as the rise of the populist right precisely in opposition to it attests. In the wake of the 2008 financial crisis, some have made the case for a third phase of "authoritarian" neoliberalism, which turns the wheel back to its conservative beginnings. This argument is assessed for what is right about it, and what is not.

Chapter 4, "*The Populist Right: Illiberal Democracy and the Economics-Culture Conundrum*," tackles two contested and unresolved issues in the literature on right-wing populism, which has exploded in the past decade. The first is the contested question of whether populism is an expression of democracy, thus restoring the victim of a neoliberal order, or whether populism is a threat to democracy. I argue that in repudiating the "liberal" in liberal democracy, the populist right amounts to a threat to democracy as we know it, rather than a cure to its current problems. Secondly, the biggest unresolved issue is to calibrate economic and cultural factors in the rise and agenda of the populist right. While the diminishing economic prospects of the lower middle classes seems to be the root cause of populist mobilization in Western societies, judged by the typical profile of its supporters, political economy issues are curiously absent from the agenda of populist right parties. Instead, opposition to immigration and the cultural changes brought by it, are central. The economics–culture conundrum is a persistent puzzle which this chapter cannot claim to resolve but hopes to throw more light on. The one safe conclusion to draw is that one-sided economic *or* cultural explanations of right-wing populism are unsatisfactory.

Chapter 5, "*The Identity Left: Antiracism and Transgender*," is about identity politics on the opposite left end of the political spectrum. The identity

INTRODUCTION 11

left has been much less covered in the social science literature than the populist right (but, see recently, Braunstein 2022; Rufo 2023; Mounk 2023), and most of the literature is either in the genre of denunciation or of foot soldiering. The focus of this chapter is on the two most vocal left identity movements active today: antiracism and transgender. What I argued with respect to the populist right is also valid for its leftist counterpart: although advocating rupture, the identity left is deeply shaped by neoliberal logic. The difference is that the identity left has found a much stronger foothold in public institutions, in the media, and in the corporate world (while the only hope of the populist right is to win the next elections, which has remained the exception so far). Particularly in higher education, the identity left has become hegemonic, branching out from there to media and corporations. Its solid legal-moral grounds are antidiscrimination laws and principles, which have outlawed formal racism and sexism for over half a century now. As a result, smaller injuries, of the immaterial and symbolic kind, take on bigger proportions. Two themes are highlighted. Much like the populist right, the identity left is illiberal. But illiberalism expresses itself not in xenophobia, as on the right, but in speech restrictions and "cancelling" opposite opinion. Secondly, and centrally, the identity left carries on neoliberal motives, "race parity" on part of the antiracists and "hyper-individualism" on the part of transgender, while both branches fail to address central neoliberal fault lines.

Chapter 6, *"End of Neoliberalism? The COVID-19 Pandemic, and After,"* turns to the biggest crisis of world society since World War II, which lasted, at its height, from 2020 to 2022, and it examines the question how neoliberalism has fared in it. Two themes are highlighted. First, authoritarianism, the original political form of neoliberalism, has had a remarkable revival in states' public health management. Not all of it, of course, is neoliberal. But the facility of side-lining democracy, the Big State–Big Firm collusion in controlling the discourse and "public–private partnership" in vaccine development while repressing cheaper therapeutic solutions, and the bit of "global governance" provided by the World Health Organization: these elements, at least, have a neoliberal ring. Secondly, when gauging the long-term effects of the pandemic, the accelerated digitalization of social life is among the most important. In particular, the pandemic highlighted the surveillance and control possibilities of the new technology, which are likely to grow further. Combining both themes, authoritarian crisis management and control-minded digitalization, one must conclude that freedom is the scarce

12 POLITICAL NEOLIBERALISM

good of the future. After equality was sacked in the pre-pandemic phases of neoliberalism, today freedom is endangered, and thus the second—and lexically prior—pillar of liberalism, ironically the one that neoliberalism had initially claimed to recover.

Chapter 1
Liberalism versus Neoliberalism

Distinguishing liberalism from neoliberalism is tricky but necessary. It is necessary because if no difference can be established, we should excise the neologism from our vocabulary and continue with its generic predecessor. But the word exists, and persistently so, even if mostly in critical, if not polemical, colors. On the assumption that "(a)ll names are names for something" (Mill 1882, 33), we should assume that "neoliberalism" stands for a distinct reality that is amenable to be charted. At the same time, the liberalism–neoliberalism distinction is tricky because it requires, in turn, a mapping of the distinct reality that the *terminus a quo*, liberalism, stands for.

Liberalism, as I argue in the first part of this chapter, has originally been a political rather than philosophical doctrine, which draws its variability and changing faces from a double opposition to the old hierarchical order of estates, on the one hand, and the millenarianism of 1789, building a new society from scratch, on the other. Liberalism thus stands in an unstable relationship with its two main political competitors, conservatism and socialism, and it oscillates between these extremes in a game of mutual attraction and repulsion. What I call the "Geuss Quartet" of toleration, freedom, individualism, and rule of law is nevertheless a good first stab at formulating a liberal core doctrine (building on Geuss 2001 and 2002). However, the Geuss Quartet does not allow distinguishing liberalism from neoliberalism. For this we need to add as explicit liberal core principles equality, democracy, and what Michael Walzer (1984) called the "art of separation" in a functionally differentiated society. As I argue in the second half of the chapter, neoliberalism is distinct from liberalism in absolutizing freedom over all other values, in a formalistic understanding of equality that entails the repudiation of social justice, in a general hostility to democracy, and in a penchant for weakening rather than strengthening functional separations.

Political Neoliberalism. Christian Joppke, Oxford University Press. © Oxford University Press (2025).
DOI: 10.1093/oso/9780197801918.003.0002

14 POLITICAL NEOLIBERALISM

Liberalism

Almost every attempt of mapping liberalism starts with the multiplicity and "fluidity" of its meanings over its two-hundred-year-and-counting lifeline (Freeden 2008, 9). Already three decades before John Rawls (1971) would reformulate liberalism as a theory of justice, which was a novel thing at the time, John Dewey (1935, 3) noted that liberalism "has meant . . . things so different as to be opposed to one another." In the same vein, Raymond Geuss (2001, 69) suggests that "no definition" of liberalism is possible, particularly as it "tends to rewrite its own past" (as he says with Rawls in mind), and "is open to very significant modification in the future." Not without paradox, Geuss draws this conclusion from a distinctly political understanding of liberalism as "a practically engaged, historically located phenomenon" (ibid.). This is surprising, considering the judicial and universalistic meaning that liberalism has acquired under the influence of Rawls.

A Political Creed . . .

Indeed, "liberal" was originally not an attribute of the modern classics in political philosophy, from Thomas Hobbes to John Locke and John Stuart Mill, who only retroactively came to be labeled thus (proto-liberal in the case of Hobbes). Instead, it was the name for a political party in Spain, 1810–1811, which fought for limiting the privileges of the king and for establishing a British-style constitutional monarchy. This political origin is even more puzzling because, from Carl Schmitt (1926) on, the unpolitical nature of liberalism, as "government by discussion," has become a commonplace. This was immortalized by the American poet Robert Frost's sardonic description of a "liberal" as "a man too broadminded to take his own side in a quarrel" (for a later academic version of the charge, see Kahn 2012). While Frost's witticism anticipated Rawls (who derived liberalism from the impossibility of knowing one's "own side" behind a hypothetical "veil of ignorance"), initially liberalism wasn't so. For Hannah Arendt, liberalism was critique of the "Roman trilogy" of religion, tradition, and authority (Alexander 2015, 984), directed against the pre-enlightenment order that was ousted by the late eighteenth-century democratic revolutions in America and France. From this angle, liberalism was *ipso facto* an endorsement of democracy—which is also implied in the fact that the Spanish early nineteenth-century *Liberales*, qua political party, were an expression of this very democracy.

However, as Geuss points out, the original early eighteenth- to early nineteenth-century liberalism was a "war on two fronts" (2001, 72). In addition to rejecting the old feudal-absolutist order, which went along with endorsing an individual-centered market society, liberals also fought on a second front, which was against the moralization and totalization of politics by the French Jacobins, post-1789.[1] With respect to the first front, it is more concise to argue that the old order's post-revolutionary *return*, qua post-1815s "reaction," was one of liberalism's energizing worries. Alan Kahan (2023, 451) thus speaks of "Liberalism 1.0," which he defines as double opposition to "Revolution & Reaction."

The fear of revolution dominates Benjamin Constant's *The Liberty of Ancients Compared with that of Moderns* (1819), one of liberalism's foundational texts, which served as a blueprint for Isaiah Berlin's (1958) famous tale of the two liberties. The liberty of moderns, favored by Constant (and later by Berlin), is what Berlin would call the "negative liberty" to be left alone by a despotic state, "the right to be subjected only to the laws, and to be neither arrested, detained, put to death or maltreated in any way by the arbitrary will of one or more individuals" (Constant 1819, 1). The ur-liberal impulse of limiting power is grounded in the sociological observation that the moderns' typical activity is not war, as it was for the ancients, but commerce, the "true life of nations," which "inspires in men a vivid love of individual independence" and requires a freedom that "consist(s) of peaceful enjoyment and private independence" (ibid., 3–4). By contrast, the ancients, whose commercial instincts were low and limited to the household where slaves did the work, invested their liberty interest all in the political realm, where freedom "consisted in an active and constant participation in collective power" (ibid.). Epitomizing liberalism's genetically lowered political temperature, Constant drew a polemical continuity between the ancients' and the contemporaneous Jacobins' (in name, Rousseau's) effusive understanding of the political. Both "furnished deadly pretexts for more than one kind of tyranny" (ibid., 5), mistaking "the authority of the social body for liberty," so that the reaches of law would not be limited to "actions" but cover "the most fleeting thoughts and impressions" also (ibid., 6). Here was a key liberal distinction, developed by Kant decades before Constant, that between morality and legality. In Constant's further articulation of the idea of public neutrality, which is yet another plank of liberal doctrine, the authorities were to

16 POLITICAL NEOLIBERALISM

be "just" but not to prescribe "happiness": "Let them confine themselves to being just. We shall assume the responsibility of being happy for ourselves" (ibid., 10). Constant's preference of modern private liberty over the "political liberty" of the ancients and their Jacobin inheritors did not mean that what Berlin (1958) rebranded "positive liberty" was irrelevant. The latter "enlarges (citizens') spirit, ennobles their thoughts," although not to worship a higher entity, like the Nation or God, but as a means to individual "self-development" (Constant 1819, 10). Accordingly, democracy needed to be for Constant, but in terms of a moderate "representative system" because citizens "do not have the time" for politics only—it would take "too many evenings," as Oscar Wilde once said about socialism.

Constant's lecture, given to the Athénée Royal in Paris, is readily identifiable as liberal two hundred years later. Importantly, Constant gave his lecture in the same year as he entered the Chamber of Deputies, where he would represent the liberal opposition of *Indépendents* to the Bourbon restoration government. So, one must assume that political positioning was never far from his mind. As one philosophical chronicler aptly summarizes Constant's pivotal role in the liberal pantheon, he was "the first person to use the word 'liberal' in print to designate a set of political positions" (Kahan 2023, 98).

. . . and its Competitors: Conservatism and Socialism

Liberalism, in fact, is the original of the three modern political ideologies, the other two, conservatism and socialism, being responses to it—what, in turn, had to change liberalism, the latter either adopting or repelling facets of their adversaries. A good description of conservative is "the felt expression of having power, seeing it threatened, and trying to win it back" (Robin 2018, 8). This makes it a movable creed, with no stable position of its own, except that history and tradition are mobilized against the liberal-cum-socialist hubris of "begin(ning) the world all over again" (Tom Paine, quoted in ibid., 51). As Robert Nisbet (1966, 23–31) pointed out, late eighteenth-century conservatives were the more radical critics of the "English system" of industrial capitalism, which they rejected root-and-branch. By contrast, the early socialists accepted the new system and merely tried to turn it to their advantage, in the form of cooperatives; later, Karl Marx and his followers would consider capitalism a "necessary" stage in the march toward socialism and communism. The arrival of socialism, the third modern ideology, which was more a response to the new market order and to industrialism than to the political revolution of 1789, but which inherited the Jacobins' utopian desire to remake society from scratch, mightily complicated the ideological landscape, and particularly the political positioning of liberalism.

Consider this definition of conservative by the British philosopher Michael Oakeshott (from whom the late Hayek borrowed much): "To be conservative . . . is to prefer the familiar to the unknown, to prefer the tried to the untried, fact to mystery, the actual to the possible, the limited to the unbounded, the near to the distant, the sufficient to the superabundant, the convenient to the perfect, present laughter to utopian bliss" (1991, 408). Made in the mid-1950s when the British political divide was between Conservatives and Labour, with "Liberals" nowhere to be seen, this definition singles out the socialists as the conservatives' opponent, and which liberal would disagree with Oakeshott's obvious preference? Not Karl Popper (1945), for instance, Oakeshott's liberal colleague at the London School of Economics, whose contemporaneous advocacy of "piecemeal social engineering" over the "historicists'" (especially Marxists') holistic experiments, has the exact same flavor.

The point is that, with the socialists in the ring, the distinction between liberal and conservative is difficult to draw. This was already the case with their Jacobin predecessors, who were the ire not just of liberals like Constant but also of who is widely considered the father of conservatism, Edmund Burke. A friend and admirer of Adam Smith, Burke supported free trade and the market order, and even denounced the British rule in India (that was endorsed by and provided employment to Mill), while he opposed the French revolution "on liberal and pluralist grounds" (Himmelfarb 2003, 72). And shouldn't one call "liberal" Burke's animosity to abstraction, and his view that "circumstances are what render every civil and political scheme beneficial or noxious to mankind" (Burke, quoted in ibid., 84)? However, calling the state a "partnership in every virtue and in all perfection," and "not only between those who are living" but including past and future generations also (Burke, quoted in ibid., 89), transcends the boundaries of the liberal: a collective entity (although still disguised as "partnership"!) is superimposed on the individual, which is anathema to the true liberal.

The liberalism–socialism distinction carries its own difficulties. Both are emancipatory and forward-looking creeds, which warrants calling socialism the "daughter of liberalism" (Crouch 2017, 225). As Joseph Schumpeter

18 POLITICAL NEOLIBERALISM

(1976 [1950], 298) put it, "the ideology of classical socialism is the off-spring of bourgeois ideology. In particular, it shares the latter's rationalist and utilitarian background." Their principled difference is to take either the individual or society as the point of departure. "Society does not consist of individuals but expresses the sum of the relations and conditions, in which individuals stand to one another," Marx writes in one of the more accessible passages in one of his least accessible works, the *Grundrisse* (1974 [1857/1858], 176). This is not liberal, at least not as originally conceived. Classic liberalism starts with the individual, which at the aggregate level entails a preference for voluntarism and contract—liberal political theory from Hobbes to Locke has envisaged society as grounded in a contract. By contrast, socialism starts with society as constitutive of the self, either deforming the latter, as under capitalism, or enabling "free, conscious activity," as under communism (Marx 1978 [1844], 76).

However, twentieth-century "new" liberalism, inspired by Mill, moved closer to a socialist position, arguing that a minimum level of not just formal equality (which is constitutive of all liberalisms) but substantive equality is prerequisite for the exercise of liberty. At the end of his famous essay, *On Liberty*, Mill suggested that government must ensure "each person's bearing his share (to be fixed on some equitable principle) of the labours and sacrifices incurred for the defending the society or its members from injury and molestation" (2003 [1859], 141). This was a cautious call for redistribution. John Dewey's was already much louder, on the assumption that a "liberalism that takes its profession of the importance of individuals with sincerity must be deeply concerned about the structure of human association" (1935, 41). Dewey thus placed on the agenda of the "new liberal school" that "the state has the responsibility for creating institutions under which individuals can effectively realize the potentialities that are theirs" (ibid., 26). In Rawls's reformulation of liberalism, this social element shines in his second principle of justice, the Difference Principle. According to it, social and economic inequalities must be "to the greatest benefit of the least advantaged members of society" (1985, 227). Rawls's case for redistribution controversially included not just class-based but also talent-based inequalities. Daniel Bell promptly called this a "socialist ethic" (1972, 57), and he rejected it as misguided and overshooting redefinition of equality, from equal "opportunity" to equality of "result" (ibid., 41).

Indeed, liberalism's co-constitutive endorsement of freedom *and* equality, even in this rank order that suggests a priority for freedom (shared by Rawls, who theorized it as "lexical priority"), opens up socialist possibilities. For Leonard Hobhouse, one of the founders of British "new liberalism" (and holder of the first sociology chair in Britain at the University of London), "individualism, when it grapples with the facts, is driven no small distance along socialist lines" (quoted by Lukes 2008, 614). In his footsteps, Walzer saw that a "consistent liberalism," which requires "wall(ing) in the market" and containing "corporate power," "passes over into democratic socialism" (1984, 322–323).

So where is the line between liberalism and socialism, the two quintessentially modern and forward-looking political ideologies that both endorse freedom and equality, even if in reverse order of priority (socialism obviously putting equality first, but with *both* of which conservatism has major issues)? A not just gradual but qualitative difference between liberalism and socialism can be found in Marx's early and eminently political essay on the *Jewish Question* (1843). Grappling with the question how "Jews" are to be integrated into a liberal but also (somewhat hopefully) post-liberal order, this tractate remains surprisingly acute for contemporary race and multiculturalism struggles. Distinguishing between merely "political" and exuberantly "human emancipation," Marx's utopian-Jacobin impulse terminally sets liberalism apart from the socialism that he prefers. Liberalism stipulates distinctions, originally and perhaps most importantly that between private and public, which first pacified the intra-Christian war of religions, later made capitalism possible, eventually also helped reigning in the latter. In the *German Ideology*, Marx traced the private–public distinction even further back, to the pre-liberal invention of the "division of labor" and of "private property." These were, to him, "identical expressions: in the one the same thing is affirmed with reference to activity as is affirmed in the other with reference to the product of the activity" (1978 [1845–1846], 160). In *Jewish Question*, the private–public distinction reappears as the more recent antagonism between (bourgeois) "civil society" and "state," which the socialism of Marx and his followers wants to undo.

What is the result of liberalism? Marx asks rhetorically, because the answer is certain to him: "(M)an was not freed from religion—he received the freedom of religion. He was not freed from property—he received the freedom of property. He was not freed from the egoism of trade—he received the freedom to engage in trade" (1843 [1992], 233). A world without religion, without property, without trade? This would be a world without institutions, functional differentiation and the respective "double lives"; a world

20 POLITICAL NEOLIBERALISM

in which the individual is transformed into a "species-being" (*Gattungswesen*), living "in community with other men," no longer separated from them through "private interest" and the "rights" protecting it (ibid., 220, 221). Indeed, the *Jewish Question* is notorious for its wholesale dismissal of the "so-called rights of man" (ibid., 227), which are liberalism's early and crowning achievement.[2] The difference between liberalism and socialism, one could argue then, is that liberalism is a negative project, drawing lines to protect the individual from other individuals and from all individuals (i.e., under a democratic regime, the state). Socialism, by contrast, is a positive project, removing these lines of separation on an optimistic, even utopian assumption of the perfectibility of human nature. In a nutshell, liberalism is about setting-up separations, while socialism is about erasing them (see Walzer 1984, and further discussion in this chapter).

While we started with liberalism's political-historical origins, and then contrasted it with the rivaling ideologies of conservatism and socialism and the imprints they left on the evolving doctrine of liberalism, we quickly slipped into philosophical waters. This is unavoidable given liberalism's multiple faces. Christoph Möllers (2020, 261) deems it "dangerous for political liberalism" to limit it to an "own liberal camp," and even in a narrowly political understanding, a feature of liberalism is that you find it affiliated with "leftist" and "rightist" positions, the former more "socialist," the latter more "conservative." That liberalism is more than exchangeable doctrine or ideology, but foundation of the socio-political, even moral world as we know it, is evident in the fact that "illiberal" is generally perceived as a threat, and even repudiated by most of those who cannot but be called illiberal (see Chapter 4 and Chapter 5). By contrast, similar negative forms of "conservative" or "socialist" do not even exist, and were they to exist, probably they would not produce the same chill.

The Geuss Quartet of Classic Liberalism

The non-negotiability, in the sense of doctrine-transcending scope of liberal tenets, is apparent when perusing the four general trends that Geuss (2001, ch. 2) found persistent over the centuries: toleration, freedom, individualism/autonomy, and limitations to discretionary power or rule of law (and all of which he traces to the early- to mid-nineteenth-century liberals Wilhelm von Humboldt, Constant, Mill, and Alexis de Tocqueville).[3]

Toleration, "the oldest layer in the liberal synthesis" (Geuss 2002, 323), in fact, was laid out more than a century earlier by Locke, in his *Letter Concerning Toleration*. For Locke, the "care of souls" was not the business of the "civil magistrate," who was merely to protect the "Safety and Security of the Commonwealth" (Locke 2016 [1689], 128, 153). Locke deemed this division due to the nature of "true . . . Religion," which "consists in the inward persuasion of the Mind" (ibid., 129) and could not be forced, neither by worldly nor by religious authorities. This was a rickety start, imbibed with Locke's Protestant persuasion, and his toleration infamously stopped at those "who deny the Being of a God" (ibid., 159). Contemporary multiculturalists find toleration wanting, even if stripped of Locke's religious and Deist limitations, because it presupposes a position of power and the disapproval of what or who is being tolerated; instead, they advocate positive recognition (Brown 2006; but see Balint 2017). The critics of toleration don't leave, however, the liberal baseline, that different religions, ethnicities, and ways of life must be able to coexist peacefully in the same society.

Similar disagreements within a shared commitment apply to the other three liberal tenets. *Freedom*, as evidenced in its synonym liberty, is arguably the one tenet most closely, if not symbiotically, associated with liberalism. Classical liberals understood it as a negative quality, most elementary, even physically Hobbes. For Hobbes, "liberty" is the "absence of opposition," something that applies only to "bodies": "that which is not subject to motion, is not subject to impediment" (1998 [1641], 139). There never was an unequivocal transition toward a positive understanding, from "freedom from" to "freedom to," and liberalism qua liberalism remained tied to a preference for the negative (see Berlin 1958). However, one understanding of freedom is non-negotiable: that freedom, in principle, is accessible to all. Conservatives, when untainted by liberal instincts, espouse freedom, too, but only "for the higher orders," while "constraint" is "for the lower orders" (Robin 2018, 4). Even Tocqueville, liberal by conviction but conservative by sentiment, waxed nostalgic about the "glory," the "heights of knowledge," and the "passionate feelings" that he associated with the aristocracy and the "old order of society," and which he deemed flattened in a democracy (1969 [1835-1840], 15f). It was above all Friedrich Nietzsche who showed that freedom could have altogether other than liberal meanings, reserving it to the heroic few who withstood the "herd's" *ressentiment* pepped-up as "morality" and "justice"—"Bad air! Bad air! This workshop where ideals are fabricated—it seems to me just to stink of lies" (2007 [1887], 28).

22   POLITICAL NEOLIBERALISM

With respect to *individualism* and *autonomy*, there may be alternatives to build a political order around in China or Iran, but not in the West. Liberals of all stripes agree that the "goal of any human society must be the well-being of individuals," who alone are the "final bearers of politically relevant value" (Geuss 2001, 97, 98). To posit God, History, Reason, or other transcendent entity like Nation as subject or object of valuation would violate liberals' instinctive "anti-paternalism," which commands that people themselves are the "final judges of what is good for them" (ibid., 101). If people's object of value is God, for example, the latter matters no more than "tea, warm baths, or string quartets if (they) appreciate them" (ibid., 99). The only disagreement among liberals, notably qua theorists not qua practitioners, is whether this individualism is metaphysical or political, to paraphrase Rawls (1992); that is, whether individualism and autonomy stand for an ethical way of life (as the earlier Rawls [1971] had assumed), or whether they are merely a political shell to be filled by many a content, religious for instance. For actually existing liberalism ("historical liberalism," as Geuss says [2001, 104]), this dispute is meaningless. But hasn't the COVID-19 pandemic, one might object, demonstrated that an altogether different value—self-preservation, bare life, or however you call it—has trumped individualism and autonomy (however understood), and proved the latter to be a rather luxurious and dispensable item (see Chapter 6)? Hopefully not, because otherwise confinement and electronic surveillance will become the new normal, as they seem to have become in China. Evidently, it is "favourable historical circumstances" (Geuss 2001, 103) that have made the "axiomatic primacy of the individual" possible, and liberals must perennially fight for sustaining or recovering it (Bobbio 1987, 106).

Finally, to *limit discretionary power*, whether from the right or the left, on the assumption that the "Committee of Public Safety can be as bad as any Louis" (Geuss 2001, 106), has been a persistent liberal trend, by way of a written constitution, separation of powers, checks and balances, the *Rechtsstaat* (rule of law) or kindred devices. Constant and the Spanish *Liberales* wanted to limit the power of the monarch by way of constitutionalism. By contrast, the whole point of the Federalist Papers was to contain the risks of democratic majority power, later described as "tyranny of the majority" by Tocqueville, in his *Democracy in America*. James Madison, in the Federalist Letter No. 10, anticipated this risk of democracy in terms of the "mischiefs of faction." As Madison identified the "most common and durable source of factions" in the "unequal distribution of property," this was perhaps the first historical moment (or document) in which the fear that democracy might destroy capitalism came to be expressed—one and a half centuries later, this would become the focal point of neoliberal reasoning and politicking.

By the measure of Federalist Letter No. 10, American liberalism has from the start been anti-democratic, *if* democracy is understood as unfettered majority rule. The American Founders made peace with democracy by calling it "Republic." The latter was a combination of representation and scale. Representation would assure that a "chosen body of citizens" would "best discern the true interest of their country"; and scale (i.e. "extend(ing) the sphere") would neutralize the danger of an "unjust and interested majority" through "tak(ing) in a greater variety of parties and interests"—in political science jargon, through the creation of "cross-cutting cleavages" (Lipset 1959).[4] Madison's Republic was a stroke of genius, maybe the biggest in the history of statecraft. The discretionary power of the demos was contained by a certain conception of democracy, as representative and large-scale, henceforth the standard across the Western world. Not to mention that Madison had also provided a compelling argument to establish a "Union" over the "States." As the irony would have it, the federal state in America, whom free market adepts have loved to hate with unbroken vigor over the centuries, was initially there to protect them from the onslaught of the plebs.

Beyond the Geuss Quartet (I): Equality

There are several absences in the Geuss Quartet of liberal core principles. The first is "equality." Perhaps Geuss felt no need to single it out because historical liberalism is an attack on the pre-enlightenment order of feudal privilege and hierarchy. Thus, a preference for equality is necessarily implied. In the light of history, that individuals are to be free and equal is the shortest summary of the liberal doctrine, and no version of it has ever dispensed with either of the two elements. The most succinct formulation of their mutual interdependence is by Tocqueville: "(M)en will be perfectly free because they are entirely equal, and they will be perfectly equal because they are entirely free. Democratic people are tending toward that ideal" (1969 [1835-1840], 503). "Full liberty implies full equality," as the early twentieth-century "new liberal" Hobhouse put it even shorter (Starr 2007, 100). Tocqueville, however, continued to argue that the "taste for freedom" was in fact "distinct" from the "taste for equality," and that freedom had

24 POLITICAL NEOLIBERALISM

always been a human ideal, while the "equality of conditions" was specific to the "(democratic) ages." And he concluded that the "chief passion which stirs men at such times is the love for this same equality" (1969 [1835-1840], 504). In the trails of Tocqueville, the realist, freedom and equality are thus "typically presented as opposing values" (Anderson 2016, 90). The "quick version" of it is the (quintessentially neoliberal) argument that "economic liberty . . . upsets substantive economic equality" (ibid.). As Möllers (2020, 40) generalized this view beyond a narrow economic context, "freedom" arises "only there where specific inequalities are possible," and he deems even "individuality, diversity, plurality" to be "phenomena of inequality." While this slights the distinction between (vertical) inequality and (horizontal) difference (see Brubaker 2015), the liberal preference for freedom renders plausible Geuss's (2001) omission of equality from his list of liberal essentials.

This omission also follows from classical liberalism's penchant for being a "negative phenomenon" (Geuss 2002, 322). Humboldt, for instance, rejected the older "cameralist" notion in Prussia that the state was obliged to provide for the welfare of its subjects (Geuss 2001, 72). This was not primarily, as one might think, in defense of markets. Instead, it stemmed from Humboldt's Romantic idea, influential on Mill and even the young Marx, that the goal of human striving is individual "self-activity" (*Selbstaktivität*) that alone allows full individuation, and which would be undermined if the state went beyond a minimalist mandate of the "control of violence and fraud" (ibid., 82). Factoring in the reality of early capitalist markets makes the historical liberals' muteness on equality all the more plausible. The rise of "self-regulating markets" in early nineteenth-century England, which required the "fictitious" commodification also of the three goods that cannot be "produced for sale": land, labor, and money, went along with a brutish revocation of the Speenhamland welfarism of the early 1800s, which had guaranteed a minimum income and the "right to live" to the poor (Polanyi 1944, 85). The Poor Law Reform Act of 1834 instead made poor relief conditional on being locked into workhouses, and on being deprived of one's civic and political rights (see Block and Somers 2014, ch. 2). This is *also* historical liberalism.

Indeed, somewhat sidestepped by Geuss (2001), historical liberalism has equally been a political *and* an economic movement, and particularly on the economic side equality was definitely not high on its agenda (except presupposing it in the thin formal sense that capitalism is founded on contract). "As an economic theory liberalism is the upholder of the market economy;

as a political theory, it upholds the principle of the state which governs as little as possible," as Norberto Bobbio (1987, 104) put it matter-of-factly. But this is committing the reverse error of understating liberalism's political dimension, or rather modeling it a touch too much on the economic one.

That there is a fundamental tension between liberalism's economic and political dimensions, if there aren't even two altogether opposite logics at work, has been acidly elaborated by Schmitt in his *Concept of the Political*. For Schmitt, liberalism was *always* a denial of politics, the latter understood as non-normative *Kampf* (struggle) between "concrete human groups," or as friend–foe relationships (1963 [1932], 66f): "There is ... no liberal politics as such, but only a liberal critique of politics" (ibid., 69). But the liberals' denial of politics, argues Schmitt, is bifurcated in a "polarity of ethical pathos and economic calculation" (ibid., 72). Thereby political *Kampf* is either transformed into economic "competition" *or* into politico-ethical "discussion" (ibid., 28). "All liberal pathos," argues Schmitt, is "directed against force (*Gewalt*) and un-freedom (*Unfreiheit*)" (ibid., 70), and it wishes to subordinate "political issues (*Gesichtspunkte*)" to "morals, law, and economy." "Ethics and economics, spirit (*Geist*) and business (*Geschäft*), education (*Bildung*) and property": these are for Schmitt not complementary but a "polarity," their only communality being to posit "the individual (*der Einzelne*) as the terminus a quo and terminus ad quem" (ibid., 69–70). Schmitt thus anticipated the diametrically opposed projects that were all possible under the umbrella of liberalism, Hayek versus Rawls at the level of theory, neoliberalism versus social democracy at the level of practice.

Schmitt also became famous for drawing a sharp contrast between apolitical liberalism and a Greek-Rousseauian conception of democracy, as identity between rulers and ruled, which he found fully compatible with his agonistic understanding of politics: "Homogeneity and repressing the heterogeneous is in the nature of democracy," in order to maintain the "substance of equality" (1926, 14). In fact, Schmitt first articulated the liberalism versus politics binary when drawing the fundamental difference between "liberal-parliamentary" and "mass democratic ideas." And he deemed the former, which he ridiculed as "government by discussion," outdated and on the way out (ibid., 13). The different origins and logics of liberalism and democracy have never been more sharply articulated, and one understands the dark fascination that Schmitt has always exercised across the political spectrum, the left arguably more than the right.

Beyond the Geuss Quartet (II): Democracy

Much like the closely affiliated principle of equality, democracy is a second conspicuous absence from Geuss's (2001) four-tenet map of historical liberalism. Through a Schmittian lens, this omission makes perfect sense. In the real world, however, liberalism and democracy have solidly evolved in tandem. Espousing a skeptical "liberalism of fear," according to which the point of political life was not to achieve a *summum bonum* but to avoid the *summum malum* of the "weak" being crushed by the "powerful," Judith Shklar (1989, 27) thought that the liberal state is "of necessity a democratic state": "(L)iberalism is monogamously, faithfully, and permanently married to democracy—but it is a marriage of convenience" (ibid., 37). This qualification was a nod to the classical understanding of democracy, artfully mobilized by Schmitt in his diatribe against liberalism and in his quest for the total state.

It is, above all, the merit of Stephen Holmes (1995) to have developed a "theory of liberal democracy" out of the liberal classics, from Bodin and Hobbes to Mill. This is in full acknowledgment that liberalism in the first has been a "constraint" on the "passions" possibly unleashed by unfettered majority rule, the first and foremost of liberal constraints being constitutionalism. From this angle, "liberalism is a necessary, though not sufficient, condition for some measure of democracy in any modern state" (ibid., 9). Importantly, Holmes suggests a pro-democracy, even pro-welfarist reading of the liberal classics, in particular Mill (ibid., ch.6, ch.8). There is a "fundamental continuity between liberal rights and welfare rights" (ibid., 266), which he deduces from a "deep liberal commitment to psychological security" that evolves, with increasing wealth, from a "physical" into a "social" direction (ibid., 37). Holmes thus arrives at an understanding of liberalism as most fully realized in the liberal-democratic synthesis: "(T)he highest political values, from a liberal perspective, are psychological security and personal independence for all, legal impartiality . . ., the human diversity fostered by liberty, and collective self-rule through elected government and uncensored discussion" (ibid., 16).[5] From this angle, Berlin's dichotomy of negative versus positive liberty is flawed because both elements are necessary and mutually reinforcing, negative liberty being a precondition for collective self-rule (that Berlin "wrongly" equated with overbearing "individual self-fulfilment"): "Citizens will not throng voluntarily to the public square if their homes can be ravaged at will by the police"

(Holmes 1995, 31). Indeed, as Jan-Werner Müller crisply describes the logical connection between liberalism and democracy, "without political rights no democracy, and without democracy no possibility to struggle fairly over the development (*Ausgestaltung*) of rights" (2019, 148).

This is not to deny that the liberal-democratic synthesis, which has dominated Western societies from the late nineteenth to the late twentieth century, and in which democracy functioned as "natural progression of liberalism" (Bobbio 1987, 114), has rested on a normatively thin or "realist" understanding of democracy as based on competitive fiduciary representation. The classic formulation is by Schumpeter: "The democratic method is that institutional arrangement for arriving at political decisions in which individuals acquire the power to decide by means of a competitive struggle for the people's vote" (Schumpeter 1976 [1950], 269). Schumpeter models democracy on the market place, which made him a progenitor of the "economic theory of democracy" (Downs 1957). Politicians are engaged in a "free competition for a free vote" (Schumpeter 1976 [1950], 271), much as market actors compete for market shares. And, as in Smith's metaphor of the market as "invisible hand," the common good is not directly intended but merely the byproduct of the competition for votes. As Schumpeter put it, in his usual style, "the democratic method produces legislation and administration as mere by-products of the struggle for political office" (ibid., 286). This is also an understanding of democracy as defined by procedure (*modus procedendi*) rather than by purpose, because a dictator can just as easily usurp the common good as the people (ibid., 270). This possibility is precisely what had attracted Schmitt to the classical (Greek) theory of democracy, which Schumpeter on his part deftly denounced as naïve in assuming a "rationalist scheme of human action and of the values of life" (Schumpeter 1976 [1950], 296). Much like liberalism does, Schumpeter's realist doctrine of democracy takes people as they are and not as they should be, as vulnerable to "sudden eruption of primitive impulses, infantilisms and criminal propensities" (ibid., 257). Most importantly, this doctrine clarifies the relationship between "democracy and individual freedom": the "free competition for free votes" requires a "considerable amount of freedom of discussion *for all*" and related individual rights (ibid., 272). In other words, democracy-on-earth requires liberalism.

In one respect, however, Schumpeter's healthily realistic view went a notch too far down the cynical road. For Schumpeter, representative democracy simply meant "rule of the politician": "Democracy means only that

28   POLITICAL NEOLIBERALISM

the people have the opportunity of accepting or refusing the men who are to rule it" (1976 [1950], 284–285). What voters do is merely "install" but not "control" government; he deemed control "contrary to the spirit of the democratic method" (ibid., 272). This is oblivious of the mechanism of "retrospective voting," enabled through the fact that elections are not one-time but repeated events. Retrospective voting establishes a link between rulers' decisions and voters' preferences, however indirectly: "Voters . . . influence public decisions through the retrospective judgment that representatives anticipate voters will make" (Manin 1997, 179). In this thin but important sense, liberal democracy is still democratic.

Beyond the Geuss Quartet (III): The Art of Separation

Next to equality and democracy, there is a third liberal tenet that needs to be added to the Geuss quartet. This one is less obvious but of great importance for our purpose of contrasting liberalism and neoliberalism. One could call this tenet, with Walzer (1984), the "art of separation." Of course, it is implicit in the liberal arch-impulse of limiting power, which is transversal to the Geuss quartet and to a degree present in each of its elements. But it is important enough to state it explicitly. It was, again, Schmitt who first noticed that liberalism "(recognizes) the 'autonomy' of the diverse areas of human life" (1963 [1932], 70). He mentions the realm of art: art as the "daughter of freedom," the aesthetic value judgment as "unconditionally autonomous," and the artistic genius as "sovereign"—all these are liberal ideas. Moreover, Schmitt continues, it is the work of liberalism to separate morality from metaphysics and religion, science from religion, art, and morality, and so on. Finally, Schmitt mentions the "economic" as the "by far most important case of an autonomous sphere (*autonomen Sachgebiets*)" (ibid., 71). As Paul Starr (2007, 54) expressed the underlying idea, liberal separation is "a means of protecting values specific to particular institutions and spheres of life."

Alas, the only sphere *not* "respected" in its autonomy, laments Schmitt (1963 [1932], 70), is the political, which liberalism has sought to "annihilate" through law, among other means. Schmitt suspects that this is because the political, as understood by him, is the only sphere in which not "abstract orders" but "concrete human beings" rule over other human beings. This is sharply observed and confirming Schmitt's own transcendent view of the political as not a separate sphere parallel to the others, but as the "most intensive and extreme" (ibid., 30) of all human associations that tops the others and can be reached from any of them. "Every religious, moral, economic, ethnic or other opposition (*Gegensatz*) can be transformed into a political opposition," argues Schmitt (ibid., 37), "if it is strong enough to effectively group human beings according to friend v. foe." Interestingly, liberalism and the Schmittian political have in common to consider human beings as "distance-taking," as geared to *Abstandnahme* (German anthropologist Helmuth Plessner, cited by Schmitt), only that radically opposite conclusions are drawn from it: containing and regulating versus aggressively embracing and letting this quality run, respectively.

In Walzer's less toxic language, "(l)iberalism is a world of walls, and each one creates a new liberty" (1984, 315)—church versus state, civil society versus political community, public versus private, and so on. Ideally, "success in one institutional setting isn't convertible into success in another," which guarantees to Walzer that "liberty and equality go together" (ibid., 321). This is a slightly different take on liberal separation than Schmitt's: what's in it for the individual versus protection of sector-specific values. In both respects, liberalism is not optional but required by "social differentiation" (ibid., 319). Niklas Luhmann, leading theorist of functional differentiation, has understood liberalism in the exact same terms (without, however, calling it by the name). He considers civil and human rights, with their core principles of freedom and equality, the "semantic correlate" to an "order of inclusion" (1995, 246), in which individuals are partially included in all of modern society's functional subsystems (economy, polity, family, education, etc.), but never exclusively in only one (as in the hierarchical society of estates).

The most sustained reflection on liberalism as correlate of a functionally differentiated society has been made by Holmes (1985). He follows Walzer in underlining the egalitarian and social-democratic implications of liberal separation: "A society of equality is a society of separations (*Grenzen*)," in which there are "barriers against the convertibility" of social goods like public offices, money, faith, knowledge, or loyalty (ibid., 24). Moreover, whereas classical liberalism saw its highest good of freedom threatened mainly by the state, under developed capitalism the biggest threat emanates from "others"; that is, capitalists. Accordingly, "compensating for the incompetence of the market became a central competence of the liberal state." In the process, the liberal concern about "security" has shifted from political "peace" to socio-economic "inequality," leading to an "expansion of the concept of security" (ibid., 33).

30   POLITICAL NEOLIBERALISM

If the "end" of liberalism is "the liberation of individuals so that realization of their capacities may be the law of their life" (Dewey 1935, 56), it had to turn into social liberalism. As Starr summarized the process, "(l)iberalism invited democracy, then democracy changed liberalism" (2007, 82).

Neoliberalism

To roll back the marriage of liberalism and democracy is the whole purpose of neoliberalism. In the late Pierre Bourdieu's (1998) *cri de coeur*, the "essence of neoliberalism" is "destruction of all the collective institutions capable of counteracting the effects of the infernal machine (of capitalism), primarily those of the state." Capitalism liberated from "collective" (i.e., democratic) constraints, and thereby allowed to roam globally and, in turn, impose its terms on domestic society, is a very good first shot at neoliberalism. Where Bourdieu erred is his optimistic view of the state, which as "nation state," or "better yet" as "supranational state" (in Europe), eventually as "world state," would always be on the side of "counteracting . . . the infernal machine" (ibid.). As we shall see, not the diminution but the refashioning of the state, at all levels, national to supranational, has been part and parcel of the neoliberal transition. When musing about "neoliberalism and its prospects," Milton Friedman (1951) stressed that the "new faith" must "explicitly recognize that there are important positive functions that must be performed by the state," the most important being the provision of "a framework within which free competition could flourish." As Quinn Slobodian put it aptly, the "neoliberal project" focused on designing institutions that both required and affected the state, the point of it being "not to liberate markets but to encase them, to inoculate capitalism against the threat of democracy, to create a framework to contain often-irrational human behaviour" (2018, 2).

Importantly, the neoliberal project *can* be seen as reverting to the original liberal tenets, as laid out by Geuss (2001). Indeed, none of the four Geuss tenets—toleration, freedom, individualism/autonomy, and limiting discretionary power—is incompatible with neoliberalism. Its chief theorist, Hayek (1960, 1966), exactly understood his project in these terms: as recovering the empiricist-individualist British tradition of liberalism, while discarding its French rationalist-collectivist aberration (that ran along the tracks of Constant's "liberty of ancients" and Berlin's "positive liberty" and can be squeezed into the Geuss quartet only with difficulty, if at all).

What makes neoliberalism "neo" is thus not its conflicting with the Geuss quartet. Instead, liberalism turns "neo" when cutting down on or even negating the three additions that we made to it: equality, democracy, and the art of separation. First, neoliberalism is about cutting down to size liberalism's equality dimension, which had expanded from formal to substantive, particularly in the second half of the twentieth century, the golden era of the welfare state. Secondly, neoliberalism is about neutralizing democracy, which had allowed the taste for equality to get into the way of capitalist profitmaking. This is to be achieved by building or strengthening non-majoritarian institutions at domestic, regional, and global levels—"world governance," as advocated today by the World Economic Forum, the Geneva-based global billionaire club, is of neoliberal colors. The result has been the rupturing of the liberal-democratic synthesis of the post-World War II period (see Chapter 2). And, thirdly, neoliberalism is separation-busting, a functional sphere- and sector-transcending comprehensive governing and life-shaping rationale. Various authors have captured this last and crucial point in various terms: "market fundamentalism" (Block and Somers 2014), "homo oeconomicus" (Foucault 2008), "human capital citizenship" (Ellermann 2019), among others. Equality-, democracy-, and separation-busting are interconnected and mutually implicated projects and processes that cannot be neatly kept apart and retold in linear and additive fashion.

All three themes are prominent in the work of Hayek, despite the variety of its strands, the neoliberal movement's towering and integrative figure. While, much like historical liberalism, neoliberalism is an eminently political project, it is still useful to approach it, in the remainder of this chapter, mainly from the theoretical or doctrinal angle, as we did for liberalism, but now laying out their common ground while identifying neoliberalism's specific departures.

A Political Creed, Again

The historical background of neoliberalism has been widely explored in recent years, and there is no need to repeat that here (e.g., Burgin 2015; Mirowski and Plehwe 2009; Slobodian 2018; Stedman Jones 2012). But it needs to be restated upfront that neoliberalism was born as a political fighting creed, not unlike its historical progenitor, liberalism. The difference is that liberalism entered a world still to be remade in its image, from feudal to modern, and just a little ahead in time of its socialist competitor that had

32   POLITICAL NEOLIBERALISM

the same ambition. When self-called "neoliberals," including Hayek, Ludwig von Mises, Wilhelm Röpke, and Alexander Rüstow, first met at the *Colloque Walter Lippmann* in Paris in August 1938, to discuss the French transla-tion of a pro-market book by American journalist Walter Lippmann (who reportedly preferred to chase women over sticking to the academic proto-col), they lived in a profoundly different world. This was a world in which economic liberalism had been tried and crushed by the Great Depression of 1929, while collectivist alternatives, in the form of fascism and communism in Europe and Russia, but also of Roosevelt's New Deal in the United States, predominated.

Accordingly, this was a world profoundly shaped in the image of liber-alism and socialism, although liberalism was on the losing end. Neolib-eralism was defined at the Colloque in narrowly economic terms, as "the priority of the price mechanism, the free enterprise, the system of com-petition," but also—and this was a novelty—"a strong and impartial state" (quoted by Plehwe 2009, 14). In fact, there was a rift among participants between strong statists, in particular Röpke and Rüstow, who would become known as "ordoliberals" and co-founders of the postwar German *Soziale Marktwirtschaft* (social market economy), on the one side, and strident free market advocates, especially Hayek and Mises, on the other.[6] What both factions shared was a heroic self-perception as marginal intellec-tual elite that had to assume positions of power to fend off the threat of mass democracy, in its totalitarian *and* soft social-democratic versions alike.

The sense of mission by an isolated few (bolstered by the fact that the early neoliberals were nearly all living in exile) was even stronger at the first meet-ing of the Mont Pèlerin Society, on a mountain overlooking Lake Geneva near Lausanne, in 1947. Its attendants included again Hayek and Mises, but also Friedman and Popper, among others. It is worth to quote the society's founding Statement of Aims at length:

> The central values of civilization are in danger. Over large stretches of the
> Earth's surface the essential conditions of human dignity and freedom have
> already disappeared. In others, they are under constant menace from the
> development of current tendencies of policy. The position of the individ-
> ual and the voluntary group are progressively undermined by extensions of
> arbitrary power. Even that most precious possession of Western Man, free-
> dom of thought and expression, is threatened by the spread of creeds which,
> claiming the privilege of tolerance when in the position of a minority,

seek only to establish a position of power in which they can suppress and obliterate all views but their own.

The group holds that these developments have been fostered by the growth of a view of history which denies all absolute moral standards and by the growth of theories which question the desirability of the rule of law. It holds further that they have been fostered by a decline of belief in private property and the competitive market; for without the diffused power and initiative associated with these institutions it is difficult to imagine a society in which freedom may be effectively preserved.[7]

The statement bears the strong signature of the society's first president (until 1960), Hayek.[8] "Freedom," "rule of law," "private property and the competitive market," and "civilization in danger," while the strong state rhetoric that had been present at the Colloque Lippmann was toned down— these were all central themes of Hayek's gloomy and missionary bestseller *Road to Serfdom*, published a few years earlier (Hayek 1944). Since the Colloque Lippmann, the mood had further darkened. Central planning, as legacy of the war economy, had become the dominant state approach in the Western world as well, not only in the Communist east. New Deal Democrats ruled uncontested in the United States, and a Labour government in the United Kingdom set out to build the welfare state—the latter henceforth was to become the main enemy.

However, the neoliberals had to hang out in the cold for thirty more years after the end of World War II, the period that was to become the high moment of social liberalism. Their moment came only after 1973, when the first serious economic recession of the postwar period, with simultaneous high unemployment and skyrocketing inflation, knocked off the Keynesian economic orthodoxy, whose Phillips Curve (stating an inverse relationship between unemployment and inflation) had ruled out such situation. What happened then has been inimitably told by Friedman: "There is an enormous inertia . . . in private and especially governmental arrangements. Only a crisis . . . produces real change. When that crisis occurs, the actions that are taken depend on the ideas that are lying around" (1982 [1962], iv).

Among the ideas "lying around" at the time were those of the economist Friedman, of course, but also those of his previous faculty colleague at the University of Chicago, Hayek (now at the University of Freiburg). Hayek's ideas are less technically economic and more society-encompassing, thus especially relevant for our purpose of mapping the difference between liberalism and neoliberalism. Hayek's main purpose had always been to "elaborate the general principles of a liberal order" at large, not only of the economy, as he pronounced in his opening address to the first Mont Pèlerin Society meeting in 1947 (Plehwe 2009, 16). Thirty years later, the newly elected British Conservative Party chief, Margaret Thatcher, interrupted a presentation at a party meeting in the mid-1970s with the resolute words: "This is what we believe!" while pulling a copy of Hayek's *Constitution of Liberty* (1960) out of her briefcase and banging it on the table.[9] That there is "no such thing as society," to quote one of Thatcher's two neoliberal neologisms that immortalized her, is certainly a lesson she could have taken out of that book, as of many other of his writings.

Absolutizing Freedom

Hayek's main work, *The Constitution of Liberty* (1960), from whose basic tenets he never departed despite repeated reformulations and amendments (in particular, in 1982a,b,c and in 1989), is all a defense of the liberal core concept of freedom, which "certainly has made little progress during the last hundred years and is now on the defensive" (1960, 7). He invokes the legacy of Madison, Mill, Tocqueville, and von Humboldt for his project—basically the same progenitors of liberalism as understood by Geuss (2001). However, a first departure is to posit more stridently the "value of freedom" above all other values; freedom is "not merely one particular value but . . . the source and condition of most moral values" (Hayek 1960, 6). No liberal had ever put it so aggressively, positing freedom as an absolute value that trumped all others. Mill's harm principle, to remember, while in substance providing a maximum reach to freedom, in form is a principle to *restrict* freedom (COVID-19 restrictionists would gleefully make use of it; see Chapter 6). From Hayek's absolutizing of freedom, it follows that he, more than any of his predecessors, pushes the fact that the pursuit of freedom must lead to inequality. Moreover, Hayek insists that not only is there no remedy to it, but that inequality is productive, that "progress" hinges on it. So far, liberals had taken inequality as a calamity that grudgingly had to be accepted to let freedom reign, although inequality also had to be contained as much as possible. Hayek's feast was to make inequality a positive value in itself.

Of course, what Hayek shares with classical liberals is that freedom proper is "negative": "(I)t describes the absence of a particular obstacle—coercion by other men." Truthful to the canon, he distinguishes this from "political freedom," which is "the participation of men in the choice of their government" (Hayek 1960, 13). Neither is negative freedom the "identification of freedom with power," which he associates with the "socialism" of Dewey (but should more properly be called social liberalism) (ibid., 17). Importantly, despite the absolutist rhetoric, the Hayekian case for freedom is not freestanding but tacitly functionalist. Freedom is a supra-individual tool to advance "civilization." Curiously, and absolutely central to Hayek, freedom is not to give space to knowledge and rationality at the individual level; on the contrary, the point of freedom is in recognition of the "inevitable ignorance" of people (ibid., 26). Without quoting Tocqueville, Hayek invokes his famous quip about the inverse relationship between individual and collective knowledge: "The craft improves, the craftsman slips back" (Tocqueville 1969 [1835-1840], 556). Given the inherent limitation of individual knowledge, freedom is "essential ... to leave room for the unforeseeable and unpredictable" (Hayek 1960, 29). Without freedom, "the craft could not improve."

While markets are not mentioned in this context (as, in fact, they rarely are in the *Constitution of Liberty*), this is why markets are so important. Because "no human mind can comprehend all the knowledge which guides the actions of society," there is the "need for an impersonal mechanism not dependent on individual human judgements, which will co-ordinate the individual efforts" (Hayek 1960, 4). This mechanism is the market. As Philip Mirowski put it to the point, while slightly sarcastic, Hayek conceives of the market as "information processor more powerful than any human brain" (2009, 435). The "price system" contains "all the relevant information," fixing the problem of the "unavoidable imperfection of man's knowledge," which is always local and contextual and thus best exercised at that level—this is the simple message of one of the twentieth century's most influential economic papers, which helped Hayek win the Nobel Prize thirty years later, in 1974 (Hayek 1945).[10] The uneven dispersal of knowledge in society, which can never be concentrated in any one individual, explains why markets are intrinsically superior to planning, which is the state's (and by implication, socialism's) mode of processing information. Central planning, done by individuals writ large, merely repeats the limits of the individual at aggregate level. The market is the answer to the anthropological fact that "(c)ertainty we cannot achieve in human affairs" (Hayek 1960, 30). Hayek agrees with his rationalist opponents that "the use of reason aims at control and predictability." But he chides them for ignoring how we

36 POLITICAL NEOLIBERALISM

arrive at reason: "the process of the advance of reason rests on freedom and the unpredictability of human action" (ibid., 38), which is best organized in the market form.

From the inherent limitation of human knowledge, and the need for markets to compensate for it, Hayek follows that "(p)rogress by its very nature cannot be planned" (1960, 41). Like his starting point of freedom, this seems to be liberal common sense. But, again, he immediately makes a surprising leap that leads him into new territory: progress "must take place in echelon fashion, with some far ahead of the rest" (ibid., 42). That there is no freedom without inequality is commonplace. But, to repeat, no liberal so far had turned this vice into a virtue. In a "progressive society, some must lead, and the rest must follow" (ibid., 45). That pushes freedom beyond the liberal pale into Nietzschean territory. Except that Nietzsche was honest (and freakish) enough to despise the weak, those "tame and civilized animal(s), ... household pet(s)" (2007 [1887], 24). Hayek, by contrast, is paternalistic. He considers the riches' "experimenting with new styles" a "necessary service without which the advance of the poor would be very much slower." In fact, take away "progress at the top," and "soon (you) prevent it all the way down" (1960, 45, 51).

Here is the origin of one of the core tenets of neoliberalism: that the purpose of state policy must be to make the rich richer, because their riches will "trickle down" in terms of employment and economic progress for all. In his furious and fact-filled attack on 21st century billionaires, *Davos Man*, Peter Goodman (2022, 8) called it the "Cosmic Lie", "the alluring yet demonstrably bogus idea that cutting taxes and deregulating markets will not only produce extra riches for the most affluent, but trickle the benefits down to the lucky masses—something that has, in real life, happened zero times." When applying his elitist conception of freedom to social policy, Hayek drew a consequence that even by his own admission is "harsh": "(U)nder a free system those with full earning capacity should often be rapidly cured of a temporary and not dangerous disablement at the expense of some neglect of the aged and mortally ill" (Hayek 1960, 299). This would "probably (be) in the interest of all," assuming the same trickle-down effect being at work. To cure the light ailment of a rich person ahead of the cancer of a poor person. This is no longer liberalism, which stipulates the equal dignity of all human beings, but Social Darwinism of the crudest kind. One must say that neoliberal social policy has never dared to go even remotely as far (see Chapter 3).

Hayek ties an elitist conception of freedom to an austere and individualistic understanding of responsibility. "Responsibility," he concedes, "has become an unpopular concept." This was a hint at what he was writing against at the time: the "cold" socialism of the welfare state, after the real beast of socialism was declared "killed . . . by the example of Russia" (Hayek 1960, 254f). The consequence of "choice" is to "bear its consequences." Further, "responsibility, to be effective, must be individual" (ibid., 83). He did not say it this way, of course, but there could be "no such thing as society" to step in. With respect to social policy, Hayek advocated a "limited" conception of "security," as "minimum . . . sustenance," presumably just to prevent death by starvation, which he distinguished from an "absolute" conception of security, as "assurance of a given standard of life" (ibid., 259). Around that time, T. H. Marshall had declared the latter the fulcrum of "social citizenship": "Social rights imply an absolute right to a certain standard of civilisation . . . Their content does not depend on the economic value of the individual claimant" (1950, 43). That, notably, wasn't socialism but social liberalism (or social democracy, which I take to be the same thing) because Marshallian social citizenship wasn't meant to abolish class and capitalism but merely to soften their edges and thus to legitimize the inequalities that remain.

In the meantime, however, while never going to a Social Darwinist extreme, social policy has decisively moved away from Marshall into Hayek's direction. Yascha Mounk (2017, ch.2) called the new logic "responsibility-tracking." According to it, (minimized) welfare is no longer distributed on the basis of individual-blind mutualization of risk but of case-by-case scrutiny that no element of choice was involved in a bad outcome (like sickness or unemployment). Twenty years after Hayek's *Constitution of Liberty*, Ronald Reagan heard the message: "We must reject the idea that every (time) a law's broken, society is guilty rather than the lawbreaker. It is time to restore the American precept that each individual is accountable for his actions." And when his Democrat successor, Bill Clinton, finally accomplished where Reagan failed, to "end welfare as we know it" at the federal level, it was in a law that carried the words "Personal Responsibility" in its name (see Joppke 2021a, 16).

Formal Equality

Despite Hayek's positive valuing of material inequality, as necessary for progress, he advocates "equality before the law" (1960, 85). This has been, after all, the "great aim of the struggle for liberty." However, formal equality

38   POLITICAL NEOLIBERALISM

is the "only kind of equality conducive to liberty," and he immediately adds: "From the fact that people are very different it follows that, if we treat them equally, the result must be inequality" (ibid., 87). The "rule of law" under which people are to be equal, and which binds the state also, is not the result of legislation, which would require a rational and centered intervention into the decentered flow of things that he abhors. Instead, the rule of law is "a limitation of all legislation" (ibid., 205). Hayek models it partially on private law in the Roman law tradition, which is the product of law-finding by jurists; but, more importantly, he models it on the English Common Law, which likewise is the decentralized and piecemeal product of courts and lawyers, and in addition was to limit the power of the king. Law, and Common Law in particular, in this sense has evolved over time, no one has deliberately made it, much like language or the market (1982a, ch.4). Its spirit is *isonomia*, "equality of laws to all manner of persons" (1960, 164). "True law," says Hayek, makes "no references to particular persons, places or objects"; it is "known and certain"; and it does not claim to be "just" but to be "equal" to everyone (ibid., 209). Finally, what is rather a first, this law is "negative," imposing no positive duties but "aim(ing) only at preventing injustice" (1982a, 110), unlike "legislation" that entails positive commands to be "carried out" and "executed" (ibid., 127).

In his later work, Hayek contrasts "rules of just conduct," which is the law properly understood, with "social justice," which to him is a fundamentally misguided enterprise (Hayek 1982b). He now defines "rules of just conduct" as "end-independent rules which serve the formation of a spontaneous order," aka the market (ibid., 31). They express the "nomos" of a "private law society," another word for market society, and they "essentially (consist of) the private and criminal law" (ibid., 34). Crucially, and this is a position clearly directed against Rawls, as is probably the entire tirade against the *Mirage of Social Justice*,[11] to be "just" is exclusively a quality of persons, not of a system. Nature cannot be just, but neither can "society" be just, understood as a "spontaneous order" of markets and the law, which has evolved without anyone having made it: "The particulars of a spontaneous order cannot be just or unjust . . . what is called 'social' or 'distributive' justice is indeed meaningless within a spontaneous order and has meaning only within an organization" (ibid., 33).

Repudiating Social Justice

The problem of social justice is twofold. First, it denies the nature of society, which is not an organization but an evolved order. "Society . . . is incapable of acting for a specific purpose," argues Hayek (1982b, 64). In this respect, "social justice" is a pleonasm, like "social language" (ibid., 78). And if social justice is tried, on the false assumption that society is an organization, the result is the destruction of the rule of law because it requires to treat different people differently. As Hayek already put it in his classic *Road to Serfdom*, "(t)o produce the same result for different people, it is necessary to treat them differently" (1944, 87f). In effect, this amounts to favoritism, "the protection of entrenched interests" (1982b, 96). This is all derived from logical argument, and from a certain understanding of what "society" is. Nevertheless, one is astounded by the cascade of pejoratives fired against social justice. As in a fit of rage, Hayek attacks it as "(w)holly devoid of meaning or content," "dishonest insinuation that one ought to agree to a demand of some special interest," "the mark of demagogy or cheap journalism," "dislike of people who are better off than oneself, or simply envy" (ibid., 96–99), "revolt of the tribal spirit" (ibid., 144). When Thatcher stated about society that "there is no such thing," she added: "There are individual men and women and there are families and no government can do anything except through people and people look to themselves first."[12] This is precisely Hayek's understanding of "welfare": "(E)ach capable adult is primarily responsible for his own and his dependents' welfare" (ibid., 99).

Except from political adrenalin, Hayek arrived at this attack on social justice, as mentioned, from a certain view of society. It bears strong resemblance with the view of the conservative British philosopher Oakeshott (2006: ch. 31, 32), who distinguished in his lectures between society as naturally evolved order (*nomocratic*) versus society as purposeful organization (*teleocratic*), with a clear preference for the former. This distinction reappears in Hayek as *kosmos* versus *taxis*.[13] A nomocratic order (*kosmos*) is a "rule-governed" spontaneous order, with the market as prime example (Hayek also refers to it as *catallaxy*). A teleocratic order (*taxis*) is an "end-governed" organization, most importantly the state (1982b, 14). One might think that, as societies modernize, they move from nomocratic to teleocratic (this is the point of James Coleman's rational-choice-based grand social theory [1998]). As we know from Max Weber, formal-

40   POLITICAL NEOLIBERALISM

rational organization (i.e., "bureaucracy") is a modern and modernizing phenomenon. More emphatically, it was the ambition of the French revolution not just to create the world anew (religious revivalism had tried that before), but to do so by human design with secular goals in mind, most famously the French tryptic *Liberté, Égalité, Fraternité* (notably in that order). For Hayek, this is all hubris and the heart of the problem that he is working against, first in its hard and degenerated version of communism and fascism, and later in its milder version of social liberalism or social democracy.

Opposed to what common sense might suggest, the *real* transition, in Hayek's view, is from "end-connected tribal society" to "rule-connected open society" (also referred to as "Great Society") (1982b, 38). The assumption is, not without plausibility, that tribal societies were composed of "small groups" with a common purpose and "instincts of solidarity and altruism" (1989, ch. 1), while in open (i.e., modern Western) societies "common concrete ends were replaced by general, end-independent abstract rules of conduct" (ibid., ch. 2). Therefore, his understanding of social justice as "revolt of the tribal spirit": this is not just a swearword, but the assumption that, deep down in collective memory, there is a longing for returning to the communal past and persistent unease with "the abstract requirements . . . of the Great Society with no such visible common purpose" (1982b, 144). In his latest work, *The Fatal Conceit* (1989), which returns to his earliest preoccupation with the "errors of socialism," Hayek depicts the transition from tribal society to modern capitalism as a result of plain evolutionary selection, a "competitive process in which success decides"—and "(e)volution cannot be just" (ibid., ch. 5).[14]

So, there *is* "society" for Hayek. But to the degree that it is modern and "progressive," it is market, and the market cannot act. And to the degree that society is "state," it arrogates to itself a knowledge that it cannot have, and if it acts on it, it can only do wrong. Throughout his work, from *The Use of Knowledge in Society* (1945) onward, there is also a populist strand of rejecting "expertise" in favor of the local knowledge of ordinary people, which is best coordinated through the "brain" of the market. Hayek dismisses "society" as a "weasel word." As he points out, its Latin root words *societas* and *socius* mean "the personally known fellow or companion." This suggests to him "a concealed desire to model (the) extended order on the intimate fellowship for which our emotions long" (1989, ch. 7).

Ultimately, Hayek's rejection of substantive equality, as social justice, rests on an ahistorical picture of society as arising each time anew with every market transaction. Hayek is absolutely silent on the original distribution of assets that people bring to the market (what Marx had called *ursprüngliche Akkumulation*, not quite accurately translated as "primitive accumulation"). And Hayek is silent on the asymmetries generated by repeat transactions, which systematically must favor some and disfavor others, at the latest in the next generation that always starts from highly unequal positions—this is the whole point of "class," and not only as Marx understood it.[15] This denial of history is deeply ironic, considering Hayek's commitment to the British tradition of liberalism, including Burke, for which "a successful free society will always . . . be a tradition-bound society" (Hayek 1960, 61). For his ahistorical and idealized lens on the market, it is worth to quote at length a passage from his synopsis of the *Constitution of Liberty* (1966, 612):

> (T)he market order does not bring about any close correspondence between subjective merit or individual needs and rewards. It operates on the principle of a combined game of skill and chance in which the results for each individual may be as much determined by circumstances wholly beyond his control as by his skill or effort. Each is remunerated according to the value his particular services have to the particular people to whom he renders them, and this value of his services stands in no necessary relation to anything which we could appropriately call his merits, and still less to his needs.

If an economic reward reflects the "value" of a service for someone willing to pay for it, this rules out to be rewarded for "merit" or desert—and with it any claim for redistribution. It also rules out the most prominent justification of neoliberal capitalism today: that it is a meritocracy (see Markovits 2019; Sandel 2020). For Hayek, market outcomes are chance outcomes, which cannot be "deserved" in any meaningful way. But more important is to describe market participation as a "combined game of skill and chance." The notion of "game" is deliberate, because "(a) game according to rules can never know justice of treatment" (Hayek 1982c, 141). The game metaphor doubles down on the pointlessness of bringing justice claims to market outcomes: "it would be nonsensical to demand that the results for the different players be just" (Hayek 1982b, 71). Justice on markets reminds one of Dodo's dictum in *Alice in Wonderland*: "Everybody has won, and all must have prizes."

42   POLITICAL NEOLIBERALISM

"Game" is important in yet another respect (to be explored later): for Hayek, as for all neoliberals, the market in its ideal form is not about exchange, which presupposes and reinforces equality, and which had been the assumption of Smith and eighteenth-century liberal economics. Instead, the market is about competition, whose result must be inequality (the change from liberal "exchange" to neoliberal "competition" is brilliantly observed by Foucault [2008]).

Leaving this last point aside for a moment, a "game" it may be for those who can withdraw from the market, or who can "play" the market on a comfortable asset cushion. But is this a fair or realist description of people without property or other "marketable" assets, today education? Alain de Benoist, main thinker of the French New Right, rightly objects to Hayek's "game" metaphor: "What is one to think of a game where, as if by chance, the winners keep winning, while the losers keep losing" (1998, 101). Hayek simply assumes that each person has something of value to bring to the market, usually conceived of as "property," and that each game is a new game, without bias or unequal starting points. But what about "the effect of property on the market liberties of those who have very little of it," as Charles Lindblom (1977, 50n) objects. It is cynical advice for repeat losers to have no one but themselves to blame.

In the beginning, the market may have been "left" (in the political sense), as Elizabeth Anderson (2017, ch. 1) put it provocatively, a "free society of equals" in the vision of Adam Smith that emancipated people from feudal shackles. "Masters fraternized with their journeymen. Alcohol passed freely between masters and journeymen even during work hours," Anderson describes this bucolic past (which seems exaggerated) (ibid., 34). But the "economies of scale" arriving with the Industrial Revolution put an end to it, whether the Smithian small market society of independent property-holders ever existed or not. The standard situation today is people without property facing heavily concentrated property in the form of big and ever bigger firms. What sort of competition should *that* be, to switch from the liberal to the neoliberal register? Firms are "private government," which is as hierarchical if not dictatorial as the old order had ever been (only half tongue-in-cheek, Anderson calls it "communist" because "the government— that is, the establishment—owns all the assets"; ibid., 39). This reality is blithely ignored in Hayek's (1982b, 96) sundry picture of "a society of free men whose members are allowed to use their own knowledge for their own purposes," while laughing the scarecrow of "social justice" out of court.

Fear of Democracy

Summing up so far, Hayek's views on freedom, equality, and justice can be called "neoliberal" in the literal sense of the word: sharing ground with the liberal tradition yet also making radical departures. But what about democracy? Hayek dreads democracy as an inroad for the "myth of social justice" (1982c, 10). Worse still, it is "the name for . . . vote-buying, for placating and remunerating those special interests which in more naïve times were described as the 'sinister interests'" (ibid., 32). Underneath the polemic, Hayek's main issue with democracy can be found in one caustic statement in the *Constitution of Liberty*. Liberalism, he says there, is about "limiting the coercive powers of *all* government." The "democratic movement," by contrast, cares about "only *one* limit to government—current majority opinion" (1960, 103). In another place, he said this about majority rule: "(I)f democracy is taken to mean government by the unrestricted will of the majority I am not a democrat" (1982c, 39).

At the same time, professions of his democratic commitments are sprinkled throughout his writings, almost as strong as his aversion. But squaring them with the latter, they ring hollow: "I profoundly believe in the basic principles of democracy as the only effective method . . . of making peaceful change possible" (Hayek 1982a, xx). Or: democracy is "an ideal fighting for to the utmost, because it is our only protection . . . against tyranny" (1982c, 5). In other places still, he takes a pragmatic middle position: democracy is "not an ultimate or absolute value and (to) be judged by what it can achieve" (1960, 106). That is not far from Shklar's "marriage of convenience," although decisively without the "monogamous" part (1989, 27).

Cutting through the decorum, the following statement again reveals Hayek's essentially antagonistic take on democracy (1966, 601):

> Liberalism and democracy, although compatible, are not the same. The first is concerned with the extent of governmental power, the second with who holds this power. The difference is best seen if we consider their opposites: the opposite of liberalism is totalitarianism, while the opposite of democracy is authoritarianism. In consequence, it is at least possible in principle that a democratic government may be totalitarian and that an authoritarian government act on liberal principles.

While Hayek starts here with a pragmatic middle position, not far from Shklar's, for the gallery one must suspect, the rest of the statement moves

44 POLITICAL NEOLIBERALISM

decidedly toward the antagonistic pole. First, liberalism is about limiting the "extent" of power, while democracy is merely about "who" holds it. Anyone vaguely familiar with Schumpeter's realist theory of democracy will agree that the liberalism part is rather more important than who temporarily may have won the competition for votes and in this sense "holds" the power. Even if the classic (Greek) theory of democracy is the measure, Hayek is Schmittian enough to know that "the people" or someone claiming to speak for them is of secondary importance. In sum, the question "who holds" power is largely academic; what matters is to restrict it, and that is thumbs up for liberalism. As he says himself, in the *Constitution of Liberty*, not "who governs" but "what government is entitled to" is the "essential problem" (1960, 403). But Hayek *really* puts his cards on the table in the second step, when drawing the strange antonyms liberalism versus totalitarianism and democracy versus authoritarianism. Because from this follows, thirdly, that democracy, qua unrestricted majority rule, can turn out totalitarian and kill liberalism, while an authoritarian government can happily co-exist with liberalism, which for Hayek never was anything else than capitalism.[16]

This is where reality kicks in, the ultimate litmus test. Hayek's support of the Pinochet dictatorship in Chile, where Chicago-style economic neoliberalism was first tested in the mid-1970s, is well-known. Hayek visited Chile in this period several times. On one occasion, in 1981, he was asked about Pinochet, in an interview with *El Mercurio*, Chile's leading conservative newspaper. His answer was:

> Dictatorship may be a necessary system for a transitional period. At times it is necessary for a country to have, for a time, some form or other of dictatorial power. As you will understand, it is possible for a dictator to govern in a liberal way. And it is also possible for a democracy to govern with a total lack of liberalism. Personally, I prefer a liberal dictator to democratic government lacking liberalism.[17]

This famous statement should not surprise anyone. It is consistent with Hayek's considered views on democracy, as laid out above, minus the decorum. Later in the same interview, however, there is a statement that is rather striking:

> When a government is in a situation of rupture, and there are no recognized rules, rules have to be created in order to say what can be done and what

cannot. In such circumstances it is practically inevitable for someone to have almost absolute powers.[18]

In one paper, Hayek referred to Schmitt as "Adolf Hitler's 'crown jurist'" (1966, 609), a man of teleocratic rather than nomocratic order, taxis rather than cosmos, organization rather than spontaneous order; that is, the exact opposite type of animal from Hayek. But on that one occasion Hayek outed himself as a Schmittian, not just replicating Schmitt's trademark antagonism between liberalism and democracy, but moving into Schmitt's camp in the decisive moment, both endorsing the authoritarian, if not totalitarian state ("almost absolute"). "Sovereign is who decides about the exception (*Ausnahmezustand*)," Schmitt famously wrote in his *Politische Theologie* (1934 [1922], 11). In the "exception," Hayek—like most neoliberals—proved to be a partisan of "authoritarian liberalism." This is incidentally the label that Hermann Heller, leading Social Democratic jurist of the Weimar period, once attributed to no one else but Schmitt himself (although with a question mark). In an address to German industrialists in November 1932, Schmitt had spoken out for a strong and "authoritarian" state that alone could sever the "excessive" connections between state and economy, and accomplish the economy's liberalization (*Entstaatlichung*) (Heller 2015 [1933], 300).

Perhaps one should not make too much of these hidden communalities between the neoliberal Hayek and the anti-liberal Schmitt. Hayek and his fellow neoliberals' qualms about democracy are strongly rooted in their fear of majority power. This is a genetic liberal Leitmotif shared by Madison, Tocqueville, Mill, and others, but also one that makes them difficult to distinguish from conservatives. In a typical passage, Hayek warns: "If we proceeded on the assumption that only the exercises of freedom that the majority will practice are important, we would be certain to create a stagnant society with all the characteristics of unfreedom" (1960, 32). This echoes Burke, who dreaded the thought that "the mob should have liberty to govern us" (quoted by Robin 2008, 8). That "the rich pay all the taxes, and the poor shall make all the laws" (the nineteenth-century Lord Robert Cecil, quoted in Ziblatt 2017, 28) is the conservative's gut anxiety that is not foreign to the liberal mind. Accordingly, Hayek is often called a conservative liberal, and rightly so. In his postscript to the *Constitution of Liberty*, Hayek himself refused to be labeled "conservative": "I can have no sympathy with the anti-democratic strain of conservatism," and on that occasion he praised the "advantages of democracy as a method of peaceful change

46 POLITICAL NEOLIBERALISM

and of political education" (1960, 403). But the conclusion that Mirowski draws from Hayek's dubious double proximity to Schmitt and Pinochet, in my view, is the last word on the matter: "If freedom becomes confused with the neoliberal utopia, then power necessarily devolves to an elite of 'freedom fighters' wo can decide when to invoke the 'exception' to traditional mass notions of democracy, justice, and morality" (2009, 446).[19]

Excursus on Moral Traditionalism

The conservative side of Hayekian neoliberalism merits further attention because it goes deeper than shared political fears. It helps explain why, in the early 1980s, neoliberalism-on-earth was closely associated with conservative political parties and with nationalism—even though it wouldn't stay that way (which is why I call this section "excursus"). In her second work on neoliberalism, Wendy Brown (2019, ch.3) demonstrates that "moral traditionalism" is a constitutive element of Hayek's thinking, as well as— to a degree at least—of neoliberalism in practice. As she aptly summarizes Hayek's position, "markets and morals . . . are rooted in a common ontology of spontaneously evolved orders borne by tradition" (ibid., 96). Already markets, as "spontaneous order," are a form of tradition. Like all evolved orders, they are not intended or designed. They are neither rational nor irrational, but qua tradition occupying a space that Hayek called "between interest and reason" (1989, ch.1). Like language, people have created markets without knowing it. Hayek quotes the seventeenth-century Italian philosopher Vico to bring out the logic: "*homo non intelligendo fit omnia*" (man became all he is without understanding it) (ibid., ch.5).

With respect to morality, Hayek has always been fond of aligning himself within the "antirationalist, evolutionary tradition" of David Hume, for whom "the rules of morality are not the conclusions of our reason" (1960, 63). When comparing the British "empirical and unsystematic tradition of liberty" with the French "speculative and rationalistic" school, the latter on the despised side of "political" as against "individual" liberty, Hayek praises the former for understanding that freedom requires tradition, in the form of "grown institutions, . . . customs and habits." Accordingly, "(a) successful free society will always in a large measure be a tradition-bound society" (ibid., 61). The "rules of conduct" underlying the rule of law derive from tradition. A key function of them is to secure "a person's right to dispose over a recognized private domain," which is the domain of family and "several property" (Hayek's strange word for private property, borrowed from H. S. Maine) (Hayek 1989, ch.2). Not all, but the most important of these rules are "moral rules." Moral rules are so important because they obviate coercion, ensuring conformity on a voluntary basis: "(F)reedom has never worked without deeply ingrained moral beliefs and . . . coercion can be reduced to a minimum only where individuals can be expected as a rule to conform voluntarily to certain principles" (1960, 62). As if from the pages of Talcott Parsons, Hayek holds that "the system of values into which we are born supplies the ends which our reason must serve" (ibid., 63). The "value framework" can never be remade "as a whole," but people must "work inside" it.

But what if this framework is not "beneficial" for all and leading a society not to bliss but to doom? This is where freedom kicks in. Only if people are "free to choose" (Hayek 1960, 67), "'impractical' ideals" can decline so that wrong turns become "self-corrective." But this requires that "freedom" is accepted as the "supreme principle," even if "the consequences in the particular instance will be (not) beneficial" (ibid., 68). Here again we encounter neoliberalism's trademark, the absolutizing of freedom and its cancelling out all other values. At the same time, freedom "did not arise from design" (ibid., 54), but is the result of "social evolution," the "selection by imitation of successful institutions and habits" (ibid., 59). What in the end meets the evolutionary test is a strange combination of freedom and traditional morality, the latter with family and property at its core. The confessed non-believer Hayek[20] closes his last work, *The Fatal Conceit* (1989), with a surprising celebration of religion as conduit of morality: "We owe it partly to mystical and religious beliefs . . . that beneficial traditions have been preserved and transmitted"; and "the only religions that have survived are those which support property and the family" (ibid., ch.9).

As it rests on "the role of traditions and the value of all the other products of unconscious growth proceeding throughout the ages" (1960, 61), Hayek's case for the "British tradition" of liberalism is nearly undistinguishable from conservatism. The conservative tilt gets stronger still through being peppered with unrelenting broadsides against the "French tradition," associated with Descartes, Condorcet, and Rousseau, whose "design theories" tried to "make the world anew," but ended in "'social' or totalitarian democracy" (ibid., 58).

48   POLITICAL NEOLIBERALISM

These broadsides evidently include yet another fiery attack on the concept of the "social," which for Hayek was a favorite of the French rationalists. Whenever the word "social" is used, as in "social good" or in "social conscience," it does two things, Hayek laments. First, it suggests an "explicit consideration of the particular consequences of the action in question" (1960, 65). It is an appeal that "individual intelligence, rather than rules evolved by society, should guide individual action" (ibid.). This is paradoxical because the social by definition "exceeds the capacity of the individual human mind." In effect, the social is "contempt for what *really* is a social phenomenon" (emphasis supplied), which is something that evolved without being intended; and it expresses "a belief in the superior powers of individual human reason" (ibid.). As Hayek points out in an earlier paper, this usage of social (that he detests) is the exact opposite of its original meaning, where it referred to the "unforeseen results of the haphazard activities of countless individuals and generations" (as in the notions of "social forces" or "social structures," with which he has no issue) (1967[1957], 241). Secondly, or perhaps the first in importance, the "social" carries the halo of "'moral' or simply 'good'" (ibid., 239). Whoever claims to speak "in the interest of society" or of the "majority," posits themself in a position of moral superiority.

These cognitive and moral elements of "social" constitute a kind of speaker's benefit: one can "claim to be endowed with a more profound insight or to possess a stronger sense of moral values," while rendering opponents as "anti-social" by definition (Hayek 1967[1957], 243). Further considering that reference to the "social" is a popular excuse to release oneself of "personal responsibility," Hayek's "open hostility" to things social is overdetermined (ibid., 245, 238).

Putting these elements together, Brown (2019, 108) gives a compelling description of the "Hayekian dream": "Installing markets and morality where society and democracy once were, through the principle of freedom from state regulation." Furthermore, Brown shows that this is not just a dream but, to a degree, descriptive of reality. Of course, "real-existing neoliberalism," in many respects, looks different from what Hayek imagined it to be. The state sucked out and dominated by plutocrats and traditional values being "weaponized" by the Christian Right, as is the situation in the United States today, is a far cry from Hayek's idyllic markets-cum-morality picture of a "successful free society" (1960, 61). On the other hand, what Brown is entirely silent about, and as I shall discuss later in this book (Chapter 3), the Third Way left embraced neoliberalism, pushing it in "progressive" directions.

But what Brown (2019) very convincingly shows is that recently "neoliberal" US Supreme Court jurisdiction *does* stand in for the Hayekian duality of protecting markets and morality, while opposing democratic legislation and with it (formally speaking) society's current majority preferences (as enshrined in statutory law). Concretely, the court has generously extended 1st Amendment free speech and religious free exercise rights to Evangelists and corporations, to the effect of "empower(ing) traditional gender and sexual norms against constraints by equality or antidiscrimination law" (ibid., 124). Indeed, a major target of these court rules are so-called SOGI laws that have added "sexual orientation" (SO) and "gender identity" (GI) to existing antidiscrimination statutes in some progressive US states. Brown documents an astounding expansion of legal techniques, such as granting corporations free speech rights, designating cakes, money, ads, and other items as "speech," and holding certain democratic laws and social practices as "controversial" for those with "deeply held beliefs." All these techniques have the Hayekian effect of "replacing democratically governed society with one organized by markets and traditional morality, under the sign of freedom" (ibid., 125). To repeat, this is not the entire face of neoliberalism-in-practice (that has rather turned more leftist over time). But it is a legal reality nevertheless, at least in the contemporary United States.

Weakening Functional Separations

A final element of neoliberalism, which clearly sets it apart from liberalism, is to weaken rather than to strengthen functional separations. From their first meeting on a Swiss mountain top, the neoliberals never had anything less in mind than "(remaking) the entire fabric of society" (Mirowski 2009, 431). As Hayek pronounced the grand ambition of the Mont Pèlerin Society at their first meeting in April 1947, "what to the politicians are fixed limits of practicability imposed by public opinion must not be similar limits to us. Public opinion on these matters is the work of men like ourselves . . . who have created the political climate in which the politicians of our time must move" (ibid., 431–432). Ever since the creed was crafted in sectarian insulation in the early postwar years, it wasn't meant to be narrowly economic but a comprehensive ideology to change the world in the image of the market. Brown (2015, 176) is thus faithful to the creed when describing neoliberalism as not simply an "economic policy" but "a governing rationality that disseminates

50 POLITICAL NEOLIBERALISM

market values and metrics to every sphere of life and construes the human itself exclusively as *homo economicus*."

Foucault, in his 1978 Collège de France lectures on the *Birth of Biopolitics* (2008), was the first to have seen this, in an extraordinary feast of foresight, because at that moment the neoliberal "ideas" were still "lying around" and waiting to be picked-up. Foucault distinguishes in these lectures between the German Ordoliberals and the "much more radical" American Anarcho-Liberals, above all Gary Becker and his "human capital" idea (ibid., 243). The Ordoliberals had made "competition" the "principle of order in the domain of the market economy," as Foucault quotes one of their main figures, Röpke (ibid., 242f). This was a fundamental departure from classic economic liberalism, whose main principle had been not competition but "exchange." Exchange was premised on and reinforced equality. By contrast, competition takes inequality not just to be inevitable outcome of market processes, but as one of the "strongest motor forces for progress" (Mirowski 2009, 438). Brown called the turn from exchange to competition a "tectonic shift" because "inequality becomes legitimate, even normative, in every sphere" (2015, 64). As Mirowski projects this turn into the present, "(t)he vast worldwide trend toward concentration of incomes and wealth since the 1990s is therefore the playing out of a neoliberal script" (2009, 438).

However, the Ordoliberals shrank back from "erect(ing) the whole of society" on the basis of competition, as the latter "dissolves more than it unifies"; for them, there needed to be a compensating "political and moral framework" to ensure "a community which is not fragmented" (Röpke, quoted by Foucault 2008, 243). The radicalism of American neoliberalism was exactly not to know such scruples and to ram the principle of competition all the way through, thus "generalizing (the economic form of the market) throughout the social body" (ibid.). Chicago economist Becker's theory of human capital provided a "strictly economic interpretation of a whole domain previously thought to be non-economic" (ibid., 219). It depicts the human being as "homo oeconomicus," who is not just "entrepreneur" but "an entrepreneur of himself," as Foucault famously specifies (ibid., 226). No personal or social domain was to be exempt from an economic lens: mating, parenting, educating, caregiving, all sorts of "non-rational conduct," even criminality and the law to restrain the latter (ibid., 268–269). As Richard Posner, leading theorist of the Chicago Law and Economics school and member of the Mont Pèlerin Society, explicates the "function of criminal sanction in a capitalist market economy": it is "to prevent individuals from bypassing the efficient market." And he added that it was "designed primarily for the nonaffluent," because the "affluent" were sufficiently kept in check by pecuniary "tort law" (in Mirowski 2013, 66).

Against liberalism's "art of separation" (Walzer 1984), neoliberalism allows the market and its competition logic to roam freely. "Market fundamentalism" is the right label for this (Block and Somers 2014). "There is no separate sphere of the market, fenced off, as it were, from the sphere of civil society," Mirowski argues, "Everything is fair game for marketization" (2009, 437), from the state down to the individual.[21] If classical liberals had conceived of the state as correcting the dysfunctions of laissez-faire, neoliberals hold that "the market ... can always provide solutions to problems seemingly caused by the market" (ibid., 439)—a contemporary example being markets for trading the right to emit pollutants. The result of economizing everything is "everyday neoliberalism" (ibid., ch.3). So deep has "neoliberalism as worldview ... sunk its roots into everyday life," down to the individual and her strategic "likes"-maximizing presentation of self on Facebook and other social media, that neoliberalism passes as "ideology of no ideology" (ibid., 28). The high-browed's rejection of the label as so yesteryear may be the exact proof of its pervasiveness.

Conclusion

While neoliberalism shares certain tenets of classic liberalism, it departs from it sharply with respect to an absolutized and elitist conception of freedom, a strict rejection of material equality and social justice, an antagonistic relationship to democracy and society at large, and its propensity to be separation-destroying rather than separation-enforcing.[22] We discussed these trends along the work of Hayek. This raises two questions: how representative it is, but also why ideas matter in the first. In his lectures on neoliberalism, Foucault (2008) covers Hayek only peripherally, while acknowledging his pivotal role of "linking" the European and American strands of neoliberalism (see Brown 2015, 59). Mirowski's authoritative account of the "Neoliberal Thought Collective" lists Hayek as its central figure (2009, 2013). From the first meeting of the Mont Pèlerin Society in 1947 onward, whose opening address was given by Hayek and whose first president he was, Hayek has been the neoliberal movement's central and integrating figure. He also stood out through his command of a wider

52 POLITICAL NEOLIBERALISM

array of disciplines than mastered by most other members of the club: law, economics, philosophy, political science, and several more.

Quite another question is the import of neoliberal ideas for real-existing neoliberalism, which is the topic of the following two chapters. The Marxist historian Perry Anderson (2000, 17) called neoliberalism "the most successful ideology in world history," which seems only mildly exaggerated. One of the movement's most erudite chroniclers took it to be a "thorough re-education effort for *all parties* to alter the tenor and meaning of political life: nothing more, nothing less" (Mirowski 2009, 431).

Mirowski (2009, 444f) noticed a further important feature of the neoliberals assembled in and around the Mont Pèlerin Society, which is their proclivity for "double truth":

> An elite would be tutored to understand the deliciously transgressive Schmitttian necessity of repressing democracy, while the masses would be regaled with ripping tales of "rolling back the nanny state" and being set "free to choose"—by convening a closed Leninist organization of counter-intellectuals.

Indeed, a peculiar contradiction in Hayek's thinking is to preach the charms of spontaneous order (*cosmos*) and to stress the limitations of individual knowledge, while plotting a strategy to save the world (via *taxis*) and arrogating to itself the capacity to theorize about society as a whole, providing a kind of theory to end all theories.

By the late 1950s, the neoliberals dropped the "neo," and to the outside world, they claimed to be nothing but "liberals" in the Smith tradition (Mirowski 2013, 29). Inside, however, judged by the secretive ways of the handpicked Mont Pèlerin Society, they continued to be a small and closed elite, self-conscious of a world-changing mission, its reach ever widening. That the "neo" attached to "liberalism" is so controversial today and tends to be rejected as tendentious, among learned folks in particular, gives a glimpse of their extraordinary real-world successes.

I
ORDER

Chapter 2
End of the Liberal-Democratic Synthesis

An Inventory

Wolfgang Streeck (2022) quipped that Margaret Thatcher, who was the first to implement neoliberalism in a liberal democracy, was a "much underrated social theorist." He meant her dictum, pronounced in an interview, that "There is no such thing (as society)! There are individual men and women and there are families and no government can do anything except through people and people look to themselves first."[1] Not mentioned by Streeck, but equally important, is her second, or rather first, neoliberal dictum, this one repeated on several occasions: "There is no alternative." Also known under the acronym TINA, it signals the Iron Lady's defense of a Hayekian market economy, unfettered by state constraints. In their combination, the two dicta fully encompass the neoliberal phenomenon, its sociology as much as its political science. The rest are academic footnotes.

"There is no such thing" is the sociology part. It flags the disappearance of society and the thinning of collective responsibilities under a neoliberal regime. One can loudly hear Friedrich Hayek's aversion to all things social, from "society," that "weasel word," to "social justice" (see Chapter 1). No longer should people be able to say, "I have a problem, it is the Government's job to cope with it!," as Thatcher further explicated her famous notion.[2] Importantly, Thatcher mentions not just one but two types of surrogate actor for the demoted state, "individual men and women" *and* "families," at least a nuclear form of society. As any wise theorist, she remains vague about her master concepts, leaving the filling-in to the herd of scribblers. But she seems to suggest the possibility of opposite political actors and projects to assemble under one broad neoliberal tent. As we know in retrospect, the focus on the individual is easily broadened into individuality, and it accordingly has attracted not only market libertarians but also left liberationists.[3] The family, of course, is dear to a conservative agenda, initially pushed by Thatcher herself and by her American complement, Ronald Reagan. But, as Melinda

---

Political Neoliberalism. Christian Joppke, Oxford University Press. © Oxford University Press (2025).
DOI: 10.1093/oso/9780197801918.003.0003

Cooper (2017) has surprisingly demonstrated, it has been effortlessly carried on by their "Third Way" leftist successors. The unifying factor between the neoliberal right and left is the doctrine of personal responsibility, on which all have come to agree, and which can be found not only in politics and public policy (above all, social policy) but also in philosophy (as luck egalitarianism) and in the social sciences (as the return of agency) (see the excellent overview by Mounk 2017, ch. 1). Personal responsibility, aptly described by Yascha Mounk (ibid., 1) as "breezing common sense and a barely concealed threat," is the doxa of neoliberal societies. It opens up a broadened understanding of neoliberalism as not just political economy doctrine but individual- and society-shaping rationale, which was again brought to the point by Thatcher as a social theorist: "Economics are the method; the object is to change the heart and soul."[4]

TINA is the political science part of neoliberalism. It is especially relevant for the task of this chapter and the following chapter, to map the institutional[5] forms of neoliberalism, synchronically and over time, respectively. Empirically, liberalism morphed into neoliberalism when there was no longer a serious alternative to it. The collapse of communism is the decisive moment in Gary Gerstle's story of the rise of the "neoliberal order" in the United States, because it "removed what remained . . . of the imperative for class compromise" (2022, 137). TINA also helps explain the populist discontent raised against this order. In their soul-searching review of "today's worldwide anti-liberal revolt," Ivan Krastev and Stephen Holmes (2019) found the "absence of alternatives" to liberalism, its being alone in the world after the demise of the communist alternative, as the heart of the malaise.[6] In post-communist societies, "this absence of alternatives, . . . even more than the gravitational pull of an authoritarian past or historically ingrained hostility to liberalism, best explains the anti-Western ethos dominating . . . today" (ibid., 5). At first, the Easterners imitated the West. But conversion fatigue and "being looked down up for the supposed inadequacy of the attempt" (ibid., 12) made them drift to nationalist and resentment-laden shores. And in the West, liberalism, while at least indigenous, has become "complacent" after 1989. Liberalism is "not the winning ideology," argues Michael Freeden (2008,14) against Francis Fukuyama's (1992) more optimistic view, but it "needs constantly to struggle against opposing ideologies." As Krastev and Holmes note with irony, "liberal theory would have predicted . . . that monopoly suppliers, freed from competitive pressures, begin to behave wastefully" (2019, 152). The reader is free to put content into "behaving wastefully." But income and wealth stagnation and a dimming future for the bottom 90 percent of society, counterpointed by gargantuan wealth concentration at the very top—not even the top ten but the top 1 percent—is an obvious candidate.

This is the story of the most influential social science work of the past half-century (Piketty 2014). And it is graphically depicted on Branko Milanovic's (2016) famous Elephant Curve, which shows changes in the global income distribution over the past thirty years, the period of globalization-cum-neoliberalization. Liberalism, alone post-1989, is in reality "Capitalism, Alone" (Milanovic 2019), and its result in the West has been a "self-perpetuating upper class and polarization between the elites and the rest" (ibid., 11). As the Chinese "alternative" fails to catch fire in the West, there is no real alternative here to "hypercommercialized capitalism." In Milanovic's dystopian view, this capitalism even "does away with alienation": "(W)hen economic agency is within ourselves, the order of things is internalized in such a way that there is nothing jarring anymore" (ibid., 193). This would be a world of TINA 2.0, where opposition not only has a harder time, but where it has become unthinkable.

Against this bleakest of scenarios, it is worth recalling that the early TINA days were optimistic, even euphoric. When communism collapsed, Fukuyama (1992) famously found that we had reached the "end of history." Now there was no serious competitor to the "ideal of liberal democracy" as political organizing principle of advanced societies (ibid., xi). In a condition of generalized "peace and prosperity," the residual problem would be "boredom" (ibid., 330), perhaps, at worst a Nietzschean "nihilistic war against liberal democracy" (ibid., 332). The suffix "neo" is notably absent from Fukuyama's description of liberalism at that time; there was simply "economic liberalism" (i.e., capitalism), which now was without rival and would provide the "prosperity" that is necessary for liberal democracy to prosper. Thirty years on, pace Milanovic, the "discontents" of liberalism have become epidemic and the typical regime change is not from authoritarian to democratic but in the reverse direction (Fukuyama 2020, 2022). Fukuyama now concedes that the rise of "neoliberal" economics is a major source of the problem, bringing about unprecedented levels of inequality and middle-class decay in the West (already noticed by him in 2014, ch. 30).

When, in 1992, Fukuyama pronounced the "ideal of liberal democracy" as without competition, he overlooked that the liberal-democratic synthesis was already in the third decade of being battered in its Western heartland,

58 POLITICAL NEOLIBERALISM

at that moment less by the political right than in the subtler form of Third Way leftism, from the New Democrats in the United States to New Labour in the United Kingdom (see Chapter 3).

Before elaborating on this development, it is helpful to have a second look at the liberal-democratic synthesis itself. Judith Shklar (1989), we noted in Chapter 1, called liberal democracy a "marriage of convenience," which points to the ambiguity of this synthesis. Having treated the friendlier "marriage" factor in the previous chapter, it is apposite to also throw light on the less comforting "convenience" factor. From a radical perspective, the democracy-part of liberal democracy has *always* been a diluted version of the real thing. But then the transition from liberal to neoliberal is small and unsurprising: "Liberal democracy has provided a depoliticized framework that nurtures neoliberalism, while providing it with a cloak of legitimacy" (Vázquez-Arroyo 2008, 127). Similarly, Roberto Unger thinks that liberal democracy is "relative democracy: democracy but not too much" (quoted in ibid., 130), democracy robbed of its egalitarian and participatory dimension.

We noticed this when discussing Joseph Schumpeter's and the American Federalists' theorizing and implementing, respectively, of the elite kind of democracy that has become associated with "liberal." But the charge that democracy's dilution is not only unintended outcome but intentional input factor in "liberal democracy," needs further attention. Because then, indeed, the transition to neoliberalism is less of a departure from liberalism than one might think. Even in John Rawls's liberalism, we find a "reduction of democracy" (Vázquez-Arroyo 2008, 149), despite his advocacy for redistribution, which distinguishes Rawls's liberalism from that of the neoliberals. Rawls favors "constitutional democracy," with legally curtailed majority powers. The reasoning of the Supreme Court, he writes in *Political Liberalism* (1992, 231), is "the exemplar of public reason," which is his favored mind-set for the conducting of democratic affairs. Sheldon Wolin (1996, 100) calls Rawlsian democracy "guardian democracy," which echoes the anti-majoritarian views of the Federalist Papers, and whose participatory element is reduced to the act of voting. In an even nastier note, Wolin dismisses Rawlsian justice as "constitutional equality tempered by *richesse oblige*," worse still, as "lobotomiz(ing) the historical grievances of the desperate." These grievances, so states Wolin, disappear behind the aseptic "veil of ignorance" from where the Rawlsian justice principles are construed (ibid., 112, 106).

In a nutshell, for its radical critics, liberal democracy falls short of "substantive democracy," where "ordinary people actively participate in power" (Vázquez-Arroyo 2008, 156). However, one must ask, did such democracy ever exist? This is not to deny that the *fear* of ordinary people is very much present in classical liberalism, which provides a direct link to its neoliberal succession. As Eric Hobsbawm pointed out in his *Age of Revolution* (1962), the early eighteenth-century liberal was no defender of democracy but a constitutionalist and advocate of government by tax- and property-owners only. "Liberalism with an aristocratic cast" is a fair description of classic liberals from Benjamin Constant to Alexis de Tocqueville, even John Stuart Mill (Vázquez-Arroyo 2008, 145). As we noted earlier, Hayek is in direct continuation of this line. But he is also in the surprising company of Carl Schmitt, as I shall further elaborate below. And this is where the liberal line is crossed.

In this chapter, I discuss six political forms of neoliberalism, from the point of view of order. We begin with the oldest, most austere, recurrent, and perhaps genetically inscribed political form of neoliberalism, which is *authoritarianism*. And we continue with neoliberalism's newest and diametrically opposed political form, which is *governance*, meant to bring back a modicum of democracy, deceptively as we shall see. *Technocracy* provides much of the content and guiding principles of governance, which likes to fashion itself as rational problem-solving, beyond the right-left distinction. *Federation* and *constitutionalism* are closely allied favorites on the legal design board of the Geneva School of "Globalists" (Slobodian 2018), but they are also conjoined in the real world, as I illustrate with a look at the European Union, the model case of a neoliberal polity. We close with a discussion of *meritocracy*, which was rejected by Hayek at the theoretical plane but has become neoliberal society's central legitimizing formula.

Authoritarianism

Authoritarian Liberalism

If we push the Hayek–Schmitt communalities, already mentioned in Chapter 1, a bit further, we arrive at "authoritarianism" as the first and crudest institutional form of neoliberalism. In Renato Christi's (1984, 1998) unconventional interpretation, Schmitt was not so much anti-liberal

60 POLITICAL NEOLIBERALISM

as anti-democrat, articulating an "authoritarian liberalism" (Heller 2015 [1933]) that is very similar to Hayek's, *both* of them embracing a deep anti-democratic strand in the liberal tradition.[7] Classic liberalism, to remember, had favored a strict distinction between civil society and state, which was the object of Karl Marx's ire in his *Jewish Question*. While the state-part of the state–society relationship is usually filled with citizenship, as in Marx's critique, this isn't necessarily so, not even for classic liberals. Constant, for instance, favored constitutional monarchy, which suggests that people are subjects rather than citizens, at least in the political realm. This may be seen as an early instance of authoritarian liberalism. Indeed, authoritarian liberalism's most succinct formulation, in past and present, is by Constant: "The government outside its sphere must not have any power; in its sphere, it cannot have enough of it" (quoted in Christi 1984, 526). An early review of the "political thought of neo-liberalism," by Carl Friedrich (1955, 513), noted that the "neo-liberals" were"fond of quoting" this strident Constant passage.[8] This demonstrated to Friedrich the neoliberals' preference for a "strong state": "To maintain the primacy of the political (the neo-liberals) want the state to be strong so that it can assert its authority via-à-vis the interest groups that press upon the government and clamor for recognition of their particular needs and wants" (ibid., 512).

But this was exactly the position of Schmitt in late Weimar. He disliked its "pluralist party state" (see Scheuerman 1997, 174), with the combination of politicized civil society and a state weakened in its autonomy by being in the grip of competing interest groups. Of course, this was the price to pay for the "historic compromise between liberalism and democracy" (Christi 1984, 526), first tried though quickly aborted in Weimar, and coming to full fruition only in the post-World War II era. The way out of the "quantitative total state," as Schmitt called the Weimar quagmire of a state seized by the struggling masses and seeking to intervene everywhere, was a "qualitative total state." Its sole purpose was to protect the autonomy of private capital, which was the one part of liberalism to which Schmitt was fully committed (see Scheuerman 1997, 176).[9] This state was possible under the Weimar constitution, argued Schmitt, in the figure of the elected *Reichspräsident*, who would rise above civil society and become unaccountable to it, a "plebiscitary dictator" expressing the unity of the people: "(T)he election of the *Reichspräsident* . . . is more than any ordinary democratic election. It is the grandiose acclamation of the German people" (Schmitt, quoted in Christi 1984, 528).[10]

Hayek did not go quite so far. But he shares Schmitt's categorical state versus civil society distinction, which is the easy because liberal part. More delicately, Hayek also shares Schmitt's distaste for the destruction of this distinction in the "pluralist party state." Hayek affirmatively quotes this pejorative notion, now referring to its author (without naming him) as that "extraordinary German student of politics" (Hayek 1982c, 194–195). Minted by Schmitt for Weimar, the epithet "pluralist party state" supported Hayek's critique of the "weakness" of the 1970s' "government of an omnipotent democracy" that must "satisfy the demands of all interested parties" (the last part is again Schmitt's phrase, quoted affirmatively by Hayek).

Hayek's way out of the conundrum was not dictatorship, as for Schmitt, but the "dethronement of politics" in a castrated democracy. To get there, Hayek proposed the curious model of a small upper house of mature-to-elderly representatives (between forty-five and sixty years of age), elected one time for fifteen years, by an equally one-time electorate of the same age bracket. This upper house would have the narrow mandate of passing "general rules," never specific laws that would draw government into the mud of clientelism. The chamber's limitations in terms of composition and scope should guarantee "probity, wisdom, and judgment" (Hayek 1982c, 112) and insulate the little legislating that was necessary from special interest politics. In effect, these limitations meant protecting *Besitz und Bildung* (property and education), a favorite notion of Hayek (Scheuermann 1997, 183). William Scheuerman ridiculed this strange arrangement as "rule by a narrow group of citizens with substantial gray hair but a rather insubstantial democratic base" (ibid., 188).

Authoritarianism, whether openly embraced (Schmitt) or hidden behind a perfunctory democracy façade (Hayek), is the first and foremost institutional form of neoliberalism. This is because authoritarianism is the straightest avenue for reining-in democracy, which is the signature—intended or unintended—of *all* institutional forms of neoliberalism.

Its intimate connection to authoritarianism suggests that neoliberalism is more at ease with politics in its nuclear form than its liberal predecessor had ever been. This is particularly the case when looking at liberalism through a Schmittian lens, as dissolving the political in favor of "discussion" and "competition" (see Chapter 1). Stefano Bartolini, more Hobbesian than Schmittian, characterizes the essence of politics as "explicit intention to achieving compliance by others" (2018, 45). Applied to government, politics is thus understood to be about providing "physical security" to a "territorial

62 POLITICAL NEOLIBERALISM

group" (ibid., 106).[11] To make the point, Bartolini quotes Macbeth's "To be thus is nothing, But to be safely thus." In politics, "(h)ands are visible . . . and . . . often armed" (ibid., 1). Authoritarian rule comes closer to this description of politics than democratic rule, which is politics mellowed by other (in particular, ethical) considerations.

Post-Democracy

Juan Linz, in an extraordinary exercise of inductive theorizing, defined authoritarian regimes through the elements of "limited . . . political pluralism," the absence of an "elaborate and guiding ideology" but presence of a "distinct mentality," the lack of "extensive (or) intensive political mobilization," and a "leader or . . . a small group exercis(ing) power within formally ill-defined limits but actually quite predictable ones" (1975, 264). Linz uses only two of these elements—limited pluralism and political apathy (ibid., 179)—to arrive at a typology of authoritarian regimes, the most important of which is "bureaucratic-military." It would be absurd to claim that neoliberally thinned Western democracies have ever fallen into such a condition. It is more a metaphor for the primary *intention* of political neoliberalism, and for its preferred *mentality*. Democratic regimes, to use Linz's own succinct definition, are formally characterized by the "free formulation of political preferences, through the use of basic freedoms of association, information, and communication, for the purpose of free competition between leaders to validate at regular intervals by nonviolent means their claim to vote" (ibid., 182f). Linz thus recognizes the dependence of a democratic regime on liberal rights: "liberal political rights are a requirement for . . . competition for power" (ibid., 183). Importantly, this formal condition remains intact in the liberal-to-neoliberal transition.[12]

Having said that, some elements of Linz's description of authoritarian regimes eerily resemble what Colin Crouch (2004) has called "post-democracy," and by which Crouch meant the political condition of Western societies in the grip of neoliberalism. In post-democracy, "elected governments and elites . . . overwhelmingly . . . represent business interests," both sectors intimately related by "revolving doors," while they meet a "passive citizenry" (ibid., 4). There is an "atmosphere of cynicism about politics and politicians," while the "close control of their scope and power . . . suits the agenda of those wishing to rein back the active state" (ibid., 23). In post-democracy, "politics once again becomes an affair of closed elites, as it was in pre-democratic times" (ibid., 104). In a restatement of the post-democracy hypothesis, Crouch (2020) emphasizes that formal democracy stays intact while political pluralism atrophies: "(A)ll the forms of democracy continue, including ... the rule of law, but ... the electorate has become passive ... and not generating a civil society vibrant enough to produce awkward counter-lobbies that try to rival the quiet work of business interests in the corridors of government" (ibid., 39).

In institutional terms, the attenuation of pluralism that in effect (not in legal form) resembles authoritarianism, is brought about by political parties that have moved their location from civil society to the state. Richard Katz and Peter Mair (1995, 2009) called it the "cartelization" of political parties. It signifies a "double withdrawal": the withdrawal of political elites into the state; and the withdrawal of citizens, who abstain even from their minimal involvement in the political process, which is voting.[13] Citizens become passive observers of a political life that takes on the form of mediatized spectacle—"audience democracy," in the words of Benard Manin (1997, ch. 6). For a more sarcastic mind, post-democratic politics is "a combination of legal state (*Rechtsstaat*) and public entertainment" (Streeck 2013, 28). Whatever you call it, this is "a new form of democracy, one in which the citizens stay at home while the parties go on governing" (Mair 2013, 98).

The post-democratic condition, not in a legal-institutional sense but as public attitude and disposition, resembles the authoritarian condition described by Linz (1975). Note that Linz speaks of "mentality" rather than "ideology," when describing the ideational underpinnings of an authoritarian regime. It is "formless, fluctuating," "more emotional than rational," and marked by the "absence of an articulate ideology, of a sense of ultimate meaning, of long-run purposes, of an a priori model of ideal society" (ibid., 268f). This mentality leads to the "alienation of intellectuals, students, youth"—which would have to be extended to larger segments of the population in post-democracy. The other Linzian markers of authoritarianism—concentration of power in a "small group," the "depoliticization" and lack of political mobilization, and the narrowed range of political pluralism—also would be a fair description of post-democracy.

In neoliberal theory and practice, the authoritarian element has found its earliest and clearest expression in Ordoliberalism's advocacy of a "strong state" that was to accompany and guarantee a "free economy" (see Bonefeld 2016). Their main representatives, Walter Eucken, Alexander Rüstow,

64   POLITICAL NEOLIBERALISM

and Wilhelm Röpke, all agree on Schmitt's critique of democratic pluralism in late Weimar, espousing the "vision of a depluralized state" (Biebricher 2020, 10), of a state "above the interested parties" (Rüstow, in ibid.), to counteract the debilitating tendencies of mass democracy. While Hayek was reluctant to empower the state, his concession that liberalism might well coexist with authoritarianism (see Chapter 1), as well as his actual support for the military dictatorship in 1970s Chile and also Portugal's, show the same attachment to the strong state–free economy binary. This binary is not limited to a formally authoritarian regime; a major study of Thatcherism is appositely entitled *The Free Economy and the Strong State* (Gamble 1988).

Thomas Biebricher (2019) argues perceptively that the political theory of neoliberalism is caught in a performative self-contradiction: its picture of "rent-seeking" politicians in a democracy does not allow the possibility of neoliberal reform, such as balanced-budget amendments (as postulated by public choice theorist James Buchanan).[14] Accordingly, there is a need for "disruptors," of the populist-authoritarian kind, using "exceptionalist conditions" to accomplish the transition. Donald Trump—not a neoliberal but an expert in disruption—called the exercise "draining the swamp" (Biebricher 2020, 14). As Biebricher concludes, "neoliberal thought is more or less inadvertently driven toward an authoritarian politics capable of cutting through the institutional red tape that supposedly locks in the democratic status quo" (ibid., 15).

Not without hyperbole, but supported by numerous real-world examples, from the Pinochet coup in Chile to the post-communist transition in eastern Europe and the American Iraq war under George Bush Jr., Naomi Klein finds that the "power of shock" is the main mode for neoliberal "disaster capitalism" to operate. She describes it as "orchestrated raids on the public sphere in the wake of catastrophic events, combined with the treatment of disasters as exciting market opportunities" (2007, 6). In her "bleakonomic" view,[15] "shock therapy" is inflicted by a "corporatist state" in which "political and corporate elites have simply merged," with "huge transfers of public wealth to private hands, often accompanied by exploding debt, an ever-widening chasm between the dazzling rich and the disposable poor and an aggressive nationalism that justifies bottomless spending on security" (ibid., 15). Tellingly, Thatcher's Falkland Islands war was called "Operation Corporate" (ibid., 138), as if to express the fusion of genres. In the United States, the "disaster capitalism complex" reached its apex under President George Bush Jr. and his diabolic deputy, the war-industrialist Dick Cheney. They established "a full-fledged new economy in homeland security, privatized war and disaster reconstruction tasked with nothing less than building and running a privatized security state, both at home and abroad" (ibid., 299). Government in such conditions is "to act as conveyer belt for getting public money into private hands" (ibid., 355).

The Punitive Turn

Not limited to shock-like transition moments, of which the COVID-19 pandemic might serve as yet another example (see Chapter 6), a kind of everyday authoritarianism is "neoliberal penality" (Harcourt 2010, 2011). This is the propensity of contemporary states to respond to small infractions with the hard hand of penal law. It is a striking coincidence that the period from 1973, when "free market ideas and privatization flourished," has also been "a period of massive expansion of the carceral sphere." By 2008, no less than 1 percent of the adult US population had been put behind bars, which is by far the highest incarceration rate of all Western countries (Harcourt 2011, 42). As if from the notebook of Constant, Reagan concisely caught the connection between removing the state from "outside its sphere" and filling it in "in its sphere": "(R)emove (the state) from interfering in areas where it doesn't belong, but at the same time strengthen its ability to perform its constitutional and legitimate function . . . In the area of public order and law enforcement, for example, we're reversing a dangerous trend of the last decade" (ibid., 40).

Neoliberal penality is not limited to the United States. With "some lag and a lot of attenuation," it arrived in Western Europe. This meant that mental institutions were replaced by prisons, zero tolerance policies were to counteract the presumed spiral of small crime breeding bigger crime (the so-called broken windows theory), youth offenders were treated more harshly, and video surveillance and biometric data collection were systematized (Harcourt 2011, 225–231). Another element of the punitive turn is "actuarial" (risk assessment) methods of jailing likely offenders. This was "warmly embraced" in France in 2008 as *rétention de sûreté*, which is a precautionary detention after an offender, considered dangerous for the public, has served his prison term (Harcourt 2010, 75).

The combination of harsh punishment and free market is no neoliberal invention. Bernard Harcourt (2010) traces its origins to mid-eighteenth

66 POLITICAL NEOLIBERALISM

century liberal Physiocrats. François Quesnay had married a conception of the market as "natural order," which was to be kept free from government intervention, with "legal despotism" against "thieves and maligns" (*des voleurs et des méchants*) (ibid., 78). The recovery of this binary in neoliberal times, also in Chicago School Law and Economics,[16] has allowed the state to amass power in criminal matters while it "naturalizes" market outcomes and the huge inequalities generated by them (Harcourt 2011, 241).

A celebrated work in the sociology of crime control (Garland 2001) situates the post-1970 transition from "penal welfarism," which had aimed at the rehabilitation of the offender, to the "re-emergence of punitive sanctions and expressive justice" (ibid., 8), within a context of "late modernity." David Garland thus avoids the moniker "neoliberalism." But the parallels are plain to see. With a sharper sociological eye, Loïc Wacquant (2009, 4) identifies the root cause of the "punitive upsurge" in the "generalized social insecurity" under a neoliberal regime. Because a de facto "right to employment" can no longer be guaranteed in the economy, the "right to security" steps into its place, "to shore up the deficit of legitimacy suffered by political decision-makers" (ibid., 7). Moreover, the turn from a re-integrationist to a "prisonfare" approach in penal policy is the flipside of the turn from welfare to "workfare" in social policy, both being "integral components of the neoliberal Leviathan" (ibid., xviii), conjoining in their "authoritarian moralism" (ibid., 311).

There are three more important elements to the "punitive turn," as observed by Wacquant (2009):

- First, in the United States at least, it occurred in a period when crime was "stagnant," in the 1980s, or even "declining," in the 1990s (ibid., 125). Violent crime was never the primary target. Instead, from Reagan on, minor infractions, in particular drug dealing, were punished with greatly stiffened sentences, including life-long prison terms for repeat offenders (ibid., 125–127).
- Secondly, there is a sharply discrepant treatment of people at the top and at the bottom of the social order. In the United States's War on Drugs, for instance, lower-class crack possession is punished severely, while upper-class cocaine is met with lenience (see Gerstle 2022, 131). Such discrepant treatment is no neoliberal invention. But it is perhaps refined and optimized today like rarely before. Wacquant calls the neoliberal state "liberal-paternalist," which is small and big in tandem,

"liberal and permissive at the top" while "paternalist and authoritarian at the bottom" (2009, 8).[17] As we shall see in the next section, "governance," not mentioned by Wacquant but the preferred self-description of the neoliberal state and boosted by policy scholars as neoliberalism's central political invention, opens up an entirely different vista on this state, one that is more commensurate with its "liberal and permissive" top-end dealings.

- Thirdly, the punitive turn, along with its workfarist complement in social policy, may have started with the political right, as under Reagan in the United States, but it continued under the Third Way political left, as in the United States under Clinton. It is *pensée unique* in a neoliberal regime. "The root cause of the punitive turn is not late modernity," as Wacquant (ibid., 302–303) objects to Garland (2001), "but neoliberalism, a project that can be indifferently embraced by politics of the Right or the Left."

The Real Thing

Having spotted authoritarian trends in formally democratic regimes, it should not be surprising that neoliberalism thrives in authoritarian regimes *stricto sensu*. Examples are Singapore, which is selling itself as a meritocratic "talent capital," and the oil states of the Middle East, above all the United Arab Emirates. As Gulf autocrats worry about a post-petrol future, they have embarked on a campaign of entrepreneurial "citizen-making" to beat the passive "rentier mentality" of their spoiled non-working youth, with "the boys . . . focused on fast cars and high salaries, the girls on going to the mall and buying luxury goods" (Jones 2017, 47). Calvert Jones describes the United Arab Emirates's "neoliberal citizenship ideal" (ibid., 114) as "love of country by making choices that align with this ideal, such as starting business, seeking private sector work, taking on volunteer work." The sheiks have tried to inculcate this ideal through a combination of "education reform, public symbolism, spectacle" (ibid., 3). One element of it is hiring highly paid Western educators to train the Gulf youth in math and science (preferably in English), curiously even introducing the latter to Oxbridge "critical thinking" (ibid., 91). Interestingly, what in Western societies is mainly associated with "neoliberal structural changes": cutting public-sector jobs and salaries and reducing social benefits, is considered "too risky" and anathema

68 POLITICAL NEOLIBERALISM

in Gulf autocracies. Instead, "softer" social engineering is preferred, working through "hearts and minds" (ibid., 19), "encouraging and teaching citizens to be entrepreneurial rather than forcing them" (ibid., 3).

Have the Gulf sheikhs been successful? Not really. Jones (2017) describes the outcome as "entitled patriots." They show "love of country" but continue to be risk-averse and "preoccupied with status" and display a strong sense of "deservingness" (ibid., 183, 184). At least the sheikhs need not fear that their "making of citizens, 2.0" (ibid., 196) is breeding democratic leanings that could endanger autocratic rule. "For that, the people would have to get out of their (air-conditioned) cars," joked one sheikh (Jones 2015, 33).

Governance

The relationship between neoliberalism and the state is "inherently unstable" (Harvey 2005, 81) because neoliberalism simultaneously requires and refutes the state. The crudest expression of the "require" part is authoritarianism. But the latter, I suggested, is better seen as a metaphor for post-democratic rule than a concise institutional description. For the "refute" part, political scientists prefer to speak of "governance." Wendy Brown (2015, 14) sees it as nothing less than neoliberalism's "primary administrative form."

The notion of authoritarianism, from Hermann Heller (2015 [1933]) on, has been a polemic against a (neo)liberalism that requires the state yet repudiates its democratic form. By contrast, governance is at heart an apology of a neoliberalism that refutes, or at least relativizes the state, while claiming to make the polity "more democratic," by "(b)ringing different interests together" (Stoker 2019, 4). In reality, as Gary Stoker admits, governance means "profits before people," "dodgy deals," and "only the few benefit" (ibid., 13). While they offer radically opposite pictures of the neoliberal state, authoritarianism and governance convene in neutralizing democracy, the first with a bang and the second with a whimper.

The point of governance is to decenter the state, and to suggest that actors other than the state are increasingly part of public policy making. Governance is reflex of the "neoliberal reforms of the public sector," as a result of which there is a "shift from a hierarchic bureaucracy towards a greater use of markets, quasi-markets and networks, especially in the delivery of public services" (Bevir 2011, 459). Whereas govern*ment* connotes hierarchy and rule by command, governance connotes networks and rule by consensus. The old world of government was one of "power, conflict, or opposition"; the new world of governance is one of "dialogue, inclusion, and consensus" (Brown 2015, 130).

But the semblance of democracy, which is the selling-point of governance, is deceptive. In reality, the arrival of governance marks the rupture of the twentieth-century nexus between society and state, which had consisted of social cleavages (especially class) being mobilized by modern "mass politics" (Flora 1999). Political life now becomes self-referential and less an expression of group conflict and cleavages. Governance is more in the idiom of problem-solving than of interest mediation, its ethos is technocratic not democratic (to be discussed later in this chapter). In Brown's critical description, "public life is reduced to problem-solving and program implementation, a casting that brackets or eliminates politics" (2015, 127). The key protagonists are no longer "classes," whose power consisted of the possibility to obstruct through their large membership, but "stakeholders," whose power is more intangible and individualized, in the form of knowledge and information (ibid., 129; also Esmark 2020, 134). The thrust of governance, one could say, is to depoliticize politics. While this may be "the oldest task in politics" (Jacques Rancière, in Flinders and Wood 2014, 4), it is still a paradox.

A classic paper by R. A. W. Rhodes (1996) aptly described governance as "governing without government." It distinguishes between six different "uses" of governance. Let me discuss them here less by their different functions, as Rhodes does, than as elements or features of the same phenomenon.

First, governance denotes a "minimal state" that realizes the neoliberal agenda of privatizing public assets, spending cuts, civil service reduction, and regulation becoming the preferred form of public intervention, favorably by non-majoritarian expert bodies.

Secondly, and significantly, before it became applied to public bodies, governance was "corporate governance" in the private sector. The private-to-public move of governance epitomizes the economization-of-everything logic of neoliberalism, the first and foremost candidate for which has been the state. As governance transits from private to public, "a more commercial style of management" replaces the "traditional public service 'ethos,' and its values of disinterested service and openness."[18] At the theoretical plane, transaction cost economics considers firms (or hierarchies) and markets as "alternative modes of governance," whose "allocation of activity . . .

is not taken as given but is something to be derived" (Williamson 1996, 7). Crucially, the direction in which the "activity" goes is determined only by efficiency and cost–benefit calculation. Efficiency thus becomes the master of the state as well, cancelling out other values, such as equality and justice.[19] This is at great cost to institutions like schools or hospitals, whose primary function clearly is not to produce a profit.

Appearing first at the firm level, governance replaced the old model of "ethical managerialism" (Chamayou 2019). Under the old model, which peaked in the 1950s, the modern corporation was a "state-like entity" (Walter Rathenau, in ibid., 59). Managers understood themselves as "trustees" of a multitude of social groups (ibid., 64), including their employees and the larger community. In the United States, the "Treaty of Detroit," in which firm-level health and retirement benefits, life-long employment, and above all wages climbing with productivity were traded against labor peace, had made General Motors, and the large corporation in general, the welfare state that the political state never was (Krugman 1999, 138).

For Adolph Berle and Gardiner Means (1932), the key feature of the "modern corporation" is the separation between property and control, as a result of which managers no longer have the same interests as shareholders. This opened up the possibility of an alliance between the "managerial classes" and the "popular classes," which, in one account, was the fundament of the post-World War II "social democratic compromise" that came to be undone by neoliberalism (Duménil and Lévy 2011, 17). At the firm level, neoliberalism meant disciplining managers by remunerating them through bonuses and share options, thus shifting their allegiance from the "popular" to the "capitalist classes" (ibid., 19). The principal-agent problem arising from the separation between ownership and control was resolved by obliging the firm and its management to "shareholder-value" as singular goal.[20] For Grégoire Chamayou (2019, ch. 8), "governance" is identical to the new rein of "shareholder-value." Echoing Rhodes's (1996) language for state-level governance, Chamayou calls the firm-level original "governing without government," in which deregulated financial markets do the government part by making underperformers vulnerable to hostile takeovers. The identical language used for both types of governing points to an ominous inversion: if industrial companies in the age of "ethical managerialism" had borrowed their models of bureaucracy and quasi-welfarist employee relations from government and even the military, today's "market-" or "vendor-states," which are no longer in military conflict but in economic competition with one another,[21] have come to "look more like shareholder-oriented corporations" (Davis 2009, 177).

Public governance's origins in corporate governance is blatantly visible in New Public Management (NPM), which is the third entry in Rhodes's (1996) list of the "uses" of governance. NPM is private-sector methods branching out to the public sector: explicit standards of performance, which is constantly monitored; value for money; and satisfying customers' interests (ibid., 655). Importantly, citizens, the constituent power of the state, are demoted in NPM to "customers"; that is, consumers, whose choices and welfare are allegedly enlarged and maximized, respectively. NPM also means introducing incentive structures into public service provision, which is contracted-out to private providers through competitive tenders. The lead metaphor is "steering" versus "rowing." Governance is to reduce the role of the state to "steering," while "rowing" (i.e., actual service provision) is farmed out to the market. Steering, not rowing, is *ipso facto* more governance and less government.

While "competition and markets" is the leitmotif of NPM, as of governance in general (Rhodes 1996, 661), the reality is quite different. Crouch shows, for the United Kingdom, that "usually only a small number of firms is involved in the sub-contracting ... There is therefore no true market here, just a series of deals between public officials and corporate representatives" (2013, 9). This means that service recipients are not truly "customers," which involves the possibility of choice, but merely "users." Moreover, against the rhetoric that "private firms bring more expertise," the same firms tend to operate across sectors, which throws their "expertise" into doubt. In the United Kingdom, for instance, a firm called Serco has procured state contracts in the domains of transport, prisons, and security, and for the management of research centers, leisure centers, defense, and schools. Its sole expertise, Crouch dryly notes, "lies in knowing how to win governments contracts" rather than "in the substantive knowledge of the services" that it provides (ibid., 10).[22] NPM illustrates Crouch's larger point that "(a)ctually existing political neoliberalism, as opposed to the models of economics textbooks, is about enhancing the power of great corporations and wealthy individuals" (ibid., 8).

A fourth feature of governance is to be wrapped in the ethical cloth of "good governance." The World Bank, for instance, has long tied its development loans to Third World countries to the "good governance" moniker (Rhodes 1996, 656), and it was followed in this by the International

72   POLITICAL NEOLIBERALISM

Monetary Fund (IMF). While "good" connotes ethics, in effect it implies that governance is intrinsically a competitive thing, in line with the contemporary "quantification of the social" and its ubiquitous rankings and ratings (Mau 2017). Governance is steeped in the rhetoric of benchmarking and best practices. Some states do it better than others, and in the absence of hard law it is the moral force of shame and pride that furthers the cause of "good governance." In the European Union, it held entry with the Open Method of Coordination (OMC). Introduced as part of the Lisbon Strategy (2000), OMC uses inter-governmental "peer pressure" with respect to "best practices"[23] in domains that fall outside the European Union's economic core competences, such as social policy, as substitute for the supra-national "community method" on which the member states have long cooled in this respect: "By entering into a system of open coordination, member states, their bureaucracies, their agencies and civil servants, have also subjected themselves to the surveillance, scrutiny and evaluation of others in new domains, with a view to arriving at certain common objectives" (Haahr 2004, 220).

A fifth feature of governance is to operate as a "socio-cybernetic system" (Rhodes 1996, 656–658). The idea is that order is achieved not through a sovereign center but through the negotiations of the involved actors. This resonates with Hayek's idea of spontaneous order (see Chapter 1). Because no single actor can claim to have all the relevant knowledge to make a policy work, all actors "need one another" (Rhodes 1996, 657). This also resonates with Niklas Luhmann's picture of a functionally differentiated society that has neither "peak" nor "center" (1986, 167–168). If you apply this picture to the state, you arrive at the idea of governance.

Closely connected to a cybernetic is a sixth and final understanding of governance, as "self-organizing networks" (Rhodes 1996, 658–659). In fact, network is perhaps the first and key category for understanding governance, which is often connected to the vision of a rising "network society" (Castells 1996). "Governance is about managing networks" (Rhodes 1996, 658), and "network" is central to Rhodes's own definition of governance as "self-organizing, interorganizational networks" (ibid., 660). As he illustrates with changes in British policymaking in the 1990s, the "British government can choose between 'governing structures'. To markets and hierarchies, we can now add networks" (ibid., 653). This is a puzzling statement because wasn't the thrust of governance to remodel government according to a market logic? But networks are not markets; they operate based on trust, not on prices. At the same time, networks share with markets a logic of "sociability," in which power operates indirectly through the accumulation of decentralized individual choices (Grewal 2008, 8). This makes both different from a logic of "sovereignty," in which power works directly through collective decision-making (ibid.). As David Singh Grewal argues more sweepingly, economic globalization means that the "relations of sociability tend to outstrip the relations of sovereignty" (ibid., 11); and neoliberalism as the "philosophy" of globalization likewise "privileges relations of sociability and mistrusts those of sovereignty" (ibid.).

Accordingly, the state, which is tied to the logic of sovereignty, is the loser of the shift toward network-based governance. While eventually undecided about the pluses and minuses of governance, Rhodes (1996) has no doubt about its "hollowing out the state." Because many hands are involved, no one is accountable. "Steering" is a fine metaphor, but it sits on complex public–private relationships that are only "vaguely" understood (ibid., 662). And how to manage "interorganizational networks" in the absence of a hierarchy of control? Rhodes cautiously affirms Theodore Lowi's (1969) famous US-focused diagnosis of classic liberalism degenerated into "interest group liberalism." Indeed, Lowi had already argued that policy networks amount to private government, "shutting out the public," "creat(ing) privileged oligarchies," and overall "favour(ing) established interests" (Rhodes 1996, 666).

Demoting Citizens to Consumers

Rhodes (1996, 667) finally warns that the positing of "citizens as users" should not be equated with their empowerment. As the democracy-enhancing credentials of governance centrally rest on the figure of citizens as customers or consumers, this requires a closer look. In a prescient think piece, Joseph Monson and Anthony Downs (1971, 76) mused about the causes of "private affluence amidst public squalor." John Kenneth Galbraith (1958) had diagnosed it for the America of the late 1950s, but it can be generalized, to varying degrees, to all Western societies after half a century of neoliberalism. Intriguingly, Monson and Downs find the "chief villain" not to be the "large business corporation" but "modern consumers." Only in the private sector do they find an adequate playing field for the "propensity to emulate" that Thorstein Veblen (2009, 75) identified as "the strongest

74   POLITICAL NEOLIBERALISM

and most alert and persistent of the economic motives proper." By contrast, public or "government goods" are "designed with an eye to uniformity," which "accord with the ideal of equality," but "cannot be used for status differentiation" (Monsen and Downs 1971, 65). To the degree that rich societies get richer, "modern consumers are biased against the public sector in favour of the private sector" (ibid., 76). Hence the "misallocation" between public and private goods is "not due to corporate manipulation but to consumer preference" (ibid., 65). To remedy the situation, Monsen and Downs propose measures that seem to be from the notebook of public sector reform in the age of neoliberal governance: design "government goods . . . to permit consumer differentiation," remove from the public ambit goods "that don't need to be publicly provided," and engage "(p)rivate producers . . . as purveyors of government goods in order to encourage greater diversity of products" (ibid. 75).

To the degree that Fordist mass production gives way to "flexible specialization" and that an affluent middle class evolves with ever more refined and individualized tastes, "sociation by consumption" (Streeck 2012, 35) takes a mighty leap forward. So does the notion that "only private firms would be able to satisfying the rising expectations of more exacting consumers" who crave for "customized products" (ibid., 37), not just in the private consumption economy but also in a marketized public space. The very paper that coined the term "new public management" grounds the latter in "a shift to a more white-collar, socially heterogeneous population less tolerant of 'statist' and uniform approaches in public policy" (Hood 1991, 7). With respect to its political carriers, Streeck (2012, 39) notes that NPM, with its democratizing ethos, was the way of Third Way leftist governments to embrace the neoliberal bandwagon. Indeed, for Labour Prime Minister Tony Blair's Strategic Unit, NPM reform aimed at a "public service characterised by competition and contestability on the supply side and by user choice and voice on the demand side" (quoted by Sadian 2022, 10).

To act in the interest of citizens as consumers, and to enlarge their range of choice in the public sector as well, is a key legitimation in the move from government to governance. Through the "post-Fordist consumption model," Streeck (2012, 43, fn.8) arrives at a demand-side description of "politics as consumption", which closely resembles the condition of "post-democracy" that Crouch (2004) had depicted from the supply side of a polity dominated by producer interests.

But the point of this reflection on citizens as consumers is not to adjudicate the causality in the rise of neoliberal governance, even though the complicity of affluent middle classes and of "post-Fordist generations" who "provide for themselves individually in the market" (Streeck 2012, 46) is an often-overlooked factor.[24] The point is rather to question the democracy and citizenship credentials of "consumer sovereignty" (see Aberbach and Christensen 2005). The rhetoric of NPM and governance is to allow citizens to "participate directly in defining public policy" and to render public services "more transparent" and "more clearly responsible towards citizens" (ibid., 232).

The reality, however, is different. First, it is not clear who the "customers" of public services are. In the case of broadcasting, for instance, is it broadcasters themselves or their listeners? The generic notion of customers "glosses over ... the distribution of power and benefits" (Aberbach and Christensen 2005, 236). Secondly, the defining mark of citizenship is to be "entitled to equal treatment," whereas customers "are not equal and it is widely accepted that the level of service they get is a function of what they pay" (ibid.). Note that the verb to customer is "customizing." There is no equivalent for this on the part of citizens. In trivial ways, customized citizenship services have long been in place—think of expedited passport delivery against an extra-fee. Going further down that road, however, wouldn't it mean "gold card" citizens being "entitled to go to the front of the line in a post office" (ibid.), simply because of their high income and tax-paying capacity? "At the limit," argues a critical review of the shift from citizen to customer, "the state becomes a provider of services in exchange for a proportion of taxes" (Fontain 2001, 71). Finally, because of the profit motive dominating the private sector, there is a natural propensity to shape and manipulate customer preferences, whereas democratic government cannot but be legitimated as being responsive to rather than formative of citizen preferences; otherwise, it would slip into "guardianship" (ibid., 68). The blurring of the private versus public sector distinction that is the hallmark of governance allows entry for a "much higher level of customer manipulation" than is commensurable with democracy (Aberbach and Christensen 2005, 237).

In sum, what the 1993 Gore Report, commissioned under the first Clinton Administration to reform the US government, called "putting customers first" and giving them "a voice—and a choice" (quoted in Aberbach and Christensen 2005, 235), undermines citizenship and democratic legitimacy as we knew it before neoliberalism.

Excursus on Governmentality

What is the relationship between "governance" and "governmentality"? This is a kindred and influential neologism introduced by Michel Foucault in his posthumously published Collège de France lectures on the "genealogy of the modern state" (2007, 2008). "Governmentality" is a composite of "govern" and "mentality," which suggests a focus on "meaning and discourses," whereas "governance" is more about "institutions and policies" (Bevir 2011, 457). They conjoin in their attention to the "diffusion of power and ruling throughout civil society," yielding the picture of a "stateless state" (ibid., 458, 464). Accordingly, what Foucault-inspired scholars call "governmentality" is little different from what non-Foucauldians, as previously discussed, have called "governance." For Nicolas Rose and Peter Miller (1992, 174), for instance:

> (p)olitical power is exercised today through a profusion of shifting alliances between diverse authorities in projects to govern a multitude of facets of economic activity, social life and individual conduct. Power is not so much a matter of imposing constraints upon citizens as of 'making up' citizens capable of bearing a kind of regulated freedom. Personal autonomy is not the antithesis of political power, but a key term in its exercise.

They call the "new technologies" of governing "action at a distance" (ibid., 180), and credit Foucault's "governmentality" for having seen it first. But "governance" scholars, who are mostly uninfluenced by Foucault, would concur with Rose and Miller's description of political power. If there is an added value to governmentality, defined by Foucault as "the way in which one conducts the conduct of men" (2007, 186), it is to show the intimate connections between "governing the self" and "governing others," so that "governing" is no longer exclusively a political matter but something that individuals do to themselves (Lemke 2001, 191). "Governmentality" theorizes what already Thatcher had known, when she debunked society: "no government can do anything except through people."[25] If governance primarily shifts the picture of the mode of governing from hierarchy to networks then the added attention in governmentality is on who is being governed to show their active role in the process.

Unlike its cousin, governance, which has a concise historical index and is clearly set apart from government, the problem with governmentality is that no clear line can be drawn between liberal and neoliberal. On one occasion, Foucault defined "government" as "the contact point, where the individuals are driven by others is tied to the way they conduct themselves" (quoted in Lemke 2001, 204). This (ungrammatical)[26] definition of government is notably not different from that of governmentality, as "conduct of conduct," and Foucault uses both concepts interchangeably, and more often with the adjective "liberal" than "neoliberal." The most positive to say about this (con)fusion is that the arrival of neoliberalism marks no real rupture for Foucault; it is merely a mid-twentieth-century "aggiornamento" of liberalism; that is, its adjustment to a changing context (Donzelot 2008, 124). In the same vein, Barry Hindess called neoliberalism "a liberal response to the achievements of the liberal mode of government" (quoted in Lemke 2001, 205, fn.7). That would be in line with the "no alternative" rhetoric of neoliberalism. But it would also undercut its nature as a political project that calls for a change of direction in society and history—the whole point of the "Neoliberal Thought Collective" since its beginnings (see Mirowski and Plehwe 2009).

One prominent Foucauldian, Mitchell Dean (2002, 121), characterized as "neoliberal" "indirect" forms of government, which are "facilitative and preventive rather than directive and distributive," and he traced this notion back to Foucault's governmentality as "conduct of conduct." But that makes neoliberal equal liberal, as understood by Foucault himself. In his 1978 lectures on "Security, Territory, Population," Foucault (2007) distinguished between the old (Machiavellian) logic of sovereignty exercised over a territory, and the new (liberal) logic of government, which is exercised over a population. The first "regulates everything," whereas the latter "lets things happen" (ibid., 45). The sovereign logic, which is concerned with the "safety (sûreté) of the Prince and his territory," for instance, calls for towns to be fortified, scarcity to be countered by restricting peasants' grain prices and trade, and contagious disease to be contained by isolating the affected. The logic is centripetal. The governmental logic, by contrast, is centrifugal. Centered around the "security (securité) of the population," it is to open towns to the circulation of people and air, to meet scarcity by the free flow of commodities, and—qua vaccination—to permit disease to enter the body so that the latter can fight it (the quotes are from Foucault 2007, 65; the enumeration follows the concise summary by Donzelot 2008, 117–122).

78 POLITICAL NEOLIBERALISM

In the transition, the state ("territorial sovereign") moves from being "architect of the disciplined space" to becoming "regulator of a milieu" (Foucault 2007, 29). Foucault describes the "game of liberalism" as "letting things follow their course," as "acting so that reality develops, goes its way, and follows its own course according to the laws, principles, and mechanisms of reality itself" (ibid., 48). This is almost identical with Michael Walzer's (1984) description of liberalism as functional-sphere-respecting and -protecting "art of separation." The old logic of sovereignty, exemplified by Machiavelli's "advice to the prince," pursued an end that is "internal to itself," while the new "art of government," which Foucault compares to the steering of a ship but also (deeper down in the annals of Christianity) the pastoral care for a flock, pursues an end that is "internal to the things it directs" (Foucault 2007, 99). He thus arrives at his famous definition of governmentality as "power that has the population as its target, political economy as its major form of knowledge, and apparatuses of security as its essential technical instrument" (ibid., 108).

What Foucault calls the "governmentalization of the state" (2007, 109), started in the eighteenth century with the birth of liberalism, although it can be traced back to the "Christian pastorate," as the notion of a "beneficient power" over a "flock" (or "multiplicity in movement") (ibid., 126, 125). This raises the question how "liberal governmentality," frequently used by Foucault although essentially a pleonasm, can be distinguished from "neoliberal governmentality," a term he used only twice and rather perfunctorily in his second lecture series on neoliberalism proper (2008, 91, 193). Foucault seems to have realized that the key distinction between liberal and neoliberal is that of boundary-maintaining versus boundary-erasing, and the latter in terms of an economic competition logic both invading the state in its internal operation *and* directing the state's relationship to the governed individuals. From the German Ordoliberals, Foucault takes the notion of an "active" and "vigilant" neoliberal state, which he sets against the laissez-faire state of classic liberalism (2008, 132f). The neoliberal state is one that works not *against* the market, in the sense of correcting its dysfunctions through market-foreign equality measures (welfare and redistribution), but that works in *favor* of the market, to guarantee its competition function, so that "(i)nequality . . . is the same for all," as Ordoliberal Walter Röpke put it ingenuously (Foucault 2008, 143). Foucault also anticipated, and this before the "governance" train went into full steam, that "political power" itself would be "modelled on the principles of the market economy" (ibid., 131).

But with respect to governmentality, whose main point is the constitutive involvement of the governed in their being governed, Foucault's decisive input was from the American neoliberals, and their economization of human beings and society. When discussing the Chicago School's "anthropological erasure of the criminal" (Foucault 2008, 258), Foucault depicts their view of society as "field . . . left open to fluctuating processes," and their criminological interventions as "action . . . brought to bear on the rules of the game rather than on the players," and being of "an environmental type" instead of aiming at "the internal subjugation of individuals" (ibid., 259–260). Furthermore, he describes the *homo oeconomicus* of human capital theory as a person who "accepts reality," "responds systematically to modifications in the variables of the environment," and as someone who "must be let alone" (ibid., 270). While he adds the "paradox" that his rationality makes *homo oeconomicus* "manageable" and "eminently governable," this approach is in no way distinct from what he had earlier described as *liberal* governmentality. *Homo oeconomicus* is merely "the correlate of a governmentality which will act on the environment and systematically modify its variables" (ibid., 271).[27]

As if to nail down the continuity between liberal and neoliberal, after having discussed the German and American neoliberals, Foucault returns to Adam Smith's "invisible hand" as eluding the possibility of an "economic sovereign," and he closes his 1979 lecture cycle on "The Birth of Biopolitics" with a discussion of the "liberal art of governing" as one that targets "civil society" (Foucault 2008, ch. 12). Foucault's basic insight is undisputed, which is that neoliberalism "extend(s) the rationality of the market . . . to domains which are not exclusively or not primarily economic" (ibid., 323). But how this affects "liberal governmentality" remains elusive; in fact, neoliberalism does not seem to have changed it at all.

The reason for this is, as highlighted by Brown (2015), a democratic deficit in Foucault's thinking. Foucault depicted the (neo)liberal citizen as being simultaneously a "subject of interest" (*homo oeconomicus*) and a "subject of right" (*homo juridicus*), and he found the two "absolutely heterogeneous" and not to be "superimposed on one another" (2008, 275–276). By the same

80   POLITICAL NEOLIBERALISM

token, Foucault never saw subjects as citizens who constitute the demos, not even in liberally mellowed ways. As Brown (2015, 86) brilliantly observes, Foucault's sovereignty "never circulates through the people" but remains "allied to the state." He forgot to "cut off the King's head in political theory" (ibid.). Foucault thus could not see "the most important casualty" of the rise of neoliberalism: "homo politicus" (ibid., 87), another word for which is democracy.

Technocracy

Its origins reaching back to the Platonic philosopher-king who ruled the city state on the basis of absolute knowledge, technocracy is "political decision-making based on technical and scientific expertise" (Esmark 2020, 4). This couldn't be further away from the (neo)liberal thought world. Hayek, who started from the "Socratic maxim that the recognition of our ignorance is the beginning of wisdom" (1960, 22), despised experts and held that "(k)nowledge and ignorance are very relative concepts" (ibid., 378). But knowledge is the ubiquitous input in governance, so that "technocratic governance" is really a pleonasm. On the other hand, "technocrat-led governments" in the narrow sense, where political leadership and decision-making no longer pass through political parties but are explicitly based on expertise, have been an extremely rare event—an empirical study of post-World War II Europe identified only twenty-four of them, and that in a small range of countries, mostly in post-communist and other transition moments (McDonnell and Valbruzzi 2014).

For technocracy to become allied with governance, it had to undergo a change in meaning and orientation. Anders Esmark (2020) described it as an alliance shift from "bureaucracy" to "democracy," at least in technocracy's self-perception. As a practical claim, this is both right and wrong. It is right because the new technocracy shares with governance the rhetoric of transparency, accountability, and stakeholder involvement, which at least has the semblance of democracy. Knowledge in the new form of digital "informationalism" is the key input in the rise of the "network state," which Esmark describes as a "new technocratic partnership with democracy against bureaucracy" (ibid., 114). Metaphorically speaking, whereas the iconic old technocrat was an engineer who thrived in the mechanic world of bureaucracy, the iconic new technocrat is an ex-hippie bent on "mak(ing) the world more open and connected," to quote Facebook-founder Mark Zuckerberg (Dijck 2013, 45).

At the same time, and this is where the equation of the new technocracy with democracy goes wrong, Silicon Valley pioneered "solutionism," which is the notion that for every social problem there is a technical fix (Morozov 2013). "Show me a problem and I'll look for technology to fix it," is the motto of Microsoft-founder and philanthropist Bill Gates (quoted in Acemoglu and Johnson 2023, ch. 8). If knowledge becomes the basis of political choice, which is the ultimate technocratic hubris, then there is no choice, and the respective issue is precisely removed from the pluralism of interests that is the medium and the idiom of democracy. Technocracy, whether new or old, cannot but depoliticize, not just in effect but in its ideology (see the further discussion in this chapter). This is incompatible with democracy as we know it, which presupposes interest pluralism, and hence conflict and choice; that is, politics.

Technocracy's high water mark was in the 1960s and 1970s, after which it succumbed to "sustained academic silence" (Esmark 2020, 9). In its golden years, which incidentally are also the golden years of the labor-capital compromise and the welfare state, Galbraith spoke of a "technostructure," an "association of men of diverse technical knowledge, experience and other talent which modern industrial technology and planning require" (in Esmark 2020, 55). Galbraith found technostructure to be the "new locus of power" in the private and public sectors alike, yet at the same time it was "strongly inhibited in (its) political role" (ibid., 68). Calling the technostructure the "extended arm of the bureaucracy" (ibid., 59), Galbraith followed the Weberian equation of technical expertise and bureaucracy, depicting the latter as tool but not the holder of political power. So did Daniel Bell (1973), who identified theoretical knowledge as the "axial principle" of the coming post-industrial society, but for whom "it is not the technocrat who ultimately holds power, but the politician" (ibid., 360). Jürgen Habermas (1968) went one step further, calling technology and science a new "ideology" that replaced the old ideology of "free and just exchange" to legitimize capitalism, leading the subaltern away from class struggle through the promise of state-guaranteed "welfare minima, (and) the prospect of secure work and a stable income" (ibid., 77).

Habermas did not see that it was class struggle itself, though in the institutionalized form of strong labor unions and mass parties beholden to their demands, and no automatist technocratic state interventionism,

82   POLITICAL NEOLIBERALISM

which guaranteed welfare, work and income in the golden age of welfare capitalism. Conservatives had a keener sense for this, most influentially the Trilateral Commission (Crozier et al. 1975, 8) that spoke of a "crisis of democracy" and "ungovernability" due to "an overload of demands on government, exceeding its capacity to respond." Double-digit inflation, the "monetary expression of distributional dissent" (John Goldthorpe, in Bickerton 2012, 93) and the result of organized labor power in the early 1970s, could no longer be contained by Keynesian demand management. This was the moment of neoliberal supply-side economics and their political propagandists. They argued that the main task of the state was not full employment and well-paid workers but to secure a profitable business environment as a lexical first, whose benefits would "trickle down" to the rest (for a critique of this part of "zombie economics," see Quiggin 2010, ch. 5). In the United States, soon followed by other countries, "organized economic interest" shifted "towards employers and the affluent" (Hacker and Pierson 2010, 176). It has remained there ever since. A comparative study of Western countries' industrial relations, which more than a free-standing technocracy must be seen as the fundament of welfare capitalism, depicted the former as "transformed in a neoliberal direction" (Baccaro and Howell 2011, 521). This meant a sharp decline of union density and strike activity, plus business-friendly deregulation. The "tripartite" corporatist structures that formally persisted, especially in continental Europe, became "mostly about extracting macro concessions from trade unions for the implementation of largely market-conforming policy reforms" (ibid., 530).

Depoliticization

The neoliberal turn, which had to be entirely surprising for Habermas and the Frankfurt School, who located the frailty of "late capitalism" on the societal demand rather than the economic supply side, has changed the role of technocracy. Previously a productive force associated with "planning and social engineering" (Esmark 2017, 501), a distinct new function of technocracy is to lock-in and remove from political choice the neoliberal turn itself. Political scientists have discussed this trend under the rubric "depoliticization." One of the first and widely quoted studies to use the term, referred to it as "the process of placing at one remove the political character of decision-making" (Burnham 2001, 128). Peter Burnham's chief example was "economic management" in the United Kingdom in the 1990s and, most importantly, the New Labour government's delegation of fighting inflation to an "operationally independent" Bank of England that was no longer beholden to the Treasury but "free" to set interest rates. The tracks for this were laid by its Tory predecessor's temporary joining of the European Exchange Rate Mechanism (ERM), which was to guarantee monetary stability by limiting currency exchange variations. The point of this "technocratic form of governance" was to replace "discretion" in monetary policy with "binding rules," thus lowering or even removing the government's responsibility for high interest rates and a high value of the pound sterling, while boosting the country's "credit ranking" for international investors (ibid., 144). Curiously, what was essentially a measure of "build(ing) counterinflationary mechanisms into the economy," thus perpetuating on the part of New Labour the supply-side economics that had started under Thatcher, was "cloaked in the language of inclusiveness, democratization, and empowerment" (ibid., 129), by linking it with NPM measures to "increase the accountability, transparency and external validation of policy" (ibid., 141).

Depoliticization is the "denial of political contingency and the transfer of functions away from elected politicians," which two British political scientists see as nothing less than the "dominant model of statecraft in the 21st century" (Flinders and Wood 2014, 1). What the naïve mind would consider a negative, the removal of an issue from the ambit of political choice, is typically converted into a positive, poaching on the starkly negative image of "rent-seeking" and "special-interest" politicians in the neoliberal demonology of democratic politics. While the objective function of depoliticization is to remove choice, its proponents, perversely, hail it as a democratizing measure. For a New Labour official, for instance, there was "a clear desire to place power where it should be: increasingly not with politicians, but with those best fitted in different ways to deploy it . . . This depoliticising of key decision making is a vital element in bringing power closer to the people" (ibid., 2).

The "rise of the unelected" (Vibert 2007) is wider than the use of technocratic bodies to lock-in neoliberalism. Frank Vibert, who welcomes the trend, distinguishes between five types:

- "service providers" (which dubiously includes central banks);
- "risk assessors" (like the US Environmental Protection Agency);

84   POLITICAL NEOLIBERALISM

- "boundary watchers" (policing the boundary between state and market, such as the US Federal Commerce Commission);
- "inquisitors" (like the US General Accounting Office); and
- "umpires and whistle-blowers" (like the US Commission on Civil Rights).

All of these "unelected bodies," of which Vibert counts some two hundred in the United States, 250 in the United Kingdom, and about seventy at the international plane, are supposedly "assessing the facts" rather than "applying values" (ibid., 3). In this function, Vibert thinks, these bodies do not just make democratic government "more robust," but are even on demand by "an informed citizenry" (ibid., 4, 14).

That much public policy today requires complex knowledge and, in this respect, is "not a danger to democracy" (Vibert 2007, 2) is undisputed. From this perspective, the European Union, which is "anchored in a technocratic vision and not a democratic one" (ibid., 129), has been influentially described as a "regulatory state" whose nature is to deal with non-majoritarian "rule-making" rather than redistributive "taxing and spending," and which in this function cannot get into the way of democratically accountable member states (Majone 1994).

However, what Christopher Bickerton (2012) has pointedly called the demotion from "nation states" to "member states," and which incidentally occurred by way of the "technocratization of political life" (ibid., 15), has reduced the power of parliament and increased that of the executive, thus impairing democracy and locking-in neoliberalism with the help of "Europe." In an important corrective to a usually Brussels-fixated Euroliterature, Bickerton characterizes "member states" as a "distinct kind of state where national power is exercised in concert with others. National executives seek to bind themselves and their domestic publics through a growing body of rules and norms created by national governments... at the EU level" (ibid., 4).

These "rules and norms" are plainly neoliberal ones. They were first tried out at national level, and often unsuccessfully. This is why Europe was called to the rescue. Examples are the focus on monetary stability, the reduction in inflationary expectations (to beat the wage-price spiral), the fixing of external rules to "credibly commit" national governments in the view of financial markets, and the severing of ties between national governments and organized societal interests, especially labor, which had been the signature feature of the "national corporatist state" boosting the equality of European societies from the 1950s to the early 1970s. Bickerton (2012) shows that all these neoliberal policies or policy objectives *preceded* the making of the Single European Act of 1985, which merely formalized and enshrined them at the supranational level, as the best way of breaking domestic resistance to implement them (ibid., 136). The same logic applies to the 1992 Maastricht Treaty establishing the European Union, whose low-inflation, balanced-budget, and debt-reduction conditions for joining the European Economic and Monetary Union (EMU) meant prescribing to member states fiscal austerity and its inevitable companion features: welfare retrenchment, wage compression, and privatization of public assets. In the case of recalcitrant Italy, the EMU criteria were readily embraced by the "technocratic" government of the day (that sported Mario Draghi as chief of the Treasury) "as a way of isolating social partners and weakening opposition to the reform process" (ibid., 134).[28]

"Member statehood" (Bickerton 2012, 182f) is a fruitful lens for understanding technocracy as a dominant political force in Europe today, and why, against its own contemporary claim, technocracy is not democracy-enhancing but reinforcing neoliberalism as political program without alternative.

Technopopulism

Furthermore, because member statehood means "limiting the power and discretion of national populations" (Bickerton 2012, 188), it *also* explains the rise of populism as counterforce to technocracy. However, that technocracy and populism are antagonistic forces is not as obvious as it seems. Consider the following statement by Blair, made at the 1999 British Labour Party Conference:

> We know what a 21st century nation needs. A knowledge-based economy. A strong civil society... The challenge is how? The answer is people... People are born with talent and everywhere it is in chains. Look at Britain. Great strengths. Great history. English, the language of the new technology... But wasted ... Arrayed against us: the forces of conservatism, the cynics, the elite, the establishment. On our side, the forces of modernity and justice. Those who believe in a Britain for all the people ... And now, at last, party

86 POLITICAL NEOLIBERALISM

and nation joined in the same cause for the same purpose: to set our people free. (Mair 2002, 92)

This statement is remarkably technocratic and populist in tandem. Bracketing its (more implicit) technocratic element ("knowledge-based," "talent," "new technology"), Mair takes it as exemplar of a "respectable" (as against protest) form of populism, which he calls "populist democracy." The latter is "a means of linking an increasingly undifferentiated and depoliticised electorate with a largely neutral and non-partisan system of governance" (ibid., 84). But the New Labour chief was also an exponent of technocracy and of governance, as the second half of Mair's brief description suggests. Because Blair's posture is simultaneously technocratic and populist, one could call it "technopopulist," which is Bickerton and Carlo Accetti's (2021) evocative term.

This sounds paradoxical because populism indeed, especially its rightwing variant, is conventionally considered an opposition to technocratic elite rule—"the people in this country have had enough of experts," yelled a leading Brexit advocate (incidentally an Oxford graduate like the one who "got it done," Boris Johnson).[29] This overlooks that technocracy and populism have something in common: an unmediated conception of the common good, as something that can be found either by "reason" (on part of the technocrat) or by listening to the popular "will" (on part of the populist). And both are equally opposed to the logic of party democracy, in which the common good can only be achieved indirectly by "voicing and aggregating plural . . . interests" (Caramani 2017, 62). "Technopopulism," the unlikely combination of technocracy and populism, sheds new light on shared features of parties and movements that are usually treated separately and in opposition to one another, such as the Italian *Cinque Stelle* on the populist end, and Blair's New Labour and Emmanuel Macron's *La République En Marche* (LREM) on the technocratic end (Bickerton and Accetti 2021).

Like "member statehood," "technopopulism" rests on an analysis of the linkage between state and society being ruptured.[30] That linkage was once provided by mass parties that mobilized and represented the major social groups and cleavage structures. Now there is an "individualized" social structure "beyond estate and class" (Beck 1983), marked by the "absence of coherent and relatively enduring social constituencies" (Mair 2013, 57). Bickerton and Accetti (2021, ch. 3) register the new situation as the end of the "ideological political logic" of left versus right, fueled (among other factors) by the 1970s economic crisis, the "cartelization" of political parties, and regional integration (in Europe)—all three also doing their share in the rise of neoliberalism.

Technopopulism is a useful lens for making sense of a variety of political phenomena that are characteristic of the neoliberal condition, and some of which we already encountered: polarization, authoritarianism, and audience-fixated posturing.

First, there is an increasing polarization and "disparaging" of the political opponent, who is not just opponent but enemy (Bickerton and Accetti 2021, 146). This logically follows from the technocratic-cum-populist claim to be in possession of truth or the popular will, which tolerates no deviation from the correct line. Macron, in (neo)liberal hagiography the "centrist, broadly liberal, pro-European" who braves the dark "forces of nationalism and populism,"[31] claims to be "*en même temps de droite et de gauche*" (at the same time of the right and of the left). This makes for a "velvety form of populism," as political philosopher Marcel Gauchet acutely observed (ibid., 60, 61). Macron's 2017 surprise victory over the "political establishment" (ibid., 5) was a victory for "France": "France has won! . . . What we represent, what you represent tonight, here . . . is France's fervour, its enthusiasm, the energy of the French people" (ibid., 63). The "technocratic slayer of populism"[32] doesn't even hesitate to call himself a populist. When Macron assembled the country's mayors in the Elysée palace in November 2018, he said: "(W)e are the real populists, because we are the people, every day" (ibid., 62). In a political universe beyond left and right, those who disagree are "imbeciles" and "do-nothings" (Macron, the technocrat) or they are "enemies of the Republic" (Macron, the populist) (ibid., 147). Playing on both registers, EM (the man and his movement, the latter sharing his acronyms not by accident) like to refer to their motley opponents as "extremists."

But if opponents are "extremists" (refashioned as *complotistes* during COVID-19) (see Mucchielli 2022a), attacks on the leader and his government become "attacks against the State," or what Macron called "perversions (*détournements*) of democracy" (Bickerton and Accetti 2021, 158). This signals a second key feature of technopopulism, which is authoritarianism. If intermediary organizations and institutions have either withered or are ideologically dismissed as "blockages" (Macron, ibid., 62), there remains only brute force to assure the compliance of distrustful and recalcitrant citizens. Bickerton and Accetti (ibid., 160f) refer the "punitive turn" less to "neoliberal ideology" than to a "deficit in democratic representation," but it is difficult to

88 POLITICAL NEOLIBERALISM

keep both elements apart, the latter being (in part) an effect of the former. Always staying with the emblematic case of France in the thrall of LREM, Macron maintained the state of emergency, which dated back to his predecessor François Hollande's anti-terrorism campaign, over five years into his rule, until August 2022. This not only allowed him to pass legislation without much parliamentary scrutiny, but to meet opposition in the street with considerable brutality. Already *En Marche*'s 2016 campaign manifesto had called for massively enforced police forces, because "proximity is the only way to collect information, and to identify and monitor dangerous individuals" (ibid., 163). When the *gilets jaunes* (yellow vests), a provincial lower middle-class revolt against higher fuel prices that sat oddly with the Macronist vision of France as "start-up nation," took to the streets over weeks and months in 2019, they encountered unprecedented police violence, with ten deaths and 2,500 serious injuries (including eyes shout out by rubber bullets that the police were newly authorized to use).

Thirdly, while technopopulism eschews the ideological left–right binary, it does not really replace it with a substitute—it is low on substance and more of a "mode of political action" (Bickerton and Accetti 2021, 2). It is a "politics of doing" (Ilvo Diamanti, ibid., 12), where doing something, and doing it effectively, trumps the question of what is being done. Macron, for instance, described himself "not interested in politics . . . I am interested in doing" (ibid., 64).[33] And he deems "the French people . . . less concerned with representation than action. They want politics to be efficient, and that's all there is to it" (ibid., 68). Because substantive issues, particularly about the political economy, have largely been removed from the political agenda, questions of image, personality, and competence loom large. This has also been described as "post-democracy" (Crouch 2004) or "politainment" (Streeck 2012, 56), a mixture of politics and entertainment. Bickerton and Accetti (2021, 150) speak of the predominance of "valence" over (ideological) "position" issues, whose mark is agreement on the "ends" of policy. Today, the ends agreed is "market-conforming democracy" (German Chancellor Angela Merkel, quoted in Tooze 2018, ch. 17). The only question that remains is who is the most competent to deliver.

Bickerton and Accetti (2021) mention the neoliberal credentials of technopopulism only in passing. This is consonant with their message that technopopulism is more style than program. But neoliberalism is all over it. Technopopulism is perhaps neoliberalism's most refined form because it uses the imagery of democracy only to neutralize it in effect. Exhibit A, again, is LREM in France. In its rhetoric, it is a democratic grassroots movement. "Change will not be dictated from above. It will be driven at the grassroots level," as Macron put it in his 2017 presidential campaign autobiography (quoted in Bickerton and Accetti 2021, 61). The central message of this campaign book, with the immodest title *Révolution*, is to wage a "democratic revolution" (Macron 2016). In reality, the Macronist "grassroots" has a distinct elite flavor. LREM was literally "made" by the McKinsey consultancy, which followed it into government, also steering the latter through the COVID-19 pandemic (see Aron and Michel-Aguirre 2022). The inner circle of "Macron Boys" are mostly *grandes écoles* graduates (and of the two most important schools at that, École nationale d'administration [ENA] and École des hautes études commerciales [HEC]), like the leader himself. With respect to the "civil society" that was allegedly recruited into Macron's first-term parliament in 2017, by means of a glossily orchestrated "Hand-in-your-CV" campaign, 90 percent of elected LREM members were in the professional/managerial category, which represents only 13 percent of the French workforce (Bickerton and Accetti 2021, 65). In early 2020, Macron's Labor Minister, Muriel Pénicaud, previously Human Resources chief of the multinational Danone, rejected as too costly for employers a smallish extension, from five to twelve days, of paid leave for parents in grief over the loss of their child, and the proposal was subsequently voted down by the LREM "civil society" majority in parliament. This left the "impression of coldness, of technocratic stubbornness, and . . . an absence of political sense" (ibid., 207, fn.6), which has followed the "president of the rich" ever since.

Federation and Constitutionalism: The European Union as Neoliberal Polity

Federation and constitutionalism are covered together in this section, for two reasons. First, they tend to be combined in the influential Geneva School of neoliberal thought, which Hayek belonged to. Secondly, they entered a unique practical synthesis in the European Union, which I shall discuss here as exemplar of a neoliberal polity.

The idea of federation held together by an "economic constitution"[34] that protects the market from democratic inferences (i.e., the idea of property-guarding supranational order ruled by law rather than people), is one of the oldest and most consequential political forms in the arsenal of neoliberals.[35]

More as an "is" than "ought," Schmitt had described the world of nineteenth-century capitalism as divided in two, the bordered world of "imperium," in which states rule over people, and the borderless world of "dominium," in which property is protected by contract that is valid across jurisdictions. What Schmitt rejected as impairment of national sovereignty was picked up by neoliberals as "best description of the world they wanted to conserve" (Slobodian 2018, 10). Born and growing up in the Habsburg Empire, the late Hayek remembered his very first paper being about "double government, a cultural and an economic government" (ibid., 105). Quinn Slobodian summarizes the idea as "large but loose federations within which the constituent nations would retain control over cultural policy but be bound to maintain free trade and free capital movement between nations" (ibid., 95).

A prescient early paper by Hayek, entitled *The Economic Conditions of Interstate Federalism* (1939), is considered by many as "blueprint for today's European Union."[36] Hayek cites again the model of Habsburg. Rather than economic, he argues, the main purpose of "interstate federation" is political: to "secure peace" (1939, sec. 1). This may have been an echo to his front experience during World War I, where he served in the Austro-Hungarian Army. It does prefigure Europe's founding idea post-1945, which was to reconcile Germany and France and prevent war in the future. However, that "peace" was no priority for Hayek is suggested by the fact that he spent no more than one sentence on it. Instead, his main point is another one: "The central government in a federation composed of many different people will have to be very restricted in scope if it is to avoid meeting an increasing resistance on the part of the various groups which it includes" (ibid., sec. 3). In other words, the "diversity of conditions" in the constitutive states "will raise serious obstacles to federal legislation." As Hayek asks rhetorically, "Is it likely that the French peasant will be willing to pay more for his fertilizer to help the British chemical industry?" (ibid.). The sociodemographic heterogeneity of federation will make sure that the limited purpose of federal power is guaranteeing "free movements of men and capital" (ibid., sec. 2). But this is only one causal path to minimize rule, from unit states to federation. Conversely, the direction being from federation to unit states, free movement of capital across states will make the latter abstain from anti-competitive social legislation. In a race to the bottom, "even the restriction of child labor or of working hours becomes difficult to carry out" (ibid.). This makes for a neoliberal win–win in both directions, not just from unit states to federation, but also from federation to unit states.[37] Both processes seal "less government all round" (ibid., sec. 4). Hayek even anticipated the notion of state-level "negative" integration that could never be compensated by federal-level "positive" integration, which Fritz Scharpf (1999) influentially developed for the European Union (although not liking what he saw): "(T)he federation will have to possess the negative power of preventing individual states from interfering with economic activity in certain ways, although it may not have the positive power of acting in their stead" (Hayek 1939, sec. 4).

Hayek avoided the Ordoliberal notion of "economic constitution," perhaps because it was associated with state and legislation, both of which he disliked. Instead, Hayek spoke of an "international order of law," which he deemed the "logical consummation of the liberal program" (Hayek 1939, sec. 5). Hayek realized that this was rather hopeful at a time that "nationalism" and "socialism," then even fused as "national socialism," dominated the world (ibid.).

Hayek captured the evolution of the European Union "in reverse order" (Scharpf 2009, 6) because, in reality, European economic integration came to antedate a forever anemic political integration. What he got right, however, is that "the integration of previously sovereign nation-states in Europe would reduce the capacity of states to regulate the capitalist economy and to burden it with the costs of an expensive welfare state" (ibid., 30).

This was certainly not intended by the "European Saints"—the German Konrad Adenauer, the French Robert Schuman, the Belgian Paul-Henri Spaak, and the Italian Alcide de Gasperi, all of whom were Catholic democrats and patriots, interestingly each one from his respective country's borderlands (Milward 1992, ch. 6). They were Europeans-by-necessity, "Europe" being antidote to the demon of nationalism that had destroyed the Continent twice in thirty years. Mainly, they were intent on "rescuing" rather than overcoming their respective nation-states, through putting them on a broader social basis than before, including workers and the lower middle classes, by means of the economic prosperity that a common market promised for all strata, not only for the elites. As Alan Milward put it acutely (ibid.), Europe's founders believed in the "mutual reinforcement" of the nation-state and Europe. At the same time, the first stabs at Europe were taken through attempts at political and military integration, and only their quick failure started the economic route. Not by accident, the first industries to be Europeanized were coal and steel, which had fed the German war machine. "Peace," little more than a cover for Hayek's market-focused

92 POLITICAL NEOLIBERALISM

"interstate federation," was the actual motive force of building Europe after World War II.[38]

Accordingly, it would be absurd to insinuate neoliberal design or logic to what, in the 1957 founding Treaty of Rome, was called European Economic Community (EEC). "It took a bit longer," so said Scharpf in a sarcastic nod to Hayek's "blueprint." Scharpf even concedes that "European social market economies reached the peak of their development and institutional diversity during the first two decades of the Community's existence" (2009, 30).

The mechanism that helped turn Europe neoliberal was "integration by law," originally the name of a research project at the Florentine European University Institute, but considered by many the key to understanding the peculiarly non-demotic and non-political driving forces of European integration.[39]

This is how, in addition to federation, constitutionalism, the notion of higher law that restricts democratic majority power, enters the picture. In Joseph Weiler's (1991) classic account, the European Court of Justice (ECJ), created in 1952 as highest legal organ of the (then) European Coal and Steel Community, took the 1957 Rome Treaty, establishing the EEC, in the Court's own words, as "basic constitutional charter" (ibid., 2407) that stands above national law. In the process, the ECJ "transformed" the EEC from an international organization to a fully-fledged federal state, from a legal (not political) point of view. In two benchmark decisions in the early 1960s, the Court established that European legal norms have "direct effect," which could be mobilized by individuals—most often firms—against their national governments; and it established that European norms enjoyed "supremacy," trumping conflicting national law (even if the latter had been passed earlier). Supremacy included the Court's heroic (and subsequently contested) assertion of "*Kompetenz-Kompetenz*," which is the competence to determine the competence of the Community. The combination of the Direct Effect and Supremacy Doctrines, writes the foremost European lawyer, "means that Community norms that produce direct effects are not merely the law of the land but the 'higher law' of the land" (Weiler 1994, 514). The Court's double strike made the European "constitutional order (indistinguishable) from that found in ... federal states" (ibid., 512f). More concretely, it made European competition law, the spearhead of its market-enhancing powers, "a life weapon in the hands of supranational actors" (Höpner and Schäfer 2010a, 17). Several decades later, it helped privatize public goods and services provision, like telecommunications, energy, and transportation, one of the

END OF THE LIBERAL-DEMOCRATIC SYNTHESIS 93

main thrusts of the neoliberal dismantling (or rather, marketizing) of the state agenda.

How this feast of self-made European *Richterherrschaft*[40] was possible is contested among scholars. A crucial factor, highlighted again by Weiler (1994), is the preliminary ruling procedure under Article 267 of the Treaty on the Functioning of the European Union (TFEU). According to it, national courts *can* (on the part of lower courts) or *must* (high courts) refer uncertain legal matters that touch upon EU law to the European Court, whose "preliminary rulings" the same national courts are then obliged to implement domestically. This mechanism created or activated a transnational camaraderie of judges. In particular, it boosted the prestige of lower courts that now engaged in a judicial review of higher-level executive and parliamentary acts. Most importantly, the fact that national courts had to implement the ECJ preliminary rulings meant that recalcitrant governments had to disobey their own courts, which is a no-go in a liberal-constitutional state.

There is nothing in itself neoliberal in the empowerment of the judicial branch. "Governing with judges" has been a common feature of European (in fact, all) liberal states after World War II (for Europe, see Stone Sweet 2000; beyond Europe, see Hirschl 2007)—one could even call it a badge of their liberalness. The difference is that the ECJ is tasked with advancing the four common market freedoms (of goods, capital, services, and persons), so that it naturally tilts in a pro-market direction.

In the European polity's first three decades, this was contained by a "legal-political equilibrium," in which "legal federalism" coexisted with "political confederalism": "(Member states) could accept constitutionalization because they took real control of the decision-making process" (Weiler 1991, 2429). In Euro-jargon, this is referred to as "intergovernmentalism." It was hammered down in the Luxembourg Accord of 1965, which requires unanimity in the (state-representing) Council of Ministers that thus became the dominant institution and legislator of the emergent Euro polity. Little noticed in the beginning, this equilibrium was first undermined, in 1970, by the Court-produced Doctrine of Implied Powers. It stipulates that whenever "legitimate ends" are to be pursued (such as, initially, treaty-making with third states) (ibid., 2416), European institutions can go beyond their "enumerated powers" (as stated in the European Community treaty).[41] Henceforth, entirely new domains fell under the Euro grip, including the environment, energy, consumer protection, health, education, research and development, and why not "defense," as Weiler quipped (ibid., 2446, fn.119):

94 POLITICAL NEOLIBERALISM

"Constitutionally, no core of sovereign state powers was left beyond the reach of the Community," argues Weiler (ibid., 2435).

But what really broke the "legal-political equilibrium" of the first three decades in favor of the legal side, was not so much "implied powers," which initially occurred with the connivance of states. Instead, the break was the introduction, in the 1985 Single European Act (SEA), of majority voting in the so-far lead institution of the Euro polity, the state-dominated Council of Ministers. This had become unavoidable after successive enlargements. But it tilted the power balance toward the European Commission (the executive organ of the Euro polity), which so far had been a subordinate player in Brussels, and toward the other supranational organs. Now that their veto power was gone, "member states are . . . in a situation of facing binding norms adopted wholly or partially against their will, with direct effect in their national legal orders" (Weiler 1991, 2462). Weiler called this an "eruption of significant proportions" (ibid., 2455). It indeed brought to a new level the notorious debate over Europe's "democratic deficit," and Weiler feared that Europe was pushed from its original promise of a pluralistic "community" into a diversity-crushing "unity," a super-state of sorts (ibid., 2479).

Post-1985, that is, after the SEA, there has been persistent politicization of the Euro polity. Liesbet Hooghe and Gary Marks (2008) speak of a transition from "permissive consensus" to "constraining dissensus." In academic terms, this was the moment of their "multi-level" approach to Euro politics, a hugely successful and by now dominant academic product that replaced the exhausted paradigms of "neofunctionalism" (betting on an unstoppable, market-originating "spillover" logic of expanding Euro powers) and "intergovernmentalism" (stubbornly deeming sovereign state power superior to the supranational tide), both of which limited their attention to things happening in Brussels. By contrast, Hooghe and Marks (ibid., 14) describe their new approach thus: "The European Union is no longer insulated from domestic politics; domestic politics is no longer insulated from Europe. The result is a greater divergence of politically relevant perceptions and a correspondingly constricted scope of agreement." Indeed, the SEA's "Internal Market Programme," which was its substantive innovation (although, in fact, it only formalized established ECJ case law), affected an ever-wider range of interests. As a result, the number of lobbying groups in Brussels exploded from six hundred in 1986 to three thousand by 1990 (Hooghe and Marks 1999).[42]

Hooghe and Marks (1999) describe the Euro-institutions torn between, on the one side, a "Neoliberal Project," which seeks to insulate markets from politics, rejects Euro-democracy, and endorses race-to-the-bottom member state competition; and, on the other side, a "Regulated Capitalism" project, symbolized by the mythologized Jacques Delors presidency of the European Commission (1985–1994) and its ideas of a Social Europe that is citizen friendly and democratic. While they concede that the Regulated Capitalism project has been "unimpressive by comparison," they curiously conclude that "(n)either project is hegemonic" (ibid.).

This is questionable. Regarding Delors, who in his prior jobs as French finance and economics minister had helped engineer French President Mitterand's neoliberal turn in the early 1980s, he went on record, in 1985, his first year in Brussels, with the rather Hayekian views that "society progresses also thanks to its inequalities," that "the social protection system . . . constitutes . . . a powerful incentive not to work," and that "the French must convert, as a matter of urgency, to the spirit of the market."[43] As Perry Anderson (2021) put it sarcastically, for the advocate of "Social Europe," whenever "there was a conflict between the adjective and the noun, the noun came first"—and that noun was more deeply steeped in neoliberal colors just because of Delors's single biggest achievement in Brussels, which was the 1985 SEA.

More importantly, the notion of competing political projects in Brussels overlooks that "integration by law" had long stacked the cards in favor of the "neoliberal project." The decisive moment in this was the famous *Cassis de Dijon* decision of the ECJ in 1979, which was merely formalized in the SEA's "Internal Market Programme." In *Cassis*, the issue was that the German government had prohibited the import of this sweet French alcoholic beverage made of black currant, commonly mixed with white wine to produce the popular *Kir*, because its alcohol percentage was too low to pass as "liquor"—that it certainly was by its look, taste, and effect. The German government, whether they pretended or not (i.e., in reality protecting its liquor industry), feared that *Cassis* might be abused by youngsters as gateway to hard alcohol. Previously, the ECJ had fought for the free movement of goods by reigning in protectionism that discriminated on grounds of their national origins, while hoping that for the remaining non-tariff barriers a "harmonization of standards" could be achieved (dubbed "positive integration" by Scharpf [1999]). In *Cassis*, the Court dealt with these non-tariff barriers in the negative by simply erasing them. If generalized, this invalidated with one

96 POLITICAL NEOLIBERALISM

strike all the national regulations with social content that states had passed for the sake of public health, safety, order, or morals, even if these measures were non-discriminatory. The vehicle for this was the Court invention, in its *Cassis* judgment, of the principle of "mutual recognition." According to it, anything that is considered safe or orderly in the origin country *ipso facto* passes as "safe" in the destination country.

What Martin Höpner and Armin Schäfer (2010a, 17) called the move from "non-discrimination" to "non-restriction," strongly resembles at European level what Dani Rodrik (2011) refers to as "hyperglobalization." The latter arrived with the creation of the World Trade Organization (WTO) in 1995. Now, as Rodrik put it (ibid., 76), "(d)omestic economic management was to become subservient to international trade and finance rather than the other way around." Trade disputes, resolved by the WTO's own judicial organs, came to reach deeply into domestic areas, like corporate taxing, food safety and health rules, labor law and environmental norms. The result was lower standards and protections and a friendlier business environment, in the process undermining democracy.

Europe's equivalent to hyperglobalization was the extension of the "mutual recognition" principle from goods, where it originated, to capital, firm establishment, and services. Höpner and Schäfer (2010b) call the result a "post-Ricardian Europe." In it, free trade is no longer good for all "varieties of capitalism" but detrimental to the more protective "coordinated" variant, at home in Continental Europe and Scandinavia, pushing the latter toward the meaner and leaner "liberal" variant known in the United Kingdom and North America (for "varieties of capitalism," see Hall and Soskice 2001). Examples abound. In company law, the ECJ, in a series of rules between 1997 and 2001, attacked the old "company seat" or "real seat" doctrine, according to which a company should operate under the law of the state in which it mainly does business. In a broad application of the mutual recognition principle, this doctrine was declared a violation of the freedom of establishment. Companies now could do legal-regime-shopping by establishing foreign letterbox "headquarters." German firms, for instance, if they were large enough, could now escape the worker-friendly "co-determination councils," one of the pillars of the German *Soziale Marktwirtschaft*, by claiming to be headquartered elsewhere. A second example is service provision and labor dispute law, which were at stake in the ECJ's controversial *Viking* and *Laval* decisions of 2005. These cases involved foreign "posted" workers performing services under the less costly and protected conditions of their (mainly Eastern European) origin states. The Court, first, lowered the wage and protection standards to be observed for posted workers abroad; second, it subordinated the union right to strike against these postings to the right of firms to provide the contested services. "(T)rade unions are obliged not to hinder or block transnational economic activity by collective action," as Höpner and Schäfer (2010a, 19) summarize this particularly scandalized aspect of the Court decisions.[44] This was again applied "mutual recognition," because the country of origin was declared responsible for the modalities of the service provided, and the other member states simply had to accept them, even if they harmed domestic labor by underbidding its protection and wage standards.[45]

The Cologne School of Scharpf, Höpner, and Schäfer interprets these trends as "conversion to the liberal model" (in the sense of Hall and Sokice 2001), and one that was "under the legal compulsion of ECJ jurisprudence" (Scharpf 2009, 27), and not, as Hayek (1939) had expected, the result of market competition. While there is truth to it, it ignores the uncomfortable fact that the SEA (1985), which merely acknowledged what the Court had established in its "mutual recognition" jurisprudence, was consented by all member states (as is formally required for treaty revisions). In particular, to hold the ECJ alone responsible ignores that the "nation-states" of Europe were only too willing to be reduced to "member states," and to see their "power (limited) through external frameworks of rule" (Bickerton 2012, 15). This helped them, whatever the political color of the respective government, to push through the neoliberal transition that was tried by most of them (even Mitterand's France in 1983, and in Germany under Kohl in the early 1980s), but that hit upon domestic obstacles. Bickerton has shown that "member state" governments, associating more with one another than with their respective societies that they preferred to keep at bay, happily presented as "required by Brussels" certain neoliberalizing measures that met particularly strong domestic resistance, such as breaking-up the public sector or labor market reforms, and later austerity to contain inflation and reduce public debt (although the latter was not always voluntary, as we will see below). The result is what Bickerton, only slightly sarcastically, described as "consensual policymaking within committees of national experts, ratified at the level of government ministers and heads of state and then presented to domestic populations as a fait accompli" (ibid., 149)—in effect, technocracy.

In a provocative intervention, Jim Caporaso and Sidney Tarrow (2009) countered that, over time, the ECJ shed the image of neoliberal villain

98 POLITICAL NEOLIBERALISM

that it may have been in the past. Instead, starting around 1986, it moved toward a Polanyian "social embedding of the labor market," in decisions that "(protect) the rights of workers and their families" (ibid., 608, 595). This seems exaggerated. Worker mobility, as one of the four market freedoms, has always been strongly protected under European law. In combination with the prohibition of national-origin discrimination, this entailed mobile workers, including their families, being successively included on equal terms in the national welfare systems of member states. Accordingly, this is not a turn from "reinforcing market structures" toward the "social embedding of markets," as Caporaso and Tarrow argue (ibid., 593). Instead, it is an "extension of negative integration" (Scharpf 2008, 91), and at the likely cost of the "underproduction of public goods" and "erosion of solidary orientations" in the member states at that (ibid., 93–94), much as Hayek (1939) had expected of his "interstate federation."

This objection holds even more against a short moment in the evolution of EU citizenship, which had been created with great fanfare in the 1992 Maastricht Treaty on European Union, in which it seemed that "citizenship" alone, irrespective of one's economic ("worker") status, would qualify Euro migrants for full and equal access to the social rights established in the member state into which they move. This "will trigger welfare state retrenchment," Höpner and Schäfer (2010a, 23) warned in the wake of the ECJ's famous *Grzelczyk* decision of 1999 that had opened this avenue, because "those who finance social security cannot be treated differently from those who do not." As Agustin Menéndez and Espen Olsen (2020, 134) explicate the dilemma, "the very same decisions that seemed to be extending social and economic rights to non-nationals were undermining the collective goods and collective rights that make possible the forms of solidarity proper of Democratic and Social states."

However, the moment that "Union citizenship" was "destined to be the fundamental status of nationals of the Member States," as boldly stipulated by the ECJ in *Grzelczyk*,[46] was short. It ended with the ECJ's *Dano* decision in 2014, in which EU citizenship snapped back to its original position of "market citizenship." According to the latter, rights of residence and access to social benefits are conditional on being economically active (i.e., "worker"). This raised yet another dilemma. The fact that a young Romanian woman moving to Germany without taking up work was denied basic social aid (*Sozialhilfe*), and thus essentially was forced out on the street (legally even out of the country, as her right of residence was denied—although this is rarely enforced), meant that "the very fact of being in need is what justifies (her) being denied access to the full enjoyment of European citizenship" (Menéndez and Olsen 2020, 113). Conversely, "a Union citizen is only entitled to social assistance in the host state, if he/she has sufficient resources (which triggers her right of residence under EU law; CJ) and therefore not in need of any social assistance" (Verschueren 2015, 381). Such is the reality of Social Europe and of European citizenship.

The fact remains that even a non-conditional European citizenship, in which the status itself creates residence and social rights, cannot but be parasitic on the resources that non-mobile citizens have provided for nominal and, more importantly still, *perceived* non-nationals. Short of these resources being directly provided at European level, and short of a European identity and solidarity that have never been more than academic constructs and the pious hope of some "good Europeans," even the most perfectly equipped European citizenship cannot escape the trap of "negative integration" in which nationally protective obstacles to free movement are raided without being compensated for at European level. Scharpf (2008, 94) thus aptly concludes that the "socially liberal" as much as the "economically liberal" jurisdiction of the European Court, are both "*Kampfansagen*" (declarations of battle) against the economic and social order of member states.

However, what Scharpf and other Social Democratic critics don't sufficiently consider is that member states are being hollowed out *internally* under a neoliberal order that has everywhere grown in strength over the past half-century, which diminishes the role that Europe can have in this. The stark binary of solidary nation-states threatened by neoliberal Europe is wrong. Also consider that the free movement right is exercised by only a small number of Europeans (see Recchi 2015). In the early millennium, just 0.1 percent of the European working-age population changed their country of origin, which is thirty times less than in the United States (Bickerton 2012, 117). As the bulk of them move for work or study, they are unlikely to be a threat to national welfare states. More importantly, these movers meet welfare states that are increasingly transformed into workfare states, in which even domestic citizen rights are conditional on having work or actively looking for work. The Hartz IV benefits, which Mrs. Dano was denied by the ECJ in 2014, are no horn of plenty but flat-rate social aid that is the same for recently arrived asylum-seekers as for unemployed Germans who lose the right to status-preserving unemployment benefits after only one year.

100   POLITICAL NEOLIBERALISM

As Lydia Morris (2016) observed, the citizen-migrant distinction loses traction in neoliberal social policy. The reinstatement of market citizenship in Europe mirrors exactly the neoliberal thinning of citizenship rights in the member states (see Joppke 2021a, 230–246).

Tocqueville had described the "individualism" that is bred by democracies as "withdraw(ing) into the circle of family and friends" (1969, 506). While sharing this individualism's apolitical thrust, the "mobile individualism" bred *and* protected by Europe is, on the opposite, to "typically leave family and friends behind" and to "lead a nomadic life" (Skrbic 2019). The social policy most attuned to protect this individualism is antidiscrimination, which happens to be the European Union's genuine social policy, geared to "create free access to the market" (Höpner and Schäfer 2010a, 25). More generally, antidiscrimination reflects a new function of the state, as it transforms from social democratic into neoliberal, which is not protecting people from the market but making them ready for it. While not a state, the European Union is the world's most advanced neoliberal polity. Imaginatively described by Alexander Somek (2014), the European Union is not in the image of a city in which people live, but of an airport in which everyone wants to be safely on the move. Its "normative core" is mobility and the antidiscrimination that undergirds it, this antidiscrimination being strong on nationality and gender from Europe's earliest to early hours and expanding from there to race and other ascriptive markers in the early millennium. The European Union envisions "a world without boundaries . . . not a place where people live together . . . a template that facilitates and stabilizes self-interested interaction within the bounds of reciprocity" (ibid., 152). In this respect, the Europe that is, is not far apart from the Europe that could be—there is only limited normative appeal to it.

Meritocracy

In his presidential campaign biography, Macron (2016, 243) calls himself "a product of the French meritocratic system," and his story starts with his provincial family's "Republican ascension" from "modest milieus" into the "bourgeoisie" through "work and talent" (ibid., 11). He concludes: "So I have chosen my life" (*J'ai donc choisi ma vie*) (ibid., 12). This is an astonishing statement because a chosen life is not one that is socially conditioned (a "product," as he says). Such is the paradox of meritocracy: it hides the social conditions that enable it. Moreover, "meritocracy" obscures that it is still a form of rule (as the Greek-rooted suffix "cracy" suggests), and in this sense a *political* phenomenon.

However, unlike the previous institutional forms, meritocracy is only indirectly a *political* form of neoliberalism, through legitimizing the social structure that neoliberalism aims to build, one in which the individual chooses (and in return alone is held responsible for) their place, on the basis of their own efforts and talents.

Friedrich Hayek (1960, 100) sharply rejected the principle of merit, deeming it a Trojan horse for distributive justice that, "once introduced, would not be fulfilled until the whole of society was organized in accordance with it. This would produce . . . the opposite of a free society—a society in which authority decided what the individual was to do and how he was to do it." The principle of merit, argues Hayek, "presumes that some human beings are in a position to determine conclusively what a person is worth and are entitled to determine what he may achieve" (ibid., 97). Accordingly, the determination of merit conflicts with his denial of an Archimedean point of knowledge and the inherent limitations of the latter. But his key objection is that market outcomes are chance outcomes that indicate the "value" of a service or a good to someone willing to pay for it, not the "merit" of those offering or producing them (Hayek 1966, 612). The market order is a "game of skill and chance," and once we agree to play it, the result stands to be accepted with no possibility of redress (ibid., 614). Market outcomes are "morally blind," the result of "trial-and-error," much like evolution "cannot be just" (Hayek 1989, ch. 5). In his earlier work, Hayek even anticipated the dystopian consequences of "meritocracy," as laid out by Michael Young (1958) who had invented the term (that is not used by Hayek): "A society in which it was generally presumed that a high income was proof of merit and a low income the lack of it, . . . would probably be much more unbearable to the unsuccessful ones than one in which . . . there was no necessary connection between merit and success" (Hayek 1960, 98).[47]

When reflecting on the principles of justice, David Miller (1999, ch. 2) noted that "desert," in which an individual is rewarded according to her contributions, is specific to only one type of human relationship, "instrumental association." He distinguishes it from two other types of relationship, "need"-based "solidaristic community" (with family and nation as typical examples), and "equality"-based community, which he equates with citizenship. The distinction between need and equality and their respective forms

102   POLITICAL NEOLIBERALISM

of community is fuzzy because citizenship is closely tied to the semantics of nationhood. But the linking of desert (or merit) to instrumental association bears a message that is loud and clear: meritocracy models society along economic relations and voluntary organizations; that is, as contract-based. Instrumental association thus shows the unmistakable handwriting of neoliberalism. As Jonathan Mijs (2016, 16) extrapolates from Miller, merit "crowd(s) out need and equality as principles of justice."[48]

Miller (1999, 177) further noticed that meritocracy, which rewards "talent and effort," has "cross-party support," and has "usually been understood as a progressive ideal." This surprises only through the negative lens of Young (1958), a British Labour intellectual, who had a premonition that meritocracy would be a viciously self-immunizing new form of class rule.[49] In the larger history of human societies, meritocracy is clearly an advance over nepotistic tribalism, and it resonates with the great modernizing stories, from Henry Maine's status to contract to Talcott Parsons's ascription to achievement.

More recently, meritocracy has been the hook for the Third-Way left to embrace the neoliberal ideal of the market, as "giv(ing) people what they deserve" (Sandel 2020, ch. 3). Michael Sandel (ibid.) called it the "rhetoric of rising," of which the previous US President Barak Obama has been an undisputed champion. Obama used to admonish his audiences to "work hard and play by the rules" (the term was borrowed from Bill Clinton), which would allow them to rise "as far as their talents will take them" (quoted in ibid.). This posture entails a state commitment to racial and sexual non-discrimination, to establish the equality of opportunity that is necessary for the logic of meritocracy to unfold, and which has become the poster call of the neoliberal left. But it entails, now on part of the individual, the direct obligation to be common-good conformant through self-responsible behavior (such direct obligation is foreign to the liberal tradition, where the common good is only indirectly achieved, as the unintended outcome of self-interested behavior)[50]. Accordingly, progressive equal opportunity speak is paired with that of paternalistic responsibility. Bill Clinton pioneered this combination in the United States, when promising (and simultaneously threatening) a welfare reform that would "(o)ffer more opportunity to all and demand more responsibility from all" (ibid.). Tony Blair carried merit talk into the United Kingdom, when describing his New Labour as "committed to meritocracy. We believe that people should be able to rise by their talents, not by their birth or the advantages of privilege" (ibid.). With respect to welfare, using terms that are nearly identical with those of Clinton,

Blair called for a "new settlement . . . for a new age, where opportunity and responsibility go together" (ibid.). On the European continent, German SPD Chancellor Gerhard Schröder mixed the progressive and paternalistic elements into one stew, in his semantically challenging advice that "everybody has the duty to seize their opportunities" (ibid.).

Underneath meritocracy's progressive equal-opportunity veneer, its crude function is to legitimize the vast increases of inequality in the neoliberal era,[51] in which (as in the United States) the bottom 90 percent saw their income stagnating while the top 1 percent had it increased exponentially (see Stiglitz 2012, ch. 1). Larry Summers, an elite economist in the Clinton and Obama cabinets, has expressed it bluntly: "One of the reasons that inequality has probably gone up in our society is that people are being treated closer to the way they're supposed to be treated" (quoted in T. Frank 2016, 173). To be simultaneously class-constituting and class-obscuring is a distinctive feature of the Western "liberal meritocratic" variant of a capitalism that, since 1989, is "alone" in the world (except for the "political" or "authoritarian" variant in China and other Asian countries) (Milanovic 2019). Compared with its social-democratic predecessor, which was a compressed middle-class society, liberal meritocratic capitalism is marked by greatly increased inequality and the rise of a "self-perpetuating upper class" (ibid., ch. 2).

The meritocratic new upper class is simultaneously more open and more closed than past upper classes. It is more open because its members are not rentiers, but they tend to work and access to privileged work positions is usually based on educational credentials that are in principle accessible to all. Milanovic (2019, 34) calls this condition *homoploutia*, which is the concentration of high capital and high labor income in the same individual. With a look at the United States, and with a good measure of hyperbole,[52] Daniel Markovits (2019) speaks of a "superordinate working class" because the top 1 percent of earners "today own perhaps two-thirds or even three-quarters of their total incomes to their labor and therefore substantially to their education" (ibid., 13). Accordingly, rising economic inequality is not due to a shift of income from labor to capital, as one might think in analogy to the capitalist past, but due to a "shift of income away from middle-class labor and toward superordinate labor" (ibid.). Because the rich of today work, and because they do so on the basis of diplomas, they are in a condition to sport their privileged position as "earned advantage."[53] Markovits calls this posture "ultimately . . . a moral error. But it rests on economic facts" (ibid., 94).

104   POLITICAL NEOLIBERALISM

The "moral error" derives from the fact that, as Markovits (2019) *also* shows, the access to elite education, particularly in the United States, is heavily skewed in favor of the very upper class that is boastful of its individual merits. At his alma mater, Yale Law School—the most elite of America's elite-(re)producing educational institutions—there are "more students from households in the top 1 percent of the income distribution than from the entire bottom half," and this is despite the fact that Yale has waived its legacy admissions that are alive and well in most other Ivy Leagues (ibid., 17). This data suggests that the meritocratic upper class, underneath its self-presentation of getting and being there through effort and hard work alone, is, in reality, tightly closed. This closure is only secondarily the result of prohibitively high university fees, which is a novelty of the past few decades—the latter due to neoliberal "human capital" reasoning for which higher education is not a public but a private good that needs to be financed by the individual who is profiting from it.[54]

No, primarily, meritocratic closure is achieved through a greater degree of homogamy or assortative mating, which is the propensity of highly educated males to marry highly educated females. In early 1960s America, only 3 percent of marriages were between two college graduates; fifty years later, this was the case for 25 percent (Markovits 2019, 48). As a result, the current US upper class is the "least gendered" in history, with homogamy accounting for one-third of the inequality increase in the United States between 1967 and 2007 (Milanovic 2019, 66, 39). Meritocratic homogamy seals the upper class through their investing more effort and resources than ever before in the production of high-achieving children—sometimes referred to as "helicopter parenting."[55] As Markovits put it dryly, "(m)eritocracy sustains dynasties by reconstructing the family on the model of the firm, the household on the model of the workplace, and the child on the model of the product" (2019, 116).

Young (1958) had erred that modern meritocracy would replenish itself through an ever more accurate and earlier testing of *natural* talent. In reality, *nurtured* talent is of the essence, its natural production site being the family that—as Schumpeter (1953, 158) knew—is the "true individual of class theory." By contrast, Young's (1958, 106) expectation that in a meritocracy "the gap between the classes (would) inevitably become wider" was on target. However, one underestimates meritocracy's class nature if not nurtured but natural talent is seen as the sorting device. As Markovits corrects

Young, meritocracy sustains itself through "more and more intense cultivation of *nurtured* talent," in the homogamous family (2019, 259, emphasis supplied). The truth of meritocracy is to "launder" prior inequality rather than constituting a new type of inequality (ibid., 73). The founder of Sciences Po, a classic academic reproduction machine of France's elite since the late nineteenth century, expressed this in all openness: "Obliged to submit to the law of the majority, the classes that call themselves superior can preserve their political hegemony only by invoking the law of the most capable."[56] It is only half-jesting to call meritocracy an "aristocracy," because it "comprehensively isolates an elite caste from the rest of society and enables this caste to pass its advantage down through the generations" (Markovits 2019, 260f). The inevitable intervention of the family gives a lie to the progressive equality-of-opportunity garb of meritocracy, which is "coherent with the idea of meritocracy, yet not with its practice" (Mijs 2016, 25).[57]

Meritocracy is evidently Janus-faced. In its self-perception, "status is never fixed, no success ever final," its "overclass convinced that it is composed of scrappy underdogs"; and all have a "personal story about how it was through grit, talent, and determination that you fought your way inside" (Hayes 2012, ch. 5). In reality, the elite has run away from the rest, in the contemporary period in particular from the middle class.[58] This yields a new variant of Disraeli's "two nations," in which economic inequality "distinctively concerns not poverty but wealth" (Markovits 2019, 78; see also Savage 2021). With an eye on the United States, Sandel speaks of "skyboxification": "At a time of rising inequality, the marketization of everything means that people of affluence and people of modest means lead increasingly separate lives. We live and work and shop and play in different places. Our children go to different schools. You might call it the skyboxification of American life" (2012, 205).[59]

Mijs (2019, 1) observed the paradox that rising inequality under neoliberalism goes along with strengthened popular beliefs in meritocracy—about two-thirds of surveyed people in twenty-three OECD countries, between 1987 and 2012, "attribute success to meritocratic factors." Mijs attributes this paradox to something akin to Sandel's skyboxification, as people on both sides of the income divide simply cannot see the width of the gap that separates their lives: "Growing levels of income inequality mean that experiences and interactions with people across income, wealth and racial fault lines

106 POLITICAL NEOLIBERALISM

are becoming more seldom" (ibid., 6). As a result, "growing inequality goes together with a strengthening of citizens' meritocratic beliefs" (ibid., 23).

Steffen Mau and colleagues (2023), in an instantly acclaimed mixed-method study of "consent" and "conflict" in contemporary Germany, confirm and further refine this finding. According to them, there is a paradoxical simultaneity, particularly among production workers and the less educated, of strongly criticizing inequality, especially from the top, *and* exceptionally strong beliefs in meritocracy, both reconciled by a certain satisfaction with their own economic situation, however modest it is. As they argue, the lower classes' "acceptance of a society based on achievement (*Leistungsgesellschaft*) is one of the most important obstacles to the political mobilization for more equality" (ibid., 87).

In perfect circularity, meritocracy justifies the inequality whose growth is unimpeded due to the very workings of meritocratic beliefs. An experimental study found that "educationism," a neologism modeled on racism and sexism to denote categorically negative attitudes toward less-educated people, is strong among highly educated *and* less educated people, trumping the traditional class markers of income and occupation: "Less educated people are seen as more responsible and blameworthy for their situation, as compared to poor people or working class people" (Kuppens et al. 2018, 429). Educationism is "one of the last bastions of 'acceptable' prejudice," and, astoundingly, it is prevalent "to an even greater extent" among lower-educated than among higher-educated people (ibid., 429, 444). This data confirms Young's dystopian foreboding of a smug meritocratic upper class "los(ing) sympathy with the people whom they govern," while "(f)or the first time in human history the inferior man has no ready buttress for his self-regard" (1958, 107, 108).

Some fifty years ago, neo-Marxists thought that a combination of political "legitimation crisis" and sociocultural "motivation crisis," emanating from rising democratic and post-materialist lifestyle aspirations, respectively, would undermine the competitive work ethic of "late capitalism" (Habermas 1973). The general acceptance of the merit principle and its inequality-legitimizing logic, even by the losers, suggests otherwise. Far from opposing capitalism, "people" themselves "have become capitalistic calculating machines" (Milanovic 2019, 195).

Conclusion

The six political forms of neoliberalism distinguished in this chapter are mutually implicated: one cannot describe one without making use of (some of) the others. At the same time, there is tension between some, while there is strong compatibility if not exchangeability between others.

The most extreme case of tension is between authoritarianism and governance. This reflects a fundamental ambiguity of neoliberalism, to simultaneously require and refute the state. A red thread of *all* institutional forms of neoliberalism is to negate democracy. This is most obvious in the case of authoritarianism, not so much in a formal as informal sense, in terms of a mentality that Crouch (2004) has called "post-democracy." Governance, in contrast, which is the closest that any of the institutional forms comes to an official self-description of political neoliberalism, is exactly meant to reinstate democracy under conditions of a state in retreat. A closer look, however, reveals that governance demotes citizens to consumers of revamped (ideally privatized and competition-imbued) state services. Of course, it is to be conceded that finding fault with the notion of citizens as consumers requires a participatory and perhaps romanticizing understanding of citizenship and democracy in (neo)liberal times, that perhaps had never been the reality even in the best of times.[60]

Let me add one further self-critical note, on authoritarianism. A more dramatic understanding of it, as prominently advanced by Klein (2007), challenges our distinction between institutional and counter-institutional political forms of neoliberalism, between order and rupture, the latter to be explored in later chapters. In such reading, neoliberalism *in toto* operates by way of rupture and exception, from its first appearance in mid-1970s Chile to the European Union's democracy-bashing imposition of austerity on southern member states, post-2008, to, perhaps, the COVID-19 crisis.

In contrast to the tension-riddled authoritarianism-governance pair, the case of strongest overlap, verging on exchangeability, is between governance and technocracy. They convene in their depoliticizing effect, pushing aside a liberal understanding of politics as interest mediation in favor of politics as problem-solving. Democracy is still meant to be enhanced by both, including by a novel, post-bureaucratic (self-)understanding of technocracy in the digital age. Technocracy's democratic pretension is both expressed

108 POLITICAL NEOLIBERALISM

and exposed as false in the phenomenon of "technopopulism" (Bickerton and Accetti 2021), which rests on an understanding, correct in my view, of populism not as an expression of but as threat to democracy (see Chapter 4).

None of the discussed institutional forms of neoliberalism are *exclusively* neoliberal—even governance, while presented here as most closely aligned with neoliberalism, might as well be understood as the generic noun to "governing" in whatever context. Instead, they may also be found in other constellations, from liberal to not so liberal, antedating the arrival of neoliberalism. The one concept whose association with neoliberal is most jarring, is constitutionalism. At its origins a bulwark against monarchs, in democratic times it became one against mobs. Since John Hart Ely (1980), constitutionalism has been associated with minority protection from the Tocquevillian risk of majority despotism, at least in the motherland of judicial review, the United States. However, neoliberals have not shied away from fashioning their claims in a language of rights. The most hilarious example is when some of them opposed the capital controls under the Bretton Woods regime (1944–1971), the international bedrock of the golden age of Social Democracy, as violation of the "right to emigrate," the "basis of all ... other human rights." This right to emigrate, so the argument went, would be void for people without the right to take their belongings with them, their "capital" included (Slobodian 2021, 135).

While we discussed the European Union from the angle of federation and constitutionalism, it exhibits also the other institutional forms of neoliberalism (except meritocracy),[61] and this in purer form than any other polity. An element in point is authoritarianism. Some deem it inherent in the European Union's structure (Wilkinson 2021), as not least the never-ending debate on the "democratic deficit" suggests—that indeed appears entirely pointless if the European Union at heart is "authoritarian liberalism" (ibid.).[62] For others, authoritarianism describes only the most recent "post-political" phase of the European Union (Dani 2017), in form of the "Troika" (consisting of the European Commission, European Central Bank, and the IMF) imposing austerity on recalcitrant southern member states. This included forced government changes in Greece and Italy, during the prolonged Sovereign Debt Crisis, which is the starkest example yet of Brussels-imposed neoliberalism at the cost of democracy (more on this in Chapter 3).

Finally, we noticed that the political left, as it embraced neoliberalism, has been stronger allied with some of its political forms than with others—particularly strong with governance, but also with the meritocratic legitimation of a neoliberal order that, as we shall see, entails a strong commitment to antidiscrimination and diversity. To better understand the shifting left-right balance and political support structure of neoliberalism, it is necessary to move from inventory to genealogy.

Chapter 3
From Right to Left, and Back?

A Genealogy

In the most complete analysis yet of the "rise and fall" of neoliberalism in a single country, Gary Gerstle (2022, 11) argues that, in the United States, neoliberalism matured from "political movement" into "political order" when the political left, which was originally allied with the welfare capitalism or social democracy that preceded the neoliberal era, bought into its principles. "A key attribute of a political order," according to Gerstle, "is the ability of its ideological dominant party to bend the opposition party to its will" (ibid., 2). Following this insight, the focus of this chapter is on this crucial transition point, when a movement initially associated with the political right turned into an order by the political left getting on board. The chapter maps some of the expressions of Third Way leftist neoliberalism, such as "social investment" welfare restructuring and a "neoliberal multiculturalism" surrounding diversity and antidiscrimination. Moreover, as further chapters will show, once there was agreement among the political center forces about the political economy, which had originally provided the gist of the right versus left distinction, political conflict shifted toward identity politics at the extreme right and left ends of the political spectrum.

When neoliberalism arrived in the United Kingdom and the United States, 1979 and 1980, respectively, it was the project of the political right—Tories in the United Kingdom and Republicans in the United States. One critic called it "vanguard" neoliberalism (Davidson 2017). It pushed crude "capitalist class" interests, such as keeping (asset-threatening) inflation down at the cost of mass unemployment, union-bashing (miners in the United Kingdom, air controllers in the United States), deregulating finance, undoing highly progressive tax systems, and privatizing the public sector. Neoliberalism's initial association with the political right suggests a conspiratorial view of its arrival as "restoration of class power" (Harvey 2005, 16). Along such lines, Wolfgang Streeck (2013, 41) corrected "late capitalist" crisis theories, which had deemed the source of trouble on the popular side: "(N)ot

Political Neoliberalism. Christian Joppke, Oxford University Press. © Oxford University Press (2025).
DOI: 10.1093/oso/9780197801918.003.0004

the masses . . . but capital has renounced its loyalty to the (welfarist) capitalism of the post-war era." Similarly, Jacob Hacker and Paul Pierson (2010, 176) argued for the United States that the neoliberal turn has been the result of "organized combat" by business, starting with the famous 1971 letter of the later Supreme Court Justice Lewis Powell to the Chamber of Commerce, which warned that the "American economic system is under broad attack."

One should not be naïve about the powers of business, which have increased to a point that "today one does not know what is state and what is market" (Streeck 2013, 72). But it is still fact that, unlike Augusto Pinochet in Chile, Margaret Thatcher and Ronald Reagan arrived by democratic acclamation, and that both stood the re-election test, by huge margins, Thatcher even twice (until a coup in her own party felled her). This points to the uncomfortable factor of lower- and middle-class complicity in the rise of neoliberalism. It is crucial for understanding why the political left could not stay aloof forever. As Michael Mann (2013, 141) summarized the dynamic, Keynesianism, which helped bring about broad middle-class prosperity in the 1960s and 1970s, "produced its grave diggers through its very successes."

In a pioneering work of continued relevance, Monika Prasad (2006) refutes a top-down explanation of neoliberal policies, which sees the latter as a result of globalization and business power instigating a race to the bottom. If that were the case, she objects, neoliberal policies should have arrived everywhere at the same time and with equal force. But, in reality, initially at least, neoliberalism succeeded only in the United Kingdom and the United States, not in Germany and France. This suggests a bottom-up explanation, which is centered on the democratic process. One important factor in her scenario is different tax-welfare linkages that sharply divided the increasingly prosperous middle classes from the poor in the Anglo-Saxon countries, while this division remained muted in Continental Europe. For instance, a "reverse-redistributive" French welfare state (ibid., 22), financed in large part by invisible regressive sales taxes and benefiting the middle classes more than the poor, is much less vulnerable to attack than a US welfare state that is financed by highly visible progressive income taxes and that targets the poor with smallish but easily politicized benefits. Prasad's main point, however, is a different and rather surprising one: the greater strength of the left in the United Kingdom and the United States over much of the postwar period, and their "adversarial" policies that included more steeply progressive tax systems and more redistributive social policies for the poor than in continental Europe, made both countries ripe for a radical backlash by increasingly affluent voters.[1]

In Prasad's footsteps, Steffen Mau (2015) has raised the question "why did the European middle classes accept neo-liberalism," and he comes to similar conclusions. With a sharper edge though, he speaks of the middle classes' "self-disempowerment" (ibid., 96). This is because half of their growth[2] post-World War II, in his calculation, is due to welfare states that redistribute more across the life cycle and *within* social classes than between them. Neoliberal austerity policies then went after the pensions, education, and health care that had mainly benefited the middle class. Why should the middle classes favor such self-harming policies? His answer is their "structural and mental transformation" by postwar prosperity: "The collective upward mobility, the increase in security and property, the spread of homeownership, the interest in providing the best education possible to one's children, and also the investment of one's own monetary resources to increase one's wealth . . . loosened ties to the state and increased affinity to the market" (ibid., 12).

Two telling elements in this list are homeownership and shareholding. By 2013, 60 percent of the housing stock in Western Europe was owner-occupied.[3] But homeowners tend to vote conservative. This nexus was cunningly exploited by Thatcher's strategy of building a "property-owning democracy." It is a centerpiece in her vision of Britain, which she appositely grounded in the past, as "British inheritance": "Let me give you my vision . . . a man's right to work as he will, to spend what he earns, to own property, to have the state as servant not as master: these are the British inheritance" (quoted in Hall 2011, 706). After passing the 1980 Housing Act, her government sold one million council flats below market value to their previous tenants. As a result, the rate of British home owners increased from 55 percent in 1980 to 67 percent in 1990 (Prasad 2006, 141). By 1987, eight years into Thatcher's reign, 57 percent of British manual workers owned their homes, 66 percent did not belong to a union, 40 percent lived in the prosperous south, and 38 percent worked in a private sector that had greatly expanded in the meantime due to the busy privatization of state firms. Here was a partially Tory-engineered "new working class" that also voted Tory (ibid., 159).

A second element to boost middle-class neoliberalism is their increased involvement in the financial sector. His eye on the United Kingdom, Mau speaks of "Machiavellian privatization" because the selling of state firms, again under market value, was "geared toward turning average voters into shareholders" (2015, 34). Employee stock ownership plans created "ambivalent interests" on the part of wage earners, who might "become shareholders of their own employer" (ibid., 37). Overall, "financialization" sucked ordinary people into the engine room of neoliberal capitalism. This happened not only through stockholding, so that by the year 2000 more than half of Americans were invested in the stock market, mostly through mutual funds, with "portfolio thinking" becoming commonplace (Davis 2009, 3, 25)[4]. In addition, stagnating wages made the middle-class dependent on more easily available credits, dubbed "privatized Keynesianism" by Colin Crouch (2011, 114), with privately owned (and itself credit-financed) housing as the collateral of choice. The perplexing outcome is that "all became complicit in the financial model" (ibid., 110).[5]

This chapter first lays out, with the help of Anthony Giddens' *Programmschrift* (1998), the ideological contours of the "Third Way," which repositioned the left in a pro-capitalist direction after the fall of Communism. The second part shows the policy import of Third Way thinking in a new conception of the welfare state, as "social investment," whose purpose is no longer the *de-* but *re-*commodification of the individual. Thirdly, the right-to-left turn of neoliberalism has also expressed itself in a thin multiculturalism surrounding diversity and antidiscrimination. Finally, some have argued, with special attention to the European Union, that after the 2008 Financial Crisis neoliberalism has recovered its original authoritarian and democracy-thumping face. With respect to the European Union, where this tendency has been strongest, I argue that the EU is not only lately but structurally authoritarian, thus moving the previous chapter's EU analysis as model neoliberal polity forward in time. Overall, authoritarianism is less a distinct third phase than an ever-present possibility or even aspect of a neoliberal order.

Third Way

The political left, originally wedded to "old-style social democracy" (Giddens 1998, 8–11) that was statist and collectivist, could not stay apart from the market turn of increasing segments of the population. This raises the question how a transformed left might distinguish itself from the neoliberal right. This turned out not as obvious as it seems because the meanings

114 POLITICAL NEOLIBERALISM

of "left" and "right" became unstable. Certainly, on the right side, "neoliberals link unfettered market forces to a defense of traditional institutions, particularly the family and the nation," and their appearance entailed "severest strictures for multiculturalism" (ibid., 12). In Gerstle's account, Reagan neoliberals, next to their free market commitment, embraced "neo-Victorian" values, lining up with the anti-new-left Neoconservatives and the evangelist Moral Majority (2022, 12). On the opposite side of what became known as "culture wars," Gerstle locates a "cosmopolitan" or "multicultural" moral perspective, which has become the trademark of the market- and globalization-friendly New Democrats from Bill Clinton on. Gerstle thus makes a larger point about the logic of political conflict in the neoliberal order, which is the "coexistence of cultural polarization with a broad agreement on principles of political economy" (ibid., 14).

However, the symbiosis of "market fundamentalism" and "conservatism" is tension ridden. "Nothing is more dissolving of tradition than the 'permanent revolution' of market forces," Anthony Giddens remarks (1998, 15). Thatcher promptly rejected to be called "conservative": "We are not a 'conservative' party; we are a party of innovation, of imagination, of liberty, of striking out in new directions, of renewed national pride and a novel sense of leadership . . . That's not 'conservative'. The name is wrong" (quoted in Fawcett 2020, part VI). Thatcher was in good company. Friedrich Hayek himself had loudly refused the label. The liberalism that he endorsed was "to let change run its course even if we cannot predict where it will lead" (1960, 400), and he expressed zero-sympathy for the conservatives' penchant to "distrust . . . the new and the strange" (ibid., 405).

The uncertain positioning of the neoliberal right is mirrored in that of the neoliberal left. Giddens, whose *The Third Way* (1998) must be considered the manifesto of the neoliberal left, would be offended by the moniker "neoliberal," which he wholly associated with "Thatcherism" and the "new right" (ibid., 8). Accordingly, in his list of "third way values," one looks in vain for a celebratory reference to the market—"freedom as autonomy" is as close as it gets, and the top two entries on his list are "equality" and "protection of the vulnerable" (ibid., 66). Throughout, the market figures mostly in the negative, in combinations like "unfettered market," "market fundamentalism," and so on, all attributed to the "neoliberals." Giddens' *Third Way* is a second-order, reflexive manifesto that already meant to answer the immediate charge that the Third Way is "warmed-over neoliberalism" (ibid., 25),[6] "Thatcher in trousers" as Eric Hobsbawm inimitably referred to Tony Blair.

FROM RIGHT TO LEFT, AND BACK? 115

At the same time, Giddens astonishingly mentions as the "prime motto" of "third way politics" that there are "no rights without responsibilities" (1998, 65). This is in distinction to "old-style social democracy," which he described as "inclined to treat rights as unconditional claims" (ibid.). While this may be correct, certainly if T. H. Marshall's (1950) social citizenship is the benchmark, this "prime motto" leaves little space, if any, to distinguish the Third Way from the "moral authoritarianism" that Giddens attributes to the neoliberal right (1998, 8). Striking the same chord, "moral regeneration" informed restrictive welfare reforms under New Labour, which signals an intention to change behavior in a patronizing way, in deviation from the "non-judgmentalism" of the past (Clasen 2000, 99). Fully on that line, Giddens endorses certain moralist and punitive aspects of neoliberalism. A first is the "obligation to look actively for work" when receiving unemployment benefits (1998, 65). A second is his implicit acceptance of the controversial "broken windows" theory of harshly punishing minor crime, because small digressions "tend to have a cumulative effect" (ibid., 86). A third is the call for "legally binding" obligations of children to look after their parents, which is a rather coercive and wishful way of producing "strong families," but which Giddens considers "a notion whose time has come" (ibid., 97f).

Giddens is silent about the fact that family (as expansion to individual) responsibility, which is part of the Third Way's understanding of "no rights without responsibilities," had been a plank of the old Poor Law tradition that came to be replaced by the modern notion of welfare "as a right, not as a charity," to quote Harold Wilensky's classic definition (1975, 1). Under Blair, parental responsibilities were also mobilized to tackle "anti-social behaviour," by withdrawing universal child benefits from the parents of juvenile offenders. Blair's Work and Pensions Secretary, Alistair Darling, expressed the underlying philosophy: "There is no unconditional right to benefit . . . we should look at making sure the social security system and the benefit system are matched by responsibility" (in Lister 2002, 2). In the United States as well, the Poor Law idea of family responsibility has been guiding principle of the 1996 Personal Responsibility and Work Opportunity Reconciliation Act (PRWORA), with which Third Way pioneer Clinton delivered on his promise to "end welfare as we know it." The title of the new law is incomplete, because not only "personal" but also "family" responsibility is enforced in it. This is still neoliberal, if one follows Thatcher's dictum that in lieu of "society," there are only "individual men and woman *and there are families*." However, the irony is that Third Way leftists, from Giddens

116 POLITICAL NEOLIBERALISM

in theory to Clinton and Blair in law and policy, would push the family element.

This confirms Melinda Cooper's (2017) argument that "social conservatism" has undergirded not only the neoliberalism of the right but of the left also. PRWORA abolished federal cash payments for single mothers, known as Aid for Families with Dependent Children (AFDC), already hated by Reagan for its production of "Welfare Queens." Its replacement, called Temporary Assistance for Needy Families (TANF), next to limiting its benefits to five years over a claimant's lifetime and imposing strict work requirements, is a state-level system of legally enforced private family responsibility. As the law's preamble says, "Marriage is the foundation of a successful society . . . Promotion of responsible fatherhood and motherhood is integral to successful child-rearing" (ibid., 107). "Promotion" is a euphemism for the sub-federal states' new task of policing paternity obligations. As Cooper comments, PRWORA recovered the "poor law tradition" in that it erases the "distinction between the emotional and financial bonds of kinship" (ibid., 69). Clinton's Democratic successor, Barak Obama, shared the "responsible fatherhood" approach in social policy, which underlined to him the "role that values and culture play in addressing some of our most urgent social problems" (ibid., 113). As Cooper further observes, the conservative streak is constitutive of neoliberal doctrine itself, as laid out by University of Chicago academics Richard Posner and Gary Becker, who argued that the "freedom of contract cannot exist without the . . . noncontractual obligations of family" (ibid., 117). Of course, they endorsed family values not for sentimental reasons, but to minimize the financial cost to society.

Despite these difficulties of distinguishing left from right neoliberalism, much of Giddens' *Third Way* is a serious reckoning with the dilemmas and the meaning of "left" after the "death of socialism." When capitalism, for the first time in history, stood to be accepted as a system without alternative, what more could be done but to smoothen its edges? His continental Critical Theory colleague, Jürgen Habermas, came to the same conclusion, arguing that the "only remaining option is to civilize and tame the capitalist dynamic from within" (quoted in Wilkinson 2021, 187). At the same time, the "blue-collar working class," the classic clientele of leftist parties, was in "steep decline" (Giddens 1998, 23), and there was a need to cater to the interests of a new "affluent majority" (ibid., 19). And who would want a return to "old-style social democracy," which never was a golden era of democracy anyway but an "elitist state, with small groups of public-spirited experts in the state bureaucracy monitoring the fiscal and monetary policies to be followed" (ibid., 16), a "post-democracy" before the word as one could add? There is truth to this, and a false romanticization of whatever preceded "neoliberalism" is concededly one of the weakest spots of using and running with the term, as tried in this book.

Moreover, Giddens's ambition not to "shrink the state" and of "democratizing democracy" (1998, 70–78) is identifiably leftist and foreign to the neoliberal DNA. Furthermore, unlike real-existing neoliberalism, particularly that of Clinton and Obama, Giddens is head-on when rejecting meritocracy as "highly unequal" and a "self-contradictory idea" (ibid., 102). Even his stress on "responsibility" is perfectly logical, on the assumption that "(w)ith expanding individualism should come an extension of individual obligations" (ibid., 65). What is the alternative, one must ask, if the binding powers of society are in decline? Finally, Giddens's gist of the family as "basic institution of civil society" is not a return to its traditional form. Instead, he favors the "democratic family" (ibid., 89) that accommodates equality and unconventional sex constellations. Overall, a distinct mark of Giddens's *Third Way* is to strengthen the democratic element that has been slighted by paleo-neoliberalism.

Other, and expressly political Third Way manifestos were less ambitious and more straightforwardly pro-market than Giddens's. In a neoliberal context, the word "third way" is actually first mentioned in the 1992 platform of the US New Democrats. It is a glowing endorsement of "free enterprise":

> Our Party's first priority is opportunity—broad-based, non-inflationary economic growth . . . and jobs for all . . . We reject both the do-nothing government . . . and the big government theory that says we can hamstring business and tax and spend our way to prosperity. Instead we offer a third way . . . (W)e honor business as a noble endeavor, and vow to create a far better climate for firms and independent contractors . . . We believe in free enterprise and the power of market force. (in Mudge 2018, 57)

For Europe, consider the Schröder–Blair Paper of 1999. While tapping into many themes, including the "responsibility of the individual for family, neighbourhood, and society," this programmatic statement of *Neue Mitte* German Social Democrats and British New Labour is self-labeled a "supply-side agenda for the left." Resembling the 1992 New Democrat platform, it is enthusiastic about "economic dynamization (*Dynamisierung*)

118 POLITICAL NEOLIBERALISM

and the release of creativity and innovation," and the forging of a "new entrepreneurial spirit in all sectors (*auf allen Ebenen*) of society."[7]

Proudly noting that "in almost all countries of the European Union Social Democrats rule," the end-of-millennium Schröder–Blair Paper proclaims that "the past two decades of neoliberal laisser-faire are over." This turned out to be wrong. At least in economic policy, Third Way governments mainly continued the line set by their rightist predecessors, and often more insistently. The first Third Way government, under Clinton in the United States, is a case in point. This "first left-leaning, pot-smoking, and free-loving baby boomer" (Gerstle 2022, 154) to move into the White House:

- signed the North American Free Trade Agreement (NAFTA) in 1993 that turned North America, including Mexico, into a single market, speeding-up the deindustrialization that helped Donald Trump in his first-time win in 2016;
- established the World Trade Organization (WTO) in 1994, which would implement neoliberal principles worldwide, most gallingly erasing non-tariff barriers that expressed democratic majority preferences;
- deregulated the telecommunications industry in 1996, which laid the foundation for Big Tech and the digital economy; and
- repealed, in 1999, the Glass Steagall Act that had separated commercial from investment banking, removing a major hurdle for the rise of finance with its giant inequities and disruptive powers, not to mention its cataclysmic crisis a few years later.

Reflecting neoliberalism's graduation from political movement to political order, the Third Way took the market economy less as something to be shaped to meet the public interest than as a natural thing that society had to adjust to. Clinton considered markets "akin to natural law": "We cannot stop global change. We cannot repeal the economic competition that is everywhere. We can only harness the energy to our benefit" (quoted in Gerstle 2022, 157). To his Third Way follower in the United Kingdom, Blair, the idea of "stop(ping) and debat(ing) globalization" was as pointless as "debat(ing) whether autumn should follow summer," and he praised the new global age as "replete with opportunities, but they only go to those swift to adapt, slow to complain, . . . willing and able to change" (quoted in Goodhart 2017, 7).

In Europe, the Third Way left's peak moment was the so-called Lisbon Strategy, given out during (socialist-ruled) Portugal's EU presidency, in

March 2000. Within just ten years, this was the hope, Europe would become "the most competitive and dynamic knowledge-based economy in the world, capable of sustainable economic growth with more and better jobs and greater social cohesion." This is a mouthful that was missed by more than an inch. But the Lisbon Strategy's combination of the economic and the social, of "competition" and "cohesion," though with a clear sense that cohesion had to be at the service of competition, was quintessentially Third-Way leftist.[8] Even more optimistic was the new Article 3.3 of the Lisbon Treaty, which obliged the Union to "combat social exclusion and discrimination" and to "promote social justice and protection."

At the time of the Lisbon summit, twelve of the (pre-enlargement) European Union's fifteen member states were governed by the left, most of them endorsing Third Way values. Whereas in the first stage of neoliberalism, dominated by the political right, constraints on capital and markets were removed, the second stage, dominated by the left, was under the star of "renew(ing) the 'social' realm in an entrepreneurial direction" (Davies and Gane 2021, 5). Only now, neoliberalism branched out from narrow economic policy into a more general "remaking of subjectivity around the ideal of enterprise" (Davies 2016, 127), as it had first been laid out in Foucault's visionary interpretation of the Chicago School's human capital idea.

Social Investment

A main plank in the Third Way policy agenda is the rebuilding of the welfare state in terms of "social investment." This notion is revealing because it reasserts the social, which was slighted by earlier neoliberals from Hayek to Thatcher, but it does so only in economic colors, as "investment." Its advocates understand social investment as alternative to a neoliberalism that is associated with "welfare retrenchment" (e.g., Hemerijck 2013). However, by conceiving of the social not as in opposition to the economic, as in the social-democratic tradition of Karl Polanyi (1944) or Marshall (1950), but trying to adjust the social to what the economy commands, social investment partakes in the "attenuation of the 'social'" that is neoliberalism's bottom line (Hall 2011, 723).

The term "social investment" itself was first used by Giddens, who meant by it a new welfare system geared toward "investment in human capital

120 POLITICAL NEOLIBERALISM

wherever possible, rather than the direct provision of economic maintenance" (1998, 117). Gøsta Esping-Andersen (2000) provided flesh to it, in a report to the Portuguese EU presidency that gave out the Lisbon Strategy. The report is a full turn from his famous, classically social democratic or social liberal idea that the ideal welfare state was to "decommodify" the individual (Esping-Andersen 1990). Instead, the point of social investment is the opposite, "recommodification." The idea is simple: rather than protect people from the market, social policy should help them to compete on the market. This requires the move from "passive maintenance" to "social investment": "The new terminology mirrors a growing consensus that social policy must become 'productivist'... That is, social policy should actively mobilize and maximize the productive potential of the population so as to minimize its need for, and dependence on, government benefits" (Esping-Andersen 2000, 22).[9] Concretely, this means adopting the Scandinavian recipe of supporting "families and children" (ibid., 3), this one in continuity with classic welfare, Nordic-style, which has always been costly and thus requiring the full mobilization of the workforce, women included. Supporting families and children allows mothers to work, thereby increasing the labor supply, and—this is the new human-capital layer with a leftist tick—push the young from early on onto an equal-opportunity track.[10] More generally, the dual family-cum-child orientation epitomizes the dual thrust of social investment to reshape the work-family life balance and to invest in human capital, also in later phases of the life-cycle, both for the sake of greater productivity.

"Equity," yes, but in the service of "maximiz(ing) efficiency" (Esping-Andersen 2000, 20): this is the essence of Third Way neoliberalism. As Esping-Andersen rather obliquely notes, it entails a "different notion of equality than that which has applied to the past" (ibid., 19). "Low-end service jobs," for instance, are to him an inevitable consequence of a "knowledge-extensive economy," and even functional for "the new needs of families" (ibid., 1). The challenge is rather to avoid "entrapment" (ibid., 27). While one may find this entirely reasonable, it follows the neoliberal playbook, in which inequality is a necessary and legitimate element of a competitive market order. The distinct Third Way response is not to eradicate inequality but to soften its edges, by "combating social exclusion" (ibid., 22). As two Canadian political scientists aptly noted, the underlying Third Way concern for "social cohesion" makes for a social policy that is more "fight against social exclusion than for social equality"; and instead of "equity now," the focus is on "equality of opportunity for *future* success" (Jensen and Saint-Martin 2003, 91, 92).

Despite his Third-Wayish U-turn, Esping-Andersen has set the normative bar high. He calls it "Rawlsian," according to which "the greatest advantage of any gains in efficiency should accrue to the poorest and weakest," thus endorsing the Difference Principle (2000, 22). By contrast, actual welfare reforms by Third Way governments have often not even met the weaker "Paretian" standard, which is "greater efficiency without anyone losing as a result" (ibid., 21). For instance, welfare-to-workfare transitions in the United States, Britain, and Germany, under Clinton, Blair, and Schröder, respectively, sought to "activate" the unemployed, yes, but more by reducing benefits and forcing them to accept low-paid jobs than by retraining them.[11] A review of Europe found the "social investment glass ... almost empty," with an "overriding focus on activation without proper attention to quality and to adequate protection in most countries" (Morel, Papier, and Palme 2012). The main exception are the Nordic countries, whose "flexicurity" schemes combine traditional social protection with activation and human capital promotion. The United Kingdom, by contrast, was high on social investment rhetoric, while reducing benefits and increasing their conditionality (ibid.).[12]

However high or low the benefit standard, the decisive Third Way move has been to deploy the efficiency rationale to a domain that had previously been dominated by an equality concern. "Social rights imply an absolute right to a certain standard of civilisation" (Marshall 1950, 43) is the old approach that came to be replaced. The irony is that conservative welfare retrenchment, as under Thatcher or Reagan, at least had kept the old "social rationale intact while imposing cost reduction" (Laruffa 2022a, 154). To conservatives, welfare was the opposite of work, and therefore it had to be reduced. By contrast, the leftist "variant of neoliberalism is more 'social' than welfare retrenchment precisely because it downplays social logic, rendering the social an economic object" (ibid., 150f). The result may be "improvements in social policy generosity," as in "social investment" proper, yet at the price of a "deeper economization" than before (ibid., 151).

A good illustration is the European Commission's 2013 "Social Investment Package." It goes to bizarre lengths in economizing the social, addressing poverty or homelessness less as intrinsic social ills than as mundane cost factors. "Social marginalisation," for instance, is said to imply "higher public health costs, increased policy and crime costs, foregone economic activity, lost wages and productivity, lost tax revenues," to which is added "the intergenerational costs that flow from the likelihood that a significant number of children from disadvantaged families will remain disadvantaged over their lifetimes" (quoted in Laruffa 2022b, 476). This is a compulsive calculation in money terms of something that is bad in itself. Similarly, the prevention of homelessness is praised as "investment" with a "high rate of return," and it is again calculated in monetary terms, even with a precise figure (whose computation is left in the dark, but a figure is a figure): "for every 1 Euro spent on preventing homelessness, about 2.20 Euros in costs are saved elsewhere" (ibid., 479). In the nine documents that constitute the European Commission's Social Investment Package, the words "efficient," "efficiency" etc. appear no less than 400 times (ibid., 478).

The neoliberal pedigree of social investment must not obscure that it may be the adequate response to "new social risks" that traditional welfare schemes are ill adapted to meet (Bonoli, 2005). In particular, the Bismarckian welfare state of continental Europe, which protects the income of male breadwinners on the basis of their prior social security payments, is premised on employment and the traditional family form that has seen its days. "New social risks" or needs arising in "postindustrial economies" (Esping-Andersen 1999, ch. 8), such as reconciling work with family obligations, lone parenthood, or low-paid work and long-term unemployment, concentrate in new risk groups, such as women, the young, and the low-skilled, which often stand outside the labor market and, indeed, wish to be included in the first. The problem is that their heterogeneity makes them difficult to organize politically.

How could the new risk groups ever be accommodated? By way of "modernising compromises," as Giuliano Bonoli (2005) has shown. This means that, primarily under Third Way governments, "old" welfare slack was cut, such as disproportionate disability or pension benefits, while the freed resources went to the new risk groups.[13] This not only increased the labor supply in low-fertility societies, and was welcome by business; it was also "much cheaper," because spending on family services or activation and training rarely exceeds 2 percent of GDP, while healthcare and pensions are more in the 10 percent range (ibid., 441). Jonah Levy (1999) called the trick turning "vice into virtue." He showed how "left-progressive" governments in France, Italy, and the Netherlands, all plagued by Bismarckian welfare states, managed to "enhance equity and efficiency simultaneously," by going after abusive disability pensions

FROM RIGHT TO LEFT, AND BACK? 123

(in the Netherlands) or excessive retirement privileges (in Italy) while upgrading the wages and benefits of part-timers and other labor market outsiders. The important message is that welfare retrenchment and welfare expansion can go hand-in-hand, one enabling the other. This yields the complex picture of welfare states "neither dismantled nor frozen" but "undergo(ing) complex processes of reconfiguration" (Häusermann 2010, 22).

The moment in which "in almost all countries of the EU Social Democrats rule(d)," to quote again the enthusiastic opening line of the 1999 Schröder–Blair Paper, turned out to be just that, a moment. Barely two years after the 2000 Lisbon European Union summit, most of these left governments were removed from office. But their social investment idea quickly became part of a "new consensus that draws support from across party lines" (Bonoli 2004). It has become a pillar of "post-industrial welfare reform," which is "not only about retrenchment but also about a plurality of constraints, needs, and demands" (Häusermann 2010, 24).

Neoliberal Multiculturalism

The rise of political neoliberalism coincided with the rise of multiculturalism, broadly understood as a minority rights movement that raises claims of cultural recognition rather than of material redistribution. As Nancy Fraser argued in a programmatic essay, "cultural recognition displaces socioeconomic redistribution as the remedy for injustice and the goal of political struggle," which is conducted by groups "under the banners of nationality, ethnicity, 'race,' gender, and sexuality" (1995, 68). The side-lining of "socioeconomic redistribution" obviously suits the neoliberal agenda, as pointed out by the social democratic critics of multiculturalism from early on (the fiercest and sharpest remains Barry 2001).

What multiculturalism shares with neoliberalism is not just their common origins in historical time and their complementarity in lowering the focus on redistribution, although each for different reasons. More substantively, both endorse the radical opening of nation-state societies that since 1989 has occurred under the flag of globalization. The early political dalliance of neoliberalism with conservative nationalism proved to be short-lived. Already Hayek had despised nationalism almost as much as he hated socialism, deeming them the "two greatest threats to a free civilization" (1982b,

124 POLITICAL NEOLIBERALISM

111), and he endorsed a cosmopolitanism in which "the stranger and even the foreigner" enjoyed the "same protection" as the "members of one's own small group" (ibid., 88). "Xenos rights," the rights of a guest-friend "who was assured individual admission and protection within an alien territory," were to Hayek a decisive mechanism to break through from tribal to market society (Hayek, quoted by Slobodian 2018, 123).

In his grand diagnosis of the contemporary "society of singularities," by which he means a society of hyper-individualism geared toward authenticity, German sociologist Andreas Reckwitz sees economic and cultural liberalism (that is, neoliberalism and multiculturalism) as dual pillars of a new regime of "apertistic liberalism," which he describes as the "opening, delimitation (*Entgrenzung*), and deregulation of the social" (2017, 375). Its carrier group is a "new middle class" of the highly educated, which subscribes to "expressive individualism," but which is internally divided between "socio-ecological" (multicultural) and "performer" (neoliberal) milieus (Reckwitz 2021). That an alliance between both groups is possible, is the claim of Fraser's "progressive neoliberalism" (2017a), developed for the United States but applicable elsewhere. It consists of an "alliance of mainstream currents of new social movements (feminism, anti-racism, multiculturalism, and LGBTQ rights)," on the one side, and "high-end symbolic and service-based business sectors (Wall Street, Silicon Valley, and Hollywood)," on the other, and she finds it realized in the New Democrats in the United States. Invented by Clinton in his 1991/1992 presidential campaign, progressive neoliberalism means "talking the talk of diversity, multiculturalism, and women's rights, even while ... walk(ing) the walk of Goldman Sachs" (Fraser 2017b).

Looking at the changing support structure of leftist parties across the major European countries, Thomas Piketty (2020) comes to a similar conclusion. He sees leftist parties no longer supported by workers but by a "Brahmin Left" of the highly educated, which "values scholastic success, intellectual work, and the acquisition of diplomas and knowledge" (ibid., 766).[14] While center-right parties continue to be dominated by a "Merchant Right" that "emphasizes professional motivation, a flair for business, and negotiating skills" (ibid.), the important matter is that both the left and the right are variants of meritocracy. They consequently share "a certain conservatism when it comes to maintaining the existing inequality regime" (ibid., 773). Under their joint reign, argues Piketty, issues of "property" are cast aside, while issues of "borders," ranging from immigration to security and multiculturalism, have entered center-stage. Piketty finds this new ruling-class constellation analogous to the "power-sharing between intellectual and warrior elites" in a feudal "trifunctional society," with the possibility of a Brahmin-Merchant fusion "as the highly educated become wealthier" (ibid., 774).

These analyses, from Fraser to Piketty, carry an important message. Contrary to its oppositional self-image, multiculturalism has become the *doxa* in a neoliberal order, if not the "ideal form of ideology" of "global capitalism," as already Slavoj Zizek (1997) had put it puckishly. Indeed, as Zizek argues, the "new multinationals" take "towards the French and American local population exactly the same attitudes as towards the population of Mexico, Brazil or Taiwan," and they share with the multiculturalists "a kind of empty global position, treat(ing) each local culture the way the colonizer treats colonial people—as 'natives' whose mores are to be carefully studied and respected" (ibid., 44).

While Zizek's view is contestable, it is incontrovertible that multiculturalism is an offshoot of the "age of human rights." But Samuel Moyn (2018, 2) has shown the latter to be "also an age of the victory of the rich." This is because human rights strive for "status equality," while pushing aside concerns over "distributive equality."[15] They establish a floor of protection under which no individual should sink, while distributive equality sought a ceiling on inequality. Distributive equality is fundamentally relational, involving society and concerned with "how far individuals are from one another," while the status equality of human rights is individualistic, worried about "how far an individual is from having nothing" (ibid.). It is easy to see that the move from "equality" proper to "sufficiency" as justice standard, which happened under the hegemony of human rights, is homologous to the ethics of neoliberalism, and "why the age of human rights (is) also the age of neoliberalism" (ibid., 180). A contemporary neoliberal of the Geneva School confirms that "the general relationship between economic liberty and human rights is productive and strong, so much so that promoting the former and latter are the selfsame enterprise" (Ernst-Ulrich Petersmann, ibid., 191).

Human rights, of course, are not minority rights, but they "have become . . . a banner for campaigns against discriminatory treatment on the basis of gender, race, and sexual orientation" (Moyn 2018, 6). Both abhor disadvantages for which the individual cannot be held responsible. As neoliberalism greatly increases the scope of "personal responsibility" in social policy (referred to as "responsibility-tracking" by Mounk 2017), it must be particularly sensitive to disadvantage outside the ambit of responsibility, arising from unchosen characteristics, such as sex and race. Neoliberal responsibilization even left its imprint in the world of progressive activism. The early gay rights movement, for instance, held that homosexuality is a matter of choice, to fend-off a prevailing nineteenth-century view of it as disease. More recently, coinciding with the rise of neoliberalism, gay activists have pushed the opposite notion that one is "born this way" (see Murray 2019, ch. 1), and they analogize homosexuality to ethnicity and race, in order to take advantage of entrenched antidiscrimination law and multiculturalism (see the early perceptive account by Epstein 1987).

The affinity between a thin multiculturalism, where multiculturalism is reduced to antidiscrimination, and neoliberalism is loud and clear in one of neoliberalism's earliest programmatic statements, Milton Friedman's *Capitalism and Freedom* (1962). In a chapter entitled "Capitalism and Discrimination," Friedman celebrates capitalism for its "substitution of contract arrangements for status arrangements." As a result, in capitalism there has been a "major reduction in the extent to which particular religious, racial, or social groups have operated under special handicaps in respect of their economic activities" (ibid., 108). Discrimination, for Friedman, is a result of monopoly, "whereas discrimination against groups of particular color or religion is least in those areas where there is the greatest freedom of competition" (ibid., 109). It simply does not pay to discriminate: "a free market separates economic efficiency from irrelevant characteristics" (ibid.). Discrimination is like tariffs that limit foreign trade, as irrational as "a 'taste' of others that one does not share" (ibid.).

One also arrives at the affinity between a thinned multiculturalism and neoliberalism through the angle of meritocracy, which is perhaps the dominant ideology of a neoliberal society. Meritocracy requires ascriptive discrimination to be suppressed. As Daniel Markovits (2019, ch. 3) put it, from the point of view of neoliberal elites, "prejudice that has no meritocratic gloss—based on race, ethnicity, gender, or sexuality—(is) . . . a cardinal and unforgivable sin that must be suppressed absolutely and without regard for the cost." This suggests that a market freedom logic works in favor of multiculturalism, not just a democratic equality logic, on which multiculturalists of all stripes have hedged their bets. In the economist's language, the combination of merit and antidiscrimination appeals to "new entrants," which immigrant minorities by definition are, while it repels "incumbents," the

FROM RIGHT TO LEFT, AND BACK? 127

natives who have other sources of advantage: "(N)ew entrants will be 'naturally' inclined to adopt a system of values that promotes competition and the constant questioning of established positions, whereas incumbents will be more prone to emphasize the dangers of 'excessive' competition" (Amable 2011, 27). Hence a multicultural immigrant society, Bruno Amable argues, will tend toward a thin understanding of equality as opportunity rather than outcome, equality as "levelling the playing field" (ibid., 24). This is exactly what neoliberalism prescribes.

Multiculturalism, of course, is a broad tent, and its advocates vehemently deny the charge of being bedfellows of neoliberalism. Will Kymlicka (2013), for one, has denounced "neoliberal multiculturalism" as "inclusion without solidarity." This is a concise description of cohesion and inclusion rhetoric growing stronger under Third Way leftist neoliberalism, as a substitute for redistribution and substantive equality demands that have fallen by the wayside. Of course, Kymlicka considers this a deviation from "multiculturalism" proper, which to him is "public recognition and support for minorities to express their distinct identities and practices" (ibid., 101), and which in his view is not separatist but integrationist ("citizenizing," he says), growing out of the 1960s civil rights struggles.

By the same token, Kymlicka (2013) has conceded that "neoliberal multiculturalism" exists. This raises the task of mapping it adequately. We must distinguish in this respect between two different understandings of the multiculturalism-neoliberalism linkage: either as historical twins contingently co-evolving in time, sharply separated in their causes and agendas; or as mutually implicated phenomena, with neoliberal precepts molding multiculturalism itself, yielding a *neoliberal* multiculturalism that differs from other variants of multiculturalism. Only the second understanding is of interest here.

But to distinguish neoliberal from other variants of multiculturalism requires a basic model of multiculturalism as a reference point. One finds one in Kymlicka (2019, 971), who makes the case for a "deschooled"[16] elementary multiculturalism that is about "reinterpret(ing) (core liberal values) in a more even-handed way." Its starting assumption is that Western liberal democracies, underneath their façade of liberal neutrality, are not "ethnoculturally neutral." They favor the "majority nation" in practice, for which minority groups stand to be compensated. The result is a "variable geometry" of different rights for different groups, which relate to the state in

128 POLITICAL NEOLIBERALISM

different ways. This is an important qualification to distinguish multiculturalism from mere antidiscrimination, which tends to be symmetric (the same
for all) and in this sense universalistic.

Kymlicka's (2019) elementary multiculturalism, which happens to be
indistinguishable from his own "liberal" theory of multiculturalism
(Kymlicka 1995), importantly entails a "shared commitment to a liberal
multicultural nationalism" (Kymlicka 2019, 972). This is because nationalism, in his view, is a "progressive political project" (Kymlicka 2015), which
provides the boundaries for democratic practice and for the solidarities that
are required for redistribution. In this view, which is simultaneously liberal nationalist and multiculturalist, the whole point of multiculturalism is
to "mitigate" nationalism's cost for minorities. Consequently, a neoliberal
multiculturalism would have to be one that denies both: the need for democratic practice and redistributive solidarities, and hence nationhood and the
premise of a closed society.

Such a "Hayekian" multiculturalism has been theorized by Chandran
Kukathas (2003), as an anarchic "archipelago of competing and overlapping
jurisdictions," in which the only right to be upheld is the "freedom to associate." Kukathas throws overboard the orthodox multicultural "politics of
recognition" in favor of a "politics of indifference," because the minimal state
pursues "no collective projects; it should express no group preferences . . . Its
only concern ought to be with upholding the framework of law within which
individuals and groups can function peacefully" (2003, 249). Kukathas' multiculturalism evidently builds on the austere modus vivendi liberalism from
Hobbes to Hayek, for which "diversity" is "not the value liberalism pursues
but the source of the problem to which it offers a solution" (ibid., 29).

Real-existing neoliberal multiculturalism departs from Kymlicka's
"deschooled" (in fact, liberal) model of multiculturalism in three respects.
First, it is not state-focused but multi-sectoral, a particularly important site
for it being the economy. Secondly, the majority-minority binary fades from
view. The thrust is symmetric and individualist rather than asymmetric and
groupist. Thirdly, and most importantly, multiculturalism's core concern
of justice for historically wronged minorities, from its earliest gestation
in the US civil rights struggles onward, is entirely absent in neoliberal
multiculturalism. Instead, an efficiency rationale moves to the fore.

I shall illustrate these elements along two prominent expressions of
neoliberal multiculturalism: diversity and antidiscrimination.

Diversity

Its first in-depth academic treatment, by Peter Schuck (2003, 14), considered the "diversity ideal" something "distinctively, if not uniquely American." By that time, the European Union had just made "United in Diversity" its official motto. Accordingly, far from being limited by geography or sector, diversity is the fungible master slogan of neoliberal societies, omnipresent in about all of its spheres,[17] in particular the corporate world where "diversity management" has long been a standard entry in the business school curriculum. Unlike traditional multiculturalism, opposition to which has been frequent and vocal (for an early version, see Schlesinger 1992), and cross-cutting political camps, diversity is something that nobody can reasonably object to. Diversity has modified multiculturalism in two crucial respects. First, it shifts the focus from the group to the individual—there is little if any society in it, in particular the "majority–minority" binary is eschewed. Secondly, liberal justice is pushed aside by a neoliberal efficiency orientation, tailored to the requisite sphere or sector in which diversity claims are raised.

Both trends are readily visible where diversity first emerged as a hard legal term, which is in the seminal *Regents of the University of California v. Bakke* decision of the US Supreme Court in 1978.[18] This was a delicate case because a white student claimed on equal protection grounds that the preferential admissions of black students to college was "reverse discrimination" against him (the plaintiff, Allan Bakke, not being admitted, while a black student with a lower test score was). Giving in to this claim would mean that the 14th Amendment's Equal Protection Clause, which so far had protected "discrete and insular minorities" only, in particular blacks, could not be read in a race-conscious way; it was there to protect everyone, whites included. This is precisely what the Court established in *Bakke*: "The guarantee of equal protection cannot mean one thing when applied to one individual and something else when applied to a person of another color. If both are not accorded the same protection, then it is not equal."[19] Accordingly, "(r)acial and ethnic distinctions of any sort are inherently suspect"[20], even if they are meant to be positive and remedial.

Justice Powell's swing opinion saved a diminished, non-quota-based form of affirmative action for decades to come.[21] But it rested on a peculiar sociological picture of the United States, as a symmetric "nation of minorities," without a fixed majority, and which ruled out that there could be a

130   POLITICAL NEOLIBERALISM

legal "recognition of special wards entitled to greater protection."[22] Who is "majority" and "minority," Powell argued, now at least conceding the existence of the former, is not cast in stone, marked by stable sociodemographic reference groups. Instead, whatever they are at a given point in time "necessarily reflect(s) temporary arrangements and political judgment."[23] Certain whites *also* suffered in the past, as did the non-Anglos from southern and eastern Europe. Retaining the static majority–minority binary, on which a race-conscious interpretation of the Equal Protection Clause rested, would require "variable sociological and political analysis necessary to produce . . . rankings,"[24] for which the court qua court just was not equipped. And such rankings "well may serve to exacerbate racial and ethnic antagonisms, rather than alleviate them,"[25] which has been the standard conservative invective against multiculturalism. Paradoxically, Justice Powell thus engaged in sociological reasoning, of sorts, to deny its possibility on part of the court.

Furthermore, and crucially, with respect to the legitimate purposes that the (subfederal) states pursued in their affirmative action programs, among these purposes could impossibly be the countering of "societal discrimination" and "historic deficit." Understood in this general way, discrimination would imply "an amorphous concept of injury that may be ageless in its reach into the past."[26] If the state insisted on its classification as remedy to discrimination, it had to be concretely "identified" discrimination,[27] and no "unnecessary burden" must ever be imposed on "innocent" third parties, like in this case on the white medical school applicant, Allan Bakke. Overall, "(p)referring members of any one group for no reason other than race or ethnic origin is discrimination for its own sake. This the Constitution forbids."[28]

With these considerations, Justice Powell ruled out that justice for historically wronged minorities, which had been the original impetus of the civil rights laws, their affirmative action sequel, and multiculturalism in general, could ever be a viable foundation for affirmative action, America's strongest legal expression of multiculturalism. But a weaker form of affirmative action could be saved if, in the case of college admissions, the state purpose was not elusive "justice" but the "attainment of a diverse student body" that helped in the "robust exchange of ideas,"[29] and thus served the purpose of the educational enterprise. However, "ethnic diversity" was "only one element in a range of factors"[30] in this endeavor, others being class or geography. In this context, Powell approvingly quoted the Harvard College admissions brief, according to which a "farm boy from Idaho" could bring something to Harvard College that a "Bostonian" could not. Diversity is not limited to race, and with respect to the latter, it is perfectly symmetrical, possibly including whites also. Most importantly, race should be at most a "plus" factor in judging an applicant's file, and it was "not (to) exclude the individual from comparison with all other candidates."[31] The bottom line, Powell hammers down, is to "treat() each applicant as an individual."

Thus, the concept of diversity was born, which is rigorously individualistic and retools multiculturalism from a justice to an efficiency rationale. In the United States, where the concept quickly expanded from higher education to corporate human relations management, diversity was the way for "race (to get) folded into a celebratory American multiculturalism and taken up in neoliberal agendas" (Berrey 2015, 5). Ellen Berrey (ibid., 8) calls the outcome "selective inclusion," because it is limited to the "upper rungs of the class ladder." In the multinational "Starr Corporation"[32] that she investigated, for instance, "diversity management," practiced there since the early 1990s, applied only to so-called exempt employees. These are non-unionized employees above a certain salary threshold and tasked with administrative, professional, managerial, or executive responsibilities (ibid., ch. 6). Accordingly, in its reach limited to "high-status people of color and women," diversity management amounts to "pushing against glass ceilings while ignoring dirty floors" (ibid., 14). It is "symbolic politics" that "largely leaves untouched persistent racial inequalities and the gulf between rich and poor" (ibid., 9). By 1998, 75 percent of Fortune 500 companies had such "diversity programs," which were not just selectively inclusive but also "routinely decoupled from the core technical functions of a company" (ibid., 202), their bloated diversity personnel being without "real power over hiring and firing" (ibid., 224).

One European review found the "diversity field itself . . . not very diverse and . . . dominated by US-centric research" (Jonsen et al. 2021, 35; see also Köllen 2021, 268). It is thus apposite to dwell a bit more on the best-studied US case. Diversity management has replaced affirmative action and equal employment opportunity policies that became politically inopportune with the onset of neoliberalism in the early Reagan years. If the point of affirmative action had been to "reduce the negative effects of exclusion," targeting "minorities," the rather different thrust of diversity management became to "promote the positive effects of inclusion," targeting "all employees" (Jonsen

132   POLITICAL NEOLIBERALISM

et al. 2021, 39). While the focus continued to be race and sex, due to its origins in civil rights law, diversity management, with "economic benefit" as its key objective, is in principle "open to any category" (Köllen 2021, 259). This brought certain curiosities. One review of the management literature, for instance, in which "diversity rhetoric" held entry in the late 1980s, found that things such as "thinking style" and to "mix quiet with talky people" are considered instances of diversity for corporate purposes. Such diversity naturally has a place for "whites" and "males" (Edelman et al. 2001, 1617). Diversity's retooling as "profitable resource" might even entail not just a silencing but explicit negative distancing from civil rights, with diversity praised for "unleash(ing) performance energy that was previously wasted in fighting discrimination," as one can read in one management manual (ibid., 1621).

The cited curiosities notwithstanding, to do something that is "simultaneously morally good and profitable" constitutes the "stable narrative" of diversity management, in and outside the United States (Köllen 2021, 267). The moral component, which in the form of "diversity training" may even incorporate the radical tenets of "critical race theory,"[33] reveals the constitutive linkage of diversity management with the multicultural minority problematic. In organizational terms, looking again at the American case, the linkage is human resource specialists in large companies saving their jobs and professional interests after the Reagan onslaught on affirmative action: "Practices designed to achieve legal compliance (with civil rights laws) were retheorized as efficient when the original impetus for adopting them was removed" (Kelly and Dobbin 1998, 962). In order not to have their offices closed, the new human-resource speak was that "(a) more diverse workforce will . . . bring greater access to new segments of the marketplace" (ibid., 973). Frank Dobbin and John Sutton (1998, 455) argue that an American propensity for "paint(ing) state domination of private enterprise as illicit" led to personnel managers' reorientation from an equality concern to "productive efficiency." However, an easier, and generalizable, explanation is the neoliberal Friedman Doctrine, according to which "the social responsibility of business is to increase its profits."[34]

In the American "weak state," companies rushed ahead to define the concrete meaning of "fair employment" that vaguely formulated and implemented civil rights laws had failed to do (see Dobbin 2009). Therefore, it does not surprise that "the civil rights movement at work has largely

FROM RIGHT TO LEFT, AND BACK? 133

failed," as an authoritative review by Dobbin and Alexandra Kalev (2021, 296) established. If managers of the industries that are to be regulated write the rules that are merely "rubber-stamped" by courts and other state agents (ibid., 295), no other outcome is to be expected.

But there is a paradox. On one side, diversity training and programs have become a "booming industry" in the United States, worth some $8 billion per year (Divine and Ash 2022, 4), and the number of people working in it has quadrupled since 2010.[35] On the other side, the effects are from meager to nil to even negative. True to neoliberal precepts, after the killing of George Floyd and the antiracist movement went viral in 2020, there has been a "hyper focus around black leadership" in the corporate world,[36] which confirms Ellen Berrey's critique of diversity as "selectively inclusive" (2015, 258). But there are other deficiencies. When employees sue for discrimination, the United States's "legal system rarely protects them from retaliation and rarely rights employers' wrongs" (Dobbin and Kalev 2021, 282). Moreover, "antibias" training alienates managers by insinuating sinister motives (ibid., 295). Such training, which often follows upon "implicit association tests" (between concepts, images, and words) that "almost invariably prove" test-takers to be "biased" (Noon 2018, 198), is punitive and re-educative by nature, and thus predictably alienates those who are required to undergo it. All is often event-driven show: after an incident involving two black customers in a Philadelphia outlet in 2018, Starbucks (the real firm), with big fanfare, closed all of its 175,000 stores worldwide to subject its (notoriously underpaid) employees to a four-hour "antibias training" (Divine and Ash 2022, 403). It is little surprise that Dobbin and Kalev (2022, 11) can show, on the basis of US data, that the individual-"bias"-scrutinizing logic of corporate diversity training has been a "spectacular failure."

In Europe, corporate diversity is mainly a branding device, in the form of "labels," "charters," and so on, that big companies are well advised to adopt, not to lose socially conscious customers (LOHAS in business school jargon, which is the initials of "Lifestyles of Health and Sustainability"). In France, corporate diversity has been promoted by the neoliberal think tank *Institut Montaigne* (Doytcheva 2009, 107). For obvious reasons, race is less central to diversity in Europe than in the United States. A report of the Council of Europe (2011) shows a rather different coloring of diversity, as a frontal rejection of orthodox multiculturalism while purporting to prolong its progressive impulse. Published shortly after the noisy good-byes to multiculturalism by the leaders of Europe's Big Three, the report deploys the word "diversity" as a substitute for the discarded "multiculturalism," and it is peppered with passages that serve the thinly concealed purpose of disciplining

134 POLITICAL NEOLIBERALISM

Europe's more than twenty-million strong Muslim immigrant population. Interestingly, however, while multiculturalism is repudiated for its separatist and group-mongering implications, "laws against all forms of discrimination in all areas of public life" are strongly endorsed, in keeping with the European Union's Race Equality and Employment Equality Directives of 2000.

Antidiscrimination

Indeed, antidiscrimination is the close legal complement to diversity rhetoric, and the second pillar of neoliberal multiculturalism. Whereas traditional multiculturalism has been continuously attacked over the past two decades, antidiscrimination is on the rise and rise, equaling diversity in its importance for the Third Way shaped neoliberal order. Whoever supports diversity, and who would not, supports antidiscrimination. Both the rhetoric and its legal fundament are necessary to support the meritocratic justification of neoliberalism. In the language of Talcott Parsons's "pattern variables" (Parsons and Shils 1951, ch. 1), meritocracy is a eulogy of "achievement" that cannot tolerate disadvantage that results from an individual's "ascribed" markers, most notably race and sex. "Meritocracy," writes one of its most astute critics in the United States, "makes elites . . . excessively sensitive to harms associated with unmeritocratic discrimination and numb to the harms produced by meritocracy itself" (Markovits 2019, ch. 3). Particularly Third Way leftist parties, as they embraced the neoliberal gospel of markets, have been staunch supporters of antidiscrimination. "We don't have a person to waste," said Clinton. To repudiate discrimination is a necessary backup to the neoliberal "rhetoric of rising," colloquially to "work hard and play by the rules," to quote the ex-US President again (Sandel 2020, ch. 3).

The relationship between traditional multiculturalism and antidiscrimination is complex, even contradictory (see Joppke 2022). On one side, both require one another. The starting point of multiculturalism is the experience of group-level disadvantage on the basis of stigmatized ascribed markers, such as race—tall people are not known to be a multicultural claims-maker.[37] But, as we saw, multiculturalists also distinguish their project from mere non- or antidiscrimination through insisting on "variable geometry" or "group-differentiated rights"; that is, rights that are not the same for all (Kymlicka 2019). This reveals that, on the other side, multiculturalism and

FROM RIGHT TO LEFT, AND BACK? 135

antidiscrimination follow different logics: particularistic versus universalist. The point of multiculturalism is the recognition of positively valued difference; the opposite point of antidiscrimination is the riddance or rendering invisible of negatively valued difference.[38]

This tension has worked itself out differently in North America and Europe. In the United States, originally race-blind civil rights law quickly turned race-conscious. This was less a philosophical than a pragmatic change because the bureaucrats in charge of implementing the civil rights laws pushed for results that were more easily obtained when interpreting these laws in a race-conscious manner (see Skrentny 1996). Supreme Court Justice Harry Blackmun expressed the logic crisply: "(I)n order to get beyond racism, we must first take account of race . . . And in order to treat some persons equally, we must treat them differently" (in Joppke 2017, 117). However, an increasingly conservative Supreme Court retracted from this logic, which came to be scandalized for constituting "reverse" discrimination for whites, thus moving back to a color-blind and symmetric understanding of antidiscrimination. This has been mainly to the disadvantage of blacks, whose improvement had been the original impetus of the 1960s' civil rights laws.

In Europe, the absence of a historical victim group has delayed the rise of antidiscrimination, which some exceptions, such as the United Kingdom. Moreover, with the partial exception of sex discrimination, there has been less impetus to push antidiscrimination into an orthodox multicultural, that is, group-specific and asymmetric direction. Tellingly, the breakthrough of antidiscrimination in Europe arrived with the European Union's Race Equality and Employment Equality Directives in 2000. By that time, the European Union had become a bastion of neoliberalism, ramming through Hayekian "common market" imperatives against state-level obstacles that stemmed from an opposite, Polanyian social protection logic. In the process, as previously discussed, "nation states" were cut down to "member states" (see Bickerton 2012). Interestingly, the activist, pro-immigrant Starting Line Group (SLG) had shrewdly advocated these measures, which were mainly meant to protect non-EU migrants, as "logical extension" of existing bans on nationality and gender discrimination, and as necessary for the completion of the single market (Guiraudon 2009, 531). Virginie Guiraudon argues that "(n)on-discrimination policy has also brought multiculturalism back through the back door by celebrating diversity in Europe" (ibid., 543). In light of this, this has been a neoliberally slimmed multiculturalism at best, which indeed has become a trademark of the European Union. Confirming the intimate connection between antidiscrimination and diversity, it was in the very same year that the two Race Equality and Employment Equality Directives were passed, in the year 2000, that the European Union also adopted its motto United in Diversity. This certainly referred to the internal diversity of historically variegated member states, but also, and with increasing urgency, to the externally imported diversity that is associated with multiculturalism.

Alexander Somek (2011, 2f), in a characteristically thoughtful reflection on European antidiscrimination law, places the latter in the context of a changing role of the state, as it transforms from social democratic into neoliberal, that is, "from sheltering people . . . against the peril of unemployment to coaching everybody into performing successfully in an increasingly rougher business environment." The European Union, while not a state, is still a prime example, also because it never possessed the fiscal tax-and-spend powers to "shelter" people in the first. As social policy more generally moves from "alleviating market dependence" to "making dependence more sustainable through enhancing the inclusive fitness of individuals," antidiscrimination is an indispensable element in this agenda. Somek (2011) calls antidiscrimination "concomitant to neoliberalism" with its strategy of making the market "not merely . . . one sphere among others but rather . . . the fundamental law governing our social existence" (ibid., 13, 14). As he further observes (Somek 2012, 12), the "inclusion" rhetoric that accompanies antidiscrimination and its thinned multiculturalism, "is a specification of the equality principle that leaves morally unexamined the domain from which someone must not be excluded."[39] In short, antidiscrimination helps camouflage and divert attention from the massively increased socioeconomic (class) inequality under neoliberalism.

An Authoritarian Third Phase of Neoliberalism, post-2008?

Most periodization of neoliberalism works not with two but three phases, a third phase setting in after the 2008 Financial Crisis (e.g., Davidson 2017; Davies 2016; Davies and Ganes 2021). As this crisis was met by states socializing the losses of an allegedly "efficient" and self-regulating financial system, one would have thought it to mean the end of neoliberalism, at least as a political economy doctrine (see Slattery et al. 2013). This is not what happened. In one influential account, a "living dead" neoliberalism trucked on, as "authoritarian neoliberalism" (Bruff 2014). Ian Bruff (2014) sees it marked by a "shift toward constitutional and legal mechanisms and the move away from seeking consent for hegemonic concepts" (ibid., 116). In his view, the Third Way left failed to democratize neoliberalism; that is, to make neoliberalism work by "seeking consent" to it. Instead, the new thrust of the "authoritarian" variant, argues Bruff, is to "insulate certain policies and institutional practices from social and political dissent" (ibid., 115).

What should we make of this? To "insulate" the market economy from democratic interference had been the thrust of neoliberalism all along, which in this sense is structurally and not merely contingently authoritarian. Furthermore, the electoral ebb and flow of the political left, which in Europe post-2008 happened to be more an aggravating ebb and the occasional flow (see Ryner 2010), must be kept apart from the persistent hold of some of their ideas, such as social investment and the neoliberal multiculturalism sketched previously. Striking a similar chord, Philip Mirowski, when asking how neoliberalism could "come through the crisis unscathed," points to an "everyday neoliberalism" that has "sunk . . . deeply into the cultural unconscious." He describes it as "narcissism of a thoroughly unmoored personality, unhinged aspirations oblivious to layers of social determination" (2013, ch. 3). This is at heart a psychic disposition, a hyper-individualism that Foucault captured in his notion of "entrepreneur of himself." It crystallizes in the combination of meritocracy and antidiscrimination that, we argued, helped the political left to get on the train of neoliberalism. Mirowski aptly calls this everyday neoliberalism "almost . . . the ideology of no ideology" (ibid., ch. 2), thus marking the point at which neoliberalism gestates from political movement to political order. For sociological institutionalists of John Meyer's Stanford School, neoliberalism is even a "world cultural ideology," stipulating "choices . . . disembedded from communal structures," and they see it operating, for instance, in school curricula that socialize students "to a generalized personhood, not citizen membership in a defined political order" (Lerch et al. 2022, 97, 116, 109, respectively). In Neil Davidson's periodization (2017, 621–625), these are all attributes of a second "social" phase of neoliberalism, which he dates between1992 to 2007.[40] Borne of the marriage of "liberation and libertarianism" (ibid.), this social neoliberalism is the making of the Third Way left.

138 POLITICAL NEOLIBERALISM

After the 2008 Financial Crisis, Davidson continues (2017, 625), neoliberalism has morphed from a progressive "social" into a conservative "preserve" mode, marked by a "regime of exception" that is authoritarian not in name but content.[41] That the financial crisis is a turning-point is undisputed. It ushered in a "striking convergence across the world in the implementation of neoliberal austerity measures, the growing support for right-wing xenophobic sentiments, the deployment of repressive state practices and the normalization of illicit financial transactions" (Fabry and Sandbeck 2019, 109f). But this description obviously involves a different understanding of neoliberalism than in its "social" phase: not as cultural template but as political economy doctrine, which indeed it had originally been. Both understandings of neoliberalism need to be kept apart, as they have different lifelines and fields of application. From its invention on, by Bruff (2014), the notion of "authoritarian neoliberalism" is exclusively used with a political economy inflection, denoting the state response to the 2008 Financial Crisis.

The authoritative account of the American response to the "first crisis of a global age," by economic historian Adam Tooze (2018), does not use the term of authoritarian neoliberalism, but it confirms its content. Tooze notices that "(i)n the event of a major financial crisis that threatened 'systemic' interests, it turned out that we lived in an age not of limited but of big government, of massive executive action, of interventionism that had more in common with military operations . . . than with law-bound governance" (2018: intro). Even the "crisis fighters" themselves, in the US Federal Reserve Bank and the Treasury Department, all of them past or future captains of the finance industry that these bodies are meant to regulate,[42] "liked to speak in military terms, about 'bazookas' and 'shock and awe'" (ibid., ch. 8), to the exact tune of Naomi Klein's "disaster capitalism" (2007). The "bazookas" was the unprecedented sum of $7 trillion of public money to bail out the banks—the year 2009 turned out to be "one of Wall Street's best years of all" (Vogl 2021, 29), with the bankers' bonuses topping those of the pre-crisis year 2007 by more than one-fourth.[43] A grotesque highpoint in Tooze's day-by-day account of the financial crisis is when President Obama advised the assembled bankers that "(my) administration is the only thing between you and the pitchforks" (2018, ch. 13). His plea for "voluntary restraint" on their bonuses obviously went unheard, while the involuntary part was allotted to ordinary Americans, several millions of whom lost their homes to foreclosure. But *all* were asked to exercise "fiscal responsibility," aka austerity,

FROM RIGHT TO LEFT, AND BACK? 139

because the money lost on the banks had to be recovered elsewhere. Obama blithely ignored the causal order of things, when he declared in the 2010 State of the Union address: "(F)amilies across the country are tightening their belts and making tough decisions. The federal government should do the same" (quoted in Tooze 2018, ch. 15: sec. 1).

But the poster child of authoritarian neoliberalism is the European Union. The case of the European Union also helps to draw the line between the authoritarian element that is intrinsic to neoliberalism, and its indisputable foregrounding after the 2008 Financial Crisis. Our account of the European Union as neoliberal polity, in Chapter 2, stopped short of the arrival of monetary union around the new millennium, that is, the making of the euro currency. But its peculiar architecture as "currency without a state" (Wilkinson 2021, 181) is decisive for understanding the Union's aggressively authoritarian posture during the Financial Crisis, which in Europe was experienced as a protracted Sovereign Debt Crisis.

The euro's origin is the 1992 Maastricht Treaty. This treaty brought several innovations, only one of which is the Economic and Monetary Union (EMU) that paved the road to the new currency. The other major innovation is European Union citizenship. This double innovation—one economic and one political—reflects the two prongs of Francis Fukuyama's (1992) euphoric "end of history," when it seemed that free-market capitalism and liberal democracy would go hand-in-hand, as triumphant economic-cum-political order without alternative. In co-inventing both a common money and a common citizenship, the European Union saw itself as the beacon of both capitalism *and* democracy. But "it would be money rather than citizenship that would come to symbolize the Europe of the twenty-first century," as Michael Wilkinson dryly comments (2021, 274).

The common currency was wanted by France to contain the hegemony of the Deutsche Mark (DM), which is a calculation that went badly wrong. Germany accepted abandoning its beloved DM as the price for national reunification, but only under its conditions: monetary without fiscal union, to be overseen by a European Central Bank (ECB) modeled on the German Bundesbank, with a democratically unaccountable technocrat at the helm whose only mandate was to keep inflation down.[44] Crucially, the ECB was constitutionally prohibited from "bailing-out" member states in financial difficulties by purchasing their sovereign bonds. This conservative construction of monetary union served German interests as a low-inflation and export-oriented economy with a frugal and savings-minded public

140 POLITICAL NEOLIBERALISM

household philosophy. And Germany brutally pushed these interests against southern debtor countries in the Euro-crisis.

However, the "asymmetric" EMU construct was also typical for the European Union at large (Menêndez 2013, 484) because state-level negative integration was not accompanied by EU-level positive (i.e., political) integration. In the words of then president of the Deutsche Bundesbank, Karl Otto Pöhl, the EMU would "necessitate the surrender of sovereignty by the individual member states, but this need not mean corresponding gains in Community authority" (in Lokdam and Wilkinson 2021, 10). The ECB, with its narrow mandate, "in Europe is the only agency engaged in economic policy worthy of the name" (Tooze 2020). Accordingly, the EMU was a further step in the "de-democratization of the economy" that had guided the European Union all along (Wilkinson 2021, 180–181). Next to the micro-control of its famous four market freedoms (of goods, services, capital, and people), now also the macro-control of money was taken away from the state—incidentally, a "common monetary policy" had already been an element of Hayek's vision of interstate federation (ibid.).[45] The European Union, in Wilkinson's persuasive reading, is structurally authoritarian, as it is built on the Ordoliberal principle of replacing popular sovereignty with individual economic freedom, that is, political with economic constitutionalism, as source of legitimacy (ibid., 272). Maastricht's EMU aggravated the intentional "disconnect between rulers and ruled" in binding member state governments to the *vincolo esterno* of externally controlled money. Through the Stability and Growth Pact (SGB), which was among the German conditions for abandoning the Deutsche Mark, the *vincolo esterno* extended from monetary policy to member states' fiscal policy, which nominally remained autonomous but factually was subjected to strict budgetary discipline, austerity before the word (ibid., 144–145).[46] In sum, the EMU "locked-in" austerity by its very structure (Schneider and Sandbeck 2019, 139).

The problem of the asymmetric monetary union, in which competences were withdrawn from member states without being compensated at European Union level, is that it was imposed on highly different economies that fared rather differently—although the differences were complementary—under this regime. The main profiteers were the low-inflation, export-oriented northern economies, Germany in particular. The main victims, as revealed in the Euro-crisis, were the high-inflation, import economies of the south, with much less competitive industries. In the early 2000s, Germany also benefited from the harsh Agenda 2010 labor market and welfare reforms that were introduced, incidentally, under the Third Way left-green government of Gerhard Schröder. Their effect was to freeze wages throughout the decade. More than enhanced productivity, this wage restraint was the reason for the German successes in these years. A "neo-mercantilist" strategy of keeping domestic demand low by suppressing wages and seeking growth through exports, aided by a chronically undervalued Euro, piled-up one of the world's largest current account surpluses, ahead even of China's (see Lapavitsas 2019, ch. 3). The bulk of these surpluses, partially drawn from selling goods to southern member states, also flew back to the south to finance its growing deficits: "The mirror image of Germany's exporting triumph has been the emergence of a Southern Eurozone periphery that has faced enormous deficits on its current accounts" (ibid.).

The immediate cause of the Eurozone crisis was the rupture, in late 2009, of capital flows into the south after Greece had disclosed its huge (and previously falsified) budget deficits, which were three times over the SGP limit. By that time, indebted states were less accountable to the "state people" who lived and worked in them than to the "market people" who financed them, in particular global financial investors and private credit rating agencies that rank states according to their creditworthiness and so decide about their collective fate (Streeck 2013). The existence of the euro had deprived the southern states in difficulty of the possibility to devaluate their local currency and thus to make their exports more competitive and put a brake on imports. The only alternative left was internal devaluation, which is wage depression and radical cuts in public expenditures.

Also known as austerity, this is what the so-called Troika, composed of the European Commission, the ECB, and the International Monetary Fund (IMF), and under the informal leadership of Germany as Europe's main financier and strongest economic power, brutally imposed on southern states as price for averting their bankruptcy. This was the moment for neoliberalism in Europe to turn blatantly authoritarian, in at least two respects. First, and most drastically, the process involved forced government changes in Italy and Greece, and overriding a public referendum in Greece that had overwhelmingly rejected the terms of the third bail-out in summer 2015. On this occasion, Germany's Finance Minister, Wolfgang Schäuble, the wheel-chaired lead figure of the Troika, lectured his Greek counterpart, motorbiking Yanis Varoufakis, that "elections cannot be allowed to change economic policy" (quoted in Tooze 2018, ch. 22).

142 POLITICAL NEOLIBERALISM

Second, as the fiscal and monetary competences of EU institutions were nil to tightly limited by design, these rescue operations involved the creation of new ad hoc instruments and agencies that were (and are) outside of EU law and devoid even of indirect democratic legitimacy. An example is the European Stability Mechanism (ESM), created as a private company with seat in Luxembourg. This is the European Union's own "mini" IMF, disposing of some 500 billion euros of bail-out funds. However, they are available only under the condition of strictly implementing the standard neoliberal reform package of fiscal austerity, wage suppression, deregulation, and privatizing the public sector (Lapavitsas 2019, ch. 4). Furthermore, Maastricht's SGP, which had been toothless so far, was hardened, among other measures, through the so-called European Semester. Under its auspices, the European Commission screens national budgets *before* they are ratified by their respective national parliament. It is part of the 2012 Fiscal Compact, a treaty of Eurozone members (plus three more member states), which also asks for the passing of national laws that require a balanced budget, following the German model of *Schuldenbremse* (debt brake) (that even enjoys constitutional status in Germany since 2009).

Interestingly, the European Semester is in the ex-ante mode of "code" rather than the mode of "law," which is ex post because a transgression needs to occur first for a punishment to follow (see Lessig 2006). Instead, "member states are to be administratively prevented from exceeding the targets for deficits, rather than having sanctions imposed on them after registering deficits" (Lapavitsas 2019, ch. 4). The new EU budgetary regime arising out of the financial crisis has been justified in the political terms of an emergency to be met—"if the euro fails, Europe fails" (German Chancellor Angela Merkel). In reality, it has brought a primary object of sovereign choice, the determination of the national budget, under technocratic EU control. As Merkel (perversely, for a democratic leader) celebrated it, "new majorities in a parliament will not be able to change the fact that those (budget) caps apply" (quoted in White 2013, 305).

Wilkinson argues that in the Euro crisis, the European Union's "soft, permissive authoritarianism was mutating into a harder, more coercive variety," and he calls the Troika's presence in Greece and elsewhere "occupation" rather than "receivership," as the latter word would be "too mild" (2021, 221, 223). As in the first round of the financial crisis in the United States, military language and metaphors abounded when the crisis hit Europe. The "bazookas" had their second coming, not in name but in meaning, in ECB chief Mario Draghi's famous warning, made in 2015 to a crocodile pool of hedge fund managers in London, that "the ECB is ready to do whatever it takes to preserve the euro." As if that language wasn't strong enough, Draghi immediately added: "And believe me, it will be enough" (quoted in Tooze 2018, ch. 18). These words alone, not (yet) followed by action, were enough to calm the markets, and that had been the purpose.

Through a Foucauldian lens, Will Davies (2021, 95–99) considers the logic at work as "revenge of sovereignty on government," and thus a regression into a bygone monarchical era. "Sovereignty," argues Davies with Foucault, is "circular" in taking life (what else are bazookas for?)[47] rather than "teleological" in making life. And it functions with an "excess of power" (the bazookas, again) rather than with "precision" and "economy," as had been the thrust of (liberal) "government." In sum, the European Union, post-2008, to Davies, is "authoritarian neoliberalism," operating by "exceptional and extra-democratic means."

Importantly, the ECB's financial rescue actions that preceded and followed upon Draghi's military-style rhetorical intervention, were not only outside the central bank's legal purview, and thus strictly speaking illegal.[48] They were also falsely billed. Formally, these rescue actions were presented as bailing out governments and helping their economies to get back in shape. In reality, they primarily protected exposed northern banks, especially German and French banks, which were major lenders in the south. For public consumption, northern lenders (especially Germans and their public and media outlets) spread the morality tale of inefficient and wasteful southern governments and societies that needed to be taught the proper habit of saving. In reality, the "sovereign debt crisis" was the mutation of a private banking crisis, the "implosion in interbank credit" (Tooze 2018, intro) brought about by hubris and malfunctioning of a deregulated financial system. This was most obviously the case in Ireland and Spain, whose budgets had even been "in surplus" until governments had to rescue their overcommitted banks after the bursting of local housing bubbles (Scharpf 2015, 388). Here as elsewhere in Europe, the affected (mostly southern) states being summarily and pejoratively called PIIGS,[49] "the private debt of highly leveraged financial institutions became the public debt of states" (Blyth 2013, 52). Mark Blyth speaks of the "greatest bait-and-switch operation in modern history," because "private-sector debt problems" were rechristened as "the Debt" generated by "out-of-control" public spending (ibid., 73). As Streeck (2011, 28) grasped

144 POLITICAL NEOLIBERALISM

the essence of the European debt crisis, it is "the drama of democratic states being turned into debt-collecting agencies on behalf of a global oligarchy of investors." With the good help of the European Union, one must add.

Critical minds, like Habermas, have not stopped defending "Europe" as democratic "bulwark" against global capitalism. To see democratic potential in the European Union is not difficult for Habermas because he deems already the nation-state to be the site of a "post-sovereign constitutionalism" (the wording is by Wilkinson 2021, 166). For Habermas, popular sovereignty no longer "circulate(s) in a collectivity" but appears "in the circulation of reasonably structured deliberations and decisions," from which he draws the "harmless" conclusion that there's no longer a sovereign in the constitutional state (Habermas, quoted in ibid.).

Against a democratic hope for Europe, however watered down in "post-sovereign" constructions like these, stands not least Article 63 of the European Union Treaty (TFEU). It stipulates that "all restrictions on the movement of capital between Member States *and between Member States and third countries* shall be prohibited" (emphasis supplied). To Streeck (2021, fn.272), plausibly, this treaty article "exemplifies the especially blatant, not only neoliberal but explicitly globalist orientation of the European Union as a political economy." Article 63 TFEU reveals the single market as "section of the global market," "eroding the idea of a European juridicial space," as Stefano Bartolini put it concisely (quoted in Wilkinson 2021, 188). The European Union, to quote Bartolini again, "bring(s) to an end the historical phase characterized by the close grip of politics on the economy through law" (ibid., 177). Hayek would have smiled.

Conclusion

Most genealogies of political neoliberalism waffle about its current state. So does Gerstle's *Rise and Fall of the Neoliberal Order*, which finishes with the message that "the neoliberal order . . . is broken" (2022, 293), but which fails to point at an alternative. In the blueprint for his book, Gerstle (2017) had still adjoined the notion of neoliberalism's "fall" with a question mark. But there is no question about the fact that the consent of the political left has lent stability to neoliberalism, turning it from political movement into political order. This consent arrived one decade into political neoliberalism's existence, when the collapse of communism made the world bereft of an alternative to capitalism:

> In a post-communist world, . . . leftists turned . . . to identity politics. The resulting battles over race, gender and sexuality generated considerable conflict, but they did not threaten regimes of capital accumulation as communism had done. Multi-culturalism and cosmopolitanism could thrive under conditions of neoliberalism, and they did. The pressure on capitalist elites and their supporters to compromise with the working class had vanished. This is the moment when neoliberalism . . . went from being a political movement to a political order. (Gerstle 2017, 256)

This statement is about the United States, but it applies more generally. In this chapter, I traced the moment of the left's conversion, which was in terms of the Third Way, and I mapped the kind of multiculturalism that is not only compatible with neoliberalism but fulfilling positive functions for it, under the rubrics of "diversity" and "antidiscrimination." Of course, there are, in addition, unrulier forms of leftist "identity politics" proper, which will be explored in Chapter 5.

After the 2008 Financial Crisis, there has been no change to the basic constellation of "capitalism, alone" (Milanovic 2019). Even the finance system that has caused the crisis has survived unscathed. As if accepting insult after injury, most people and parties in most countries gave in to the socializing of the costs of this crisis, in the form of austerity and aggravated inequality. These three facts alone: the consent of the left, the lack of a systemic alternative, and its Teflon-like immunity to crisis, suggest that no end to the neoliberal order is in sight.

However, the authoritarian handling of the crisis, particularly in the European Union, has raised the question whether we have entered a third phase of neoliberalism, after its rightist first and leftist second phases. While the first shift, from right to left (more precisely: the left *also* embracing neoliberalism), is undeniable, the second "shift" is more doubtful, for two reasons. First, the authoritarian turn only foregrounded an element of neoliberalism that had been constitutive of it from the start; we shall see, in Chapter 6, that the pandemic crisis of 2020–2022 would have much the same effect. Secondly, the authoritarian turn recalls attention to the fact that neoliberalism has several faces, that of a political economy doctrine shielding markets from

146 POLITICAL NEOLIBERALISM

democratic interference, but also that of a socio-cultural doctrine tending toward hyper-individualism and malleable subjectivity. Only the first face of neoliberalism was involved in the authoritarian turn post-2008. The second face simply has different fields of application, which are not affected in this context. Our account of neoliberal multiculturalism, with its diversity and antidiscrimination expressions, certainly does not suggest that second-phase (and—face) "social" neoliberalism is at low ebb. Quite the contrary, in fact.

When discussing the "authoritarian" EU response to the financial crisis, Davies (2021) similarly highlights the "ambivalence" of neoliberalism, even as a narrower political economy concept. He sees it combining *both* parts of Foucault's sovereignty versus government binary, and eventually he steps back from conceiving of the latter as phases, but rather as synchronic aspects of contemporary rule. Accordingly, Davies calls the European Union a "hybrid sovereign-governmental power," while adding that "neoliberal political reason" in general "weaves between the zones of government and sovereignty, muddying the distinction itself" (ibid., 106).

Without drawing any such distinction, Jens Beckert (2019, 5) identifies neoliberalism's "moral vision for society" as "not . . . a collective project, but rather as an infinite number of individual projects for which the state sets the frame."[50] And he calls this vision "largely exhausted," diagnosing a "loss of faith," particularly after the failure to regulate financial markets after 2008. At the same time, Beckert admits that "there are currently no politically strong narratives that would point to alternatives to the neoliberal logic of competition, markets, and coercion" (ibid., 10). Bradford DeLong, in his "long" twentieth-century history of American capitalism, finds that neoliberalism failed to deliver for the popular classes on the employment and income side. But, often overlooked, neoliberalism lowered the prices of consumption goods, so that on balance "the American working and middle classes were richer in 2010 than their counterparts had been in 1979" (2022, ch. 15). This may explain the high level of acquiescence despite neoliberalism's overall negative report card for ordinary folk, which was out as early as the mid-1980s. But to his own question why neoliberalism lasted, DeLong's lapidary six-word answer is: "because Ronald Reagan won the Cold War" (ibid.).

The picture that emerges in this chapter is that of a right–left consensus on the core parameters of neoliberalism, even extending from economic to social policy. The political economy being voided as a source of conflict and rupture, identity politics has moved to the fore.

II
RUPTURE

Chapter 4
The Populist Right

Illiberal Democracy and the Economics–Culture Conundrum

The gist of political neoliberalism, from the point of view of order, is to undermine the liberal-democratic synthesis, not just by protecting the market from democratic interference but by helping its principles to spread across societal sectors, the state in particular. Accordingly, the friendliest reading of populism is to resurrect this synthesis's badly battered democratic component. In one such reading, although without specifying the neoliberal context, "populisms have a legitimate place in liberal and social democracies. One could even say that they are inevitable given the likelihood of entropy inherent in these regimes" (Schmitter 2019, 80). The plural form in this formulation points to the variety of populisms in past and present. One of the earliest social-scientific discussions even wondered whether populism is a "unitary concept" or "simply a word wrongly used in completely heterogeneous contexts" (Ionescu and Gellner 1969, 3)—in effect, Ghita Ionescu and Ernest Gellner leaned toward the latter alternative. The least to agree on is that there are left-wing and right-wing forms of populism—which still leaves "populism" undefined.

There is no agreement in this respect whether populism is "ideology" (Mudde 2004), "strategy" (Weyland 1996), or "style" (Moffitt 2016). In the single most influential account, by Cas Mudde (2004), populism is a "thin-centered ideology," in which a "pure people" opposes a "corrupt elite" and favors a politics that is "expression of the *volonté générale* (general will) of the people" (ibid., 543). Qua "thin-centered," the populist ideology needs to be complemented by something thicker, most importantly nationalism or socialism. Otherwise, the right versus left distinction could not be made.

A critic of the "myth of global populism" (Art 2020), who prefers a more differentiated vocabulary for the "disparate phenomena" packed under the populist label, nevertheless finds Mudde's definition the one that he "cannot improve upon" (ibid., 1, 10). Indeed, the normatively loaded people versus

Political Neoliberalism. Christian Joppke, Oxford University Press. © Oxford University Press (2025).
DOI: 10.1093/oso/9780197801918.003.0005

150   POLITICAL NEOLIBERALISM

elite dichotomy is the minimal content of all known expressions of populism, left and right, past and present: "(P)opulism *always* involves a critique of the establishment and an adulation of the common people" (Mudde and Kaltwasser 2017, 5; emphasis supplied). Mudde presents his as an "ideational approach" (2021, 573), and thus as distinct from other approaches. However, rivaling political-strategy or political-style approaches are derivative because they can't do without this minimal "ideational" input. After all, the root word of populism is the Latin *populus*, the people (*demos* in Greek), who nominally rule in a democracy. For Margaret Canovan (1999), one of the first and most incisive students of populism, the latter is a "shadow cast by democracy itself"; it articulates the aspirational ("redemptive," she says) face of democracy that is undercut by its "pragmatic" realities.

The populism to be examined in this chapter is the one that had its apex in the *annus miserabilis*, 2016, with the double shock of the Brexit referendum that would lead the United Kingdom to leave the European Union, followed by the victory of Donald Trump in the US presidential elections of the same year. Both events have been widely interpreted as the breakthrough of populism in the West, and of a populism that is distinctly right-wing and nationalist, and in the Trumpist version at least not the resurrection of but a threat to democracy (see Levitsky and Ziblatt 2018). The Brexit and Trump upheavals feed on widely different sources, including a chronic unhappiness about Europe in the United Kingdom and a diminishing white majority in the United States. However, a conspicuous communality of both is that they happened in the two Anglo-Saxon pioneer countries of neoliberalism, and where the latter has gone to its most extreme. Promptly, the Brexit–Trump tandem has been taken as expression of a deep crisis, if not the end, of liberalism and the liberal order, both domestically and at the international plane (among the many crisis accounts, Krastev and Holmes [2019] stands out).

Much of this crisis talk has been hyperbole. The populist juggernaut tottered as early as 2017, when Brexit and Trump were *not* followed by populist victories in the Netherlands and France, as many had feared. Post-Brexit Britain likes to fashion itself as "truly Global,"[1] and Trump went down in 2020 (although he was re-elected in 2024). In Europe, with the exception of Italy where populists have governed twice since 2018 (and do so at the time of writing), populism-in-power is mainly limited to its eastern half, helped by non-consolidated post-communist party systems and by lesser constitutional and cultural obstacles. A recent study of "right-wing populist parties" in sixteen European countries, East and West, found an average vote share of 16 percent in 2021, up from 12.6 percent in 2001 (Bartels 2023, 13, fn.22). This is significant but hardly ground for alarmism. Most importantly, Larry Bartels attributes this moderate growth "not to increased demand for right-wing populism among ordinary Europeans, but to the increased ability and willingness of populist entrepreneurs to mobilize and cater to that demand" (ibid., 150). Judged by their (often inept) leadership, an *Economist* editorial found populist right parties limited by a "clown ceiling," with "a rapid ascent, a noisy thud against the ceiling and a swift retreat."[2] It cites the example of the German AfD (*Alternative für Deutschland*), which became Germany's "biggest opposition party in parliament" in the wake of the Syrian Refugee Crisis, but since has been diminished by "far-right extremism and infighting."[3] Given their relatively small size, the policy impact of the populist right is limited. In their preferred docket, which is migration policies, there has been "no or limited impact" (Caiani and Graziano 2022, 573); the same applies to their preference for "welfare chauvinism" (to be discussed later in this chapter).

The populist right still represents the "single most successful" new political party family in postwar Europe (Wolinetz and Zaslove 2018, 12). Its gradual ascent coincides with the rise of political neoliberalism since the 1980s, and it has been gaining momentum with the onset of globalization post-1989. While its most dramatic "moment" so far was 2016, populism has also become a "chronic" feature of the neoliberal order (see Brubaker 2017a, 357, 369–373). It thus requires a closer examination.

The fact that populism in the West, with some exceptions,[4] tends to be on the political right, tells us something important about the changing neoliberal order. Considering that populism by nature is counter-establishment and counter-elite, a populism that is on the political right logically *must* visualize the opposed establishment in leftist colors. But this attests to the shift of political neoliberalism from the right to the left, and to the hegemonic position that the Third Way left has acquired in the neoliberal order. In one account (Putzel 2020, 418), the populist right is entirely in response to "phase two" neoliberalism, which consists of "neoliberal social policies based on the recognition of the rights of women, minorities, migrants and the poor."

But what is "right" to begin with? Its meaning has greatly changed since its first appearance in the French Revolution, when it was simply a spatial notion for the monarchic forces seated on the right side of the new republican parliament. Later, with the rise of capitalism, "right" became the

152 POLITICAL NEOLIBERALISM

name of its defenders, and it has never lost this association until the present day. Accordingly, the roots of many populist radical right parties in Europe, such as the French Front National, the Austrian FPÖ (*Freiheitliche Partei Österreichs*), even the more recent AfD in Germany, are as free market musketeers against bureaucratically bloated and tax-mongering states (in the shape of "Brussels" for the early AfD). One of these parties' earliest analyses identified as their "winning formula" the combination of "free market" and "authoritarian" orientations—labeled "right-authoritarian" (Kitschelt and McCann 1995). In this formula, "right" stands for "neoliberal economic policies," while "authoritarian" refers to "nationalist, particularist sociocultural policies" (ibid., 275).

Some have even attached the adjective "populist" to mainstream neoliberalism's earliest political articulations in the West, which were on the political right. Stuart Hall (1979) famously did this for Margaret Thatcher, calling her brand of politics "authoritarian populism." One can drive this to the point that neoliberal doctrine itself bears populist possibilities. Note that Milton Friedman presented himself to a larger American television audience as "leading a revolt of the poor against the rich" and defending the cause of "the ordinary worker and the ordinary consumer," who for him were the true winners of "less government" (in Brandes 2019, 78, 71, respectively).[5] A previously unrecognized case of neoliberal populism is the Dutch Pim Fortuyn. Better known for bringing a peculiarly bohemian and culturally liberal variant of right-wing populism to the Netherlands that built itself in opposition to an "illiberal" (and gay-hostile) Islam, Fortuyn had earlier been a neoliberal zealot, spreading the notions that workers had to become "entrepreneurs of the self" and learn that "if a man will not work, he shall not eat."[6]

Over time, the populist right muted its neoliberal roots and embraced "centrist economic" (Lange 2007, 411) and pro-welfare positions, yet only for natives—"welfare chauvinism" (Jennser-Jedenastik 2018). This was a strategic choice to cater to the working-class defectors of leftist parties that had adopted Third-Way neoliberalism. In the process, right-wing populist parties became "a new type of working-class party" (Oesch 2008, 350).[7] In an analysis of European Social Survey Data from 2002/2003, Daniel Oesch (2008) found that the support for these parties by "production workers" exceeded their average support by a factor of 1.3 in Switzerland, 1.4 in France, 1.6 in Austria, 1.7 in Belgium, and 1.9 in Norway (ibid., 356). But he also found that working-class voters' main concern was not with "economic grievances" but with "questions of community and identity," especially surrounding immigration, opposition to which also became their preferred parties' signature on the political supply side (ibid., 349). Colin Crouch (2020, 97) has a simple explanation for the relative absence of economic concerns among the populist right: "Since by definition the political right is anti-egalitarian, rightist populism has to define its enemies in terms other than wealth and power." While compelling in its simplicity, this explanation has the whiff of circularity. To avoid it, we need to place the populist right in the larger context of political and social transformation.[8]

A first round of change conducive to the rise of the populist right precedes the arrival of political neoliberalism. For the generation growing up in the late 1960s to 1970s, especially its more affluent parts, Ronald Inglehart (1977) had diagnosed a "silent revolution" in the personal values held by them, from "materialist" to "post-materialist," their political expression becoming the new social movements and green parties of the late 1970s and 1980s. In return, one can look at the emergent populist right as a (somewhat delayed)[9] "silent counter-revolution" (Ignazi 1992) on that same new values dimension, which is more about culture and lifestyle than the economy, seeking a "non-materialistic answer to the agenda of the New Politics" (ibid., 19). Accordingly, the aging and numerically shrinking materialists responded to the "New Politics" of the left with a rightist program of "law and order enforcement" and "immigration control" (ibid., 25).

To this domestic-level values change needs to be added a second round of structural change brought about by globalization, which kicked in a decade later, post-1989. Globalization, qua "denationalization," has fundamentally transformed the national political space, dividing "winners" and "losers" on a new "integration-demarcation" cleavage that is superimposed on the established left–right cleavage (Kriesi et al. 2008). Martin Lipset and Stein Rokkan (1967) had argued that mid-twentieth-century European party systems were the "frozen" product of the two late-nineteenth- to early-twentieth-century "national" and "industrial" revolutions, generating four cleavages: center/periphery and state/church as a result of the national revolution, rural/urban and capital/labor as result of the industrial revolution. In principle, political party formation *could* revolve around all four cleavages and their corresponding interests and identities. In reality, the two cleavages connected to the national revolution, expressed in oppositional territorial and religious identities, cooled down in most (not all) places, leaving mainly the capital/labor cleavage as the gist of party

154 POLITICAL NEOLIBERALISM

formation and political conflict (landed interests and the rural/urban cleavage disappeared with the shrinking of the agrarian sector). This is the origin of the economic left versus right distinction in politics as we knew it, until the arrival of neoliberalism. The left stood for social protection and market regulation, the right for competition and free markets. Globalization, which is merely the spatial expression of neoliberalism, amounts to a reopening of the national, in essence cultural and identity-related, cleavage type.

This story has been instructively told by Hanspeter Kriesi et al. (2008), including its often-perplexing national variations (that have to be left aside here). Refuting a view that globalization has "added" a new dimension to political space,[10] the authors hold that political space has *always* been two-dimensional, economic and cultural, at least if one follows the Lipset–Rokkan model. Through this lens, globalization's new cleavage, which divides the proponents of (international) "integration" and those of (national) "demarcation," becomes "embedded" into the two-dimensional basic structure. Because political space's cultural dimension was already reshaped by the post-materialist value changes brought by the "silent revolution" and its new social movements and green parties, globalization amounted to "transforming it once again" (Kriesi et al. 2008, 13). This means that the previously intra-domestic defense of traditional values, mostly around morality and lifestyle issues, turned ethnic and nationalist, bringing to full bloom the combination of opposition to the European Union and to immigration that is the trademark of the populist right across Europe (see Hobolt and Tilly 2016, 977–978, 983).

Importantly, the mainstream political parties, defined by taking opposite positions on the old economic left/right cleavage, have come to "view . . . economic denationalization both as inevitable and beneficial," and they "converged on moderately pro-integration positions" (Kriesi et al. 2008, 15, 16). This description implies the Third Way transformation of the left and its adoption of neoliberalism, discussed in the previous chapter. In principle, the neoliberal all-party consensus *could* have provided an opening for a new opposition force with a strong economic focus, on the now vacant leftist pole of the old class cleavage. But it hasn't,[11] except for the flicker of leftist populism in southern Europe after the 2010 Sovereign Debt Crisis (see Borriello and Jäger 2023), and the welfare chauvinism of rightist populism in western Europe, which has always remained subordinate to its cultural focus on immigration (see Ivarsflaten 2008).

Instead, the action has all been on the cultural front, where the "driving force" have been the new populist radical right parties assembling the "losers" of globalization (Kriesi et al. 2008, 19). Their focus on culture, while downplaying the fact that "losing" from globalization has a very material meaning, is not accidental. This is because the new "integration-demarcation" cleavage as such, for which Liesbet Hooghe and Gary Marks (2018) have proposed the simpler label "transnational," is "at its core a cultural conflict," pitting "libertarian, universalistic values against the defense of nationalism and particularism" (ibid., 123). Hooghe and Marks point out that this new cleavage has "greater salience" (ibid., 127) for new parties that are undivided on this cleavage's specific issues and thus take more extreme positions on them. These new parties are, next to the populist right parties, green and new left parties on the other end of the political spectrum. By contrast, mainstream parties face internal divisions in this respect, having to reconcile opposite positions on the old and new cleavage types: conservative parties are globalist in economic but not cultural respect; while (traditional) social democratic parties are culturally liberal but economically statist and welfarist. Accordingly, the result of globalization has been the fragmentation of (non-majoritarian, proportional representation) political party systems in Europe, with the arrival of new left and right parties on the new cleavage axis. This fragmentation shows in the fact that the average voting share of the three traditional party families (social democratic, conservative, liberal) has decreased, from 75 percent in 2000 to 64 percent in 2017 (ibid.), and the trend continues.

Hooghe and Marks (2018, 127) further argue that the new transnational cleavage will endure because it is "grounded in educational opportunities that have persistent effects over a person's life and which are conveyed to offspring." Indeed, the level of education is the main line separating the "losers" from the "winners" of globalization: it tends to be low on the part of losers, and high on the part of winners. Education increases options for exit, which are better for individuals with higher skill levels, while a lower skill level makes you immobile and consequently experience the opening of national boundaries as a threat. Fleshing out the profiles of winners and losers from globalization, Kriesi et al. (2008) further distinguish between "exposed" and "traditionally protected" sectors of the economy. Globalization winners are entrepreneurs and qualified employees in the exposed sectors, plus the "cosmopolitan citizens" who culturally favor a borderless world. Its losers are entrepreneurs and qualified employees in the traditionally protected sectors,

156   POLITICAL NEOLIBERALISM

all unqualified employees, in whatever sector, and "citizens who strongly identify themselves with their national community" (ibid., 8). As Paul Collier (2018, 53) simplified this complex picture, strong national identifiers tend to be people who lack "skill" as alternative source of self-esteem, which makes them draw more on "nationality."

This is a good first stab at the demographic basis of the new-cleavage parties. On part of the populist right (TAN in political science jargon: Traditional, Authoritarian, Nationalist), this demographic basis is a fairly broad spread that reaches well into the middle class, but on average with lower skill levels. On part of new left and green parties (GAL: Green, Alternative, Libertarian), it contains the expanding category of "social and cultural specialists" (Kriesi et al. 2008, 12). This is a subtype of professional who identifies "not only with their professional community" (which is a mark of *all* professionals, distinguishing them from managers who identify with their organization), but who identifies "also with their clients" (ibid.). Overall, education matters not only for its personal economic benefits in a meritocratic society, but also for its "'liberalizing' effect," those endowed with it tilting toward "cultural tolerance and openness." In reverse, the "poorly educated are usually less tolerant" (ibid.). Hooghe and Marks (2018, 116) similarly see in education a "powerful structuring factor" for the transnational cleavage, not only as skill and mobility provider, but also because it "allows a person to see things from the other side," thus becoming "a key to empathy for those who have a different way of life."

In the remainder of this chapter, I first return to the political thrust of right-wing populism, which can be summarized as "illiberal democracy." As such, this is not a solution to democracy's problems in a neoliberal order but an aggravation of them. In a second step, I argue that the economic backdrop of populism is massively increased inequality and economic insecurity as a result of neoliberalism, and the concomitant decline of the vision and reality of middle-class society. Third, less these economic woes than cultural change, particularly that brought by immigration, has set the agenda of the populist right. Because the latter is also nationalist, the question arises what kind of nationalism it is and how it expresses itself in policy terms. With a focus on Europe, I argue that in the West populist nationalism has expressed itself, among other areas, in welfare chauvinism, which however had only limited impact. In Eastern Europe, by contrast, populist nationalism has fueled the rise of a self-declared "illiberal state," as the case of Viktor Orbán's Hungary eerily demonstrates.

Illiberal Democracy

The 2016 party program of the German AfD, which preceded its *völkisch* turn by only one year, presented the party as one of "liberals and conservatives," "free citizens of our country," and "convinced democrats" (AfD 2016: preamble). It wants to be "an alternative to what the political class believes it can impose on us as 'without alternative' (*alternativlos*)." It opposes the "political class of professional politicians," which primarily cares about itself and constitutes a "political cartel" (ibid., 8). Only the "state people" (*Staatsvolk*) of the Federal Republic "can put an end to this illegitimate situation."

This party statement not only confirms Mudde's (2004) "ideational" definition of populism, that is, the pure people versus corrupt elite binary; it also replicates, down to the word, Richard Katz and Peter Mair's (1995) "cartel theory" of political parties that no longer represent civil society but have become colluding and self-serving parts of the state apparatus. Confirming its neoliberal roots that would be quickly shed in favor of *völkisch* nationalism,[12] the 2016 AfD program curiously favors the privatization of state institutions (AfD 2016, 9), and it approvingly cites Friedrich Hayek's views on the imperfectability of human knowledge and political action (ibid., 10). Apart from this, the critique of an atrophied political process dominated by a "small and powerful political clique within the parties" (ibid., 8) closely resembles leading academic diagnoses, not only of "cartel party" but also of "post-democracy" (Crouch 2004), discussed in Chapter 2. Takis Pappas (2019), an astute comparativist of populism, understands populism entirely as endogenous response to a "democratic representation crisis" (ibid., 124), or "liberal decay" (ibid., 262), which is not far from the AfD's 2016 views: "Increased bureaucratization and institutional rigidity in politics, the recycling of political elites and the rise of technocracy, the entrenchment of interest groups, the lack of transparency, widespread corruption, and spreading cynicism" (Pappas 2019, 262).

However, Pappas (2019, 190) also concludes, on the basis of detailed historical case studies of populists in power, from Juan Perón in 1940s' Argentina to Orbán in 2010s' Hungary, that "in the long run and almost without fail, populism is calamitous for liberal democracy": "It decimates old established institutions, generates intense social polarization, and produces economic and political crisis; sometimes, it even morphs into autocracy." In line with most recent key contributions (Mudde 2004; Müller 2016;

158 POLITICAL NEOLIBERALISM

Galston 2018; Mounk 2018; Urbinati 2019a, 2019b), Pappas argues that populism, while "always democratic," which distinguishes it from fascism or communism, is "never liberal" (2019, 35). In short, populism is "democratic illiberalism" (ibid., 33). Merely inverting the words, Mudde (2004, 561) speaks of "illiberal democracy" because populism "rejects all limitations on the expression of the general will, most notably the constitutional protection of minorities and the independence . . . of key state institutions."

Against Pluralism and Constitutionalism

In particular, pluralism and constitutionalism, and thus the dual pillars of the "liberal" in liberal democracy, meet the ire of populists. This is because these principles dilute the direct and unmediated expression of the general will, either as expression of its impossibility (pluralism) or as hindrance to its approximation qua majority will (constitutionalism). With respect to pluralism, party government rests on a realistic understanding of society as divided by interests and cleavages that compete for political expression. "There is no unitary vision of a volonté générale," as Daniele Caramani (2017, 63) acutely describes the philosophy of party government, "nor is there a unitary vision of a society's common interest. There are societal cleavages that must be articulated and aggregated." Part of the pluralist vision is a probabilistic understanding of democratic politics that is undercut by populist certainties. A literary giant, Samuel Beckett, found the right expression for the pluralist view: "Ever tried. Ever failed. No matter. Try again. Fail again. Fail better" (quoted in Müller 2016, 35).

Constitutionalism is the second pillar of "liberal" in liberal democracy that is defied by populism. It is disliked for constraining the general will. In Yascha Mounk's (2018) synoptic account of contemporary populism, the latter conducts an "illiberal democracy" attack on "undemocratic liberalism," elements of which are "bureaucracies as lawmakers" (independent commissions without democratic oversight), democratically unaccountable central banks that prioritize inflation control over full employment, "judicial review" proper that "protects individual rights and the rule of law," and the proliferation of international treaties and organizations. This is apparently a mix of liberal and neoliberal realities. The bottom line of "undemocratic liberalism" is that "people no longer have a real say in all these policy areas" (ibid., ch. 2)—which, of course, implies the questionable counterfactual that they ever had. And constitutionalism as a generic word for these matters,

THE POPULIST RIGHT   159

cuts both ways. It unquestionably helped enshrine neoliberalism, as we see in Chapter 2. But successful populism also tries to "constitutionalize its particular majority" (Urbinati 2019a, 119), the rewriting of the constitution being the means for cutting the democratic ladder on which populist leaders climbed into office (see the discussion of Orbán's Hungary).

Opinions are divided whether democracy minus the liberal element is still democracy. On the optimist side, Mounk is impressed by the "democratic energy" of populism, which to him makes its contemporary incarnations distinct from "older far-right movements": "today's populists claim . . . to deepen the democratic elements of our current system. That matters" (2018, ch. 1). On the pessimist side, Jan-Werner Müller argues, convincingly in my view, that "democracy can only exist on a liberal basis" (quoted in Blokker 2022, 263). This is because without pluralism and constitutionalism the "institutionalized uncertainty" that "real democracy" requires cannot be guaranteed (Müller 2021, 71, borrowing the idea from Adam Przeworski). From this follows that "illiberal democracy" is an oxymoron.

The Paradox of Direct Representation

A compelling case why populism fails the democratic test has been made by Nadia Urbinati (2019b). To her, populism is not what it claims to be, a return to the classic idea of direct democracy. Instead, populism is a "new form of representative government, but a disfigured one," one that entails "direct representation" (ibid., 4). This contradiction in terms captures the fact that populism requires a leader and thus is itself a "representative form of politics" (ibid., 115). However, it is a particular form of representation, not "mandate representation" as in party government, which is replaceable, but "representation as embodiment," which is fixed. This "creates an irresponsible leader," "jeopardiz(ing) pluralism by principle" (ibid., 116). Moreover, true representative democracy is "diarchic," consisting not just of "will" (expressed in elections and decision-making) but also of "opinion" (the pluralist element), both "remain(ing) independent" (ibid., 7). Populist direct representation tilts the pluralist element, yielding "illiberal democracy"— which is "not democracy at all" (ibid., 10). The populist leader faces the dilemma that he (it is rarely a she) "must become an insider," if he succeeds, "without ever appearing to be one" (ibid., 156). This is why populists in power are in permanent campaign mode, like Trump. They "must be able to collapse the difference between movement and power, and between inside and outside" (ibid.).

160   POLITICAL NEOLIBERALISM

Urbinati's case for populism as a threat to democracy is evidently on the assumption that populism is less "ideology and style" than "strategic movement to remake political authority" (2019b:115). It requires to be in power to release its poisonous effects. However, she also makes a compelling argument why already qua "ideology and style" populism cannot be the fix to democracy's deficits that it claims to be. This is because its claim to represent the "people" as a whole, and thus to express the "general will," is false to begin with. In reality, populism "is a phenomenology that involves replacing the whole with one of its parts" (ibid., 13). This was already entailed, but not reflected on, in Mudde's pure people versus corrupt elite binary (2004). In populist imaginary, the people are always qualified by an adjective: "pure," "real,"[13] and so on. But this makes them part of a whole, already because the "elite" is not included (that, technically speaking, cannot but be part of "the people," unless it is imagined as of foreign origins). Even more clearly in form of "the majority," typically the "silent" one that populists claim to be or speak for, "the part erases the whole and makes politics a question of partiality" (ibid., 37). Real-existing populism thus entails factionalism and polarization. Of course, representative democracy also, in its party government form, implies the majority principle. But its logic is *pars pro toto*, and the assumption is that the constitution of the majority can—even must—change over time. In populism, the logic shifts to *pars pro parte* (ibid., 15), and the majority is fixed and always the same. The "majority principle" morphs into "majority rule," or from "procedure" into "a force" (ibid., 95). Populism rests on a "possessive conception of politics," as Urbinati put it concisely (ibid., 14). It seeks a "regime of rather than by the majority" (Urbinati 2019a, 123).

Another way of putting the matter is that populist politics is "like a war rather than a game, a matter of winners and losers, with no fiction of universalism" (Urbinati 2019b, 192). Reviewing the "grand dichotomy of the 20th century," which is the left–right division structuring that century's politics, Steven Lukes (2008) noted that this dichotomy embodies the "principle of parity." It means that "political alternatives are legitimately equal contenders" (ibid., 606, 607). The arrival of identity politics, in which the opponent is demonized as illegitimate and to be overcome or even erased, and of which right-wing populism is only *one* variant, falls short of the parity principle. This is why populism "cannot answer the problems that populists are reacting against" (Urbinati 2019b, 207).

The Difference that Power Makes

Despite these principled objections, to be in power makes all the difference for releasing the illiberal threat of populism. Poland, ruled between 2015 and 2023 by the populist Law and Justice Party (PiS), moved one category down from full "liberal democracy" to "electoral democracy," with restricted media and courts.[14] Hungary, under Orbán's Fidesz party, in power since 2010, fell even further down into the "electoral autocracy" category, with "no real choice over their leader."[15] The United States under Trump's first presidency (2017–2020) might have joined Poland or even Hungary if it were not blessed by stable democratic institutions and strong constitutional norms. Steven Levitsky and Daniel Ziblatt (2018, ch. 8) eerily demonstrated that after only one year, the Trump presidency, at least by way of expressed intention, fulfilled all four of Juan Linz's criteria of the "breakdown of democratic regimes" and turn to authoritarianism: it rejected the democratic rules of the game (including election results), denied the legitimacy of political opponents, encouraged violence, and curtailed the civil liberties of opponents.

Globally, "competitive authoritarianism," which is a "hybrid regime" in which authoritarian governments "coexist indefinitely with meaningful democratic institutions" (Levitsky and Way 2002, 58), has been the most rapidly growing regime type since the 1990s, and it is almost by definition the *terminus ad quem* for populists in power (who cannot totally dispense with democracy but are also authoritarian at heart). As Przeworski pointed out, the problem today is "subversion of democracy by stealth" (2019, 15), or "democratic backsliding" as a "process of gradual erosion of democratic institutions and norms" (ibid., 172), which often occurs with "continued popular support" (ibid., 187). The main agent in Przeworski's scenario of "subversion by stealth" is "right-wing populism," which he interestingly considers "an ideological twin of neoliberalism" in its hostility to institutions: "Both claim that social order is spontaneously created by a single demiurge: 'the market' or 'the people'" (ibid., 87).

At the same time, Przeworski (2019, 203) concedes that "electoral victories of the radical Right are not on the horizon in most European countries," as these parties have reached a plateau of "about one-fourth" of potential voters. Moreover, as electoral survey data suggest, their increasing share has been "due more to the abstention of centrist voters than to an increase of extreme voters" (ibid., 94). This has been confirmed by other analysts of

162 POLITICAL NEOLIBERALISM

survey data. Kriesi (2020, 242) reports that a "clear decline" of support for democracy among younger age cohorts in the United States is *not* happening in Europe, where "the democratic ideal is alive and well." While this contrasts with "widespread democratic dissatisfaction" there (ibid., 246), specifically related to a "lack of responsiveness" by political elites in north-west Europe and "performance failures" in south and east Europe, this is "no time for panic" (ibid., 256). In north-west Europe, Kriesi concludes, the "illiberal potential" of the populist right "has been curbed so far by . . . proportional electoral systems and the need to form coalitions when getting into power" (ibid.), which has a moderating effect. In the same vein of refuting the "crisis of democracy" talk in Europe, Bartels even reads from European Social Survey data that "Europeans were just as satisfied with the working of democracy in 2019 as they had been fifteen years earlier" (2023, 2). To Bartels, populist successes are not due to demand-side but to supply-side factors: "charismatic leadership, over-the-top media coverage and the stumbles and scandals of mainstream competitors" (ibid., 14). The illiberal turns in Poland and Hungary, for instance, only happened *after* populists gained power; the latter were brought in power by voters who were mainstream "conservative" rather than radical "populist" in their leanings, and they stayed in power because "ordinary Hungarians and Poles flourished" (ibid., 209).

Endogenous political and elite-focused accounts of populism are a useful antidote to alarmist warnings of a populist "wave" inundating Western democracies. However, they are incomplete. Not on the side of alarmists, Przeworski is still "moderately pessimistic," as he cannot see "what would get us out of the current discontent": "This crisis is not just political; it has deep roots in the economy and in society" (2019, 206). This is why we need to turn to the economic root causes of populism.

Inequality and Middle-Class Decline

Middle-Class Myth . . . and Reality

In 1953, the US weekly *Time* sent an editor on a national tour to review "people who seldom see a reporter." He found that "(e)ven in the smallest town and most isolated areas . . . the U.S. is wearing a very prosperous middle-class suit of clothes . . . People are not growing wealthy, but more of them than ever before are getting along" (quoted in Krugman 2009, 37). This was only the beginning of the "Great Compression" (ibid., ch. 3) between rich and poor that brought America closer to the vision of middle-class society, and thus to a post-class society, than probably any other society in history. The vision continues to matter because, since Aristotle, a prosperous middle class has been considered the basis of a functioning democracy (see also the update by Lipset 1959). But the reality is no longer.

A 2019 OECD report found the middle class in rich societies "under pressure,"[16] even "squeezed," as its members "have seen their standard of living stagnate or decline, while higher income groups have continued to accumulate income and wealth" (OECD 2019, 3). At that time, the top 10 percent in the income distribution held almost half of total wealth, while the bottom 40 percent held just 3 percent. Accordingly, there was the need for a "new growth narrative that puts people's wellbeing at the centre" (ibid.). This is a questionable (and jargonizing) conclusion because symbolic change ("new narrative") is unlikely to fix the structural dissipation of the middle of society, judged by the OECD report's own findings. The share of middle-income households fell from 64 percent to 61 percent between the mid-1980s and the mid-2010s. This sounds small. The shrinkage is easier to see in generational terms: 70 percent of Baby Boomers (born between 1943 and 1964) were middle-income (and thus middle–class) in their 20s, while only 60 percent of Millennials (born between 1983 and 2002) today are in this income bracket. Moreover, in the past three decades, median incomes increased one-third less than the average income of the richest 10 percent—and they would pale even further if the top 1 percent was the benchmark. At the same time, house prices grew three times faster than household median income in the past twenty years, while education costs also grew much faster than income, in particular in the United Kingdom and the United States. As a result, home ownership and college, the two pillars of middle-class aspiration, are increasingly out of reach or they come at the price of crushing individual and family debt (see Zaloom 2019).

Despite these sobering data, no less than two-thirds of OECD populations unabashedly "think of themselves as part of the middle class," even 80 percent in Scandinavia, the Netherlands, and Switzerland, which are traditionally rich and egalitarian societies (OECD 2019, 18). However, the alarm signal is rampant pessimism about the future: 60 percent of parents in twenty-one OECD countries list the risk that their children won't achieve the same "level of status and comfort" as one of their top three concerns (ibid., 26). In the face of similar Pew Research data for 2015, Przeworski finds the "collapse of the deeply ingrained belief in intergenerational progress . . . a phenomenon at a civilizational scale" (2019, 107).

The pessimism is well-founded. In the United States, 80 percent of those born in the 1970s into an average-income household would achieve a higher income than their parents; for those born in the 1980s, this chance has shrunk to 50 percent (Baldwin 2019, 213). Moreover, what Richard Baldwin calls the "globotics upheaval," which is job loss due to automation, stretches well into professional categories (including "Robo lawyers"); his estimate of globotic labor shrinkage for the United States is "between big and enormous"; that is, between one and six of every ten jobs lost due to automation (ibid., 161). In sum, "(d)igital technology is driving mass job displacement at a furious pace, but it is doing little to foster mass job creation" (ibid., 187).

Western middle-class decline is visualized on Branko Milanovic's (2016) famous "elephant curve." Depicting the evolution of the global income distribution since the late 1980s, the graph shows income stagnation or even decline around the eighty-fifth to ninetieth percentiles—these are people who are globally rich but among the middle-incomers in OECD societies. They are the losers of globalization. The two winners are the people in the fortieth to sixtieth percentiles of the global income distribution, which are mainly the emergent (although nominally much poorer) middle classes in China and India; and the top 1 percent of global incomers (half of them in the United States, but increasing numbers in Russia, China, and India), whose income and wealth has virtually exploded over the past thirty years. Kicking off the debate over the richest 1 percent in the United States, economist Joseph Stiglitz (2011) noted that the upper 1 percent now takes one-fourth of national income every year while controlling 40 percent of wealth, up from 12 percent and 33 percent, respectively, twenty-five years earlier. Over the same period, men with only a high-school degree, once sufficient for a job that was both blue collar and middle class, saw their incomes fall by 12 percent. "All the growth in recent decades," Stiglitz concludes, "has gone to those at the top."

US Congressional Budget Office data are even more drastic (see Therborn 2013, 122). They show that between 1979 and 2007, the top 1 percent of earners more than doubled their income (after taxes and transfers); the next 19 percent kept their share (36 percent of the total); but all others, the bottom 80 percent, lost. After the Great Recession in 2008, which might have been the doom moment of finance capitalism, the wealthiest 1 percent of households had 225 times the wealth of the typical American household—which is almost double the ratio as in 1962 or 1983 (Stiglitz 2012, 8). The Walton family alone, consisting of just six members and owning the low-cost Walmart supermarket chain, commanded $70 billion USD, which corresponds to the combined wealth of the bottom 30 percent of US society. Refuting the myth of "trickle-down economics," Stiglitz argues that "the riches accruing to the top have come at the expense of those down below," and that in the process the "middle class is being hollowed out" (ibid., 7). And this is not the result of anonymous market logic, but of "government policy" and successful "rent-seeking" by the rich (ibid., 8). For instance, the top marginal tax rate decreased from 70 percent under Jimmy Carter in the mid-1970s to merely 35 percent under George Bush Jr. in the early 2000s; in 2007, the average tax rate in the top four hundred households was as low as 16.6 percent, whereas taxpayers in general had to pay an average of 20.4 percent (ibid., 72).

As a result, the middle-class no longer forms a continuum with the rich, and its standard movement is no longer upward but downward. The middle class and the rich now live in separate worlds, and the middle-class continuum is with the lower levels of society. Fear of falling has become the new normal. As Daniel Markovits (2019, 105) notes for the United States, the "poor/middle-class income gap" has narrowed by 25 percent since the mid-twentieth century, whereas the "middle-class/rich income gap" has nearly doubled.

At the same time, meritocracy is the main justification for the widening gap between the rich and the rest. Note that even Markovits, a stern critic of the "meritocracy trap," holds that for the rich today, unlike for the rich in the past, "work has become the dominant path to wealth" (2019, 13). While the bottom also seems to believe in this (see Mau et al. 2023, ch. 3), French economist Thomas Piketty (2014), in his famed longitudinal analysis of tax returns in the United States and Europe, disagrees, showing that it is the nature of capitalism, with a short mid-twentieth-century exception, to be "patrimonial," with the rate of return on capital exceeding the rate of growth of output and income—expressed in the formula "$r > g$" (ibid., 25). This means that "inherited wealth grows faster than output and income" (ibid., 26). Put more simply: growth feeds wealth inequality, which "undermine(s) the meritocratic values on which democratic societies are based" (ibid., 1).[17]

166   POLITICAL NEOLIBERALISM

Inequality from the Top

Unlike in the past, inequality today works from the top. At least since Stieglitz (2011), the focus of critical attention has been on the richest 1 percent, replacing the previous concern about poverty. This is also the starting point of British sociologist Mike Savage's impressive review of the "return of inequality" (2021). Over the past half century, Pierre Bourdieu (1984) had set the standards for a "culturalist" class analysis, giving much to the internal composition of capital, economic versus cultural, and the requisite (intra-elite class) struggles for dominance. Savage (2021, 67) notes that this has become anachronistic as the importance of the volume of capital today greatly exceeds that of its composition. "(T)he secondary distinction between intellectuals and industrialists has waned as economic inequality has increased and the capital volume axis has therefore become more drawn out," Savage observes. And "(t)hese days, hip artists are also effective businesspeople, while rich people are also investing heavily in the art world" (ibid.). But most importantly, mounting inequality and elite riches "ha(ve) the effect of eroding the very principles of field contestation," which had been Bourdieu's main contribution to class theory. As Savage concludes, "(t)hose with large amounts of capital often don't see themselves as operating in the same social space or competing with those who are much poorer than they are. Those who are on the poorer fringes of society often see the rich as a world apart. They are no longer playing the same game" (ibid., 67–68).

Curiously, inequality from the top has been picked up at the 2017 World Economic Forum in Davos, the rich world's annual meeting place, as a potential source of "profound social instability." As Savage (2021, 16) sarcastically notes, this is in contrast to "populist politicians," who have been slow if not failing to put it on their agenda, preoccupied as they are with "immigration and threats to national sovereignty".

But the connection between mounting inequality and the rise of the populist right is incontrovertible. Sheri Berman (2021, 75) detects a "clear connection between the divisive and destabilizing economic trends of the last decades and rising support for populism."[18] More concretely, an analysis of European voting data has shown that "shocks from trade and migration," the usual triggers of the national sovereignty and cultural preservation agenda of the populist right, "elicit populist opposition only where the top 1 percent have gained the most" (Flaherty and Rogowski 2021, 495). This suggests that "top-heavy inequality" is at least indirectly related to the "persistence of public support for antiglobalization parties, especially those on the Right" (ibid.).

The Role of Education

Thomas Flaherty and Ronald Rogowski (2021, 496) further notice that education, or rather the lack of it, more than low or precarious occupational status, predicts support for antiglobalization parties. Education, in fact, especially the possession of a college degree, as Kriesi et al. (2008) were among the first to point out, figures centrally when trying to divide the "winners" from the "losers" of globalization. US statistics show that education has emerged as "the differentiator between economic precarity and success."[19] Americans with a college degree now have real wages 86 percent higher than those without. And not having a degree means little to no real wage increase since 1979.

Not holding a four-year college degree also is the main cause of the epidemic surge of "deaths of despair" (Case and Deaton 2020) in the American white working-class. Anne Case and Angus Deaton have shockingly revealed that the life expectancy of American whites without a bachelor's degree has decreased by 25 percent over the past decades, the three main causes of "death of despair" being suicide, drug overdose (doctor-prescribed pain-killing opioids), and alcoholic liver disease (ibid., 3). Case and Deaton note that this is "not the poorest group in the United States" (ibid., 8). Worse than wage decline is the outsourcing of low-education work to business-service firms that "do not bring the sense of pride"—one is "no longer invited to the holiday party" (ibid.) and is likely to remain stuck down low over one's working life. Key to the deaths of despair is "a long-term and slowly unfolding loss of a way of life for the white, less-educated, working class" (ibid., 146).[20] Not having a college degree has also been the gateway to voting for Trump in 2016: 72 percent of white non-college males and 62 percent of white non-college women did so.[21]

The same rift by education, even down to the numbers, has marked the Brexit vote earlier that year: 73 percent of British voters without a college degree voted for leaving the European Union, while 75 percent with a degree voted for staying.[22] Accordingly, two British political scientists interpret Brexit as the outcome of a long-brooding struggle between "two politically conscious opposing tribes" (Sobolewska and Ford 2020, 11): "identity liberals," assembling "graduates," on one side, and "identity conservatives," drawing disproportionately on "school leavers," on the other side, both locked in a "pure identity conflict, pushing the old economic class conflict into the background" (ibid.). As Maria Sobolewska and Robert Ford further point out, this has also been a rift between generations: postsecondary education in the United Kingdom expanded not before the 1990s, when the 1992 Education Act transformed polytechnics into universities. As a result, university attendance skyrocketed, from barely 15 percent in 1988 to 40 percent by the mid-2010s (ibid., ch. 2). This makes for an education divide between those born before and after the 1970s. The tragic of Brexit is not really that the non-educated prevailed over the educated, but that the old and dwindling prevailed over the young and growing who might have looked for opportunity on the "continent," as "Europe" is known on the island.

Beyond the Trump and Brexit examples, the importance of education for understanding changing political cleavages in Western democracies, and for right-wing populism in particular, has been demonstrated by French economist Piketty and collaborators (most recently, Gethin, Martínez, and Piketty 2021). For the 1950s and 1960s, they identify a "class-based" pattern of voting, in which the combination of education and income—"two strongly correlated measures of socioeconomic status" (ibid., 42)—made people vote either left (with a low level of both) or right (high level of both). From then on, however, there has been a continuous trend of the highly educated to vote left, while high incomers continue to vote right. This trend is "accelerated," not caused, by the rise of green and radical right parties, which concentrate the high- and low-educated voters, respectively (ibid., 1f). The authors call the new pattern "multiple elites," because the educated now vote for the left (dubbed "Brahmin Left"), while the rich continue voting for the right ("Merchant Right")—the novelty being that the elites are no longer united in their preference for the right. At the same time, the voting turnout of the bottom 50 percent least educated and poorest "has fallen sharply" (ibid., 5). The political system simply does not speak for them any longer. Instead, "political systems ... increasingly oppose two coalitions embodying the interests of two kinds of elites" (ibid., 42).

The multiple-elite structure helps explain why massively increased inequality over the past few decades did not lead to calls for redistribution: the educated, while mostly not rich, still are well-endowed materially, so they care less about getting more and about redistribution in general.[23] Instead, the "reversal of the education cleavage" is "tightly associated" with the rise of a "new sociocultural axis of political conflict" (Gethin, Martínez-Toledano, and Piketty 2021, 42), on which the educated and less-educated, or rather their preferred parties (left-green and right-populist, respectively), occupy opposite poles. The authors' parallel analysis of party manifestos, added to that of voter demographics, reveals that polarization on economic issues has "remained remarkably stable," while polarization on sociocultural issues "has dramatically risen since the 1970s" (ibid., 30). While the data don't allow the authors to establish the direction of causality, from parties to voters or vice versa, one important factor on the political demand side is "growing educational attainment."[24] Whereas in the 1950s less than 10 percent of voters in Europe and the United States had a college degree, there are more than three times as many today. This made catering to educated voters, "who often put living in a liberal society above lowering their tax bills,"[25] inevitable. Thus described, who but leftist parties would take the educated in?

While this demographic trend would make the Third-Way reconstruction of left parties inevitable, Piketty (2020), in a prior version of the education-cleavage hypothesis, does not hold back from lashing out against the left for having "abandoned the working class" (ibid., 40). He holds the left's "ideological failure" responsible for the workers' turn to the "social nativism" that is nourished by emergent populist right parties. In this reading, there was choice in the left's addressing either (economic) "property" or (cultural) "border" issues, and only the misguided preference for the latter (that could not but be cosmopolitan from a leftist position) opened the gateway for nativism on the part of abandoned workers: "(I)dentity conflicts are fueled by disillusionment with the very ideas of a just economy and social justice" (ibid., 831). As a man of the left, Piketty has an axe to grind, and he turned it against his own kind, perhaps exaggerating the degree of voluntarism in the decline of the left.[26]

Class and Occupational Specifications

It is undeniable that a low level of education, and thus to be on the losing end of globalization and technological change, is a major support factor for right-wing populism. Negatively formulated, "support for the radical right

170　POLITICAL NEOLIBERALISM

is weakest among highly educated professionals" (Kitschelt 2007, 1199). In addition, one can make more fine-grained class and occupational specifications. In a ten-country comparison, Oesch and Line Rennwald (2018, 784) found that "class voting" is "very much alive and kicking" in a West European party system that, due to the revival of the cultural conflict axis, has moved from "bipolar" to "tripolar." In addition to "left" and "centre right," the two antagonists on the established economic conflict axis, there is now the "radical right," which forms one pole on the new cultural axis. With respect to the classes and occupational groups that these party families compete for, Oesch and Rennwald distinguish between "preserves," "contested strongholds," and sites of "open competition." Notably, the only "preserves," where there is basically no competition, are the highly educated, who either, as "sociocultural professionals," vote for the left (green parties included); or, as "managers" (also liberal professionals and employers), vote center-right (ibid., 787).[27]

The radical right, as the newest of the three party families, by definition needs to fish in other waters. But it acquired "strongholds," if "contested" ones, the first being the "working class" (in competition with the left), the second being "small business owners" (now in competition with the center right). A third site, "open competition," is fishing ground for *all* parties, and it consists of (lower-) middle class "clerks" and "technical specialists" (Oesch and Rennwald 2018, 787). The radical right made the strongest middle-class inroad in the (however tiny) small-business-owner segment, yet yielding the "highest score among production and service workers" (ibid., 794); in consequence, its electorate is the one with the "strongest working-class bias of the three party poles" (ibid., 800). Overall, "party competition continues to be firmly rooted in the social structure," which affirms the grander cleavage-structure diagnoses. However, the "small size of the different classes," particularly if subdivided by occupational profile,[28] creates the need for coalition-building and accounts for increased fragmentation and "instability" of the party system (ibid., 801).

The picture of an "increasing proletarianisation" (Oesch and Rennwald 2018, 801) of the populist right electorate must not ignore its significant middle-class component. Importantly, the latter kicks in qua "squeezed" or "declining middle," although more through its members' "fearing" than actually "experiencing" economic adversity (Kurer 2020, 1800). Therefore, this middle-class component of the populist right is often taken as an argument against the view that populists assemble the losers of globalization. But

THE POPULIST RIGHT   171

this would entail a rather narrow understanding of "losing." Thomas Kurer showed that "semiskilled routine workers" in the lower middle class have a strong propensity for voting radical right. "Routine work" is performed by 25 to 30 percent of the workforce in the examined countries (Germany, Britain, and Switzerland), the main examples being blue-collar jobs in industry and basic white-collar work in administration. Being "codifiable," routine work is replaceable by automation,[29] thus constituting a particularly "vulnerable occupational environment" (ibid., 1801, 1804). Nevertheless, this old "central pillar of the lower middle class" (ibid., 1804) is shrinking mainly indirectly, not through being fired but through not being replaced when retiring—"natural turnover" (Kurer and Palier 2019, 3).[30] Accordingly, routine workers experience only "relative economic decline," not real "impoverishment" (Kurer 2020, 1798). Kurer calls them "survivors." Unlike job losers, who turn left or abstain, survivors vote right, especially populist right: "(A) perception of relative societal decline and concerns about one's position in the social hierarchy—not unemployment or acute material hardship— . . . drives support for right-wing populist parties" (ibid., 1800). The surviving but declining middle is marked by "status anxiety," "with an emphasis on the values and virtues of an idealized past" (ibid., 1805).

The importance of "status anxiety" and of "nostalgia" or "societal pessimism," which mixes economic and cultural motives and where direct personal concern is submerged to or embedded in larger societal concern, has been affirmed in many studies of the populist right in Western Europe and the United States.[31] The Brexit vote has been explained in these terms, as expression of the "social malaise of intermediate classes" (Antonucci et al. 2017). So has the 2016 Trump vote, with a racial inflection, as driven by dominant-status "white Americans . . . under siege" (Mutz 2017, 4330).

The sociotropic motivation revealed in these analyses also has a geographic dimension. One study of the United States and Europe argued that not the "individual" but "community" is the proper unit for studying populism, because "populist support is strongest in communities that experienced long-term economic and social decline" (Broz et al. 2021, 464). A study with an even broader scope found populism less a matter of "interpersonal inequality," but "revenge of the 'places that don't matter,'" in developing countries as much as in the developed world (Rodriguez-Pose 2017).

To the degree that status anxiety is driving the declining middle, they espouse an "identity politics" that cannot be alleviated by "more welfare" and

172   POLITICAL NEOLIBERALISM

"financial support from governments"; instead, they "want their perceived relative decline in the social hierarchy addressed" (Kurer 2020, 1826). As Kurer concludes, "right-wing populist parties have long realized this" (ibid.). It is therefore important to take a closer look at the non-material, cultural motives that are driving the populist right and its supporters.

Cultural Deflection

To deflect means to "change direction." The notion of cultural deflection addresses the crucial fact that the economic root causes of populism, previously discussed as inequality and middle-class decline, find little direct expression in the preferences and programs of the populist right, which nevertheless is the main haven for the losers of these processes. Mudde stated in 2007 that "the economic program is a secondary feature in the ideologies of populist right parties" (ibid., 119), and that economic concerns are "also secondary to their electorates" (ibid., 120). This remains true today (see Noury and Roland 2020). When tackling the question why the economic wounds inflicted by neoliberalism have not led to the strengthening but decline of the left, while the star of the populist right has risen, Francis Fukuyama (2018, ch. 8) cites Gellner's famous "wrong address theory." For Gellner (1983, 129), this was one of the "false theories of nationalism," espoused by Marxists in response to 1914, when nation triumphed over class: "The awakening message was intended for classes, but by some terrible postal error was delivered to nations." Then and now, Fukuyama (2018, ch. 9) sees the root of the deflection from class to nation, or from economics to culture, in human psychology: "(T)he pain of poverty is felt more often as a loss of dignity." Without denying the importance of dignity and recognition—the status-anxiety diagnosis for the dwindling middle pointed in this direction—by that logic class should *never* have stood a chance over nation, which does not correspond to the historical facts.

What Dani Rodrik (2021) calls the "economics versus culture question" in the explanation of the populist right, requires a composite answer, one that eschews a simplistic either-or as much as settling on only *one* mechanism when combining the two. A strikingly simple bridge from economic root causes to cultural deflection builds on the fact that populist right parties draw support from two heterogeneous occupational groups, "blue-collar workers" and "owners of small businesses" (Ivarsflaten 2005). Their economic interests are diametrically opposed, pro-state-interventionist the workers' and anti-interventionist the small owners' interests. This raises the paradox that the two groups that give "disproportionate" support to the populist right are also the ones that are "the most divided" on economic issues (ibid., 489). Hence, as Elisabeth Ivarsflaten shows along case studies of the French Front National and the Danish People's Party, the need to bridge the economic differences by "issues cross-cutting the economic dimension" (ibid., 471): restricted immigration, law and order, EU skepticism, anti-corruption; that is, the cultural "position" and political "valence" issues that populist right parties hold in ample storage.[32] However, this political supply-side explanation dodges the question why these (and not other) non-economic issues could arise in the first, and why they should appeal precisely to these groups. For this, we need something akin to the cleavage theories discussed earlier.

Starting with the assumption that "globalization shocks" are driving the rise of the populist right, Rodrik (2021) has laid out a "conceptual framework" of the multiple channels through which these shocks (that he further differentiates into trade, immigration, and finance shocks) help amass populist votes. In this framework, culture is merely "an intermediate variable rather than the ultimate driver," only "amplifying the political effects of globalization shocks" (ibid., 135). That means, there *is* the possibility of the "economic dislocations" brought by globalization shocks *directly* shaping "individual policy preferences" on the demand-side, or "party programs" on the supply-side, *without* the detour of culture. However, this would amount to the leftist class voting and class politics that has taken a nosedive under neoliberalism, and that only in some places (and limited times) has found a left-populist successor. Instead, the more likely causal paths are indirect, working through the variable set of "culture, racial attitudes, social identity" (ibid., 140). This may again happen on either the political demand-side or supply-side, the culture set directly shaping individual voting preferences, or these preferences being indirectly elicited by party programs that first adopted the culture set. The two culture-mediated paths are the more likely today, as the fortunes of the populist right attest to. Overall, Rodrik's "conceptual framework" suggests that a "comprehensive analysis" needs to reckon with four causal channels for globalization to fuel populism, two each on the demand- and supply-side of politics.[33] Needless to say, this is a "tall order" that no single analysis has yet pulled off (ibid., 141).

174   POLITICAL NEOLIBERALISM

However, despite the complexity, Rodrik (2021, 162) offers a simple reason, equally working for the supply *and* demand sides of politics, why the globalization backlash has taken the "right-wing, nativist form" that works through culture. This is because globalization by definition generates "'outsider' targets": "foreign exporters, culturally different workers, international banks," which allow economic distress to be "recast as threats on the dominant group's traditional way of life, deepening the divide between 'us' and 'them.'"

Both Ivarsflaten (2005) and Rodrik (2021), in different ways, operate with the assumption of cultural deflection, and of a propensity of the political right to engage in it. This has historical predecessors. Ziblatt (2017, 34) has addressed the "conservative dilemma" in the making of nineteenth-century European democracies, which is that playing "the numbers game" to win elections required conservative parties to compromise their "inegalitarian and hierarchical views." The solution was to "find and exploit issues that cross-cut and diminish the impact of social class as an electoral cleavage, supplanting it with issues such as nationalism, religion, and patriotism" (ibid., 49). A contemporary variant is the US Republican Party, which already preceding Trump had mobilized white identity to defend (or rather deflect from) wealth inequality (Hacker and Pierson 2020; see also Frank 2004).

The right's penchant for cultural deflection is affirmed in a comprehensive study of the programs of 450 political parties (right and left) in forty-one democracies (including some non-European), from 1945 to 2010: "Increasing inequality shifts the proportion of the population falling into lower socioeconomic categories . . . In the face of rising inequality, . . . leftist parties will emphasize economic issues in their manifestos. By contrast, the nonredistributive economic policies often espoused by rightist parties will not appeal to this burgeoning constituency. Rather, . . . rightist parties will opt to emphasize values-based issues" (Tavits and Potter 2015, 744). As the authors further argue, values-issues "distract" voters, drawing them away from their economic interests, and rightist parties have understood to exploit this. The rightists' politicization of values is especially strong in "more diverse and more religious countries, as well as in those countries that are experiencing high inflows of foreign-born individuals" (ibid., 745). This analysis does not factor-in the "neoliberal consensus in economic and social policymaking" (Kriesi et al. 2012, 17), which made the Third-Way left take distance from economic redistribution, but also take a progressive stance on the cultural cleavage generated by globalization. This was a godsend for the right, which is always economically inegalitarian, yet ready to fulfil the new need to be "socially and culturally opposed to opening the borders" (ibid., 19).

In sum, cultural deflection has been a strategy of the political right in past and present, to wash over the economic inegalitarianism that happens to define it but that locks it into a minority position.

Ethnopluralism

What makes the populist right "right" is a "specific form of nationalism," which Mudde called "nativism": "an ideology, which holds that states should be inhabited exclusively by members of the native group" (2007, 19). Nativism is another word for ethnic nationalism, which is usually distinguished from civic or liberal nationalism.[34] It is a well-known fact that, unlike their historical antipodes of class and socialism, nation and nationalism have not been theorized "from within" to the same degree (see Szporluk 1988). This applies even more to the ethnic variant of nationalism.

To the limited degree that an intellectual doctrine can be attributed to the ethnic nationalism that circulates today within the populist right, the closest candidate is the "ethnopluralism" developed by the French *Nouvelle Droite*, in particular Alain de Benoist.[35] It has been influential not only for the French Front National, but also for other populist right parties in Europe (see Rydgren 2018, 3–4).[36] Confirming these parties' location on a new cleavage axis, New Right thinking indeed is a response to a prior multiculturalism, which in France has figured as the "right to difference" (*droit à la différence*) on the part of minorities. Now this right is claimed for the majority as well. "What is good for the Bororos or the Guayaquis, should be no less good for us": "the right of peoples to be themselves" (Benoist 2017 [1985], 103). Benoist calls this borrowing from multiculturalism "mutual decolonization," in which "White Power" is the logical progression from "Black Power." At the same time, "racism" is nominally rejected: "I am for non-discrimination, for de-colonization, for the self-determination of peoples," says Benoist (ibid., 102). Unlike classic racism, which was hierarchical, the novelty of ethnopluralism is to be horizontal; it stipulates the "equal value of homogenous peoples in their native territories" (Benoist, quoted in Weiss 2017, ch. 1).

176 POLITICAL NEOLIBERALISM

Indeed, a manifesto entitled *The French New Right in the Year 2000* (Benoist and Champetier 1999), is over long stretches indistinguishable from a radical leftist multiculturalism. It finds the "true wealth of the world" in "the diversity of its cultures and peoples" (ibid., 11), while opposing the "homogenizing universalism" of the West that it sees embodied in liberalism, "the main enemy" (ibid., 3). The French New Right is even (self-)depicted in this manifesto as allied with the "peoples struggling against Western imperialism" and "racism," in a posture called "differentialist anti-racism" (ibid., 13). Already long before this statement, the intellectual historian of the (New) Right, Pierre-André Taguieff, spoke of the "third-worldism of the right," and he mocked Benoist as "one of the last French leftists" (1993, 21).

The problem is that the endorsement of inequality and hierarchy as natural and ineradicable features of human society, is a definitional element of the political right since its birth, post-1789 (Bobbio 1996). However, positively valued inequality and hierarchy are not easily matched with the "pluralism" element in ethnopluralism, which borrows from multiculturalism and suggests symmetry and equality. As a result, classic racism slips back in.[37] It is barely suppressed in the claim that "all races are superior," and that "all races have their own genius" (Benoist 2017 [1985], 85). It is out in the open when "racial differences in intelligence (IQ) . . . cannot be denied," and when Benoist oddly distinguishes the "intuitive reasoning" of "blacks" from the "discursive reasoning" of others (ibid., 97).

Most importantly, ethnopluralism rejects the mixing of races and peoples, each is to stick to their "own" territory without interference by the others. Next to the endorsement of inequality and hierarchy, the rejection of mixing is a second feature of classic racism that pops up in the New Right. From the rejection of mixing follows a principled rejection of immigration, which can only lead to "discrimination, segregation, the loss of culture, and crime" (Benoist 2017 [1985], 99).[38] The rejection of immigration, for primarily cultural reasons, is the perhaps strongest communality between the New Right doctrine of ethnopluralism and the agenda of populist right parties (for the latter, see Ivarsflaten 2008, 3).

Also central to New Right thinking is its frontal opposition to liberalism (as well as to Christianity, as its historical roots). This replaced an earlier anti-communist stance, which became anachronistic post-1989 (see Taguieff 1993, 14). However, what Benoist calls "liberal" is perhaps better called "neoliberal"—a notion that never took off in a French intellectual culture that

THE POPULIST RIGHT   177

has not liked liberalism much, the latter doing much of the pejorative work that in other places only the prefix "neo" does.[39] Liberalism, Benoist argues, "destroys community"; it reduces social life to the "care of material things"; it "does not defend liberty but the right to be private"; and politics is reduced to "a kind of service for economic bosses, administration replaces leadership, nations are reduced to mere markets" (Benoist 2017 [1985], 190). Overall, "liberalism," as Benoist understands it, is to him the "main enemy" (ibid., 198), rather than "communism" or "Islam," which take rather subordinate roles in this respect.

Here is an important difference between New Right theory and practice. The anti-(neo)liberal motif, while central to New Right thinking, is rather subdued in the programs of populist right parties. As previously mentioned, this is due to many of these parties' neoliberal pasts, and their prior endorsement of anti-tax and anti-welfare positions, in this faithful to their earliest core constituency in the old middle class of small shop-owners and artisans. As they turned anti-immigrant, some populist right parties, especially in the small liberal western and northern states of Europe, have even complemented their trademark ethnic nationalism with a defense of liberal values, such as gender equality and the freedom of speech (see Halikiopoulou et al., 2013). But they did so for entirely opportunistic reasons, to denounce an "illiberal" Islam (see Brubaker 2017b).

Welfare Chauvinism

The nasty reality of ethnopluralism, of course, is that "pluralism" is not meant to apply to domestic society. After all, it is an intellectual articulation of ethnic nationalism, despite the left-multiculturalist rhetoric. In policy terms, welfare chauvinism is this nationalism's perhaps most pertinent expression, at least in Western Europe. It "promotes nativism as the main organizing principle of social policy," and has been embraced by populist radical right parties as they moved away from "neoliberal economic views" (Ensser-Jedenastik 2018, 294).[40] Considering that these parties assemble an "anti-state petite bourgeoisie" and a "traditionally left-leaning working class" clientele (Röth et al. 2018, 328), to become pro-welfare, in however constricted ways, is not an obvious move for them. But populist right parties have been shown to support "deregulation," perhaps, especially if in coalition with the center-right; but not "welfare retrenchment" (ibid.).

178   POLITICAL NEOLIBERALISM

In colloquial language, welfare chauvinism thrives on the image that "Henk and Ingrid pay for Ali and Fatima," as has been the slogan of Dutch populist Geert Wilders's PVV party. This choice and distribution of names (two Dutch against two Muslim) suggests that not just shared citizenship but co-ethnicity should be the condition for welfare entitlement, from which all immigrants are thus to be categorically excluded. While welfare chauvinism is one of the rare socioeconomic (as against cultural or identity) planks in populist right programs (see Röth et al., 2018), it is of interest here as an applied form of ethnic nationalism. Or rather, it shows how little space there is for it in a liberal state.

Indeed, welfare chauvinism, whose thrust is plain ethnic exclusion, runs against severe constitutional obstacles. Not even formal citizenship, in itself a rather imperfect proxy for co-ethnicity in liberal states, provides a shell for limiting social benefits. "The principle of equal treatment is simply sacred. Period," said a senior civil servant in the Dutch Department of Social Affairs when pressed about the issue (Koning 2019, 189). As a result, it is "impossible in the Netherlands," as in other liberal-constitutional states, "to implement any policy that directly discriminates between native-born citizens and legal immigrant residents" (ibid., 188). The populist right has adjusted to these constraints in betting on excessive residence requirements as a proxy. The Dutch PVV, for instance, demands ten years of legal residence as condition for social benefits (five years more than required for legal residence, which usually triggers equal treatment), or to exclude temporary migrants altogether (what has long been the practice in the United Kingdom, even without any radical right input). The Netherlands, where the populist right has been a strong political force for two decades, shows the reach *and limits* of welfare chauvinism: only immigrants with "the most robust status" are entitled to benefits today, after considerable residence time and tough integration tests and requirements (ibid., 147).

Welfare chauvinism *sensu stricto* is thus non-implementable. Next to the toughening of residence time, one finds two further proxies for welfare chauvinism in the populist right. The first is to exclude on the basis of "contribution history," which is directed against asylum-seekers and undocumented migrants (Ennser-Jedenastik 2018, 307). So, there is little opposition to including immigrants in pension and unemployment schemes, simply because these schemes operate on the basis of reciprocity and prior insurance payments. By contrast, the strongest opposition is to including migrants in tax-financed social aid or health care, which is the gist of the "Henk and Ingrid" polemic. But in insisting on reciprocity and prior contribution, the populist right, not different in this from majority views, in fact takes a neoliberal position, and one that has long found its way into law and policy. Accordingly, a May 2011 report of the Dutch Council for Social Development bears a neoliberal handwriting, but populists, as plain ethnic exclusion is not on offer, can easily subscribe to it: "Who does not contribute ... to welfare and innovation cannot stay and is not allowed to make a claim on the welfare state" (quoted in Koning 2019, 158). The same neoliberal-populist congruence is the "duty to integrate" and the responsibility to "maintain oneself independently," which the Dutch government laid out as its "new vision on integration" in the same year (ibid., 161).

Secondly, while right populists have come to oppose welfare retrenchment and austerity, they also oppose positive measures for new risk groups and social investment policies, as discussed in Chapter 3. This proxy for welfare chauvinism is not a neoliberal position but "welfare nostalgia" (Fenger 2018, 190). Its gist is to protect male and working labor-market insiders, the classic beneficiaries of Bismarckian welfare states. Conversely, welfare nostalgia hits "not only migrants, but also women and perhaps even other non-traditional workers like self-employed and temp workers" (ibid.). As their main clientele is not actual but prospective losers, who still *have* something to lose, including relatively secure jobs, populist right parties often support harsh workfare programs for the unemployed, who (irrespective of their ethnicity or nationality) are considered outside the pale of "hard-working people." And these parties stand in for a traditional "transfer-oriented welfare state that downgrades those social investments on which new social risk groups rely" (Rathgeb and Busemeyer 2022, 10). These populist party positions exactly mirror their voters' preferences. The latter have been shown to be "pro-welfare" not across the board, but only for the "deserving" (the elderly and handicapped at the top, and the unemployed at the bottom, just above immigrants), within a "particularistic-authoritarian welfare state" (ibid.).

Orbán's Nation[41]

As the case of welfare chauvinism shows, populist nationalism has limited reach in Western Europe. In the East, by contrast, with populists in power, their ethnic nationalism has been the blueprint for building a self-conscious

180   POLITICAL NEOLIBERALISM

"illiberal state," curiously under the roof of the European Union that has proved impotent to stop the process.[42] Orbán has used his trademark notion of illiberal state only seven times, which makes it more of a "short-term marketing slogan" (Pap 2018, 62). However, short of the word, illiberal content permeates the new Hungarian constitution, passed in 2011, which helped "the Dictator"[43] and his Fidesz party to "cement[] themselves in" (Kornai 2015, 299), for three consecutive election victories so far.

Before scrutinizing this remarkable new constitution, which allows us to see in minutia how ethnic nationalism changes liberal law in fundamental ways, it is first necessary to put Hungary into its proper neoliberal context. Hungarian populism is a model case of populist backlash in a region, post-communist Europe, which has embraced neoliberalism more "enthusiastically and persistently" than any other region in the world (Appel and Orenstein 2016, 313), at least at elite level. This elite enthusiasm included the post-communist left, which was eager to go the extra-mile "to prove they were bona fide capitalists" (ibid., 318). After the social distress caused by initial "shock therapy" brought the left back to power in the mid-1990s, they "held on" to neoliberal reforms with steady nerve (Ther 2016, 83). Their "second-wave neoliberalism" (ibid., ch. 5) even went beyond the expectations of international financial institutions or the European Union, in including the privatization of pensions and health care, and introducing flat income taxes and reducing corporate taxes to record lows. The cross-party zeal was due to a logic of "competitive signaling" (Appel and Orenstein 2016, 316), by means of which post-communist states sought to "impress potential investors and attract capital."

The neoliberal bonanza came to an abrupt halt with the global financial crisis of 2008–2009. Unlike in the West, this crisis was a real game-changer. The foreign capital influx, on which a highly indebted Hungary was particularly dependent, suddenly stopped. Hungary was also the only country in the region in which foreign banks (like the Austrian Raiffeisenkasse) had offered easy loans in Euro and Swiss Franc, for common people to buy housing. Lured by their low interest rates (which were thus transferred from West to East), one million Hungarians (one of every ten!) took advantage of this possibility (Ther 2016, 222–225). The rub was that the monthly instalments fluctuated with the value of the local currency, the Forint. The Forint's dramatic decline after 2008, in particular against the Swiss Franc, made these mortgages unpayable for many or most. This was the moment for Orbán, who had been a center-right neoliberal during his first stint as prime minister, from 1998 to 2002,[44] to return triumphantly in 2010, now with the pledge to "put the international banks in their place" (ibid., 225). This is what he did, converting the foreign currency loans into Forint at a low rate determined by his government, with two-thirds of the cost to be swallowed by the banks that loudly protested. No government in the West, from Washington, DC, to Berlin, had dared to make the banks pay for the calamity they were responsible for—although neoliberalism's "popular dimension" (ibid., 226), of which the Hungarian foreign-currency mortgage craze was one example, must not be overlooked.

Reining in international banks was only one element of Orbán's economic nationalism. The latter also included renationalizing oil, gas, utilities, and the private pension funds that he himself had introduced a decade earlier; it further included special taxes on foreign firms, a public work program,[45] and pro-natalist policies.[46] Although building a kleptocratic "Mafia state" at the same time, diverting large sums of EU money into the pockets of family and friends, it is fact that Orbán brought "jobs, growth, and gains for the lower and middle classes" (Orenstein and Bugarič 2020, 8, 9). Like in Poland, where Jaroslaw Kaczyński's PiS explicitly adopted Orbán's model, at least the populist-nationalist part of it, it has been less the "appeal of radical nationalism" to their respective electorate that has sustained these parties and their leaders over time (PiS until 2023), than the "fact that they presided over substantial increases in prosperity and subjective well-being" (Bartels 2023, 15).

Orbán and Fidesz's return to power in 2010 is out of the populist playbook, as it thrived on a grotesque "corrupt elite" blunder of their socialist predecessors. Five months after winning narrowly in 2006, socialist Prime Minister Ferenc Gyurcsány was audiotaped in an internal discussion with party hacks, admitting that "we lied throughout the last year-and-a-half, two years . . . We lied in the morning, we lied in the evening" (quoted in Bartels 2023, 193). Huge protests notwithstanding, the socialists sat it out for the remaining three-and-a-half years. But Orbán's victory in 2010 was preordained. Most importantly, it came with a two-thirds majority in parliament, which allowed him to introduce far-reaching constitutional changes. These maintained a democratic façade while pushing Hungary to the brink of autocracy. Ironically, constitutional law, whose normal function in a

182 POLITICAL NEOLIBERALISM

democracy is to prevent the "tyranny of the majority," was used to erect just such a majority tyranny (Pap 2018, 19), which of course is the tyranny of the man himself, Orbán.

The first step in this direction was the pronunciation of a grand System of National Cooperation (SNC), which is striking for its millenarian vision of a "new political community" (renamed "Hungary," in lieu of "Hungarian Republic") and complete rupture with the old. As Trump would trumpet in his 2017 inauguration speech, that "today we are not merely transferring power from one administration to another . . . but . . . back . . . to you, the people"[47], Orbán claimed that the "voting booth revolution" of 2010 had entitled him to establish a "new social contract." While there was credence to Trump's claim, in Orbán's case there was not, because nothing of the sort had been part of his campaign. "Hungarians," one can read in the government's post-election SNC declaration, "have authorized us . . . to establish a new political, economic, and social system built on new rules in every area of life. They *expect me with all my strength and ability* to help the Hungarian community dispose of the old system and create, consolidate, and operate a new one . . . Through this declaration we *acknowledge the will of the people*, and make it the compass of the future" (quoted in Pap 2018, 51; emphasis supplied). This passage, which stresses the separateness but co-importance of leader and popular will, affirms Nadia Urbinati's (2019b, 4) sharp observation that populism is not so much "direct democracy," which it claims to be, as "direct representation," a "disfigured" form of representative government.

Previously, the SNC declaration continues, "Hungary . . . was controlled by elite agreements and invisible pacts" (quoted in Pap 2018, 53)—the socialists' 2006 audiotape blunder comes to one's mind. But the charge and the remedial ambition go deeper:

> The new social contract calls for cooperation instead of divisiveness, service of the public good instead of the advocacy of private interests . . . In the future, instead of private aims and interests, politics must serve common aims and interests . . . work, home, family, health and order are the solid pillars of the System of National Cooperation . . . it shall establish the primacy of public good over private interests, the primacy of order over lawlessness, the primacy of safety over unpredictability and governmental chaos, and the primacy of economic advancement over debt and vulnerability. (in ibid., 54)

This was simultaneously a frontal attack on neoliberalism, in which private interest prevails over the public good, while remaining in its ambit, because "work" and to "free up the energies of individual ambition" (ibid.) were still central. The celebration of work was subtly contrasted to a "'decadent' West," as Mitchell Orenstein and Bojan Bugarič observe (2020, 8); but work also contrasts with "speculation," the mark of finance capitalism (and his later arch enemy, George Soros).[48]

Orbán's vision is that of a "work-based state" (Pap 2018, 57), but one in which work and private initiative *directly* serve the public good, without the liberal detour of the "invisible hand." His new constitution, the Fundamental Law of 2011, contains two curious work-related clauses that simultaneously stipulate that "(e)veryone shall be responsible for him- or herself, *and* shall be obliged to contribute to the performance of state and community tasks according to his or her abilities and possibilities" (Article O; emphasis supplied); and that "(e)veryone shall have the right to choose his or her work," while being "obliged to contribute to the enrichment of the community through his or her work, in accordance with his or her abilities and potential" (Article XII). This resembles the common-good individualism underlying neoliberal workfare programs, in which individuals are required to be self-providing not to become a burden to the public purse. And the nation is conceived of as community of the thrifty—call it "neoliberal nationalism" (Joppke 2021b).

Orbán's infamous pronunciation of the "illiberal state," which came three years after the SNC (a notion he had long dropped by then), is closely tied to the idea of a "work-based state":

> The work-based state is approaching. We want to organise a work-based society that is not liberal in character . . . we must break with liberal principles and methods of social organisation . . . The Hungarian nation is not simply a group of individuals but a community that must be . . . constructed. And . . . the new state that we are constructing in Hungary is an illiberal state, a non-liberal state. (quoted in Pap 2018, 57f)

Having read politics at Pembroke College, Oxford (piquantly as a Soros Scholar), Orbán is aware that "liberal" and "democratic" are not of the same cloth. His plain understanding of "illiberal" or "non-liberal" is a system in which the national or public interest stands above that of the individual, but that nevertheless "does not reject the fundamental principles of liberalism

184 POLITICAL NEOLIBERALISM

such as freedom" (ibid., 59). Isaiah Berlin (1958), not quite believing that this is possible, would call it a system of "positive liberty."

While the notions of the SNC and illiberal state quickly disappeared, their underlying idea of public trumping individual interest in a "work-based state" made it into the new constitution of 2011, the Fundamental Law.[49] So did an unabashedly ethnic understanding of "Hungary," as prior to its Republican form. Both elements combined make the new Hungary an illiberal state, indeed. The Fundamental Law opens with a "National Avowal," which differs from usually ceremonial constitution preambles in being equipped with legal force (Article R). Ahead of the preamble, the new constitution's first words are "God bless the Hungarians." This is the first line of the national anthem, written in 1823. This opening entreaty, which in its religious commitment might have been consensual two hundred years ago, prefigures what is most unusual about this "constitution." Instead of laying out a "bill of rights" and a "plan of government," which has been the double function of liberal state constitutions since the 1776 Constitution of Philadelphia (see Sartori 1962), Orbán's constitution lays out, and prescribes as obligatory for all, a particular form of life, not even a morality but an ethics, a *Sittlichkeit* as Kant would say. Call it "Orbán's nation." Because it has little resemblance with the Hungarians' *actual* ways of life, of which there are several, as everywhere (see Pap 2018, ch. 4).

The first words of the preamble, "We, the Members of the Hungarian Nation, . . . hereby proclaim" introduces an even narrower, not only Christian but ethnic definition of the constituent power. This becomes clear further down, when one of several "We . . . proclaim" is "that the national minorities *living with us* form part of the Hungarian political community and are constituent parts of the State" (emphasis supplied). While the multicultural thrust is commendable,[50] this formulation implies that the "we" that is the constituent power of Orbán's constitution (and members of his nation) is (or are) smaller than the citizenry on whose behalf this constitution must be formally issued. As the Council of Europe's Venice Commission critically commented, the formulation "intimat(es) that members of the 'national minorities living with us' are not part of the people behind the enactment of the constitution," and it added that the properly liberal formulation would be "We, citizens of Hungary."[51] In a word, Orbán's constitution enshrines ethnic nationhood. The ethnic nationalism that is driving the populist right everywhere, has uniquely acquired constitutional status in this astounding document.

Having understood this, the first of nineteen "we proclaim" stanzas in the National Avowal, strange as it is, does not raise eyebrows: "We are proud that our king Saint Stephen built the Hungarian State on solid ground and made our country a part of Christian Europe one thousand years ago." Neither does the fourth stanza: "We are proud that our nation has over the centuries defended Europe in a series of struggles and enriched Europe's common values with its talent and diligence." The first part of it is indirect reference to the historical role of Hungarians in fighting Ottoman invasions. This trope would become central after the 2015 Syrian refugee crisis, when opposition to Muslim immigration, along with opposition to a Brussels that is suspected of imposing this migration on Hungary, advanced as one of Orbán's two main campaign motives, in the 2018 and 2022 national elections (for 2018, see Bos and Pállinger 2018). The fifth part of the National Avowal also, although seemingly repetitive at this point, is noteworthy: "We recognise the role of Christianity in preserving nationhood." Zoltán Fleck et al. (2011), in their legal *Opinion on the Fundamental Law of Hungary*, observe that this declaration is "not as a statement of historical fact, but also with respect to the present" (ibid., 7). Moreover, as most other elements of the (to repeat, legally binding) National Avowal, this element brings "private life under . . . regulatory purview in a manner that is not doctrinally neutral, but is based on a Christian-conservative ideology . . . it prescribes for the members of the community a life model" (ibid., 17). It is a violation of state neutrality, and anathema to a liberal constitution.

Particularly noteworthy in this respect is the thirteenth stanza in Orbán's constitution preamble: "We hold that the family and the nation constitute the principal framework of our coexistence, and that our fundamental cohesive values are loyalty, faith and love." Two elements stick out. First, the "fundamental values" of Orbán's nation are cultural, not political: "loyalty, faith and love" (whatever these ill-defined things are). Of course, it is the point of all nationalisms and national identities to be historically singular.[52] But nowhere has this so far been attempted to be put into law, not to mention constitutional law. The second element, the equation of nation and family, is not unusual in the annals of nationalism. Unusual, however, for a constitution passed in the twenty-first century, is the definition of "family" that is given in the second, "Foundation" part of the Fundamental Law: "Hungary shall protect the institution of marriage as the union of one man and one woman established by voluntary decision,

186 POLITICAL NEOLIBERALISM

and the family as the basis of the survival of the nation. Family ties shall be based on marriage or the relationship between parents and children. The mother shall be a woman, the father shall be a man" (Article L). This rules out gay marriage, while the last sentence gives Orbán a firm (although circular because self-engineered) constitutional hand in his current row with the European Union over gender identity and transsexual rights.

Let me mention one last curiosity of Orbán's nation as laid out in the Fundamental Law, which goes to the heart of its inherent illiberalism: "The right to freedom of expression may not be exercised with the aim of violating the dignity of the Hungarian nation or of any national, ethnic, racial or religious community. Persons belonging to such communities shall be entitled to enforce their claims in court against the expression of an opinion which violates their community, invoking the violation of their human dignity, as provided for by an Act" (Article IX). András Pap (2018, 129) rightly calls this an "utterly disturbing" clause, because "dignity" in "classic constitutional doctrine in Europe is generally intended to protect the individual rather than the community." Although some might endorse this clause as a properly "symmetric" kind of multiculturalism that protects minorities *and* majority alike (see Koopmans and Orgad 2023), this freedom-of-speech restriction brings to a peak the paternalism and individual-rights thumping that permeates this entire "constitution." The statutory law giving flesh to this clause, passed in 2014, penalizes "conduct constituting a needlessly serious violation in an attempt to damage that community's reputation," and a charge can be filed even if one is not a member of the respective "community," minority or majority (Pap 2018, 12). In a competent dictator's hands, which Orbán's certainly are, this is a formidable tool to restrict elementary freedoms.

Pap (2018, 67) succinctly summarizes the standard members' profile of Orbán's nation, combining their work-related, ethnic, and life-style features: "ethnically Hungarian individuals who belong to the middle class; are active in the labor market; are not unemployed; are practicing Christians . . . ; are heterosexuals, married and living with their spouses; are sexually monogamous and are able to conceive naturally."[53] Needless to say, this dreamed-up Hungarian—the dream national of all the populist right in Europe—is a rare find in the streets of Budapest, of any European city at that.

Conclusion

A proper analysis of the populist right in the neoliberal order needs to combine political, economic, and cultural elements, and perhaps more.[54] Qua populism, populism is in the first a political movement addressing the deficit of democracy that is endemic to neoliberalism. However, as it crosses out the liberal elements of democracy, in particular pluralism and constitutionalism, populism, especially the right-wing variant, cannot but be a threat to democracy itself. The economic backdrop to populism is middle-class decline, even though its dominant claims, both on the political demand and supply sides, are cultural. Next to throwing light on the "right" in "populist right," cleavage theory in the Lipset–Rokkan tradition is the most plausible explanation of this "cultural deflection." It suggests that globalization has revitalized the cultural cleavage that had first appeared in the late nineteenth-century "national revolution" (Lipset and Rokkan 1967). The calibrating of economic and cultural factors in the rise of the populist right remains the explanatory challenge of the day, which needs to be met in a context-sensitive way. The least to say is that one-sided, either economics- or culture-focused explanations, are insufficient.

This becomes clear when looking at two prominent examples on either side of the economics-culture divide. A self-consciously economics-focused analysis of "anti-system politics," right *and* left, by Jonathan Hopkin (2020), has argued that globalization-affected "creditor countries" generate right-wing populism, while "debtor countries" produce the left-wing variant: "The ways in which welfare systems distribute exposure to economic risks predict whether anti-systems politics takes a . . . left-wing or right-wing direction" (ibid., 17). However, if part of the explanation why populism in (south European) debtor countries is leftist, is that it is carried by "more progressive-minded" youngsters (ibid.), the question arises where this "progressive-mindedness" is coming from in the first. It does not appear to be endogenous, so that one would need to factor-in the cultural value or cleavage changes that Hopkin explicitly rules out: "exposure to inequality and financial insecurity predicts anti-system politics better than cultural changes" (ibid., 51). Moreover, the claim that "(m)ost anti-system right-wingers addressed economic grievances head-on, identifying migration as an economic threat as much as a cultural one" (ibid., 251), with its stress on economics, does not seem to hold empirically. This is even by Hopkin's own admission, when he argues, correctly in my view, that populist right parties "(lack) credible programs of reform or strategies for fundamental institutional change" (ibid., 252).

On the opposite end, a decidedly culture-focused account of the populist right, as proposed by Pippa Norris and Inglehart (2019), also runs into problems. They claim that "cultural values," better than "economic indicators," predict populist voting (ibid., 20). While not denying the role of "economic conditions," as having "deepened the cultural backlash" (to the post-materialist value revolution of the new left) (ibid., 17), their central notion of "cultural backlash" suggests a one-factor explanation that discards economics. Sheri Berman (2021, 74–75) noted that individual-level surveys, as conducted by Norris and Inglehart (2019), tend to support a cultural explanation of populism, while macro-level analyses support an economic explanation. This is a strong reason for ecumenical thinking on populism. Discarding economic factors faces the difficulty that globalization, which clearly fueled the rise (and the nationalism) of the populist right, is in the first an economic (plus technological) phenomenon with dismal economic consequences for the core support groups of the populist right. The cleavage theory of Kriesi et al. (2008, 2012), which stresses the "cultural logic" (as against "economic logic") of populist mobilization (Kriesi et al. 2012, 17), nevertheless agrees with the view, favored by most, of culture as only an intermediate variable, because the first mover, after all, is "globalization."

Norris and Inglehart's "cultural backlash" theory rests on a narrow understanding of who are the "losers" of globalization. The "economic grievance theory" they dismiss is said to identify as losers "the *least prosperous* citizens" who provide "strongest support for authoritarian and populist values" (2019, 132; emphasis supplied). However, when summarizing their findings, Norris and Inglehart concede that "both authoritarian and populist values are consistently stronger among *less well-off* people, who are most likely to feel a sense of economic insecurity" (ibid., 166; emphasis supplied). The "least" versus "less" well-off distinction seems to be nit-picking. True, the "least" well-off have long been known to either abstain from the political process or to vote for the left (or for the Democrats in the United States, as in the 2016 presidential elections, as Norris and Inglehart confirm [ibid., 139]). But in their focus on the "less" well-off, Norris and Inglehart in fact support the argument of the "squeezed middle" that we presented above, the "middle" that has not yet lost but is in fear of losing and inflicted by "social pessimism and nostalgia" (ibid., 21). Accordingly, Norris and Inglehart describe Trump support as "concentrated among socially conservative older white men, non-college graduates, and residents in small-town America" (ibid.). This, indeed, qua "non-college" and "small-town," is the declining middle class that has been the main loser of globalization *and* support group of the populist right.

Overall, the populist right is certainly a disruptive political force *in* the neoliberal order, but hardly a force *against* it. The populist right is "neoliberalism's scorpion tale," as Wendy Brown (2020) calls it. In her furious critique, which mixes Freudian and Nietzschean motives, the "demonized status of the social and the political in neoliberal governmentality," which she sees epitomized in the thinking of Hayek, has laid the groundwork for the "profoundly antidemocratic form of the (populist right) rebellion" (ibid., 42). Brown correctly depicts the populist right as preoccupied more with the cultural than the economic face of the neoliberal order, as "decry(ing) 'social justice warriors' (SJWs) for undermining freedom with a tyrannical agenda of social equality, civil rights, affirmative action, and even public education" (Brown 2019, 28). Positively phrased, Brown sees the "Left" engaged in an honest combat to "make visible the complex histories and social forces reproducing white male superordination and hegemony" (ibid., 43). This, indeed, is the perspective of left identity politics, and the reality it fights may well exist (although its pervasiveness is subject to doubt). However, as I argue in the next chapter, much like the populist right, although in different ways, left identity politics is more the expression of than movement against the neoliberal order.

Chapter 5
The Identity Left

Antiracism and Transgender

Much like the notion of "populist right," that of "identity left" is not self-designation but third-party attribution, and often with polemical intent.[1] Unlike the populist right, which has a clearly demarcated organizational expression in radical right parties, the identity left is spread over a more diffuse spectrum. This includes political parties, especially Green parties and Third-Way reformed Social Democratic parties; social movements and campaigns, which is the preferred expression and self-presentation of antiracism and transgender, the focus of this chapter; and not least, administrative, professional, and corporate elites, whose boundaries with movements and campaigns are notoriously blurred.

The pairing of "left" with identity politics implies that the left has turned its back on the class politics with which it was historically associated. Accordingly, one widely quoted review article defines "identity politics" as "political practice that is cultural, symbolic, or psychological in nature, distinct from class politics and class movements" (Bernstein 2005, 66). While "left" is not mentioned in this definition, the association of identity politics with the post-1960s "civil rights and women's movements" (ibid., 49) marks it as a politics of the left, at least originally.[2]

By the same token, the implied move of the left, from "challenging the class structure" to being "more concerned with culture and identity" (Bernstein 2005, 49), is not merely a change of topic. Rather, it is a change in the nature of its politics, from universalist to particularistic, and thus a betrayal of its original impulse. The notion of identity left is jarring because the left thus enters a terrain that was initially occupied by the political right. The right qua right made its first appearance as the particularizing critique of the universalist pretensions of the French Revolution, which had been meant not just for the French but for humankind. In this key, the anti-enlightenment conservative and founder of the "antiliberal tradition" (Holmes 1993, ch. 1), Joseph de Maistre, declared that "the human being as such does not exist."

Political Neoliberalism. Christian Joppke, Oxford University Press. © Oxford University Press (2025).
DOI: 10.1093/oso/9780197801918.003.0006

And he memorably added that "(i)n my lifetime I have met French, Italians, Russians, etc . . . But as for man, I declare that I have never in my life met him" (in Furedi 2018).

Indeed, modern history's first identity politics was nationalism. By contrast, socialism and the left inherited the universalism of the French revolution, according to which the only "foreigners in France are the bad citizens," in the famous words of journalist and revolutionary Jean-Lambert Tallien (quoted in Brubaker 1989, 44). Therefore, Marxist historian Eric Hobsbawm pithily phrased the tension between "Left" and "identity politics" as follows: "The political project of the Left is universalist: it is for *all* human beings . . . And identity politics is essentially not for everybody but for the members of a specific group only" (1996, 43). Hobsbawm has no mercy with those who argue that nationalism might as well be a cause of the left, which indeed it sometimes was or is: "The nationalist claim that they are for *everyone's* right to self-determination is bogus" (ibid.).

The particularistic thrust of left identity politics stands out in one of its first documents, the 1977 Collective Statement of the Combahee River Collective, a small but influential American East Coast activist group of black lesbian feminists that set the tone for the future: "We believe that the most profound and potentially most radical politics come directly out of our own identity, as opposed to working to end somebody else's oppression."[3] It is true, this statement *also* claims that "To be recognized as human, levelly human, is enough,"[4] which makes it identifiably left. One contemporary advocate of left identity politics thus refers to it as "rebellious universalism," to fend off the standard reproach of particularism and of fragmenting emancipatory movement and society at large (Dyk 2019, 13). While Silke van Dyk obviously makes much of the universalist element, she immediately buries it under the competing notion that "the 'normal', the 'general', and the 'human' was and is determined as particularly white, male, healthy, and heterosexual" (ibid., 5). How both notions go together, "universalism" and the debunking of "the 'general'", she does not say. In the Combahee statement, the trademark particularism of left identity politics appears in the charge that the "American political system" is "a system of white male rule."[5] And to the degree that there is a group-transcending impulse, it is directed toward other oppressed groups. "The major systems of oppression are interlocking," the Combahee feminists argue, so that the goal is "struggling against racial, sexual heterosexual, and class oppression."[6] The notion of "interlocking oppression," essentially on the grounds of race and sex (including sexual

192 POLITICAL NEOLIBERALISM

orientation), with class as of only secondary (if any) importance, anticipates "intersectionality," one of the key concepts of the identity left (the word
invented two decades later by Crenshaw 1991).

Much like the populist right, the identity left advocates political rupture.
The Combahee River Collective, for instance, aims at nothing less than "the
destruction of the political-economic system of capitalism and imperialism as well as patriarchy" (to which would need to be added "racism").[7]
Albrecht Koschorke, a German literary scholar who has written briefly
but incisively about identity politics, has noted that the identity left shares
with the populist right an "anti-hegemonic impulse" and a "rhetoric of the
subaltern"—both essentially pose as victims (2022, 469, 473). However, he
also points to an important difference between the two. Unless it manages
to enter parliament or even to win elections (i.e., through the democratic
route, which has remained the exception so far), the populist right is an outsider to public institutions, if not a pariah for polite society. By contrast,
despite its oppositionist-cum-victim posture, the identity left, its adherents
generally educated and rich in cultural capital, is "mostly situated within
institutions and fighting with the means of these institutions." The identity left shows a "penchant for the statist" (*Zug ins Etatistische*), Koschorke
notes with a bit of sarcasm. The American culture warrior Christopher Rufo
(2023) even thinks that the "radical left" has "conquered everything," first
the universities, and from there the media, the state (qua bureaucracy), and
corporations. The populist right's constitutive anti-elite disposition shows
that they have understood this. Accordingly, they may lean toward a "radical critique of institutions if not the system" even more than the identity left,
as Koschorke finds (2022, 474).

The institutional lever of the identity left is civil rights law[8] and the norm
of non-discrimination that no one can legitimately put in question today,
not even the populist right. Accordingly, openly defended or legally codified
racism and sexism (and related disparagement of sexual orientation) have
become anathema. By the same token, as the material injuries of presumably inferior race or sex or tabooed sexual orientation and identification
have receded, smaller injuries on these grounds, which are suspected to
persist in the anonymous workings of language and institutions, take more
weight. Because these persistent injuries are principally in the realm of the
symbolic and language, even in people's unconscious, it is no accident that
the institutional spheres that are constitutively linguistic and mind-shaping,
like education and the media, have become primary sites of contestation.

A prominent example of these new injuries are "microaggressions," which are minor verbal or behavioral "indignities" that are mainly in the eye of the beholder, but qua "aggression" become subject to regulation and sanctioning, especially on college campuses (Campbell and Manning 2014, 694). Because the thrust of these interventions is speech-censoring and thus not only behavior-correcting but mind-controlling, with a rather broad and subjective understanding of the "harm" that is meant to be countered by them (see Haslam 2016), it does not surprise that the identity left has often been charged with illiberalism.[9] If disdain for "the liberal habits of tolerance, dissent, debate, (and) openness" is the heart of the "antiliberal idea," as Stephen Holmes (2022, 3) put it in the words of the great German American historian of Nazism, Fritz Stern[10], it certainly is not absent from the identity left.

But more important for our purposes is the situating of the identity left within the neoliberal order. The Austrian philosopher Robert Pfaller (2018) noticed a "strange discrepancy" in "rich Western states" between "economic brutalization and de-democratization," on the one hand, and "increasing cultural sensibilization," on the other. This is a concise description of a strange asymmetry in the neoliberal condition, in which culture is screened for the inequities and injustices that are ignored in the economy. Perhaps over the top, Pfaller deems the identity left not merely a bystander but "active contribut(or) to the neoliberal production of inequality." More to the point may be his claim that "postmodernity," as advanced by the identity left, "is the cultural program of neoliberalism" (ibid.). This is a cognitive and political relativism of standpoints and refutation of objectivity and universalism, which are unmasked as the particularism of the dominant.

The identity left's relativism withdraws the distinction between private and public, which had been liberalism's contribution to resolving Europe's confessional wars, and much later helped counter-balance the market with democratic imperatives, citizenship as remedy to capitalism in T. H. Marshall's (1950) classic tale. Neoliberalism and identity politics, the rightist variant included, are complementary in undermining this fundamental distinction of liberal societies. Neoliberalism furthers the "privatization of public space" (Pfaller 2018) by infusing market principles in non-market spheres, particularly the political and the state. Pioneered by the second-wave feminist notion that "the personal is political," the identity left complements the neoliberal privatization with placing the public under the *Generalverdacht* of camouflaged (white male) group power. The "civic public," argues Iris Marion Young (1990:10), "exclude(s) . . . persons identified

194   POLITICAL NEOLIBERALISM

with the body and feeling—women, Jews, Blacks, American Indians, and so on." As Koschorke (2022, 476) sees the matter, the identity left erases the distinction between "empirical person" and "persona"; it refutes the abstractions beyond the individual and their group, such as "citizen" and "human being," which signals to Koschorke nothing less than the "closing of the bourgeois age" (ibid., 481). Even if flawed with respect to historical detail,[11] Richard Sennett (1977) had argued insightfully that the capacity to step back from one's empirical person and slip into a public role had a civilizing and even protective function. If things public and universalist are suspected of being "Eurocentric" or kindred particularisms, society fragments into competing groups without a common tie. "How can one build a symbolic order," Koschorke (2022, 477) worries, "if all positions . . . are particularistic?"[12]

This group fragmentation endorsed and furthered by the identity left, is an ironic echo to the neoliberal aversion to the social and to society, which has been characteristic of neoliberal theory and practice alike, from Friedrich Hayek to Margaret Thatcher. One finds this echo in Nancy Fraser's pointed critique of Polanyian "social protections" against the risks of "marketization," which she finds "oppressive" and "premised on majority religious or ethnocultural self understandings, which penalize members of minority groups" (Fraser 2017c, 37). "Protections . . . are . . . also predations," as Fraser (2011, 147) puts it, on the bases of "gender, nationality, and race." Unlike the neoliberal's debunking of the social, the identity left's debunking of it is not in the service of the individual but of the groups that have been wronged by society. With the denunciation of the social and its abstractions as site of group power and oppression, not only the possibility of shared norms gets lost, but also the "capacity for empathy" (Koschorke 2022, 477). Hence the sharpened polarization between left and right identity politics that is a signature of the neoliberal order.[13]

On both ends of the political spectrum, the right included, the rise of identity politics marks a "crisis of representation" (Koschorke 2022, 475–480). The "mischiefs of faction," which is the main risk of democracy that was meant to be fixed by Madisonian elite representation, return under the pretext of resurrecting democracy. On the right end, there is the curious novelty of "direct representation" (Urbinati 2019a, 4), in which a populist leader irreplaceably incorporates an unchangeable and reified majority, which is a "group" no less than the groups on the left. On the left end, there is the new concept of "mirror representation," according to which political representatives need to share the empirical features of the represented, especially their

THE IDENTITY LEFT 195

race and sex (Phillips 1998). In both variants, a new logic of *pars pro parte* replaces the old logic of *pars pro toto* (Urbinati 2019a, 15). This removes an abstraction that is usually associated with the institution of citizenship, and that is required for liberal democracy to function.

In the identity left, the withdrawal of a common ground shows in its aversion to "cultural appropriation." The *Cambridge Dictionary* defines it as "the act of taking or using things from a culture that is not your own," and it is tabooed if it involves presumed domination.[14] In cultural appropriation, the wrongfully appropriated is in the position of victim. To be a victim is constitutive of left identity politics, which in this respect inherits the left's sympathy for the underdog. Bradley Campbell and Jason Manning (2014, 723) speak of a "culture of victimhood," which they describe as a "concern with status and sensitivity to slight combined with a heavy reliance on third parties." The "third-party" reliance hints at the paradoxical coexistence of the victim posture with a strong elite presence in and authority support for left identity politics, by corporate managers, HR officers in universities and big firms, and by state bureaucrats and politicians.

While the emphasis on "oppression and social marginalization" is "congenial to the leftist worldview" (Campbell and Manning 2014, 723, 724), the victim posture is easily copied by the political right.[15] Philip Manow (2019, 37) calls this the "open flank of left identity politics." As he asks, "How can one deny to majority society a positive self-image as racist or nationalist, if this is conceded to each minority as a progressive act?" The logical consequence from "Black Lives Matter" is that "White Lives Matter" too, especially if the latter happen to be looked down upon by the elites as a "basket of deplorables"[16] or as "hillbillies" (Vance 2016). Campbell and Manning (2018, 161–170) appositely speak of "competitive victimhood," which includes the possibility of "conservative victims." To stay with the mentioned "hillbillies," who are lower-class white people of the depressed Appalachian region, they are "the only group of people you don't have to be ashamed to look down upon" (ibid., 165). Hence, victims they are all.

It follows that there is a left–right identity politics spiral, each side responding to and reinforcing the other. Cleavage theory, as discussed in the previous chapter, and the fact that multiculturalism preceded the populist right in historical time, suggest that the beginnings of this identity spiral are on the left side. Francis Fukuyama confirms that "the right has adopted the language and framing of identity from the left: the idea that my particular group is being victimized" (2018, ch. 11). Tellingly, the French New Right

196 POLITICAL NEOLIBERALISM

intellectual Alain de Benoist (2017 [1985]) depicts his advocacy of "ethno-pluralism" as a Gramscian "cultural revolution from the right." Down to the reference to Gramsci, cult author of the left, this closely resembles the rhetoric of the multicultural left.

The left-to-right "rhetoric of the subaltern" is tied up in social structure with "recognition struggles within middle class milieus" (Koschorke 2022, 472–475). These struggles signal a fragmenting of the middle class that, in the preceding age of Social Democracy, had been the herald of a post-class society. The middle classes' differently successful sections now take sharply opposite positions on the left versus right axis. The upwardly mobile "new" middle class, boosted by advanced college degrees, espouses an "inclusive" posture toward minorities, whereas the downwardly mobile "old" middle class dwells in resentment and the "exclusion" of minorities. With the "tearing up" of the middle class, which once had been the centrist backdrop to the postwar catch-all or people's parties (*Volksparteien*), "hostility" returns to "the inner fabric of society" (ibid., 482). As Pfaller (2018) put it darkly, and again somewhat over the top, the "upper ranks (*die Oberen*) have set themselves apart from the middle ranks (*die Mittleren*), while unleashing the lower ranks (*die Unteren*) against the middle ranks." The element of truth in this polemic, which conjures up the populist demon of cosmopolitan elites allied with immigrant minorities (for an authentically populist confirmation, see Gauland 2018), is the dominant position of the identity left in the left versus right contest, which sits oddly with its self-defining victim posture.

Next to withdrawing the private–public distinction, whose social-structural side is to leave the political scene to competing particularisms within a decomposing middle class, a second neoliberal element in left identity politics is what Wendy Brown has aptly called "loss of futurity" (Brown 1995, 74). Indeed, a mark of the neoliberal order is the loss of the future, both in institutional and attitudinal respects—one historian called neoliberalism "the best ideological system for breaking promises" (Bartel 2022, 19). Institutionally, the demise of communism, post-1989, has ushered in a condition in which "there is no alternative," to quote again Thatcher. Attitudinally, societal pessimism and the loss of belief in a better future for the next generation take hold of the falling or at least stagnating sections of the middle class (see Chapter 4). The socialist politics of class had inherited from liberalism a "faith in progress,"[17] and with it a preference for becoming over being. Identity politics inverts this preference, back from becoming to being: "Who has no future needs more origins. And who can no longer hope to *become* anything interesting needs to stress that she *is* something precious and vulnerable *already*" (Pfaller 2018; emphasis supplied).

Identity politics is congenial to a neoliberal order of "broken promises" (Bartel 2022) in being simultaneously backward-looking and presence-fixed, while the future dissipates. "When the future collapses," which is the neoliberal condition, "the past rushes in," as John Torpey (2006, 24) describes the point of departure for the politics of reparations that he sees prospering in the "progressive left." Similarly, for John Gray (2020), the "wokes," as he calls them, have "no vision of the future" other than a "cathartic present" in which the discriminatory "sins" of the past are expunged. Therefore, the preoccupation of antiracism with removing from the public square historical monuments or names that carry ignoble associations. These are "symbolic actions" that seek to "sever the present from the past, not policies designed to fashion a different future," as Gray put it (ibid.).

If "controlling the past" becomes more important than "hoping in a better future" (Braunstein 2022, ch. 1), a deep pessimism must follow. It marks, in particular, the antiracist movement, the most extreme expression being "Afro-Pessimism," according to which "Blackness is coterminous with Slaveness. Blackness *is* social death" (Wilderson 2016). Not quite as bleak but in the same direction, "The Permanence of Racism" is the title that Derrick Bell (1992), one of the antiracist movement's chief theorists and founder of Critical Race Theory (CRT), has chosen for an influential collection of his papers. When still in a critical mode toward the identity left, Brown (1995, 74) captured the paradox well: "politicized identity . . . becomes attached to its own exclusion . . . because it is premised on this exclusion for its very existence as identity." That pessimism must result from the antiracists' constitutive fixation on their opposite, the racists, is readily visible in one of this movement's central documents, by Ibram X. Kendi. In his *How to Be an Antiracist*, Kendi rejects a gradualist view of "racial progress" in lieu of a constant "duel of antiracist and racist progress," with a neutral position of "not racist" declared impossible, or rather "a mask to hide racism" (2019: ch. 16 and intro).

The loss of futurity, and turn to past certainties, is paradoxically counterpointed by a greatly enlarged range of individual choice. If the loss of futurity is a distinctly neoliberal context factor shaping identity politics, with respect to the enlargement of choice, no clear line between "liberal" and "neoliberal" can be drawn: both conjoin in making the individual and her choices the lynchpin of morality and political order. As Rogers Brubaker (2016a, 6)

198   POLITICAL NEOLIBERALISM

perceptively noted, in an "age of unsettled identities" there is a "sharpened tension" between the "language of choice" and "that of givenness."[18]

The tension between givenness and choice is constitutive of all instances of left identity politics to be discussed in this chapter.[19] However, their relative weight differs across types of identity politics, in particular race versus sex. Given the prevailing notion that "races do not exist," which has been propagated by UNESCO since the 1950s,[20] one would expect racial identities to be high on choice and low on givenness. Conversely, considering the biological underpinnings of sex, which until recently was backed by the distinction between sex (as biological) and gender (as cultural), one would expect sex-related identities to be high on givenness and low on choice. In reality, the exact opposite is the case. This is demonstrated by the general acceptance of changing one's sex and the inverse tabooing of changing one's racial affiliation.[21] Brubaker (2016a, 7) attributes this counterintuitive constellation to the "authority of ancestry" over racial classifications—at least in the United States, where this "authority" was first the result of a racist state and later of the antiracist movement, and for which there is no equivalent on the part of sex. But "authority of ancestry" is a rather anodyne term for the "guild-protective agenda" that drives this asymmetry (Reed 2015). As Adolph Reed (ibid.) argues, "There is no coherent principled defense of the stance that transgender identity is legitimate but transracial is not." At the same time, he finds that in both instances of "entitlement based on extrasocietal, ascriptive identities," we are dealing with "neoliberalism's critical self-consciousness" (ibid.).

This chapter probes deeper into the similarities and differences of antiracism and transgender as prominent instances of left identity politics in the neoliberal order. The focus throughout is on antiracism and transgender as "political projects" of activists and intellectuals, not as "lived experiences" of real (black or transgender) people,[22] which are unquestionably often hurtful and causes of distress. Antiracism, which I discuss in the first part, with an unavoidable focus on the United States, shares with its 1960s Black Power predecessor a profoundly negative view of American race relations, which are said not to have improved much, if not to have worsened in the post-civil-rights era. But antiracism is distinguished from Black Power, which had been a street-level movement, in being mainly an elite movement with a firm grounding in the world of education, in particular universities. This may also explain its "postmodernist" focus on language and perceptions as sites of oppression and of fighting it. Antiracism endorses a relativism of standpoints and perspectives that is in tension with its claim that racism is "structural" or "systemic," which suggests non-positional objectivity. Distinctly neoliberal about antiracism is its practical focus on "race parity," as Reed (2016) calls the movement's demand for equal racial representation in positions of social privilege. This removes attention from non-racial sources of inequality, which has greatly increased under neoliberalism. Transgender, which I look at in the second half, shares with antiracism its postmodernist relativism and elite basis. But transgender pushes the rather opposite notion that people are not irreversibly caught in their bodies; instead, the body is deemed either irrelevant or modifiable in accordance with one's felt "gender identity." I discuss the three main conflict issues surrounding transgender: access of transwomen to separate female spaces; the expansion of gender identity into the pre-puberty phase, often with dire consequences for remorseful transitioners; and that all of society is asked to adopt a view that biological sex does not exist, which remains implausible to most. Transgender's neoliberal pedigree is an exalted individualism that abstracts jointly from the constraints of society and nature. And it is pushed, in an "intersectional" alliance with the antiracists, by the elites and protagonists of the neoliberal order, including large corporations who detect in the movement a convenient (because inexpensive) way to dispense "social justice."

Antiracism

Still a Racial Caste System?

Perhaps the most dramatic case of persistent, if not increased, disadvantage that black people do face in the United States is their disproportionate imprisonment. "Mass incarceration," which has exploded in the wake of the post-1980s War on Drugs, is the "New Jim Crow," as Michelle Alexander has denounced it in a widely acclaimed study (2020 [2010]). By the end of 2008, black men were imprisoned at 6.5 times the rate of white men (Forman 2012, 102), and the trend was for one of three black males born in 2001 to serve prison time at one point in their lives (Alexander 2020 [2010], 11). A big part of black imprisonment is for relatively light offenses that are met with disproportionate brutality under new drug laws, passed from Reagan on, which have targeted crack cocaine as particularly "dangerous to society"

200 POLITICAL NEOLIBERALISM

(ibid., 141). Over 90 percent of those convicted of crack offenses at the time of Alexander's study were black, and only 5 percent white. Considering that a crack offense was punished hundred times more severely than one related to powder-cocaine offense[23], which is more expensive and more in use among white people, it is not far-fetched to suspect racial animus at work. According to Alexander, the "design of the drug war," which targeted the (black-populated) inner cities rather than schools (where drugs also widely circulate), and with its focus on cheap crack rather than more expensive drugs, "effectively guarantees that those who are swept into the nation's new undercaste are largely black and brown" (ibid., 129). Black "entrapment" (ibid., ch. 5) is Alexander's word for the procedural sequence of:

- extraordinary (Supreme-Court approved) police discretion to stop-and-frisk, which disproportionately hits black people under the blanket of probability;
- the predominance of plea-bargaining in the conviction phase, where the threat of stiff mandatory sentencing makes it rational to "'convict yourself' in exchange for . . . leniency," even if one is innocent (ibid., 111); and
- the "invisible punishment" of "felony" status that follows upon prison time, which entails sometimes permanent exclusion across the main aspects of civic life, from housing to work to welfare to voting, in effect from citizenship.

"Mass incarceration," Alexander grimly concludes, "defines the meaning of blackness in America: black people . . . are criminals. That is what it means to be black" (ibid., 244).

However, the "New Jim Crow" differs from the old in one crucial respect: it does not hit all black people equally, but only "provided they are first labelled felons" (Alexander 2020 [2010], 238). The New Jim Crow is still a "racial caste system," Alexander insists, but it is "colorblind." This leaves two possibilities of further reasoning: either to spell out the difference that colorblindness makes, or to flatten this difference. Typical of the antiracism to be charted in this section, which also typically blurs the boundaries between scholarship and activism, Alexander opts for flattening the difference. While she distinguishes between "slavery," "Jim Crow," and "mass incarceration" as three distinct "racialized systems of control" (ibid., 17), the polemical thrust is to relativize their differences. Hence the notion of "New Jim Crow": "The

THE IDENTITY LEFT   201

decision to wage the drug war primarily in black and brown communities rather than white ones . . . *has had precisely the same effect* as the literacy and poll taxes of an earlier era. A facially race-neutral system of laws has operated to create a racial caste system" (ibid., 250, emphasis supplied). In conclusion, "African Americans, as a group, are no better off than they were in 1968 in many respects" (ibid., 284).

Alexander's specification, "in many respects," suggests reservation about a blanket continuity claim, but the elements that don't fit this claim are still folded back into it. Most blatantly, she belittles as "collateral damage" the fact that mass incarceration "directly harms far more whites than Jim Crow ever did"; to her, this damage to white people is "essential to preserving the image of a colorblind criminal justice system" (Alexander 2020 [2010], 254). This glosses over the fact that 60 percent of US prisoners are *not* black; one-third of them are white and 20 percent are Hispanic, the latter with an incarceration rate that is double the rate of white people (Forman 2012, 136–138). If the "War on Drugs was declared as part of a political ploy to capitalize on white racial resentment against African Americans," as Alexander (2020 [2010], 255) thinks, the significant Latino component in this war is not easy to integrate. Furthermore, the focus on drug-related imprisonment overlooks that over one-half of US prisoners are violent offenders, with drug offenders representing only one-fourth of the total prison population (Forman 2012, 125f). As homicide is disproportionately involving black people, not just as perpetrators but as victims also, there happens to be strong support for punitive crime policies among ordinary black people and their civic leaders. This likewise has no place in the Jim Crow analogy (ibid., 121f; see also Gottschalk 2015, ch. 7).

But the most important shortcoming of the racist continuity claim is the blending-out of growing class differences within the US black population. Mass incarceration is "largely confined to the poorest, least-educated segments" of American black people (Forman 2012, 132). As James Forman points out, a black male born in the late 1960s has a nearly 60 percent chance of going to prison at one (or more) point(s) in his life, while for a black with a college degree this probability shrinks to just 5 percent. In short, a college degree protects you from prison, which is a cross-race constant. At the same time, the share of college-educated black people has greatly increased since the 1970s: while only 4 percent of black people above twenty-five years of age had a college degree in 1967; by the late 2010s, 20 percent had one (ibid., 134). Accordingly, the rise of a college-educated black middle class is the

202 POLITICAL NEOLIBERALISM

strongest objection to the Jim Crow analogy. As Forman (ibid., 136) reinforces a distinction that Alexander herself has introduced, if only to flatten it, "mass incarceration" is "much less totalizing" than Jim Crow: "In 2011, *no* institution can define what it 'means to be black' in the way that Jim Crow or slavery once did."

As if to wash away Forman's (not to forget, friendly) critique,[24] Alexander doubles down in the preface to the tenth anniversary edition of her celebrated work. A hardened tone suggests that she got it right after all (Alexander 2020 [2010], ix–xlv). Almost with a sigh of relief, she pronounces that, in the age of Donald Trump, the "colorblind veneer" is off, allowing her to step back from the modicum of differentiation that marked her earlier work. "Everything has changed. And yet nothing has," she writes laconically in 2020, "The politics of white supremacy, which defined our original constitution, have continued unabated" (ibid., xiv). Significantly, the notion of "white supremacy," which she used barely four times in the rest of the book (its main text left unchanged from its first edition in 2010), and exclusively in reference to the past not the present, and which has no index entry, appears eleven times in the new 2020 preface, and now always in reference to the present. This is because with the rise of Trump, "We are now living in an age of unabashed racialism, a time when many white Americans feel free to speak openly of their nostalgia for an age when their . . . dominance would be taken for granted" (ibid., xi). Her book was written "in a different world," she now says, when "the politics of white supremacy had been driven temporarily underground" (ibid., xiv). The new-old world is both "more terrible and more beautiful," more "beautiful" because of the rise of "vibrant racial justice movements led by new generations of activists" (ibid., xiii). These movements, with Black Lives Matter (BLM) at the forefront, would indeed make the racist continuity claim in much less qualified ways than Alexander had done in 2010, encouraged by the fact that in the meantime the "dog whistles have been replaced by bullhorns" (ibid., xiv).

From Black Power to Antiracism

It is striking how much the pessimist vision and radical demands of today's antiracists resemble those of the 1960s Black Power movement, although more than half a century is separating them.[25] In a classic text, Robert Blauner (1972) had depicted "racial minorities" (Asians and Hispanics included) as "internal colonies of American capitalism" (ibid., vii), who were forever denied the "immigrant" path of integration and had to remain wedded to a "Third World perspective" of ultimately violent "anti-colonial politics" (ibid., 89). He later modified his view, removing assimilation-bound Asians and Hispanics from the status of "colonized," while giving more space to coalition-minded "class analysis and class politics." Importantly, this class politics should include "white people" in "our muddled strivings toward a better society" (Blauner 2001, 191). Twenty years before the BLM movement made antiracism a global phenomenon, Blauner criticized "(t)oday's overheated racism discourse": "(I)f racism is everywhere, then effectively nothing can be done about it" (ibid., 216).

The notion of "institutional racism," which inspires today's antiracists (often with exchangeable adjectives, like "structural" or "systemic"),[26] was invented in Stokely Carmichael and Charles Hamilton's 1960s Black Power manifesto (Ture [Carmichael] and Hamilton 1967). Carmichael and Hamilton demarcated "institutional" from merely "individual racism," to suggest that racism is not just an evil attitude but deeply cast in a "white power structure" and "white supremacy" (ibid., 7, 54) that oppress black people as a group. The only way out for black people was to "lead and run their own organizations" (ibid., 46), with the aim of "the necessarily total revamping of the society" (ibid., 60f). "There is no 'American dilemma,'" as Carmichael and Hamilton dismissed the famous notion by Gunnar Myrdal, "because black people in this country form a colony, and it is not in the interest of the colonial power to liberate them" (ibid., 5). This vocabulary has remained amazingly constant.

Consider the founding text of CRT, by Harvard law professor Bell (1980). It sublimates the Black Power view into an "interest convergence" theory of black emancipation in post-1950s America. Accordingly, "the interest of blacks in achieving racial equality will be accommodated only when it converges with the interests of whites" (ibid., 523). In Bell's somber optic, the 1954 *Brown v. Board of Education* decision of the US Supreme Court, which desegregated America's southern schools, was primarily motivated by the Cold War confrontation with the Soviet Union.[27] And he took subsequently revisionist decisions of the Supreme Court, which no longer acknowledged indirect or "disparate impact" discrimination, as evidence that this interest convergence ceased quickly. In fact, one of the most convincing parts in Alexander's critique of black mass incarceration is her analysis of the "closing (of) the courthouse doors" to "claims of racial bias at every stage of the criminal justice process, from stops and searches to plea bargaining and sentencing" (2010 /20:241). In its seminal *McCleskey v. Kemp* (1987) decision, for instance, the Supreme Court refused to consider, in a death penalty case, statistical evidence as proof of racial bias in penal sentencing. Instead, it demanded clear evidence of intent. But proof of "intent" is systematically unavailable given the nature of the penal process, including the occluded jury system. It is thus tempting to read into such court decisions the "desire to immunize the entire criminal justice system from claims of racial bias" (Alexander 2020 [2010], 139).

Bell's founding text set the dark and pessimistic tone of CRT and of the activism that is inspired by it, both of which assume one continuous line of racism from the past into the present.[28] In the field of sociology, the influential "racial formation" perspective by Michael Omi and Howard Winant (1986) makes much the same claim: "The hallmark of this (American) history has been *racism*, not the abstract ethos of equality . . . Race will *always* be at the center of the American experience" (ibid., 1, 6)—the latter a strange statement that is more in the range of belief than of cognition. Even worse, in the 2014 edition of their work, Omi and Winant claim that "American society has . . . become more segregated and more racially unequal" (quoted in Wimmer 2015, 2192).

More recently, the racist continuity claim has moved from sociological abstraction to historical concretion, in the debatable assertion that America's founding moment, the Revolutionary War of 1776 against Britain, was not fought for the idea that "all men are created equal," but on the opposite to defend slavery. This is the controversial claim of the 1619 Project, a 2019 *New York Times* initiative for a "new origin story." This new American origin story starts with the arrival of the first African slaves in the English colony of Virginia, in 1619. The notion of "new origin story" clearly shows the different nature of identity politics if compared with class politics. Whereas class politics "built the identity of the working class on an image of the future," and as one in which "class" would be no longer, "identity politics treats past victimization as a renewable resource in disputes about the present," as Torpey (2023, 46) put it aptly.

In her opening essay to the 1619 Project, Nikole Hannah-Jones makes two controversial statements: first, that the colonists "decided to declare their independence from Britain . . . because they wanted to protect the institution of slavery"; and, secondly, that in the past as in the present, "black Americans fought back alone" (both quoted in Torpey 2023, 48). The critical intervention of renowned historians forced the *New York Times* editors to reduce the first claim, so that in the final (book) version only "some of" the colonists seceded for keeping their property in humans (ibid., 56). However, the second—no less controversial—claim, which blithely ignores the participation of white people in black emancipation, from Lincolnian abolition to the 1960s civil rights struggles,[29] remained unchanged. Both claims, America's founding in injustice and categorical white hostility, provide a red thread from 1960s Black Power to contemporary antiracism. As Carmichael and Hamilton (1967, 34f) nonchalantly anticipated the thrust of the 1619 project, "Our basic need is to reclaim our history and our identity from what must be called cultural terrorism, from the depredation of self-justifying white guilt." With respect to the involvement of America's leading newspaper in this enterprise, which was once committed to "All the News That's Fit to Print," Torpey finds the "conclusion . . . unavoidable that the *Times* has abandoned any pretense of journalistic objectivity in its support for the 1619 Project and its principal creators" (ibid., 62).

Of course, the racist continuity claim must reckon with the fact that in the age of civil rights openly expressed racism has become delegitimized—hence the distinction between "individual" and "institutional racism," introduced already by the authors of *Black Power* (1967). The critical race sociologist Eduardo Bonilla-Silva calls the "new" form of racism "color-blind racism." It arises in a situation where "subtle, seemingly non-racial practices have replaced the brutal tactics of racist domination of the past as the primary instrument for maintaining white privilege. Yet these practices are as effective as the old ones in preserving the racial status quo" (Bonilla-Silva 2022, 38). However, there is one conceded difference between now and then: the move from "overt" to "covert behaviour" on the part of unrepentant racists, or what Bonilla-Silva calls "smiling face" discrimination (ibid., 3). This is less a matter of law and institutions—these are all explicitly non-discriminatory now—than of language and representation. Therefore, the struggle has moved from the street to the academy, and one of the defining features of contemporary antiracism is that no clear line can be drawn between scholarship and antiracist practice. Pierre-André Taguieff (2021, 13) is right: "The confusion was never bigger between the visions of militants and scholarly investigations." In this respect, contemporary antiracism departs from its 1960s Black Power predecessor, which arose out of the mid-1960s ghetto riots and was fought by ordinary people who were deemed to

206 POLITICAL NEOLIBERALISM

no longer afford "a 'non-violent' approach to civil rights" but to have to "fight back" (Carmichael and Hamilton 1967, 53).

In this context, Torpey (2023, 34) notices an important "shift in terminology concerning inequality from the 1960s to the present." In Blauner's classic indictment of "racial oppression," the direction of oppression was vertical, top to bottom. Those subject to oppression were "burdened and pushed down into the lower levels of the social order (Blauner quoted in Torpey 2023, 34). By contrast, a central notion in contemporary antiracism is for oppression to consist of "marginalization" and to produce "marginalized communities." Here the spatial connotation of oppression is not vertical but horizontal. Marginalization "brings to mind the idea of being pushed *aside* rather than down—as having a distant relationship with the 'mainstream' rather than with the top" (ibid., 34). The remedy to this oppression is not in the realm of the material, "redistribution," but in the realm of the symbolic, "recognition," in Fraser's (1995) terms. As Torpey (2023, 34) concludes, "The marginalized ... are people who need more *attention*; the poor and oppressed need more *money* and more *power*." This certainly overstates the difference between old and new antiracism, because "marginal" without "down" is hardly thinkable. But it catches the new centrality of language and the symbolic in today's antiracist theory and practice—which thereby, as Torpey draws the link to neoliberalism, "deflects attention from the massive increases in economic inequality that have burdened and pushed people down in American life over the past half-century" (ibid.). Of course, there *is* an important material resource element to antiracist claims-making, which Kendi (2019) calls "equity." While never precisely defined, it asks for equal outcomes between racial groups, in accordance with their population share, resembling quotas. As I discuss later, such equity leaves unexamined the absolute level of inequality; only the racial group's relative positioning in the distribution of important resources (like money and wealth) matters. The equity claim indirectly legitimizes a neoliberal order in which the absolute level of inequality has greatly increased.

Enter Postmodernism

Kimberlé Crenshaw (1991) attributes the "identity politics" turn in the conceptualization of, and struggle against, racism to the "postmodernist idea that categories we consider natural or merely representational are actually socially constructed in a linguistic economy of difference" (ibid., 1296). Accordingly, contemporary antiracism differs from its 1960s Black Power precursors in the move from "materialism to "idealism."[30] Language and perceptions become central to the operation of racism, as well as to effective opposition against it. This pays tribute to a post-civil rights context, argues Crenshaw (ibid., 1276), in which "the most egregious discriminatory laws have been eradicated." As a result, racism today works more by way of "popular discourse" and lingering perceptions on the part of individuals than through laws and institutions (ibid.). One could say that 1960s Black Power had targeted physical macro-aggression, while much of today's antiracism addresses symbolic "micro-aggression" (see Campbell and Manning 2014)—"much of," because the videotaped police brutality that incited BLM is an altogether different matter.

At the same time, the focus on language implies a radicalization that explicitly catapults antiracism outside the orbit of liberalism. Consider for this Crenshaw's illustration of her "identity politics" of race (and gender), which she distinguishes sharply from the "dominant conception of social justice" in "mainstream liberal discourse." Crenshaw draws a distinction between "I am Black" and "I am a person who happens to be Black" (1991, 1297). "Happens to be Black," she says, "achiev(es) self-identification by straining for a certain universality"; "I am Black," by contrast, is a "positive discourse of self-identification" that springs from one's concrete "social location," and it leads straight to "social empowerment." A strict linguistic analysis may reveal that the asserted distinction between both perspectives, groupist versus universalist, is faulty and that "we are told the exact same thing" (Church 2020). The important matter is the declared break with "liberal discourse" and its assumption of a common ground, which indeed is the point of departure of all identity politics, that of the right included.

Delving further in the "postmodernist idea(s)" that according to Crenshaw (1991, 1296) underlie left identity politics, we may distinguish between a postmodernist "knowledge" and a postmodernist "political" principle (Pluckrose and Lindsay 2020, ch. 1). The postmodernist *knowledge* principle is the denial of the possibility of objective knowledge, and the intrinsic linkage of knowledge to social position. To begin with, postmodernism is "skepticism towards metanarratives" (Lyotard 1984), such as science, Enlightenment, and Marxism. It connotes pessimism and fragmentation, after the failure of the 1960s movements to bring about grand change, and the failure of the communist alternative two decades later. In contradiction

208   POLITICAL NEOLIBERALISM

to its later American applications, the original "*La French theory*," in French philosopher Jean-François Braunstein's (2022, intro) succinct summary of the thought of Jean-François Lyotard, Michel Foucault, and Jacques Derrida, takes distance from political action; it effaces the possibility of "identity" and "subject"; and it adopts a stance of irony and humor. "There is always something in us that struggles against something other in us," as Foucault captured the loss of certainty that is the postmodern condition (quoted in ibid.). Postmodern knowledge is "ultimately a form of cynicism," argue Helen Pluckrose and James Lindsay (2020, 22). "There is nothing outside the text," is Derrida's famous diction (quoted in ibid., 40), there is no stable "signified" behind floating "signifiers," so that there cannot be objectivity and truth but only the playful "deconstruction" of the internal relationships between signs and symbols. Hence the centrality of language in postmodern thinking. This thinking is well summarized, by Pluckrose and Lindsay (ibid., 43), as "ultimate meaninglessness, lack of direction, and concern only to deconstruct, disrupt, and problematize without providing any resources for rebuilding."

Braunstein (2022, intro) notices the paradox that the key postmodern tenets—the apolitical stance, the abdication of subject and identity, and humor and irony—would be turned into their exact opposite by the identity left. The most important departure from *La French theory*'s defining relativism, never entirely clarified because in contradiction with the underlying social constructivism, is the assumption that subaltern or victim positions or identities allow a wider and deeper range of knowledge than dominant positions. Critical Race legal theorists Richard Delgado and Jean Stefancic (2017, 11) call it the "unique voice of color," which, they admit, "coexist(s) in somewhat uneasy tension with antiessentialism." Accordingly, a privileged access to truth is available to the oppressed who speak in one voice: "Minority status . . . brings with it a presumed competence to speak about race and racism" (ibid.). As Bonilla-Silva expresses the idea, "We have always been the ethnographers of whiteness" (2022, 27). This suggests that, in addition to the notion that only the racially (and otherwise) dominated can speak authentically about their oppression, they also have the unique cognitive tools to decipher the ways of their oppressors, who are depicted as ignorant or in a state of denial.

From this follows that legitimate disagreement with antiracist precepts is not possible. Disagreement even becomes a proof of racism. Robin DiAngelo (2018) calls "white fragility" the unhappy condition of white people, in particular "progressive" white people, who are in a chronic state of denial. She describes this as "a state in which even a minimum amount of racial stress becomes intolerable, triggering a range of defensive moves. These moves include . . . anger, fear, and guilt, and behaviors such as argumentation, silence, and leaving the stress-inducing situation" (ibid., ch. 7). In her view, to be white makes you "racist" by definition (ibid., ch. 1), and white people cannot but profit from "white supremacy" that "elevates white people as a group" (ibid., ch. 2). Accordingly, "white" cannot be a position from which to talk legitimately about race and racism, including (and above all) in academia.[31]

Some[32] have attributed this cognitive illiberalism, which calls for the "cancelling" of opposite views, to the influence of Frankfurt School philosopher Herbert Marcuse, who had penned, in the heat of the 1960s movements, a fiery indictment of "repressive tolerance" (Marcuse 1969 [1965]). Marcuse, indeed, propagated the "withdrawal of toleration of speech and assembly from groups and movements which promote aggressive policies, armament, chauvinism, discrimination on the grounds of race and religion," and in an Orwellian key he called this intolerance "true tolerance" (ibid., 100, 106). Marcuse even anticipated, by half a century, the notorious word of "cancellation," namely, "of the liberal creed of free and equal discussion" (ibid., 106). Different from postmodernism, however, Marcuse, as a Marxist and inheritor of the Enlightenment tradition, held to the possibility of objective truth: "(T)here is an objective truth which can be discovered," he held (ibid., 89). This allowed Marcuse to distinguish with ease between "stupid opinion" and "the intelligent one," between "false" and "true consciousness," and subsequently between "false" and "true tolerance," which perversely meant to him to be "intolerant toward the protagonists of the repressive status quo" (ibid., 85). And with more than a bit of *chuzpe*, Marcuse cites the "authentic" liberalism of John Stuart Mill to justify his illiberal views, yet only adopting from Mill his questionable defense of "despotism" for "barbarians" and his proposal of "plural voting" (which would give more numerical weight to the votes of the educated) (ibid., 82, 86, 123). If truth is with the intellectuals, Marcuse concludes, they must also rule. Borrowing the notion from Plato, Marcuse asks for a "dictatorship of intellectuals," no tongue in cheek (ibid., 106, 121). Obviously, Marcuse was in the thrall of the great "metanarratives," from Plato to Mill, that postmodernists would rail against. Stunningly, one also sees that Marxism and postmodernism yield the same illiberal outcomes. Marcuse dedicated *Repressive Tolerance* to "my students at Brandeis University" (ibid., 81).

210 POLITICAL NEOLIBERALISM

One must wonder how well these students were served by a teacher for whom "the restoration of freedom of thought may necessitate new and rigid restrictions on teachings and practices in the educational institutions" (ibid., 100f).

Turning from the postmodernist knowledge to its *political* principle, this is a conception of society as a closed system of "power and privilege," as Ilke Adam (2022, 1) put it affirmatively. From this follows that change can come not by reform but only by rupture, and not by compromise but by putting "the others" in charge. This is a direct challenge to political liberalism, if the latter is understood as "search for an ethically acceptable order of human progress among civic equals without recourse to undue power" (Fawcett 2014, xiv). CRT explicitly rules out this possibility, and thus positions itself outside of and against liberalism. Two advocates describe CRT as "question(ing) the very foundations of the liberal order, including equality theory, legal reasoning, Enlightenment rationalism, and neutral principles of constitutional law" (Delgado and Stefancic 2017, 3). CRT, as described by Delgado and Stefancic (ibid., ch. 1), further stipulates that racism is an "ordinary, not aberrational" phenomenon deeply engrained in "everyday experience" and the "usual way society does business"; that racism "serves important purposes . . . for the dominant group," "psychic" purposes for the poor and "material" ones for the rich; and, of course, that race is at the same time "socially constructed" and the product of "social thought and relations," adequately comprehended only by the "unique voice of color" (ibid., 8). In sum, "racism is present everywhere and always, and persistently works against people of color, who are aware of this, and for the benefit of white people, who tend not to be, as it is their privilege" (ibid., 120).

The postmodern political principle entails that polarization and the impossibility of compromise is the mark of (this kind of) identity politics. Left identity politics thus does its part in the conflict spiral with the populist right, which results from the lack of a "generally accepted balancing mechanism" (Koschorke 2022, 471). America's current culture wars offer plentiful illustration. Among the more recent is the "weaponizing" of CRT by the populist right. By July 2022, forty-two Republican-ruled states have introduced bills or other action to limit CRT in public schools. The most prominent is Florida's Stop the Wrongs to Our Kids and Employees (W.O.K.E.) Act, which also applies to companies and their diversity, equity, and inclusion (DEI) training schemes.[33] The Florida law's (and similar anti-woke laws') chief strategist, Rufo, operates on the alarmist assumption that "(t)he corporation no longer exists to maximize profit but to manage 'diversity and inclusion'. The state no longer exists to secure natural rights, but to achieve 'social justice.'"[34] This hyperbolic claim is disproved by the fact that Rufo-inspired and -instructed Republican states—twenty-two on his count by 2023 (Rufo 2023, preface)—have successfully fired back with Florida-type anti-woke laws.

Trump: First White President?

Critical race thinking assumes that all black people and all white people think and act alike, as if they were members of a tribe. In this vein, Ta-Nehesi Coates (2017) seeks to dispel the notion that the "white working class" voted for Trump in 2016 out of "cultural resentment" against liberal elites, and in the hope of "economic reversal." He dismisses this view as "raceless antiracism" of the "modern left," from Bill Clinton to Bernie Sanders, which wrongly prioritizes class over race. Instead, Coates argues, Trump "assembled a broad white coalition that ran the gamut from Joe the Dishwasher to Joe the Plumber to Joe the Banker," in a show of "dominance among whites across class lines." As a result, "whiteness brought us Donald Trump," which makes him "America's first white president." However, an analysis of election data shows that Coates' view of a "tribe of white people" installing Trump, distorts the facts (al-Gharbi 2018). First, because many white Trump voters in 2016 had voted for Obama in 2012, particularly in America's mid-Western rustbelt, the question arises as to why the "white tribe" had not installed Republican candidate Mitt Romney as president in 2012—obviously these "whites" did not mind voting for a "black" candidate. Second, not only did Trump get a smaller share of the white vote in 2016 than Romney had got in 2012, but Trump *also* got more Hispanic and Asian votes than Romney in 2012; Trump even received the "largest share of the black vote of any Republican since 2004" (ibid., 5).[35] The perplexing but inevitable conclusion is that "people of color . . . put Trump in the White House" (ibid.) in 2016, and they would do it again, in an even bigger way, in 2024.[36] Third, and perhaps most damning, Coates's "white coalition" thesis is undermined by the fact that 63 percent of non-Hispanic white voters did *not* vote for Trump in 2016. Musa al-Gharbi concludes that "the 'white supremacy' thesis . . . is confounded by the very data it seeks to explain" (ibid., 8).

The Problem of Race-Centrism

A paradox of antiracist epistemology is, on the one side, its "constructivist" focus on language and perception, which amounts to screening and policing the (white) mind for the racism that the latter stubbornly denies;[37] while, on the other side, this racism is deemed to be "structural," "institutional," or "systemic." As it were, the antiracist conception of racism is maximally subjectivist and objectivist at the same time, while doing little to identify the mechanisms that may link both. Leaving out the subjectivist part for a moment, evidence for the objectivist part is rarely provided, and its workings stay in the dark. Instead, it is simply assumed that gaps between the number of black people (and other minorities) and their representation in socially desired positions (of wealth, income, education, etc.) is the result of racism, and of racism alone.[38] In a trenchant critique of "race-centrism," Andreas Wimmer (2015, 2188) points out that the assumption of race as "master category" for explaining inequality would require to "systematically (compare race) to other inequality-producing processes," which is not so much an exercise of "reduction" but of understanding "conjunction." Alas, in critical race analysis, "reduction" prevails over "conjunction."

Take the example of Bonilla-Silva (1996, 470), who speaks of a "racialized social system" in which "racial practices" have "changed from overt and eminently racist to covert and indirectly racist." "(T)he unchanging element," he argues, is that "Blacks' life chances are significantly lower than those of Whites." To him, the persistent "difference in life chances" is due to "a racialized social order": "Generally, the more dissimilar the races' life chances, the more racialized the social system, and vice versa" (ibid.). When Bonilla-Silva discusses other factors—in particular, class and gender—that might explain black disadvantage, he does not deny their effect but relativizes them on methodological grounds, for instance, because "racial data cannot be retrieved through surveys" (ibid., 471). While this may well be the case, Bonilla-Silva thus unwittingly admits the leap of faith that his assumption of a "racialized social system" requires.

Through the more practice-minded and therapeutic lens of DiAngelo (2018, ch. 3), "(a)ttributing inequality between whites and people of color to causes *other than* racism" (emphasis supplied) is itself a form of racism. She dubs this racism "aversive," and "a manifestation of racism that well-intentioned people . . . exhibit." Due to contemporary antiracism's emphasis on language and perceptions, it is *here*, in deep-seated subjectivity (including the unconscious) rather than in the objective workings of society's institutions, that the real sources of racial disadvantage are sought. This applies also to Bonilla-Silva's (2022) understanding of "systemic racism." He identifies it with "color-blind racism," which is a "new racial *ideology*" (sic!) that reproduces racial inequality through "covert behaviour." He gives the example of realtors who are "not showing all the available units" to black buyers (ibid., 3).[39] However, this "smiling face" discrimination (ibid., 38) is not even in the realm of the unconscious but of the strategic. If this is how "white privilege" is maintained today, it is entirely by way of "linguistic manners and rhetorical strategies" (ibid., 105). Only with difficulty can this racism, which qua language can never be far from an individual's mind and intent, be called "systemic" (ibid., 32) or "structural" (Bonilla-Silva 1996). The least to say is that such an expanded understanding of "systemic" or "structural" belittles the difference of today's racism from past forms of racism, from slavery to Apartheid, which had been formally inscribed in society's institutions.

Wimmer (2015, 2186) also detects a problem with the related assumption that racial inequality is perpetuated by the "racist inclination of the white majority which operates as a collective, strategic actor." This runs into the "free rider" problem that prevents large groups from becoming a collective actor (Olson 1965). At a minimum, one would need to know the "coordination mechanisms" to make this happen, because "hundreds of millions of members" are involved (Wimmer 2015, 2195). And such improbable collective action would face the additional hurdle of formal institutions that are "meant to combat racial discrimination" (ibid., 2196).

While it has become de rigueur, even outside antiracist circles, to call racism "systemic" or "structural,"[40] how reasonable is it as the standalone that it is mostly (and originally had been) meant to be, decoupled from (bad) intentions? The eminent American historian of comparative race, George Fredrickson (2000, 85), defined racism as "an ethnic group's assertion . . . of a privileged . . . status vis à vis members of another group . . . who are *thought*, because of *defective ancestry*, . . . to possess a set of socially relevant characteristics that disqualify them from full membership in a community or citizenship in a nation-state" (emphasis supplied). "Defective ancestry" does not reduce racism to phenotype-based discrimination; antisemitism, the second type of classic racism, is captured by it too. Qua

214 POLITICAL NEOLIBERALISM

ancestry, the reference is still biological in both, in color racism and in antisemitism. This follows the lead of Max Weber (1976 [1922], 234), who defined racism as a pejorative stance directed against "*auffällig Anders-geartete*" (conspicuously different-in-kind). At the same time, again as for Weber,[41] racism according to Fredrickson is entirely a product of the mind: *belief* (qua "thought") in defective ancestry is implied in his definition of racism, which in my view is, together with Weber's, the most compelling in the literature. "Institutional racism," as something decoupled from belief and attitude, is difficult to reconcile with this. Decoupling racism from "individual attitudes," Fredrickson (2000, 80) argues, "would undermine the conception of racism as an ideological construction and make it synonymous with the statistical inequality . . . of any group with a sense of racial . . . identity, whatever the actual causes of its situation might be." The phrase "whatever the actual causes" suggests that, ironically, institutional racism is more in the realm of postulate and belief than of empirical proposition.

As the "new racism" claim of CRT has moved from biology to culture, the underlying reasoning tilts even more to the notion that "race doesn't exist, but racist identities exist, within a social system that is intrinsically racist" (Taguieff 2021, 74). How this combination, linguistically speaking, of adjectives without a noun, should be possible, is a "mystery," at least to Taguieff (ibid.). Particularly the assumption of a "social system" as "intrinsically racist" (i.e., of "institutional racism"), which since the 1960s must operate in a context of institutionalized non-discrimination and delegitimized racist attitudes and conduct, is difficult to uphold. Mara Loveman (1999, 894) rightly rejects as "circular" Bonilla-Silva's definition of "racialized social system" as a system that operates "along racial lines." A similar objection applies to Kendi (2019), when he argues: "'(I)nstitutional racism' and 'structural racism' and 'systemic racism' are redundant. Racism itself is institutional, structural, and systemic" (ibid., intro). This asks for a categorical decoupling of racism from mental disposition, even wiping out the possibility of subjective racism—which must be the starting point of any meaningful concept of racism, without, of course, wanting to deny the objective knock-on effects that W. I. Thomas captured in his famous theorem (that subjective definitions of the situation are "real in their consequences").[42] A purely objectivist understanding of racism is also incommensurable with Kendi's Manichean view of society as divided between "racists" and "antiracists"—social types defined by their attitudes.

A New Religion?

The circularity of antiracist reasoning, and the fact that the institutional racism that is central to it cannot be seen (other than by statistical disparities, which may well have other causes), have moved some critics to call it a religion, no kidding (Braunstein 2022; Gray 2020a; McWhorter 2021; Wood 2021). For Peter Wood (2021), for instance, "systemic racism" is formally akin to "theology," because it states a reality that cannot be disproved. While this may be a jaundiced view, its kernel of truth is that the "systemic racism" formula took off just when systemic racism in the vernacular sense, as backed by "the complicity of law, the approval of society, the power of economics, and the reinforcement of culture" (ibid.), has largely disappeared. A religious dimension is inadvertently present in Kendi's *How to be an Antiracist*, which is the story of an "awakening" to racial injustice, with a sinful before[43] and a cathartic after, resembling the act of conversion in sectarian Protestantism. In one revealing passage, Kendi compares his "strivings" to be an antiracist to his parents' "strivings to be Christian": "I cannot disconnect my parents' religious strivings to be Christian from my secular strivings to be an antiracist" (2019, ch. 1). This and other parallels with sectarian Protestantism make (black) linguist John McWhorter (2019, ch. 1) claim, though not without an element of jesting, that antiracism "actually *is* a religion" (McWhorter 2021, ch. 2): it has its own clergy,[44] rituals (including the washing by white people of black feet or footballers' "taking the knee" as atonement for racial injustice), original sin (white privilege), and temptation to "ban the heretic" and to expurgate. While the religion analogy will remain with a question mark, at a minimum, antiracism shares with Marxism and with psychoanalysis the existence of an unverifiable core, and to be more a lens to interpret the world than a scientific theory of the world, with mind-changing and emancipatory effects that make their adepts emotionally invested in these systems of thought, or rather, belief.[45]

Seizing the English Department

Todd Gitlin once remarked that "While the Right has been busy taking the White House, the Left has been marching on the English Department."[46] As one would expect from antiracism's first element, its focus on language and perceptions, a second element that distinguishes it from Black Power is its institutional venue and constituency. Torpey (2023, 80) describes the antiracists as "rooted chiefly in the academy and other cultural and philanthropic institutions." This also applies to antiracism's target audience. Bonilla-Silva (2022, 3), for instance, singles out "progressive whites," because he deems them particularly captive of a "new racism" that "defies facile racial readings." "Systemic racism is you!" (ibid., 27), he tells his readers (most likely college students, as this pronouncement is in a leading American race studies text). This racism, Bonilla-Silva continues, is "you claiming to be color-blind." And, as if from the pulpit, he thunders: "Liberal and progressive Whites, the moment you absolve yourself of your racial sins, is when whiteness has seeped deeper into your souls" (ibid., 32). Similarly, DiAngelo (2018, intro) considers "white progressives" the primary target of her interventions (under her professional hat of "diversity trainer") because they "cause the most daily damage to people of color," and "indeed uphold and perpetrate racism."

"White liberals" have been receptive to these messages. If 35 percent of them thought in 2011 that racism was "a big problem" in the United States, the figure was up to 61 percent in 2015, and even 77 percent in 2017 (Goldberg 2020). From about 2010 on, white liberals are even stronger leaning toward this view than non-white liberals. In 2016, national polling found a (small) majority of 52 percent of white liberals disagreeing with the statement: "Blacks should work their way up without special favors." The corresponding figure for non-white liberals in that year was only 29 percent (ibid.). Accordingly, what Matthew Yglesias (2019) famously called "The Great Awokening," is primarily one of white liberals, whose "opinion has moved to the left of black Americans."

In a perceptive analysis of left and right "identity politics" challenges to contemporary liberalism, Fukuyama (2020) notes that the right, where it was successful, "seize(d) political power," as in Hungary, India, or the United States. By contrast, the left has come to dominate "cultural institutions," in particular the media and academia—places that were "liberal" before, in the left-progressive American sense, but that now have moved even further to the left. A quantum leap in this respect was after the Minnesota police murder of George Floyd in May 2020, which caused the BLM movement to go viral and global. At North American elite universities, long devoted to diversity, antiracist mobilization rose to fever pitch. One among many, Montreal's McGill University hastily developed an "Action Plan to Address Anti-Black Racism," which previously had not been much of an issue on Canada's physically frozen but racially milder grounds. A few thousand miles southwest, at UCLA, just ten days after Floyd's death, an open letter by "non-Black graduate students" addresses a "pervasive culture of anti-Blackness," of all places, in the university's acclaimed sociology department. The charges against faculty, one of the most diverse in the United States,[47] include a "(n)on-black professor reading the n-word from a quote in lecture" and "failing . . . Black students while passing non-Black students" in field exams. With respect to students, examples of "internalized anti-Blackness" are "(n)on-Black students touching Black students' hair" and "white women . . . crying in class because Black students held them accountable." Among the demands for change are cash transfers to and lighter exams for "Black students," and "(n)o mandatory TAing for all Black graduate students until Black graduate students determine our classrooms a safe work environment."[48]

The concern about "safety" in a setting that one would not expect to be dangerous, points to further elements of academy-based antiracism, which have become known under the rubrics of "trigger warnings," "deplatforming" and "cancel culture," and "microaggressions." All of them seek to restrict or repress speech that is non-conformant with the favored view.[49] Greg Lukianoff and Jonathan Haidt (2018, ch. 10) speak of "concept creep,"[50] from "physical" to "emotional safety," calling the result "safetyism." They attribute it to a new "Generation Z" of over-parented and digitally socialized upper-middle-class youth arriving on campus after 2010,[51] exactly when academic antiracism took off. On campus, they meet a fast-expanding university "bureaucracy of safetyism" which treats their students as fee-paying "consumers," while showing a penchant for "overreaction" and "overregulation" (ibid.). In fact, even more than a leftist faculty, especially in the humanities and social sciences (see Haidt 2016 for this), bloated university administrations are a major factor in the spreading of left identity ideology and practice. In the public University of California system, for instance, administrative staff has more than doubled since 2010. The growth of administration has even been twice as high in private colleges and universities. And administrators, predominantly equipped with degrees in education studies, tend to be even more left-leaning than academic staff.[52]

The Media and Woke Capital

Next to finding its way into higher education, and the education sector in general, left identity politics has taken hold of the media and big corporations.[53] As Zach Goldberg (2021) argues for the United States, the media, long before the arrival of Trump, "dramatically increased coverage of racism and embraced new theories of racial consciousness." In America's two leading newspapers, *The New York Times* and *The Washington Post*, the use of the terms "racist" and "racism" increased by 700 percent and 1000 percent, respectively, between 2011 and 2019; between 2013 and 2019, the terms "white" and "racial privilege" even increased by 1200 percent in the *Times* and 1500 percent in the *Post*. Accordingly, Goldberg identifies in these papers "a worldview sometimes abbreviated as 'wokeness' that combines the sensibilities of highly educated and hyperliberal white professionals with elements of Black nationalism and academic critical race theory."

When, in March 2021, a white man killed eight people in an Atlanta massage parlor, six of them Asian-descent women, the *New York Times* was quick to construe the event as sitting on a wave of "anti-Asian hate crime" because this was in the logic of expanding antiracism.[54] A few hours after the massacre, *New York Times* lead journalist Hannah-Jones, known from the 1619 Project, wrote on Twitter: "Last night's shooting and the appalling rise in anti-Asian violence stem from a sick society where nationalism has been stoked and normalized."[55] Kendi did not stand back, when tweeting: "Locking arms with Asian Americans facing this lethal wave of anti-Asian terror. Their struggle is my struggle. Our struggle is against racism and White Supremacist domestic terror."[56] However, immediately publicized police evidence pointed in a rather different direction, because the young killer, a frequent customer of the site of his shooting, was described by a close friend as a "deeply religious person" tormented by a sex addiction, who even had spent time in a rehab facility to get rid of the latter (Torpey 2023, ch. 6). A *New York Times* journalist nevertheless dismissed this explanation as "incredulous" in the eyes of "many Asian American women, for whom racism and sexism have always been inextricably intertwined." Accordingly, she took "the shooting rampage" to be "the culmination of a racialized misogyny," which may well exist but perhaps not provide the right explanation for this particular event.[57]

As I argued in Chapter 3, the dominant face of neoliberalism today is leftist. This is not as novel as it seems. Capitalism has been recognized as a progressive instead of conservative force by none other than Karl Marx and Friedrich Engels, in their *Communist Manifesto* of 1848, which includes the famous stanza "all that is solid melts into the air, all that is holy is profaned." More recently, Luc Boltanski and Eve Chiapello diagnosed a "new spirit of capitalism" (2005), which is the Bohemian "artistic critique" of the 1968 generation incorporated into capitalism's motive forces. *New York*

Times editorialist Ross Douhat even observed the "rise of woke capital."[58] This notion stands for big firms, especially in the information technology and entertainment sectors, that have not only embraced the mainstreamish diversity discourse, as described in Chapter 3, but even sided with the more radical expressions of antiracism and transgender (the latter to be discussed in the next section).

If the Fordist "Treaty of Detroit" had traded high wages for labor peace, the new "Peace of Palo Alto" dispenses a "certain kind of virtue-signaling on progressive social causes," in the hope that this will "blunt efforts to tax or regulate our new monopolies too heavily," as the inventor of the notion of "woke capital" finds.[59] This progressive posture applies not only to the High Tech and Hollywood usual suspects, but to most Fortune 500 corporations, including Starbucks, Nike, General Motors, BlackRock, and the Bank of America. Corporate progressivism first showed its muscle in the 2016 struggle surrounding the so-called Bathroom Law (HB2) of North Carolina. It was followed by similar bills in other states, which prescribed sex-segregated public toilet use according to birth-registered biological sex. The threat by some big companies to withdraw their operation from North Carolina, including PayPal and Deutsche Bank, forced the Republican majority in the state to repeal this legislation in 2017. Later, Coca-Cola and Delta criticized racially tinged voter-suppression laws in Georgia and other Republican-ruled states (Fraser 2022).[60] Generally, in the age of Trump, big business has turned away from the "right-wing rowdyism" of the Republican Party (ibid., 8). This is in full knowledge that on tax and deregulation, business would always sit in one boat with the Republicans—a "win–win scenario for woke capitalism."[61]

Race Parity as Neoliberal Ideology

Antiracism fulfils a legitimizing function for a neoliberal order that distributes privilege more by way of class than of race. At least this is the critique by Adolph Reed, a renowned and outspoken political scientist at the University of Pennsylvania, who "happens to be black" (in the Crenshawian sense) and an avowed socialist (see Brubaker 2020). According to Reed (2016), antiracism's exclusive focus on race helps camouflage the massively increased economic inequality from the top that marks the neoliberal order. In particular, Reed criticizes the antiracist focus on "race parity" that finds fault only with the unequal representation of black people *within*

220   POLITICAL NEOLIBERALISM

socially desired positions, while blending out the greatly increased inequalities *between* these positions, especially with respect to income and wealth, over the past thirty years.

While the original impetus of the BLM movement has been lethal policing, the more ephemeral goal of race parity is not absent from it. What matters in this regard is getting the "right" people into high-status positions, irrespective of how these positions are defined and remunerated. "Black people need to run the transit board. Black people need to run the water board. Black people need to run the school board," postulates Alicia Garza, one of the three (all-female) BLM leaders (quoted by Szetela 2020, 1369). At the same time, neoliberal fault-lines are ignored. According to Adam Szetela's inside account of BLM, the prominent black activist and Democrat millionaire, Al Sharpton, for instance, is faulted more for his insensitivity to LGBT issues than for his political ties to fast food giant McDonalds and low-wage employer Walmart, or any other of his neoliberal engagements (such as a corporate-minded rebuilding of New Orleans after the tropical storm Katrina destroyed much of it in 1999). In intersectionality terms, race parity is just more easily interwoven with the "gender" than the "class" component of the "race, class, gender" triad, so that "Sharpton's interests as a millionaire neoliberal are, literally, erased from the narrative" (ibid., 1370).

The race-parity focus hides significant intra-group disparities of black people. Bringing them into view reveals "race reductionist" politics as the enterprise of "black professional middle-class agenda-setting strata" (Reed 2020, 39). Note that the "racial wealth gap" is largely one in the top 10 percent of the US income distribution. If one eliminates the gap between the bottom 90 percent of each racial group, white people and black people, this still leaves more than three-fourth of the gap intact, according to the calculation by Reed and Touré Reed (2022, 121). From this angle, the call for race parity, as applied to income, is relevant only for a small subgroup of the one-third of employed Black people in the United States who, in 2019, worked in management, the professions, and in related occupational categories (ibid., 132, fn.24). Adolph Reed concludes that "black politics is thoroughly embedded within the neoliberal regime" (2016, 268), and he calls antiracism the "left wing of neoliberalism."

It is no wonder that the class-focused propositions of Democrat socialist Sanders have stirred little enthusiasm in black leadership circles. John Lewis and James Clyburn, two long-term black Democrats and Student Nonviolent Coordinating Committee veterans who are broadly sympathetic to BLM, flatly rejected Sanders's propositions for free public higher education as "irresponsible": "There's not anything free in America. We all have to pay for something. Education is not free. Health care is not free. Food is not free. Water is not free. I think it's very misleading to say to the American people, we're going to give you something free" (John Lewis, quoted in Reed 2016, 279). In Reed's critical eyes, the black denial of class politics, ironically, is a "class politics" itself. It is enabled by the institutionalization of civil rights, which has led to the rise of a "stratum of race relations engineers and administrators who operate in Democratic party politics and as government functionaries, the punditry and commentariat, educational administrators and the professoriate, corporate, social service and non-profit sectors, and the multibillion-dollar diversity industry" (Reed 2018, 111).

Hillary Clinton, in a speech during the 2016 presidential campaign that attacked her "single issue" rival for the Democratic nomination, Sanders, unwittingly expressed the legitimation function, not just of antiracism but of left identity politics at large for the neoliberal order: "Not everything is about an economic theory, right? If we broke up the big banks tomorrow . . . would that end racism? Would that end sexism? Would that end discrimination against the LGBT community?" (quoted in Reed 2018, 113). Each of her rhetorical questions, which were addressed to a largely minority and women audience, was answered with a roaring "No!"[62]

Transgender

Parallel to race, gender has become a second focus of left identity politics. This is in both opposite and joint ways. On the opposite end, if the thrust of race is to depict the individual as inescapably caught in her bodily condition, up to a point that shared humanity fades from view, the opposite thrust of (trans)gender is to liberate the individual from her bodily condition in the most radical way, as modifiable in any direction one chooses, or rather is intrinsically forced to choose. Transgender, one might say, is a variant of blending out what all humans have in common, this time by denying their link with nature, not the ties beyond one's particular group. Philip Mirowski (2013, ch. 9) uses transgender to illustrate "new neoliberal personhood," because it envisions "(a) world where you can virtually switch gender, imagine you can upload your essence separate from your somatic self, assume any set of attributes." In this respect, the possibility to change one's gender is often part of a broader "transhumanist" agenda, such as "enhancing" the species

222 POLITICAL NEOLIBERALISM

through gene therapy, technologizing human reproduction, and, ultimately, beating death itself.[63]

With respect to their communalities, antiracism and transgender both reinforce the neoliberal order, each in their own way: antiracism, indirectly, through its class-obscuring focus on race parity; transgender, directly, through its hyper-individualism that negates not only nature but also societal conventions surrounding sex and gender. With Brubaker (2023a), one might also argue that transgender's "hyper-individualism," which in the famous terms of Albert Hirschman entails "exit" over "voice" strategies in the case of dissatisfaction with existing social conditions, removes attention from "distributional concerns and structural inequalities," and thereby stabilizes the neoliberal order.[64]

Postmodernism, Again: Queer Theory

As variants of left identity politics, antiracism and transgender are linked through the construct of "intersectionality," which "challenge(s) all forms of discrimination" (Crenshaw 1989, 145). It is not incidental that all three female leaders of BLM have credentials on the gender front, and not in the conventional feminist sense. More fundamentally still, both movements share the postmodernist epistemology. The notion that language is performative, and that the politics of the subaltern is, above all, the playful and parodic subverting of the dominant categories that marginalize them, has found its apotheosis in queer theory, which is the main intellectual resource of transgender. Queer theory's import for transgender is the destruction of the sex versus gender binary, in which sex was seen as biological and gender as social or cultural, and which had oriented second-wave feminism since the days of Simone de Beauvoir.

In particular, the philosopher Judith Butler has destroyed the gender versus sex binary in two crucial steps: first, by denying the possibility of causality between the two; and, secondly, in arguing that sex also is a "variable construction" (Butler 1999 [1990], 10). With respect to causality, it is logically compelling to argue with Butler: "If gender is the cultural meanings that the sexed body assumes," which had been second-wave feminists' point of entry, "then a gender cannot be said to follow from a sex in any one way" (ibid.). As Butler stated elsewhere (1993, 313), gender is "a kind of imitation for which there is no original." If conceived of as "radically independent of sex," which of course is more than a touch more radical than second-wave feminists would condone, "gender . . . becomes a free-floating artifice" (Butler 1999 [1990], 10). And she anticipates the possibility of transgender *before* it was politically on the map: "*man* and *masculine* might just as easily signify a female body as a male one, and *woman* and *feminine* a male body as easily as a female one." Moreover, the radical decoupling of sex from gender renders obsolete the assumption that, if sex is binary, gender also must be binary: "there is no reason to assume that genders ought also to remain as two" (ibid.). Hence, Butler also prefigures the "non-binary," who today go under the preferred pronouns "they/them."

Up to this point in her argument, Butler left "sex" untouched. But "what is 'sex' anyway?," she continues (Butler 1999 [1990], 10). For the postmodernist thinker that she is, sex surely cannot be "natural, anatomical, chromosomical, or hormonal" (ibid.). Instead, sex also is "discursively produced," this time by "scientific discourses in the service of other political and social interests" (ibid.). Foucault had shown the way, deeming "sex" a nineteenth-century artifice of a new form of population management, which he called "bio-power" (1980, 140–147). But then, somewhat stepping back from her assumption that gender and sex vary independently, Butler concludes that the very distinction between sex and gender must be void. If even sex is "culturally constructed," she speculates, "perhaps it was always already gender, with the consequence that the distinction between sex and gender turns out to be no distinction at all" (Butler 1999 [1990], 10–11).[65] Having denaturalized sex and subsumed it under gender, we are in the realm of gender identity. Here, a man or a woman is purely someone who performs, in the extreme: merely declares, manhood or womanhood. Performance, with the barren illocutionary speech act "I declare" as its nuclear form, is the essence of Butlerian queer theory. This theory is "the purest form of applied postmodernism" (Pluckrose and Lindsay 2021, 19), whose general thrust Martha Nussbaum (1999) appositely described as to shift the focus from the "material side of life" to "verbal and symbolic politics."

The Paradox of Gender (and Trans) Identity

Butler's *Gender Trouble* (1999 [1990]) provided intellectual impetus to the transgender movement and its central claim of "gender identity" being determinative of a person's "sex." An authoritative source put it thus:

"'Gender identity' . . . refer(s) to each person's deeply felt internal and individual experience of gender, which may or may not correspond with the sex assigned at birth."[66] Accordingly, gender identity is a human universal; transgender kicks in when there is a non-correspondence between "gender" and "sex." Two aspects of this on-the-ground definition of gender identity are puzzling, because they contradict the tenets of queer theory à la Butler.

First, as something that is "deeply felt" and "internal" to a person, to which is often added that this identity is immutable and experienced early on in a person's life, gender identity is clearly outside the ambit of culture, society, anything "constructed." On the contrary, it seems to be an "inner essence" (Brubaker 2016a, 136) to which only the individual has access—a "sexed soul," "innate and ineffable," as Helen Joyce put it felicitously (2021, intro). Some have thus argued, not to denigrate it but to defend its existence, that gender identity is found in a part of the brain, so that there are female and male brains after all—which lets biology return through the backdoor.[67] Such essentialist reasoning is entirely outside the hyper-constructivist tenets of queer theory, which "ignores biology nearly completely" (Pluckrose and Lindsay 2020, 89). "To queer," after all, is to reject identity, to "disrupt seemingly fixed categories, and to problematize any 'binaries' within it" (ibid., 94). By contrast, "gender identity," qua identity, requires the binaries that queer theory repudiates.

Secondly, even if gender is determinative of sex, it still requires sex as its other. This is because only the mismatch between both triggers trans. In this respect, too, biology slips back in, although relativized as "assigned" (at birth), or rather as falsely assigned. In some (activist) definitions of gender identity, the apparent contradiction is meant to be muted by speaking of "gender assigned at birth," thus simply avoiding the word "sex." However, such initial "gender" cannot be determined but by inference from a person's bodily shape or equipment, which in common parlance is biological sex. As Structuralism 101 suggests, the other of a category is always required to attribute meaning to the latter, in this case "gender" requiring "sex." One must even argue that trans identity requires non-trans as a norm, and thus the matching of biological sex with one's gender, which is notionally rejected for its oppressive and marginalizing effects. In an interesting reflection on being "alone in my apartment," which was the sad condition for most during the two-year COVID-19 pandemic, a self-declared "transgender-nonbinary" admits that they were also bereft of the non-transgender, non-nonbinary mainstream that is required for their identity to assert itself: "With the gender binary all but gone, what did it mean to be nonbinary? How do I define my gender when I—accustomed to how visible my gender usually makes me—am no longer being watched?"[68] This statement concedes the necessity of the norm ("gender binary") for the possibility of breaking it ("nonbinary"), and visibly so. The binary trans are caught in an even more vexing paradox. Because they are necessarily denied biological markers to assert their gender identity, they must resort to—and thereby affirm—rather crude stereotypes[69] of "male" or, more often, "female," such as hairdo, skirt, and lipstick,[70] which have been rejected by most feminists as sexist and demeaning[71]—and by the cognizant everyday traveler are immediately recognized as either authentic or fake. In a world that is overwhelmingly and perpetually non-trans—and must be so for the trans person to *be* in the first—the latter is in a genuinely tragic situation, as he/she/they must simultaneously presuppose *and* reject a world that is constitutively other.

Legal Recognition of Gender Identity: From Dramaturgical to Illocutionary

Since the days of Lili Elbe, alias Einar Wegener, a Danish early twentieth-century artist settling with his wife in Paris and who was the first person to undergo a series of sex-change surgeries in Berlin and Dresden (and sadly died after the fourth intervention),[72] the lot of people trapped in a body they do not want has mainly concerned medical doctors, sexologists, and clinical psychologists. What is medically referred to as "gender dysphoria" is a rare condition that (while precise counts do not exist) afflicts well under 1 percent of people in the world. Only from the 1990s on, in the wake of the gay rights movement that incorporated the "T" to become LGBT, did transgender emerge as a political actor, fighting for the legal recognition of changing one's birth-attributed sex *without* having to undergo a surgical intervention that continues to be loaded with discomfort and great risk. Joyce (2021, ch. 1) attributes the politicization of transgender to "long-term societal trends," away from considering transsexualism as "anomaly" or "disease," and—importantly—as part of a "shift to individual, rather than communal, conceptions of personhood." In a "communal" (i.e., conventional) conception, the person is never abstracted from their reproductive capacity—hence, the importance of biological sex as key entry in any one

226   POLITICAL NEOLIBERALISM

person's first official document, the birth certificate. From the point of view of gender identity, by contrast, the person and the relations they engage in (including marriage) become "an individual rather than societal contract." Not only nature but society disappears in the hyper-individualist universe that gender identity construes. One might say that this is an identity geared to a condition in which there is "no such thing" as society, which we argued is the neoliberal condition (see Chapter 2).

A watershed event in the legal recognition of gender identity was the British Gender Recognition Act (GRA) of 2004. This is the first law in the world not to require sex-change surgery for being legally recognized as of the other sex, qua changed birth certificate and passport. Typical for similar reforms that soon followed in most other Western states, and which critics have described as the result of "policy capture" by the transgender lobby (see below), the GRA was written by Stephen Whittle, the head of the UK trans-activist group "Press for Change" (PFC), and who is until the present day Britain's foremost transgender activist.[73] However, a medical component is still required under the GRA, in terms of a "gender dysphoria" diagnosis. In addition, the act requires one to have "lived in the acquired gender" for two years as a precondition for changing one's legal sex.

When the GRA was debated in Parliament, Lord Tebbit called it an "objectionable farce," because he deemed "sex" determined by chromosomes that "cannot be changed" (in Whittle and Turner 2007, 1). But according to Whittle, the GRA "does exactly that": it "changes the legal sex of trans people in the UK" (ibid.). More than that, Whittle explicitly takes the GRA as putting Butler's queer theory into practice, because "the sex/gender distinction, (where sex normatively refers to the sexed body, and gender, to social identity) is demobilized both literally and legally" (ibid.). At the same time, and in obvious contradiction to this, although in recognition of what we called the paradox of gender identity, Whittle concedes that "the difference between sex and gender . . . has underpinned and made possible trans identities" (ibid., 2). The result is still, much as Butler stipulated at the level of theory, that "(g)ender then, now determines 'sex'" in British law also (ibid.). Moreover, as neither surgery nor hormonal treatment is required under the GRA, the obvious consequence is that "there may well be legal women who have a penis, and . . . men who have a vagina" (ibid., 9).

In a brilliant analysis of how queer theory drove prison reform in England, Michael Biggs (2022) calls "dramaturgical" the stage of legally recognizing gender identity as reached in the GRA. The required two-year period of living in the acquired gender entails, in language borrowed from Erving Goffman, that "the individual gives off the appearance of femininity or masculinity through body modification, clothing and gesture" (Biggs 2022, 1). But the desired endpoint of legal recognition, from the point of view of transgender activism, is to move further, from "dramaturgical" to "illocutionary" performance, where mere declaration or self-identification, short of medical diagnosis and waiting period, is sufficient. Self-identification is now a reality in a growing number of countries, including Belgium, Ireland, Denmark, Finland, Norway, Portugal, Spain, France, Switzerland, in many sub-federal states in the United States, and most recently, in Germany.

On the one hand, self-identification is the logical endpoint of legal transgender recognition, in that if fully de-medicalizes gender identity, making it exclusively a matter of the individual's choice, decoupled from a somatic basis. The European Court of Human Rights has made an important stride in this direction, in its judgment on *A.P., Garçon and Nicot v. France* (2017).[74] While this decision leaves the requirement of a medical certificate intact,[75] this is more of a realistic concession than a principled commitment. The court points out that the "vast majority" of the forty Council of Europe states still requires a psychiatric diagnosis, but that the latter "does not directly affect individuals' physical integrity."[76] Exactly this, the previous "requirement to demonstrate an irreversible change in appearance,"[77] through surgery or hormonal treatment, is outlawed with this decision, as a violation of the right to "private and family life" protected by Article 8 of the European Convention of Human Rights (ECHR). If the court considers "irreversible" interventions a human rights violation, this runs counter to the apodictic nature of gender identity, which is said to be immutably fixed early in one's life. But the gist of the court's stance is that it is only one step away from transgender recognition through self-identification alone, without a medical diagnosis. The court itself suggests as much when it is "mindful" of, and thus obviously not averse to, the view that "transgenderism is not an illness and . . . addressing gender identities from the perspective of a psychological disorder adds to the stigmatisation of transgender persons."[78] This is the key phrase that clears the path for self-identification. Further considering that *A.P., Garçon and Nicot v. France* is not the first time that the court held gender identity to fall under ECHR Article 8 protection,[79] it seems only a question of time for self-identification to become the dominant legal standard.

228   POLITICAL NEOLIBERALISM

On the other hand, Biggs (2022) has pointed to the problematic consequences of self-identification, at least when applied to the sensitive prison
sector. Prisons, it must be stated clearly, cannot be taken as representative
for *all* societal spheres; but qua "total institution" (Goffman 1961), they
raise prickly issues of individual vulnerability because their inmates are
deprived of most of their civic rights. Self-identification would provide criminal transwomen, on their say-so, without the slightest bodily modification,
access to female prison cells, and bodies, one must suppose.[80] While England
has so far legally abstained from moving toward self-identification (although
it is likely to do so under the new Labour government that entered in 2024),
its prison system has de facto already introduced it, after a 2017 reform
that was conceived and steered by a transgender organization, and whose
express motivation was the "wish to respect someone in the gender in which
they identify" (in Biggs 2022, 16). As it is difficult, if not impossible, to fulfil
in prison the two-year "living in the acquired gender" condition, the mere
application for a Gender Recognition Certificate was rendered sufficient by
this reform. On this notion, Karen White, described in a *Guardian* investigative report as "convicted paedophile and on remand for grievous bodily
harm, burglary, multiple rapes and other sexual offences against women,"[81]
while legally still a man under the name David Thompson, was transferred
at her request to an English women's prison—where she promptly sexually assaulted two more women. A member of a transgender rights group,
who had known White from civil life, described her as "insist(ing) (that)
people referred to her in her acquired gender without trying terribly hard
to present as a woman."[82] As a former (transgender) neighbor put it, she
was "more transvestite than transsexual with no real desire to be a woman";
"David just walked into his flat one day as David and walked out the next
day as Karen" (ibid., 17). Indeed, Biggs concludes, "White's performance
was illocutionary" (ibid.) in the precise sense of (Austin-inspired and Searle-
refined) speech-act theory, and Biggs dubbed her the "apotheosis of queer
theory as implemented in English prisons" (ibid., 18).

Sites of Conflict (1): Transwomen

The English prison case, though an extreme case that cannot be generalized to all sectors (and all countries)[83], still epitomizes one central conflict
surrounding transgender, which is the potential impairment of ordinary

women's rights by an unconditional and often absolutizing recognition of transwomen rights. Note that, according to 2017 data on the United Kingdom, sixty-five of 125 convicted transwomen were sex offenders, thus posing a significant risk to natal female prisoners (Asteriti and Bull 2020, 4). Their interests have simply not been considered in recent transgender-friendly UK prison reforms, which two authors, writing about the even more extreme Scottish case, call the result of "policy capture" (Murray and Blackburn 2019, 262).

Whittle does not hide the premise on which transgender rights in general are based: "With the recognition of equal opportunities and rights for women and men, there are very few circumstances left where the sex or gender of an individual might be considered legally germane" (Whittle and Turner 2007, 3). While this statement points more to the ultimate (and empirically unlikely) endpoint of transgender emancipation, which is the abolishment of legal sex for everyone, Whittle obviously assumes that "equal opportunities and rights for women and men" exist as a matter of fact, here and now, so that to be feminist has simply become anachronistic. Hence, the feminists who disagree go under the unflattering name of TERF—Trans Exclusionary Radical Feminists.

As the activist diction that "transwomen are women" has become mainstreamed, the plain word "woman" has been delegitimized out of fear of discriminating against transwomen. Hence the propensity, even in official medical language, in politics, and in the media, to speak of "bodies with vaginas," "pregnant people" or "people who menstruate" instead of "women," without much concern about the dehumanizing ring of such words. "More than a whiff of misogyny is in the air," observes a (female) editorialist, because there is no parallel campaign to "abandon the word 'men' in favour of 'prostate-havers', 'ejaculators' or 'bodies with testicles'. It is almost always women who are being ordered to dispense with a useful word they have used all their lives."[84]

The "useful word" (woman) hints at the fact that biology, once a ground to disadvantage women, has in the civil right era become a ground for compensatory advantage that is put at risk once its reality is denied, which is the astoundingly science-denying imposition that the current sensitivity for trans rights demands. Note that, in the notorious American bathroom battles, segregated facilities for females, which transwomen seek access to, have been critiqued by the Democrat left as analogous to racial segregation and privilege that need to be erased.[85] When, under the late Obama

230 POLITICAL NEOLIBERALISM

Administration, the federal Department of Justice sued North Carolina to open its female public bathrooms to transwomen, the Attorney General compared the state's opposition with the "fierce and widespread resistance to *Brown v. Board*," which would lead to the "isolation and exclusion" of transgender people. And, as if this wasn't clear enough, she continued that "not so very long ago," southern states "had signs above restrooms, water fountains and on public accommodations keeping people out based upon a distinction without a difference" (quoted in Melnick 2018, 12). The race analogy obscures that sex- and race-based segregation are grounded in fundamentally different rationales: protection versus exclusion, respectively.[86] A similar protection rationale applies to sex-segregated professional sport, which is a second site for access by (physically stronger) transwomen to produce obvious inequities—and which happens to be "perhaps the most striking place where self-ID is catching on."[87]

The interests of women tend to be negated whenever transwomen ask for equal access and treatment. Consider the May 2016 Dear Colleague Letter on Transgender Students, issued by the civil rights units of the US Department of Justice and the Department of Education, under the late Obama Administration.[88] It imposes equal treatment of transgender students in all educational institutions that receive federal funding, from schools to universities. This is on the apodictic (and legally contested) assumption that Title IX of the US civil rights laws, which was passed in 1972 to prohibit discrimination on the basis of "sex," and was clearly meant to protect girls and women, encompasses "gender identity," a concept unknown at the time. Henceforth, the 2016 Dear Colleague Letter declares, "the Departments treat a student's gender identity as the student's sex for purposes of Title IX."[89] Moreover, it bases gender identity on self-identification: "Under Title IX, there is no medical diagnosis or treatment requirement that students must meet as a prerequisite to being treated consistent with their gender identity."[90] "Gender transition" is referred to as "transgender individuals . . . asserting the sex that corresponds to their gender identity instead of the sex they were assigned at birth."[91] Obviously assuming that transitioning means to "change sex itself," the US federal government fully adopts and replicates "gender-identity ideology's self-referential nature and incoherence" (Joyce 2021, ch. 10) because the sex/gender binary is simultaneously denied *and* presupposed. Ultimately, male and female "cannot mean both biology and identity" (ibid.).

Concretely, the 2016 Dear Colleague letter orders "equal access" for transgender students to all "educational programs and activities," including sex-segregated activities and facilities: restrooms, locker rooms, shower facilities, housing, even athletic teams, among others. "When a school provides sex-segregated activities and facilities", the letter stipulates, "transgender students must be allowed to participate in such activities and access such facilities consistent with their gender identity."[92] Importantly, single-user facilities, which previously served as a compromise solution for trans-females (there almost never is conflict surrounding trans-males), are explicitly rejected as discriminatory; instead, these facilities "may" be made available for "all" (other, in fact, except trans) "students who voluntarily seek additional privacy."[93] In all of this, "the desire to accommodate *others' discomfort* cannot justify a policy that singles out and disadvantages a particular class of students."[94] The notion of "others' discomfort" studiously anonymizes, as throughout this US government pronunciation, whose interests and rights are subordinated to absolutized trans interests and rights: those of girls and women, for whom Title IX had been created in the first.

The first Trump victory in November 2016 obliterated this rather controversial measure, which shows how far some jurisdictions and public institutions have moved to accommodate trans at the cost of other interests. One must also conclude that a feminist defense against expansive trans rights requires reasserting the biological foundation of sex.

Kathleen Stock, the ultimate TERF, has understood this, and the price for her reassertion of biological sex was to be forced to resign from her post of philosophy professor at the University of Sussex, after a campaign that included not only students but many fellow academics. "(B)inary sex exists," Stock dares to say in her sharply argued yet fiercely incriminated *Material Girls* (2021, ch. 2). It exists not least in the form of chromosomic (XX vs. XY) difference on which the reproduction of the human species (and of all mammals) hangs. Even if one holds, as does the noted biologist and gender theorist Anne Fausto-Sterling, that sex is a "continuum" and that 1.7 percent of people are "intersex," this still means that 98.3 percent are *not* intersex, and thus, in a binary biological sense, are male or female. While this is a matter for biologists to decide, it is of strategic importance for feminists to insist that to be a woman has biological foundations. This is simply because "(w)hen women are limitless and formless, they can have no political demands" (Joyce 2021, ch. 7). If some radical feminists deny the biological foundation of sex, this is incoherent. Stock

232 POLITICAL NEOLIBERALISM

shows this in a compelling critique of lesbian feminist Monique Wittig's famous assertion that "there is no sex . . . It is oppression that creates sex and not the contrary." This dodges the question, argues Stock, how this oppression *started*, and *who* started it. Most likely it was "due to genetics and associated tendencies to relatively superior physical strength" (Stock 2021, ch. 2). But then, how could oppression itself have "created" such characteristics? Wittig's "dominance model" (ibid.), which is energized by the feminist impulse to refute biological determinism, is incoherent; binary sex is a reality that cannot be wished away, and this on purely logical grounds.

Not only qua feminist, but also qua lesbian, Stock has skin in the game. Because "(w)ithout a meaningful definition of sex, there can be no meaningful definition of sexual orientation" (Joyce 2021, ch. 7). Inherent in the logic of transgender is to deem lesbianism or gayness as denied or incomplete transitioning, rather than the physical preference, "beyond individual control" (Stock 2021, ch. 3), for same-sexed bodies that they probably are. While one is used to consider the T in LGBT as Gay-, Lesbian-, and Bisexual-compatible fourth letter and ally, and all of them, qua sex-based activism, to be continuous with feminism, in principle (not necessarily in reality) transgender is deeply subversive of its presumed allies. Distinguishing between "software" and "hardware" orientations in identity politics, which are colloquial terms for either choice or the absence of it, respectively, in identity matters, Douglas Murray (2019, ch. 4) has put it concisely: "(I)f a significant amount of modern rights campaigning is based on people wishing to prove that their cause is a hardware issue," which is required in a (neo)liberal context of "luck egalitarianism" (see Anderson 1999) and required by the premium on immutability in civil rights and antidiscrimination law, "then trans forces the other movements to go in precisely the opposite direction. Trans campaigners intent on arguing that trans is hardware can only win their argument if they persuade people that being a woman is a matter of software. And not all feminists," and lesbians one must add, "are prepared to concede this one" (Murray 2019, ch. 4). The software/hardware metaphor may not be entirely consistent, because transgender, as we argued, simultaneously presupposes *and* refutes the sex-gender distinction. But transgender's tension, if not incompatibility, with other sex-based politics is spot-on.

Stock's feminist- (cum-lesbian) inspired insistence that sex has biological foundations is taken by transgender activists as denying the "existence" of transgender people.[95] In reality, Stock is a self-described "moderate" who does not deny the existence of transgender people but the absolutizing of their rights, which seems to be happening in a growing number of public institutions, in particular, academia, as Stock's forced removal from it attests to. The "denial-of-existence" hyperbole is not accidental because in postmodernist epistemology speech is performative, literally calling into existence things and people. Hence the importance of "cancelling" speech that is considered a threat to dominant views. When trans activist students tried to block Stock's appearance at Oxford University in May 2023, they "refute(d) that this is a free speech issue—disinviting someone is not preventing them from speaking."[96] Hyperbole is evidently paired with euphemism because to deny a renowned academic from speaking at a place that is constitutionally dependent on "free speech" is surely no minor affair.

Sites of Conflict (2): Trans Youth

When Stock finally spoke in Oxford, a young protestor tried to glue themselves onto the podium floor, wearing a t-shirt with big capital letters: "NO MORE DEAD TRANS KIDS." This points to the second critical issue surrounding transgender, which is the transitioning of children and adolescents. If the transwoman conflict involved (mainly adult) male-to-female transitioning, in the case of youth it is, on the opposite, increasingly girls who request to become boys. A 2019 best-practice report on "legal gender recognition for youth" more generally reveals the strong institutional hold of the transgender movement: this report was written pro bono by Dentons, self-described as the world's largest law firm, and it was issued by IGLYO, an international LGBT youth and student organization that is co-funded by the European Union. The report bemoans that, contrary to the successes on legal recognition via "self-determination," "less progress" has been made "for trans youth" (by which it means people under the majority age of 18) (IGLYO 2019, 1). In the introduction to this report, an Icelandic trans youth finds that the absence of "legal gender recognition for minors . . . takes away their ability to fully enjoy and feel safe in their identity" (ibid., 8), and that "(i)t's time we respect the right of children and teenagers to self-determine their own identity" (ibid., 9). Rather delicately, the report's practical advice of how to move forward on this matter is to "get ahead of the government"

234 POLITICAL NEOLIBERALISM

with "progressive legislative proposal," to "(a)void excessive press coverage and exposure," and, not least, to "be wary of compromise" (ibid., 20, 21).

Armed with the ultimate weapon of an allegedly epidemic suicide disposition among trans youth,[97] the transgender youth and child campaign raises prickly issues of parental authority, social fad, and irreversibility. Above all, the growing number of children and youth, and predominantly girls, who ask for medical transitioning is simply staggering and unlikely to have other than social causes (that must be denied from the point of view of gender identity). If the United States had just one pediatric gender clinic in 2007, ten years later there were forty-five of them (Anderson 2018, intro); in the United Kingdom, there has been a phenomenal 4,400 percent increase of teenage girls seeking gender treatment over the same period (Shrier 2020, ch. 2). Accordingly, there is a vested professional and commercial interest in facilitating the transitioning of youth. This is further boosted by the fact that "gender-affirming care," in which essentially the patient and not the doctor makes the diagnosis, has become the gold standard in this domain.[98] This brings the transgender industry in collision course with parents, who tend to be side-lined in the process as "transphobic" obstacles. Parents are side-lined by schools that are often withholding information about internal name changes and other trans-related matters, and by their own children, who are intent on transiting, first with puberty blockers, later with cross-sex hormones, and eventually with surgery. One compliant doctor expresses the prevailing attitude thus: "For us, the diagnosis is made by the patient, not the doctor, in the same way that a patient seeking breast enlargement is the one who diagnoses her own breasts as being too small" (in ibid., ch. 9).[99] A previous "watchful waiting" approach, motivated by the fact that the majority of affected children later desist from the wish to transition,[100] is increasingly rejected, even prohibited by law in Canada, in many states of the United States, and more recently in the United Kingdom, as "conversion therapy."[101] The US educational sector, from schools on,[102] is fully enlisted in the trans youth campaign. Many colleges and universities offer "Preferred Name Change Forms" on entry, and their health plans cover hormonal treatment, and often gender surgery (ibid., ch. 8).[103]

Much like the insistence on the biological foundation of sex has been discredited for the sake of transgender accommodation, so has the assumption that there must be social causes to the sudden increase of minority-age children and youth, especially girls, who claim to be transgender. Lisa

Littman, previously a research physician at Brown University, is to the youth side of the transgender debate what Stock is to its transwoman side, the heretic who stands in the way of "social justice." And like Stock, Littman suffered serious professional consequences for her considered academic views—the US Department of Health cancelled her consultancy, and the Dean of Brown's School of Public Health condemned Littman for "discredit(ing) efforts to support transgender youth and invalidat(ing) the perspectives of members of the transgender community."[104] In her incriminated research article, Littman (2018) observes the new phenomenon of a "sudden or rapid onset of gender dysphoria," especially among female teenagers undergoing puberty, and she attributes it mainly to "social and peer contagion" (ibid., 2). While it is for others to decide whether parent reports, on which her study is based, are sufficient to establish the existence of a "potential new subcategory of gender dysphoria" (ibid., 40), Littman does assemble valuable information about the social conditions of a sudden preference for becoming trans, which up to that point no other academic had noticed (or wanted or dared to notice). First, this trans preference is highly clustered in "friendship groups," preceded by intense ("binge-watching") internet and social media use,[105] and the majority experiences "an increased popularity" after announcing to be transgender (ibid., 17). Second, while the majority of trans youth described their parents as "transphobic" or "bigoted" (ibid., 23), and tried to hide their new identity from them, over 80 percent of interviewed parents expressed rather liberal views on gay and transgender rights (ibid., 11). Third, parents reported that their affected children, nearly half of them described as "academically gifted" (ibid., 32), "seemed to focus on feeling as though they were victims," taking the problems that pile up in a trans perspective like "badges of honor" (ibid., 20). Thus, the picture emerges of trans youth as members of a Generation Z growing up as "digital natives" in "coddled," liberal, upper-middle-class environments, much as described by Lukianoff and Haidt (2018), who are predominantly white and "seeking cover" in the only "minority identity" that is available to them when arriving on campus, which is "trans."[106] In particular, it is girls, often suffering in addition from other psychic disorders, who are confused about their changing bodies and catch the "new idea" that they are not "lesbians" but "'really' boys" (Shrier 2020, ch. 1).

Littman (2018) is careful to present her study as "descriptive" and "exploratory," with its purpose being more to "generate" than to validate

236 POLITICAL NEOLIBERALISM

hypotheses (ibid., 2), and she loses few occasions to call for "more" and "further" research to corroborate her findings. But the responses to her paper have been furious—beginning with the fact that *PLoS ONE*, the noted open access journal that published it, imposed on the author a longish and humiliating (auto-) "Correction" that, in fact, did not correct or retract anything but merely reiterated the many caveats that the author had already stated in the original text. One sociological critic, a transwoman, laments that "(t)he voices of trans youth are noticeably absent" in the article (Ashley 2020, 789)—but they were never meant to be captured by the research in the first. And she calls Littman's "theory" (that also never claimed to be a theory) a "conspicuous example of epistemological violence." The latter, according to Florence Ashley (ibid., 791–792), occurs when "data interpretations that have negative consequences for marginalised groups are selected despite the existence of alternative, equally (or more) plausible interpretations." This would imply that the first imperative of science is not to improve on existing knowledge but to be political, in this case, not to offend "marginalised groups."

One might well argue that the truly marginalized in the trans youth drama are the youngsters who may later regret the irreversible choices that they are too easily allowed to make by trans-friendly and adult-peopled institutions, from schools and colleges to the medical sector. In the United States, the grip of gender-affirming care, now extended to children, seems unbreakable (except by political opposition in Republican-ruled states). "We are completely saturated with corporate influences," including "Big Pharma," on the one side, and with transgender "lobby groups," on the other, one medical critic describes the situation in the United States.[107]

At the same time, transgender in general, and the involvement of children in particular, has been drawn into the American culture wars. By 2021, sixteen Republican states introduced bills to block the prescription of puberty blockers and hormones to children,[108] and right-wing zealots call "grooming" (a term usually applied to pedophiles) the readiness of doctors to promote the gender transition of children.[109] On the other end, Democratic President Joe Biden, who from his first day in office had been intent on passing an Equality Act that would outlaw discrimination on the basis of gender identity, make the latter a matter of self-identification, and prohibit what he (or rather what the transgender lobby in his party) calls "conversion therapy," denounced as "close to sinful" Republican laws that prohibit gender-affirming care for children.[110]

By contrast, in Europe, the tide seems to be turning. In England, the High Court sided with Keira Bell, a remorseful girl-to-boy transitioner (now self-identified as a lesbian), who accused Britain's only public gender clinic at the Tavistock Hospital in London of having been too fast and one-directional in her treatment. In typical fashion, Bell's treatment had started with puberty blockers at sixteen, continued with male hormones, and ended with the amputation of both breasts in her early twenties, an intervention she now deeply regrets.[111] The court agreed with the plaintiff that under-sixteens are too immature to meaningfully consent to puberty blockers and its cascading consequences, calling the drug-related part of her treatment "experimental" and thus outside the law. Sweden, Denmark, Finland, Norway, and France followed suit, stopping or restricting blockers to minors and moving back to therapy instead.[112]

Sites of Conflict (3): Forced to be Immersed in a Fiction

In the United Kingdom, it was a pastime of journalists for a while to ask Labour leader Keir Starmer the "can women have a penis" question, in full knowledge of the impossible act for him to please both the influential transgender lobby in his party and feminists (and ordinary female voters). When first surprised by the question, Starmer stumbled and refused to answer.[113] More composed, he said this: "A woman is a female adult, and in addition to that trans women are women."[114] The "in addition" betrays the attempt to have it both ways. As did this statement a year later: "For 99.9 percent of women, it is completely biological . . . and of course they haven't got a penis."[115] Which implies that 0.1 of "women" *do* have a penis.

On this, a transwoman political activist and editorialist, Debbie Hayton, commented: "If Keir Starmer thinks that I am a woman, I am delighted to tell him the truth. Transwomen (like me) are male, while women (like my wife) are female. Biology does not lie, male is not female, and therefore transwomen are not women. Shocking that might sound to some ears, the logic is inescapable and the sky does not fall in when you admit it."[116] "Shocking" it sounds indeed, which is indicative of a "genuine revolution in the liberal intelligentsia's understanding of sex and gender"[117] that happened in very short time. And, one must assume, the fact alone that a transwoman said this, let her get away with it. Maverick activist-cum-editorialist Hayton's statement meets the definition of "transphobia," as provided by Stonewall,

238 POLITICAL NEOLIBERALISM

the world's leading LGBT advocacy group: "the fear or dislike of someone based on the fact that they are trans, including denying their gender identity or *refusing to accept it*" (quoted in Stock 2021, ch. 1; emphasis supplied). Because Hayton *refuses to accept* gender identity as defined by its central tenet, which is that "transwomen are women," she is strictly speaking "transphobic." Stonewall's trick is to equate the refusal of doctrine with the "fear or dislike" of persons, thus moving the matter into the ambit of hate speech and discrimination. It is thus no longer in the realm of the legitimate, not even the legal,[118] so that the power of the state can, in principle, be mobilized against those who "deny" and "refuse" gender identity. Much like in the case of antiracism, no disagreement with the ideological tenets of transgender is possible.

As Stock (2021, ch. 6) put it, transgender forces society to become "immersed in a fiction," the fiction that biological sex does not exist, which continues to be exotic to most people. Of course, this is on the assumption that "people can't literally change sex" (ibid.), which is still the dominant view of science but considered hate speech by Stock's opponents. The transgender movement's successes in this respect are visible when comparing the first version of the Yogyakarta Principles, issued in 2007, with their "Plus 10" version ten years later. In 2007, Yogyakarta's "Principle 3" had asked for "self-defined" gender identity, and that "changes to identity documents will be recognised" on this basis. As self-identification has become the reality in a growing number of countries, the 2017 version of the Yogyakarta Principles goes a decisive step further. Now their "Principle 31" asks for nothing less than to "end the registration of the sex and gender of the person in identity documents such as birth certificates, identification cards, passports and driver licences, and as part of their legal personality."[119] In a nutshell, the last frontier of transgender is the abolishment of legal sex for everyone.

This is unlikely to ever happen. But the society-wide imposition of the transgender "fiction" (Stock), or what transwoman Hayton called transgender's "phantasy world," has made impressive strides. For Hayton, transgender is a "matter of faith," which "can neither be proved nor falsified." However, as she continues, unlike, say, Christian transubstantiation, which in Christian doctrine is the transformation of bread into flesh, but which not even believing Christians seek to impose on the rest of society, "the evangelists of gender identity ideology are not satisfied with an agreement to disagree over whether men can be transformed into women. They take no prisoners in their zeal to change society."[120]

THE IDENTITY LEFT 239

Truthful to the postmodernist stress on the performative power of language, this "zeal" is above all directed at changing public language, where addressing people by their preferred pronouns has become de rigueur. In progressive jurisdictions, this is not merely a matter of moral obligation or decency, on which most people (including this writer) of course agree, but of the law and the police that enforce it. In California, for instance, health care workers who don't use patients' requested gender pronouns face penal law sanctions. As the initiator of California's Senate Bill 219, passed in 2017, defended the measure, "deliberately misgendering a transgender person isn't just a matter of opinion, and it's not simply 'disrespectful, discourteous, or insulting'. Rather, it's straight up harassment."[121] In New York, a similar legal obligation exists also for employers, landlords, and business owners (see Shrier 2020, intro).

In the United States, strong constitutional free speech protections are a significant obstacle to using the law to impose the transgender fiction, so that the mentioned measures have immediately become embroiled in court conflict. At the same time, a model for effectively changing the norms of society by law exists in form of Title IX of the civil rights laws, which has branched out from the ex-post correction of individual sex discrimination in public education, to a society-wide preventive program to change behavior, minds, and norms (see Melnick 2018).

It is important to trace this development because it shows the pivotal importance of the civil rights bureaucracy to push and implement ideas that show the imprint of the identity left and that clearly have illiberal implications. It started with a 2014 White House campaign against epidemic "rape and sexual assault" on campus, which claimed that "one in five" female college students were or had been the victims—a rather inflated figure, akin to a moral panic, that would require ten million sexually violated college women over a sixteen-year period (Melnick 2018, 149). According to a White House report, "(s)ex assault is pervasive because our culture still allows it to persist. According to the experts, violence prevention can't just focus on the perpetrators and the survivors. It has to involve everyone" (in ibid., 165). To avoid the risk of losing federal funding, colleges and universities have built up, in record speed, what two legal scholars call a "sex bureaucracy" (Gersen and Suk 2016). It not only goes against individual acts of sexual violence but "regulate(s) ordinary sex" for everyone, in laborious detail; in one curious instance, it includes "foreplay" instruction (ibid., 882, 929). As a result, "sexual assault" has become equated with "anything other than enthusiastic,

240   POLITICAL NEOLIBERALISM

excited, creative, and imaginative sexual agreement" (ibid., 930). Feminist lawyer Catherine MacKinnon has set the mark: "I call it rape whenever a woman has sex and feels violated" (ibid., 903, fn.105).

The important matter is an expanded understanding of what is "violence" and "assault,"[122] whose flip side is the expectation of excessive correctness on the part of everyone. Not in content but in form, this is akin to the attitude that transgender (more precisely, the elites that speak for them) expect(s) society to adopt. Similar to the world of Kendi (2019), in which there are only "racists" or "antiracists," the sex bureaucracy growing out of Title IX divides the world into perpetrators and virtuosi, with no place for the ordinary. As the US federal government describes the purpose of "primary prevention programs" on campus, they are for "the promotion of positive and healthy behaviors that foster healthy, mutually respectful relationships and sexuality, encourage safe bystander intervention, and seek to change behaviour and social norms in healthy and safe directions" (in Gerson and Suk 2016, 912).[123] The federal government's 2016 "Dear Colleague Letter on Transgender Students" is an extension of this logic. It seeks "to create and sustain inclusive, supportive, safe, and non-discriminatory communities for all students," and does so in enacting the gender identity ideology by means of state power.[124] For one of its authors, Vanita Gupta, the "project of civil rights" demands nothing less than "being bold, . . . going against the grain of current-day popular thinking . . . [This means using power] to bend the arc of history itself . . . harnessing the law as a force for positive change" (quoted in Melnick 2018, 241).

It is ironic that the Land of the Free has gone the extra mile in "harnessing the law for positive change," which is a friendly term for legislating morality, a no-go from a liberal point of view. Short of the law, the societal imposition of transgender norms, as defined by their elites, has progressed through the soft force of "moral obligation" (Stock 2021, ch. 1), whose reverse is the shaming of violators or non-followers. Stonewall's list of "Diversity Champions" is impressively long. It includes, in the United Kingdom alone, "blue-chip companies, political parties, local authorities, government departments such as the Department for Education, schools, most universities, newspapers and broadcasters, police and armed forces, arts organisations, the Crown Prosecution Service, the Equality and Human Rights Commission, and many other major national bodies" (ibid., ch. 6). Members of the Stonewall list commit themselves to "allow anyone to access facilities, spaces and groups which align with their gender identity" (ibid.), and of course to adopt the dominant view of what constitutes gender identity in the first. As to the motivation of the corporate world to be on top of the list, the answer is simple: "Rainbow lanyards, pronoun badges and 'all-gender' toilets cost little or nothing" (Joyce 2021, ch. 11). And action on the "social justice" front may divert attention from distinctly less enthusiasm for economic justice, which would require paying corporate taxes.[125]

Conclusion

A useful contrast between right and left identity politics has been drawn by Wolfgang Thierse, a senior German Social Democrat and previous president of the Bundestag: "More than ever, we live in an ethnically, culturally, and religiously plural society. In this society, diversity is not the goal but a factual basis of our democracy and our culture. To *deny this fact* or wanting to reverse it, is the fatal, even dangerous feature of right identity politics. Reversely, to *elevate this fact* into a social and cultural program, is in my view the problem of left identity politics."[126] Underneath this appositely dual critique of left and right identity politics is a concern about "societal integration" (*gesellschaftlicher Zusammenhalt*), which in Thierse's view requires the "recognition of rules and obligations," as well as the "acceptance of majority decisions." What seems both reasonable and obvious, nevertheless provoked a "shit storm" (Thierse) in the social media,[127] and the SPD leadership at the time distanced itself from Thierse's views—of course, not because of his critique of the right but of the left variant of identity politics.

This vignette impressively demonstrates the discursive hegemony of left identity politics. It also forces us to qualify seeing the latter as an expression of "rupture" rather than of the "order" of neoliberal societies. In fact, it is a mark of left identity politics that its more orderly or institutionalized forms, which we discussed earlier in terms of "neoliberal multiculturalism" (see Chapter 3), are exceedingly difficult to distinguish from its radically critical and counter-establishment forms, which have been the focus of this chapter. *Both* have taken hold *within* dominant institutions, despite the oppositionist rhetoric of the identity left. This is much in contrast to the populist right, which, for good or bad, has remained largely outside of dominant institutions (except when winning the occasional elections).[128] The "woke religion," as Braunstein may certainly exaggerate but does not miss the point, is "the official discourse of our elites" (2022, intro).

242 POLITICAL NEOLIBERALISM

A common feature of antiracism and transgender is their "social justice" orientation, which in the pejorative view of their critics is held and exercised by "warriors." The martial language deflects from the peculiarity of left identity politics to be prominently based in the least martial of all institutions, the academy. "We all live on campus now" (Sullivan 2018), because universities—in particular the best of them—are the site from which the war against "white supremacy," "white privilege," "rape culture," and so on is mainly conducted. The students who are both enlisted in and driving this war are the ruling elites of tomorrow, so that the "danger of drifting away from liberal democracy" (ibid.) is real. And "polarization has made this worse," as Andrew Sullivan (ibid.) adds with respect to the extreme (but not singular) American scene, "because on the left, moderation now seems like a surrender to white nationalism, and because on the right, white identity politics has overwhelmed moderate conservatism."

The Danish legal philosopher and European high court justice Alf Ross once noted that "(t)o invoke justice is the same thing as banging on the table: an emotional expression which turns one's demand into an absolute postulate. That is no proper way to mutual understanding. It is impossible to have a rational discussion with a man who mobilizes 'justice', because he says nothing that can be argued for or against" (quoted by Miller 1999, 274, fn.2). While friendlier to the idea of "social justice," David Miller (1995, 140) importantly observes that it requires the "trust" that one's support for a "just demand on this occasion" will be reciprocated in the future; which, in turn, requires "solidarity not merely within groups but across them." One must conclude that the "social justice" claims examined in this chapter fall short of this, and by not a few inches. Pluckrose and Lindsay call "social justice scholarship and thought" a new stage in the development of postmodernism, coming into its own not before the 2010s, and in which postmodernism freezes into capital-letter "Theory" and "Truth" that beg no compromise: "legitimate disagreement is not an option" (2020, 198). This pushes social justice scholarship closer to "religious ideology" (ibid.) than to theory as conventionally understood, that is, as necessarily in the plural form of "conjectures and refutations" (Popper 1962).

Hence, Braunstein's polemic of "woke religion" (2022), which he examined along the same examples as we did in this chapter: antiracism and transgender. Although Braunstein notices an important difference between the two: he calls antiracism a "religion against universalism," while transgender is a "religion against reality." In both directions, antiracism and

THE IDENTITY LEFT   243

transgender are recognizably products of a neoliberal order. Antiracism reflects, and reinforces, a fragmenting of society, the denigration of shared bonds and public status, such as citizenship, which might cut down to size, and reconcile, conflicting private and group interests. Daniel Rodgers (2011, 261) appositely called the post-1980s neoliberal era an "age of fracture": "Three decades in which the very language of society had grown thinner, in which the 'little platoons' of freely choosing selves commanded more and more of the social imagination, in which block identities (of race, gender) seemed to have grown more fractured and fluid."

Transgender also fits Rodgers's description of "freely choosing selves," though projecting an unbound optimism about "transhuman" and "self-made" possibilities that differs markedly from the stark pessimism of racially frozen societies whose reductive view of future is a present cleansed of the remains of past injustice. Neoliberalism, one scholar observed (Ludwig 2016, 418), has "coincided with more liberal, tolerant, inclusive, and diverse sexual policies," expressed in "rainbow" and "gay capitals" (like Berlin and Tel Aviv, respectively), and "One Love" binds on the arms of footballers who are among the highest earners on the planet. And "rainbow families," while incontrovertible from a liberal (non-discriminatory) point of view, *also* strengthen "an ideal of an anti-social society by expanding marriage and its underlying ideal of privatizing social responsibilities" (ibid., 421f).

While antiracism and transgender have their respective pieties and sacrileges, they share a tension between enlarged "choice" and a sense of "being born this way," which is the mark of the "unsettled identities" of our time (Brubaker 2016a). It is thus apposite to close this chapter with a closer look at the ultimate taboo, which is the view that if changing one's gender is possible, it should also be possible to change one's race. Rebecca Tuvel (2017), a junior philosophy professor, has made this case, on logically impeccable and strenuously "respectful" grounds, to use a favorite adjective of the identity left: "Since we should accept transgender individuals' decisions to change sexes," mainly in recognition of their right to self-identification, "we should also accept transracial individuals' decisions to change races" (ibid., 264).

The furious response to Tuvel's compelling "defense of transracialism" (2017) has been called a "modern-day witch hunt," and this is no understatement.[129] A vitriolic "open letter" signed by over five hundred academics demanded that Tuvel's peer-reviewed article be "retracted" from *Hypatia*, the academic journal that had published it, and the majority of its editorial board members issued a "profound apology" for the "harm" and "violence" that the article caused to the aggrieved transgender and racial minority "communities," stating that it "should not have been published."[130] The protest letter noted that Tuvel "used vocabulary and frameworks not recognized, accepted, or adopted by the conventions of the relevant subfields"—the cited examples being "biological sex," "male genitals," and "transgenderism" (strangely, the parallel "transracialism" in the title of her paper, which might be equally disliked for its potentially pejorative "ism," went uncommented). The obsession with words shows the identity left's belief in the performative power of language, which a critic found akin to "magical thinking" (Braunstein 2022, ch. 2).

Tuvel (2017, 272) made her case from a (John Stuart) "Millian" perspective, that "we should encourage 'different experiments in living' and not interfere with others' liberty unless doing so would prevent harm to others." Mill's classic liberal insight must be considered the main casualty of left (and right) identity politics.

III
OUTLOOK

Chapter 6
End of Neoliberalism?

The COVID-19 Pandemic, and After

When does neoliberalism end? The 2008 Financial Crisis failed to do much in this respect. Some argue that the COVID-19 pandemic, raging across much of the planet for at least two full years between 2020 and 2022, was that moment, which the philosopher John Gray (2020b) declared a "turning point in history." Barely two weeks after much of the world population was sent into "lockdown," which is a term that perversely originated in the prison sector, Shlomo Avineri, the eminent Israeli political scientist, deemed that the "coronavirus has killed neoliberalism," because now "everyone looks to the state."[1] A younger German political analyst had the same reflex, finding that "the age of neoliberalism, in terms of the primacy of market interests over all other social interests, is coming to an end."[2] After four decades of "neoliberal scepticism about the state," he marvels, it is clear that "nation states still have enormous creative power." Indeed: "(W)hen was the last time the capitalist machine was halted in order to protect the old and the sick?"[3] Even in global capitalism's premier print medium, *Financial Times*, one could read that "the administrative state is poised for a comeback," considering the urgent "necessity of public expertise, public infrastructure, brute public coercion."[4] Again in the *Financial Times*, its senior editorialist, Martin Wolf, upped the ante by pronouncing the "return to the idea of citizenship," because "the first concern of democratic states is the welfare of all their citizens."[5]

In retrospect, it is astonishing that the most severe restrictions of individual freedoms ever imposed in peacetime on liberal societies, with most of their members effectively put under some form of house arrest, would garner so much enthusiasm. Much of the end-of-neoliberalism fanfare rests on a flawed understanding of neoliberalism, as if it ever meant the absence of the state. In reality, the "strong state" had from the beginning been the guardian of the "free economy" that the neoliberal movement set out to build (Gamble 1988; applied to the pandemic, see Šumonja 2020, 215).

Political Neoliberalism. Christian Joppke, Oxford University Press. © Oxford University Press (2025).
DOI: 10.1093/oso/9780197801918.003.0007

248 POLITICAL NEOLIBERALISM

In this vein, one might argue that the state's heavy-handed crisis management, with a double strategy of lockdown followed by mass vaccination, to which "no alternative" was permitted, was a return to the "authoritarian liberalism" that some (like Wilkinson 2021) had always deemed to be the nucleus of neoliberalism (for detecting "authoritarian liberalism" in pandemic surveillance, see Tréguer 2021). The pandemic crisis also fits the picture of "disaster capitalism," in which the "power of shock" is deployed to create "exciting market opportunities" (Klein 2007, 6)—except that now we are dealing not with manufactured but natural disaster. Naomi Klein (2020) still seized the opportunity, declaring lockdown the moment of a "Screen New Deal." Indeed, in May 2020, the Governor of New York, Andrew Cuomo, partnered with tech billionaires Bill Gates and Eric Schmidt (the former Google chief and chair of the National Security Commission on Artificial Intelligence) to push for "a future economy and education system based on tele-everything." Also edging in this direction, German sociologist Richard Münch (2022, 72) sees in pandemic management a "new form of rule" fed by "ever new threats," dubbed "benevolent paternalism," which to him is "the sociologically decisive about the Corona pandemic."

There are at least three ways in which neoliberalism is implicated with the COVID-19 pandemic: with respect to its *causes*, its *political management*, and its *long-term effects*.

With respect to the pandemic's *causes*, already the earliest theory of zoonotic transmission suggested a "plague unleashed by heedless global growth and the massive flywheel of financial accumulation" (Tooze 2021, intro). The neoliberal connection is even more obvious in the alternative theory of a laboratory accident, which initially was denounced as "conspiracy" and cancelled in the social media (including Facebook and Twitter),[6] but in the meantime is back on the table.[7] According to this theory, the virus escaped from the Wuhan Institute of Virology, a biotech laboratory in Wuhan, China, that was engaged in gene-manipulating "gain-of-function" research. Such research is prohibited in the United States for its great risks but was co-financed by its federal government (and the European Union) in said laboratory under a less choosy jurisdiction—which explains why this theory had to be suppressed at all cost.[8] Gain-of-function research serves the development of new vaccines, including the one that was eventually proffered as remedy to the pandemic. If the "lab-leak" theory is confirmed, as it recently was in a report of the U.S. House of Representatives (2024), there would be a perfect circularity between the (narrowly human and vaccine-related) causes and the (vaccine-centric) solution to the pandemic, somewhat defying a grand interpretation of the latter as "first comprehensive crisis of the age of the Anthropocene" (Tooze 2021, intro).

With respect to the pandemic's *political management*, Rogers Brubaker commented that it would be a "tricky thing" to show that a "heavy-handed COVID crisis management," with its "technocratic-authoritarian elements," followed "from neoliberalism per se."[9] This is correct. Of course, there are other than neoliberal elements to it, most notably calling the state of exception to avert a perceived fundamental threat to human life and society in a context of great uncertainty. In this mode, science-and-technology studies doyen Sheila Jasanoff (2020, par. 4) argues that pandemic management per se is an instance of "public health sovereignty," in which people are demoted from acting "social and political subjects" to "biomedical subjects, more acted upon than acting." Similarly, social historian Peter Baldwin (2021, 10), in one of the first comparative studies of state responses to the COVID-19 pandemic,[10] sees pandemics as "first-order political events," in which there is an "immediate faceoff between the community's obligation to safeguard itself and individual citizens' claims not to be sacrificed in the process." In a "primordially political situation," Baldwin argues, there is simply no choice but to trample on individual freedoms. In addition, he cites an etiological factor that is specific to the Corona virus: its "highly contagious" nature, with a high degree of transmission by "asymptomatic" carriers, in his view, precluded a milder or "voluntary" approach, and instead required "the authorities to lock up everyone" (ibid., 173).

Compatible with these views, a "political sociology perspective" suggested by Austrian sociologist Klaus Kraemer (2022, 28, 5), makes the need for "action under uncertainty" the starting-point for the "overextension of pandemic management," which became generalized and sustained by cross-state "isomorphism" and intra-state "path dependency," respectively, among other mechanisms. German social theorist Münch adds to this the toolbox of Georg Simmel's sociology of conflict, according to which an external threat conditions an internal closing of ranks and eradication of critics, leading to further conflict escalation, polarization, and enforced conformity—the pandemic "erosion of democracy" and, in particular, the state-level scapegoating of the "unvaccinated" for a pandemic that would not end, are explicable in these terms.[11]

However, the drawback of such generic politics-cum-sociology master frames is to be at heart apologetic, to redescribe what happened as "without

250   POLITICAL NEOLIBERALISM

alternative," thus unwittingly affirming the dominant state rhetoric. Their nucleus is the presumption of a "deadly epidemic" (Baldwin 2021, 172). Shared by most social science accounts of COVID-19 management to this day, except a few critical ones,[12] it naturalizes the state's response to the pandemic as the only possible, at least only humanely acceptable response. This may yield highly twisted accounts, such as by political scientist Jan Zielonka (2020). On the one hand, he bemoans that "(o)ur basic rights to privacy, to work, and to move and to associate freely have been brushed aside, by states aspiring to be quasi-absolute powers," deeming this "almost . . . a revolution" (ibid., 1). On the other hand, he lets these "quasi-absolute" states off the hook, by depicting them as "combating a deadly virus" that "could not be treated in a benign manner."

It is obvious that in a strongly naturalizing account, which ignores even the modicum of constructivism that is standard in post-Weberian social science, there is not much factoring in of "neoliberalism."[13] The latter only moves into the picture, at least as a possibility, when arguing that there was nothing natural in the harsh lockdowns imposed by most Western states, and in the compulsory vaccination drive that followed. Lockdown, to begin with, was a historically novel approach pioneered by China in the earliest phase of the COVID-19 pandemic. While this does not sound "neoliberal" at all, its way of being transmitted does have the ring of it. In an unacknowledged instance of "global governance," which is central to the neoliberal playbook, and in which the recommendations of the World Health Organization (WHO) played an important role,[14] lockdown suddenly became considered best practice, in radical departure from previous pandemic practice, by—admittedly—panic-struck states.[15] And they would stick to it, increasingly against the evidence, due to a logic of blame avoidance and path dependence. A lately dissenting member of the British public health establishment called it the "lazy solution": governments "couldn't change course because to do so would be admission that they'd taken the wrong path to begin with. Instead, they doubled down and imposed lockdown again" (Woolhouse 2022, 255).

While the neoliberalism factor in lockdown is and will remain subject to debate, it is incontrovertibly in place when considering the complement to lockdown, which is rapid vaccine development and (quasi-)compulsory mass vaccination. From the start, the latter was considered the only way out of the pandemic (and out of lockdown as the first "no alternative" response). The vaccine part of the story is one of "public–private partnerships," involving "revolving doors" and interest collusion between the public and the private sectors,[16] whose dividing line is notoriously difficult to draw in the neoliberal order.

Finally, with respect to the *long-term effects* of the pandemic, we move from the question of neoliberalism "in" to that of neoliberalism "after" the pandemic. Swedish sociology polymath Göran Therborn (2022) thinks that neoliberalism has merely been an "interlude": "(A)fter four decades its hegemony is now ending," as a combined result of the 2008 Financial Crisis, the rise of China, and COVID-19 (ibid., 36). But then he *also* sees the coming of another phase of "ruthless capitalism," "yet to be baptized," although he already finds for it the words "digital-tech finance capitalism . . . within state-defined geopolitical parameters" (ibid., 37). Obviously, Therborn equates neoliberalism with "market sovereignty over the entire world," that is, globalization as we knew it before 2020. This indeed is being dented by the post-2020 surge of geopolitical rivalry, by now not only involving America and China, but a belligerent Russia also. It folds the world back from a global market to an arena of armed regional hegemons. However, at domestic level, what Therborn calls "digital-tech finance capitalism" is unquestionably of neoliberal pedigree, and not in need of further baptism. The virtualization of life during the pandemic foregrounded and pushed to a new level the "digital-tech" element in contemporary capitalism and social life at large.

This concluding chapter has two parts. The first seeks to identify and gauge the importance of neoliberal elements in the political management of the COVID-19 pandemic, while the second addresses accelerated digitalization as perhaps the major long-term effect of the pandemic—which in this respect reinforced existing trends rather than creating fundamentally new ones. In the first part, which is on COVID management, I highlight two elements that have been fairly convergent across states: a policy of (differently) strict lockdowns, complemented by state-financed vaccine development and quasi-mandatory mass inoculation. While the neoliberal element is easy to discern in the "public–private" logic of vaccine development and application, it is less obvious in the lockdown strategy. But there is at least a family resemblance of lockdown with the authoritarianism and democracy containment that thrives in a neoliberal order. In the second part, I argue that the digitalization of everything is among the pandemic's most significant long-term impacts on society. In this respect, I first highlight the nature of "digital platforms," in which public functions are served by private actors, Big Tech, which has been a driving force throughout post-1990s

252 POLITICAL NEOLIBERALISM

neoliberalism; followed by mapping the emergent dystopia of an "untact society," in which much of social life goes virtual, but with the paradoxical consequence that only a small elite may continue to enjoy what a tech mogul has cynically called "reality privilege"; and I close with looking at the makings of a "digital identity," with the barcoded COVID-19 vaccine passports as prototype. The vaccine passports may foreshadow a new form of behavior-conditional citizenship in liberal lands, which is pioneered by China's social credit system. Overall, neoliberalism is all but dead. Having long eroded liberalism's lexically second principle, equality, it is now putting at risk its first principle as well, which is freedom.

The COVID-19 Doxa

"Normal" social science accounts of state responses to the COVID-19 pandemic have stressed their variations and sought to explain them. There is nothing wrong with this. Isn't all social science variation-finding and - explaining, as it deals with a reality that is contingent and thus, in the human domain, historical; that is, a reality that is of necessity varied? Baldwin (2021: abstract) made a start, arguing that "countries have responded very differently" to the "same threat." He distinguishes between three different state responses: *targeted quarantine*, attributing this response to China, Taiwan, Singapore, and the Antipodes; attempted *suppression* of the virus, also known as lockdown, favored by "most nations" because they were "too late for targeted quarantine"; and *hands-off mitigation*, which implies minimal restrictions and the favoring of voluntarism, while betting on the arrival of natural herd immunity—the approach of a motley bunch of states, autocracies like Nicaragua, Belarus, and Turkmenistan, but also, and importantly, Sweden. In retrospect, Baldwin's quarantine versus lockdown distinction seems overdrawn, because drastic freedom restrictions are characteristic of both approaches; and quarantine eventually ended in lockdown, as in China, which invented the thing. Baldwin's scorn is for mitigation, and he misses no opportunity to attack the Swedes for it: they took the "wrong direction" (ibid., 273); to arrive at "herd immunity" through "voluntary compliance" is a "fatal contradiction" (ibid., 154);[17] and he not only calls natural herd immunity "unethical" (in this following the WHO), but also ridicules the Swedes for it: "like a dog with a bone, they would not let [it] go" (ibid.). Of course, Baldwin *must* single out the Swedes' voluntarist approach for loathing to reconcile his variation-finding social science exercise with his naturalist (and variety-suppressing) presumption that the nature of the virus itself required to "lock up everyone" (ibid., 173). Baldwin's concerted scorn for voluntarism, in turn, relativizes his distinction between quarantine and virus suppression, which on Baldwin's own premises must amount to much the same, "to lock up everyone."

Not least because COVID-19 immediately opened up lavish funding opportunities, there has been an immediate rush of political science studies, almost all of them examining "variation in policy responses" (Toshkov et al. 2022,1009). Many of them focus on the role of scientific expertise, which rarely before had played such a big role in political decision-making, the latter removed from democratic into hastily assembled and secretive executive venues.[18]

To give a flavor for the normal political science of COVID-19, Dimiter Toskhov and colleagues (2022) are interested in the "speed" of school closures and of imposing national lockdowns, explaining fast-moving by a combination of factors: a high level of centralization (even if "government effectiveness" is low, as in Eastern Europe); the existence of separate health ministries (and their political heads being doctors); and—curiously—right-wingers constituting the government. This presupposes and leaves undiscussed that schools *were* closed and that lockdowns *were* imposed, which are the *really* interesting facts without precedence that require explanation.

Similarly, Sarah Engler and colleagues (2021, 1089), when examining a "trade-off" between "public health" and "fundamental democratic principles" in thirty-four European countries, find that "variation . . . is remarkable." As one would expect, the authors also find that "strong protection of democratic principles already established in 'normal' times makes governments more reluctant to opt for restrictive policies" (ibid., 1077). However, what they leave unaddressed is that "restrictive policies" were nevertheless the norm, even if some were less severe than others, the less severe policies unsurprisingly found in countries with strong "protection of individual liberties."[19] Furthermore, in the presumed trade-off between public health and democracy, it remains unexamined what constitutes "public health" in the first; it is simply assumed that the virus concern may fill it up completely, as it did. But it is these black boxes: of "restrictive policies" in the pursuit of "public health," the latter understood by the authors in the same narrow sense as by the public authorities, that need to be filled.[20]

254 POLITICAL NEOLIBERALISM

The point of these exercises is to find out which countries did "better" or "worse" in various respects, such as efficiency ("saving lives") or compliance with democratic norms. However, the most elaborate and permanently updated exercise in describing and analyzing "variation in government responses to COVID-19," which covers 185 countries between January 2020 and December 2022 (in the latest version), by a team of Oxford political scientists (Hale et al. 2023), finds it "impossible to provide a comprehensive assessment of which countries have fared better or worse" (ibid., 20). Somewhat at odds with its variation-finding claim, the study further observes that initially "most governments implemented similar policies within a similar timeframe," namely "stringent policies," even though policies "eventually diverged, particularly in decisions to roll back measures" (ibid., 11, 12). And it argues that initially stringent policies spread by way of "copycat-effect," in a situation of "little information beyond news reports from China and northern Italy" (ibid., 12).

That states copied one another in a moment of panic is an entirely plausible assumption, on which there is agreement in the literature. A comprehensive examination of OECD countries' early pandemic responses found that "governments follow the lead of others and base their decisions on what other countries do" (Sebhatu et al. 2020, 21,201), confirming a tenet of organizational sociology that "mimicry is a common response among decision-makers when the effect of a decision is uncertain" (ibid.). These authors note that four out of five typical "non-pharmaceutical interventions" (NPI), such as school closures, business closures, and travel restrictions, spread to 80 percent of OECD countries within just two weeks in March 2020, adding that "the homogeneity in timing of adoption is striking" (ibid.).

However, this raises the question of the first move(r), and how it arrived that lockdown, a historically unprecedented measure, happened to be the first move, particularly in a liberal society.

With the mentioned exceptions, mainstream social science, in its preoccupation with variation-finding, tends to be mute on the *really* interesting aspect of liberal state responses to the COVID-19 pandemic, which is their surprising similarity. In a polemical but thought-provoking work (which led him to be "cancelled" by the media and fellow academics), the French sociologist Laurent Mucchielli (2022a) speaks of a *Doxa du Covid* (Covid Doxa). He summarizes it in five points, with a focus on France but—I submit—applicable elsewhere. First, the pandemic has been taken, from the start and with no relenting in its two-year-plus duration, as a fundamental panhuman threat, even though its lethality, also from beginning to end, was highly correlated with old age and comorbidity. Secondly, a medical solution to the virus was instantly precluded by the diction that "no therapy is possible." Thirdly, as long as no vaccine was available (whose development was in process before a pandemic was officially declared), a political solution: lockdown (an umbrella term for business and school closures and society-wide distancing rules, in the extreme confinement at home of the entire population), was favored over the medical and more proportionate and targeted measures favored in previous pandemic responses. Fourthly, this mainly political (rather than medical) crisis response was accompanied by a strategy of rapid vaccine development followed by mass inoculation, which in most places was not legally (for most) but factually obligatory because refusing to be vaccinated would lead to one's exclusion from public life. Last and not least, the lockdown-plus-mass-vaccination strategy was turned into a "doxa" by the systematic suppression of critique, which became denounced as *complotisme* and conspiracy-thinking. Apart from the new social media, which were all too eager to demonstrate their public-mindedness (as some of them, like Facebook, had just come on trial for their private-data extracting business model), the legacy media played a significant part in this. Furthermore, and curiously, the political left was everywhere more insistent on restrictiveness than the right, and opposition to the Covid Doxa was associated with "libertarian" and "right-wing" positions. What Toby Green and Thomas Fazi (2023, 98) call the "Covid Consensus," in particular on lockdown, was "an article of faith, supported by the overwhelming majority of self-defined progressive public opinion."

Surprisingly, when the pandemic was over, in late May 2022, Gates, the billionaire founder of Microsoft whose foundation money and influence had done much to make vaccine development the dominant global health strategy long before the COVID-19 pandemic, had this to say about the Corona virus: in the early days, he muses, "we didn't understand that it's a fairly low fatality rate and that it's a disease mainly of the elderly, kind of like the flu."[21] This is the exact opposite of the Covid Doxa, and the type of thinking that the latter was meant to stamp out. How this was possible in a liberal society remains a puzzle that this chapter cannot claim to resolve, but perhaps to assemble a few necessary pieces for it.

World Governance

A modicum of world governance, not in a formal-legal but informal-discursive sense of an established global public health network sounding out and circulating "best practice," was one important element in explaining states' overall similar COVID-19 responses, in particular lockdown. China's early success in bringing the first COVID-19 wave down in this way, at least in its official presentation,[22] made it the best practice for others to follow. This was hammered down by a WHO that declared the Chinese not only the "best," but, a notch stronger, "*the only measures* that are currently proven to interrupt or minimize transmission claims" (in Green and Fazi 2023, 69).

But let us step back a bit in time. On January 17, 2020, the Johns Hopkins Center for Health Security, the World Economic Forum, and the Gates Foundation jointly published a "Call to Action" that summarizes the wisdom of "Event 201," a three-hour fictional pandemic response exercise that had taken place a few months ago, in mid-October 2019, in a New York luxury hotel. It involved top corporate and political executives from around the world. The belated publication of the results—at the exact onset of the real thing and just ahead of the world's foremost business meeting in Davos—is ominous. While not mentioning the incipient COVID-19 crisis with a single word, the January 2020 Call to Action opened with words whose intended reference was obvious: "The next severe pandemic will not only cause great illness and loss of life but could also trigger major cascading economic and societal consequences that could contribute greatly to global impact and suffering. Efforts to prevent such consequences or respond to them as they unfold will require unprecedented levels of collaboration between governments, international organizations, and the private sector." In short, "Public–Private Cooperation for Pandemic Preparedness and Response" was asked for, invoking one of political neoliberalism's key notions, which is also the title of this Call to Action.[23]

Event 201 was only the latest in a series of similar biomedical crisis exercises that had taken place over the past twenty years, with scare names such as Dark Winter (in 2001), Atlantic Storm (in 2005), and Clade X (in 2018). These exercises, all American-led but with high-level international political, corporate, and media participation, marked the rise of "biosecurity" as a major focus of the US military-industrial complex, post-1989. At this precise point in time, terrorists replaced Communism as the enemy to beat or guard against—the "threat blank" left by the end of the Cold War had to be

END OF NEOLIBERALISM? 257

filled, as US Senator Sam Nunn put it (Lakoff 2017, 151f). Because biological weapons are prohibited under international law, biosecurity from the start occupied an "obscure grey zone of threat defence and threat production," as a German chronicler stated (Schreyer 2020, 41). The development of new vaccines against new viruses was unfailingly the proposed solution in these threat scenarios, whose initial focus on sinister forces gradually shifted to natural causes. The fictitious Event 201 pandemic, for instance, which almost overlapped with the real one, originated in a "zoonotic corona virus" jumping from bats to pigs to humans—life would imitate art just a few months later (or at that time had already, because the real Corona virus is suspected to have circulated in Wuhan as early as September 2019; that is, *before* Event 201). As Paul Schreyer described the Event 201 scenario, it mixes the themes of "anxiety, mass death, state of emergency, state overload, freedom restrictions, vaccine procurement, pharma regulation, and media strategy" (ibid., 97). What was then fiction eerily anticipated the unfolding COVID-19 crisis, in whose management many of the Event 201 participants would actually take active and not minor roles. In another premonition of things to come, the Event 201 recommendations include the call on "(g)overnments and the private sector (to) assign a greater priority to developing methods to combat mis- and disinformation," which "will require developing the ability to flood media with fast, accurate, and consistent information."[24] The rather cynical advice to "flood media" (reminiscent of former Trump counselor Stephen Bannon's words to "flood the zone") reads like a blueprint of the Covid Doxa that most Western states would roll-out from March 2020.

Most importantly, the pandemic war games, conducted between 2001 and 2019, helped build a US-led but global personal and organizational public health infrastructure, which included Chinese officials, as in Event 201.[25] The pre-existence of this infrastructure is an important element in explaining the remarkably similar responses when the *Ernstfall* happened, in the first trimester of 2020, particularly with respect to the immediate notion that only a vaccine could show the way out of the crisis. In April 2020, Gates, perhaps the single most influential individual in the unfolding COVID-19 drama, dwarfing the weight of most states (which itself is a noteworthy fact inseparable from four decades of neoliberalism), made this astonishing statement to BBC: "Now here we are. We didn't simulate this, we didn't practice, so both the health policies and economic policies, we find ourselves in uncharted territory" (quoted in Kennedy 2021, ch. 2). Considering Gates'

258   POLITICAL NEOLIBERALISM

active input not only in Event 201, but in some of the previous pandemic simulations as well, this statement is dubious.

The point of "world governance," of which the Geneva-based World Economic Forum (WEF) is an ardent advocate, is to include corporate actors as "equal participants," and not only as lobbyists, to constitute "multi-stakeholder groups" and "public–private partnerships," the preferred jargon not only in Geneva (see Häring 2021, part 1).

Gates is a prominent case in point. He advertised "global corporate citizenship," at a WEF meeting back in 2009. Since the mid-1990s already, Gates had embraced philanthropy of a specific sort. What since 2000 has been the "Bill and Melinda Gates Foundation," in direct and indirect ways, is today the single biggest financial contributor to the WHO, but also holding stock and bonds in the pharma companies Merck, Pfizer, Novartis, Sanofi, and others. Hence it is an instance of "philantrocapitalism," appositely described by Linsey McGoey (2015, conclusion) as "here to save the world—as long as the world yields to their interests." Investing in vaccine development, as Gates declared to a US news station at the 2019 WEF annual meeting in Davos, brings a twenty-to-one return for each dollar.[26] Through the GAVI vaccine alliance and Global Fund (the latter mainly fighting AIDS), the Gates foundation was instrumental in reorienting global health policy from a "miasmic" concern for the environmental and social causes of disease and building comprehensive health systems, particularly in less developed countries, to an obsession with a single "germ" to be eradicated by a vaccine.[27]

One immediately sees the imprint of tech "solutionism" (Morozov 2013). As a critic put it, the Gates Foundation has a "narrowly conceived understanding of health as the product of technical interventions divorced from economic, social, and political contexts."[28] Political scientist Peter Hägel (2020, 214) describes the "Gates approach" in similar terms: "(H)is 'vertical' approach to global health is concentrated on fighting infectious diseases, sidelining strategies that focus more on the socioeconomic determinants of health and the building of comprehensive primary healthcare systems."[29] Already preceding the new millennium, what initially was just the "William H. Gates Foundation" (without his wife's name attached to it) had played a "key early role" in the shift of the WHO from a focus on "primary health schemes" to "managing specific diseases" (HIV/AIDS, malaria, tuberculosis) within a "public–private partnership" frame, through supporting the organization with $1.7 billion USD between 1998 and 2000 (Lakoff 2017, 74–75).

END OF NEOLIBERALISM? 259

Since his refashioning from businessman to "Philanthropist-in-Chief"[30], Gates has acquired a controlling influence on the WHO—the chronicler of *Billionaires in World Politics* calls him the "unofficial minister of global health" (Hägel 2020, 212). In 2005, Gates became the first ever private individual to address the World Health Assembly (WHA), which consists of the WHO member states' health ministers. And he was given a second opportunity in 2011, which he used for an urgent call for vaccine development: "All 193 member states, you must make vaccines a central focus of your health systems," he admonished the audience.[31] Already a year earlier, Gates had launched the "Decade of Vaccines," with a $10 billion USD pledge at the WEF meeting in Davos (Hägel 2020, 205). After his 2011 WHA appearance in Geneva, the WHA promptly announced the "Global Vaccine Action Plan 2011–2020," as a result of which over half of the WHO budget has been diverted into vaccines.

The current WHO chair, Tedros Ghebreyesus, when appointed in 2017, may be considered Gates's candidate, considering that he previously had headed his GAVI and Global Fund initiatives. When the Corona crisis acquired momentum, Gates stepped down from the Board of Directors of Microsoft to launch a media and political campaign for fast and massive vaccine development. In an article published in the *New England Journal of Medicine* in April 2020, he described COVID-19 as a "once-in-a-century pathogen" that "can kill healthy adults in addition to elderly people with existing health problems" (Gates 2020, 1677)—this careful formulation implicitly suggesting that "elderly people" were *mostly* at risk, which in fact had been known from the beginning.[32] "Billions of dollars" were needed from governments, Gates demanded, in a "partnership between the public and private sectors," to "minimize risk for pharmaceutical companies and get them to jump in with both feet," because "pandemic products are extraordinarily high-risk investments" (ibid., 1678).

This reads like a quote from University College London economist Mariana Mazzucato's acclaimed *Entrepreneurial State* (2013), minus her critical diction. In this study, Mazzucato attacked as "parasitic" and "free-riding" the fact that in advanced technology sectors, including pharmaceutics, risks are "socialized" while rewards are "privatized," the state shouldering the high-risk venture, while companies happily take the reward (such as cashing-in on high-priced patented drugs). The reward, in turn, is mostly not reinvested but used for "share buybacks," to increase the stock market value of the company.[33]

260 POLITICAL NEOLIBERALISM

While Gates's focus was clearly on profitable vaccines,[34] he also came around in favor of lockdown. China "did a lot of things right at the beginning," Gates commented, especially to "shut down completely"; there was just "no alternative to this agenda" (quoted in Green and Fazi 2023, 162).

To calibrate the role of the WHO in shaping the COVID-19 response, it is worth recalling its problematic and widely criticized role in COVID-19's predecessor pandemic, the 2009 Hong Kong Swine Flu. Admittedly dealing with a far less contagious and dangerous virus than the one causing the 2020 pandemic, the WHO declared the Hong Kong flu a "pandemic" on the basis of a lightened definition of "pandemic," issued shortly before the contested event. According to the new definition, a pandemic no longer required "enormous numbers of deaths and illness"; instead, an extended geographic spread was sufficient. Only on that basis could the WHO declare a "pandemic" on June 11, 2009, maintaining its call over a long period, at the highest threat level of "6," which signifies a "full global pandemic" (see Lakoff 2017, 104). However, this was "against the evidence," as a 2010 Council of Europe (CoE) parliamentary assembly inquiry concluded (Flynn 2010, 2). The CoE parliamentary assembly resolution that had called for this inquiry is strongly worded: "In order to promote their patented drugs and vaccines against flu, pharmaceutical companies influenced scientists and official agencies, responsible for public health standards to alarm governments worldwide and make them squander tight health resources for inefficient vaccine strategies and needlessly expose millions of healthy people to the risk of an unknown amount of side-effects of insufficiently tested vaccines."[35]

The CoE's more cautiously worded final report noted a "disparity between the relatively mild unfolding of the influenza and the actions taken at European and national level" (Flynn 2010, 2). Foreshadowing a widespread government practice during COVID-19, the report also noted that many countries didn't distinguish "dying with swine flu" and "dying of swine flu" (ibid., 3). Mostly, however, the report queried whether the "development of new vaccines," which was immediately made the focus of state response, was "absolutely required" (ibid.). It noted the "(p)ossible influence of the pharmaceutical industry on public health decisions and conflicts of interest of scientific experts involved," considering that "(s)ome members" of the two WHO advisory bodies had "professional links to certain pharmaceutical groups"—further information about which was withheld by the WHO, to "protect their privacy" (ibid., 4). Crucially, the WHO's declaration of a pandemic triggered so-called sleeping contracts or "advance-purchase agreements" between states and "large pharmaceutical groups," guaranteeing them $7 billion to $10 billion USD profits from H1N1 vaccine sales in 2010 (ibid., 4)—small figures if compared with what was at stake in 2021–2022, but nevertheless.

Another element of the 2010 CoE report stands out: it criticized as "generally inappropriate" the fast comparison made at the time with the Spanish Flu of 1918, which promptly popped up again, and immediately, in 2020: "such comparisons ... tended to heighten fear among Europeans" (Flynn 2010, 5). Informed by hugely inflated projections by the influential mathematical biologist Neil Ferguson of Imperial College London,[36] which also would have a repeat-show in 2020, the UK Department of Health expected sixty-five thousand deaths from the swine flu in Britain alone—in reality, there were just 360 by January 2010 (ibid., 8). France counted 263 deaths, far below the seasonal influenza rates that vary between four thousand and six thousand. But huge amounts of vaccines were ordered, most of them for nothing; for instance, the French government ordered ninety-four million doses, while only five million of its citizens agreed to be injected.

The WHO and other public health institutions "'gambled away' some of the confidence the European public has in these highly reputed organisations," the CoE report (Flynn 2010, 18) summarizes what in retrospect has widely been considered a "false pandemic." At least these are the words of Wolfgang Wodarg[37], chair of the responsible CoE parliamentary assembly Health Committee, who called the matter "one of the greatest medicine scandals of the Century."[38] When COVID-19 arrived, all this was forgotten.[39]

Lockdown

At the onset of the COVID-19 pandemic, the vaccine fixation was in place. But not lockdown. This was new. To understand the enormity of it, it is worth recalling previous pandemic responses, which were altogether different. They may be summarized as "focused protection."

This is also the name of the alternative to lockdown proposed in the Great Barrington Declaration (GBD), issued in October 2020 by three well-reputed (but subsequently "cancelled") epidemiologists of Oxford, Stanford, and Harvard. The core of the GBD proposal was to "allow those who are at minimal risk of death to live their lives normally to build immunity to

262 POLITICAL NEOLIBERALISM

the virus through natural infection"—so-called herd immunity—"while better protecting those who are at highest risk," which might include targeted vaccination once a vaccine was available, and other measures that were not specified.[40] Obviously more sketch than detailed outline, GBD simply summed up the standard practice in previous pandemics: to protect those most at risk, to close worst-hit areas for short periods, and to introduce moderate distancing measures (as summarized by Green and Fazi 2023, 60). Importantly, and this was the main thrust of GBD, the principles of proportionality, broadly understood cost–benefit balancing, and minimizing the disruption of public life all were to be observed. This is exactly what lockdown did not. It assumed that COVID-19 is alone in the world, equating the entirety of "public health" with virus suppression. As GBD described the likely damages of lockdown, all of which indeed would eventually accrue: "Current lockdown policies are producing devastating effects on short and long-term public health. The results (to name a few) include lower childhood vaccination rates, worsening cardiovascular disease outcomes, fewer cancer screenings and deteriorating mental health—leading to greater excess mortality in years to come, with the working class and younger members of society carrying the heaviest burden. Keeping students out of school is a grave injustice."[41]

When GBD was published, the opposite Covid Doxa was firmly established. Major figures supporting it, especially in the US public health sector, sensed the danger. In an email exchange publicized under the US Freedom of Information Act, Francis Collins, Director of the US National Health Institute, wrote to his colleague Anthony Fauci, "America's Doctor": "This proposal from three fringe epidemiologists . . . seems to be getting a lot of attention . . . There needs to be a quick and devastating published take down of its premises." Collins promptly told *The Washington Post*, "This is not mainstream science. It's dangerous" (quoted in Green and Fazi 2023, 279f). Obviously assisting in the US-led "take down" effort, WHO chief Ghebreyesus declared herd immunity "a concept used for vaccination," and outside of it "scientifically and ethically problematic"[42]—a questionable statement that his organization had to relativize shortly, conceding the possibility of "natural" herd immunity. Much like the Swedish Public Health Authority, which implicitly followed the GBD line of "focused protection" over "lockdown," the GBD proponents, in fact, never considered herd immunity a "strategy" but a natural (although desirable) outcome, much like spring follows upon winter.[43]

But the main charge of the lockdown proponents was that GBD ignored the fate of the old and the vulnerable. This turned GBD's notion of *focused* protection on its head, as it precisely targeted these groups. The charge that GBD slaughtered the old and vulnerable on the altar of the young and healthy wanting to go on with life as normal, was made in the so-called John Snow Memorandum (JSM). This was the final coup in the Collins–Fauci GBD "take-down" effort, which supposedly expressed the "scientific consensus on the COVID-19 pandemic"[44]: "Prolonged isolation of large swathes of the population is practically impossible and highly unethical."[45] But GBD had not asked for it, and least as obligatory measure, as was insinuated in the JSM response. The JSM, which opens with the questionable statement that there were "1 million deaths" among "35 million people (infected) globally" (which would amount to a fatality rate equaling the 1918 Spanish Flu)[46], clearly expresses the double strategy underlying the Covid Doxa. This strategy consisted of "controlling community spread of COVID-19," preferably through the (hopefully) virus-suppressing lockdowns that were attacked by GBD and defended in the JSM counter-attack, "until safe and effective vaccines and therapeutics arrive within the coming months."[47] Needless to add, GBD was immediately classified and censored on Google, Facebook, and other social media as "misinformation."

It is important to note that, before lockdown arrived, NPI was not only a non-recommended, but strongly criticized measure to respond to a "high-impact respiratory pathogen pandemic" (JHCHS 2019). This was confirmed as late as September 2019, in a report published by the Johns Hopkins Center for Health Security (JHCHS), the academic cockpit of the US biosecurity sector. Instead, the emphasis was on "rapid vaccine development for novel threats," followed by "mass vaccination strategies," with special mention being made of the mRNA-based vaccines that would first come into mass operation in the second phase of the COVID-19 pandemic (ibid., 10–11). The 2019 JHCHS report does not even mention the word "lockdown." The whole thing was unknown, even inconceivable at the time, in particular if one sees the negative assessment of much lighter NPI measures mentioned in the report. The proxy to lockdown is "quarantine," defined as "separation of potentially infectious individuals from susceptible populations" (ibid., 56), and otherwise the focus is on evaluating travel restrictions or border closures. And all these measures, from quarantine to border closures, do not pass muster. NPIs, at most, "may give governments more credibility among their citizens," but they are deemed "unlikely to substantially add to

264   POLITICAL NEOLIBERALISM

disease control efforts" (ibid., 22). Among the particular NPIs considered, "travel restrictions" may "only slightly delay the epidemic peak," and otherwise "hinder response efforts." "Quarantine" is even "the least likely NPI to be effective in controlling the spread due to high transmissibility," and it is criticized as "highly disruptive to societies and economies if . . . implemented for prolonged periods" (ibid., 57, 58). Overall, NPIs are considered more a psychological tool to "abate fear" than "necessary public health measure." This is because there is a "broad lack of evidence of efficacy and a lack of understanding about secondary adverse impacts"; and "(i)t is important to communicate to political leaders"—but also the WHO is mentioned as address (ibid., 12–13)—"the absence of evidence surrounding many NPI interventions and the adverse consequences that may follow them" (ibid., 58).

Almost simultaneously but independently, the WHO came to identical conclusions in its September 2019 report on "Nonpharmaceutical Public Health Measures for Mitigating the Risk and Impact of Epidemic and Pandemic Influenza" (WHO 2019). Hardly any of the "social distancing measures" discussed in this report is approved. Contract tracing: "not recommended," and it "can lead to ethical issues" (ibid., 37). Isolation of the sick: only if voluntary (ibid., 41). Quarantine of exposed individuals: "not recommended" because there is "no obvious rationale" for it, and there are "considerable difficulties in implementing it" (ibid., 47). School closures: only "conditionally recommended," as it "raise(s) major issues for families and communities" (ibid., 51). Even with respect to "avoiding crowding," one of the main foci of lockdown, "evidence of its effectiveness is very low," and "(t)here may be cultural or religious issues." The same negative report card is issued for "travel-related measures." "Entry and exit screening" (like fever-measuring at airports): "not recommended," because of "overall ineffectiveness" (ibid., 64). "Internal travel restrictions": at best "conditionally recommended," in the "early stage of a localized extraordinarily severe pandemic for a limited period" (ibid., 66). "Border closure": "not recommended," because of "very low quality of evidence, economic consequences, resource implications, and ethical implications" (ibid., 69). These consistently negative recommendations were backed by hundreds of scholarly sources, tacked into an impressively long footnote apparatus.

Only if one calls attention to these official sources at length, issued by two central actors of global health governance, JHUCHS and WHO, one understands—and cannot but be puzzled by—the dramatic novelty

END OF NEOLIBERALISM? 265

of lockdown. How did it come about? One crucial factor was a catastrophist mathematical Corona-death projection published in March 2020 by Imperial College London epidemiologist Ferguson, who had already overestimated the expected death rate of the 2009 Hong Kong Swine Flu by a factor of about eighty (with respect to the United Kingdom). In retrospect, his COVID-19 projection (Ferguson et al. 2020), which circulated among political decision-makers already before its publication date of March 16, 2020, must be considered one of the most influential scientific interventions of all time, at least with respect to domestic policymaking. The word "lockdown" appears in the paper only once, and obliquely, but it laid the track for lockdown as near-universal COVID-19 response.

Based on a "microsimulation model," the Ferguson paper expects 510,000 COVID-19 deaths in the United Kingdom by October 2020, and 2.2 million in the United States over the same period, in case of an "unmitigated epidemic" (Ferguson et al. 2020, 7). With respect to "mitigation" (i.e., NPI, for which the paper introduced the henceforth ubiquitous neologism "flattening the curve"), the paper compares the likely outcomes of two strategies: "mitigation" proper and "suppression." "Mitigation" proper is the traditional approach of "slowing but not necessarily stopping epidemic threat," and "protecting those most at risk" (ibid., 1)—the approach that only Sweden would take, and the GBD would recommend six months later. "Suppression," by contrast, aims at "revers(ing) epidemic growth"; that is, pushing the reproduction number, "R" (the average number of new infections generated by a previous infection), "to below 1" (ibid., 3). This is to occur through "a combination of case isolation, social distancing of the entire population and either household quarantine or school and university closure" (ibid., 10)—what subsequently became known as "lockdown." But this was not all. Suppression, to be effective, would have to be upheld "until a vaccine becomes available (potentially 18 months or more)" (ibid., 2).

The game-changing dynamite in the Ferguson paper is its estimation of the comparative death and hospitalization rates of both COVID-19 responses, "mitigation" as against "suppression". Yes, the softer mitigation strategy might reduce deaths "up to half" and hospital demand by two-thirds. But this would still imply that the UK and US health care capacity would be "exceeded many times over," "at least 8-fold" in fact, and this was on the "optimistic" side (Ferguson et al. 2020, 16). Accordingly, to avoid the collapse of health systems, "we . . . conclude that *epidemic suppression is the only viable strategy at the current time*" (ibid., emphasis supplied). This is the

266   POLITICAL NEOLIBERALISM

advice that would be heeded by most governments, including the required follow-up to lockdown, mass vaccination (once the stuff was available). Only the rather insane proposition to lock-in the entire population for eighteen consecutive months or longer was not implemented anywhere.

Only Swedish health experts were not convinced—"there is so much uncertainty in (the Imperial model) that made us think it was not a realistic scenario," said one of them (Borraz and Jacobsson 2023, 86). Most other governments followed Ferguson's advice, including the British and American, which were targeted by the Imperial model, and the French, one of whose health experts on the "scientific council" newly established by President Macron had previously worked with Ferguson at Imperial College. As an authoritative study of early COVID-19 responses across OECD countries confirms, "one of the most widely shared studies cited by political decision makers was Imperial College's simulation study" (Sebhatu et al. 2020, 21,202).

In the terms of Andrew Lakoff (2017, 20), lockdown reflects a new health security approach of "preparedness" for "unpredictable but potentially catastrophic" public health events, by means of the "imaginative enactment" of the worst case to occur. Worst-case thinking also tends to be favored by democratically accountable politicians, to reduce their immense responsibilities in settings where ordinary probabilistic risk assessment fails.[48]

But, on the critical side, to base a policy of such unprecedented reach and untested consequences on one mathematical model also entailed a "fetishization of science," trusting that "data-driven models" and to "follow the science" were a better guide for "evidence-based" policy than accumulated experience (Green and Fazi 2023, 392). It is difficult to disagree with Green and Fazi that lockdown arrived through "privileging . . . computer-simulated models and data tools over the experience of medical history in the treating of new epidemics" (ibid.); hence, the Swedish exception that precisely refused to ditch "established epidemiological knowledge" in favor of "uncertain and evolving evidence" (Olofsson et al. 2022, 5).

The Ferguson paper twice refers to "experience in China," which allegedly shows that "suppression is possible in the short term" (Ferguson et al. 2020, 2). In fact, in practical terms, China invented lockdown, and with apparent success just when the pandemic took off elsewhere. An important mediator in this respect was the WHO, which, after initial reservation and hesitation, came out decidedly in favor of the Chinese method. This has two implications, which are both ironic and contradictory. First, lockdown, to a degree, was the result of world governance, not in a legal but discursive sense, as "script" to follow (Meyer et al. 1997), which for the time being is its main way of operating. A British epidemiologist, who had advised the Scottish government in its early COVID-19 response, thus speaks of lockdown as "quickly" established "international norm" (Woolhouse 2022, 255). This defies the dominant pandemic-response image of the return of borders and of the sovereign state, which was experienced with particular pain in an allegedly internally borderless Europe[49]. This, of course, *also* happened, but only as following a global-level recommendation. Secondly, and in direct contradiction to the optimistic and progressive-minded picture of world governance, "if it feels as if people around the world have been living in a totalitarian state throughout 2020, that is because they have been . . . (T)he policies of one of the most repressive countries in the world had become the global scientific consensus" (Green 2021, ch. 4). This overstates the case, but it contains an element of truth, which is related to the possibility that four decades of neoliberal democracy erosion have facilitated such a (authoritarian-cum-technocratic) consensus, as well as its ready popular acceptance.

Previously skeptical of NPIs, the WHO's turnaround occurred stepwise. On January 23, 2020, the local WHO representative in China declared that "the lockdown of 11 million people (in Wuhan) is unprecedented in public health history so it is certainly not a recommendation that the WHO has made" (quoted by Green and Fazi 2023, 57). Five days later, WHO chief Ghebreyesus visited the Chinese leader Xi in Beijing. Their mutual admiration was long-standing, and one element in a long-standing American suspicion of the WHO as being too China-friendly, which culminated in the Trump administration's controversial withdrawal from the WHO in May 2020.[50] After his return from Beijing, Ghebreyesus praised China for its "commitment to transparency and the efforts made to investigate and contain the current outbreak." But the decisive moment was a second visit of a WHO delegation in February 2020. A report published on February 24, again praises the Chinese government for "perhaps the most ambitious, agile, and aggressive disease containment effort in history," and for its "high-quality, non-pharmaceutical public health measures" (in ibid., 68)—almost all of which, we saw, the WHO had condemned wholesale only six months earlier! And, to quote at length this crucial report's central phrase, the "measures that have been employed to contain COVID-19 in China . . . are *the only measures* that are currently proven to interrupt or minimize transmission chains" (in ibid., 69). Thus "lockdown" was born, not just on the mathematical drawing board, but at the level of global governance.

In the early phase of the pandemic, the initial Chinese success to bring the virus down was widely admired, even though this was not by liberal means. Among the admirers was not only the WHO (whose China-friendly posture throughout the pandemic crisis the historian Niall Ferguson [2021: ch.9] denounced as "supine, if not sycophantic"), but many public health scientists in the West. "Solidarity with all scientists and health professionals in China" was the watchword of the time, to quote *The Lancet*'s March 7, 2020 "Statement" by a group of prominent health scientists, which also condemned as "conspiracy theory" the notion that the COVID-19 virus was human-made, at that time believed to be mainly damaging to the Chinese government.[51] Outside the medical world, economic historian Adam Tooze's first-year chronicle of the COVID-19 pandemic is full of admiration for China, which showed to him that "(b)eing willing to sacrifice normality was actually the best way to preserve normality" (2021, ch. 3). By February 2020, when the West was "wasting time" (ibid.) and not knowing how to respond, as described by Tooze in rich detail, China, "(a)fter achieving effective suppression (of the virus)," was "back to normality" (ibid., ch.4). Or so it seemed.[52] The German sociologist Armin Nassehi, who had close access to the German chancellery under Angela Merkel and advised her government during the pandemic, acknowledged that "the Chinese autocratic solution is undoubtedly efficient," and he derived from it the "sociological hope in governing with a firm and unrelenting hand (*Durchregieren*)."[53]

Green and Fazi (2023, 392) suspect a "symbiotic relationship between the Chinese model and the Western neoliberal model." This sounds shrill but is not entirely misguided. "Democracy," especially if it turned "contentious," came to be considered in pandemic times as an "inconvenience," as the French medical scientist and writer Alex Kahn put it (Stiegler 2021, 12). That democracy, and the freedoms that are necessary to practice it, was (or were) no longer a first principle but something to be dispensed with if the perceived need arises, and that this happened almost without any opposition, is one of the pandemic's eeriest experiences. While this was not to save the market but to save life, the authoritarian element in it is certainly not foreign to neoliberalism. But this isn't all. With respect to the primacy of "saving life," in which physical trumps social life, Didier Fassin (2021) detected a neoliberal motif in this as well. This is because lockdown's "sparing of physical lives . . .

END OF NEOLIBERALISM? 269

laid bare ... the indifference toward the injustices in the treatment of social life" (ibid., 171)—Fassin's example being the unequal virus risk exposures by low-wage "essential workers" and high-salaried "home office" employees.

One could arrive at China's model function not only through detecting "authoritarian tendencies intrinsic to Western neoliberal capitalism itself" (Green and Fazi 2023, 395), but, on the contrary, through imputing on China what the West allegedly lacked: collective- or civic-mindedness. In this vein, Dominique Moïsi, a prominent French political scientist, lauded the "*civisme des Asiatiques*" (civic-mindedness of the Asians) and their penchant for "prioritiz(ing) the collective interest" over the individual interest (Stiegler 2021, 58). In whatever way one arrives at the model character of the Chinese COVID-19 response, Barbara Stiegler aptly summarizes that "in the pandemic, China dominates. Not only economically, but also morally, culturally, and politically" (2021, 9f).

A positive view on China was further supported by an antiracist impulse, which was aroused in the entire first year of COVID-19 by then-President Trump's constant drumming of the racist-sounding (but also plainly descriptive) "Chinese virus" ("Kung Flu" was another of his favorites). Striking an anticolonial chord, two leading German social scientists wondered "why we do not learn from Asiatic countries," and their answer is: "Corona reveals Western arrogance."[54] As they further argue, somewhat surprisingly in the first week of "lockdown": "That Germany did not learn from the Asian successes in fighting the pandemic is mostly due to postcolonial ignorance."

In late 2020, Neil Ferguson recounts the political course of events that unfolded at numbing speed: "It's a communist one party state, we said. We couldn't get away with it, we thought ... And then Italy did it. And we realized we could" (quoted by Green and Fazi 2023, 82). This statement is significant, first, for the "we" that recalls the pre-Chinese, academic roots of lockdown that Ferguson and his Imperial College lab themselves had prepared;[55] and, secondly, for underscoring the pioneering of lockdown by the "communist one party state." But the first nation-wide lockdown in history, indeed, was declared by Italy on March 9, 2020, topping the Chinese lockdowns that never went beyond the regional level. Italy's would be one of the harshest and most protracted lockdowns, which was rapidly followed in other European countries, domino-style. Incidentally, the Italian government's history-making decision occurred under a socialist health minister who was in close contact with Chinese health officials.[56] One of these officials, when visiting Italy in late March, accused the Italian government of

270   POLITICAL NEOLIBERALISM

still being too lax: "(P)olicies unfortunately are still not tight enough by our standards. There are still too many people around . . . (I)t is time to close the economic activities and prohibit the movement of people. Everyone has to stay at home, in quarantine" (in Green and Fazi 2023, 82). These were bossy words for a visitor, which demonstrate the Chinese moral high ground in the first year of the COVID-19 pandemic.

The spring 2020 lockdowns in Europe, which were followed by several more lockdowns from the fall on, were differently strict, lighter in the Nordic countries (including Switzerland, the Netherlands, and Germany), tough in the South: Italy, Spain, Greece—and France (see Boulakia and Mariot 2023). France, under a neoliberal government, went to greater authoritarian extremes than most other countries in Europe.[57] *"Nous sommes en guerre"* (we are at war) was President Macron's opening salve, when announcing the French lockdown on March 16, 2020. As in other European countries, the French parliament immediately disempowered itself by passing an emergency health law that gave broad powers to the executive to rule by decree. And most pandemic decisions in France came to be made behind closed doors, in the reactivated "Defense and National Security Council" (CDSN), meeting weekly from March 2020 on (Bandelow et al. 2021, 125).

The war rhetoric, a recurrent presence in France since the 2015 Islamist terror attacks, and which was even more questionable if moved from a non-uniformed to a non-human opponent, was not Macron's invention. The pandemic simulation and prevention exercises, briefly discussed earlier, were all in a context of biosecurity. When a real pandemic happened, to call it "war" was a natural reflex. None other than Gates spread the war rhetoric in pre-pandemic times. For instance, at the 2017 Munich Security Conference, Gates warned his high-level NATO and state leader audience not to "ignore the link between health security and international security," and at the 2018 Malaria Summit in London, he said that "the world needs to prepare for pandemics in the same serious way it prepares for war" (in Kennedy 2021, ch. 12). The first country, of course, to fight COVID-19 in terms of a war was China, for which this was a "people's war," or even a "total war" (Knight and Creemers 2021, 8, 9). Overall, if "war" became standard language of political leaders during the COVID-19 pandemic, it is not far-fetched to argue that the purpose was to spread fear and to make people accept drastic and prolonged freedom restrictions.

The French government did not just talk but walk akin to being in a war. *"Couvre-feu,"* literally "to extinguish the fire," a wartime measure for enemy planes to miss their target at night, meant that after a certain hour, as early as 6 p.m. (to "counter the apero-effect" [*contrer l'effet apéro*], as the Macron party spokesman Stanislaus Guerini put it cynically)[58], no one was allowed to leave home.[59] This was on top of "confinement," this word, like "lockdown," more an import from prison than from martial language. Confinement meant a general prohibition to leave home during daytime also, except for walking your dog or shopping. This needed to be "self-authorized" by downloading from the internet and signing an "*attestation de sortie auto-redigées*" (self-authorized exit permit), a legal absurdity of exempting yourself from a general rule. In what the German weekly, *Die Zeit*, ridiculed as "*Absurdistan*," the French government passed 387 administrative rule changes between October 2020 and April 2021, one every four days (see Mucchielli 2022a, ch. 5). In just two months, between March and April 2021, the French police issued 2.2 million contraventions for being out when you were not supposed to, starting with a 135 Euro fine, and it could go up to 3,750 Euro for repeat offenders; reportedly, even homeless people were fined. In the first five weeks of lockdown, no less than 15.5 million police checks occurred across the hexagon (Tréguer 2021, 17), not a small number in a country of sixty-seven million. Unsurprisingly, in 2020, France was no longer counted as "full democracy" on *The Economist*'s Democracy Index.

The French "bureaucratic frenzy" (*frénésie bureaucratique*) (Mucchielli 2022a, ch. 5) was perhaps extreme, but not singular in Europe. A particularly sinister document is a "strategy paper" issued by the German Interior Ministry, entitled "How We Can Get COVID-19 Under Control."[60] The product of cross-disciplinary "expert" opinion that was convened for the purpose, the paper shows a panic-struck government in search of the best method to instill a maximum of fear in people. Obviously under the impression of Ferguson's computer simulations, there is a "worst case" assumption of "over a million deaths in 2020—in Germany alone," and to "avoid this worst case is of the highest strategic priority."[61] The paper distinguishes between four scenarios, from "Fast Control" to "Abyss" (*Abgrund*). To achieve "fast control," of course the favored scenario, the Germans needed to be told what "worst case" meant: "To achieve the desired shock effect, the concrete effects of a complete contamination (*Durchseuchung*) for human society need to be demonstrated." For instance, "(m)any gravely sick will be refused by hospitals, and they suffer a painful death struggling for air at home. Dying from suffocation is a primal fear (*Urangst*) for every human being." Darker

272   POLITICAL NEOLIBERALISM

still, children were to be enlisted in the fear campaign. "Children won't be affected by the epidemic," the paper muses. "Wrong. If they then contaminate their parents, and one of them agonizingly dies at home, they will feel guilty—for instance, if they forgot to wash their hands after playing. This is the most horrible thing that a child can ever experience."[62]

The German Interior Ministry paper also reflects on the best way to "reduce social contacts," for which the English neologism "social distancing" came into use, an import from the American health security complex. The idea is to achieve this distancing by Orwellian doublethink, in which words are given their exact opposite meaning. The concrete proposal is to spread the slogan "together distanced" (*gemeinsam distanziert*), a contradiction in terms, in the social media (#wirbleibenzuhause, "physical distance = societal solidarity"). More playfully, the "online community" is called upon for a "joint 'fact-check' of information and further Hackathons." These measures were grandly declared a "future-oriented . . . envisioning of a new relationship between society and state."[63]

This language suggests the handwriting of a sociologist, Heinz Bude, who was one of the experts recruited for this purpose. This incidentally proves that including social scientists in pandemic management (no single virologist was involved in drafting the German Interior Ministry paper), whose absence was often held responsible for the lack of attention to long-term, non-intended consequences of locking-in entire populations, did not have to yield a fundamentally different crisis response. In a later reflection "from the engine room of pandemic consultation," Bude (2022, 247–249) defended the envisaged "shock therapy," for which the explicit model indeed was "China," with its "cultural differences . . . consciously blended out": "Our challenge was how to control (*zugreifen auf*) individual behavior in a complex, modern society . . . To speak with Gramsci, the matter was to order constraints (*Zwänge zu verordnen*) and to do this with people's consent, while retaining the ideological upper hand (*Deutungshoheit*)."

Giorgio Agamben, the Italian philosopher who wrote incisively about "bare life" and the "state of exception," and a cult author of the left, was the only intellectual of name to dare to criticize lockdown, with the tools of his own philosophy. In a first blog published in late February 2020, he simply reiterates the Italian National Research Council (NRC) statement that there was "no SARS-CoV2 epidemic in Italy" *at the time*, and that in 80 to 90 percent of cases the symptoms were "moderate," "a kind of flu" (as we saw, even Gates eventually embraced this view, although only after his vaccine cause was served). On the basis of the official NRC definition of the situation, Agamben criticizes, first, the "disproportionate" and "grave" government restrictions of elementary individual freedoms, which he thinks "manifest again the growing tendency of the state of exception to become a normal governing paradigm." Secondly, and entirely plausible in view of the German Interior Ministry document cited earlier, Agamben criticizes the instilling of a "state of fear" and "collective panic." This is achieved, he argues, in a "perverse vicious circle" of fulfilling the "desire for security" that was created by this very fear campaign.[64]

After this initial critique of the disproportionate freedom restrictions by lockdown, in a second blog, Agamben focuses on the barren picture of society and public policy that transpires in the measures underway, as "no longer believ(ing) in anything but bare life." To which one could add, with Wolfgang Streeck, that the "talk of the virus that equally threatens us with death" camouflages the "permanently growing disparity of life conditions (*Lebenslagen*) according to social status and economic class position,"[65] even with respect to the risk of being hit by that virus. Moreover, Agamben insists, the protection of "bare life," or to "flatten the curve," which was the soundbite of the day, is not "something that unites people." Instead, it "blinds and separates them." This is because "other human beings . . . are now seen solely as possible spreaders of the plague whom one must avoid at all costs and from whom one needs to keep oneself at a distance of at least a meter." Agamben thus exposes the Orwellian doublethink, such as the mentioned phrase "together distant." Division, not unity, must also be the unintended result of the favored war metaphor: "a war with an invisible enemy that can lurk in every other person is the most absurd of wars. It is, in reality, a civil war. The enemy is not outside, it is within us." Moreover, Agamben condemns the inhumane practice, common during the pandemic, of the COVID-19 dead to be denied the "right to a funeral"—as every schoolchild knows, this was the theme of Sophocles's Antigone tragedy, in which moral conscience memorably trumps political obligation. "(It) is curious," Agamben throws another dart, "that the churches remain silent on the subject," which indeed they did, not only in Italy. Finally, he utters a truism about the state of exception, which came to be the state of normality between 2020 and 2022: "A society that lives in a perennial state of emergency cannot be a free society."[66]

In a third blog[67] (there were several more), Agamben dares to compare a hypertrophied notion of public health with the *salut public* whose protection had justified the *terreur* (terror) of the French revolution. Public health

274   POLITICAL NEOLIBERALISM

absolutism was also hypocritical; in Agamben's view, "panic is spread . . . also to deflect attention from past omissions of several governments." His reference is neoliberal hospital reforms, which had been pushed in particular by the explicitly "technical" governments that Italy has had in several editions over the past decades. They reduced Italian hospital capacity by 50 percent, between 1997 and 2015, and the number of hospital employees by forty-six thousand between 2009 and 2017 (Šumonja 2020, 218). As in other European countries,[68] these "reforms" shockingly continued during the pandemic. Adam Tooze (2021, ch. 1) speaks of "organized irresponsibility" in Western countries' health sectors since the 1980s: "(S)urplus capacity was viewed not as a responsible precaution but a regrettable drag on efficiency." The publicly staged need to "flatten the curve" was not natural fate but, to the degree that it wasn't exaggerated,[69] the self-generated result of decades of neoliberal health policy, in which profit-making has trumped public health as guiding principle. Agamben makes a second, equally important point: considering the "new function" that "doctors and virologists" have acquired in "governing the pandemic," he finds it "dangerous" to "let them decide on matters that are lastly of an ethical and political nature."[70] To "follow the science" also ignores that there is not, and cannot be, "agreement among scientists." As this fundamental fact was ignored, "science has become the religion of our time," which he wants to be understood "literally." If one considers the policy-making power of Ferguson's fantastical computer simulations, this conclusion does not seem exaggerated.

In retrospect, it is difficult to find fault with the three main points of Agamben's critical COVID-19 blogs: first, that lockdown's freedom restrictions were disproportionate; secondly, that "social distancing," perhaps the *Unwort* of 2020–2021, betrayed an impoverished view of society as reduced to bare life, which weirdly echoes the neoliberal motto that "there is no such thing as society"; and, thirdly, that science as speaking with one voice and brought (too) close to political decision-making implied a disfigured and self-aggrandizing understanding of science. Who could reasonably disagree with this? But Agamben, figuratively speaking, was thrown out of town, after being subjected to the equivalent of being tarred and feathered, especially by the left that had previously adored him for the same critical philosophy that he simply brought to bear on the pandemic. "Each short essay was more absurd . . . than the last," all just "right-wing . . . conspiracy theories," posted philosopher Benjamin Bratton on the leftist *Verso Blog*.[71] "Monitor and punish? Yes, please," responded Slavoj Zizek, which this time was less of

END OF NEOLIBERALISM? 275

a witticism than his previous provocations. At least, to Zizek, Agamben was not a right-wing turncoat but guilty of a "widespread Leftist stance," which is to suspect the "power exercise of social control" behind every government policy; but this "does not make the reality of the threat disappear."[72] A young Belgian philosopher, whose professional website describes him as expert on "neoliberal governmentality"[73], even demands that "society (must) be defended from Agamben," whom he finds indistinguishable from "corona denialists such as Bolsonaro or Trump."[74]

Indeed, that right-wing populists like "Bolsonaro or Trump" opposed lockdown and ridiculed distancing measures, like mask-wearing, helps explain why the left would ardently support these things. As Baldwin (2021, 164) quipped about the United States, a mask in the face "became the semiotic opposite of a MAGA hat," if not a "totemic symbol" in the Durkheimian sense of the "grouping of men into clans according to natural objects" (Klinenberg 2024, 151). But something deeper was involved in leftist support for lockdown. It seemed to recover a positive concept of freedom and resurrection of a public-good-oriented state, after forty years of neoliberal draught and Market idolization. In this perspective, lockdown was not, in however contorted ways, affine to certain neoliberal precepts, such as a disdain for democracy; on the contrary, it was a *Befreiungsschlag* against the neoliberal decimation of the public good.

If, in the process, the left did not entirely abandon the concept of freedom, this was at the price of a crooked version of it. Advocating what he calls "social liberty," sociologist Frank Nullmeier (2020, 4), for instance, argues that the "pandemic qua socio-natural condition is per se the opposite of freedom (*Unfreiheit*)." Conversely, "a shutdown is the attempt to remove the pandemic-caused *Unfreiheit* through the state-ordered restriction of freedom rights." Furthermore, "the *Unfreiheit* to be at risk to be infected at any moment is significantly reduced through freedom-of-access restrictions (*Zugangsbeschränkungen*)" (ibid., 12). In short, "the loss of freedom is answered with the loss of freedom, in order to restore the conditions of a free life in common" (ibid., 12–13). Lockdown as freedom giver, or to be deprived of freedom for the sake of recovering freedom—here is another instance of Orwellian doublethink. In response to such reasoning, a German public law professor pithily notes that "a freedom that first has to prove that it isn't dangerous, has ceased to exist (*ist abgeschafft*)."[75]

Such reasoning, of course, negates the possibility to question the proportionality of lockdown. The dilemma shines in Jürgen Habermas's ringing defense of the "strict preventive measures," which he holds up positively against a "libertarian course of opening." Notably, Habermas's COVID-19 intervention was not in March 2020, when a situation of panic might excuse him, but in September 2021, after not just one but three lockdowns in Germany, and the fourth lockdown lurking just around the corner. Ever since the first lockdown, there was a lively debate among German constitutionalists whether the "protection of life" trumped all other constitutional rights. Most stridently, Oliver Lepsius attacked a "state of exception in jurisprudence," in which an absolutized "protection of life" stamped out the usual need to carefully justify and balance the restriction of basic rights.[76] In particular, the first clause of the Basic Law, which stipulates that "human dignity is inviolable," does not allow this, argues Lepsius: "China as model. In the 'Hour of the Executive', human beings are reduced to their naked physical existence. But exactly this the Basic Law does not permit: this would be ... a violation of human dignity," protected by Article 1 of the Basic Law, and it would be a violation of other basic rights as well. To which Habermas (2021, 24) bluntly responded that "one cannot want to protect the dignity of a person and let her body rot," so that the "protection of life by the state is the implication of ... the protection of human dignity."

However, as Freiburg constitutionalist Dietrich Murswiek (2021a) objects, the "right to life" guaranteed by Article 2(2) of the Basic Law, is wrongly interpreted in such reasoning. While the right to life does have superordinate status to other freedom rights, according to Murswiek,[77] it only "obliges the state to protect the individual against acts by third parties, but not against general risks of life or natural catastrophes," such as pandemics. In legal language, the right to life protects against "*Störer*" or "*Gefährder*," hostile or dangerous third parties, either the state (qua *Abwehrrecht* [defensive right]) or private actors (qua *Schutzrecht* [protective right]). In the pandemic context, this might justify forcibly isolating infected and sick persons. But it could not justify isolating the healthy, which is the nature of lockdown. "Healthy people are no *Gefährder*," Murswiek puts it plainly (2023, 484). Unless, of course, and that was the brachial yet mostly unspoken gist of the lockdown advocates, one considered *all people*, the sick *and* the healthy, as *Gefährder*; that is, "potential spreader of the virus."[78] This, however, would not meet the constitutional proportionality test, at least in Murswiek's view (2021b, 11).

The legal validity of these arguments cannot be adjudicated here.[79] But it is striking how much Habermas, Germany's foremost public intellectual and critical conscience since the founding of the Federal Republic in 1949, embraced the Covid Doxa, even down to the word. And in this, he was representative of the left at large. This was a "war of species against species," Habermas adopts the official government line (2021, 2). To him, the "relatively strict, even if not consequently implemented course" of the German government was backed by the "consensual council of scientific experts"—thus invoking the questionable image of science as speaking with one voice (ibid., 5). On the other end, Habermas rejects the "noisy polemic" of the "pro-opening lobby" (*Lockerungslobby*) (ibid., 7). Only in brackets, he mentions a "seriously worrisome phenomenon for the near future", which is "the politically aggressive and conspiracy-theoretical denial of the pandemic infection and mortality risks." To him, as for most other leftists, there was a "radical right core" to the "fake-liberally (*scheinliberal*) justified protests of the Corona deniers"—which he calls, fashionable among certain German social scientists at the time, "extremism of the middle" (ibid.).

At the same time, Habermas (2021) plausibly argues that, at the level of constitutional theory, the COVID-19 crisis throws into sharp relief the inherent tension between the two components of "liberal democracy," its liberal component pushing for "the guarantee of subjective freedoms," while the democratic element points at the "self-empowerment of citizens for the political pursuit of collective goals." More concretely, lockdown meant to him the "asymmetric insistence on the solidarity of citizens *at the cost of* equally guaranteed subjective freedoms" (ibid., 3; emphasis supplied). However, what sounds fine at the level of theoretical abstraction looks a lot less innocent in the real world. The constitutional argument obscures that, during lockdown, "citizen solidarity" was rather easy to afford for the laptop class doing "home office" in their countryside houses; it was less comfortable for a working-class family crammed into a small city apartment for extended periods and several times over. And the heft of the "freedom cost" was likewise not shouldered equally across social categories but selectively, by the young (deprived of school and often subject to violence at home by stressed fathers), by women and mothers (doing home schooling, in addition to their habitual double shift), and by the poor (either deprived of work and income or toiling as "essential workers" on the virus front) (see Green and Fazi 2023, ch. 6–8).

The Habermasian construct of "democracy" and "citizen solidarity" being exercised qua lockdown buys into the notion that there was no alternative, while putting a halo on the brute force with which it was implemented.

278 POLITICAL NEOLIBERALISM

Claus Offe, eminent political sociologist (and surely no rightist but incidentally a former assistant of Habermas at the University of Frankfurt), dared to call the spade by its name.[80] In ethical respect, he finds it "doubtful" to put the "right to life" above all other basic rights—this was a formula that might lead to the "irreversible establishment of authoritarian regimes," and he cites the example of Hungary where Viktor Orbán was busily doing just that. With respect to the "Corona problem," Offe continues, in medical terms this was mostly a "geriatric" one, and the "generalized interventions" (his word for lockdown) effectively aimed at "prolonging the lifetime of multi-morbid seniors," at the cost of the "younger and middle generations," who faced unemployment and the loss of welfare (*Wohlstandseinbussen*). Instead of lockdown, he favored a "group-specific differentiation of regulation"—the medical pre-Corona standard and anticipating the GBD (that was issued several months later). But, as we saw, this was the alternative that was effectively and systematically suppressed during the pandemic. While Offe does not use the word that made Agamben persona not grata: "The Invention of an Epidemic," which was the super-incriminated title of Agamben's first Corona blog,[81] Offe's position boils down to the exact same. It questioned the "deadly" nature of the virus to which only "one" answer was possible—the premise on which the Covid Doxa rested. Offe was lucky enough to be spared Agamben's fate of being expelled from polite society.

In one respect, however, Habermas (2021, 6) was exactly right: lockdown was "supported by the large majority of the population," in Germany as elsewhere.[82] In this (technopopulist?) sense, one might call the political Covid management a "*Sternstunde der Demokratie*" (golden hour of democracy).[83] Green (2021, ch. 4) is "baffled . . . as to why citizens of liberal democracies were so willing to give up their freedoms to fight a disease which, it quickly became clear, the vast majority of them were not in danger from." If most people gave in to the drastic freedom restrictions, some even eagerly following the vile government advice to spy and report on neighbors who violated lockdown rules, which resembles the *Blockwart* practices of the Nazis, one must suspect that two decades of continuous "crisis" drumming, accompanied by states' promotion of "security" from secondary to primary value, have contributed to this. At least, this is the suggestion by Green and Fazi (2023, 396), who describe the new millennium as in a "perennial state of 'crisis,'" from the terrorist attacks of 9/11, the Financial Crisis of 2008, to the climate crisis and COVID-19, and continuing today with the wars in Ukraine and Israel. Crisis-in-permanence reinforces the loss of future, which

END OF NEOLIBERALISM? 279

we argued earlier is a feature of the neoliberal order. "Permanent crisis," Green and Fazi argue perceptively (ibid), "means being stuck in a perpetual present where all energies are focused on the fight against the 'enemy' of the moment."

A particularly drastic example of accepting freedom restrictions for the sake of absolutized security comes from the land of John Bull (an early nineteenth-century cartoon figure that stood for "English liberty"). If the British government initially hesitated to impose lockdown, this was out of fear that the "British public would not accept (it)"—which proved to be "completely wrong," as the Prime Minister's chief advisor, Dominic Cummings, later told a parliamentary review committee (House of Commons 2021, 44). Indeed, when after sixteen months of lockdown, in July 2021, the British government restored what Prime Minister Boris Johnson satirized, only half-jesting, as the "ancient, inalienable right of free-born people of the United Kingdom to go to the pub," the majority of the British were not amused.[84] A poll found that two-thirds thought that "masks, social distancing and travel restrictions" should rather continue, and still a majority supported these measures until COVID-19 is "controlled worldwide." More astoundingly still, "a sizeable minority would like personal freedoms to be restricted permanently," and almost 20 percent supported a permanent ban on leaving home after 10 p.m. "without good reason." The pandemic "revealed John Bull's authoritarian streak," *The Economist* concluded.[85] However, such attitudes were prevalent elsewhere. Two German critics called Western states' political COVID-19 management a "real Milgram experiment" (Lütge and Esfeld 2021, 91), in which unrelenting fear-mongering had to bear strange fruits.[86]

Of course, not everyone agreed with or gave in to lockdown. In Germany, lockdown critics became known as *Querdenker* (lateral thinkers). They drew support from the independent *Mittelstand*, small business owners and entrepreneurs who were disproportionately affected by the mandated closure of stores and in-person services. But the "lateral" logo also points to the involvement of the artistic milieu, which likewise suffered from the closing of physical-presence-requiring theatres, galleries, clubs, etc. William Callison and Quinn Slobodian (2021) see this motley bunch of lockdown critics united by "the conviction that all power is conspiracy," and they depict them beholden to an understanding of freedom as "defined in the negative, reduced to individual license and shorn of any sense of mutual responsibility or solidarity." These formulations show that the authors did

280 POLITICAL NEOLIBERALISM

not like what they saw. Similarly, Carolin Amlinger and Oliver Nachtwey (2022) call the *Querdenker* attitude "libertarian authoritarianism," whereby the "authoritarian" element in this remains in the dark. "Their only authority are they themselves [*sie selbst*]," the authors say at one point (ibid., 292). But this seems to suggest that "libertarian" *is* "authoritarian," which makes their pairing a tautology.

Offering a "critical theory" framework for deciphering the *Querdenker*, Amlinger and Nachtwey depict them as pathological "side effect (*Nebenfolge*) of late modern society," whose "promise of individual self-realization bears a potential for injury (*Kränkungspotential*) that may turn into frustration and resentment" (2022, 13). But what the authors call critical theory is uncritical affirmation of the government's lockdown policy. If *Querdenker* show an "overbearing intellectual critique of the state measures," and if they "contest the danger of the virus and the proportionality of the measures" (ibid., 22), it is implied that these measures *are* "proportionate" and all right in light of the "danger." The state is rational, only its critics are not—this is the message.

Lockdown critics were generally depicted as "arching toward far-right beliefs" (Callison and Slobodian 2021). In this respect, the empirical part of Amlinger and Nachtwey (2022), which is based on an online survey of 1,150 Lateral Thinkers, contains a surprising finding, but one that is contrarian to dismissing them as far right: 41 percent of surveyed *Querdenker* had recently voted for the Greens and the radical Left Party, while the preference for the radical right party, AfD, was only at third place, with 15 percent. The authors immediately seek to relativize this finding, when arguing that while "arriving mainly from the left," the *Querdenker* "are now moving toward the right" (ibid., 23). And they read a deep authoritarian disposition into this move, attributing to it "a radically individual understanding of the right to freedom that tips over to the authoritarian" (ibid., 24)—again, the meaning of "authoritarian" staying in the dark.

But there is a simpler explanation for lockdown critics' move to the right, which is rooted in a political demand-supply logic. Amlinger and Nachtwey (2022, 245) themselves hint at it: "Progressives are asking for regulation (*Normierung*), while conservatives are emphasizing the right to free self-determination." This was the main pandemic cleavage on the political supply side (particularly strong in the United States with its Democrat versus Republican polarization), though the Covid Doxa did much to delegitimize and subdue it. Most radical right parties, including the German AfD, initially supported border closures, what silenced them for a moment because this was happening anyway. Over time, however, these parties positioned themselves as freedom defenders and critics of government "authoritarianism" (see Kaltwasser and Taggert 2022).[87] "*Liberté, liberté*" was the chant at rallies organized by French Front National dissident Florian Philippot in spring and summer 2021, and he presented himself at the French 2022 presidential election contest as opponent to the Macron government's "*dictature sanitaire*" (health dictatorship).[88] No wonder that lockdown critics were trending toward such political offers. If this was the pull factor, German political scientist Philip Manow plausibly describes the reverse push dynamics: "If one denounces people long enough as right fringe, they will eventually move into this corner."[89]

How effective were the lockdowns in saving lives and containing the virus? A ten-country comparison by a team of Stanford virologists (Bendavid et al. 2021, 4)[90] found "no evidence that more restrictive nonpharmaceutical interventions ('lockdowns') contributed substantially to bending the curve of new cases in England, France, Germany, Iran, Italy, the Netherlands, Spain or the United States in early 2020." The United States, with its polar Democrat–Republican divide, offers a natural experiment to assess the effectiveness of lockdown, which tended to be opposed in Republican-ruled and happily implemented in Democrat-ruled states. But the US state with perhaps the harshest lockdown policy, Democratic California, had no significantly better health outcome than the Republican "Free State of Florida" (measured by the number of COVID-19 deaths, but correlated with the two states' different age structure) (Nocera and McLean 2023, ch. 15). A multi-country meta-analysis by researchers of the University of Lund and Johns Hopkins University, which summarizes the results of twenty thousand studies of state responses to the COVID-19 pandemic, found that "the policy of lockdowns represents a global policy failure of gigantic proportions" (Herby et al. 2023, 20). In their conclusion, "lockdowns in the spring of 2020 in Europe resulted in 6,000 to 23,000 deaths avoided. To put those numbers into context, during an average flu season, approximately 72,000 deaths are recorded in Europe" (ibid., 19).[91] Two Lund University economists, who point at the fact that "most of Swedish society remained open" while combining "low excess death rates with relatively small economic cost," call lockdown "the greatest policy failure of modern times"

(Andersson and Nonung 2024, 4, 3, 14). An early British supporter of lockdown, who later criticized most states' repeated and persistent use of it, is even convinced that "history will judge lockdown as a monumental mistake on a truly global scale," considering its "damage . . . to lives and livelihoods" and its "overestimated" public health benefits (Woolhouse 2022, 238).

If the final jury on lockdown is nevertheless out, this is also due to its self-immunizing nature. Mucchielli (2022b, 18) succinctly identifies the "circular reasoning" behind lockdown that shields it from criticism: "(C)atastrophist previsions permit to justify unprecedented political measures; in turn, reference to these measures is made to explain why the catastrophist previsions have not materialized."

Mass Vaccination

Two advocates of "global health governance" list the factors that drive "public–private partnerships" (PPP) in this domain: the rise of transnational corporations with market power, the privatization of government services, the rise of private philanthropy, and the concentration of power in the pharmaceutical industry (Clinton and Sridhar 2017, 15f).[92] An astute critic, Mazzucato, concisely summarizes what PPP boils down to: "prioritise the interests of business over the public good."[93] Writing in the first days of lockdown, Mazzucato is hopeful that the "COVID-19 crisis" offers a "chance to do capitalism differently."[94] As the second half of the Covid Doxa suggests, which is rapid vaccine development followed by mass inoculation, her hopes were dashed.

In fact, more than lockdown, the neoliberal imprint on which will remain doubtful to many, perhaps most, the vaccine part of the story is unreconstructed political neoliberalism. At the same time, implied in the assumption of a deadly virus roaming globally, is the rather opposite notion, incidentally propagated by the WHO, that "no one is safe until everyone is safe." This would call for vaccine being considered a public good, and not "intellectual property" (IP), which it was at the onset of the pandemic, and, as we shall see, continued to be. IP is the "blood of the private sector," as Pfizer chief Albert Bourla defended it,[95] denouncing as "nonsense" and "dangerous" the opposite notion, propagated by the WHO, that vaccines are "global public goods."[96] Like blood is necessary for life, IP proved to be untouchable. Bourla also provided the standard industry justification for IP, when

END OF NEOLIBERALISM? 283

suggesting that "companies are risking billions of dollars on development programmes despite the chances of recouping investment not being good."[97] This is a rather inaccurate picture of the pharma industry's business model, though the one offered for public consumption.

If socialization of risk and privatization of reward was the outcome of the 2008 Financial Crisis, the same can be said about the vaccine part of the pandemic crisis. One important difference is that "free-riding" (Mazzucato 2013, 32) had been the routine functioning of the pharma industry all along, in terms of publicly funded research and development whose fruits (new drugs and therapies) are privately appropriated as patents or intellectual property rights (IPRs). Before COVID-19 arrived, the pharmaceutical industry showed "extreme reluctance" (Durisch and Hertig 2021, 9) to get involved in vaccine development, preferring instead more lucrative investment in longer-term chronic-disease drugs, such as against cancer or diabetes. The sheer size of the pandemic and the "billions of dollars" of government money that Gates had asked for and that instantly arrived, changed the game. The one thing that did not change is pharma's business model. In a context of "financialized" capitalism (see Krippner 2011), much like General Motors has shifted its focus from selling cars to selling car insurance, the large pharmaceutical companies, Big Pharma, has moved away from developing and manufacturing drugs, particularly novel and risky ones, toward operating as "private equity funds" (Durisch and Hertig 2021, 29). This means the redirection of profits to the financial market, and to buy up the small biotech start-ups that (in addition to public-sector and university laboratories) are the drivers of innovation, the purpose of these acquisitions being not to push innovation further but to reap the small firms' IPRs.

Between February and December 2020, governments threw the enormous sum of 93 billion Euros into the development of COVID-19 vaccines and therapeutics, 32 percent of it on part of the US government and 24 percent by the European Union (Durisch and Hertig 2021, 20, 22). This public money was handed out as "blank cheques," with "no strings" attached in terms of conditionality on pricing and access, transparency, and, of course, IPRs (ibid., 24). In the case of Moderna, initially a small Boston-based biotech start-up, its entire COVID-19 vaccine development was financed externally, about three-fourth by the US government and the rest by CEPI, a Gates-Foundation-led "global partnership" for vaccine development. But then its vaccine also became the most expensive on the market. If Moderna's pre-COVID-19 revenue was $60 million USD (in 2019), in 2021 its revenue

284 POLITICAL NEOLIBERALISM

exploded to \$13.2 billion USD, while the value of its shares grew by 700 percent in 2020 (ibid., 6). As in all vaccine development, taxpayers were charged twice: first for R&D, and then for the vaccines that resulted from it.

The bilateral procurement contracts between Big Pharma and governments were kept away from the public eye by strict confidentiality agreements—the European Union haughtily declared that there was "no overriding public interest in transparency" (Durisch and Hertig 2021, 17). The little that is known about the contracts, some of which made it into the public in heavily redacted (i.e., blackened) form, shows strong pharma companies imposing *their* conditions on weak and compliant states, with respect to pricing, clinical testing (raw data being treated as property not in need to be revealed), and, most crucially, the distribution of responsibility for negative side effects of the vaccines. Indeed, the perhaps most galling feature of the vaccine contracts is the complete exemption of pharma from civil liability for the adverse effects of vaccination. Moreover, as in the contract between Pfizer and South Africa, the company did not just relieve itself of any responsibility but obliged the government to "create, dedicate, and maintain a no-fault compensation fund sufficient to undertake and completely fulfil the indemnification obligations," and this by a tight deadline.[98] A private company reaping all of the benefit yet delegating all responsibility for a bad outcome to the state, even daring to prescribe the details of state responsibility—this is the reality of public-private partnership, at least in the pharma sector in times of COVID-19.

One may think that in the unequal "partnership" between public-good-obliged governments and profit-oriented pharma companies, the non-negligible third player in the game, which is philanthropic foundations, might tilt the balance in favor of the public good. Aren't these foundations "non-profit"? Aren't they "philanthropic"? The exact opposite turned out to be the case. Gates, "an inspiration for all" (Pfizer's Bourla), threw his and his foundation's mighty weight solidly in favor of profit-making, which is tantamount to IPR protection (Zaitchik 2021).

Consider the case of AstraZeneca's COVID-19 vaccine. One of the early frontrunners in developing a COVID-19 vaccine was Oxford University's Jenner Institute. Its initial commitment was to make the vaccine publicly available through "open licensing." The rub is that the Gates Foundation was, for a long time, a major donor to the institute, and it also supported its present vaccine research, "to the tune of some USD 384 million."[99] The foundation pushed the institute to partner with the Anglo-Swedish pharma giant AstraZeneca, to be in charge of global manufacturing and distribution. In the process, open licensing was withdrawn. AstraZeneca pledged "no-profit" sales, but only during the "pandemic"—its ending set beforehand as July 2021, barely half a year after the vaccine was available. True, AstraZeneca's COVID-19 vaccine was by several times the most affordable. But the principle of intellectual property rights was maintained.

Beyond his Oxford engagement, Gates launched the WHO-based "Covid-19 ACT-Accelerator," a global vaccine-development "partnership," its main purpose being IPR protection. This was in a moment when the notion of vaccine as "global public good" had tailwind. Even the *Financial Times* came around in favor of a vaccine that is "universally and cheaply available" (Zaitchik 2021).[100] The Gates Foundation's pharmaceutical share-holdings are known, which in common sense (although not in law) would make it "for profit." But Gates's private investments in the sector are not known, and when asked about them, he refused to lay them open.[101] Remarkably, no one bothered. When Gates penned his influential April 2020 call to action in the *New England Journal of Medicine* (previously discussed), a journal that otherwise is ultra-pedantic about its authors' "conflict-of-interest" declarations, Gates got away with perfunctorily stating that these conflicts are "numerous," without specifying what they were. Obviously, this "(gave) readers no sense of the size, scope, or type of his financial stake in the pandemic."[102]

Summing up so far, governments, philanthrocapitalists, and pharma jointly put their eggs into the basket of accelerated vaccine development. This helps explain one peculiar element of the "Covid Doxa" (Mucchielli 2022a), which is a negative complement to its double focus on lockdown and vaccines: the stubborn denial that therapy was possible. It started, in France (but not much different elsewhere), with the strange government advice, "*je dois rester chez moi jusqu'à ma guèrison*" (I need to stay at home until my recovery) when feeling sick, at most to take a painkiller against fever, and to call a doctor only when breathing became difficult—which may have contributed to the rather high 20 percent mortality rate of hospitalized COVID-19 patients in France (Mucchielli 2022a, ch. 4).

Equally strange, already in the first half of January 2020, two months before there was an official "pandemic," the French government turned hydroxychloroquine (HCQ), an anti-inflammatory in use for sixty-five years to prevent and cure malaria and classified as "essential medicine" by WHO, from a freely accessible over-the-counter drug into a prescription drug. This made it a "List II poisonous substance," without citing any recent study

286 POLITICAL NEOLIBERALISM

or data to justify the unusual move. HCQ, an unpatented and accordingly cheap drug, would move into the picture when Didier Raoult, France's most internationally recognized virologist,[103] began successfully using it on early-phase COVID-19 patients in his Marseille hospital, IHU, France's leading university hospital for infectious diseases. The attack that followed, conducted at the highest level of the French government, against this, never to forget: non-Parisian, maverick doctor with the undefinable-age looks of Asterix, has been told elsewhere.[104] The chase was even joined by Anglo-Saxon social-science writers: Baldwin (2021, 17) ridiculed Raoult as "off-piste French clinician" indulging in "quackery."

What was going on? A plausible explanation is that the vaccine lobby, spearheaded by the American public health elite, saw the risk of a nearly cost-free vaccine alternative, which led it to commission some twenty clinical trial studies to shoot down HCQ.[105] Some of these studies used extreme overdoses, and applied HCQ in the late phase of COVID-19, in deviation from Raoult's IHU protocol, with the alarming finding of 10 to 20 percent more deaths than in the control groups (see Kennedy 2021, ch. 1). One of the anti-HCQ studies, published in May 2020 in *The Lancet* (together with the *New England Journal of Medicine* the medical world's leading journal), was outed as "fabrication" and "monumental fraud,"[106] and it quickly had to be withdrawn. The paper was based on a completely invented data set, compiled by an obscure Chicago-based organization, Surgisphere, among whose twelve employees were a science fiction writer and an "adult-content model."[107] Surgisphere's chief executive, Sapan Desai, a vascular surgeon who was involved in three medical malpractice suits in the United States (two of them filed as recently as November 2019), figured as one of the authors. But so did Mandeep Mehra, a "widely published and highly regarded professor of medicine at Harvard."[108] This is common practice in the pharma industry: clinical trials studies are conducted, the results ghost-written by "contract research organizations," and the papers then sent to "recognized scientists" to dignify them with their names (Deruelle 2022, 4). This seems to have happened here. *Lancet* editor Richard Horton is well aware of the problem, stating that "journals," his own apparently included, "have devolved into information laundering operation for the pharmaceutical industry" (Kennedy 2021, ch. 1). To Green and Fazi (2023, 146), the Surgisphere scandal shows "Big Pharma's breathtaking power." While no direct link was established in this case, Big Pharma is known for serial misconduct that is then resolved by negotiated settlements.[109] But the damage was done. After Surgisphere's *Lancet* publication, the French government, which seems to have just waited for it, instantly banned HCQ for COVID-19 treatment, as did the Portuguese, Italian, and Belgian governments. And the WHO immediately withdrew HCQ from its large-scale Solidarity Trial, which tested a variety of anti-COVID-19 drugs for their effectiveness.

A similar story can be told about Ivermectin (IVM), a Nobel-Prize winning drug originally used against human parasites, which, like HCQ, was classified as "essential medicine" by the WHO, and since 1996 has been unpatented and thus inexpensive and readily available—and of zero interest to pharma. Previously praised as "wonder drug," reports of successful early-phase COVID-19 treatments with IVM, especially in India where it was widely in use from April 2021 on, brought up the pharma lobby against it. This included the pharma giant Merck, which had developed the drug but lost interest once it was no longer patented. In early February 2021, Merck suddenly discovered "a concerning lack of safety data in the majority of studies," which was followed by negative statements by the WHO, the US Federal Drugs Administration (FDA), and the EU European Medicines Agency (EMA),[110] the latter two responsible for the licensing of drugs in their respective jurisdictions (Kennedy 2021, ch. 1). With the US public health establishment at the forefront, which, in this case, in addition to the FDA, included the National Institute of Health (NIH) and the Centers for Disease Control (CDC), the previous wonder drug was slandered as "horse dewormer." Again, social scientists followed the lead. For historian Simon Schama (2023, ch. 10), IVM was the "next populist panacea" (after HCQ), "ideal for anyone harbouring suspicions about Deep State medicine," and—weirdly—he thinks that for right-wingers "its associations with the guts of animals made it somehow more authentically homestead."

Intrinsic medical justifications for either of these views cannot be adjudicated here. But one motivation, which links both campaigns and the ultra-vituperative tone in which they were conducted, is obvious: as preventive and early-disease-phase drugs, and basically cost-free, HCQ and IVM had to threaten the multi-billion vaccine enterprise. More concretely, no vaccine could be fast-tracked for emergency-use approval, called "Emergency Use Approval" in the United States and "Conditional Market Authorization" in the European Union, by the FDA and the EMA, respectively, if there was an existing approved drug on the market that was deemed

288   POLITICAL NEOLIBERALISM

effective against the same disease, in this case COVID-19. In short, cheap prevention-cum-therapy drugs threatened the extravagant, and as yet unfinished, vaccine drive.

However, some element of therapy had to be. Complementary to the vaccine drive, the medicament of choice became Remdesivir, a repurposed antiviral, originally used against the Ebola virus, and—crucially—with an active patent owned by Gilead. As it was a late-disease-phase drug, it was not in competition with the vaccines. And, most importantly, as a patented drug, eventually sold for as high as $3,000 USD per treatment course (production cost being under $10 USD per dose), Remdesivir was no threat to pharma's business model. Of course, intrinsic to this model is a hefty public-funding component: the US National Institute of Allergy and Infectious Diseases (NIAID), since 1984 headed by Fauci, and the CDC paid Gilead $79 million USD to develop Remdesivir, which covered most of its development costs. Accordingly, these public agencies had a stake in fast-tracking the drug through the regulatory process.[111] The rub is that none other but the WHO itself, in a study published in mid-October 2020, found the expensive drug to be ineffective in lessening the severity of COVID-19 infections, and in lowering the risk of death; the WHO study even detected serious adverse effects for lungs and kidneys. These findings from the huge WHO Solidarity Trial did not prevent the European Union to sign a $1.2 billion USD contract to acquire five hundred thousand treatment courses of Remdesivir, and the FDA to approve the drug two weeks later. "This is a very, very bad look for the FDA," which had not even consulted its external expert group on the controversial drug, "and the dealings between Gilead and European Union make it another layer of badness," said Eric Topol, a leading American cardiologist and director of the Scripps Research Translational Institute in La Jolla, California.[112] Despite the fact that, in November 2020, the WHO officially recommended *not* to use Remdesivir, the "useless" drug continues to be prescribed, its US sales being $2.7 billion USD in 2020 alone (Durisch and Hertig 2021, 28).

Once the COVID-19 vaccines were ready and rolled out at unprecedented scale, from early 2021 on, it soon transpired that mass inoculation would not stop the pandemic. On the contrary, as registered, and to a degree self-produced, by freely available (although highly expensive) PCR tests and cheaper (self-)testing methods, wave after wave of mass infection rolled in, fueled by ever new virus variants (the best-known being Delta and Omicron). While the majority of the newly infected showed only light or no symptoms at all, each wave was nevertheless accompanied by a new lockdown. Governments and their expert councils now spread the message that only a complete vaccination of the entire population, reaching ever further down in the age hierarchy, even to children, and which after a while included the necessity of ever renewed injections (so-called boosters), could stop the pandemic. The German virologist Christian Drosten, advising the German government and with his curly hair a highly popular television presence, like many others, liked to use the brutish neologism *Durchimpfung* (complete vaccination) for this (the German word echoing the military *Durchmarsch*). West of the Rhine, the government drumbeat was "*le virus est toujours là*" (the virus is always there), followed by the request "*protégez-vous et protégez les autres*" (protect yourself and protect the others). This alarm was repeated at least every full hour on public radio, each time preceded by two brief and highly unpleasant sounds—it was "war," after all. That vaccination was not just self-protection but that it had to be done for the public good, to reduce the risk of infecting others, became the order of the day.

In retrospect, it had to be known to the responsible public authorities that the impact of the vaccines on the risk of infection was a complete unknown because they were never tested for it. By October 2020, long before the first vaccines were on the market, it was public knowledge, at least in expert circles, and openly stated by the industry, so impossibly unknown to governments that were all heavily advised by medical experts at the time, that the COVID-19 vaccines were never tested for two things: first, that they reduce the likelihood of severe illness; secondly, that they prevent infection, and thus the possibility to infect others (see Doshi 2020). But these were the exact two reasons why being vaccinated came to be considered a public duty: first, to prevent hospitals from being overrun; and secondly, and mainly, to reduce the risk of infecting others. Tal Zaks, chief medical officer of Moderna, stated with respect to the first objective of preventing serious illness: "The trial"—he was reporting on Moderna's all-important Phase III trial (involving thirty thousand cases), the last hurdle to take for emergency use authorization—"is precluded from judging (hospital admissions), based on what is a reasonable size and duration to serve the public good here" (in ibid., 3). The second half-sentence sounds obscure, but it isn't. The Moderna medic referred to the very low rate of COVID-19 hospitalization in the United States, which was a mere 3.4 percent of all cases (even lower, 1.7 percent, in the zero to forty-nine years age group, although ascending to 7.4 percent among the 65+). There simply weren't

290 POLITICAL NEOLIBERALISM

enough cases around for testing the more serious conditions, and the "public good" required to act fast. "Operational realities" were also in the way of testing the second, decisive vaccine objective that would become central to the later government propaganda: "Our trial will not demonstrate prevention of transmission . . . because in order to do you would have to swab people twice a week for very long periods" (Tal Zaks, quoted in ibid.).

When asked at a 2022 Congressional hearing, "When the government told us the vaccinated could not transmit (Covid), was that a lie or was that a guess?," Deborah Birx, the coordinator of the US Coronavirus Task Force, answered evasively: "I think it was a hope" (quoted by Green and Fazi 2023, 201). Alas, that was not communicated at the time. Instead, the public rhetoric was that of Pfizer chief Bourla, who stated in June 2021, evidently against his own better knowledge, that "widespread vaccination is a critical tool to stop transmission" (in ibid., 200).

The campaign against the non-vaccinated, who were mischievously held responsible for the fact that the pandemic didn't stop, shifted to high gear in the fall of 2021. At this moment, about three-fourths of Western populations were vaccinated at least once.[113] But a new virus variant, Omicron, arriving from South Africa via Amsterdam's Schiphol Airport, brought a new peak of infections, with the threat of a fourth lockdown looming on the horizon (that soon became reality). However, Omicron, it quickly turned out, was the least dangerous of the Corona virus variants so far. Further, it was plain to see that high levels of *Durchimpfung* were ineffective to stop the virus. Finally, negative side effects of vaccination increasingly became public, especially on young people whose COVID-19 risks were small to nil.[114] Also consider that, technically, all of the COVID-19 vaccines were still in the experimental and emergency authorization phase, with their adverse effects notoriously under-reported or not reported at all, and their long-term effects completely unknown. In this context, it was entirely reasonable for the (on average) one-fourth of vaccine resisters across Western countries to refuse the offer they were not supposed to refuse. Not just the epidemiological facts, but international human rights law was on their side. Building on the 1947 Nuremberg Code, Article 7 of the International Convention on Civil and Political Rights requires "free consent to medical and scientific experimentation." It sounds sensationalist but is hard to refute that Covid vaccination was "a vaccine experiment of a grand scale that is unprecedented in the history of medicine" (Ségur 2022, 464).

END OF NEOLIBERALISM? 291

So, this was a moment that suggested being skeptical about the wisdom of (mass) vaccination, while the notion of a deadly virus equally dangerous to all was by now anachronistic (as it had been from the start).[115] This needs to be recalled to gauge the magnitude of the ensuing "witch hunt" against the non-vaccinated, as the German sociologist Münch called the campaign without overstating (2022, 57). It happened when the pandemic approached its third (and final) year, between late 2021 and early 2022. More than driving the authoritarian and freedom-impairing political management of the COVID-19 crisis to its ignoble extreme, this episode shows the thin crust that separates civilization from barbary. From Henri Tajfel's Social Identity Theory, we know how fast random external labeling, like being called "blue" or "red," can become touchstones of group identity and aggression against those who are of the other assigned color. Something similar happened in this final round of the COVID-19 saga. Except, of course, that hatred against the "non-vaccinated" by the "vaccinated," the equivalent of blue and red, *seemed* to be different in one respect, which is that a substantive ground and justification of the binary existed. The non-vaccinated were considered "*Gefährder*" (Münch 2022, 57); that is, "potential offenders who constitute a threat to public safety," which of course they were not.

It is no exaggeration to say that the "unvaccinated" became the "target of institutionally sanctioned hate speech" (Green and Fazi 2023, 188). In early 2022, French President Macron reached deep into the vulgar register: "*Les non-vaccinés, j'ai grand envie de les emmerder*" (my strong desire is to piss-off the non-vaccinated). He had a forceful tool at his disposal, the EU Digital Covid Certificate, a barcoded vaccination pass that had been in place since June 2021. It came to be used in France (and other European countries) not just for crossing borders, its original purpose, but to exclude all who did not possess that document from bars, restaurants, public transport, and other public places, even hospitals. The new frontier of "pissing them off" was to make it more difficult for vaccine skeptics to sneak in with a negative COVID-19 test. In France, this happened through making the test self-paying and thus prohibitively expensive. This time, Germany even went one nasty notch further, formally excluding the merely tested who had neither a prior COVID disease nor a vaccination credential—the so-called 2G rule (either *genesen* [recovered] or *geimpft* [vaccinated], tertium non datur). The Minister President of Saarland, Tobias Hans, defended the harsh 2G on television: "(This) is sending a clear message to the non-vaccinated: you are now kicked out of society (*raus aus dem gesellschaftlichen Leben*). Therefore,

292 POLITICAL NEOLIBERALISM

we are doing 2G without compromise" (Kostner 2022, 133). Other German politicians, notably across the party spectrum, theorized "freedom" in a way that would have pleased George Orwell for his foreboding. "Freedom means obligatory vaccination for all, instead of restrictions for all," said the general secretary of the Bavarian CSU. "It is a vulgar understanding of freedom to equate freedom with . . . physical integrity (*Unversehrtheit*)," said an SPD member of the Bundestag (ibid., 136), thus inadvertently suggesting that vaccination might be a health threat.

Never before in the history of liberal democracies have political leaders dared not just to aggress, but to factually expel a sizeable portion of society that simply insisted on their own considered judgement, without harming anyone. To repeat, the favored justification for this expulsion, that "no one has the freedom to endanger others" (Kostner 2022, 129), which was meant to be an application of John Stuart Mill's Harm Principle,[116] was simply false. The non-vaccinated were no threat to anyone, not even to themselves. This did not prevent US President Biden from claiming, "(t)his is the pandemic of the nonvaccinated," and like an Old Testament prophet he foresaw "a winter of severe illness and death for yourselves, your families, and the hospitals you may soon overwhelm." For Italian Prime Minister Mario Draghi, "the appeal not to get vaccinated is an appeal to die, basically. You don't get vaccinated, you get sick, you die. Or you kill" (quoted by Green and Fazi 2023, 189). That the non-vaccinated "kill," which legally speaking should have put them behind bars, was the summit of this oratory of hate.

Political talk was followed by action. In November 2021, the Austrian government effectively placed the non-vaccinated under house arrest, and parliament passed a law that made vaccination obligatory (but that was never implemented for constitutional reasons). In Greece, from December 2021, vaccine refuseniks above sixty years of age were fined 100 Euros per month, not a small amount in a country impoverished by more than a decade of EU-ordered austerity; this was the "price to pay for health," Prime Minister Mitsotakis snippily declared (in Telford et al. 2022, 47). In Italy, from October 2021, all employees had to be vaccinated, and from January 2022, the vaccine obligation applied to everyone above the age of fifty. In the same month, a "Super Green Pass" limited access to practically all public spaces and functions, from bars to transport, to those who were either vaccinated or recovered, mirroring Germany's 2G; and this requirement applied to children from the age of twelve onward. Not to let them starve, the non-vaccinated were allowed to enter Italian supermarkets, if they had a valid COVID-19 test (Green and Fazi 2023, 183f). As the Italian prime minister justified these draconian measures, "most of the problems we are facing today depend on the fact that there are unvaccinated people" (in Telford et al. 2022, 50).

Not legally but factually, not being vaccinated meant to be expelled from society. There was "such thing," after all, "society," and it was cynically deployed as a stick by the late disciples of the Iron Lady, who infamously had denied its existence. It is an interesting fact that, from Macron's heartfelt wish to "piss-off" the non-vaccinated, to Draghi's morbid phantasy that the non-vaccinated "kill," it was neoliberal "reformers" who not just sported the most graphic opinions but also were among the more uninhibited freedom cutters, from beginning to end.

But it needs to be repeated that the COVID-19 restrictions, including their bitter last moment—the campaign against the non-vaccinated—were met with large public approval. And this approval was even stronger on the left side of the political spectrum. With respect to the United States, a representative poll in January 2022 found that 48 percent of *all* American voters favored President Biden's plan of mandatory COVID-19 vaccination for the employees of large companies and government agencies.[117] But 59 percent of *Democrat* voters went a step further, favoring the confinement of people at their homes at all times if they refused to be vaccinated, and 45 percent of Democrats, difficult to believe, favored interning vaccine-resisters in "designated facilities," also known as camps.[118]

Digitalization

Today, a numbing silence surrounds the pandemic, this single most extraordinary event in postwar history, and, in particular, its ugly finale. Everyone seems to rather forget that it all happened, like in a trauma. "Denial was everywhere," as Eric Klinenberg (2024, 370) summarizes the US Democrats' reluctance to be associated with the coronavirus restrictions that they had happily ordered, once the pandemic emergency was officially ended there, which was as late as May 11, 2023. Early in the pandemic, German sociologist Rudolf Stichweh speculated that "there will be structural changes (*Strukturbrüche*), but we do not yet know what they will be."[119] Almost four years after 2020, "the year everything changed" (Klinenberg 2024), not terribly much seems changed. Of course, at least two major societal COVID-19 effects are notable: more inequality and more digitalization. Both, however, are not the "structural changes" that Stichweh had expected.

294 POLITICAL NEOLIBERALISM

Instead, they merely aggravate and accelerate, respectively, things that were long in place or in the making. Above all, they confirm Klinenberg's suspicion that "neoliberalism . . . looks likely to survive the calamity" (2024, 367), to say the least.

With respect to inequality, the wealth and income gap between the super-rich and the rest of global society, already at historical heights before COVID-19, has increased even further. Economist Joseph Stiglitz (2022) estimates that "(g)lobal billionaire wealth grew by USD 4.4 trillion between 2020 and 2021, and at the same time more than 100 million people fell below the poverty line." To get a sense of the enormity of the wealth gap increase, the 713 US billionaires saw their collective wealth increase by 60 percent in the 16 months between March 2020 and July 2021 (Fourcade 2021, 347).[120] According to an Oxfam report (2022, 9), "the world's ten richest men have doubled their fortunes, while over 160 million people . . . have been pushed into poverty" (the latter defined as earning less than $5.50 USD per day).

In terms of sector, among the biggest winners, predictably, are Big Pharma and Big Tech. After its COVID-19 vaccine was out in February 2021, Pfizer expected to sell it for a total of $26 billion USD before the end of the year, at hugely variable prices, because the company cleverly played-out individual governments against one another (Goodman 2022, ch. 14). In a cynical demonstration of the close link between vaccine development and profit-making, Pfizer chief Bourla sold 62 percent of his company stocks on the very day that the first positive clinical trial data were in, betting on the instant hike of Pfizer's share value that indeed occurred (Durisch and Hertig 2021, 29).

As most of personal and social life went virtual during lockdown, Big Tech had to be the second big winner. Jeff Bezos, the founder and CEO of Amazon saw his wealth grow by $70 billion USD between March and December 2020, to a record $185 billion USD, riding on Amazon's share value explosion of 90 percent in the same short period. Even bigger (relative) wealth increases accrued to Facebook's Mark Zuckerberg (by 80 percent, to USD 100bn) and to Google's Larry Page (growing by half to USD76bn). In this company, Bill Gates's wealth increase in this period, from USD 100bn to USD 120bn, looks paltry.[121] As so much concentrated wealth needs outlets, it is unsurprising that Bernard Arnault, the champion of French luxury brands from couture to champagne, would double his wealth, from USD 69bn to USD 148bn in these fabulous nine months,[122] and he is now among the world's three richest persons.

Covid was a bonanza for the world's super-rich, aggravating the inequality from the top that is the signature of the neoliberal order (see Chapter 4). Naturally silent about their windfall, Big Tech leaders adopted an altruist posture, most blatantly perhaps Mark Benioff, founder of the software giant Salesforce, whose company value doubled to USD 225bn in the even shorter period from March to August 2020: "In the pandemic, it was CEOs ... all over the world who were the heroes ... They're the ones who stepped forward with their financial resources ...—not for profit, but to save the world" (quoted by Goodman 2022: prologue). Appositely, Benioff performed his act of corporate selflessness at the 2021World Economic Forum meeting in Davos, in a panel on "stakeholder capitalism." Blowing into the same horn, ex-Google chief Eric Schmidt invited his American fellow-citizens to "(t)hink about what your life would be like in America without Amazon," exhorting them to "be a little bit grateful" that companies like Amazon "got the capital, did the investment, built the tools that we're using now, and have really helped us out" (quoted by Klein 2020).

In Schmidt's nasty little pique one can loudly hear the tables being turned. Because the pandemic happened to be a "godsend for the tech giants" (Brubaker 2023a: vii) just when they had come under mighty pressure, both in the US and in Europe, for their size and unfair competition practices, tax avoidance, and, not least, their obscure and privacy-imperiling data appropriations (dubbed "data colonialism" by two critics, Couldry and Mejias 2018). In early 2018, *The Economist* summarized the pre-pandemic charges in the acronym BAADD—"big, anti-competitive, addictive and destructive to democracy," and it suggested ways to "tame the tech titans."[123] Covid would call it off.

Even more than increased inequality, the digitalization of "everything" (Fourcade 2021:346) stands out as perhaps the single most important long-term societal effect of the pandemic, and this is what I will look at further in the rest of this chapter (and book). The pandemic brought home, quite literally, what digitality's dystopian endpoint might be, because for an extended moment it was already there: home office, home education, home delivery, home communication, home entertainment, home everything, the whole world through a screen. This is a world in which the public either dissolves or is sucked into the private sphere, which has long been a defining feature of the neoliberal order (even though the reverse direction, of the private being exposed to public gaze, such as unmade beds or untidy rooms awkwardly on screen in a "zoomed" business meeting or academic seminar,

296 POLITICAL NEOLIBERALISM

is quite new). The pandemic home-everything was accomplished through the smartphone applications and "infrastructural" internet platforms provided by the five tech giants:[124] Google, Apple, Facebook, Amazon, and Microsoft, collectively known as GAFAM. They are the heart of "platform capitalism" (Srnicek 2017). It pushes to a new level what Colin Crouch was the first to identify as the beating heart of "actually existing" neoliberalism: not the market v. state binary, as in Hayekian theory, but the "dominance of public life by the giant corporation" (Crouch 2011: viii).

Digital Platforms

What are "platforms," and what does "digital" add to them? A platform, literally, is a "raised level surface" on which people or things stand (Brubaker 2023a:101). As a platform raises everyone equally, this notion, if paired with the adjective "digital," echoes the utopian and countercultural expectations that were invested in the internet once it moved out of the US military-industrial complex, where it had originated. What in early days was called "cyberspace" flags a technology whose interactive nature busts the distinction between producers and consumers (yielding "prosumers" and "produsers"); that does away with elitist gatekeepers and intermediaries and thus empowers the common folk; where knowledge is free and shared by all; and whose decentralized nature makes it impossible to be controlled by the state. "We are creating a world that all may enter without privilege or prejudice accorded by race, economic power, military force, or station of birth . . ., without fear of being coerced into silence or conformity," as an early cyberspace enthusiast put it.[125] To the degree that Big Tech's digital platforms became a core feature of actually existing neoliberalism, the cyberspace utopia runs as an ever weaker but never extinguished background noise, even if thinned-down to technocratic "solutionism" (see Nachtwey and Seidl 2020).[126] Importantly, for Big Tech, the pandemic was not just a commercial boon, but also moral-political salvation, allowing it to recover the original posture of "not just . . . a business but . . . a steward of humanity" (Zuckerberg, in ibid., 26f).

The real as against ideal features of digital platforms have received ample attention elsewhere.[127] I recapture here mainly their darker aspects that *also* transpired in the pandemic, and that are likely to evolve further.

First, digital platforms are intermediaries, connecting interested parties; notionally, they are not interested parties in their own right. This makes digital platforms look like markets—except that they are privately owned, "proprietary markets" (Staab 2015). Their connecting function and notional disinterestedness allow digital platforms to remove themselves from the societal contract and thrive in a regulatory grey zone. Uber, for instance, which is not an "infrastructural" but "sectoral" platform,[128] that is, specializing in one function, in this case transport, posits itself as a "connective platform" rather than what it really is, a "transport service." This allows Uber to "withdraw from collective responsibilities" for the sector in which it operates, which is public transport, and which decays in the same measure as platform companies like Uber become predominant in it (Van Dijck et al. 2018:73 and 74). Furthermore, Uber drivers are de facto employees but legally entrepreneurs, which absolves the platform company of any social responsibility and related expenditures. Typical work in the platform economy is "gig," temporary on-demand freelancing, and thus notoriously precarious (see Crouch 2019). Finally, like all digital platforms, Uber claims to be "empowering customers" (Van Dijck et al. 2018:23). In reality, the ubiquitous ratings that follow upon and in turn condition app-provided services, in what is often referred to as "sharing economy," cut both ways. Uber drivers, but also Airbnb apartment letters, rate their customers much as customers rate their service providers, whereby "providers and clients are becoming dependent on each other's evaluation" (ibid., 91). This is a market equivalent to the state-led Chinese social credit system, and more than an inch away from the libertarian cyberspace utopia.[129]

Even further away from this utopia is a *second* feature of digital platforms, which is that they are "architectures of interaction" (Brubaker 2023a:104). Platforms are not neutral but "in a position to specify and control the forms and formats of interaction between the parties they bring together" (ibid.). US President Trump was banned from Twitter once his tweets were deemed inappropriate or inconvenient; the same happened to many critics of the Covid Doxa, and not only on Twitter but across the GAFAM range. As Facebook's Zuckerberg boasted his company's proactive role in "fight(ing) disinformation" during the pandemic, "(s)o we're removing false claims and conspiracy theories that have been flagged by leading global health organizations" (in Tréguer 2021, 13).

Lawrence Lessig (2006) famously expounded that cyberspace allows for a new and perfected form of control: "code." Code may function like law

298   POLITICAL NEOLIBERALISM

("code is law," ibid., 5), as a device to control behavior. But both differ in one important respect: code is *ex ante* while law is *ex post*.[130] In law, individuals act first, and in this basic sense they are free; at worst, they self-discipline in anticipation of the punishment for trespassing the law—*if* they get caught, which they might as well *not*. In code, there is no such freedom. Code operates "through a kind of physics. A locked door is not a command 'do not enter' backed up with the threat of punishment by the state. A locked door is a physical constraint on the liberty of someone to enter some space" (ibid., 81f).[131] In a prescient flight of imagination, Gilles Deleuze (1992) saw that the computer would herald a new type of society, "societies of control," in which individuals are demoted to data-constructed "dividuals," apparently "free-floating" in social and physical space, yet monitored by "electronic collars" and in need of an "electronic card that raises a given barrier"—that could "just as easily be rejected" (ibid., 7). Code does away with the need to discipline people, beasts can be controlled this way.

From a commercial angle, Google's former chief economist, Hal Varian (2014, 30), hailed the computer for enlarging the range of economic transactions, via "trust … but verify." This is a variation of Lenin's motto "trust is good, control is better," in which (much as in its original) the trust element has all but disappeared. "Because transactions are now computer mediated," argues Varian, "we can observe behaviour that was previously unobservable and write contracts on it." No longer, say, do car dealers need to hire a "repo man" to recover the vehicle of an insolvent buyer. Instead, "(n)owadays it's a lot easier just to instruct the vehicular monitoring system not to allow the car to be started and to signal the location where it can be picked up" (ibid.).

Required for control by code is a *third* and essential feature of digital platforms, which is to "extract, process, and control data" (Brubaker 2023a, 105). If digital platforms, most of the time, are available for free, this is because in return for using them, the platform owners appropriate the "data exhaust" that accrues in the process, not just using it to optimize the algorithms that feed their services but selling on these data to interested third parties, such as advertising companies or data brokers that sell them on to yet other parties (including politicians in campaign mode, Barak Obama being one of the first). To Varian, this is just fine. Isn't it true that "(p)eople are willing to share quite personal information if they get something they want in return"? Think of "a mortgage, medical advice, legal advice—or advice from your personal digital assistant" (2014, 30).

END OF NEOLIBERALISM? 299

Shoshana Zuboff begs to disagree, in her influential diagnosis of "surveillance capitalism" (see also Pistor 2020a, 2020b). What to the apologist is "data exhaust," is "behavioural surplus" to the critic, acquired in a "one-way process" without the consent, most often even without the knowledge, of their producers, those who click and roam the internet (Zuboff 2015, 80).[132] Worse still, these data are weaponized as "instrumentarian power" against their producers, for instance, in the form of personalized advertisement that aims at peoples' "behavioral modification" (2019, ch. 1).

For Zuboff (2015, 80), the defining feature of surveillance capitalism is the "absence of structural reciprocity between the firm and its population," which she thinks existed in the Fordist era of mass production. It is true: whereas the top three Detroit automakers employed 1.2 million people as late as the late 1990s, the top three Silicon Valley firms, in 2014, employed barely one-tenth as much, a meager 137,000 (ibid.). This may be further dramatized when comparing the "Old" versus "New Economy Business Model," following Mazzucato (2013, 181–192). The old model, valid in the Golden Era of democratic capitalism, offered stable employment in hierarchical corporations, high salaries, and subsidized health care plus old age pensions. The new model, in which "companies are footloose" (ibid., 183), is the opposite in all these respects. As Mazzucato illustrates with the example of Apple, among its forty-seven thousand directly employed, more than half (twenty-seven thousand) work in one of the 246 American Apple stores, with no sales commissions or stock options. At the top end, in 2011, the nine Apple lead executives earned 17,600 times as much as its US retail employees (ibid., 185). Apple thus perfectly matches what Zuboff (2015, 80) calls the "structural independence of the firm from its population," and the breaking-apart of the "historical relationship between market capitalism and democracy."

Evgeny Morozov (2019) rightly objects that Zuboff's "surveillance capitalism" diagnosis rests on the questionable assumption of a perfectly reciprocal "managerial capitalism" of the past. And it overlooks that a modicum of reciprocity might be recovered by upgraded consumption. Indeed, its lure to the consumer has been a central selling-point of the neoliberal order from early on. The "maximization of consumer welfare" (Robert Bork, in Khan 2017, 720, fn.37), in terms of lower prices, is the guiding principle of the Chicago "Law and Economics" School's reinterpretation of American antitrust law, paving the way for ever bigger companies—monopolization being fine as long as it makes consumers better off. This theory explicitly discards the massive wealth transfer that goes along with monopolization.[133]

300 POLITICAL NEOLIBERALISM

But it cannot be denied that what people lost as workers, they have partially recouped as consumers, making them consent to the neoliberal order, whether one likes it or not.[134] As Pepper Culpepper and Kathleen Thelen (2019, 1) argue, in a neoliberal order "citizens" morph into "consumers," and "platform power," in particular, is lastly backed by "the tacit allegiance of consumers."

Despite this valid objection, Zuboff is on target when arguing that freedom, once associated with cyberspace, is imperiled under surveillance capitalism. What Google's Varian nonchalantly described as "writing contracts on observed behaviour," is really the end of contracts as a device to mitigate uncertainty by trust, which both presupposes *and* reinforces freedom: "(C)ontracts are lifted from the social and reimagined as machine processes. Consensual participation in the values from which legitimate authority is derived, along with free will and reciprocal rights and obligations, are traded in for the universal equivalent of the prisoner's electronic ankle bracelet," as Zuboff (2015, 81) plays on Deleuze's "societies of control" metaphor. And with Hannah Arendt, Zuboff insists that "human fallibility in the execution of contracts is the price of freedom" (ibid.). Conversely, the digital control by "Big Other," situated "somewhere between nature and God," even outshines the Bentham-Foucauldian Panopticon, because, unlike the latter, "there is no place to be where the Other is not" (ibid., 81, 82). Moreover, the Panopticon was a place for punishment, whereas digital platforms are "requirements for social participation," imposing themselves with an overwhelming sense of inevitability" (ibid., 85). As Brubaker (2023a, 106–107) put it, digital platforms concentrate and exercise "infrastructural power." While akin in this respect to the public utilities of the past, the difference is that platform power is in private hands, which decouples it from democratic accountability.

Zuboff is not deaf to the element of voluntarism and complicity under this regime, conceding that "(e)veryone will expect to be tracked and monitored, since the advantages in terms of convenience, safety, and services will be so great" (2015, 82). For this very reason, to call this condition "surveillance" capitalism is a touch too dark. In an intriguing ethnography of digital self-track technology, Natasha Dow Schüll (2016) sees the latter deployed by a "passive, choosing self" that is neither externally "controlled," as in the Deleuze–Zuboff scenario, nor "self-controlled," in the late-Foucault-inspired "responsibilization" sense (see Rose and Miller 1992). Instead, the

END OF NEOLIBERALISM? 301

self-tracking individual, whose Fitbit watch will tell them when to stop exercising, is "nudged."[135] Nudging "assumes a choosing subject, but one who is constitutionally ill equipped to make rational, healthy choices." While self-tracking is merely a niche in the range of the digital, the element of complicity should never be discarded when the individual submits to digitality's dubious charms.[136]

Opinions are divided whether "rule by data" (Pistor 2020b) is still within the ambit of political neoliberalism, or something new and different. Marion Fourcade and Jeffrey Gordon (2020) find that the "dataist state" is a follow-up to the "neoliberal state," and thus is new and different. In their view, the neoliberal state was intent on "produc(ing) a rational economic subject" (ibid., 86), or, in Nikolas Rose and Peter Miller's terms (1992), governing the individual "at a distance" through the individual's own free choices. By contrast, the dataist state seeks to "obtain the desired behaviour, whether or not it is animated by rational intentions" (Fourcade and Gordon 2020, 86)— paternalist "nudging" is key to it. Similarly, Brubaker (2023a, 46) speaks of the "*post*-neoliberal self," governed not "through its choices" but "through its data," a self that is no longer free to choose but "conditioned to respond to increasingly pervasive and finely calibrated stimuli."

These observations are valid, but they don't warrant the conclusion that political neoliberalism has passed, even in terms of these authors' own analyses. Brubaker (2023a, 47), for instance, immediately steps back a little, qualifying as "not yet" his dystopian vista of the "colonization of the self," the latter with the self's full complicity to add. And Fourcade and Gordon's analysis also suggests that the dataist state is fully within a neoliberal logic, for one, because this state results from a "four-decade-long ... reorientation of the state to serve the market" (2020, 79); and, secondly, the neoliberal notion that individuals are to "take responsibility for themselves and compete for rights and benefits that are indexed to success in a market" (ibid., 96) continues to be acute. Evgeny Morozov, when looking at digital technology's latest incarnation, which is "artificial general intelligence" (AGI), is therefore on the mark that this signals not the end of neoliberalism but, on the contrary, reinforces "its main biases." Among these "biases" he finds the notion that private actors always outperform public actors ("market bias"); that "adapting to reality beats transforming it" ("adaptation bias"); and the prevalence of efficiency over justice concerns ("efficiency bias") (Morozov 2023). To all these neoliberal precepts and "biases," no alternative is in sight.

302 POLITICAL NEOLIBERALISM

Untact Society

"Untact society" is a term of South Korean provenience. Its "untact" component refers to "service that is provided without face-to-face encounters between employees and customers through the use of digital technologies" (Lee and Lee 2020, 4). Its "society" component flags the intention to turn untact from a pandemic emergency device into a program to "spur economic growth by removing layers of human interaction from society."[137] This is what the South Korean government in all seriousness did when introducing the term in 2020. Already before the pandemic, South Korea was the most AI-robotized society on earth, sporting untact boutiques, untact cosmetic stores, untact phone shops, untact convenience kiosks, untact coffee bars, untact fast food joints, untact car showrooms, and many more things untact. Even psychological counseling and treatment for depression, which one would think to flourish in such settings, is increasingly done via mobile applications, targeting the growing chunk of youngsters who "find face-to-face counselling uncomfortable" (ibid., 14). Lonely seniors can "interact with an AI speaker by asking it to play music, have a simple conversation, perform quizzes, or even call for help in an emergency."[138]

Before the South Korean government made the untact society an economic program, it grew out of societal demand and circulated as a marketing device. A business-minded report (Lee and Lee 2020, 10) identified the demand side as "customers' preference for a 'comfortable cut-off' from communication over 'uncomfortable communication' ... Many young consumers who are accustomed to digital devices tend to feel uncomfortable around people and prefer 'solo shopping.'" In short, "interpersonal fatigue" among the young is among "the main drivers for the proliferation of untact technology in the market" (ibid.).

It is still paradoxical that the South Korean government would support "untact" because, for years, it had been alarmed by and tried to work against with big money and program effort several trends that can only get worse as a result of untact: the country's dwindling birth rate, which is the lowest in the world (0.78 in 2022), its exponential growth of single-person households (from 4.8 percent in 1980 to 33.4 percent by 2021),[139] and most worrisome, the highest suicide rate in the OECD. The government now seems unmoved by this, pumping $7.6 billion USD into an "untact growth fund" for an envisioned twelve hundred untact startups by 2025.[140] At a minimum, untact is simply popular: a poll found that 80 percent of Seoul residents wished the pandemic restrictions on face-to-face interaction to be maintained in the future.[141]

Compared with South Korea's enthusiasm, Western audiences seem more reserved about the virtues of untact, which is not a term in use here. There is a strangely ambivalent entry on something akin to untact in Klaus Schwab and Thierry Mallet's *Great Reset* (2020), taken by some as a conspiratorial blueprint by the global tech and money elite to revamp all of society in their interest. What this report dubs "e-things," it takes to be the inevitable result of the "digital transformation." "(A) cycling class in front of a screen at home doesn't match the conviviality and fun of doing it with a group in a live class," the authors concede, "but is in fact safer (and cheaper!)" (ibid., 63). Similarly, compared with "driving to a distant family gathering for a weekend" (which by its very formulation seems to be a nuisance), "the WhatsApp family group is not as fun but, again, safer, cheaper and greener" (ibid.). And with respect to "flying to a meeting" or "attending an academic course," flying may be more "fulfilling," but "Zoom is safer, cheaper, greener and much more convenient" (ibid.). In this mishmash of cost, safety, and greenery, not only the conspiracy theorist can sense the Big State–Big Tech mobility restrictions (only for ordinary people, of course) that are looming on the horizon, once what in the European Union is known as "Green Transition" shifts to high gear.[142] No big fantasy is required to get to this point. The Davos authors' chips are down when they conclude that "personal health and well-being will be a much greater priority for society, which is why the genie of tech surveillance will not be put back into the bottle."

During the pandemic, the "digital divide" was mainly experienced as the privilege of the well-to-do and educated to withdraw with their laptops to their country retreats, while the plebs had to perform "essential work" in full exposure to the virus. The opening lines of star academic Simon Schama's history of pandemics and vaccines, which touches on COVID-19 only spottily, and in sarcastic disdain of anyone who deviates from its doxa that he adopts wholesale, wax lyrical about "peepers" and "wood frogs" approaching "our house in the Hudson valley," in the "13th month of the COVID confinement"—"the more we retreated into digitally numbed companionship, the more brazenly the company of animals advanced towards us" (Schama 2023, ch. 1).[143] A younger and lesser known academic did not even find much difference between pandemic and ordinary times: "(Q)urantine is just a raw, surprising name for

304   POLITICAL NEOLIBERALISM

the condition that computer technologies have brought over the last two decades: making almost everything possible from the quiet isolation of a desk or a chair illuminated by an internet-connected laptop or tablet."[144] Pandemia merely brought home to him the "banal normality of this reality." And with the help of Netflix, "the last thing anyone might worry about is getting bored at home"—given the streamlined correctness of this entertainment machine, one must wish him good luck with this. At the same time, like most in the laptop class, he was aware of, and guilt-plagued by, the "massive power imbalance" dividing remote and frontline workers.

However, the post-pandemic digital divide is likely to be the exact opposite. Sociality, mobility in space, and person-to-person services will become the preserve of the elite, while the rest will inhabit the Ersatz reality that Meta, Facebook's follow-up, is already building for them (and which, incidentally, the WEF is heavily invested in). Marc Andreessen, the chatty tech billionaire who invented the Netscape browser, has a precise vision of this. When asked, by a very hip "retard," in the second year of the pandemic, "Are we *too* connected these days," unprepared "for constant, instantaneous contact," Andreessen ridiculed his questioner as suffering from "Reality Privilege." It is worth quoting his response at length:

> A small percent of people live in a real-world environment that is rich, even overflowing, with glorious substance, beautiful settings, plentiful stimulation, and many fascinating people to talk to, and to work with, and to date . . . Everyone else, the vast majority of humanity, lacks Reality Privilege—their online world is, or will be, immeasurably richer and more fulfilling than most of the physical and social environment around them in the 'real world'. The Reality Privileged, of course, call this conclusion dystopian, and demand that we prioritize improvements in reality over improvements in virtuality. To which I say: reality has had 5000 years to get good, and is clearly still woefully lacking for most people, I don't think we should wait another 5000 years to see if it eventually closes the gap. We should—and we are building—online worlds that make life and work and love wonderful for everyone, no matter what level of reality deprivation they find themselves in.[145]

In short, to be locked behind a screen, in work and free time alike, is likely to be the lot of the unprivileged multitude, and they will not even notice it.

Digital Identity

A Frenchman stranded in Wuhan in the winter of 2020 found memorable words for what he saw: "A cyber-securitized world where each individual is suspect (of being sick), registered, traced, bar-coded. Green code: you circulate. Red code: you are halted."[146] His reference, of course, is to the Chinese "Health Code," a voluntary (but factually required) smartphone application that uses algorithms and big data technology to assess its user's health profile, and to control their behavior on this basis (see Cong 2021). The Chinese Health Code also includes a third, perhaps most heinous color: orange, which requires its recipient to go into (naturally, digitally controlled) quarantine after having come too close to an infected person. The Chinese Health Code, whose simultaneously punitive and enabling logic grew out of the country's notorious Social Credit System (see Knight and Creemers 2021), could also be used outside the health context, to play "dirty tricks" on politically suspect individuals, who suddenly saw the orange or red light blinking when embarking on something not liked by the authorities.[147] The Health Code has still enjoyed "widespread support" by the Chinese, who—like most people in the West—voluntarily "are giving up some rights in return for absolute security."[148]

While a good deal less dystopian, the vaccine passports introduced in Western countries in the second year of the pandemic may differ in degree, but not in kind from the Chinese Health Code. Their communality is to give up rights (in the West many more than in China) for the lure of safety. The French philosopher Stiegler described the authorities of her country "fascinated by the Chinese model and its techno-securitarian approach where everything is numerical and the authorities distribute citizenship permits accordingly. This is exactly the spirit of this pass that is pretended to be 'sanitary.'"[149] In July 2021, the French government pioneered the extension of the EU Digital Covid Certificate, which originally was meant to register one's vaccination status for unrestricted traveling within and beyond the European Union, into a *passe sanitaire* (Sanitary Pass), to limit access to most functions and spaces of public life to fully (first double-, later triple-) vaccinated, recovered, or recently tested persons, from the tender age of twelve years onward. Italy, under the neoliberal technocrat Draghi, even used its "Green Pass" (one wonders: is the "green" a reference to the Chinese Health Code, to ecology, or to both?) to control access to supermarkets and all public transport, the local kind included. This was, as Stiegler and

François Alla (2022, 46) concisely argue, nothing less than the creation of a "new type of society." Citizenship or legal residence no longer suffice to participate equally in society. Instead, by means of the health pass, "the authorities could directly modify, through numerical applications, the range of rights and obligations of each citizen" (ibid., 53).

Citing a range of examples, from digitally "smartened" Western cities where "good deeds" give you privileged access to infrastructure, to the darker Chinese Social Credit world where facial recognition techniques publicly shame jaywalkers on giant public screens, among other oddities, Wessel Reijers, Liav Orgad, and Primavera de Filippi (2023) speak of the rise of "cybernetic citizenship." This is a citizenship that moves "from status to process": "Cybernetic citizenship is a dynamic, adjustable process that turns citizenship from an unconditional legal status to a historically lasting process, subject to fault and correction" (ibid., 224). The key is that rights no longer automatically and equally derive from status but need to "be constantly earned" (ibid.). Cybernetic citizenship, indeed, is "earned citizenship," yet for everyone, not only for immigrants (who are the focus in Joppke 2021c). Behavioral modification in the service of what public authorities consider the common good is of the essence. Cybernetic citizenship is "republican," but in an instrumental sense because digitally registered civic virtue (like getting COVID-19 vaccine jabs as many times as the authorities want) is required to get along individually, and the "good citizen" is "conformist, rule-abiding," not "active, vigilant" (Reijters et al. 2023, 225). This is not only a description of China. A (Macronist) French health official, in an appeal for "national unity" addressed to his "fellow-citizens," expresses the notion that a good citizen is one who faithfully follows her government: "In these difficult times, we don't need polemics about the government measures; we don't need grandstanding by good-thinkers (*tribunes bienpensantes*) who unduly put freedom and science in opposite corners and who put at risk the most elementary of all human values, which is to protect yourself and your family."[150]

Already preceding the pandemic, Big Tech and international organizations, including the United Nations, World Bank, the WEF, and the European Union, had been promoting digital identities, with health and "known traveler" passports as their points of entry. One of the most prominent identity projects is ID2020, which was initiated by the Rockefeller Foundation in 2010 and supported by Microsoft, Accenture, the GAVI vaccine alliance, and the United Nations High Commissioner for Refugees (UNHCR). It

END OF NEOLIBERALISM? 307

is all couched in progressive speak. Identity is a "human right" (Kruchem 2021), and the ambitious goal is to bestow that right on all people on the planet, especially in its most precarious zones, like refugee camps, by providing them with a digital ID by 2030. This electronic identity is supposedly a "self-sovereign identity" (Allen 2016), about which only the individual is in control, with the help of decentralized blockchain technology that was first put in use for state-bypassing cryptocurrencies.

However, what may be of great help to people in underdeveloped places without birth registers and regular access to identity documents and passports, may carry significant risks in more developed parts of the world, especially with respect to freedom. Blockchain, while less centrally controllable than data stored on big private servers, requires that no single entry can ever be erased—the logic being that of a correct bank statement requiring all prior transactions to be traceable, to the very first. And the idea of all personal data concentrated in one barcode, which is also driving the current EU "Digital Identity Wallet" project, inheres the obvious risk that a lapse on one dimension, say, not to get a required vaccination in time, could impair you on some other dimension, say, to open a bank account. Overall, what is billed as giving you "access to services," might as well "be 'switched off' at any moment" (Green and Fazi 2023, 427), as Deleuze anticipated in his society of control. And even if, formally speaking, "(c)itizens will at all times have full control of the data they share," as the European Commission promises with respect to its Digital Identity Wallet,[151] how can it be avoided that the factual power imbalance between, say, apartment owners and prospective renters, employers and aspiring employees, banks and clients in need of a bank account, or governments and aspiring travelers, is *not* resolved in favor of the former, and to hand out the information that *they* want, even if it exceeds what they are legally entitled to ask for?

In Europe, digital identity projects are also pursued at the national level. Examples include France, which is about to register all citizens biometrically, offering them the carrot of moving annoying administrative encounters, like for passport renewals, from crowded city halls to your smartphone; and Germany, which plans to transform its tax ID into a generic "personal identification number" (Kruchem 2021). None of these projects has ever been subject to democratic debate. Far-reaching change of life in society is presented, and apparently accepted, as the necessary course of things. Everything digital seems to be as inevitable as the course of the seasons, and the current measure of progress is how much of it a society has or not. In a

308   POLITICAL NEOLIBERALISM

decision about the "microcensus", back in 1969, the German Constitutional Court had condemned as a violation of human dignity the "forced register-ing and cataloguing of human beings in their whole personality and thus treating them like a thing that is in every respect accessible."[152] In the digital age, such concern seems to have evaporated.

The same absence of debate applies to the perhaps most far-reaching of all digital state projects in current times, which is the abolition of cash money (see Häring 2021, part 3). All G-20 states are committed to it, in the form of the US-initiated "Global Partnership for Financial Inclusion." A "Better than Cash Alliance" even enjoys the status of a UN-based organization and is self-described as "partnership of governments, companies, and international organizations that accelerates the transition from cash to digital payments in order to help achieve the Sustainable Development Goals."[153] This is the sing-sang of global elites, who dress themselves simultaneously green and anti-poverty. Never to miss out on anything global and to "change the world to the better," which in reality means all that is good for big business, the WEF, of course, is advocate of a "cashless society" that will "help to close the financial inclusion gap," whatever that is.[154] It is unclear how digital pay-ment will be of help to someone out in the street begging for a coin; note that social aid in Australia is already dispensed in the form of digital pay-ment cards—that do not give you access to alcohol and other "unnecessary" items (Häring 2021, part 3). This is paternalism, but not of the liberal sort.

Conclusion

Some think that the COVID-19 pandemic, which happened to be far less lethal than most pandemics of the past two thousand years, marks the arrival of "post-neoliberalism" (Davies and Gane 2021). Indeed, considering the return of the state, with borders, surveillance, and fiscal expansion, "it is hard to classify the present political conjuncture as 'neoliberal'" (ibid., 22). Post-pandemic states, as *The Economist* registers with alarm, are into "indus-trial policy" and managing "green transitions," yet in terms of protectionist "home economics," so that "free markets" seem to be "history."[155] For two unlikely cheerleaders, the pandemic "sound(s) the death knell of neoliberal-ism, a corpus of ideas and policies ... favouring competition over solidarity, creative destruction over governmental intervention, and economic growth over social welfare" (Schwab and Malleret 2020, ch. 1).

While the state is clearly more proactive in post-pandemic times, it is not exactly reversing the neoliberal order of priorities. Closer to the truth is Tooze when judging the immediate impact of the pandemic: "(T)he entrenched influence of wealth over politics, the law and the media, the disempowerment of workers—all perdured" (2021, intro). Green and Fazi's otherwise identical conclusion, that "the world's wealthiest people accumulated vast amounts of capital, while the poorest were flattened" (2023, 286), is a tad more bitter because of their focus on the global south. The predominantly informal global south economies were much more brought to the brink than those in the north because, without luxurious furlough schemes to their rescue, people were simply locked-in and sent to starvation when their commercial street activities were locked-down—what the WHO nevertheless insisted on because of the absence of "test and trace" systems in these less developed places (ibid., 302). And lockdowns under authoritarian governments were a lot worse than those in liberal democracies. In the Philippines, those under eighteen years of age and over sixty-five years of age were not allowed to leave their homes for twenty long months. In Angola, it was illegal for children to go outside and play for seven months. The list of global south government atrocities could be continued (see ibid., ch. 8).

These ugly facts throw a sour light on the spate of utopian thinking that was unleashed by the same pandemic. Walther Benjamin once wrote that "the concept of progress must be grounded in the idea of catastrophe."[156] It is thus no accident that leftist thinkers would read all sorts of positives into the pandemic. In the record time of little more than a week after the first Western lockdowns were in place, Zizek (2020) was on stage with the very first (small) book-length COVID-19 reflection. It opens with a hilarious vignette of freshly resurrected Jesus Christ's "Touch me Not" to Mary Magdalene, into which Zizek reads "a hope that corporal distancing will even strengthen the intensity of our link with others" (ibid., 3). This was the opening salve in the Orwellian doublethink that accompanied the pandemic from beginning to end. And, for a change, the Slovenian provocateur was not funny. He finds that now it is time for a "new form of what was once called Communism" (ibid., 56), but unlike the moral-ideological original, a "bare survival" variant (ibid., 92). He derives it from the negative fact of viral transmission interconnecting everyone in a most elementary way: "(I)f one group is affected, the other will inevitably also suffer" (ibid., 14f).

Interconnectedness, mutual dependence, ethic of care, the common good in lieu of the hyper-individualism of the neoliberal order: this is why the

310 POLITICAL NEOLIBERALISM

left loved COVID-19, and lockdown in particular. In this mode, Judith Butler (2022) denounced "personal liberty" as "death drive," and the pandemic taught her to give precedence to "mutual care" and "understanding ourselves as interdependent creatures."[157] Her equally famed fellow intellectual, the late Bruno Latour (2021, ch. 1), deemed himself irretrievably transformed into a beetle like Kafka's Gregor Samsa: "Once locked down, always locked down." The pandemic showed Latour that humans, qua terrestrial beings, are "interdependent," "heterotrophs," as he says, not the individualized "autotrophs" that we grew up as, and he welcomes lockdown as "helping terrestrials flee beyond the flight out of this world" (ibid., ch. 11). For Latour, the pandemic lockdown is smallish anticipation of the "general lockdown" that he considers necessary to save the climate (ibid., ch. 5).

It is unsurprising that the left, in particular, embraced "public health authoritarianism."[158] The authoritarian COVID-19 management was in a paradoxical way overdetermined. On the one hand, it shows a certain *affinity* with neoliberal precepts, such as a disdain for democracy in lieu of the correct solution. With a little bit of phantasy, building on Fassin's idea that the "recognition of life as the highest of all values" (2012, 249), while of long (Christian) pedigree, thrives especially in neoliberal times, one might also argue that lockdown brought such "biolegitimacy" to a "climax" (as Fassin 2021, 156, does himself): in putting "physical lives" over "social life," lockdown continued in the eroding and denigration of the social that is a hallmark of the neoliberal order.

On the other hand, and exactly contrary to this, leftist supporters of lockdown read into the latter a correction to the perceived *deficits* of a neoliberal order, above all its disdain for the public good—or rather its equation with whatever is profitable and efficient. To quote Zizek again, lockdown and kindred measures showed that "our first principle should be never to economize but to assist, unconditionally, irrespective of costs, those who need help, to enable their survival" (2020, 86). The paradox is that in its support for lockdown (and the Covid Doxa at large), the left had to endorse or even double-down on lockdown's (more or less tacit) neoliberal affinities, making it, indeed, a matter of "no alternative."

However, a third and perhaps decisive factor explaining an authoritarian COVID-19 management is never to forget: this was an exceptional measure not meant to last, and panic-struck states plainly seeking to save lives in a moment of unprecedented uncertainty is unrelated to anything "neoliberal." Note that all health-related restrictions and obligations have long been lifted.

In this crucial respect, life has returned to normal, as if nothing had ever happened. Who would have believed, at the height of the crisis in 2020 or 2021, that international travel without health passes would ever be possible again, as indeed it now is?

At the same time, none of COVID-19's "transformational benefits" have arrived. If one looks around, what is there to see but "war, inflation, instability, and rising inequality"?[159] Political neoliberalism is trucking on, propelled by an ever-closer alliance of Big State and Big Firms that have been the pillars of neoliberalism-on-earth all along, and that are also the two big winners of the COVID-19 crisis. A quarter century ago, Perry Anderson described "neo-liberalism as a set of principles (that) rules undivided across the globe: the most successful ideology in world history" (2000, 17). While the world has changed in many ways, this is as true today as it was then. But the pandemic experience also suggests that freedom, neoliberalism's original North Star, will be the scarce good of the future.

Endnotes

Introduction

1. Milton Friedman had advocated something similar, in terms of a negative income tax to beat poverty, in one of neoliberalism's classic manifestos, *Capitalism and Freedom* (1962).
2. Certainly, Marshall (1950, 43) added that social rights were "conditional . . . on the discharge of the general duties of citizenship." But in the short section where these duties are addressed (ibid., 78), there does not appear to be much spike to them. The "general obligation to live the life of a good citizen," for instance, faces the odds that "the community is so large that the obligation appears remote and unreal" (ibid.).
3. See, however, the spirited counterpoint by Kieran Healy (2017, 126), to "fuck nuance," mainly because it "inhibit(s) the process of abstraction that makes theory valuable."
4. Of course, there is the motley multitude that gathers under the umbrella of anti-globalization, and which has been a regular sight at rich state summits since the 1999 Battle of Seattle. But they cannot even agree on the "anti," which is a difficult position to take considering that the global south, next to the proverbial 1 percent at the top, has been the second winner of globalization, lifting billions of people out of poverty. Too many diverse groups, individuals (including Nobel Prize winners), and causes fall under the rubric of anti-globalization, so that it will not be further considered here.
5. A brilliant exploration, on the basis of German survey and interview data, that political polarization along certain "trigger points" is not necessarily grounded in social-structural polarization and the division of society into *Grossgruppen* (classes), is Mau, Lux, and Westheuser (2023).

Chapter 1

1. "A hatred of Jacobin radicalism," which branched out into a hostility to the Enlightenment, universal reason, and progressivism at large, is also at the origins of "Cold War liberalism" (Moyn 2023, 21). In Moyn's account, it included Judith Shklar as its central (although ambiguous) figure, Isaiah Berlin, Karl Popper, and others, and eventually "collapsed into neoliberalism and neoconservatism" (ibid., 171).
2. For a trenchant critique of Marx's wholesale dismissal of rights, see Steven Lukes (1985, 66): "Even under altruism there will be a need to protect people from others' mistakes about what altruism requires."
3. Elif Özmen (2023) reduces the Geuss quartet to three (individualism, freedom, equality). But in effect she gives a very similar description of classic liberalism (although from a philosophical and Rawlsian perspective, which is the one that Geuss repudiates).
4. The German sociologist Georg Simmel (1992 [1908], ch. 6) was the first to articulate Madison's idea in academic discourse, in his notion of the "crossing of social circles" (*Kreuzung sozialer Kreise*).
5. In his "incomplete history of liberalism," the French philosopher Alan S. Kahan (2023, 3) makes the identical point, even though he phrases it differently: "Liberalism is the search for a society in which no one need to be afraid. Freedom from fear is the most basic freedom."
6. Plehwe takes this disagreement, to which many more can be added, as proof of the "variety of neoliberalisms" (2009, 3). This is undoubtedly true. However, by definition there must be less disagreement under the neoliberal than under the liberal tent because otherwise the term would be meaningless. A brilliant summary of the neoliberal creed in eleven tenets is the conclusion of the same volume, by Philip Mirowski (2009), to which the mentioned Plehwe (2009) serves as the introduction. And Mirowski's Eleven Commandments, as you could call them (later expanded to thirteen, Mirowski 2013, ch. 2), have "fairly clear origins" in the "Hayekian" version of neoliberalism (2009, 442).

ENDNOTES 313

7. Mont Pèlerin Society, *Statement of Aims*, Mont Pèlerin (Vaud, Switzerland), April 8, 1947, https://www.montpelerin.org/statement-of-aims/.
8. After disagreements on the first draft, which had been co-written by Hayek, the preparation of the final Statement of Aims was actually delegated to Lionel Robbins, a leading economist at the London School of Economics. However, Robbins was close to Hayek (they were faculty colleagues at LSE), and he retained the Hayekian key terms of the first draft (Plehwe 2009, 24). Plehwe called the final statement a "nonspecific and anodyne" version of the first draft (ibid.).
9. John McDonough, "The Tortured Saga of America's Least-Loved Policy Idea," *Politico*, May 22, 2021, https://www.politico.com/news/magazine/2021/05/22/health-care-individual-mandate-policy-conservative-idea-history-489956.
10. The 1974 Nobel Prize committee mentioned among Hayek's contributions "(h)is conclusion . . . that knowledge and information held by various actors can only be utilized fully in a decentralized market system with free competition and pricing" (https://www.nobelprize.org/prizes/economic-sciences/1974/hayek/facts/).
11. In the *Constitution of Liberty* (1960), written before Rawls was on the map, "justice" is only a minor entry.
12. https://newlearningonline.com/new-learning/chapter-4/margaret-thatcher-theres-no-such-thing-as-society.
13. In the *Constitution of Society*, the same distinction appeared as two traditions of liberalism, the empiricist British (that he preferred) versus the rationalist French (Hayek 1960, ch. 4).
14. This late Hayekian view is *grosso modo* confirmed in a monumental assembly of empirical studies, many of them experimental, by Harvard human evolutionary biologist Joseph Henrich (2020).
15. As Joseph Schumpeter (1953, 158) put it in a classic paper, "The family, not the physical person, is the true individual of class theory."
16. This also follows from Hayek's dismissive view of "positive freedom." In the *Constitution of Liberty*, he distinguishes his "own" (negative) view of freedom from "political freedom," which is "the participation of men in the choice of their government." He continues: "But a free people in this sense is not necessarily a people of free men; nor need one share in this collective freedom to be free as an individual" (1960, 13). In the *Road to Serfdom* (1944), Hayek argues that economic freedom is a precondition for political freedom, but *not* vice versa. This also betrays, at best, an instrumental attitude toward democracy, which coexists with a principled aversion to it.
17. Extracts from an interview with Hayek in *El Mercurio*, April 12, 1981, https://puntodevistaeconomico.com/2016/12/21/extracts-from-an-interview-with-friedrich-von-hayek-el-mercurio-chile-1981/.
18. Ibid.
19. In the terms of Thomas Biebricher's (2023) brilliant reconstruction of conservatism, Hayek's political thought incorporates the two "core concepts" of conservatism, the substantive idea of a "normative naturalness" (that Hayek understood mainly historically, but with a strategically embraced element of the religious), and the procedural idea of "experience-based incrementalism" (ibid., 29, 38). Moreover, Hayek's later sympathies for the Chilean dictatorship *also* reflect the risk of a "moderate conservatism" to slip into authoritarianism: "There is nothing inherent in conservatism to make it resistant against authoritarian temptations" (ibid., 55).
20. In the 1981 *El Mercurio* interview, Hayek was asked whether he "believe(s) in God," and his answer was: "I have never understood the meaning of the word God. I believe that it is important in the maintaining of laws." In his opening address to the first meeting of the Mont Pèlerin Society, Hayek said this: "I am convinced that unless the breach between true liberal and religious convictions can be healed, there is no hope for a revival of liberal forces" (quoted in Mirowski 2009, 440).
21. This includes putting a price on everything, including human life. Early twentieth-century US progressive reformer Irving Fisher, who was also "the nation's first neoliberal," estimated the price of an "eight-pound baby . . ., at birth, USD 352 a pound" (Cook 2016, 257).
22. Moral traditionalism, while not of liberal pedigree at all but central to Hayek's thought, is a separate matter, because it did not prove as enduring and pervasive as the other four neoliberal tenets (see Chapter 3 of this volume).

314 ENDNOTES

Chapter 2

1. https://newlearningonline.com/new-learning/chapter-4/margaret-thatcher-theres-no-such-thing-as-society.
2. Ibid.
3. Pointing to hidden continuities between the 1960s counterculture and 1980s Reaganism, Christopher Caldwell (2020, 93) cites the novelist Kurt Andersen, who finds that "Do your own thing" is "not so different than 'every man for himself.'" Similarly, Mark Lilla called "identity politics," taking hold of the US Democratic Party, "Reaganism for lefties": "(T)hese are just two tired individualistic ideologies intrinsically incapable of discerning the public good" (2017). The related phenomenon of neoliberal multiculturalism or "progressive neoliberalism" (Fraser 2017) is explored in Chapter 3. Gary Gerstle's history of neoliberalism in America stresses the appeal of Hayekian "freedom, spontaneity, and unpredictability" to the New Left, which was born in the Bohemian quarters of lower Manhattan (2022, 98f).
4. Margaret Thatcher interviewed by Ronald Butt ("Mrs. Thatcher: The First Two Years," *Sunday Times*, May 3, 1981).
5. As this and the following chapters discuss the political forms of neoliberalism from the vantage point of order, I call these political forms here "institutional." That is, the notions "political forms" and "institutional forms" are used interchangeably.
6. Krastev and Holmes (2019) is the most erudite and imaginative of an avalanche of "crisis of liberalism" diagnoses in the wake of 2016, the *annus miserabilis* of Brexit and Trump. Among many others, see also King (2017), Deneen (2018), Luce (2017), Ash (2021), and Fukuyama (2020, 2022). A red thread in these diagnoses is the failing of "economic liberalism" (Ash 2021) to deliver "prosperity for all" (King 2017, 12).
7. This interpretation is contestable, not only because of Schmitt's recurrent diatribes against liberalism, but also because it ignores his endorsement of the "constituent" power of the demos and of a Rousseauian model of democracy, which made him a grey eminence for a radical theory of democracy (see Kalyvas 1999, 109f). Christi's interpretation is still helpful for mapping communalities between Schmitt and Hayek's conceptions of liberalism.
8. Indeed, in Christi (1984, 526) and Friedrich (1955, 513), the mentioned Constant quote is taken from a work (in French) by Ordoliberal Wilhelm Röpke.
9. "Schmitt rejected *political* liberalism but felt quite comfortable with *economic* liberalism" (Kalyvas 1999, 108).
10. This position, incidentally, was compatible with Article 48 of the Weimar Constitution, which gave license to Schmitt to equate democracy (properly understood) with dictatorship. See Roth (2005, 151).
11. Of course, next to the Hobbesian, there is also the Rousseauian conception of politics, which goes back to the Greek classics. In this view, "the political defines a distinct kind of association that aims at the good of all" (Wolin 1983, 16). Bartolini (2018) leaves it aside because it dissolves politics into ethics. It is obvious that the order of states does not listen to the Greek tune, and neoliberalism is congenitally deaf to it.
12. Whereas Linz (1975) keeps authoritarian and democratic regimes strictly apart, Steven Levitsky and Lucan Way (2002) have diagnosed the rise of "hybrid regimes" in 1990s Africa, post-communist Eurasia, Asia, and Latin America. These regimes "combined democratic rules with authoritarian governance," and not just in a temporary transition moment but "indefinitely" (ibid., 51, 58). Levitsky and Lucan call this new regime type "competitive authoritarianism."
13. By the 1990s, average voting turnout in Europe sank below 80 percent, the lowest in half a century (Mair 2013, ch. 1).
14. This paradox has been noted by Andrew Gamble: "Their (the neoliberals') revolution in government requires that a group of individuals be found who are not governed by self-interest, but are motivated purely by the public good of upholding the . . . market order" (1988, 28). Where Biebricher (2020) suspects cynical populists at work, for Gamble it seems to be more for true believers to resolve the paradox by a "wholesale dismantling of the state" (1988, 28).
15. See the skeptical review of Klein (2007) by economist Joseph Stiglitz, "Bleakonomics," *New York Times*, September 30, 2007.
16. According to Chicago School scholar Richard Posner, the "major function" of criminal sanction is "to prevent people from bypassing the system of voluntary, compensated exchange—the 'market'" (quoted by Harcourt 2010, 74). Gary Becker (1968) argued that sentences are the

ENDNOTES 315

"price of crime," so that harsh sentencing reduces crime much as high prices reduce demand. Chicago neoliberals break with the Physiocratic logic of market and penal system as "mutually exclusive and noncontinuous (spaces)" (Harcourt 2011, 147) when proposing market solutions to organizing the prison system (see ibid., ch. 6).

17. In later publications, Wacquant (2010, 217; 2012, 68) speaks of a "centaur state," borrowing the image of the half-horse half-human creature in Greek mythology. In her "rereading Foucault in the shadow of globalization," Nancy Fraser (2003, 169) similarly observes a "new kind of segmented governability," which is "responsibilized self-regulation for some, brute repression for others."

18. Rhodes (1996, 654) is quoting the UK-based Chartered Institute of Public Finance and Accountancy (CIPFA), a fourteen thousand-member professional body of people working in public finance.

19. The *locus classicus* is the famous Coase Theorem, presented in the most-cited law journal article of all times that kick-started the Chicago "Law and Economics" school (Coase 1960). According to it, the gold standard for the "treatment of harmful effects" is to "maximise the value of production," irrespective of other considerations (ibid., 42). According to this influential line of thinking, which helped Ronald Coase, a Chicago law professor, to win the Nobel Prize in Economics in 1991, to achieve the "social good" is merely a "maximization problem in aggregate market value," and the function of the law—the state's constitutive medium—is no longer to resolve issues of "harm and restitution" but to serve "market efficiency" (Rodgers 2011, 58).

20. The imposition of "shareholder values" at the firm level, argues Natascha van der Zwan similarly (2014, 187), allowed "reuniting ownership and control: disciplining corporate managers through shareholder activism."

21. For a damning critique of the "competitiveness agenda," as "extracting wealth from poorer, smaller, less mobile elements of the economy, and handing it to bigger, more mobile global players," see Paul Krugman (1994).

22. The British mismanagement of the COVID-19 crisis, 2020–2022, offers ample material for Crouch's critique: "COVID-19 has revealed the depth of cronyism and clientelism in British public life. More than almost any comparable state, Britain—or, more accurately, England—has outsourced swathes of its pandemic response, often to companies with strong links to Conservative politicians but little obvious relevant experience" (Geoghegan 2020). Serco, again, played a major and dubious role in this (ibid.). Absurdly, in November 2020 the British government hired management consultants for advising them how the government could "manage without management consultants" (Jones and Hameiri 2021, 1047).

23. https://eur-lex.europa.eu/EN/legal-content/glossary/open-method-of-coordination.html.

24. Streeck's (2013) own seminal work on the rise of neoliberal capitalism wavers between stressing the demand-side role of middle-class consumer interests and supply-side "financialized" capitalist class interests.

25. See endnote 1.

26. The quote is from one of two lectures that Foucault gave at Dartmouth College in November 1980, so that it is not a translation (error) from French but the original (flawed) English.

27. The "liberal paternalism" of "nudging" works in the same indirect manner, through shaping individuals' "choice architecture" (Thaler and Sunstein 2008). The difference is that nudging works on unconscious "heuristics and biases" as revealed by behavioral economics, whereas governmentality (somewhat naively) counts on the "rational behaviour of those who are governed" (Foucault 2008, 312).

28. For the long and torturous history of the "*vincolo esterno*" in Italy, that is, the uses of Europe as "external tie" by successive "technical governments" to push through neoliberal reforms, see Thomas Fazi (2021). Fazi's conclusion applies more generally: "(T)he *vincolo esterno* should be understood first and foremost as a process of self-imposed diminution of sovereignty by national elites aimed at constraining the ability of popular-democratic powers to influence economic policy, thus enabling the imposition of neoliberal policies that would not have otherwise been politically feasible."

29. Michael Gove, quoted in "Britain Has Had Enough of Experts, Says Gove," *Financial Times*, June 3, 2016, https://www.ft.com/content/3be49734-29cb-11e6-83e4-abc22d5d108c.

30. This case is overstated. See my discussion of cleavage theory in Chapter 4.

31. "Macron Rolls Up His Sleeves," *The Economist*, April 30, 2022, 19.

316 ENDNOTES

32. "Charlemagne: Macron 2.0," *The Economist*, May 11, 2022, 28.
33. Macron's model, Tony Blair, likewise said about himself that he "never really (was) in politics" (Joppke 2021a, 25).
34. The concept of economic constitution stemmed from the 1930s German Ordoliberals, and they meant to see it realized by and within a "strong state." What Slobodian (2018) calls the "Geneva School," Hayek amongst them, shifted the concept to the level of federation—making them "Ordoglobalists" (ibid., 12).
35. The neoliberal idea of federation is very different from the common understanding of the term, especially in reference to the European Union. Reinforced in the early millennium debate over the "finality" of Europe, kicked off by then German Foreign Minister Joschka Fischer, "European federation" has meant more quasi-state powers (a "European government") and stronger democratic institutions at EU level (a two-chamber "European Parliament"). See *From Confederacy to Federation—Thoughts on the Finality of European Integration*, speech by Joschka Fischer at Humboldt University Berlin, May 12, 2000, https://ec.europa.eu/dorie/fileDownload.do?docId=192161&cardId=192161, at 9.
36. Wolfgang Streeck, quoted by Slobodian (2018,105). See also Biebricher (2018, 187) and Scharpf (2009).
37. Scharpf (2009, 6) sharply observes, however, that no "(neoliberal) ideological preferences" are required for this double logic to work: "the structural factors associated with the integration of heterogeneous nation states" are sufficient. This is also Scharpf's own take on the (dis)functioning of the European Union. Against the "good Europeans," who believe in a "social" or "democratic" Europe, he holds that they "should understand that the socioeconomic asymmetry of European law is caused by structural conditions whose effect does not depend on the ideological orientations of members of the Court or the Commission" (ibid., 34).
38. See Perry Anderson's masterful review of two of Alan Milward's major works on the making of European Union: "The High Politics of the Franco-German Axis Tell a Story Older than that of Voters in Pursuit of Consumer Durables and Welfare Payments" (1996, 14). In a later review essay, Anderson (2021) gives more credit to NATO for the peace function: "The truth ... is that after 1945 there was never any risk of another outbreak of hostilities between Germany and France, ... because the Cold War made the whole region an American security protectorate."
39. The main alternative, of course, is Andrew Moravcsik's theory of "liberal intergovernmentalism," which conceives of European integration as intended outcome of national governments' strategies of "manag(ing) economic interdependence" (1993, 474).
40. This is Scharpf's disparaging term (2008, 97).
41. The treaty basis of the "implied powers" doctrine is Article 235 of the EEC. It is activated whenever "objectives of the Community and this Treaty" are to be pursued. Expansively interpreted by the Court, it provides "unlimited discretionary powers to Community organs" (Tschofen 1991, 489).
42. By 2021, the number of registered lobbyists in Brussels was even at thirty thousand, 63 percent of them "corporate and consultant." This is 2.5 times more than the number of lobbyists in Washington, DC (Anderson 2021).
43. The citations are from a book that Delors co-wrote with the TV journalist Philippe Alexandre just before his Brussels appointment (Amable and Polambarini 2021, ch. 2).
44. This contradicted Article 153(5) of CTFEU, which declares the "right to strike" outside its purview (Höpner and Schäfer 2010a, 19).
45. This was in direct opposition to a labor-protective provision in the Treaty (Article 50 TEC). See Höpner and Schäfer (2010b, 352f).
46. ECJ, *Grzelczyk* decision, C-184/99, at par. 31.
47. Hayek (1960, 442) mentions Young (1958) in a footnote, confessing "not yet" having read the book but that it "appears to bring out these problems very clearly."
48. For a different critique of merit as justice principle, finding it "fundamentally derivative" because "contingent on our views of a good society," see Amartya Sen (1999, 5). At the same time, Sen argues that "we can scarcely dispense with incentive systems altogether" (ibid., 9).
49. Even though in Young's fable (1958) it is socialists pushing meritocracy. That their progressivism goes astray is the main point.
50. This difference has been acutely observed by Claus Offe (2001).
51. For national variations of meritocracy as "legitimizing inequality," see Heuer et al. (2020).

ENDNOTES 317

52. See Leonard (2019), who criticizes Markovits (2019) for "neatly omitting capitalists from his story."
53. An alternative argument that grounds deep down in the human psyche a propensity to attribute success in life to one's skill and hard work, rather than to the "luck" that it mostly is, while explaining failure as "bad luck," is made by behavioral economist Robert Frank (2016, esp. ch. 5).
54. In the United States, the "sea change" was in 1981, under Reagan. His budget director, David Stockman, said: "I do not accept the notion that the federal government has an obligation to fund generous grants to anybody that wants to go to college" (quoted in Zaloom 2019, 12). In the United Kingdom, the same reasoning, which conceives of higher education as private "human capital" good, prevailed in 2010 under the Tory government of David Cameron, which introduced hefty university fees (see Marquand 2013, ch. 4).
55. Perhaps first observed by Annette Lareau, who called the phenomenon "concerted cultivation" (2002). More recently, Paul Collier (2018, 110) speaks of the rise of the "nuclear dynastic family."
56. Émile Boutmy (1872), quoted in Piketty (2020, 711).
57. As Jonathan Mijs (2016, 26) further argues, to really work, the merit principle would require "equal outcomes," for instance, through disallowing parents to interfere in their children's education and prohibiting homogamy—which is obviously an "unattainab(le) . . . approach."
58. Markovits (2019, 131f) reports that the "achievement gap" of middle school children in the United States, while almost non-existent between the "rich" and the "middle class" in 1970s America, is now 25 percent greater than that between middle-class and "poor" children. With respect to income, the gap between the poor and the middle class has narrowed, while that between the middle class and the rich has widened even more (ibid., 105). Accordingly, the new dividing line is no longer between the poor and the middle class, but between the middle class and the rich.
59. One of the earliest diagnoses of the "secession of the symbolic analysts" is by Robert Reich (1992), which is also one of the earliest and enduringly relevant analyses of globalization; see also Lash (1995, ch. 2).
60. For a case that democracy, at least in Europe post-1945, has always been "highly constrained" and "deeply imprinted with a distrust of popular sovereignty" (that had brought the Nazis to power in Germany), see Jan-Werner Müller (2011, 128). In his view, "disciplining democracy," to avoid an authoritarian backsliding, has been the essence of the "post-war constitutional settlement" (ibid., 146). Martin Conway (2020, 8) speaks of "formal democracy," with "limited opportunities for popular control of rulers and for expressions of dissent."
61. This is because meritocracy is primarily a description of social structure, more precisely: an ideology of attributing status positions therein. This does not fit the European Union, which is a polity but not a society.
62. For contrary positions on the European Union's democratic deficit, see Majone (1994), who denies the relevance of democratic ambition in the non-majoritarian "regulatory state" that the Union is to him; see Moravcsik (2008, 332), who deems the democratic deficit a "myth," among other reasons, because a "perfect democracy" is nowhere to be found; and see Follesdal and Hix (2006, 533), who argue against *both* Majone and Moravcsik that even on a "thinnest" understanding of democracy, the European Union falls short because it does not allow "contestation for political leadership and over policy."

Chapter 3

1. On the weaker side, however, Prasad (2006) boxes herself into an unconvincing refutation of the role of "ideas" and "national cultures" for explaining neoliberal polices. This includes the rather odd statement that the "power of structure" (in this case, visible taxes in the United States) "called forth the necessary ideology" (the so-called "Laffer Curve," which claims that tax reductions would be "self-paying" by spurring economic growth). This has the sound of witchcraft. As Vivian Schmidt notes in a perceptive review, Prasad's rejection of the role of ideas conflicts with her own approach of political actors trying to "win over electorates" through "deliberation and debate" (Vivien A. Schmidt, Review of *The Politics of Free Markets* by Monica Prasad, *Perspectives on Politics* 6, no. 1 [2008]: 193).

318 ENDNOTES

2. Mau (2015, x) defines as "middle class" a household whose income is between 70 percent and 150 percent of the median income. Middle-class "growth" then means more households in this income bracket.

3. This figure of home ownership hides huge national variations: about 40 percent in Germany, but double as much or more in the United Kingdom and Spain (Mau 2015, 54).

4. Davis (2009, 27) reports that, in 2004, 39 percent of shareholders in the United States identified themselves as Republican Party voters.

5. An Australian group of political economists make "asset democratization" pursued with particular vigor by the Third Way left, the revolving axis of an original theory of neoliberalism, which is centered less on the logic of advancing commodification and market exchange than the speculative logic of credit and debt (Adkins, Cooper, and Konings 2020).

6. Judged by the result, this strategy was not successful. Most European social democratic parties, including the Swedish that had adopted several Third Way positions many years before the word (such as active labor market policies), avoided or even openly repudiated the "third way" label. This is despite the fact that many of these parties, like in Spain, the Netherlands, Germany, Belgium, and Portugal, adopted even stronger Third Way positions than the British Labour Party (Bonoli 2004, 200).

7. Schröder-Blair Paper, *Der Weg nach vorne für Europas Sozialdemokraten*, June 8, 1999 (London).

8. Magnus Paulsen Hansen and Peter Triantafillou (2011) speak of an "alignment of economic and social concerns" in the Lisbon Strategy. As we shall see below, this misses the one-directional sense of this alignment, in which the economic is prior to the social.

9. However, against "contemporary fashions in policy," often under the Third Way flag, Esping-Andersen (2000, 22) warns against "ignoring income maintenance," the need for which "will not disappear, not even in the best designed, 'productivist' welfare state."

10. While Esping-Andersen's EU report is clear enough in giving the "absolute highest priority to ensuring the welfare of children" (2000, 3), in a later report to the progressive UK Policy Network, entitled *Against Social Inheritance*, he even calls to "abolish social inheritance," because "life-chances are powerfully over-determined by what happens in children's life prior to their first encounter with the schools system" (quoted in Lister 2004, 159).

11. For the drastic German case, whose Hartz IV reform under *Neue Mitte* SPD Chancellor Gerhard Schröder followed the Anglo-Saxon model of "making work pay," see Fleckenstein (2008).

12. See also Christopher Deeming and Paul Smyth (2015), who distinguish between "heavy" social investment in Nordic countries, delivering on "promotion" and "protection" in tandem, and "light" social investment in the United Kingdom and Australia, combining low protection with some (and reversible) human capital investment. More recently, Horn et al. (2022, 8) depict the UK as "atypical" in its "one-sided focus on punitive measures." By the same token, the other fifteen OECD countries examined in their study showed a "significant trend towards more punitive *and* enabling measures" (ibid.), from c. 1997 on—the high moment of "third way" social democracy in Europe.

13. This pattern has been confirmed by Tarik Abou-Chadi and Ellen Immergut (2019). They show for ten OECD countries, from 1980 to 2011, that "(l)eft parties in government become more likely to cut pension rights generosity and to recalibrate social policy in favour of social investment when electoral competition increases" (ibid., 714), while the opposite pattern, that is, to favor old over new welfare claimants, holds for center-right parties in power. The social investment policies covered in their analysis are parental leave, day care, and labor market activation.

14. That workers simply walked away from Third-Way leftist parties is contested in the literature (opposite views are assembled in Häusermann and Kitschelt 2024). For a critique of Piketty (2020), which argues on the basis of European Social Survey data (2002–2018) that there is "little empirical evidence that social democratic parties represent the educational elite," and that the new middle classes that support leftist parties are still "largely in favour of economic redistribution," see Abou-Chadi and Hix (2020).

15. Such thin and formalistic understanding of human rights evolved over time. The 1948 Universal Declaration of Human Rights included a list of social and economic rights, which was enough reason for Friedrich Hayek to reject the document as derived from "the Marxist Russian Revolution" (Whyte 2019, intro.). Only in the 1970s, not least under the influence of

ENDNOTES   319

Amnesty International and similar NGOs, did human rights campaigning adopt a minimalist neoliberal line of "embrac(ing) law to restrain politics, while avoiding engagement with those social and economic rights that could only be achieved through political action" (ibid.). See also Samuel Moyn (2018, ch. 5), who squares the post-1970s thinning of human rights with the fixation on "basic needs" in development thinking, emblemized by Amartya Sen's "Human Development Index."

16. Kymlicka's (2019) notion of "deschooled" multiculturalism is a critical response to Brahm Levey (2018), who spoke of a "Bristol School of multiculturalism." Kymlicka adds to the Bristol School an "Australian" and a "mainstream" liberal multiculturalism but sees all of them converging in a "liberal multicultural nationalism." Hence, his is a plea for "deschooling" multiculturalism.

17. For diversity's arrival in the German *Aussenministerium* (Foreign Office), see the sarcastic commentary by Berthold Kohler, "Diplomatische Diversität," *Frankfurter Allgemeine Zeitung*, June 18, 2021.

18. 438 U.S. 265 (*Regents of the University of California v. Bakke*), June 28, 1978.

19. This and the following quotes are from the decisive swing opinion of Justice Lewis Powell in *Bakke* (ibid., 289f).

20. Justice Powell, ibid., 291.

21. On June 29, 2023, in its *Students for Fair Admissions, Inc. v. President and Fellows of Harvard College* decision, a Trump-recomposed, ultra-conservative Supreme Court rejected even the thinned-down diversity variant of affirmative action, as in violation of the Constitution's Equal Protection Clause. Ahead of this widely-anticipated decision, Emily Bazelon (2023) rightly noted that the diversity rationale "allowed affirmative action to endure but left it vulnerable, stripping away history and the moral underpinning to remedy racism."

22. Opinion of Justice Powell (in *Bakke*), 294.

23. Ibid., 295.

24. Ibid., 297.

25. Ibid., 298f.

26. Ibid., 307.

27. Ibid., 309. By the time it decided on *Bakke*, the Supreme Court had already negated, in its *Washington v. Davis* decision (1976), an understanding of discrimination as "disparate impact," which obliterated the need to establish the intention to discriminate.

28. *Bakke*, 307.

29. Ibid., 312.

30. Ibid., 312.

31. Ibid., 317.

32. One must suspect Starbucks Company to lurk behind the "Starr" label, which was chosen for anonymity reasons (Berrey 2015, ch. 6).

33. "Unconscious bias training," for instance, rests on the dubious assumption that "almost everyone is a suppressed racist" (Noon 2018, 200).

34. See the article by Milton Friedman, under this title, in *New York Times Magazine*, September 13, 1970.

35. "Diversity Training," *The Economist*, August 27, 2022, 73.

36. "Diversity Consulting," *The Economist*, November 28, 2020, 62.

37. For a (only half-joking) case that "short guys" should be protected, see "Short Guys Finish Last," *The Economist*, December 23, 1995, 21–24.

38. See Robert Post (2000), who identifies the "logic of American antidiscrimination law" as making appearance invisible.

39. See already Hugh Collins (2003, 22ff), who sharply distinguished between the welfarist "equality" and antidiscrimination's "social inclusion" objectives, the first targeting "relative" and the latter "absolute" disadvantage of particular groups in society.

40. See also Davies (2016, 127–128), who calls this phase "normative neoliberalism."

41. Davies (2016, 132) calls this third phase of neoliberalism "punitive."

42. About the US Federal Bank's "motivated favouritism," see the critical account by Jacobs and King (2016).

43. The increase of bonuses was from $117 billion in 2007 to $145 billion in 2009 (Tooze 2018, ch. 13).

320   ENDNOTES

44. Note that the US Federal Bank has two mandates: "price stability" *and* "maximum employment."
45. However, when a common European currency was first proposed in the 1970s, Hayek rejected it for its implicit statism, and he preferred "free markets in money" (Lapavitsas 2019, ch. 3).
46. The SGP stipulates that a member state's budget deficit must not exceed 3 percent of GDP, and its indebtedness must not be above 60 percent of GDP. These conditions, formally controlled by the threat of fines, were chronically violated, even by core member states like France and Germany itself.
47. In addition, austerity, whose effectiveness in generating economic growth is questioned even by some of the organizations that are prescribing it (like the IMF), is "circular": it is "exercised simply because it must be, not because of its effects" (Davies 2021, 107).
48. See Martin Höpner and Florian Rödl's (2012) strident critique of "governance in the sovereign debt crisis," calling it "illegitimate and illegal."
49. PIIGS stands for Portugal, Ireland, Italy, Greece, and Spain, which were the five European countries most exposed to the financial crisis.
50. See also Daniel Rodgers's *Age of Fracture* (2011).

Chapter 4

1. Prime Minister Theresa May, in a speech on January 17, 2017, https://time.com/4636141/theresa-may-brexit-speech-transcript/.
2. "The Clown Ceiling," *The Economist*, January 9, 2021, 23. In an earlier review, Herbert Kitschelt (2007) noted the "self-limiting" performance of radical right parties, winning a maximum of 25 percent of the electorate, and less in most countries, and "quickly punished by their own voters" when in government (ibid., 1177). This remains true for most of western Europe, though not for its eastern part.
3. "The Clown Ceiling." Most recently, however, a combination of costly ecological transition and persistently high numbers of asylum seekers has lifted the AfD above the 20 percent mark, making it Germany's second most popular party (after the conservative CDU), and arguably the dominant party in the post-communist eastern Länder.
4. For (short-lived) left populism in southern Europe after the 2008 Financial Crisis, in this case more of a "moment" indeed, see Borriello and Jäger (2023).
5. In a sarcastic exchange with Friedman, Marxist economist Samuel Bowles called it the "lemonade stand capitalism myth": "Charlie Brown and Linus are gonna have a lemonade stand, and Lucy's gonna have another lemonade stand and that's your idea of capitalism" (quoted by Brandes 2019, 72).
6. Merijn Oudenampsen, "The Forgotten Fortuyn," *Sidecar*, July 22, 2022, https://newleftreview.org/sidecar/posts/the-forgotten-fortuyn. For a brief discussion of "neoliberal populism," see Tugal (2016).
7. However, it would be far too simplistic to argue that disgruntled working-class voters moved straightaway from leftist to populist-right parties. For the variety of electoral pathways and the changing composition of "working class" to begin with, see the excellent overview by Abou-Chadi, Mitteregger, and Mudde (2021). Despite apparent complexities, the authors conclude that it remains true that "radical right parties do disproportionately draw support from working class voters" (ibid., 18). However, these are more likely to be previous non-voters than previous social-democratic-party voters, whose shift toward the radical right a recent study found "absolutely marginal" (Häusermann and Kitschelt 2024, 396).
8. Crouch (2020) does that too, with an amended version of Lipset–Rokkan's theory of cleavage structures, discussed in the following.
9. This delay is because of the generational factor: the "materialists" socialized in the interwar period (1900–1945) grow old and die, while the "post-materialists" growing up in affluence post-World War II gradually increase in number and influence. As Norris and Inglehart (2019, 47f) formulated it later, this trend reaches a "tipping point" in which "social conservatives have become . . . resentful at finding themselves becoming minorities stranded on the losing side of history."
10. This view has recently been reiterated by Armin Schäfer and Michael Zürn (2021, 79), who speak of the "*creation* of a two-dimensional political space *as result of* a new conflict line" (emphases supplied), in addition to that between capital and labor. They call the new conflict

ENDNOTES   321

line "cosmopolitan v. communitarist" (that is identical with Kriesi et al.'s [2008] "integration v. demarcation" cleavage). Also building their argument on the Lipset–Rokkan cleavage theory, Schäfer and Zürn (2021) might respond that the pacification of the cleavages connected with the national revolution had made political space de facto one-dimensional, leaving mainly the capital-labor cleavage. Kriesi et al. (2008) nevertheless is conceptually more accurate.

11. The concluding chapter of Kriesi et al. (2008), written by Edgar Grande, speculates that the "politics of security" (economically understood), as advocated by left-wing populist parties, "might gain in attractiveness in the coming years" (ibid., 341). This has not materialized.

12. The 2017 AfD party program rails against the German "trend toward self-abolition" (*Selbstabschaffung*) through Islamic immigration, borrowing the title of a controversial bestseller (Sarrazin 2010), and it advocates "national population policy" (*nationale Bevölkerungspolitik*) for the "preservation of the own state people" (*Erhaltung des eigenen Staatsvolks*).

13. Nigel Farage, leader of the pro-Brexit UKIP party, celebrated the referendum outcome as "a victory for real people" (Noury and Roland 2020, 423).

14. "Economic Freedom v Political Freedom," *The Economist*, March 19, 2022, 61–63, at 62.

15. Ibid.

16. "Middle-income households" are those holding between 75 percent and 200 percent of median national income (OECD 2019: executive summary).

17. The relative share of income and wealth inequality differs from country to country. In France, there is more wealth than income inequality. In the United Kingdom, it is the opposite. The United States "stands out in having exceptionally high amounts of both income *and* wealth inequality" (Savage 2021, 79). In denying the wealth inequality component in the United States, Markovits (2019, ch. 2) draws a somewhat teary picture of American high-earners suffering from "deep alienation," "exploiting themselves and deforming their personalities."

18. However, as Berman (2021, 75) concedes, this macro-level connection is less visible at the micro-level of individual attitudes and preferences. Hence, many analysts have stressed the importance of future-related and "sociotropic" (as against "egotropic") concerns at individual level. Steenvoorden and Harteveld (2018), for instance, argue on the basis of the European Social Survey that "societal pessimism," which is "concern that society is in decline," and which is different from "grievances over personal circumstances" (ibid., 29), is the driving force of voting for populist radical right parties.

19. "Stuck in Place: The Democrats' Social-Spending Package Cannot Repair the American Dream," *The Economist*, November 6, 2021.

20. Note, however, that from around 2010, the kind of death Case and Deaton wrote about "can ... be found among nearly every demographic group," in particular blacks, youth, and native Americans. Moreover, such death is ever more due to drug overdoses than due to the other two causes, which suggests that this "now looks more like a medical crisis than a social one" ("Deaths of Despair: The Narrative is Out of Date," *The Economist*, January 5, 2024).

21. William Galston and Clara Hendrickson, "The Educational Rift in the 2016 Election," *Brookings*, November 18, 2016, https://www.brookings.edu/blog/fixgov/2016/11/18/educational-rift-in-2016-election/.

22. See previous endnote.

23. This finding is contested in the literature. Based on German survey data, for instance, Helbling and Teney (2017, 127) find that "stronger cosmopolitan identities," which one finds predominantly among the educated, do "not negatively impact their commitment to national redistributive solidarity." And "people who support solidarity will show solidarity towards everyone" (ibid., 147).

24. "Brahmins v Merchants," *The Economist*, May 29, 2021, 81.

25. Ibid.

26. See the entirely different picture in the empirical studies on changing leftist parties in Western Europe assembled by Häusermann and Kitschelt (2024). They refute the existence of an "economic-cultural trade-off" on the political supply *and* demand side (ibid., 401); find that "voter flows remain overwhelmingly and narrowly constrained within the ideological-left field" (ibid., 405); and argue that "transformative and irreversible structural changes" (ibid., 394), in particular the change from "industrial" into "knowledge societies," rather than "mistakes" of party leaders, are responsible for the changing fortunes of classic leftist parties.

322 ENDNOTES

27. In the attempt to fine-tune the link between class position and political preferences, Oesch (2006) has pioneered a "work logics" distinction within the middle class, essentially "managers" versus "sociocultural professionals" (ibid., 263), finding that the latter tend to support new left parties while the former prefer the center-right.

28. As Kitschelt and Rehm (2014, 1681) note, intra-class "occupational task structures" matter for political preference formation only at higher-skill level, as already laid out by Oesch (2006).

29. The focus of Kurer (2020) is evidently technological change, not globalization (see also Im 2019). As Kurer and Palier (2019, 2) argue, globalization mainly hits low-skilled workers, while technological change hits "the middle of society." Because the latter, with "routine workers" at the forefront, respond with endorsing an "exclusive understanding of the nation state and citizenship," as propagated by the populist right, they don't seem to distinguish between endogenous (technological) and exogenous (globalization-related) sources of change. While economists tend to treat both separately (e.g., Rodrik 2021), technological change and globalization are in reality closely connected.

30. The literature is divided whether there is "polarization away from middle-skill jobs to low- and high-skilled employment," as an OECD report claimed in 2017 (Oesch and Piccitto 2019, 441). Oesch and Piccitto deny this for Western Europe, where they find "clear-cut occupational upgrading" (while conceding that "the traditional working class and subordinate white-collar employees lost ground") (ibid., 443, 461, respectively). Kurer (2020, 1814), despite his case for the "declining middle," also observes that occupational "upgrading is slightly more common than downgrading." A differentiated picture is by Peugny (2019), who finds "a very clear trend" toward polarization in seven of twelve examined (non-eastern) European countries (ibid., 4), along with a general "decline in the proportion of middle-skilled jobs" (ibid., 5). At the same time, "the jobs that remain in (the) area of middle-skilled employment continue to offer relatively good employment (conditions)" (ibid., 6). The United States seems to be a clear case of polarization, particularly with respect to earnings. Markovits (2019, ch. 6) reports that one-fourth of mid-skilled jobs have disappeared since 1980, including the death of the entire "middle management" category, while high-skilled jobs have increased by over one-third. He sees a parallel expansion of "glossy" and "gloomy" jobs, which makes for a "labor market epitomized by Walmart greeters and Goldman Sachs bankers" (ibid.).

31. For "status anxiety," see Gidron and Hall (2017); for "nostalgia" and "societal pessimism," see Steenvoorden and Harteveld (2018) and Gest et al. (2018).

32. See also Kriesi et al. (2012, 4), who argue that the populist right's appeal to the "cultural anxieties" of globalization losers provides the "lowest common denominator for their mobilization," "given their heterogeneous economic interests."

33. The alternative, of course, is taking culture as free-standing and not merely "intermediate variable" (Rodrik 2021, 135). Norris and Inglehart (2019) have done this. See my discussion in the conclusion.

34. The classic work is Kohn (1944). The most important contemporary reformulation is Brubaker (1992).

35. Taguieff (1993), in a critical review of French New Right thinking, calls it "ethno-differentialism."

36. However, Benoist distanced himself from the FN in 1990 (Taguieff 1993, 11), among other reasons because he did not share the party's increasingly anti-Islamic orientation.

37. As Taguieff (1993, 6) shows in his authoritative review, Benoist had earlier endorsed a biologically racist kind of nationalism, centered around the alleged virtues of "Indo-Europeans." This included his support of eugenics. Only from the mid-1970s on, did "cultural differentialism" replace "biological determinism" in Benoist's thinking (ibid., 14).

38. The 2000 French New Right manifesto, which in many other respects reads like a new left manifesto, does not deny the New Right's stance "against immigration," but pairs it with "cooperation" with the "Third World" (Benoist and Champetier 1999, 14).

39. See Judt (1992, ch. 12). See also the tendentious characterization of "liberalism" by Thomas Piketty (2020, 795, fn.132), as "sacraliz(ing) the market and the disembedding of the economy."

40. An exception to this trend is the Swiss People's Party (Schweizer Volkspartei, SVP), one of the earliest and persistently strongest West European populist parties, whose socioeconomic policy positions have remained staunchly neoliberal (Lefkofridi and Michel 2017, 251).

41. This section profited from a critical reading by Szabolcs Pogonyi.

42. Article 7 TFEU, on paper the "nuclear option" that allows to expel a member state that violates the "values" of the European Union, is in reality lame-duck because it requires unanimity in the European Council, the head-of-states cockpit of the European Union. In this way and respect, populist-ruled Poland and Hungary happily relied on one another (until the PiS election loss in 2023).

43. "The Dictator is coming," with these words, loud and clear to hear in front of running television cameras, European Commission chief Jean-Claude Juncker welcomed Orbán at a 2015 EU summit in Riga, somewhat alcoholized, it seems, and jovially with a High Five and a friendly slap on Orbán's (properly chosen) right cheek (https://www.theguardian.com/world/video/2015/may/22/hello-dictator-european-commission-president-juncker-jokes-hungarian-orban-video). There is strange camaraderie in the European State Nobility.

44. Orbán, a political animal if there ever was one, went through several incarnations, always grasping the opportunity of the moment: bearded youthful dissident daring the apparatchiks before a Budapest crowd in June 1989, and moving on to center-right once his previously left-liberal Fidesz party did not do well electorally in the mid-1990s. The extreme right was only his third stop, post-2002, always with Fidesz, the party he founded. This was when his previous coalition partner, a small conservative party, with which he had ruled Hungary as Europe's youngest prime minister between 1998 and 2002, entered into a government coalition with the socialists. That coalition would last eight years, leaving Fidesz in the opposition wilderness (https://dossiers-bibliotheque.sciencespo.fr/une-vie-politique-europeenne-european-political-life/metamorphosis-thirty-years-viktor-orban). In a famous speech in 2009, Orbán had a foreboding that Fidesz would have to win only one more time, but then decisively, to rule the country alone in the "next 15 to 20 years," without "unnecessary" debates (Pap 2018, 58). This is exactly what happened.

45. The public work program was criticized as inefficient and brutish, offering only "rock-bottom wages," at 31 to 33 percent of the national average (Kornai 2015, 286). More successful was Orbán's recruitment of European manufacturers, like Volkswagen-Skoda, which liked the country's low wages in comparison with rising wages in China and other Asian countries.

46. This economic nationalism wasn't all of one cloth. In 2011, Orbán also introduced a flat income tax at the low level of 16 percent (currently 15 percent), and, in 2017, he brought the corporate income tax down to 9 percent (also flat), which is Europe's lowest. In addition, unemployment benefits were limited to ninety days, and between 2008 and 2017 family allowance was frozen. When Orbán added a "punitive" public works scheme and the criminalization of homelessness to the bill, Stubbs and Lendrai-Bainton (2020, 542) call the result an instance of "authoritarian neoliberalism." Boasting his tax credentials, Orbán presented himself as a mini-Reagan in the opening speech of the US Republicans' 2022 Conservative Political Action Committee (CPAC) conference in Dallas, Texas (https://www.youtube.com/watch?v=IANho_dp_BI). Philipp Ther (2016, 157) is on the mark, when he characterizes Orbán's program as an unorthodox combination of "right-wing US Republicanism and the collectivist heritage of state socialism." Szabolcs Pogonyi calls it a "very mixed bag that (one) cannot easily describe either as neoliberal or populist" (personal communication).

47. https://www.politico.com/story/2017/01/full-text-donald-trump-inauguration-speech-transcript-233907.

48. The "work" versus "speculation" contrast is made in Orbán's 2022 CPAC speech (see above). Soros being Jewish, this contrast inevitably panders to antisemitic sentiments.

49. *The Fundamental Law of Hungary* (as in force on December 23, 2020), https://www.parlament.hu/documents/125505/138409/Fundamental+law/73811993-c377-428d-9808-ee03d6fb8178. I will leave out the patently unconstitutional way of ramming through this "constitution," without any participation of the opposition parties (which unitedly voted against it) or public debate. I will also leave out its dismantling of the Constitutional Court, which had been one of the most powerful in the world, and the prodigious use in it of "cardinal laws" (known in other countries, like France, as "organic laws"). Cardinal laws need to be passed by a two-thirds majority *present* in parliament (still a lighter hurdle than passing or amending the constitution itself, which requires a two-thirds majority of *all members* of parliament). The required supermajority petrifies issues of family policy, social policy, or tax and budget policy that in regular democracies are left to the government of the day to decide, that is, by way of simple parliamentary majorities. See Fleck et al. (2011) and Venice Commission (2011), and the excellent account by Pap (2018).

324 ENDNOTES

50. Hungary—although ethnically homogenous at 97 percent—has long subscribed to a multiculturalism for national minorities, though one that has been criticized as "illiberal" and "dishonest" (Pap 2018, ch. 5). When Orbán declared in 2015, in an interview with the German daily *Frankfurter Allgemeine Zeitung*, that "we do not want a multicultural society," this was new speak in Hungary. Of course, Hungarian "multiculturalism" had never been meant for immigrants, which was Orbán's point of reference (motivated by the Syrian refugee crisis).

51. "We, the citizens of Hungary" *does* appear in the preamble, but only in its second-last line, and more as an afterthought (or pseudo-liberal concession).

52. This is the point even of "liberal nationalism," which David Miller (1995), dubiously in my view, distinguishes from a universalistic "civic nationalism" (that he attributes to Jürgen Habermas's notion of constitutional patriotism).

53. The "able to conceive naturally" element of this constitutionally prescribed membership profile of Orbán's nation follows from Article 2 in the "Freedom and Responsibility" part of the Fundamental Law. It protects the "life of the foetus . . . from the moment of conception." A unique provision in Europe (except Ireland), this might rule out not only abortion, but also in-vitro fertilization (which requires the killing of embryos).

54. One important factor not addressed here is new social media. For more on this, see Empoli (2019).

Chapter 5

1. This chapter profited from a critical reading by David McBride.

2. See also Hobsbawm (1996, 39): "(T)he civil rights judgments of the 1950s, which were first applied to blacks and then extended to women, provid(ed) a model for other identity groups."

3. Combahee River Collective, "The Combahee River Collective Statement" (1977), https://www.blackpast.org/african-american-history/combahee-river-collective-statement-1977/.

4. Ibid.

5. Ibid.

6. Ibid.

7. Ibid. With respect to the favored notion of "racial capitalism," see the devastating critique by Wacquant (2023).

8. Tracing the "origins of woke" in the United States, Richard Hanania (2023, ch. 2) calls civil rights law the "skeleton key of the left." See also Caldwell (2020).

9. "The Threat from the Illiberal Left," *The Economist*, September 4, 2021, 7–8.

10. Stern's statement was directed against the ultra-right "Germanic ideology" of the early twentieth century intellectual Moeller van den Bruck and kindred thinkers, who championed the notorious notions of "Third Reich" and "Third Way," and who fused cultural pessimism, Slavic mysticism, and virulent rejection of Western liberalism. See Stern (1961).

11. See the damning review of Sennett (1977) by Cambridge historian John Plumb, "When Did Citizens Become Strangers?," *New York Times*, January 23, 1977.

12. Cognitively, we need the universal as "the horizon of understanding between two particulars," which would not be "intelligible" without it (Todorov 1993, 12).

13. In the United States, the polarization between Democrats and Republicans, labeled "partyism" by Cass Sunstein, has become notorious (see Joppke 2021a, 52–53). For Europe, see Herold et al. (2023) and Münch (2023). An intelligent rebuttal that society is "polarized," with a focus on Germany, is Mau et al. (2023).

14. https://dictionary.cambridge.org/dictionary/english/cultural-appropriation. Charges of cultural appropriation have multiplied in fashion (such as dreadlocks worn by whites) and in the performing arts. Even Reggae has recently been questioned if performed by whites (https://www.swissinfo.ch/eng/business/how-a-white-swiss-reggae-band-forced-switzerland-to-question-cultural-appropriation/47789954). But then there is no reason to exempt from this taboo Jazz and Blues, which are the quintessentially (black) American art forms.

15. Tellingly, the intellectual New Right, originating in France but spreading from there to Germany, Italy, and Austria, likes to call itself "identitarian right" (see Weiss 2017, 2018). Much like the identity left, it depicts itself in a defensive position, as in the inflammatory notion of a "population replacement" by Islamic migration.

16. This is Democratic Party presidential candidate Hillary Clinton's much-publicized denigration of "half of" Donald Trump supporters in 2016, whom she further called "racist, sexist,

ENDNOTES 325

homophobic, xenophobic, Islamophobic" (https://time.com/4486502/hillary-clinton-basket-of-deplorables-transcript/).

17. According to Fawcett (2014), "faith in progress" is one of liberalism's "grand ideas."
18. See also the more extended discussion in Brubaker (2016a, 135–141).
19. Note that Brubaker (2016a) does not discuss right identity politics. Given its propensity for ethnic nationalism, including the right would tilt the balance strongly to the pole of "givenness."
20. https://en.unesco.org/news/races-do-not-exist-but-racism-does.
21. See for this, in the United States, the simultaneous condemnation of Rachel Dolezal, a white-to-black transitioner, and celebration of Caitlyn Jenner, a male-to-female transitioner (Brubaker 2016b).
22. I owe this distinction to David McBride.
23. Under Obama, the ratio was reduced to 18:1.
24. A similarly friendly critique is Gottschalk (2015, ch. 6). While critiquing Alexander's single-minded focus on "racial disparities," which obscures other (demographic, economic, social, etc.) factors that may cause black overrepresentation in the US prison system, Gottschalk still calls hers a "masterful" work (ibid., 120, 127).
25. This similarity is also noticed by Rogers Smith and Desmond King in their recent account of "America's New Racial Battle Lines" (2024, 28), who otherwise see a new radical "repair" versus supremacist "protect" fault line having replaced the earlier race-blind versus race-conscious dichotomy in American race relations.
26. In her analysis of mass incarceration, Michelle Alexander (2020 [2010], 228) speaks of "structural racism." Commendably free of "complicated theories and obscure jargon" (ibid.), she likens it to the wires of a bird cage, whose intricate connections and arrangement "serve to enclose the bird and . . . ensure that it cannot escape."
27. Bell would later receive empirical ammunition for his bleak theory by historian Mary Dudziak (2011).
28. See the *New York Times Magazine* of August 14, 2019, which is devoted to the topic.
29. For the overwhelmingly white participation in the 1964 Mississippi Freedom Summer project, see the classic sociological study on "high risk activism" by McAdam (1986).
30. The materialism-idealism distinction, marking different stages of CRT, is made by Delgado and Stefancic (2017, ch. 1).
31. As DiAngelo is white herself, it is not clear how this diagnosis is possible in the first. When reflecting "what to be done," her lapidary advice is "I strive to be 'less white'" (2018, ch. 12).
32. "Out of the Academy," *The Economist*, September 4, 2021, 14; see also Rufo (2023, ch. 1).
33. "The Culture War in Education: Schools for Scandal," *The Economist*, July 16, 2022, 33–35.
34. "The Great Leap Backward," *The Economist*, July 29, 2023, 62.
35. In 2020, Trump's popularity with minority voters (Asian, Hispanic, and African American) increased even further. See "US Election 2020: Why Trump Gained Support Among Minorities," *BBC News*, November 22, 2020, https://www.bbc.com/news/world-us-canada-54972389. Between 2016 and 2020, Hispanic voters, once loyal Democrats, moved eighteen points towards the Republicans, and by 2024 they were almost as likely to vote Republican as Democrat. Also "(b)lack men are . . . slowly peeling away from the Democrats" ("Biden or Bust," *The Economist*, January 6, 2024). These trends were confirmed by the 2024 presidential election outcome. For the particularly striking case of "Latinos", 42 percent of whose eligible voters opted for Trump, see David Signer, "Ausgerechnet die Latinos haben genug von der demokratischen Identitätspolitik", *Neue Zürcher Zeitung*, 22 November 2024, p.5.
36. See "Poll Position," *The Economist*, November 25, 2023, 75.
37. Dobbin and Kalev (2022, 11) show, on the basis of US data, that the individual "bias-" scrutinizing logic of corporate "diversity training" has been a "spectacular failure."
38. This objectivism is not a prank of antiracist reasoning. It has legal grounding in the "disparate impact" doctrine of US civil rights law, which likewise assumes (without further examining) that racial disparities (in the workplace) are the result of discrimination, and of discrimination alone. Richard Hanania (2023) thus boldly argues that there is a straight line from civil rights law to "wokeness."
39. In their account of persistent residential "hypersegregation" in America, Massey and Denton (1993) highlight strategic behavior of this sort. Accordingly, they ultimately "anchor their institutionalist account in collective psychology" (Reed and Chowkwanyun 2012, 156), such as white fear for the value of their property.

326   ENDNOTES

40. See the European Commission's "Anti-Racism Action Plan" (2020), issued in the wake of the killing of George Floyd, which talks about "structural racism."
41. Weber (1976 [1922], 234) speaks of "race membership" as *"subjektiv... empfunden"* (subjectively perceived).
42. https://en.wikipedia.org/wiki/Thomas_theorem.
43. There is a good deal of self-berating in Kendi's biographic description of his pre-conversion self, such as his youthful enthusiasm for Martin Luther King Jr.'s civic inclusion gospel, or his earlier preference for women with light-brown skin, both of which he now regrets. See Andreas Kilb, "Ibram X. Kendi in Berlin," *Frankfurter Allgemeine Zeitung*, July 11, 2022.
44. Without drawing the religion analogy, Szetela (2020, 1374f) noticed the standard academic celebration of BLM as "prophetic," the treating of their queer feminist leadership with "reverence and honour," and the reluctance to publicly criticize the movement.
45. I owe this parallel to a conversation with Graham Hill.
46. https://www.nytimes.com/2022/02/05/us/todd-gitlin-dead.html.
47. Among thirty-eight "core faculty" in the UCLA sociology department at present, at least fourteen are a visible minority, and even more specialize in areas like migration studies and ethnic and race relations, for which the department is internationally known. It should also be mentioned that seventeen of its thirty-eight faculty members are women.
48. "UCLA Sociology's Obligation to Tangibly Address Anti-Blackness", email by two "non-Black graduate students," sent on June 5, 2020, and circulated in the UCLA sociology department (copy on file with the author). A much better-known post-Floyd academic mobilization is a "Faculty Letter" at Princeton University, dated July 4, 2020. It was signed by around 350 faculty members, who deplore the "indifference to the effects of racism on this campus." The letter asks for a new faculty committee "that would oversee the investigation and discipline of racist behaviours, incidents, research, and publication on the part of faculty," with the definition of "what counts as racist" to be determined by the future committee ("Faculty Letter," July 4, 2020, Princeton University, copy on file with the author). As this initiative immediately received the support of Princeton's president, Christopher Eisgruber, Trump's Department of Education deviously and hypocritically opened an inquiry against the university, because under the 1964 Civil Rights Act no federal money can be given to institutions that are guilty of racial discrimination. See Conor Friedersdorf, "How Princeton Opened Itself to the Ultimate Troll," *The Atlantic*, September 25, 2020.
49. Much like the notion of institutional or structural racism, the penchant for speech restrictions has grounding in the evolution of US civil rights law, particularly the courts' inclination "to define discrimination in the broadest possible sense," as an influential 1971 Court of Appeals decision on race discrimination at the workplace asserted (Hanania 2023, ch. 2). The result has been "harassment law," which is built on the notion that civil rights are violated "when women or minorities are made to feel uncomfortable," the threshold for it being in the eye of the beholder or even of uninvolved third parties. The ensuing speech restrictions are one prong in Hanania's straight-line story from civil rights law to "wokeness."
50. The notion of concept creep is by psychologist Nick Haslam (2016). One of his examples is "prejudice," whose expanding scope "primarily reflects an ever-increasing sensitivity to harm, reflecting a liberal moral agenda" (ibid., 1). While "often well motivated," concept creep "runs the risk of pathologizing everyday experience and encouraging a sense of virtuous but impotent victimhood." For a trenchant exploration of the "culture of victimhood," and its grounding in a "more egalitarian society in which members are much more sensitive to those inequalities that remain," see Campbell and Manning (2014, 717).
51. The "concerted cultivation" style of (white) upper-middle-class parenting has first been observed by Annette Lareau (2002).
52. A political scientist publishing these data "faced a campaign by outraged students aiming to revoke his tenure" ("Out of the Economy," *The Economist*, September 4, 2021, 14).
53. A more complete analysis would have to include state bureaucracies, which of course overlap with the education sector. State bureaucracies are the focus of Rufo (2023, ch. 17). Later in this chapter, I touch on the role of the US civil rights bureaucracy in implementing transgender norms.
54. Even at the height of the COVID-19 pandemic, which President Trump liked to see as caused by the "Chinese virus," the number of anti-Asian hate crimes in the United States, while going

ENDNOTES 327

up "substantially" in percentage terms, remained "quite small" in absolute numbers (rising from 158 in 2019 to 279 in 2020), and it remained five times below the share of the "largest group hit by hate crimes," which are blacks (Torpey 2023, ch. 6).

55. Andrew Sullivan, "When the Narrative Replaces the News," *The Weekly Dish*, March 19, 2021.
56. Ibid.
57. Shaila Dewan, "How Racism and Sexism Intertwine to Torment Asian-American Women," *New York Times*, March 18, 2021.
58. Ross Douhat, "The Rise of Woke Capital," *New York Times*, February 28, 2018.
59. Ibid.
60. However, corporate opposition to Republican voter-suppression laws, which target black people and other minorities as more likely to vote Democrat, was less pronounced. The reason is that "the voting bills are being driven by mainstream Republican lawmakers, rather than lesser-known right-wing figures," as was the case in the bathroom bills (David Gelles, "Corporations, Vocal About Racial Justice, Go Quiet on Voting Rights," *New York Times*, March 29, 2021).
61. Ross Douhat, "The Rise of Woke Capital."
62. https://www.washingtonpost.com/news/post-politics/wp/2016/02/13/clinton-in-nevada-not-everything-is-about-an-economic-theory/.
63. Because transhumanism "entails modifying a complex, interlinked package of traits," with uncertain "ultimate outcome," and as it abandons any sense of "humility concerning our human nature," Francis Fukuyama (2004) calls it "the world's most dangerous idea."
64. Brubaker himself suggested this, in his review of the manuscript.
65. Of course, this does not mean that "bodies don't exist prior to culture" but only that "our understanding" of bodies, through whatever category one choses, is "mediated by culture" (Sharpe 2021). This friendly reading of Butler still leaves open the meaning of "sex" if stripped of its biological reference. Hence Butler's cautious "perhaps" when subsuming sex under gender.
66. *The Yogyakarta Principles: Principles on the Application of International Human Rights Law in Relation to Sexual Orientation and Gender Identity*, Geneva, March 2007, at 8, https://yogyakartaprinciples.org/.
67. The British activist organization "Press for Change," founded by transman Stephen Whittle, speaks of an "intersex condition of the brain" (quoted in Thomas 2020, 4).
68. Alex Marzano-Lesnevich, "How Do I Define My Gender if No One Is Watching Me?," *New York Times*, April 2, 2021.
69. There is an interesting parallel in the case of antiracism, where the need for stereotypes follows from its epistemological standpoint relativism. For instance, the Smithsonian National Museum of Afro American History and Culture, in one of its exhibitions, controversially described "white culture" as "rational thinking," "scientific method," "hard work as key to success," and "plan for future"—thus unwittingly reinforcing the racist stereotype of black people as not capable of or at least extraneous to such things (see Rod Dreher, "Smithsonian's Anti-White Propaganda," *The American Conservative*, July 15, 2020). While the Smithsonian list of racial stereotypes was withdrawn after protests, they live on, for instance, in the educational program of "equitable mathematics," funded by the Gates Foundation. It refutes for black kids the notions of a "good response" or "right answer," and condemns as racist if teachers ask their black students to "show their work" (*A Pathway to Equitable Math Instruction*, 2021, equitablemath.org).
70. Note that in progressive jurisdictions, such as Australia, where teachers ask school children to "explore gender," this is by crude stereotypes: for boys, "building things, liking action films and playing with toy cars"; for girls, "cooking, dancing, shopping and gossiping" ("The Body of Law," *The Economist*, October 27, 2018, 21–22).
71. As Brubaker (2023b) pointed out, gender transitioning reinforces traditional gender binaries and stereotypes. Because it tends to be the most critical members of established gender categories who "exit" from these categories, while conservative members stay, gender transitioning necessarily has "stabilizing consequences for the traditional gender order" (ibid., 154).
72. Elbe was in the mistaken belief, perhaps conveyed to her by the German sexologist Magnus Hirschfeld who treated her, that surgery would make her a real woman with the ability to bear children (the fourth and last surgery is believed to have been a uterus transplantation).

328 ENDNOTES

Hirschfeld, like Elbe, was a gay and transvestite, known in Berlin's drag bars as Aunt Magnesia. See Joyce (2021, ch. 1).

73. Whittle is an academic lawyer. Personally, he is a former lesbian who transitioned from female to male in 1975.

74. ECtHR, *Case of A.P., Garçon and Nicot v. France*, decision of April 6, 2017.

75. Hence a queer critic of the judgment lamented the continued "pathologisation of trans identities" (Gonzalez-Salzberg 2018, 538).

76. *Case of A.P., Garçon and Nicot v. France.*, at 40.

77. Ibid., 44.

78. Ibid., 39.

79. First in *Case of Christine Goodwin v. The United Kingdom* (July 11, 2002), the ECtHR decided that the lack of a legal recognition procedure for a transwoman who had undergone gender re-assignment violated her right to privacy under Article 8 of ECHR. The case was argued for the plaintiff by UK transgender activist and lawyer Stephen Whittle, and it moved the UK government to pass the 2004 Gender Recognition Act.

80. While the rate of surgical gender reassignment is higher among natal males than females, "(a)t most a third of transgender people have any surgery . . . Most rely exclusively on cosmetics or changes in how they dress. Most trans women are anatomically male" ("The Body of Law," *The Economist*, October 27, 2018, 20). Their number can only increase further as gender self-identification becomes the norm.

81. Nazia Parveen, "Karen White: How 'Manipulative' Transgender Inmate Attacked Again," *The Guardian*, October 11, 2018.

82. Ibid.

83. However, for very similar problems in the United States, where recently liberalized policies for transgender prisoners are "endangering" female inmates, see "Hard Cell," *The Economist*, September 28, 2024, 42. A Freedom-of-Information request of May 2024 revealed that 48 percent of the 1.433 inmates in US federal male prisons who identify as women are there for sex offenses, which is "nearly four times the share in the general prison population."

84. "She Who Must Not Be Named," *The Economist*, October 2, 2021, 13.

85. On the dangers, and absurdities, of "racism by analogy," see the excellent account by Ford (2009, ch. 2).

86. Of course, one should not romanticize the protective function of sex-segregated facilities. Public bathrooms, for instance, were first segregated in the nineteenth century in the pursuit of "Victorian values that stressed the importance of privacy and modesty" for women who moved from "their" destined place, which was home, to the workplace (Terry Kogan, "How did Public Bathrooms Get to Be Separated by Sex in the First Place?," *The Conversation*, May 27, 2016). However, their patriarchal origins do not delegitimize their protective (as well as hygienic) functions today, which few women would want to give up.

87. "The Body of Law," *The Economist*, October 27, 2018, 22. In 2016, the International Olympic Committee (IOC) stopped requiring Olympic athletes to have undergone gender-reassignment surgery and hormonal treatment when competing in the acquired gender—in the case of male athletes now competing as women, only the lowering of testosterone levels is asked for. While the resulting inequities are widely resented, "few elite female athletes (are) willing to speak publicly about the topic, lest they lose sponsorship deals or team places" ("Women's Sport: Swimming in Controversy," *The Economist*, March 19, 2022, 35). An exception is tennis icon Martina Navratilova, who spoke out without inhibition against self-identification in sports as "insane" and "cheating" (Joyce 2021, ch. 9).

88. US Department of Justice (Civil Rights Division) and US Department of Education (Office for Civil Rights), "Dear Colleague Letter on Transgender Students," May 13, 2016, https://www2.ed.gov/about/offices/list/ocr/letters/colleague-201605-title-ix-transgender.pdf.

89. Ibid., 2.

90. Ibid.

91. Ibid.

92. Ibid., 3.

93. Ibid.

94. Ibid., 2 (emphasis supplied).

95. When Stock gave a talk in Oxford in May 2023, one hundred academics and staff objected to her invitation: "We believe that trans students should not be made to debate their existence"

(Matthew Weaver, "Kathleen Stock Says She is a 'Moderate' as Protests Planned Over Oxford Debate," *The Guardian*, May 29, 2023).

96. Ibid.
97. "There is little or no evidence for this" ("The Body of Law," *The Economist*, October 27, 2018, 21).
98. In the American medical profession, including the American Academy of Pediatrics, gender-affirming care is expected to be followed "uncritically and unquestionably" ("Medical Education and Gender: Identity Problems," *The Economist*, January 8, 2022, 30).
99. The affirmative care principle is also a sign of de-professionalization. Ray Blanchard, a leading sexologist at the University of Toronto (who came under fire by transgender activists for arguing that "autogynephilia"—heterosexual men being aroused by cross-dressing—is a form of transsexualism), put it this way: "I can't think of any branch of medicine outside of cosmetic surgery where the patient makes the diagnosis and prescribes the treatment" (quoted by Shrier 2020, ch. 7).
100. Several medical studies have shown that between 61 percent and 98 percent of children diagnosed with gender dysphoria were later reconciled to their natal sex ("Trans Rights: Boys and Girls," *The Economist*, December 12, 2020, 54).
101. For a critical discussion, see "Conversion Therapy: Missing the Mark," *The Economist*, December 4, 2021, 28–29. The notion of conversion therapy, if applied to transgender people, is a deliberate polemic, fusing it with conversion from homosexuality that, of course, has long been delegitimized. The matter is altogether different with trans people, in particular children, who often suffer from psychological disorders like depression, anxiety, and autism, and who face irreversible choices that have no parallel in the case of "ordinary" homosexuals. One might rather call fast-ordered transition "in effect conversion therapy," because (in most cases) previous homosexuals are turned into members of the opposite "sex" ("Trans Rights: Lost in Conversion," *The Economist*, June 25, 2022, 39).
102. California, New Jersey, Colorado, and Illinois have laws mandating LGBTQ history in school, and the curriculum material is provided by activist organizations. The National Education Association, the US teachers' syndicate, recommends to "affirm" transgender students and not to inform parents about their kids' coming out in school. "Bullies are forever circling trans-identified students," these bullies including parents, as Shrier (2020, ch. 4) summarizes the dominant mind set.
103. Obama's Affordable Care Act of 2010 prohibits discrimination based on sexual orientation and gender identity. Accordingly, health insurance companies must cover hormones and surgeries—the logic being that if hormones are provided to the non-transgendered (e.g., for birth control), the (rather more expensive) cross-sex version must be made available to trans people (see Shrier 2020, ch. 9).
104. Bess Marcus, quoted in Meredith Wadman, "New Paper Ignites Storm Over Whether Teens Experience 'Rapid Onset' of Transgender Identity," *ScienceInsider*, August 30, 2018, https://www.science.org. A former dean of Harvard Medical School called Marcus's statement "anti-intellectual" and "completely antithetical to academic freedom" (ibid.).
105. For the scene of "influencers," such as YouTuber Chase Ross who has set up his own "Uppercase Chase 1" channel, see Shrier (2020, ch. 3).
106. In his recent and instantly acclaimed work on the detrimental effects of iPhone and social media on children and youngsters, Jonathan Haidt (2024, ch. 6) cites the work of Lisa Littman for the notion that "gender dysphoria may also be related in part to social media trends," and that it "appears in social clusters."
107. "Transgender Health Care for Children: In Search of Evidence," *The Economist*, July 30, 2022, 38.
108. "Transgender Treatments: Blocked," *The Economist*, April 24, 2021, 33.
109. "Treating Gender Dysphoria in Kids: Trans Substantiation," *The Economist*, April 8, 2023, 16.
110. Ibid.
111. "Trans Rights: Bellwether?," *The Economist*, December 5, 2020, 29.
112. "Treating Gender Dysphoria in Kids: Trans Substantiation," *The Economist*, April 8, 2023, 16. In the United Kingdom, a report by pediatrician Hillary Cass, which was commissioned by the National Health Service and published in early 2024, is a real game-changer. According to it, "we have no good evidence on the long-term outcomes of interventions to manage gender-relating distress," and it suggests that "for the majority of young people, a medical pathway may

330 ENDNOTES

not be the best way (to alleviate this distress)" (quoted in Helen Lewis, "Britain is Leaving the U.S. Gender-Medicine Debate Behind," *The Atlantic*, April 12, 2024). As Helen Lewis writes, "(t)his is a million miles away from prominent American medical groups' recommendations to simply affirm an adolescent's stated gender—and from common practice at American gender clinics" (ibid.).

113. https://www.facebook.com/thedarrengrimes/videos/keir-starmer-do-women-have-a-penis/671964703925814/.

114. Interview with Keir Starmer, *The Times*, March 12, 2022.

115. Interview with Keir Starmer, *Sunday Times*, April 1, 2023.

116. Debbie Hayton, "Keir Starmer's Gender Identity Muddle," *The Spectator*, March 13, 2022.

117. Jesse Singal, Review of *Trans* by Helen Joyce, *New York Times*, September 7, 2021.

118. While their lines are often blurred (as in US civil rights law), laws against hate speech must in principle be distinguished from antidiscrimination laws. Hate-speech laws raise the problem of the "heckler's veto," if the *perception* of being offended becomes the defining criterion, as in some of these laws. As Timothy Garton Ash (2016, 228) draws the line, somewhat provocatively, "the *advocacy* of discrimination should be allowed by law—and then heavily criticized in public debate—but *actual* discrimination should definitely not be."

119. *The Yogyakarta Principles Plus 10*, Geneva, November 10, 2017, at 9, https://yogyakartaprinciples.org/principles-en/yp10/.

120. Debbie Hayton, "Keir Starmer's Gender Identity Muddle."

121. Greg Burt, "CA Supreme Court to Decide if the State Can Jail a Person for Refusing to Use Someone's Preferred Pronouns," *California Family Council*, November 14, 2021, https://www.californiafamily.org/2021/11/ca-supreme-court-to-decide-if-the-state-can-jail-a-person-for-refusing-to-use-someones-preferred-pronouns/.

122. According to a student manual at the University of Michigan, "sexual violence" includes "criticizing the partner sexually" and, incredibly, the negative of sex, "withholding sex and affection" (Melnick 2018, 151).

123. "Safe bystander intervention" is an anodyne description for involving third parties in a Homeland Security-style spying operation of "see something, hear something, know something, say something" (Joffe 2018), in the extreme against the alleged "victim's" own wishes (Joffe 2017).

124. "Dear Colleague Letter on Transgender Students," 1.

125. Salesforce, a Silicon Valley "tech behemoth" known for "championing social-justice causes," paid no federal taxes on its $2.6 billion USD profits in 2020 ("The Illiberal Left: Out of the Academy," *The Economist*, September 4, 2021, 15).

126. Wolfgang Thierse, "Wie viel Identität verträgt die Gesellschaft?," *Frankfurter Allgemeine Zeitung*, February 22, 2021.

127. Interview with Wolfgang Thierse, *Neue Zürcher Zeitung*, March 10, 2021.

128. In Germany, the AfD has even become the target of the *Verfassungsschutz* (Office for the Protection of the Constitution).

129. Jesse Singal, "This is What a Modern-Day Witch Hunt Looks Like," *New York Magazine*, May 2, 2017.

130. Rogers Brubaker, "The Uproar Over 'Transracialism,'" *New York Times*, May 18, 2017.

Chapter 6

1. Shlomo Avineri, "Coronavirus has Killed Neoliberalism," *Haaretz*, March 30, 2020.

2. Marc Saxer, "COVID-19: How Corona Broke the System," *International Politics and Society*, March 23, 2020, https://www.ips-journal.eu/regions/global/how-corona-broke-the-system-4180/.

3. Ibid.

4. Janan Ganesh, "The Administrative State is Poised for a Comeback," *Financial Times*, March 12, 2020.

5. Martin Wolf, "Democracy Will Fail if we Don't Think as Citizens," *Financial Times*, July 6, 2020. See also Wolf (2023).

6. See the "Statement in Support of the Scientists, Public Health Professionals, and Medical Professionals of China Combatting COVID-19," *The Lancet* 375, no. 7 (March 2020): e42. Signed by a group of leading "public health scientists" from various countries, the statement "strongly condemn(s) conspiracy theories suggesting that COVID-19 does not have a natural origin." As if this wasn't clear enough, the statement continues that "(c)onspiracy theories do nothing

ENDNOTES 331

but create fear, rumours, and prejudice that jeopardise our global collaboration in the fight against the virus," notably with the "scientists, public health professionals, and medical professionals of China." First appearing online on 18 February 2020, the letter later turned out to be "organized and drafted" (Wade 2021) by the controversial British zoologist Peter Daszak, whose New-York based EcoHealth Alliance for several years already had received United States government funding for conducting Coronavirus research in the Wuhan Institute of Virology. While four more signers of the *Lancet* letter had direct ties to the EcoHealth Alliance, none of them declared "competing interests".

7. In late February 2023, the Director of the FBI, Christopher Wray, considered a laboratory accident in Wuhan the "most likely" cause of the COVID-19 pandemic ("Covid Origin: Why the Wuhan Lab-Leak Theory is So Disputed," *BBC News*, March 1, 2023).

8. Email communication between leading US health officials, including Anthony Fauci, which was obtained under the US Freedom of Information Act, reveals their instrumental role in suppressing the lab-leak theory (see Green and Fazi 2023, ch. 1; Kennedy 2021, ch. 11).

9. Personal communication, March 8, 2022.

10. Also one of the first comparative studies of state responses to COVID-19, and of continued value, is the unpublished report by Jasanoff et al. (2021).

11. Richard Münch, *Ruling by Numbers: What Can be Learned from the Corona Pandemic?*, Presentation at the Institute of Sociology, University of Bern, April 24, 2024.

12. For critical accounts, see Mucchielli (2022a, 2022b), Stiegler (2021) (written in French), Green and Fazi (2023), and Münch (2022) (written in German). Promptly, on his French Wikipedia site, Laurent Mucchielli is accused of spreading "false information" about the "danger of the virus," and of being a "participant in disinformation about the COVID-19 pandemic" (https://fr.wikipedia.org/wiki/Laurent_Mucchielli). Green and Fazi (2023), a cautiously argued and impressively detailed and comprehensive English-language account of the COVID-19 pandemic that covers the Global North and South in tandem, was dismissed in *The Guardian* by a self-described "political activist" as making a "travesty of the facts" (https://www.theguardian.com/commentisfree/2023/mar/23/lockdown-sceptics-history-academics-left-covid), and the book was otherwise ignored. Richard Münch, one of Germany's most prominent social theorists, has been (so far) spared public denunciation. By far the most fact-filled critical account of the US COVID-19 response centering around the enigmatic figure of "America's Doctor," Anthony Fauci, is Kennedy (2021). The author, Robert F. Kennedy, of the famous Kennedy clan, is slandered, in the very first sentence of his Wikipedia entry, as "advocating anti-vaccine misinformation and public health-related conspiracy theories." Wikipedia, in fact, has been on the frontline of propagating a government-conformant line on the COVID-19 pandemic (supported by most social media and platforms, including Twitter, Facebook, YouTube, and Google). Wikipedia thus blithely abandoned its cherished principle of "neutrality" and of representing the "sum of all human knowledge."

13. An exception is Cafruni and Talani (2023). They share the "deadly virus" line, but also highlight the "neoliberalism" factor. However, the latter is not engaged by them to problematize the double strategy of lockdown plus mass vaccination; instead, they use it to explain, for instance, the "lethal inequalities and injustices of the American health care system" (as in Cafruni's chapter on the United States, ibid., 27). This does not diminish their findings. A neoliberally hollowed-out administrative state is undoubtedly an important factor in explaining a deficient crisis response. Next to the United States, a particularly blatant case is the United Kingdom, where the pandemic amounted to an "enormous bonanza for private-sector contractors," from testing and tracking to the provision of masks, all incompetently done, so that the military had to be called in to fix the private-sector blunders (Jones and Hameiri 2021, 1041–1044). Jones and Hameiri sarcastically speak of "'failed states' in the global north" (ibid., 1047). However, this does not exhaust the involvement of neoliberalism in state responses to the COVID-19 pandemic. Leaving out the neoliberalism factor in explaining the overarching "double strategy" amounts to apologizing the latter, as simply required by the circumstances.

14. This is not to deny that the role of the World Health Organization, particularly in the early phase of the pandemic, was widely criticized, mostly for making its calls too late (Woolhouse 2022, ch. 15), apparently not to offend China (Ferguson 2021: ch.9), and sometimes for being inconsistent (as with respect to mask-wearing) (see Klinenberg 2024, ch. 6).

332 ENDNOTES

15. "I could see Troy burning," recalls a senior *New York Times* journalist who had covered pandemics for twenty-five years (McNeil 2024, 11). This was in consideration of the earliest reported fatality rates, which seemed to be "very close to what the world had seen in 1918" (ibid., 6).

16. For "revolving doors," see David Marquand's (2013, ch. 6) vivid description of Britain. More generally, and borrowing for this condition Charles Lindblom's notion of "circularity," Frank Pasquale (2015) argues that the "blurring" of the market versus state distinction is "at the core" of a "black box society" ruled by "proprietary algorithms" (ibid., 207, 215, 4), the key players being tech companies, finance, and governments.

17. "Aiming at herd immunity meant assuming that voluntary compliance had broken down" (Baldwin 2021, 55). Of course, in the extreme, and in an ideal world of perfect voluntary compliance, this is true. In the real world, Sweden was redeemed by a long-term relatively low COVID-19 death rate, which was much below the mortality rate of countries with harsh and protracted lockdowns, such as Italy, France, Spain, or Belgium, and also well below the Western European average (see Wang et al. 2022).

18. For the role of expertise, see, for instance, Hodges et al. (2022). In their four-country comparison (Germany, Italy, Netherlands, and Britain), these authors argue that the high level of "uncertainty" and need for "drastic intervention" led to a strong reliance of politicians on scientific advice, particularly in the early stages of the pandemic. In later stages, by contrast, "gaps emerged between scientific advice emphasising caution, while politicians increasingly became inclined to promote a relaxation of restrictions to serve economic and social values" (ibid., 265). A detailed and insightful comparison of the "organization of expertise" in Sweden and France, by Olivier Borraz and Bengt Jacobsson (2023, 103), notes that the "dominant discourses in 2020, among academics, experts, and political officials alike" in most countries were pro-lockdown—but that, with an eye on Sweden, "alternative courses were possible."

19. Engler et al. (2021, 1082) hypothesize and confirm that of three determinants of "democratic quality": "protection of individual liberties," "cheques and balances," and "rule of law," the first factor has the strongest effect.

20. Sweden, the one exception from lockdown in Europe, for instance, was also the country where the leading actor in its COVID-19 response, the expert-constituted Public Health Agency, would balance "current *and future* health risks" (emphasis supplied), overall taking a "broad and long-term perspective on public health" (Olofsson et al. 2022, 1, 7), instead of the narrow and short-term view that prevailed elsewhere.

21. Green and Fazi (2023, 162f). The entire conversation between Gates and Fareed Zakaria is available on YouTube at https://www.youtube.com/watch?v=cuNWRoHRzkU.

22. For the improbability that, in China, "the infection was stopped dead in its tracks, completely contained by April 1, 2020," see George Calhoun, "Part 1: China is Underreporting the Covid Death Rate," *Forbes*, January 2, 2022.

23. Johns Hopkins CHS, WEF, and BMGF, *Event 201. Public-Private Cooperation for Pandemic Preparedness and Response. A Call to Action*, https://centerforhealthsecurity.org/sites/default/files/2022-12/200117-publicprivatepandemiccalltoaction.pdf. The event itself is fully documented on YouTube at https://centerforhealthsecurity.org/our-work/tabletop-exercises/event-201-pandemic-tabletop-exercise.

24. Johns Hopkins CHS, WEF, and BMGF, *Event 201*.

25. The Chinese participant in Event 201, George Gao, Director-General of the Chinese Center for Disease Control and Prevention, may well have been aware that the fictitious scenario was already real in his country.

26. https://www.cnbc.com/video/2019/01/23/bill-gates-and-the-return-on-investment-in-vaccinations-davos.html.

27. For the distinction between "miasma" and "germ" theories of disease, see McGoey (2015, introduction) and Kennedy (2021, ch. 9). It overlaps with the distinction between "horizontal" and "vertical" approaches to public health, the first focusing on the creation of comprehensive health systems, the second on fighting specific diseases (Hägel 2020, 200).

28. University of Toronto public health professor Anne-Emanuelle Birn, quoted in Lakoff (2017, 77).

29. This had detrimental effects on Global South health systems, where Gates-funded vaccination programs homed in on a "few diseases" while "shortchang(ing) basic needs such as

ENDNOTES   333

nutrition and transportation" (Charles Piller and Doug Smith, "Unintended Victims of Gates Foundation Generosity," *Los Angeles Times*, December 16, 2007).

30. As Gates is referred to by Nicola Twilley, "The Terrifying Lessons of a Pandemic Simulation," *The Atlantic*, June 1, 2018.

31. https://www.gatesfoundation.org/ideas/speeches/2011/05/world-health-assembly. When Gates's wife, Melinda, was invited to give the WHA keynote address in 2014, several global health NGOs issued an unusual protest note: "It is unacceptable that the WHO, supposedly governed by sovereign nation states, should countenance that at its global conference the keynote address would be delivered thrice in ten years by individuals from the same organization, and from the same family" (Hägel 2020, 205f).

32. By April 2020, one month into the official "pandemic," the basic facts were known and they would remain constant: "the overwhelming majority of people do not have any significant risk of dying from COVID-19"; "80 percent of all cases were mild," while the risk of dying was concentrated in the above-seventy years of age group and in those with an "underlying illness"; and "(h)alf of all people testing positive for infection have no symptoms at all" (Scott Atlas, "The Data Is In—Stop the Panic and End the Total Isolation," *The Hill*, April 22, 2020). A leading British epidemiologist confirms that, by March 2020, "we knew . . . that the main risk from novel coronavirus is to the elderly, frail and infirm" (Woolhouse 2022, 121).

33. Between 2003 and 2012, the Pfizer pharmaceutical company "spent amounts equivalent to 71 per cent and 75 per cent of its profits, respectively, on share buybacks and dividends" (Mazzucato 2013, 32).

34. When the COVID-19 vaccines were released, Gates infamously insisted that their patents should not be lifted, which would have made the vaccines more accessible to the Global South: "The through-line for Gates has been his unwavering commitment to drug companies' right to exclusive control over medical science" (Zaitchik 2021). I will come back to this point later.

35. F. William Engdahl, "European Parliament to Investigate WHO and 'Pandemic' Scandal," *Healthcare in Europe*, January 26, 2010, https://healthcare-in-europe.com/en/news/european-parliament-to-investigate-who-and-pandemic-scandal.html.

36. Matthew Weaver, "Swine Flu Could Affect Third of World's Population, Says Study," *The Guardian*, May 12, 2009.

37. Wodarg's English-language Wikipedia entry includes this confused sentence, obviously meant to smear him: "(S)ome of his statements (on the Covid-19 pandemic) were neither verifiable nor falsifiable, and because the facts Wodarg presented had nothing to do with each other, his statements had proved to be misleading" (https://en.wikipedia.org/wiki/Wolfgang_Wodarg). Further down in the same entry, one reads that Wodarg expressed his views on "radical media," some of them "close to the AfD," the German radical right party. To denounce critics of the Covid Consensus as right-wing has been standard. Wodarg was member of the Social Democratic Party (SPD) between 1988 and 2021, and he left it in obvious disagreement with its partaking in the Covid Doxa.

38. F. William Engdahl, "European Parliament to Investigate WHO and 'Pandemic' Scandal."

39. A friendlier interpretation of the 2009 European swine flu controversy has been provided by sociologist Andrew Lakoff (2015, 2017, ch. 4). According to Lakoff, the WHO, informed by recent developments in the US biosecurity sector, acted on a new public health approach based on "sentinel devices," in lieu of a traditional approach based on "actuarial devices." Sentinel devices "treat unprecedented diseases that cannot be mapped over time, but can only be anticipated and prepared for," and they involve a high level of uncertainty about potentially catastrophic events that require decisive early action, often deemed unnecessary after the fact, as it turned out in 2009 (2017, 40). Accordingly, what "played out in an 'ethical' register," argues Lakoff, is better seen as "tension between these two kinds of security mechanisms" (2015, 46, 40). Note that the "new" sentinel security system is actually quite old, as Lakoff himself points out, stemming from the US Cold War civic preparations for a nuclear war (2017, ch. 1). I agree with Lakoff that the element of a new health security approach, based on "preparedness" rather than traditional "risk assessment," cannot be dismissed. But this does not mute the "ethical" (corruption) charges made by WHO critics. One week after the mentioned Council of Europe parliamentary assembly report was published, a separate joint investigation by the *British Medical Journal* (*BMJ*) and the Bureau of Investigative Journalism revealed a "system struggling to manage the inherent conflict between the pharmaceutical industry, WHO, and the global public health system, which all draw on the same pool of scientific experts." It also

334 ENDNOTES

critiqued a "somewhat incestuous approach" taken by the WHO when internally reviewing the conflict-of-interest charges raised against the organization (Cohen and Carter 2010, 1274, 1279). While Lakoff (2015, 2017, ch. 4) mentions and discusses the *BMJ* report, he does not seem to be moved by its findings.

40. https://gbdeclaration.org/.

41. Ibid.

42. "Great Barrington Declaration," *Wikipedia*, https://en.wikipedia.org/wiki/Great_Barrington_ Declaration. This entry is part of the "take down" effort demanded by Collins.

43. https://thehill.com/policy/healthcare/519727-trump-health-official-meets-with-doctors-pushing-herd-immunity/. In his otherwise critical account of Sweden's "dangerously liberal" (early) COVID-19 response, Jon Pierre correctly states that "flattening the curve" of new infections was the primary strategy in Sweden also, with herd immunity merely as "secondary outcome" (Pierre 2020, 479, 482).

44. A statistical analysis by Stanford epidemiologist John Ioannidis (2022), of course himself a prominent critic of the Covid Doxa, suggests that both the GBD and the JSM "have been signed by many leading stellar scientists with very high citation impact in the scientific literature" (ibid., 4). The difference is that JSM signatories have many more followers on Twitter. Accordingly, the "social media superiority" of JSM may have created the impression that it is "the dominant strategy pursued by the vast majority of knowledgeable scientists" (ibid., 6).

45. "Scientific Consensus on the COVID-19 Pandemic: We Need to Act Now," (also known as the John Snow Memorandum), *The Lancet* 396, no. 31 (October 2020): e71–e72.

46. In reality, in its deadly first year, the COVID-19 pandemic killed less than 0.006 percent of the world population, while the Spanish Flu overall killed approximately 2.7 percent (Schwab and Thierry 2020, conclusion). By late 2023, the officially counted seven million COVID-19 deaths corresponded to 0.09 percent of the world population (Andersson and Jonung 2024, 4). At any point in its development, the COVID-19 pandemic was several hundred times less lethal than the Spanish Flu.

47. "Scientific Consensus on the COVID-19 Pandemic," e72.

48. Lakoff (2007, 2017) shows that "preparedness" originated in the Cold War and its threat of a nuclear attack, but eventually was applied to other security threats, related to terrorism, the environment—and "emerging infectious disease" (2007, 255).

49. As Daniel Thym and Jonas Bornemann (2020, 1170) put it cautiously, the initial closure of internal Schengen borders, reopened only on the condition of possessing a valid health pass, "signalled a general distance from the European Project" (2020, 1170). The "Europe that protects, empowers and defends" (ibid., 1156), pronounced by previous European Commission chief Jean-Claude Juncker, was nowhere to be seen.

50. US membership in the WHO was immediately restored under the Biden presidency.

51. By now, the United States, the European Union, and certain European national governments (most notably the French) have reason to fear the lab-leak theory—all of them had financed (and some, like the European Union, still do finance) gain-of-function research in the suspected Wuhan Institute of Virology.

52. Tooze could not know the disastrous last act of the Chinese two-year-plus zero-COVID-19 policy, in late April 2022, when desperate residents of completely locked-down Shanghai went insane, crying out loud into the darkness from their sealed apartments for food and help (https://www.youtube.com/watch?v=3SRuKZ5P1io).

53. Jörg Phil Friedrich, "Corona-Aufarbeitung," *Die Welt*, March 22, 2024.

54. Jürgen Gerhards and Michael Zürn, "Warum wir nicht von asiatischen Ländern lernen," *Tagesspiegel*, March 22, 2023.

55. Also influential in the United State was a statistical analysis of "social distancing" measures by forty-three major US cities during the 1918 Spanish Flu—which demonstrated to a team led by medical historian Howard Markel the "value of early, combined and sustained nonpharmaceutical interventions to mitigate a pandemic" (Markel et al. 2007, 653).

56. Michael Senger, "Neil Ferguson, China and a Fanatical Socialist Health Minister: The Untold Story of How Lockdown Came to Italy and the West," *The Daily Sceptic*, August 5, 2022.

57. In pre-pandemic times, with the suppression of the Yellow Vests in mind, Bruno Amable and Stefano Polombarini (2021, preface) wrote about the Macron government that it shows "to which extent a radical neoliberal transformation of society. . . must be based on brutal police repression and significant infringement of civil liberties."

ENDNOTES **335**

58. Maxime Tandonnet, "Contrer l'effet apéro," *FigaroVox*, January 15, 2021, https://www.lefigaro.fr/vox/politique/contrer-l-effet-apero-une-formule-revelatrice-de-la-deconnexion-dramatique-des-elites-au-pouvoir-20210115.
59. As the author can testify, machine-gun equipped police squads patrolled French metropolitan bars and cafés around 6 p.m. to ensure that *apéro* was off.
60. "Wie wir COVID-19 unter Kontrolle bekommen," *Strategy Paper of the Federal Ministry of the Interior*, Berlin, March 22, 2020 (copy in author's possession).
61. Ibid., 1. A compelling critique of Germany's "continued worst-case orientation," which can be applied to most other countries, is Obermaier (2022).
62. "Wie wir COVID-19 unter Kontrolle bekommen," 13.
63. Ibid., 17.
64. Giorgio Agamben, "L'invenzione di un epidemia," *Quodlibet*, February 26, 2020.
65. Wolfgang Streeck, "Wissenschaftlern folgen? Ja doch, aber welchen?," *Frankfurter Allgemeine Zeitung*, January 11, 2021, 13.
66. The Agamben quotes are from the English translation of the Italian original published in *Quodlibet*, March 17, 2020, https://bookhaven.stanford.edu/2020/03/giorgio-agamben-on-coronavirus-the-enemy-is-not-outside-it-is-within-us/.
67. A German translation appeared as "Guest Commentary," *Neue Zürcher Zeitung*, May 5, 2020, https://www.nzz.ch/feuilleton/giorgio-agamben-der-notstand-erlaubt-alles-die-ethik-dankt-ab-ld.1553878?reduced=true.
68. In France, between 1990 and 2017, 160,000 hospital beds were removed, one-third of the national total, and the cuts continued during the pandemic (Mucchielli 2022a, ch. 8).
69. In France, for instance, in 2020, COVID-19 patients represented only 2 percent of all hospital patients, and 5 percent of intensive-care patients (Deruelle 2022, 10). In Germany, the hospital association IQM (*Initiative Qualitätsmedizin*) reported that "in 2020 our clinics were never at a capacity limit" (Lütge and Esfeld 2021, 24).
70. That experts "decided" during the pandemic is certainly not true. And if they did, as the Public Health Authority in Sweden, this was a political choice—that the government was subsequently reprimanded for by the Swedish Corona Commission, at least with respect to the early phase of the pandemic (https://www.regeringen.se/globalassets/regeringen/block/fakta-och-genvagsblock/socialdepartementet/sjukvard/coronakommissionen/summary.pdf). The literature shows a great deal of cross-national and temporal variation in the relationship between experts and political decision-makers, even in the early phase of the pandemic when expert advice was the gold standard. In some countries, like Denmark and Norway, politicians raced ahead with lockdown against the milder suggestions of their national experts (see Baekkeskov et al. 2021; Christensen and Laegreid 2022); in others, like France, expert pluralism enabled the President to "cherry-pick" and follow a line commensurate with a non-medical agenda (such as keeping schools open, which Macron courageously did) (see Borraz and Jacobsson 2023, 96). In the late phase of the pandemic, politicians increasingly distanced themselves from experts, in the pursuit of "social and economic values" (Hodges et al. 2022, 249).
71. Benjamin Bratton, "Agamben WTF, or How Philosophy Failed the Pandemic," *Verso Blog*, July 28, 2021, https://www.versobooks.com/en-gb/blogs/news/5125-agamben-wtf-or-how-philosophy-failed-the-pandemic.
72. Slavoj Zizek, "Monitor and Punish? Yes, Please," *The Philosophical Salon*, March 16, 2020, https://thephilosophicalsalon.com/monitor-and-punish-yes-please/.
73. https://www.tilburguniversity.edu/staff/t-christiaens.
74. Tim Christiaens, "Must Society Be Defended from Agamben?," *Critical Legal Thinking*, March 26, 2020, https://criticallegalthinking.com/2020/03/26/must-society-be-defended-from-agamben/.
75. Hinnerk Wissmann, quoted by Dietrich Murswiek, "Die Politik hat in ihrem Corona-Furor jedes Mass verloren," *Die Welt*, February 26, 2021.
76. Oliver Lepsius, "Vom Niedergang grundrechtlicher Denkkategorien in der Corona-Pandemie," *Verfassungsblog*, April 6, 2020, https://verfassungsblog.de/vom-niedergang-grundrechtlicher-denkkategorien-in-der-corona-pandemie/.
77. Other prominent legal lockdown critics did not agree: "the right to life (is) no '*Supergrundrecht*' (superordinate basic right), but even limited by direct state interventions (*durch direkte staatliche Eingriffe einschränkbar*)" (Heinig et al. 2020, 864).

336 ENDNOTES

78. This is the view of the prominent constitutional lawyer and former constitutional justice Paul Kirchhof, who justified lockdown by calling all people qua human being "*Gefährder*," and the non-vaccinated even "*Intensivgefährder*" (extra-dangerous) (quoted in Murswiek 2023, 488).

79. Not mentioning the legal *Störer* versus *Nichtstörer* distinction with one word, the German Federal Constitutional Court came around in favor of the Habermasian line. In March 2022, the court refused to consider a complaint that the forced closing of restaurants violated their owners' "professional freedom" (*Berufsfreiheit*), which is protected under the Basic Law. "The protection of health and life is a legitimate purpose," argued the court, "the pursuit of which justifies even severe restrictions of (the right to) professional freedom" (*1 BvR 1295/21*, "Bundesnotbremse," March 23, 2022, at para 21).

80. Claus Offe, "Pandemie-Politik: Optionen und Konflikte," *Corona Blog of the Vienna Institut für die Wissenschaften vom Menschen*, April 20, 2020, https://www.iwm.at/blog/pandemie-politik-optionen-und-konflikte.

81. Agamben, "L'invenzione di un epidemia."

82. Of course, there were cross-national variations, reflecting the "public trust" level of the population (say, high in Germany, lower in France), and over time the general trend was declining popular support for lockdown (see the French-German comparison by Bandelow et al. 2021).

83. As Udo Knapp did, with his eye on the German COVID management, when the draft chapters of this book were discussed at the Wissenschaftszentrum Berlin (WZB) in December 2023.

84. "Some Britons Crave Permanent Pandemic Lockdown," *The Economist*, July 10, 2021.

85. Ibid.

86. For a bizarrely affirmative description of a "desire for stricter controls" in the left-progressive milieu, see Novina Göhlsdorf and Harald Staun, "Kontrolliert uns!," *Frankfurter Allgemeine Zeitung*, November 19, 2021. The authors argue that "control" (through mandatory health passes for entering bars, discotheques, etc.) "need not be a force of restriction and need not mean being bossed around (*Gängelung*), but it can be an instrument of creative ordering (*Gestaltung*) and of enabling (*Ermöglichung*)." I have no idea what this means.

87. Rogers Brubaker (2020) called it one of the "paradoxes" of populism in the pandemic: in deviation from its previously protectionist leanings, right-wing populism turned "anti-protectionist" because of its "relational and oppositional" nature, "defined by what it opposes."

88. "Présidentielle 2022: Florian Philippot candidat pour rétablir la 'liberté,'" *Libération*, July 15, 2021.

89. Interview with Philip Manow, "Der Notfallmodus wurde nie verlassen," *Neue Zürcher Zeitung*, December 31, 2021.

90. It needs to be noted that among the four authors are John Ioannidis and Jay Bhattacharya, both leading critics of the Covid Doxa; Bhattacharya is one of the three main signatories of the GBD.

91. Herby et al. (2023) was immediately attacked, not least because the study was published under the auspices of the UK-based "neoliberal" or "free market" think tank Institute of Economic Affairs (IEA). See the polemical review by Ian Sample, "Revised Report on Impact of Covid Lockdowns 'Adds Little Insight,'" *The Guardian*, June 5, 2023.

92. The first author, Chelsea Clinton, daughter of Bill, is vice-chair of the Clinton Foundation.

93. Mariana Mazzucato, "The Covid-19 Crisis is a Chance to Do Capitalism Differently," *The Guardian*, March 18, 2020.

94. Ibid.

95. Quoted by Durisch and Hertig (2021, 11).

96. Thomas Meek, "Plans to Challenge IP of Covid-19 Products are 'Dangerous', Say Industry Leaders," *APM Health Europe*, May 29, 2020, https://www.apmhealtheurope.com/freestory/10/68999/plans-to-challenge-ip-of-covid-19-products-are-dangerous-%2C-say-industry-leaders.

97. Ibid.

98. *Manufacturing and Supply Agreement between Pfizer Laboratories Proprietary Limited and the Government of the Republic of South Africa* (typescript, in author's possession).

99. Tim Schwab, "While the Poor Get Sick, Bill Gates Just Gets Richer," *The Nation*, October 5, 2020.

100. See also "Everyone Wins When Patents Are Pooled," *Nature* 581 no. 240 (May 21, 2020), https://doi.org/10.1038/d41586-020-01441-2.

101. Schwab, "While the Poor Get Sick."

ENDNOTES 337

102. Ibid.
103. Raoult's current Google Scholar's citation number is a most impressive 222,000.
104. See Mucchielli (2022a, ch. 7), Kennedy (2021, ch. 1), and Green and Fazi (2023, ch. 3).
105. In addition, tech platforms, like Google (owned by Alphabet, which also owns several vaccine companies), but also Facebook and Instagram suppressed reports of successful COVID-19 cures with HCQ (see Kennedy 2021, ch. 1).
106. Roni Caryn Rabin, "The Pandemic Claims New Victims: Prestigious Medical Journals," *New York Times*, June 14, 2020.
107. Melissa Davey et al., "Surgisphere: Governments and WHO Changed Covid-19 Policy Based on Suspect Data from Tiny US Company," *The Guardian*, June 3, 2020.
108. Caryn Rabin, "The Pandemic Claims New Victims."
109. Particularly notorious in this respect, Pfizer paid over $6.5 billion USD since 1995 in penalties for forty-two cases of misconduct, including misrepresenting experimental results and concealing information about the negative side effects of drugs (Deruelle 2022, 4).
110. Both the FDA and EMA are partially funded by "user fees," which is a euphemism for the industry to be regulated financing their regulators (at 45 percent for the FDA, and at a whopping 85 percent for the EMA). The current head of EMA, Emer Cooke, previously worked for the European Federation of Pharmaceutical Industries and Associations (EFPIA), pharma's biggest lobby organization in the European Union. Public health is a notorious instance of agency capture and "revolving doors" between the private and public sectors, which is a key element of neoliberal "post-democracy" (Crouch 2004).
111. It should also be noted that the Gates Foundation had a $6.5 million USD stake in Gilead. In an August 2020 interview, Gates stated that if struck by COVID-19, he would want to be treated with Remdesivir—not mentioning his foundation's stock-holding in Gilead (Schwab, "While the Poor Get Sick").
112. Jon Cohen and Kai Kupferschmidt, "The 'Very, Very Bad Look' of Remdesivir, the First FDA-Approved COVID-19 Drug," *Science*, October 28, 2020, https://www.science.org/content/article/very-very-bad-look-remdesivir-first-fda-approved-covid-19-drug. The EU Commission, which signed the contract in early October 2020, one week before the WHO published the drug's failure in its Solidarity Trial, claims not to have been informed about the latter. Gilead, however, knew since September 23 that "the trial was a bust" (ibid.).
113. Full disclosure: The author was fully vaccinated by late July 2021, receiving his third ("booster") injection in December of the same year, all for the purely opportunistic reasons of being able to travel and eating and drinking out.
114. Accordingly, Kostoff et al. (2021) ask rhetorically, "Why are we vaccinating children against COVID-19?" The same study *also* found that for people above the age of sixty-five, "there are five times the number of deaths attributable to each inoculation vs those attributable to COVID-19" (ibid., 1665). In August 2022, *British Medical Journal* senior editor, Peter Doshi (also a professor at the University of Maryland, Baltimore), together with an international group of scientists from UCLA, Stanford, a Spanish and an Australian university, published a study showing that, irrespective of age, the risk of "serious adverse events of special interest" following Pfizer and Moderna COVID-19 vaccination surpassed the risk reduction for COVID-19 hospitalization achieved through these vaccines (Fraiman et al 2022).
115. See endnote 32.
116. Armin Nassehi is right: "It (Mill's Harm Principle) seems like written for the debates surrounding an appropriate understanding of freedom in the Corona pandemic" (2023, 54). The problem is the unquestioned assumption that harm on others is inflicted by the non-vaccinated. It is equivalent to the assumption that driving a car is harming pedestrians, because of the possibility of hitting one. No study has yet demonstrated that the possibility of being infected by a non-vaccinated person with a COVID-19 virus is bigger than being infected by a vaccinated person. In fact, the evidence suggests the opposite, and ever more as more people get vaccinated.
117. For most American colleges and universities, especially the prestigious, a COVID-19 vaccine mandate, for students included, remained in place long after the pandemic was factually over. When I asked a well-known political science professor at Columbia University, in late May 2023, "how many shots did you get?," she answered "oh, I don't know, five, six, I got my last right before leaving" (for vacationing in Europe).

338   ENDNOTES

118. Rasmussen Reports, *COVID-19: Democratic Voters Support Harsh Measures Against Unvaccinated*, https://www.rasmussenreports.com/public_content/politics/partner_surveys/jan_2022/crosstabs_heartland_covid_january_5_2022), January 13, 2022.
119. Rudolf Stichweh, "An diesem Imperativ kann die Politik scheitern," *Frankfurter Allgemeine Zeitung*, April 6, 2020.
120. A representative of the advocacy group Americans for Tax Fairness observed: "Their pandemic profits are so immense that America's billionaires could pay for a major Covid relief bill and still not lose a dime of their pre-virus riches. Their wealth growth is so great that they alone could provide a USD 3,000 stimulus payment to every man, woman and child in the country, and still be richer than they were nine months ago" (Rupert Nate, "Ten Billionaires Reap USD 400bn Boost to Wealth During Pandemic," *The Observer*, December 19, 2020).
121. Ibid.
122. Ibid.
123. "How to Tame the Tech Titans," *The Economist*, January 18, 2018.
124. For the distinction between "infrastructural" and "sectoral" platforms, the latter being for specific services (like transport, education, or health), see van Dijck et al. (2018).
125. John Perry Barlow, *A Declaration of the Independence of Cyberspace*, February 8, 1996, https://www.eff.org/cyberspace-independence.
126. For a recent recovery of the utopian-solutionist spirit of the high-tech revolution's beginnings, see Marc Andreessen's hilarious "Techno-Optimist Manifesto": "We had a problem of isolation, so we invented the Internet. We had a problem of pandemics, so we invented vaccines. We have a problem of poverty so we invent technology to create abundance. Give us a real world problem, and we can invent technology that will solve it" (Andreessen 2023).
127. Foundational texts are Staab (2015) and Van Dijck et al. (2018); Brubaker (2023a, ch. 4) is an excellent synopsis.
128. See footnote 124.
129. For certain similarities between the Chinese and Western cases, see Orgad and Reijers (2020).
130. Accordingly, it is more precise to say that code "replaces" law (Susskind 2018, 110).
131. Control through architecture is no invention of the digital age. Infamously, in the 1950s Robert Moses built extra-low bridges on Long Island to keep away from its beaches "racial minorities and low-income groups" traveling not by car but by bus from New York City (Winner 1980, 124).
132. Similarly, Frank Pasquale (2015, 10) speaks of a "one-way mirror" in a "black box society," where "powerful businesses, financial institutions, and government agencies hide their actions behind nondisclosure agreements, 'proprietary methods', and gag rules," while "our own lives are increasingly open books" (ibid., 3).
133. "The consumer welfare model, which views consumers as a collectivity, does not take this income effect into account" (Robert Bork, in Khan 2017, 720, fn.38). The main effect of the Chicago School's reinterpretation of American antitrust law, which is the circularity of declining wages and cheaper consumption, is well-described by Peter Goodman (2022, ch. 19): "This was a neat transfer of wealth from working people to shareholders—one justified by the benefits for the consumer. Shoppers needed low prices, because they were increasingly working in places like Walmart. A feedback loop of diminishing living standards for American workers turned Walmart's founders into the richest family in the land." This is also a main theme in Randall Hansen's (2023) impressive account of how the 1973 OPEC Oil Crisis changed the world.
134. Staab (2015, ch. 5) is clear on this: the winners of "proprietary markets" (apart from GAFAM who own them) are consumers; the losers are workers (but also producers whose profits are reduced by user fees, and who on top of it are often swallowed by GAFAM themselves).
135. For the "liberal paternalism" of nudging, see Thaler and Sunstein (2008).
136. This seems to be the reason why Brubaker (2023a, 163), when comparing the dystopias of Orwell and Huxley, grants "greater purchase" to Huxley. Capturing the element of digital complicity, and in a kind of Polanyi-in-reverse, Marion Fourcade and Kieran Healy (2024, 262) speak of a "double movement," in which the "convenience and . . . pleasures of connectedness . . . functionally contribute to other ends, helping an organization exert control or a business make a profit."
137. Raphael Rashid, "South Korea Cuts Human Interaction in Push to Build 'Untact' Society," *The Guardian*, December 10, 2021.

ENDNOTES 339

138. Ibid.
139. "Asia's New Family Portrait," *The Economist*, June 30, 2023.
140. Rashid, "South Korea Cuts Human Interaction."
141. Ibid.
142. https://reform-support.ec.europa.eu/what-we-do/green-transition_en.
143. Not unlike Schama's French fellow star academic, Bruno Latour (2021, ch. 3), who discovered "Gaia," the unity of all life on "Earth with a big E," when spending the pandemic in his countryside residence.
144. Ian Bogost, "You Already Live in Quarantine," *The Atlantic*, March 4, 2020.
145. Niccolo Soldo, "The Dubrovnik Interviews: Marc Andreessen—Interviewed by a Retard," *Substack*, May 31, 2021.
146. Alexander Labruffe, quoted in Stiegler (2021, 10).
147. Chris Buckley et al., "Living by the Code: In China, Covid-Era Controls May Outlast the Virus," *New York Times*, January 30, 2022.
148. Ibid.
149. Barbara Stiegler, "Les autorités détournent les questions sanitaires pour instaurer une société de contrôle," *Reporterre*, July 31, 2021.
150. Olivier Claris, author of "Appel à nos concitoyens: nous avons besoin d'union nationale" (Stiegler 2021, 16).
151. European Commission, *Commission Proposes Trusted and Secure Digital Identity for All Europeans—Questions and Answers*, Brussels, June 3, 2021, ec.europa.eu/commission/press corner/detail/en/ip_21_2663.
152. Hans Peter Bull, "Die Nummerierung der Bürger: Effizienzdenken versus Überwachungsangst," *verfassungsblog.de*, September 12, 2020.
153. https://www.betterthancash.org/.
154. https://www.weforum.org/agenda/2020/01/benefits-cashless-society-mobile-payments/.
155. "Are Free Markets History?," *The Economist*, October 7, 2023, 9.
156. Ari Gandsman and José López, "How Covid Killed Utopia," *Compact*, August 31, 2023.
157. "What Judith Butler Learned from the Pandemic," *Critical Mass*, December 21, 2022.
158. Gandsman and López, "How Covid Killed Utopia."
159. Ibid.

Bibliography

Aberbach, Joel, and Tom Christensen. 2005. "Citizens and Consumers: An NPM Dilemma." *Public Management Review* 8, no. 2: 225–246.

Abou-Chadi, Tarik, and Simon Hix. 2020. "Brahmin Left versus Merchant Right?" *British Journal of Sociology* 72: 79–92.

Abou-Chadi, Tarik, and Ellen Immergut. 2019. "Recalibrating Social Protection: Electoral Competition and the New Partisan Politics of the Welfare State." *European Journal of Political Research* 58: 697–719.

Abou-Chadi, Tarik, Reto Mitteregger, and Cas Mudde. 2021. *Left Behind by the Working Class? Social Democracy's Electoral Crisis and the Rise of the Radical Right.* Berlin: Friedrich-Ebert Stiftung.

Acemoglu, Daron, and Simon Johnson. 2023. *Power and Progress: Our Thousand-Year Struggle over Technology and Prosperity.* New York: Public Affairs.

Adam, Ilke. 2022. "Multiculturalism in Europe in the Post-2020 Black Lives Matter Era." Unpublished manuscript.

Adkins, Lisa, Melinda Cooper, and Martijn Konings. 2020. *The Asset Economy.* Cambridge: Polity.

AfD. 2016. "Programm für Deutschland." Stuttgart. https://www.afd.de/wp-content/uploads/sites/111/2017/01/2016-06-27_afd-grundsatzprogramm_web-version.pdf.

Alexander, James. 2015. "The Major Ideologies of Liberalism, Socialism and Conservatism." *Political Studies* 63: 980–994.

Alexander, Michelle. 2020 [2010]. *The New Jim Crow: Mass Incarceration in the Age of Colorblindness.* New York: The New Press.

Al-Gharbi, Musa. 2018. "Race and the Race for the White House." *American Sociologist* 49, no. 4: 496–519.

Allen, Christopher. 2016. "The Path to Self-Sovereign Identity." *Life with Alacrity*, April 25.

Amable, Bruno. 2011. "Morals and Politics in the Ideology of Neo-Liberalism." *Socio-Economic Review* 9: 3–30.

Amable, Bruno, and Stefano Polambarini. 2021. *The Last Neoliberal: Macron and the Origins of France's Political Crisis.* London: Verso.

Amlinger, Carolin, and Oliver Nachtwey. 2022. *Gekränkte Freiheit: Aspekte des libertären Autoritarismus.* Berlin: Suhrkamp.

Anderson, Elizabeth. 1999. "What is the Point of Equality?" *Ethics* 109, no. 2: 287–337.

Anderson, Elizabeth. 2016. "Freedom and Equality." In *The Oxford Handbook of Freedom*, edited by David Schmidtz and Carmen Pavel, 90–105. New York: Oxford University Press.

BIBLIOGRAPHY 341

Anderson, Elizabeth. 2017. *Private Government*. Princeton, NJ: Princeton University Press.

Anderson, Perry. 1996. "Under the Sign of the Interim." *London Review of Books*, January 4, 13–17.

Anderson, Perry. 2000. "Renewals." *New Left Critique* January–February: 5–24.

Anderson, Perry. 2021. "Ever Closer Union?" *London Review of Books* 43, no. 1: January 7.

Anderson, Ryan T. 2018. *When Harry Became Sally: Responding to the Transgender Movement*. New York: Encounter Books.

Andersson, Fredrik, and Lars Nonung. 2024. "The Covid-19 Lesson from Sweden: Don't Lock Down." *Economic Affairs* 44: 3–16.

Andreessen, Marc. 2023. "The Techno-Optimist Manifesto." https://a16z.com/the-techno-optimist-manifesto/.

Antonucci, Lorenza, Laszlo Horvath, Yordan Kutiyski, and André Krouwel. 2017. "The Malaise of the Squeezed Middle: Challenging the Narrative of the 'Left Behind' Brexiter." *Competition and Change* 21, no. 3: 211–229.

Appel, Hilary, and Mitchell Orenstein. 2016. "Why Did Neoliberalism Triumph and Endure in the Post-Communist World?" *Comparative Politics* 48, no. 3: 313–331.

Aron, Matthieu, and Caroline Michel-Aguierre. 2022. *Les infiltrés*. Allary Éditions: Paris.

Art, David. 2020. "The Myth of Global Populism." *Perspectives on Politics* 20, no. 3: 999–1011.

Ash, Timothy Garton. 2016. *Free Speech*. New Haven, CT: Yale University Press.

Ash, Timothy Garton. 2021. "The Future of Liberalism." *Prospect Magazine* January/February.

Ashley, Florence. 2020. "A Critical Commentary on 'Rapid-Onset Gender Dysphoria.'" *Sociological Review Monographs* 68, no. 4: 779–799.

Asteriti, Alessandra, and Rebecca Bull. 2020. "Gender Self-Declaration and Women's Rights." *Modern Law Review* 83, no. 3: 539ff.

Baccaro, Lucio, and Chris Howell. 2011. "A Common Neoliberal Trajectory: The Transformation of Industrial Relations in Advanced Capitalism." *Politics and Society* 39, no. 4: 521–563.

Baekkeskov, Erik, Olivier Rubin, and PerOla Öberg. 2021. "Monotonous or Pluralistic Public Discourse? Reason-Giving and Dissent in Denmark's and Sweden's Early 2020 COVID-19 Responses." *Journal of European Public Policy* 28, no. 8: 1321–1343.

Baldwin, Peter. 2021. *Fighting the First Wave*. New York: Cambridge University Press.

Baldwin, Richard. 2019. *The Globotics Upheaval: Globalization, Robotics, and the Future of Work*. Oxford: Oxford University Press.

Balint, Peter. 2017. *Respecting Toleration*. Oxford: Oxford University Press.

Bandelow, Nils, Patrick Hassenteufel, and Johanna Hornung. 2021. "Patterns of Democracy Matter in the Covid-19 Crisis: A Comparison of French and German Policy Processes." *International Review of Public Policy* 3, no. 1: 121–136.

Banting, Keith, and Will Kymlicka, eds. 2017. *The Strains of Commitment: The Political Sources of Solidarity in Diverse Societies*. New York: Oxford University Press.

342 BIBLIOGRAPHY

Barry, Brian. 2001. *Culture and Equality*. Cambridge: Polity.

Bartel, Fritz. 2022. *The Triumph of Broken Promises: The End of the Cold War and the Rise of Neoliberalism*. Cambridge, MA: Harvard University Press.

Bartels, Larry. 2023. *Democracy Erodes from the Top: Leaders, Citizens, and the Challenge of Populism in Europe*. Princeton, NJ: Princeton University Press.

Bartolini, Stefano. 2018. *The Political*. Colchester: ECPR Press.

Bazelon, Emily. 2023. "Why is Affirmative Action in Peril? One Man's Decision." *New York Times Magazine*, February 15.

Beck, Ulrich. 1983. "Jenseits von Stand und Klasse." In *Soziale Ungleichheiten*, edited by Reinhard Kreckel, 35–74. Schwartz: Göttingen.

Becker, Gary. 1968. "Crime and Punishment: An Economic Approach." *Journal of Political Economy* 76, no. 2: 169–217.

Beckert, Jens. 2018. "The Exhausted Futures of Neoliberalism." *Journal of Cultural Economy* 13, no. 3: 1–13.

Bell, Daniel. 1972. "On Meritocracy and Equality." *Public Interest* Fall: 29–68.

Bell, Daniel. 1973. *The Coming of Post-Industrial Society*. New York: Basic Books.

Bell, Derrick. 1980. "Brown v. Board of Education and the Interest-Convergence Dilemma." *Harvard Law Review* 93: 518–533.

Bell, Derrick. 1992. *Faces at the Bottom of the Well: The Permanence of Racism*. New York: Basic Books.

Bendavid, Enan, Christoph Oh, Jay Bhattacharya, and John Ioannidis. 2021. "Assessing Mandatory Stay-At-Home and Business Closure Effects on the Spread of COVID-19." *European Journal of Clinical Investigation* 51: 1–9.

Benoist, Alain de. 1998. "Hayek: A Critique." *Telos* 110: 71–104.

Benoist, Alain de. 2017 [1985]. *Kulturrevolution von Rechts*. Dresden: Jungeuropa Verlag.

Benoist, Alain de, and Charles Champetier. 1999. "The French New Right in the Year 2000." *Telos* 115: 117–144.

Berle, Adolph, and Gardiner Means. 1932. *The Modern Corporation and Private Property*. New York: Macmillan.

Berlin, Isaiah. 1969 [1958]. "Two Concepts of Liberty." In *Four Essays on Liberty*, 118–172. Oxford: Oxford University Press.

Berman, Sheri. 2021. "The Causes of Populism in the West." *Annual Review of Politics* 24: 71–88.

Bernstein, Mary. 2005. "Identity Politics." *Annual Review of Sociology* 31: 47–74.

Berrey, Ellen. 2015. *The Enigma of Diversity*. Chicago, IL: University of Chicago Press.

Bevir, Mark. 2011. "Governance and Governmentality after Neoliberalism." *Policy and Politics* 39, no. 4: 457–471.

Bickerton, Christopher. 2012. *European Integration: From Nation-States to Member States*. Oxford: Oxford University Press.

Bickerton, Christopher, and Carlo Invernizzi Accetti. 2021. *Technopopulism: The New Logic of Democratic Politics*. Oxford: Oxford University Press.

Biebricher, Thomas. 2019. *The Political Theory of Neoliberalism*. Stanford, CA: Stanford University Press.

BIBLIOGRAPHY 343

Biebricher, Thomas. 2020. "Neoliberalism and Authoritarianism." *Global Perspectives* 1, no. 1: 1–18.

Biebricher, Thomas. 2023. *Mitte/Rechts: Die internationale Krise des Konservatismus.* Berlin: Suhrkamp.

Biggs, Michael. 2021. "Queer Theory and the Transition from Sex to Gender in English Prisons." *Journal of Controversial Ideas* 2, no. 1: 1–21.

Blauner, Robert. 1972. *Racial Oppression in America.* New York: Harper and Row.

Blauner, Robert. 2001. *Still the Big News: Racial Oppression in America.* Philadelphia: Temple University Press.

Block, Fred, and Margaret Somers. 2014. *The Power of Market Fundamentalism: Karl Polanyi's Critique.* Cambridge, MA: Harvard University Press.

Blokker, Paul. 2022. "Populism and Illiberalism." In *Routledge Handbook of Illiberalism*, edited by András Sajó, Renáta Uitz, and Stephen Holmes, 261–279. London: Routledge.

Blyth, Mark. 2013. *Austerity: The History of a Dangerous Idea.* New York: Oxford University Press.

Bobbio, Noberto. 1987. *The Future of Democracy.* Cambridge: Polity.

Bobbio, Noberto. 1996. *Left and Right: The Significance of a Political Distinction.* Cambridge: Polity.

Boltanski, Luc, and Eve Chiapello. 2005. *The New Spirit of Capitalism.* London: Verso.

Bonefeld, Werner. 2016. "Authoritarian Liberalism: From Schmitt via Ordoliberalism to the Euro." *Critical Sociology* 43, no. 4–5: 747–761.

Bonilla-Silva, Eduardo. 1996. "Rethinking Racism." *American Sociological Review* 62: 465–486.

Bonilla-Silva, Eduardo. 2022. *Racism Without Racists.* Lanham, MD: Rowman and Littlefield.

Bonoli, Giuliano. 2004. "Social Democratic Policies in Europe: Towards a Third Way?" In *Social Democratic Party Policies in Contemporary Europe*, edited by. G. Bonoli and Martin Powell, 197–213. London: Routledge.

Bonoli, Giuliano. 2005. "The Politics of the New Social Policies: Providing Coverage Against New Social Risks in Mature Welfare States." *Policy and Politics* 33, no. 3: 431–449.

Borraz, Olivier, and Bengt Jacobsson. 2023. "Organizing Expertise During a Crisis: France and Sweden in the Fight Against Covid-19." *Journal of Organizational Sociology* 1, no. 1: 73–107.

Borriello, Arthur, and Anton Jäger. 2023. *The Populist Moment: The Left After the Great Recession.* London: Verso.

Bos, Ellen, and Zoltán Tibor Pállinger. 2018. "Die Parlamentswahl in Ungarn 2018." *Midem-Bericht 2018-2*, Dresden.

Boulakia, Théo, and Nicolas Mariot. 2023. *L'attestation. Une expérience d'obéeissance de masse, printemps 2020.* Paris: Éditions Anamosa.

Bourdieu, Pierre. 1984. *Distinction: A Social Critique of the Judgment of Taste.* Cambridge, MA: Harvard University Press.

344 BIBLIOGRAPHY

Bourdieu, Pierre. 1998. "The Essence of Neoliberalism." *Le Monde Diplomatique* (December).

Brahm Levey, Geoffrey. 2018. "The Bristol School of Multiculturalism." *Ethnicities* 19, no. 1: 200–226.

Brandes, Sören. 2019. "The Market's People: Milton Friedman and the Making of Neoliberal Populism." In *Mutant Neoliberalism: Market Rule and Political Rupture*, edited by William Callison and Zachary Manfredi, 61–88. New York: Fordham University Press.

Braunstein, Jean-François. 2022. *La religion woke*. Paris: Grasset.

Brown, Wendy. 1995. *States of Injury*. Princeton, NJ: Princeton University Press.

Brown, Wendy. 2006. *Regulating Aversion: Tolerance in the Age of Identity and Empire*. Princeton, NJ: Princeton University Press.

Brown, Wendy. 2015. *Undoing the Demos: Neoliberalism's Stealth Revolution*. New York: Zone Books.

Brown, Wendy. 2019. *In the Ruins of Neoliberalism: The Rise of Antidemocratic Politics in the West*. New York: Columbia University Press.

Brown, Wendy. 2020. "Neoliberalism's Scorpion Tale." In *Mutant Neoliberalism*, edited by William Callison and Zachary Manfredi, 39–60. Fordham, NY: Fordham University Press.

Broz, Lawrence, Jeffrey Frieden, and Stephen Weymouth. 2021. "Populism in Place: The Economic Geography of the Globalization Backlash." *International Organization* 75: 464–494.

Brubaker, Rogers. 1989. "The French Revolution and the Invention of Citizenship." *French Politics and Society* 7, no. 3: 30–49.

Brubaker, Rogers. 1992. *Citizenship and Nationhood in France and Germany*. Cambridge, MA: Harvard University Press.

Brubaker, Rogers. 2015. "Difference and Inequality." In *Grounds for Difference*, 10–47. Cambridge, MA: Harvard University Press.

Brubaker, Rogers. 2016a. *Trans*. Princeton, NJ: Princeton University Press.

Brubaker, Rogers. 2016b. "The Dolezal Affair." *Ethnic and Racial Studies* 39, no. 3: 414–448.

Brubaker, Rogers. 2017a. "Why Populism?" *Theory and Society* 46, no. 5: 357–385.

Brubaker, Rogers. 2017b. "Between Nationalism and Civilizationism." *Ethnic and Racial Studies* 40, no. 8: 1191–1226.

Brubaker, Rogers. 2020a. "The Danger of Race Reductionism." *Persuasion*, September 10.

Brubaker, Rogers. 2020b. "Paradoxes of Populism During the Pandemic." *Thesis Eleven* 164, no. 1: 73–87.

Brubaker, Rogers. 2023a. *Hyperconnectivity and its Discontents*. Cambridge: Polity.

Brubaker, Rogers. 2023b. "Exit, Voice, and Gender." *Sociological Theory* 41, no. 2: 154–174.

Bruff, Ian. 2014. "The Rise of Authoritarian Neoliberalism." *Rethinking Marxism* 26, no. 1: 113–129.

Bude, Heinz. 2022. "Aus dem Maschinenraum der Beratung in Zeiten der Pandemie." *Soziologie* 50, no. 3: 245–255.

BIBLIOGRAPHY 345

Burgin, Angus. 2015. *The Great Persuasion: Reinventing Free Markets Since the Depression*. Cambridge, MA: Harvard University Press.

Burnham, Peter. 2001. "New Labour and the Politics of Depoliticisation." *British Journal of Politics and International Relations* 3, no. 2: 127–149.

Butler, Judith. 1993. "Imitation and Gender Insubordination." In *The Lesbian and Gay Studies Reader*, edited by Henry Abelove, Michele Aina Barale, David M. Halperin, 307–320. New York: Routledge.

Butler, Judith. 1999 [1990]. *Gender Troubles*. New York: Routledge.

Butler, Judith. 2022. *What World is This? A Pandemic Phenomenology*. New York: Columbia University Press.

Cafruni, Allan, and Leila Talani, eds. 2023. *The Political Economy of Global Responses to COVID-19*. Basingstoke: Palgrave Macmillan.

Caiani, Manuela, and Paolo Graziano. 2022. "The Three Faces of Populism in Power: Polity, Policies and Politics." *Government and Opposition* 57: 569–582.

Caldwell, Christopher. 2020. *The Age of Entitlement*. New York: Simon and Schuster.

Callison, William, and Quinn Slobodian. 2021. "Coronapolitics from the Reichstag to the Capitol." *Boston Review*, January 12.

Campbell, Bradley, and Jason Manning. 2014. "Microaggression and Moral Cultures." *Comparative Sociology* 13: 692–726.

Campbell, Bradley, and Jason Manning. 2018. *The Rise of Victimhood Culture*. Basingstoke: Palgrave Macmillan.

Canovan, Margaret. 1999. "Trust the People! Populism and the Two Faces of Democracy." *Political Studies* 47: 2–16.

Caporaso, James, and Sidney Tarrow. 2009. "Polanyi in Brussels: Supranational Institutions and the Transnational Embedding of Markets." *International Organization* 63: 593–620.

Caramani, Daniele. 2017. "Will v. Reason: The Populist and Technocratic Forms of Political Representation and their Critique to Party Government." *American Political Science Review* 111, no. 1: 54–67.

Case, Anne, and Angus Deaton. 2020. *Deaths of Despair and the Future of Capitalism*. Princeton, NJ: Princeton University Press.

Castells, Manuel. 1996. *The Rise of the Network Society*. Oxford: Blackwell.

Chamayou, Grégoire. 2019. *Die unregierbare Gesellschaft: Eine Genealogie des autoritären Liberalismus*. Berlin: Suhrkamp.

Christensen, Tom, and Per Laegreid. 2022. "Scientization Under Pressure—The Problematic Role of Expert Bodies During the Handling of the COVID-19 Pandemic." *Public Organization Review* 22: 291–307.

Christi, Renato. 1984. "Hayek and Schmitt on the Rule of Law." *Canadian Journal of Political Science* 17, no. 3: 521–535.

Church, Jonathan. 2020. "The False Dichotomy in Kimberlé Crenshaw's Intersectionality." *Merion West*, June 16.

Clasen, Jochen. 2000. "Motives, Means and Opportunities: Reforming Unemployment Compensation in the 1990s." *West European Politics* 23, no. 2: 89–112.

346 BIBLIOGRAPHY

Clinton, Chelsea, and Devi Sridhar. 2017. *Governing Global Health*. New York: Oxford University Press.

Coase, Ronald. 1960. "The Problem of Social Cost." *Journal of Law and Economics* III: 1–44.

Coates, Ta-Nehesi. 2017. "The First White President." *The Atlantic*, October 15.

Cohen, Deborah, and Philip Carter. 2010. "WHO and the Pandemic Flu 'Conspiracies.'" *British Medical Journal* 340: 1274–1279.

Coleman, James. 1998. *Foundations of Social Theory*. Cambridge, MA: Harvard University Press.

Collier, Paul. 2018. *The Future of Capitalism: Facing the New Anxieties*. London: Allen Lane.

Collier, Stephen J. 2012. "Neoliberalism as Big Leviathan, or…? A Response to Wacquant and Hilgers." *Social Anthropology* 20, no. 2: 186–195.

Collins, Hugh. 2003. "Discrimination, Equality and Social Inclusion." *Modern Law Review* 66, no. 1: 16–43.

Cong, Wanshu. 2021. "From Pandemic Control to Data-Driven Governance: China's Health Code." *Frontiers in Political Science* 3: 1–14.

Constant, Benjamin. 1816. "The Liberty of Ancients Compared with that of Moderns." oll-resources.s3.us-east-2.amazonaws.com/oll3/store/titles/2251/Constant_Liberty1521.html.

Conway, Martin. 2020. *Western Europe's Democratic Age: 1945–1968*. Princeton, NJ: Princeton University Press.

Cook, Eli. 2016. "The Neoclassical Club: Irving Fisher and the Progressive Origins of Neoliberalism." *Journal of the Gilded Age and Progressive Era* 15: 246–262.

Cooper, Melinda. 2017. *Family Values: Between Neoliberalism and the New Social Conservatism*. New York: Zone Books.

Couldry, Nick, and Ulises Mejias. 2018. "Data Colonialism: Big Data's Relation to the Contemporary Subject." *Television and New Media* 20, no. 4: 336–349.

Council of Europe. 2011. *Living Together*. Strasbourg: Council of Europe.

Crenshaw, Kimberlé. 1989. "Demarginalizing the Intersection of Race and Sex: A Black Feminist Critique of Antidiscrimination Doctrine, Feminist Theory, and Antiracist Politics." *University of Chicago Legal Forum* 1989, no. 1: 139–167.

Crenshaw, Kimberlé. 1991. "Mapping the Margins: Intersectionality, Identity Politics, and Violence Against Women of Color." *Stanford Law Review* 43, no. 6: 1241–1299.

Crouch, Colin. 2004. *Post-Democracy*. Cambridge: Polity.

Crouch, Colin. 2011. *The Strange Non-Death of Neoliberalism*. Cambridge: Polity.

Crouch, Colin. 2013. *Making Capitalism Fit for Society*. Cambridge: Polity.

Crouch, Colin. 2017. "Neoliberalism, Nationalism, and the Decline of Political Tradition." *Political Quarterly* 88, no. 2: 221–229.

Crouch, Colin. 2019. *Will the Gig Economy Prevail?* Cambridge: Polity.

Crouch, Colin. 2020. *Post-Democracy after the Crisis*. Cambridge: Polity.

Crozier, Michel, Samuel Huntington, and Joji Watanuki. 1975. *The Crisis of Democracy*. New York: New York University Press.

BIBLIOGRAPHY 347

Culpepper, Pepper, and Kathleen Thelen. 2019. "Are We All Amazon Primed? Consensus and the Politics of Platform Power." *Comparative Political Studies* 53, no. 2: 288–318.

Dani, Marco. 2017. "The Rise of the Supranational Executive and the Post-Political Drift of European Public Law." *Indiana Journal of Global Legal Studies* 24, no. 2: 399–427.

Davidson, Neil. 2017. "Crisis Neoliberalism and Regimes of Permanent Exception." *Critical Sociology* 43, no. 4–5: 615–634.

Davies, Will. 2016. "The New Neoliberalism." *New Left Review* 101: 121–134.

Davies, Will. 2021. "The Revenge of Sovereignty on Government? The Release of Neoliberal Politics from Economics Post-2008." *Theory, Culture and Society* 38, no. 6: 95–118.

Davies, Will, and Nicholas Ganes. 2021. "Post-Neoliberalism?" *Theory, Culture and Society* 38, no. 6: 3–28.

Davis, Gerald F. 2009. *Managed by the Markets: How Finance Reshaped America*. New York: Oxford University Press.

Dean, Mitchell. 2002. "Powers of Life and Death Beyond Governmentality." *Cultural Values* 6, no. 1–2: 119–136.

Deeming, Christopher, and Paul Smyth. 2015. "Social Investment After Neoliberalism: Policy Paradigms and Political Platforms." *Journal of Social Policy* 44, no. 2: 297–318.

Deleuze, Gilles. 1992. "Postscript on the Societies of Control." *October* 49: 3–7.

Delgado, Richard, and Jean Stefancic. 2017. *Critical Race Theory*. New York: NYU Press.

Deneen, Patrick. 2018. *Why Liberalism Failed*. New Haven, CT: Yale University Press.

Deruelle, Fabien. 2022. "The Pharmaceutical Industry is Dangerous to Health: Further Proof with Covid-19." *Surgical Neurology International* 13, no. 475: 1–18.

Dewey, John. 1935. *Liberalism and Social Action*. New York: Capricorn Books.

DiAngelo, Robin. 2018. *White Fragility*. Boston: Beacon Press.

Dijck, José van. 2013. *Culture of Connectivity: A Critical History of Social Media*. Oxford: Oxford University Press.

Dijck, José van, Martijn de Waal, and Thomas Poell. 2018. *The Platform Society: Public Values in a Connective World*. Oxford: Oxford University Press.

Divine, Patricia, and Tory Ash. 2022. "Diversity Training: Goals, Limitations, and Promise." *Annual Review of Psychology* 73: 403–429.

Dobbin, Frank. 2009. *Inventing Equal Opportunity*. Princeton, NJ: Princeton University Press.

Dobbin, Frank, and Alexandra Kalev. 2021. "The Civil Rights Revolution at Work." *Annual Review of Sociology* 47: 271–303.

Dobbin, Frank, and Alexandra Kalev. 2022. *Getting to Diversity*. Cambridge, MA: Harvard University Press.

Dobbin, Frank, and John Sutton. 1998. "The Strength of a Weak State." *American Journal of Sociology* 104, no. 2: 441–476.

Donzelot, Jacques. 2008. "Michel Foucault and Liberal Intelligence." *Economy and Society* 37, no. 1: 115–134.

Doshi, Peter. 2020. "Will Covid-19 Vaccines Save Lives? Current Trials Aren't Designed to Tell Us." *British Medical Journal* 371: m4037.

Downs, Anthony. 1957. *An Economic Theory of Democracy*. New York: Harper.

348 BIBLIOGRAPHY

Doytcheva, Milena. 2009. "Réinterprétations et usages sélectifs de la diversité dans les polititiques des entreprises." *Raisons politiques* 35: 107–124.

Dudziak, Mary. 2011. *Cold War Civil Rights: Race and the Image of American Democracy*. Cambridge, MA: Harvard University Press.

Duménil, Gérard, and Dominique Lévy. 2011. *The Crisis of Neoliberalism*. Cambridge, MA: Harvard University Press.

Durisch, Patrick, and Gabriela Hertig. 2021. "Big Pharma Takes It All." *Public Eye Report*, Zürich and Lausanne, March.

Dyk, Silke van. 2019. "Identitätspolitik gegen ihre Kritik gelesen." *Aus Politik und Zeitgeschichte*, February 22. bpb.de/shop/zeitschriften/apuz/286508/identitaetspolitik-gegen-ihre-kritik-gelesen/.

Edelman, Lauren, Sally Riggs Fuller, and Iona Mara-Drita. 2001. "Diversity and the Managerialization of Law." *American Journal of Sociology* 106, no. 6: 1589–1641.

Ellermann, Antje. 2019. "Human–Capital Citizenship and the Changing Logic of Immigrant Admissions." *Journal of Ethnic and Migration Studies* 46, no. 12: 2515–2532.

Ely, John Hart. 1980. *Democracy and Distrust: A Theory of Judicial Review*. Cambridge, MA: Harvard University Press.

Empoli, Giuliano da. 2020. *Ingenieure des Chaos*. München: Blessing.

Engler, Sarah, Palmo Brunner, Romane Loviat, Tarik Abou-Chadi, Lucas Leemann, Andreas Glaser, et al. 2021. "Democracy in Times of the Pandemic: Explaining the Variation of COVID-19 Policies across European Democracies." *West European Politics* 44, no. 5–6: 1077–1102.

Ennser-Jedenastik, Laurenz. 2018. "Welfare Chauvinism in Populist Radical Right Platforms: The Role of Redistributive Justice Principles." *Social Policy and Administration* 52, no. 1: 293–314.

Epstein, Steve. 1987. "Gay Politics, Ethnic Identity." *Socialist Review* 93: 9–54.

Esmark, Anders. 2017. "Maybe It Is Time to Rediscover Technocracy?" *Journal of Public Administration Research and Theory* 27, no. 3: 501–516.

Esmark, Anders. 2020. *The New Technocracy*. Bristol: Bristol University Press.

Esping-Andersen, Gøsta. 1990. *The Three Worlds of Welfare Capitalism*. Princeton, NJ: Princeton University Press.

Esping-Andersen, Gøsta. 1999. *Social Foundations of Postindustrial Economies*. Oxford: Oxford University Press.

Esping-Andersen, Gøsta. 2000. "A Welfare State for the 21st Century, Report to the Portuguese Presidency of the EU." Prepared for the Lisbon Summit, March 2000.

European Commission. 2020. "A Union of Equality: EU Anti-Racism Action Plan 2020–2025." *COM*, September 18. https://commission.europa.eu/strategy-and-policy/policies/justice-and-fundamental-rights/combatting-discrimination/racism-and-xenophobia/eu-anti-racism-action-plan-2020-2025_en.

Fabry, Adam, and Sune Sandbeck. 2019. "Introduction to Special Issue on 'Authoritarian Neoliberalism.'" *Competition and Change* 23, no. 2: 109–115.

Fassin, Didier. 2012. *Humanitarian Reason: A Moral History of the Present*. Berkeley and Los Angeles: University of California Press.

Fassin, Didier. 2021. "The Moral Economy of Life in the Pandemic." In *Pandemic Exposures*, edited by Didier Fassin and Marion Fourcade, 155–176. Chicago: Hau Books.

Fawcett, Edmund. 2014. *Liberalism*. Princeton, NJ: Princeton University Press.

Fawcett, Edmund. 2020. *Conservatism: The Fight for a Tradition*. Princeton, NJ: Princeton University Press.

Fazi, Thomas. 2021. "The Eternal Return of 'Technical Government' in Italy." *American Affairs*, May 20.

Fenger, Menno. 2018. "The Social Policy Agendas of Populist Radical Right Parties in Comparative Perspective." *Journal of International and Comparative Social Policy* 34, no. 3: 188–209.

Ferguson, James. 2010. "The Uses of Neoliberalism", *Antipode* 41, no. s1, 166–184.

Ferguson, Neil et al. 2020. "Report 9: Impact of Non-Pharmaceutical Interventions (NPIs) to Reduce COVID-19 Mortality and Healthcare Demand." Imperial College London, 16 March.

Ferguson, Niall. 2021. *Doom: The Politics of Catastrophe*. New York: Penguin.

Fifi, Gianmarco. 2024. "From Social Protection to 'Progressive Neoliberalism': Writing the Left into the Rise and Resilience of Neoliberal Policies (1968–2019)." *Review of International Political Economy* 30, no. 4: 1436–1458.

Flaherty, Thomas, and Ronald Rogowski. 2021. "Rising Inequality as a Threat to the Liberal International Order." *International Organization* 75: 495–523.

Fleck, Zoltán, Gábor Gadó, Szabolcs Hegyi, Gábor Juhász, Zsolt Körtvélyesi, Balázs Majtényi, and Gábor Tóth. 2012. "Opinion on the Fundamental Law of Hungary (Amicus Brief)." In *Constitution for a Disunited Nation: On Hungary's 2011 Fundamental Law*, edited by Andrew Arato, Gábor Halmai, and János Kis, 455–490. Budapest: Central European University Press. Citations are from the 2011 typescript (in author's possession).

Fleckenstein, Timo. 2008. "Restructuring Welfare for the Unemployed: The Hartz Legislation in Germany." *Journal of European Social Policy* 18, no. 2: 177–180.

Flinders, Matthew, and Matt Wood. 2015. "Depoliticization, Governance and the State." In *Tracing the Political: Depoliticization, Governance and the State*, edited by M. Flinders and M. Wood, 1–20. Bristol: Policy Press.

Flora, Peter, ed. 1999. *State Formation, Nation-Building, and Mass Politics in Europe: The Theory of Stein Rokkan*. Oxford: Oxford University Press.

Flynn, Paul. 2010. "The Handling of the H1N1 Pandemic: More Transparency Needed." Council of Europe, Parliamentary Assembly, AS/soc, Strasbourg. March 23.

Follesdal, Andreas, and Simon Hix. 2006. "Why There is a Democratic Deficit in the EU." *Journal of Common Market Studies* 44, no. 3: 533–562.

Fontain, Jane. 2001. "Paradoxes of Public Sector Customer Service." *Governance* 14, no. 1: 55–73.

Ford, Richard Thompson. 2009. *The Race Card: How Bluffing About Bias Makes Race Relations Worse*. New York: Picador.

Forman, James. 2012. "Racial Critiques of Mass Incarceration: Beyond the New Jim Crow." *New York University Law Review* 87, no. 1: 101–146.

Foucault, Michel. 1980. *The History of Sexuality. Vol. 1*. New York: Vintage.

350 BIBLIOGRAPHY

Foucault, Michel. 2007. *Security, Territory, Population*. Basingstoke: Palgrave Macmillan.

Foucault, Michel. 2008. *The Birth of Biopolitics*. Basingstoke: Palgrave Macmillan.

Fourcade, Marion. 2021. "The Great Online Migration: COVID and the Platformization of American Public Schools." In *Pandemic Exposures*, edited by Didier Fassin and Marion Fourcade, 345–368. Chicago: Hau Books.

Fourcade, Marion, and Jeffrey Gordon. 2020. "Learning Like a State: Statecraft in the Digital Age." *Journal of Law and Political Economy* 78: 78–107.

Fourcade, Marion, and Kieran Healy. 2024. *The Ordinal Society*. Cambridge, MA: Harvard University Press.

Fraiman, Joseph, Juan Erviti, Mark Jones, Sander Greenland, Patrick Whelan, Robert M. Kaplan, et al. 2022. "Serious Adverse Events of Special Interest Following mRNA COVID-19 Vaccination in Randomized Trials in Adults." *Vaccine* 40: 5798–5805.

Frank, Robert H. 2016. *Success and Luck: Good Fortune and the Myth of Meritocracy*. Princeton, NJ: Princeton University Press.

Frank, Thomas 2004. *What's the Matter with Kansas? How Conservatives Won the Heart of America*. New York: Metropolitan Books.

Frank, Thomas. 2016. *Listen, Liberal*. Melbourne: Scribe.

Fraser, Nancy. 1995. "From Redistribution to Recognition?" *New Left Critique* 1, no. 212 (July/August).

Fraser, Nancy. 2003. "From Discipline to Flexibilization? Rereading Foucault in the Shadow of Globalization." *Constellations* 10, no. 2: 160–171.

Fraser, Nancy. 2011. "Marketization, Social Protection, Emancipation." In *Business as Usual*, edited by Craig Calhoun and Georgi Derluguian, 137–158. New York: New York University Press.

Fraser, Nancy. 2017a. "The End of Progressive Neoliberalism." *Dissent*, January 2.

Fraser, Nancy. 2017b. "From Progressive Neoliberalism to Trump—and Beyond." *American Affairs*, November 20.

Fraser, Nancy. 2017c. "A Triple Movement?" In *Beyond Neoliberalism*, edited by M. Burchardt and G. Kirn, 29–42. Basingstoke: Palgrave Macmillan.

Fraser, Steve. 2022. "It's Time to Take Woke Capital Seriously." *Dissent* 69, no. 1: 107–114.

Fredrickson, George. 2000. "Understanding Racism." In *The Comparative Imagination*, 77–97. Berkeley and Los Angeles: University of California Press.

Freeden, Michael. 2008. "European Liberalisms." *European Journal of Political Theory* 7, no. 1: 9–30.

Friedman, Milton. 1951. "Neo-Liberalism and its Prospects." *Farmand*, 89–93. https://miltonfriedman.hoover.org/internal/media/dispatcher/214957/full.

Friedman, Milton. 1982 [1962]. *Capitalism and Freedom*. Chicago, IL: University of Chicago Press.

Friedrich, Carl. 1955. "The Political Thought of Neo-Liberalism." *American Political Science Review* 49: 509–524.

Fukuyama, Francis. 1992. *The End of History and the Last Man*. New York: Free Press.

Fukuyama, Francis. 2004. "Transhumanism—the World's Most Dangerous Idea." *Foreign Policy*, September.

BIBLIOGRAPHY 351

Fukuyama, Francis. 2018. *Identity: The Demand for Dignity and the Politics of Resentment*. New York: Farrar, Straus and Giroux.

Fukuyama, Francis. 2020. "Liberalism and its Discontents: The Challenges from the Left and the Right." *American Purpose*, October 3.

Fukuyama, Francis. 2022. *Liberalism and its Discontents*. London: Profile.

Furedi, Frank. 2018. "Die verborgene Geschichte der Identitätspolitik." In *Die sortierte Gesellschaft: Zur Kritik der Identitätspolitik*, edited by Johannes Richardt, 13–25. Frankfurt am Main: Novo Argumente Verlag.

Galbraith, John Kenneth. 1958. *The Affluent Society*. Boston: Houghton Mifflin.

Galston, William. 2018. "The Populist Challenge to Liberal Democracy." *Journal of Democracy* 29, no. 2: 5–19.

Gamble, Andrew. 1988. *The Free Economy and the Strong State*. Basingstoke: Macmillan.

Gamble, Andrew. 2006. "Two Faces of Neo-Liberalism." In *The Neo-Liberal Revolution: Forging the Market State*, edited by Richard Robison, 20–35. Basingstoke: Palgrave Macmillan.

Gates, Bill. 2020. "Responding to Covid-19—A Once-in-a-Century Pandemic?" *New England Journal of Medicine* 382, no. 18: 1677–1679.

Gauland, Alexander. 2018. "Warum muss es Populismus sein?" *Frankfurter Allgemeine Zeitung*, October 6.

Gellner, Ernest. 1983. *Nations and Nationalism*. Ithaca, NY: Cornell University Press.

Geoghegan, Peter. 2020. "Cronyism and Clientelism." *London Review of Books* 42, no. 21 (November 5).

Gerson, Jacob, and Jeannie Suk. 2016. "The Sex Bureaucracy." *California Law Review* 104: 881–948.

Gerstle, Gary. 2017. "The Rise and Fall (?) of America's Neoliberal Order." *Transactions of the Royal History Society* 28: 241–264.

Gerstle, Gary. 2022. *The Rise and Fall of the Neoliberal Order*. New York: Oxford University Press.

Gest, Justin, Tyler Reny, and Jeremy Mayer. 2018. "Roots of the Radical Right: Nostalgic Deprivation in the United States and Britain." *Comparative Political Studies* 51, no. 13: 1694–1719.

Gethin, Amory, Clara Martínez-Toledano, and Thomas Piketty. 2022. "Brahmin Left versus Merchant Right: Changing Political Cleavages in 21 Western Democracies, 1948–2020." *Quarterly Journal of Economics* 137, no. 1: 1–48.

Geuss, Raymond. 2001. *History and Illusion in Politics*. Cambridge: Cambridge University Press.

Geuss, Raymond. 2002. "Liberalism and its Discontents." *Political Theory* 30, no. 3: 320–338.

Giddens, Anthony. 1998. *The Third Way: The Renewal of Social Democracy*. Cambridge: Polity.

Gidron, Noam, and Peter Hall. 2017. "The Politics of Social Status: Economic and Cultural Roots of the Populist Right." *British Journal of Sociology* 68, no. S1: S57–S84.

Godschalk, Marie. 2015. *Caught: The Prison State and the Lockdown of American Politics*. Princeton, NJ: Princeton University Press.

352 BIBLIOGRAPHY

Goldberg, Zach. 2020. "How the Media Led the Great Racial Awakening." *Tablet Magazine*, August 5.

Gonzalez-Salzberg, Damian. 2018. "An Improved Protection for the (Mentally Ill) Trans Parent: A Queer Reading of *Ap, Garçon and Nicot v. France*." *Modern Law Review* 81, no. 3: 526–538.

Goodhart, David. 2017. *The Road to Somewhere: The Populist Revolt and the Future of Politics*. London: Hurst.

Goodman, Peter S. 2022. *Davos Man: How the Billionaires Devoured the World*. New York: Custom House.

Gray, John. 2020a. "The Woke Have No Vision of the Future." *UnHerd*, June 17.

Gray, John. 2020b. "Why This Crisis is a Turning Point in History." *New Statesman*, April 1.

Green, Toby. 2021. *The Covid Consensus*. London: Hurst.

Green, Toby, and Thomas Fazi. 2023. *The Covid Consensus*. London: Hurst.

Grewal, David Singh. 2008. *Network Power: The Social Dynamics of Globalization*. New Haven, CT: Yale University Press.

Guiraudon, Virginie. 2009. "Equality in the Making: Implementing European Non-Discrimination Law." *Citizenship Studies* 13, no. 5: 527–549.

Gusterson, Hugh. 2017. "From Brexit to Trump: Anthropology and the Rise of Nationalist Populism", *American Ethnologist* 44, no. 2, 209–214.

Haahr, Jens Henrik. 2004. "Open Co-Ordination as Advanced Liberal Government." *Journal of European Public Policy* 11, no. 2: 209–230.

Habermas, Jürgen. 1968. *Technik und Wissenschaft als "Ideologie."* Frankfurt am Main: Suhrkamp.

Habermas, Jürgen. 1973. *Legitimationsprobleme im Spätkapitalismus*. Frankfurt am Main: Suhrkamp.

Habermas, Jürgen. 2021. "Corona und der Schutz des Lebens: Zur Grundrechtsdebatte in der pandemischen Ausnahmesituation." *Blätter für deutsche und internationale Politik* September: 1–32.

Hacker, Jacob, and Paul Pierson. 2010. "Winner-Take-All Politics." *Politics and Society* 38, no. 2: 152–204.

Hacker, Jacob, and Paul Pierson. 2020. *Let Them Eat Tweets: How the Right Rules in an Age of Extreme Inequality*. New York: W. W. Norton.

Hägel, Peter. 2020. *Billionaires in World Politics*. Oxford: Oxford University Press.

Haidt, Jonathan. 2016. "Why Concepts Creep to the Left." *Psychological Inquiry* 27: 40–45.

Haidt, Jonathan. 2024. *The Anxious Generation: How the Great Rewiring of Childhood is Causing an Epidemic of Mental Illness*. New York: Penguin.

Hale, Thomas, Anna Petherick, Toby Phillips, and Samuel Webster. 2023. "Variation in Government Responses to COVID-19." Blavatnik School of Government Working Paper, Oxford University, BSG-WP-20/032, Version 15, June.

Halikiopoulou, Daphne, Steven Mock, and Sofia Vasilopoulou. 2013. "The Civic Zeitgeist: Nationalism and Liberal Values in the European Radical Right." *Nations and Nationalism* 19, no. 1: 107–127.

BIBLIOGRAPHY 353

Hall, Peter, and David Soskice, eds. 2001. *Varieties of Capitalism: The Institutional Foundations of Comparative Advantage*. Oxford: Oxford University Press.

Hall, Stuart. 1979. "The Great Moving Right Show." *Marxism Today* January: 14–20.

Hall, Stuart. 2011. "The Neo-Liberal Revolution." *Cultural Studies* 25, no. 6: 705–728.

Hanania, Richard. 2023. *The Origins of Woke: Civil Rights Law, Corporate America, and the Triumph of Identity Politics*. New York: HarperCollins.

Hansen, Magnus Paulsen, and Peter Triantafillou. 2011. "The Lisbon Strategy and the Alignment of Economic and Social Concerns." *Journal of European Social Policy* 21, no. 3: 197–209.

Hansen, Randall. 2023. *War, Work, and Want: How the OPEC Oil Crisis Caused Mass Migration and Revolution*. New York: Oxford University Press.

Harcourt, Bernard E. 2010. "Neoliberal Penality: A Brief Genealogy." *Theoretical Criminology* 14, no. 1: 74–92.

Harcourt, Bernard E. 2011. *The Illusion of Free Markets: Punishment and the Myth of Natural Order*. Cambridge, MA: Harvard University Press.

Häring, Norbert. 2021. *Endspiel des Kapitalismus*. Köln: Quadriga.

Harvey, David. 2005. *A Brief History of Neoliberalism*. New York: Oxford University Press.

Haslam, Nick. 2016. "Concept Creep." *Psychological Inquiry* 27, no. 1: 1–17.

Häusermann, Silja. 2010. *The Politics of Welfare State Reform in Continental Europe*. Cambridge: Cambridge University Press.

Häusermann, Silja, and Herbert Kitschelt, eds. 2024. *Beyond Social Democracy: The Transformation of the Left in Emergent Knowledge Societies*. Cambridge: Cambridge University Press.

Hayek, Friedrich von. 1939. "Economic Conditions of Interstate Federation." *New Commonwealth Quarterly* 5, no. 2: 131–149.

Hayek, Friedrich von. 1944. *The Road to Serfdom*. Chicago, IL: University of Chicago Press.

Hayek, Friedrich von. 1945. "The Use of Knowledge in Society." *American Economic Review* 35, no. 4: 519–530.

Hayek, Friedrich von. 1967[1957]. "What is 'Social'?—What Does it Mean?" In *Studies in Philosophy, Politics and Economics*, 237–247. Chicago, IL: University of Chicago Press.

Hayek, Friedrich von. 1960. *The Constitution of Liberty*. Chicago, IL: University of Chicago Press.

Hayek, Friedrich von. 1966. "The Principles of a Liberal Order." *Il Politico* 31, no. 4: 601–618.

Hayek, Friedrich von. 1982a. *Law, Legislation and Liberty, Vol.1: Rules of Order*. London: Routledge.

Hayek, Friedrich von. 1982b. *Law, Legislation and Liberty, Vol.2: The Mirage of Social Justice*. London: Routledge.

Hayek, Friedrich von. 1982c. *Law, Legislation and Liberty, Vol.3: The Political Order of a Free People*. London: Routledge.

354 BIBLIOGRAPHY

Hayek, Friedrich von. 1989. *The Fatal Conceit: The Errors of Socialism*. Chicago, IL: University of Chicago Press.

Hayes, Christopher. 2012. *Twilight of the Elites: America after Meritocracy*. New York: Crown.

Healy, Kieran. 2017. "Fuck Nuance." *Sociological Theory* 35, no. 2: 118–127.

Heinig, Hans-Michael, Thorsten Kingreen, Oliver Lepsius, Christoph Möllers, Uwe Volkmann, and Hinnerk Wißmann. 2020. "Why Constitution Matters— Verfassungsrechtswissenschaft in Zeiten der Corona-Krise." *Juristen Zeitung (JZ)* 75, no. 18: 861–872.

Helbling, Marc, and Céline Teney. 2017. "Solidarity between the Elites and the Masses in Germany." In *The Strains of Commitment: The Political Sources of Solidarity in Diverse Societies*, edited by Keith Banting and Will Kymlicka, 127–151. New York: Oxford University Press.

Heller, Hermann. 2015 [1933]. "Authoritarian Liberalism?" *European Law Journal* 21, no. 3: 295–301.

Hemerijck, Anton. 2013. *Changing Welfare States*. Oxford: Oxford University Press.

Henrich, Joseph. 2020. *The Weirdest People in the World*. New York: Allen Lane.

Herby, Jonas, Lars Jonung, and Steve H. Hanke. 2023. *Did Lockdowns Work? The Verdict on Covid Restrictions*. London: Institute of Economic Affairs.

Herold, Maik, Janine Joachim, Cyrill Otteni, and Hans Vorländer. 2023. *Polarization in Europe*. Dresden: MIDEM.

Heuer, Jan-Ocko, Thomas Lux, Steffen Mau, and Katharina Zimmermann. 2020. "Legitimizing Inequality: The Moral Repertoires of Meritocracy in Four Countries." *Comparative Sociology* 19: 542–584.

Himmelfarb, Gertrude. 2003. *The Roads to Modernity: The British, French, and American Enlightenments*. New York: Knopf.

Hirschl, Ran. 2007. *Towards Juristocracy*. Cambridge, MA: Harvard University Press.

Hobbes, Thomas. 1998 [1651]. *Leviathan*. Oxford: Oxford University Press.

Hobolt, Sara, and James Tilly. 2016. "Fleeing the Centre: The Rise of Challenger Parties in the Aftermath of the Euro Crisis." *West European Politics* 39, no. 5: 971–991.

Hobsbawm, Eric. 2012. "Identity Politics and the Left." *New Left Review* 217: 38–47.

Hodges, Ron, Eugenio Caperchione, Jan van Helden, Christoph Reichard, and Daniela Sorrentino. 2022. "The Role of Scientific Expertise in COVID-19 Policy-Making: Evidence from Four European Countries." *Public Organization Review* 22: 249–267.

Höpner, Martin, and Florian Rödl. 2012. "Illegitim und rechtswidrig: Das neue makroökonomische Regime im Euroraum." *Wirtschaftsdienst* 92, no. 4: 219–222.

Höpner, Martin, and Armin Schäfer. 2010a. "Polanyi in Brussels?" MPIfG Discussion Paper 10/8, Max-Planck-Institut für Gesellschaftsforschung, Köln.

Höpner, Martin, and Armin Schäfer. 2010b. "A New Phase of European Integration: Organised Capitalisms in Post-Ricardian Europe." *West European Politics* 33, no. 2: 344–368.

Holmes, Stephen. 1985. "Differenzierung und Arbeitsteilung im Denken des Liberalismus." In *Soziale Differenzierung*, edited by Niklas Luhmann, 9–41. Opladen: Westdeutscher Verlag.

BIBLIOGRAPHY   355

Holmes, Stephen. 1993. *The Anatomy of Antiliberalism*. Cambridge, MA: Harvard University Press.

Holmes, Stephen. 1995. *Passions and Constraint: On the Theory of Liberal Democracy*. Chicago, IL: University of Chicago Press.

Holmes, Stephen. 2022. "The Antiliberal Idea." In *Routledge Handbook of Illiberalism*, edited by András Sajó, Renáta Uitz, and Stephen Holmes, 3–15. London: Routledge.

Hood, Christopher. 1991. "A Public Management for All Seasons?" *Public Administration* 69: 3–19.

Hooghe, Liesbet, and Gary Marks. 1999. "The Making of a Polity: The Struggle Over European Integration." In *Continuity and Change in Contemporary Capitalism*, edited by Herbert Kitschelt, Peter Lange, Gary Marks, and John D. Stephens, 70–98. New York: Cambridge University Press.

Hooghe, Liesbet, and Gary Marks. 2008. "A Postfunctionalist Theory of European Integration: From Permissive Consensus to Constraining Dissensus." *British Journal of Political Science* 39: 1–23.

Hooghe, Liesbet, and Gary Marx. 2018. "Cleavage Theory Meets Europe's Crisis: Lipset, Rokkan, and the Transnational Cleavage." *Journal of European Public Policy* 25, no. 1: 109–135.

Hopkin, Jonathan. 2020. *Anti-System Politics: The Crisis of Market Liberalism in Rich Democracies*. Oxford: Oxford University Press.

Horn, Alexander, Anthony Kevins, and Kees van Keersbergen. 2022. "The Paternalist Politics of Punitive and Enabling Workfare." *Socio-Economic Review* 21, no. 4: 2137–2166. https://doi.org/10.1093/ser/mwac060.

House of Commons (Health and Social Care, and Science and Technology Committees). 2021. "Coronavirus: Lessons Learned to Date." September 21. London: House of Commons.

IGLYO (International Lesbian, Gay, Bisexual, Transgender, Queer and Intersex [LGBTQI] Youth and Student Organization). 2019. "Only Adults? Good Practices in Legal Gender Recognition for Youth." November. https://www.iglyo.org/resources/only-adults.

Ignazi, Piero. 1992. "The Silent Counter-Revolution: Hypotheses on the Emergence of Extreme Right-Wing Parties in Europe." *European Journal of Political Research* 22: 3–34.

Im, Zhen Jie, Nonna Mayer, Bruno Palier, and Jan Rovny. 2019. "The 'Losers of Automation': A Reservoir of Votes for the Radical Right?" *Research and Politics* 6, no. 1. https://doi.org/10.1177/2053168018822395.

Inglehart, Ronald. 1977. *The Silent Revolution: Changing Values and Political Styles Among Western Publics*. Princeton, NJ: Princeton University Press.

Ioannidis, John P. 2022. "Citation Impact and Social Media Visibility of Great Barrington and John Snow Signatories for COVID-19 Strategy." *British Medical Journal Open* 12: 1–7.

Ionescu, Ghita, and Ernest Gellner, eds. 1969. *Populism*. London: Weidenfeld and Nicolson.

BIBLIOGRAPHY

Ivarsflaten, Elisabeth. 2005. "The Vulnerable Populist Right Parties: No Economic Realignment Fueling their Electoral Success." *European Journal of Political Research* 44: 465–499.

Ivarsflaten, Elisabeth. 2008. "What Unites Right-Wing Populists in Western Europe?" *Comparative Political Studies* 41, no. 1: 3–23.

Jacobs, Lawrence, and Desmond King. 2016. *Fed Power: How Finance Wins*. New York: Oxford University Press.

Jasanoff, Sheila. 2020. "Pathologies of Liberty: Public Health Sovereignty and the Political Subject in the Covid-19 Crisis." *Cahiers Droit, Sciences & Technologies* 11: 125–149.

Jasanoff, Sheila, Stephen Hilgartner, J. Benjamin Hurlbut, Onur Özgöde, and Margarita Rayzberg. 2021. "Comparative Covid Response: Crisis, Knowledge, Politics. Interim Report." Harvard Kennedy School of Government. https://compcore.cornell.edu/wp-content/uploads/2021/03/Comparative-Covid-Response_Crisis-Knowledge-Politics_Interim-Report.pdf.

Jensen, Jane, and Denis Saint-Martin. 2003. "New Routes to Social Cohesion? Citizenship and the Social Investment State." *Canadian Journal of Sociology* 28, no. 1: 77–98.

Johns Hopkins Center for Health Security (JHCHS). 2019. *Preparedness for a High-Impact Respiratory Pathogen Pandemic*. Baltimore, MD.

Jones, Calvert W. 2015. "Seeing Like an Autocrat: Liberal Social Engineering in an Illiberal State." *Perspectives on Politics* 13, no. 1: 24–41.

Jones, Calvert W. 2017. *Bedouins into Bourgeois: Remaking Citizens for Globalization*. New York: Cambridge University Press.

Jones, Lee, and Shahar Hameiri. 2021. "COVID-19 and the Failure of the Neoliberal Regulatory State." *Review of International Political Economy* 29, no. 4: 1027–1052.

Jonsen, Karsten, Martha L. Maznevski, and Susan C. Schneider. 2021. "Diversity and Its Not So Diverse Literature." *International Journal of Cross Cultural Management* 11, no. 1: 35–62.

Joppke, Christian. 1999. *Immigration and the Nation-State: The United States, Germany, and Great Britain*. Oxford: Oxford University Press.

Joppke, Christian. 2005. *Selecting by Origins: Ethnic Migration in the Liberal State*. Cambridge, MA: Harvard University Press.

Joppke, Christian. 2010. *Citizenship and Immigration*. Cambridge: Polity.

Joppke, Christian. 2017. *Is Multiculturalism Dead? Crisis and Persistence in the Constitutional State*. Cambridge: Polity.

Joppke, Christian. 2021a. *Neoliberal Nationalism: Immigration and The Rise of the Populist Right*. Cambridge: Cambridge University Press.

Joppke, Christian. 2021b. "Nationalism in the Neoliberal Order: Old Wine in New Bottles?" *Nations and Nationalism* 27, no. 4: 960–975.

Joppke, Christian. 2021c. "Earned Citizenship." *European Journal of Sociology* 62, no. 1: 1–35.

Joppke, Christian. 2022. "Multiculturalism and Antidiscrimination Law." *Law & Business* 25: 59–89.

Joyce, Helen. 2021. *Trans: When Ideology Meets Reality*. New York: One World.

BIBLIOGRAPHY   357

Judt, Tony. 1992. *Past Imperfect: French Intellectuals, 1944–1956.* Berkeley and Los Angeles: University of California Press.

Kahan, Alan S. 2023. *Freedom from Fear: An Incomplete History of Liberalism.* Princeton, NJ: Princeton University Press.

Kahn, Paul. 2012. *Political Theology.* New York: Columbia University Press.

Kaltwasser, Cristóbal Rovira, and Paul Taggert. 2022. "The Populist Radical Right and the Pandemic." *Government and Opposition* 59, no. 4: 977–997.

Kalyvas, Andreas. 1999. "Who's Afraid of Carl Schmitt?" *Philosophy and Social Criticism* 25, no. 5: 87–125.

Katz, Richard, and Peter Mair. 1995. "Changing Models of Party Organization and Party Democracy: The Emergence of the Cartel Party." *Party Politics* 1, no. 1: 5–28.

Katz, Richard, and Peter Mair. 2009. "The Cartel Party Thesis: A Restatement." *Perspectives on Politics* 7, no. 4: 753–766.

Kelly, Erin, and Frank Dobbin. 1998. "How Affirmative Action Became Diversity Management." *American Behavioral Scientist* 41, no. 7: 960–984.

Kendi, Ibram X. 2019. *How To Be an Antiracist.* New York: One World.

Kennedy, Robert F. Jr. 2021. *The Real Anthony Fauci: Bill Gates, Big Pharma, and the Global War on Democracy and Public Health.* New York: Skyhorse Publishing.

Khan, Lina. 2017. "Amazon's Antitrust Paradox." *Yale Law Journal* 126: 710–805.

King, Stephen. 2017. *Grave New World: The End of Globalization, the Return of History.* New Haven, CT: Yale University Press.

Kitschelt, Herbert, with Anthony McGann. 1995. *The Radical Right in Western Europe.* Ann Arbor, MI: University of Michigan Press.

Kitschelt, Herbert. 2007. "Growth and Persistence of the Radical Right in Postindustrial Democracies." *West European Politics* 30, no. 5: 1176–1206.

Kitschelt, Herbert, and Philipp Rehm. 2014. "Occupations as a Site of Political Preference Formation." *Comparative Political Studies* 47, no. 12: 1670–1706.

Klein, Naomi. 2007. *The Shock Doctrine: The Rise of Disaster Capitalism.* New York: Metropolitan Books.

Klein, Naomi. 2020. "Screen New Deal." *The Intercept,* May 8. https://theintercept.com/2020/05/08/andrew-cuomo-eric-schmidt-coronavirus-tech-shock-doctrine/.

Klinenberg, Eric. 2024. *2020: One City, Seven People, and the Year Everything Changed.* New York: Knopf.

Knight, Adam, and Rogier Creemers. 2021. "Going Viral: The Social Credit System and COVID-19." Unpublished paper (copy on file by author).

Köllen, Thomas. 2021. "Diversity Management." *Journal of Management Inquiry* 30, no. 3: 259–272.

Kohn, Hans. 1944. *The Idea of Nationalism.* New York: Macmillan.

Koning, Edward. 2019. *Immigration and the Politics of Welfare Exclusion: Selective Solidarity in Western Democracies.* Toronto: University of Toronto Press.

Koopmans, Ruud and Liav Orgad. 2023. "Majority-Minority Constellations: Toward a Group-Differentiated Approach", in R. Koopmans and L. Orgad, eds. *Majorities, Minorities, and the Future of Nationhood,* 1–34. Cambridge: Cambridge University Press.

358 BIBLIOGRAPHY

Kornai, Janos. 2015. "Hungary's U-Turn." *Society and Economy* 37, no. 3: 279–329.

Koschorke, Albrecht. 2022. "Identität, Vulnerabilität und Ressentiment." *Leviathan* 50, no. 3: 469–486.

Kostner, Sandra. 2022. "Droht ein gesellschaftliches Long Covid?" In *Pandemieprolitik: Freiheit unterm Rad?*, edited by Sandra Kostner and Tanya Lieske, 127–141. Stuttgart: Ibidem.

Kostoff, Ronald, Daniela Calina, Darja Kanduc, Michael B. Briggs, Panayiotis Vlachoyiannopoulos, and Andrey A. Svistunov. 2021. "Why Are We Vaccinating Children Against COVID-19?" *Toxicology Reports* 8: 1665–1684.

Kraemer, Klaus. 2022. "How Do State Authorities Act Under Existential Uncertainty?" *Culture, Practice and Europeanization* 7, no. 1: 5–36.

Krastev, Ivan, and Stephen Holmes. 2019. *The Light that Failed: A Reckoning.* London: Allen Lane.

Kriesi, Hanspeter. 2020. "Is There a Crisis of Democracy in Europe?" *Politische Vierteljahresschrift* 61: 237–260.

Kriesi, Hanspeter, Edgar Grande, Romain Lachat, Martin Dolezal, Simon Bornschier, and Timotheos Frey. 2008. *West European Politics in the Age of Globalization.* Cambridge: Cambridge University Press.

Kriesi, Hanspeter, Edgar Grande, Martin Dolezal, Marc Helbling, Dominic Höglinger, and Swen Hutter. 2012. *Political Conflict in Western Europe.* Cambridge: Cambridge University Press.

Krippner, Greta. 2011. *Capitalizing on Crisis: The Political Origins of the Rise of Finance.* Cambridge, MA: Harvard University Press.

Kruchem, Thomas. 2021. "Leben in der überwachten Gesellschaft." *Deutschlandfunk Kultur*, December 27.

Krugman, Paul. 1994. "Competitiveness: A Dangerous Obsession." *Foreign Affairs* 73, no. 2: 28–44.

Krugman, Paul. 1999. *The Conscience of a Liberal: Reclaiming America from the Right.* New York: Penguin.

Kukathas, Chandran. 2003. *The Liberal Archipelago.* Oxford: Oxford University Press.

Kuppens, Toon, Russell Spears, Antony Manstead, Bram Spruyt, and Matthew Easterbrook. 2018. "Education and the Irony of Meritocracy: Negative Attitudes of Higher Educated People towards the Less Educated." *Journal of Experimental Social Psychology* 76: 429–447.

Kurer, Thomas. 2020. "The Declining Middle: Occupational Change, Social Status, and the Populist Right." *Comparative Political Studies* 53, no. 10–11: 1798–1835.

Kurer, Thomas, and Bruno Palier. 2019. "Shrinking and Shouting: The Political Revolt of the Declining Middle in Times of Employment Polarization." *Research and Politics* 6, no. 1. https://doi.org/10.1177/2053168019831164.

Kymlicka, Will. 1995. *Multicultural Citizenship.* Oxford: Oxford University Press.

Kymlicka, Will. 2013. "Neoliberal Multiculturalism?" In *Social Resilience in the Neoliberal Era*, edited by Peter Hall and Michelle Lamont, 99–125. New York: Cambridge University Press.

Kymlicka, Will. 2015. "Solidarity in Diverse Societies: Beyond Neoliberal Multiculturalism and Welfare Chauvinism." *Comparative Migration Studies* 3, no. 17: 15–33.

Kymlicka, Will. 2019. "Deschooling Multiculturalism." *Ethnicities* 19, no. 6: 971–982.

Lakoff, Andrew. 2007. "Preparing for the Next Emergency." *Public Culture* 19, no. 2: 247–271.

Lakoff, Andrew. 2015. "Real-Time Biopolitics: The Actuary and the Sentinel in Global Public Health." *Economy and Society* 44, no. 1: 40–59.

Lakoff, Andrew. 2017. *Unprepared: Global Health in a Time of Emergency*. Berkeley and Los Angeles: University of California Press.

Lange, Sarah de. 2007. "A New Winning Formula? The Programmatic Appeal of the Radical Right." *Party Politics* 13, no. 4: 411–435.

Lapavitsas, Costas. 2019. *The Left Case Against the EU*. Cambridge: Polity.

Lareau, Annette. 2002. "Social Class and Childbearing in Black Families and White Families." *American Sociological Review* 67, no. 5: 747–776.

Laruffa, Francesco. 2022a. "Neoliberalism, Economization and the Paradox of the New Welfare State." *European Journal of Sociology* 63, no. 1: 131–163.

Laruffa, Francesco. 2022b. "Studying the Relationship Between Social Policy Promotion and Neoliberalism: The Case of Social Investment." *New Political Economy* 27, no. 3: 473–489.

Laruffa, Francesco. 2023. "Making Sense of (Post)Neoliberalism." *Politics and Society* 52, no. 4: 586–629. https://doi.org/10.1177/00323292231193805.

Lash, Christopher. 1995. *The Revolt of the Elites and the Betrayal of Democracy*. New York: W. W. Norton.

Latour, Bruno. 2021. *After Lockdown: A Metamorphosis*. Cambridge: Polity.

Le Galès, Patrick. 2016. "Neoliberalism and Urban Change: Stretching a Good Idea Too Far?" *Territory, Politics, Governance* 4, no. 2: 154–172.

Lee, Sang, and DonHee Lee. 2020. "'Untact': A New Customer Service Strategy in the Digital Age." *Service Business* 14: 1–22.

Lefkofridi, Zoe, and Elie Michel. 2017. "The Electoral Politics of Solidarity: The Electoral Agenda of Radical Right Parties." In *The Strains of Commitment: The Political Sources of Solidarity in Diverse Societies*, edited by Keith Banting and Will Kymlicka, 233–267. New York: Oxford University Press.

Lemke, Thomas. 2001. "The Birth of Bio-Politics." *Economy and Society* 30, no. 2: 190–207.

Leonard, Sarah. 2019. "The Fall of the Meritocracy." *New Republic*, September 5.

Lerch, Julia, Patricia Bromley, and John W. Meyer. 2022. "Global Neoliberalism as a Cultural Order and its Expansive Educational Effects." *International Journal of Sociology* 52, no. 2: 97–127.

Lessig, Lawrence. 2006. *Code: Version 2.0*. Cambridge, MA: Harvard University Press.

Levitsky, Steven, and Lucan Way. 2002. "The Rise of Competitive Authoritarianism." *Journal of Democracy* 13, no. 2: 51–65.

Levitsky, Steven, and Daniel Ziblatt. 2018. *How Democracies Die*. New York: Crown.

Levy, Jonah. 1999. "Vice into Virtue? Progressive Politics and Welfare Reform in Continental Europe." *Politics and Society* 27, no. 2: 239–273.

360 BIBLIOGRAPHY

Lilla, Mark. 2017. *The One and Future Liberal: After Identity Politics.* New York: Harper.

Lindblom, Charles. 1977. *Politics and Markets: The World's Political-Economic Systems.* New York: Basic Books.

Linz, Juan. 1975. "Totalitarian and Authoritarian Regimes." In *Handbook of Political Science. Vol. 3,* edited by Fred Greenstein and Nelson Polsby, 175–411. Reading, MA: Addison-Wesley.

Lipset, Seymour Martin. 1959. *Political Man: The Social Bases of Politics.* New York: Doubleday.

Lipset, Seymour Martin, and Stein Rokkan. 1967. "Cleavage Structures, Party Systems, and Voter Alignments: An Introduction." In *Party Systems and Voter Alignments: Cross-National Perspectives,* 1–50. New York: Free Press.

Lister, Ruth. 2002. "Investing in the Citizen-Workers of the Future: New Labour's 'Third Way' in Welfare Reform, Fostering Social Cohesion." Working Paper #5, SSHRC Canada.

Lister, Ruth. 2004. "The Third Way's Social Investment State." In *Welfare State Change: Towards a Third Way?,* edited by Jane Lewis and Rebecca Surender, 157–181. Oxford: Oxford University Press.

Littman, Lisa. 2018. "Parent Reports of Adolescents and Young Adults Perceived to Show Signs of a Rapid Onset of Gender Dysphoria." *PLoS ONE* 13, no. 3: 1–44.

Locke, John. 2016 [1689]. *A Letter Concerning Toleration.* Oxford: Oxford University Press.

Lokdam, Hjalte, and Michael Wilkinson. 2021. "The European Economic Constitution in Crisis: A Conservative Transformation." LSE Law, Society and Economy Working Papers 03/21, London School of Economics.

Loveman, Mara. 1999. "Is 'Race' Essential?" *American Sociological Review* 64, no. 6: 891–898.

Lowi, Theodore. 1969. *The End of Liberalism.* New York: W. W. Norton

Luce, Edward. 2017. *The Retreat of Western Liberalism.* London: Little Brown.

Ludwig, Gundula. 2016. "Desiring Neoliberalism." *Sexuality Research and Social Policy* 13: 417–427.

Lütge, Christoph, and Michael Esfeld. 2021. *Und die Freiheit? Wie die Corona-Politik und der Missbrauch der Wissenschaft unsere offene Gesellschaft bedrohen.* München: Riva.

Luhmann, Niklas. 1986. *Ökologische Kommunikation.* Opladen: Westdeutscher Verlag.

Luhmann, Niklas. 1995. "Inklusion und Exklusion." In *Soziologische Aufklärung, Vol. 6,* 237–264. Opladen: Westdeutscher Verlag.

Lukes, Steven. 2008. "Epilogue: The Grand Dichotomy of the 20th Century." In *The Cambridge History of 20th-Century Political Thought,* edited by Terence Ball and Richard Bellamy, 602–626. Cambridge: Cambridge University Press.

Lukianoff, Greg, and Jonathan Haidt. 2018. *The Coddling of the American Mind.* New York: Penguin.

Lyotard, Jean-François. 1984. *The Postmodern Condition.* Minneapolis: University of Minnesota Press.

Macron, Emmanuel. 2016. *Révolution.* Paris: Éditions XO.

BIBLIOGRAPHY   361

Madison, James. 1878. "Federalist Paper No. 10." avalon.law.yale.edu/18th_century/fed10.asp.

Mair, Peter. 2002. "Populist Democracy vs. Party Democracy." In *Democracies and the Populist Challenge*, edited by Yves Mény and Yves Surel, 81–98. Basingstoke: Palgrave Macmillan.

Mair, Peter. 2013. *Ruling the Void: The Hollowing of Western Democracy*. London: Verso.

Majone, Giandomenico. 1994. "The Rise of the Regulatory State in Europe." *West European Politics* 17, no. 3: 77–101.

Manin, Bernard. 1997. *The Principles of Representative Government*. New York: Cambridge University Press.

Mann, Michael. 2013. *The Sources of Social Power. Vol. 4: Globalization, 1945–2011*. New York: Cambridge University Press.

Manow, Philip. 2019. "Politischer Populismus als Ausdruck von Identitätspolitik?" *Aus Politik und Zeitgeschichte*, February 22, 33–40.

Marcuse, Herbert. 1969 [1965]. "Repressive Tolerance." In *A Critique of Pure Tolerance*, edited by Robert Paul Wolff, Barrington Moore, and Herbert Marcuse, 81–117. Boston: Beacon Press.

Markel, Howard, Harvey B. Lipman, J. Alexander Navarro, Alexandra Sloan, Joseph R. Michalsen, Alexandra Minna Stern, et al. 2007. "Nonpharmaceutical Interventions Implemented by US Cities During the 1918–1919 Influenza Pandemic." *Journal of the American Medical Association (JAMA)* 298, no. 19: 644–655.

Markovits, Daniel. 2019. *The Meritocracy Trap: How America's Foundational Myth Feeds Inequality, Dismantles the Middle Class, and Devours the Elite*. New York: Penguin.

Marquand, David. 2013. *Mamon's Kingdom: An Essay on Britain, Now*. London: Penguin.

Marshall, T. H. 1950. *Citizenship and Social Class*. Cambridge: Cambridge University Press.

Marx, Karl. 1974 [1857–1858]. *Grundrisse der Kritik der politischen Ökonomie*, Berlin (East): Dietz Verlag.

Marx, Karl. 1978 [1844]. "Economic and Philosophic Manuscripts of 1844." In *The Marx-Engels Reader*, edited by Robert Tucker, 66–125. New York: W. W. Norton.

Marx, Karl. 1978 [1845–1846]. "The German Ideology." In *The Marx-Engels Reader*, edited by Robert Tucker, 146–200. New York: Norton.

Marx, Karl. 1992 [1843]. "On the Jewish Question." In *Karl Marx, Early Writings*. New York: Penguin.

Mau, Steffen. 2015. *Inequality, Marketization and the Majority Class: Why Did the European Middle Classes Accept Neo-Liberalism?* Basingstoke: Palgrave Macmillan.

Mau, Steffen. 2017. *Das metrische Wir: Über die Quantifizierung des Sozialen*. Berlin: Suhrkamp.

Mau, Steffen, Thomas Lux, and Linus Westheuser. 2023. *Triggerpunkte: Konsens und Konflikt in der Gegenwartsgesellschaft*. Berlin: Suhrkamp.

Mazzucato, Mariana. 2013. *The Entrepreneurial State: Debunking Private vs. Public Sector Myths*. London: Anthem Press.

McAdam, Doug. 1986. "Recruitment to High-Risk Activism: The Case of Freedom Summer." *American Journal of Sociology* 92, no. 1: 64–90.

McDonnell, Duncan, and Marco Valbruzzi. 2014. "Defining and Classifying Technocrat-Led and Technocratic Governments." *European Journal of Political Research* 53: 654–671.

McGoey, Linsey. 2015. *No Such Thing as a Free Gift: The Gates Foundation and the Price of Philanthropy.* London: Verso.

McNeil, Donald Jr. 2024. *The Wisdom of Plagues: Lessons from 25 Years of Covering Pandemics.* New York: Simon and Schuster.

McWhorter, John. 2021. *Woke Racism: How a New Religion Has Betrayed Black America.* New York: Portfolio/Penguin.

Melnick, R. Shep. 2018. *The Transformation of Title IX: Regulating Gender Equality in Education.* Washington, DC: Brookings Institution Press.

Menéndez, Agustin. 2013. "The Existential Crisis of the European Union." *German Law Journal* 14, no. 5: 453–526.

Menéndez, Agustin, and Espen Olsen. 2020. *Challenging European Citizenship: Ideas and Realities in Contrast.* London: Palgrave Macmillan.

Meyer, John, John Boli, George M. Thomas, and Francisco O. Ramirez. 1997. "World Society and the Nation State." *American Journal of Sociology* 103, no. 1: 144–181.

Mijs, Jonathan. 2016. "The Unfulfillable Promise of Meritocracy." *Social Justice Research* 29: 14–34.

Mijs, Jonathan. 2019. "The Paradox of Inequality: Income Inequality and Belief in Meritocracy Go Hand in Hand." *Socio-Economic Review* 19, no. 1: 7–35.

Milanovic, Branko. 2016. *Global Inequality: A New Approach for the Age of Globalization.* Cambridge, MA: Harvard University Press.

Milanovic, Branko. 2019. *Capitalism, Alone.* Cambridge, MA: Harvard University Press.

Mill, John Stuart. 1882. *A System of Logic.* New York: Harper.

Mill, John Stuart. 2003 [1859]. *On Liberty.* Oxford: Blackwell.

Miller, David. 1995. *On Nationality.* Oxford: Oxford University Press.

Miller, David. 1999. *Principles of Social Justice.* Cambridge, MA: Harvard University Press.

Milward, Alan. 1992. *The European Rescue of the Nation-State.* Routledge: London.

Mirowski, Philip. 2009. "Postface: Defining Neoliberalism." In *The Road from Mont Pèlerin: The Making of the Neoliberal Thought Collective,* edited by Philip Mirowski and Dieter Plehwe, 417–451. Cambridge, MA: Harvard University Press.

Mirowski, Philip. 2013. *Never Let a Serious Crisis Go to Waste: How Neoliberalism Survived the Financial Meltdown.* London: Verso.

Mirowski, Philip, and Dieter Plehwe, eds. 2009. *The Road from Mont Pèlerin: The Making of the Neoliberal Thought Collective.* Cambridge, MA: Harvard University Press.

Möllers, Christoph. 2020. *Freiheitsgrade: Elemente einer liberalen politischen Mechanik.* Berlin: Suhrkamp.

Moffitt, Benjamin. 2016. *The Global Rise of Populism.* Stanford: Stanford University Press.

BIBLIOGRAPHY 363

Monsen, Joseph, and Anthony Downs. 1971. "Public Goods and Private Status." *Public Interest* Spring: 64–76.

Moravcsik, Andrew. 1993. "Preference and Power in the European Community: A Liberal Intergovernmentalist Approach." *Journal of Common Market Studies* 31, no. 4: 473–524.

Moravcsik, Andrew. 2008. "The Myth of Europe's 'Democratic Deficit.'" *Intereconomics* 43: 331–340.

Morel, Nathalie, Bruno Palier, and Joakim Palme. 2012. "Social Investment: A Paradigm in Search of a New Economic Model and Political Mobilization." In *Towards a Social Investment Welfare State?*, edited by N. Morel, B. Palier, and J. Palme, 353–376. Bristol: Policy Press.

Morozov. Evgeny. 2013. *To Save Everything, Click Here: The Folly of Technological Solutionism*. New York: PublicAffairs.

Morozov, Evgeny. 2019. "Capitalism's New Clothes." *The Baffler*, February 4.

Morozov, Evgeny. 2023. "The True Threat of Artificial Intelligence." *New York Times*, June 30.

Morris, Lydia. 2016. "Squaring the Circle: Domestic Welfare, Migrants Rights, and Human Rights." *Citizenship Studies* 20, no. 6–7: 693–702.

Mounk, Yascha. 2017. *The Age of Responsibility: Luck, Choice and the Welfare State*. Cambidge, MA: Harvard University Press.

Mounk, Yascha. 2018. *The People v. Democracy: Why Our Freedom is in Danger and How to Save it*. Cambridge, MA: Harvard University Press.

Mounk, Yascha. 2023. *The Identity Trap*. New York: Penguin.

Moyn, Samuel. 2018. *Not Enough: Human Rights in an Unequal World*. Cambridge, MA: Harvard University Press.

Moyn, Samuel. 2023. *Liberalism Against Itself: Cold War Intellectuals and the Making of Our Times*. New Haven, CT: Yale University Press.

Mucchielli, Laurent. 2022a. *La doxa du Covid: Tome 1*. Paris: Éoliennes.

Mucchielli, Laurent, ed. 2022b. *La doxa du Covid: Tome 2*. Paris: Éoliennes.

Mudde, Cas. 2004. "The Populist Zeitgeist." *Government and Opposition* 39, no. 4: 541–563.

Mudde, Cas. 2007. *Populist Radical Right Parties in Europe*. Cambridge: Cambridge University Press.

Mudde, Cas. 2021. "Populism in Europe: An Illiberal Democratic Response to Undemocratic Liberalism." *Government and Opposition* 56: 577–597.

Mudde, Cas, and Cristóbal Rovira Kaltwasser. 2017. *Populism: A Very Short Introduction*. New York: Oxford University Press.

Mudge, Stephanie. 2018. *Leftism Reinvented: Western Parties from Socialism to Neoliberalism*. Cambridge, MA: Harvard University Press.

Müller, Jan-Werner. 2011. *Contesting Democracy: Political Ideas in 20th Century Europe*. New Haven, CT: Yale University Press.

Müller, Jan-Werner. 2016. *What is Populism?* Philadelphia: University of Pennsylvania Press.

364 BIBLIOGRAPHY

Müller, Jan-Werner. 2019. *Democracy and Disrespect*. Princeton, NJ: Princeton University Press.

Müller, Jan-Werner. 2021. *Democracy Rules*. New York: Farrar, Straus and Giroux.

Münch, Richard. 2022. *Die Herrschaft der Inzidenzen und Evidenzen*. Frankfurt am Main and New York: Campus.

Münch, Richard. 2023. *Polarisierte Gesellschaft: Die postmodernen Kämpfe um Identität und Teilhabe*. Frankfurt am Main and New York: Campus.

Murray, Douglas. 2019. *The Madness of Crowds: Gender, Race and Identity*. London: Bloomsbury.

Murray, Kath, and Lucy Hunter Blackburn. 2019. "Losing Sight of Women's Rights." *Scottish Affairs* 28, no. 3: 262–289.

Murswiek, Dieter. 2021a. "Über Defizite und Fehlentwicklungen in der Lockdown-Judikatur." *Verfassungsblog*, March 16.

Murswiek, Dieter. 2021b. "Die Corona-Waage—Kriterien für die Prüfung der Verhältnismässigkeit von Corona-Massnahmen." *Neue Zeitschrift für Verwaltungsrecht* 40, no. 5: 1–15.

Murswiek, Dieter. 2023. "Die zwei Schutzgüter des Rechts auf Leben." In *Völkerrecht-Europarecht-Deutsches Recht*, edited by Peter Hilpold and Christoph Perathoner, 475–490. Wien: Nomos.

Mutz, Diana. 2017. "Status Threat, not Economic Hardship, Explains the 2016 Presidential Vote." *Proceedings of the National Academy of Sciences (PNAS)* 115, no. 19: E4330–E4339.

Nachtwey, Oliver, and Timo Seidl. 2020. "The Solutionist Ethic and the Spirit of Digital Capitalism." Unpublished manuscript (in author's possession).

Nassehi, Armin. 2023. *Gesellschaftliche Grundbegriffe*. Munich: Beck.

Nietzsche, Friedrich. 2007 [1887]. *On the Genealogy of Morality*. Cambridge: Cambridge University Press.

Nisbet, Robert. 1966. "The Two Revolutions." In *The Sociological Tradition*, 21–46. New York: Basic Books.

Nocera, Joe, and Bethany McLean. 2023. *The Big Fail: What the Pandemic Revealed About Who America Protects and Who it Leaves Behind*. New York: Portfolio/Penguin.

Noon, Mike. 2018. "Pointless Diversity Training." *Work, Employment and Society* 32, no. 1: 198–209.

Norris, Pippa, and Ronald Inglehart. 2019. *Cultural Backlash: Trump, Brexit, and Authoritarian Populism*. New York: Cambridge University Press.

Noury, Abdul, and Gerard Roland. 2020. "Identity Politics and Populism in Europe." *Annual Review of Political Science* 23: 421–439.

Nullmeier, Frank. 2020. "Covid-19-Pandemie und soziale Freiheit." *Zeitschrift für politische Theorie* 11, no. 1: 127–157.

Nussbaum, Martha. 1999. "The Professor of Parody: The Hip Defaitism of Judith Butler." *New Republic*, February 22.

Oakeshott, Michael. 1991. "On Being Conservative." In *Ideals and Ideologies: A Reader*, edited by Terence Ball and Richard Dagger, 154–162. New York: HarperCollins Publishers.

Oakeshott, Michael. 2006. *Lectures in the History of Political Thought*. Exeter (UK): Imprint Academic.

Obermaier, Robert. 2022. "Entscheidungen unter Ungewissheit: Worst-Case-Denken und die Folgen," In *Pandemiepolitik: Freiheit unterm Rad?*, edited by Sandra Kostner and Tanya Lieske. Stuttgart: Ibidem.

OECD. 2019. *Under Pressure: The Squeezed Middle Class*. Paris: OECD Publishing.

Oesch, Daniel. 2006. "Coming to Grips with a Changing Class Structure." *International Sociology* 21, no. 2: 263–288.

Oesch, Daniel. 2008. "Explaining Workers' Support for Right-Wing Populist Parties in Western Europe." *International Political Science Review* 29, no. 3: 349–373.

Oesch, Daniel, and Giorgio Piccitto. 2019. "The Polarization Myth: Occupational Upgrading in Germany, Spain, Sweden, and the UK, 1992–2015." *Work and Occupations* 46, no. 4: 441–469.

Oesch, Daniel, and Line Rennwald. 2018. "Electoral Competition in Europe's Tripolar Political Space: Class Voting for the Left, Centre-Right and Radical Right." *European Journal of Political Research* 57: 783–807.

Özmen, Elif. 2023. *Was ist Liberalismus?* Berlin: Suhrkamp.

Offe, Claus. 2001. "Wessen Wohl ist das Gemeinwohl?" In *Die Öffentlichkeit der Vernunft und die Vernunft der Öffentlichkeit: Festschrift für Jürgen Habermas*, edited by Klaus Günther and Lutz Wingert, 459–488. Frankfurt am Main: Suhrkamp.

Olofsson, Tobias, Shai Mulinari, Maria Hedlund, Åsa Knaggård, and Andreas Vilhelmsson. 2022. "The Making of a Swedish Strategy: How Organizational Culture Shaped the Public Health Agency's Pandemic Response." *SSM-Qualitative Research in Health* 2: 1–8.

Olson, Mancur. 1965. *The Logic of Collective Action*. Cambridge, MA: Harvard University Press.

Omi, Michael, and Howard Winant. 1986. *Racial Formation in the United States*. New York: Routledge and Kegan Paul.

Orenstein, Mitchell, and Bojan Bugarič. 2020. "Work, Family, Fatherland: The Political Economy of Populism in Central and Eastern Europe." *Journal of European Public Policy* 29, no. 2: 176–195.

Orgad, Liav, and Wessel Reijers. 2020. *How to Make the Perfect Citizens? Lessons from China's Model of Social Credit System*. Florence: EUI Working Papers (RSCAS 2020/28).

Oxfam. 2022. "Inequality Kills." Briefing Paper, January.

Pap, András. 2018. *Democratic Decline in Hungary: Law and Society in an Illiberal Democracy*. London: Routledge.

Pappas, Takis. 2019. *Populism and Liberal Democracy: A Comparative and Theoretical Analysis*. Oxford: Oxford University Press.

Parsons, Talcott, and Edward Shils. 1951. *Toward a General Theory of Action*. Cambridge, MA: Harvard University Press.

Pasquale, Frank. 2015. *The Black Box Society: The Secret Algorithms that Control Money and Information*. Cambridge, MA: Harvard University Press.

366 BIBLIOGRAPHY

Patterson, Orlando. 1990. *Slavery and Social Death*. Cambridge, MA: Harvard University Press.

Peugny, Camille. 2019. "The Decline in Middle-Skilled Employment in 12 European Countries." *Research and Politics* 6, no. 1: 1–7.

Pfaller, Robert. 2018. "Sprecht wie Mimosen! Handelt wie Bestien!" In *Die sortierte Gesellschaft: Zur Kritik der Identitätspolitik*, edited by Johannes Richardt, 123–137. Frankfurt am Main: Novo Argumente Verlag.

Phillips, Ann. 1998. *The Politics of Presence*. Oxford: Oxford University Press.

Pierre, Jon. 2020. "Nudges Against Pandemics: Sweden's COVID-19 Containment Strategy in Perspective." *Policy and Society* 39, no. 3: 478–493.

Piketty, Thomas. 2014. *Capital in the 21st Century*. Cambridge, MA: Harvard University Press.

Piketty, Thomas. 2020. *Capital and Ideology*. Cambridge, MA: Harvard University Press.

Pistor, Katharina. 2020a. "Statehood in the Digital Age." *Constellations* 27: 3–18.

Pistor, Katharina. 2020b. "Rule by Data: The End of Markets?" *Law and Contemporary Problems* 83, no. 2: 101–124.

Plehwe, Dieter. 2009. "Introduction." In *The Road from Mont Pèlerin: The Making of the Neoliberal Thought Collective*, edited by Philip Mirowski and Dieter Plehwe, 1–42. Cambridge, MA: Harvard University Press.

Pluckrose, Helen, and James Lindsay. 2020. *Cynical Theories*. Durham, NC: Pitchstone.

Polanyi, Karl. 1944. *The Great Transformation*. Boston: Beacon Press.

Popper, Karl. 1945. *The Open Society and its Enemies* (2 vols.). London: Routledge.

Popper, Karl. 1962. *Conjectures and Refutations*. New York: Basic Books.

Post, Robert. 2000. "Prejudicial Appearances: The Logic of American Antidiscrimination Law." *California Law Review* 88, no. 1: 1–40.

Prasad, Monica. 2006. *The Politics of Free Markets: The Rise of Neoliberal Economic Policies in Britain, France, Germany, and the United States*. Chicago, IL: University of Chicago Press.

Przeworski, Adam. 2019. *Crisis of Democracy*. New York: Cambridge University Press.

Putzel, James. 2020. "The 'Populist' Right Challenge to Neoliberalism: Social Policy between a Rock and a Hard Place." *Development and Change* 51, no. 2: 418–441.

Quiggin, John. 2019. *Zombie Economics: How Dead Ideas Still Walk Among Us*. Princeton, NJ: Princeton University Press.

Rathgeb, Philip, and Marius Busemeyer. 2022. "How to Study the Populist Radical Right and the Welfare State." *West European Politics* 45, no. 1: 1–23.

Rawls, John. 1971. *A Theory of Justice*. Cambridge, MA: Harvard University Press.

Rawls, John. 1985. "Justice as Fairness: Political not Metaphysical." *Philosophy and Public Affairs* 14, no. 3: 223–251.

Rawls, John. 1992. *Political Liberalism*. New York: Columbia University Press.

Recchi, Ettore. 2015. *Mobile Europe: The Theory and Practice of Free Movement in the EU*. Basingstoke: Palgrave Macmillan.

Reckwitz, Andreas. 2017. *Die Gesellschaft der Besonderheiten*. Berlin: Suhrkamp.

Reckwitz, Andreas. 2021. "Auf der Suche nach der neuen Mittelklasse." *Leviathan* 49, no. 1: 33–61.

Reed, Adolph. 2015. "From Jenner to Dolezal: One Trans Good, the Other Not So Much." *Common Dreams*, June 15.

Reed, Adolph. 2016. "The Post-1965 Trajectory of Race, Class, and Urban Politics in the United States Reconsidered." *Labor Studies Journal* 41, no. 3: 260–291.

Reed, Adolph. 2018. "Antiracism." *Dialectical Anthropology* 42: 195–115.

Reed, Adolph. 2020. "Socialism and the Argument against Race Reductionism." *New Labor Forum* 29, no. 2: 36–43.

Reed, Adolph, and Merlin Chowkwanyun. 2012. "Race, Class, Crisis: The Discourse of Racial Disparity and its Analytical Discontents." *Socialist Register* 48: 149–175.

Reed, Adolph, and Touré Reed. 2021. "The Evolution of 'Race' and Racial Justice under Neoliberalism." In *New Polarizations, Old Contradictions*, edited by Greg Albo and Colin Leys, 113–134. London: Merlin Press.

Reich, Robert. 1992. *The Work of Nations*. New York: Viking.

Reijers, Wessel, Liav Orgad, and Primavera de Filippi. 2023. "The Rise of Cybernetic Citizenship." *Citizenship Studies* 27, no. 2: 210–229.

Rhodes, R. A. W. 1996. "The New Governance: Governing without Government." *Political Studies* XLIV: 652–667.

Robin, Corey. 2018. *The Reactionary Mind: Conservatism from Edmund Burke to Donald Trump*. New York: Oxford University Press.

Rodgers, Daniel T. 2011. *Age of Fracture*. Cambridge, MA: Harvard University Press.

Rodriguez-Pose, Andrés. 2017. "The Revenge of the Places that Don't Matter." *Cambridge Journal of Regions, Economy and Society* 11, no. 1: 189–209.

Rodrik, Dani. 2011. *The Globalization Paradox: Why Global Markets, States, and Democracy Can't Coexist*. New York: Oxford University Press.

Rodrik, Dani. 2021. "Why Does Globalization Fuel Populism? Economics, Culture, and the Rise of Right-Wing Populism." *Annual Review of Economics* 13: 133–170.

Röth, Leonce, Alexandre Afonso, and Dennis Spies. 2018. "The Impact of Populist Radical Right Parties on Socio-Economic Policies." *European Political Science Review* 10, no. 3: 325–350.

Rose, Nikolas, and Peter Miller. 1992. "Political Power Beyond the State: Problematics of Government." *British Journal of Sociology* 43, no. 2: 173–205.

Roth, Klaus. 2005. "Carl Schmitt—ein Verfassungsfreund? Seine Stellung zur Weimarer Republik in der Phase der relativen Stabilisierung (1924–29)." *Zeitschrift für Politik* 52, no. 2: 141–156.

Rufo, Christopher. 2023. *America's Cultural Revolution: How the Radical Left Conquered Everything*. New York: Broadside Books.

Rydgren, Jens. 2018. "The Radical Right: An Introduction." In *Oxford Handbook of the Radical Right*, edited by J. Rydgren, 1–14. Oxford: Oxford University Press.

Ryner, Magnus. 2010. "An Obituary for the Third Way: The Financial Crisis and Social Democracy in Europe." *Political Quarterly* 81, no. 4: 554–563.

Sadian, Samuel. 2022. "Wolfgang Streeck on Consumption, Depoliticisation and Neoliberal Capitalism." *European Journal of Social Theory* 25, no. 4: 596–613.

368 BIBLIOGRAPHY

Sandel, Michael. 2012. *What Money Can't Buy: The Moral Limits of Markets*. New York: Farrar, Straus and Giroux.

Sandel, Michael. 2020. *The Tyranny of Merit: What's Become of the Common Good*. New York: Penguin.

Sarrazin, Thilo. 2010. *Deutschland schafft sich ab*. München: Deutsche Verlags-Anstalt (DVA).

Sartori, Giovanni. 1962. "Constitutionalism: A Preliminary Discussion." *American Political Science Review* 56, no. 4: 853–864.

Savage, Mike. 2021. *The Return of Inequality: Social Change and the Weight of the Past*. Cambridge, MA: Harvard University Press.

Schäfer, Armin, and Michael Zürn. 2021. *Die demokratische Regression: Die politischen Ursachen des autoritären Populismus*. Berlin: Suhrkamp.

Schama, Simon. 2023. *Foreign Bodies: Pandemics, Vaccines and the Health of Nations*. New York: Simon and Schuster.

Scharpf, Fritz W. 1999. *Governing in Europe*. Oxford: Oxford University Press.

Scharpf, Fritz W. 2008. "Individualrechte gegen nationale Solidarität." In *Die politische Ökonomie der europäischen Integration*, edited by Martin Höpner and Armin Schäfer, 89–99. Frankfurt am Main: Campus.

Scharpf, Fritz W. 2009. "The Double Asymmetry of European Integration." MPIfG Working Paper 09/12. Cologne: Max-Planck-Institut für Gesellschaftsforschung.

Scharpf, Fritz W. 2015. "After the Crash: A Perspective on Multilevel European Democracy." *European Law Journal* 21, no. 3: 384–405.

Scheuerman, William. 1997. "The Unholy Alliance of Carl Schmitt and Friedrich A. Hayek." *Constellations* 4, no. 2: 172–188.

Schlesinger, Arthur. 1992. *The Disuniting of America*. New York: Norton.

Schmitt, Carl. 1926. *Die geistesgeschichtliche Lage des heutigen Parlamentarismus*. Berlin: Duncker und Humblot.

Schmitt, Carl. 1934 [1922]. *Politische Theologie*. Berlin: Duncker und Humblot.

Schmitt, Carl. 1963 [1932]. *Der Begriff des Politischen*. Berlin: Duncker und Humblot.

Schmitter, Philippe. 2019. "The Vices and Virtues of 'Populism.'" *Sociologica* 13, no. 1: 75–81.

Schneider, Étienne, and Sune Sandbeck. 2019. "Monetary Integration in the Eurozone and the Rise of Transnational Authoritarian Statism." *Competition and Change* 23, no. 2: 138–164.

Schreyer, Paul. 2020. *Chronik einer angekündigten Krise: Wie ein Virus die Welt verändern konnte*. Frankfurt am Main: Westend.

Schuck, Peter. 2003. *Diversity in America*. Cambridge, MA: Harvard University Press.

Schüll, Natasha Dow. 2016. "Data for Life: Wearable Technology and the Design of Self-Care." *BioSocieties* 11, no. 3: 317–333.

Schumpeter, Joseph. 1953. "Die sozialen Klassen im ethnisch homogenen Milieu." In *Aufsätze zur Soziologie*, 147–213. Tübingen: Mohr.

Schumpeter, Joseph. 1976 [1950]. *Capitalism, Socialism, and Democracy*. New York: George Allen and Unwin.

BIBLIOGRAPHY   369

Schwab, Klaus, and Tierry Mallet. 2020. *Covid-19: The Great Reset*. Little Island: Forum Publishers.

Sebhatu, Abiel, Karl Wennberg, Stefan Arora-Jonsson, and Staffan I. Lindberg. 2020. "Explaining the Homogeneous Diffusion of COVID-19 Nonpharmaceutical Interventions Across Heterogeneous Countries." *Proceedings of the National Academy of Sciences (PNAS)* 117, no. 35: 21,201–21,208.

Ségur, Philippe. 2022. "Pourquoi la vaccination obligatoire anti-covid viole l'État de droit." In *La doxa du covid. Tome 2*, edited by Laurent Mucchielli, 461–470. Paris: Éoliennes.

Sen, Amartya. 2000. "Merit and Justice." In *Meritocracy and Economic Inequality*, edited by Kenneth Arrow, Samuel Bowles, and Steven Durlauf, 5–16. Princeton, NJ: Princeton University Press.

Sennett, Richard. 1977. *The Fall of Public Man*. New York: Knopf.

Sharpe, Alex. 2021. "Review of Helen Joyce's *Trans* and Kathleen Stock's *Material Girls*." *Critical Legal Thinking*, October 8.

Shklar, Judith. 1989. "The Liberalism of Fear." In *Liberalism and the Moral Life*, edited by Nancy Rosenblum, 21–38. Cambridge, MA: Harvard University Press.

Shrier, Abigail. 2020. *Irreversible Damage: The Transgender Craze Seducing Our Daughters*. New York: Regnery.

Simmel, Georg. 1992 [1908]. *Soziologie*. Frankfurt am Main: Suhrkamp.

Skrbic, Aristel. 2019. "Mobile Individualism: The Subjectivity of European Union Citizenship." *Netherlands Journal of Legal Philosophy* 48, no. 1: 15–28.

Skrentny, John. 1996. *The Ironies of Affirmative Action*. Chicago, IL: University of Chicago Press.

Slattery, David, Joseph Nellis, Kosta Josifidis, and Alpar Losonc. 2013. "Neoclassical Economics: Science or Neoliberal Ideology?" *European Journal of Economics and Economic Policies: Intervention* 10, no. 1: 313–326.

Slobodian, Quinn. 2018. *Globalists: The End of Empire and the Birth of Neoliberalism*. Cambridge, MA: Harvard University Press.

Smith, Rogers M., and Desmond King. 2024. *America's New Racial Battle Lines: Protect versus Repair*. Chicago: University of Chicago Press.

Sobolewska, Maria, and Robert Ford. 2020. *Brexitland: Identity, Diversity and the Reshaping of British Politics*. Cambridge: Cambridge University Press.

Somek, Alexander. 2011. *Engineering Equality: An Essay on European Anti-Discrimination Law*. Oxford: Oxford University Press.

Somek, Alexander. 2012. "From Workers to Migrants, from Distributive Justice to Inclusion: Exploring the Changing Social-Democratic Imagination." *European Law Journal* 18, no. 5: 711–726.

Somek, Alexander. 2014. "Europe: Political, not Cosmopolitan." *European Law Journal* 20, no. 2: 142–163.

Srnicek, Nick. 2017. *Platform Capitalism*. Cambridge: Polity.

Staab, Philipp. 2015. *Digitaler Kapitalismus: Markt und Herrschaft in der Ökonomie der Unknappheit*. Berlin: Suhrkamp.

370 BIBLIOGRAPHY

Starr, Paul. 2007. *Freedom's Power: The True Force of Liberalism*. New York: Basic Books.

Stedman Jones, Peter. 2012. *Masters of the Universe: Hayek, Friedman, and the Birth of Neoliberal Policy*. Princeton, NJ: Princeton University Press.

Steenvoorden, Eefje, and Eelco Harteveld. 2018. "The Appeal of Nostalgia: The Influence of Societal Pessimism on Support for Populist Radical Right Parties." *West European Politics* 41, no. 2: 28–52.

Stern, Fritz. 1961. *The Politics of Cultural Despair: A Study in the Rise of the Germanic Ideology*. Berkeley and Los Angeles: University of California Press.

Stiegler, Barbara. 2021. *De la démocracie en pandémie*. Paris: Éditions Gallimard.

Stiegler, Barbara, and François Alla. 2022. *Santé publique année zero*. Paris: Éditions Gallimard.

Stiglitz, Joseph. 2011. "Of the 1%, By the 1%, For the 1%." *Vanity Affair*, May.

Stiglitz, Joseph. 2012. *The Price of Inequality*. New York: W. W. Norton.

Stiglitz, Joseph. 2022. "COVID Has Made Global Inequality Much Worse." *American Prospect*, March 1.

Stock, Kathleen. 2021. *Material Girls: Why Reality Matters for Feminists*. London: Fleet.

Stoker, Gerry. 2019. "Can the Governance Paradigm Survive the Rise of Populism?" *Policy and Politics* 47, no. 1: 3–18.

Stone Sweet, Alec. 2000. *Governing with Judges: Constitutional Politics in Europe*. Oxford: Oxford University Press.

Streeck, Wolfgang. 2011. "The Crises of Democratic Capitalism." *New Left Review* 71: 5–29.

Streeck, Wolfgang. 2012. "Citizens as Consumers: Considerations on the New Politics of Consumption." *New Left Review* 76: 27–47.

Streeck, Wolfgang. 2013. *Gekaufte Zeit: Die vertagte Krise des Kapitalismus*. Berlin: Suhrkamp.

Streeck, Wolfgang. 2016. *How Will Capitalism End? Essays on a Failing System*. London: Verso.

Streeck, Wolfgang. 2021. *Zwischen Globalismus und Demokratie: Politische Ökonomie im ausgehenden Neoliberalismus*. Berlin: Suhrkamp.

Streeck, Wolfgang. 2022. "In the Superstate." *London Review of Books* 44, no. 2 (January 27).

Stubbs, Paul, and Noémi Lendrai-Bainton. 2020. "Authoritarian Neoliberalism, Radical Conservatism and Social Policy within the European Union, Croatia, Hungary and Poland." *Development and Change* 51, no. 2: 540–560.

Sullivan, Andrew. 2018. "We All Live on Campus Now." *New York Magazine*, February 9.

Šumonja, Miloš. 2020. "Neoliberalism is Not Dead—On Political Implications of Covid-19." *Capital and Class* 45, no. 2: 215–227.

Susskind, Jamie. 2018. *Future Politics: Living Together in a World Transformed by Tech*. Oxford: Oxford University Press.

Szetela, Adam. 2020. "Black Lives Matter at Five." *Ethnic and Racial Studies* 43, no. 8: 1358–1383.

Szporluk, Roman. 1988. *Communism and Nationalism*. New York: Oxford University Press.

Taguieff, Pierre-André. 1993. "Origines et metamorphoses de la nouvelle droite." *Vingtième Siècle* 40: 3–22.

Taguieff, Pierre-André. 2021. *L'antiracisme devenu fou*. Paris: Hermann.

Tavits, Margit, and Joshua Potter. 2015. "The Effect of Inequality and Social Identity on Party Strategies." *American Journal of Political Science* 59, no. 3: 744–758.

Telford, Luke, Mark Bushell, and Owen Hodgkinson. 2022. "Passport to Neoliberal Normality? A Critical Exploration of Covid-19 Vaccine Passports." *Journal of Contemporary Crime, Harm, Ethics* 2, no. 1: 42–61.

Thaler, Richard, and Cass Sunstein. 2008. *Nudge: Improving Decisions about Health, Wealth and Happiness*. New York: Penguin.

Ther, Philipp. 2016. *Europe Since 1989: A History*. Princeton, NJ: Princeton University Press.

Therborn, Göran. 2013. *The Killing Fields of Inequality*. Cambridge: Polity.

Therborn, Göran. 2022. "The World and the Left." *New Left Review* 137 (September–October): 23–73.

Thomas, Jane Clare. 2020. "The Political Erasure of Sex. Appendix: A Brief History of Transgender Ideology." *Political Erasure of Sex*, October. www.thepoliticalerasureofsex.org.

Thym, Daniel, and Jonas Bornemann. 2020. "Schengen and Free Movement Law During the First Phase of the Covid-19 Pandemic." *European Papers* 5, no. 3: 1143–1170.

Tocqueville, Alexis de. 1969 [1835–1840]. *Democracy in America*. New York: Harper and Row.

Todorov, Tzvetan. 1993. *On Human Diversity*. Cambridge, MA: Harvard University Press.

Tooze, Adam. 2018. *Crashed: How a Decade of Financial Crisis Shaped the West*. New York: Viking.

Tooze, Adam. 2020. "The Death of the Central Bank Myth." *Foreign Policy*, May 13.

Tooze, Adam. 2021. *Shutdown: How Covid Changed the World's Economy*. New York: Viking.

Torpey, John. 2006. *Making Whole What Has Been Smashed: On Reparations Politics*. Cambridge, MA: Harvard University Press.

Torpey, John. 2023. "On Race and Class: Refocusing the Progressive Agenda". Unpublished Manuscript.

Toshkov, Dimiter, Brendan Carroll, and Kutsal Yesilkagit. 2022. "Government Capacity, Societal Trust or Party Preferences: What Accounts for the Variety of National Policy Responses to the COVID-19 Pandemic in Europe?" *Journal of European Public Policy* 29, no. 7: 1009–1028.

Tréguer, Felix. 2021. "The Virus of Surveillance." *Political Anthropological Research on International Social Sciences* 2, no. 1: 16–46.

Tschofen, Franziska. 1991. "Article 235 of the Treaty Establishing the European Economic Community." *Michigan Journal of International Law* 12: 471–509.

Tugal, Cihan. 2016. "Neoliberal Populism as a Contradictory Articulation." *European Journal of Sociology* 57, no. 3: 466–470.

Ture, Kwame (Stokeley Carmichael), and Charles Hamilton. 1992 [1967]. *Black Power*. New York: Random House.

Tuvel, Rebecca. 2017. "In Defense of Transracialism." *Hypatia* 32, no. 2: 263–278.

Urbinati, Nadia. 2019a. *Me the People: How Populism Transforms Democracy*. Cambridge, MA: Harvard University Press.

Urbinati, Nadia. 2019b. "Political Theory of Populism." *Annual Review of Political Science* 22: 111–127.

U.S. House of Representatives. 2024. *After Action Review of the COVID-19 Pandemic: The Lessons Learned and a Path Forward*. Select Subcommittee on the Coronavirus Pandemic, Washington, D.C., 4 December.

Vance, J. D. 2016. *Hillbilly Elegy*. New York: HarperCollins.

Varian, Hal. 2014. "Beyond Big Data." *Business Economics* 49, no. 1: 27–31.

Vázquez-Arroyo, Antonio. 2008. "Liberal Democracy and Neoliberalism: A Critical Juxtaposition." *New Political Science* 30, no. 2: 127–159.

Veblen, Thorstein. 2009 [1899]. *The Theory of the Leisure Class*. New York: Routledge.

Venice Commission. 2011. "Opinion on the New Constitution of Hungary." Opinion No. 621/2011. Strasbourg: Council of Europe.

Verschueren, Herwig. 2015. "Preventing 'Benefit Tourism' in the EU." *Common Market Law Review* 52: 363–390.

Vibert, Frank. 2007. *The Rise of the Unelected: Democracy and the New Separation of Powers*. Cambridge: Cambridge University Press.

Vogl, Joseph. 2021. *Kapital und Ressentiment*. München: C. H. Beck.

Wacquant, Loïc. 2009. *Punishing the Poor: The Neoliberal Government of Social Insecurity*. Durham, NC: Duke University Press.

Wacquant, Loïc. 2010. "Crafting the Neoliberal State: Workfare, Prisonfare, and Social Insecurity." *Sociological Forum* 25, no. 2: 197–220.

Wacquant, Loïc. 2012. "Three Steps to a Historical Anthropology of Actually Existing Neoliberalism." *Social Anthropology* 20, no. 1: 66–79.

Wacquant, Loïc. 2023. "The Trap of 'Racial Capitalism.'" *European Journal of Sociology* 64, no. 2: 153–162.

Wade, Nicholas. 2021. "The Origin of COVID: Did People or Nature Open Pandora's Box?", *Bulletin of the Atomic Scientists*, 5 May (https://thebulletin.org/2021/05/the-origin-of-covid-did-people-or-nature-open-pandoras-box-at-wuhan/).

Walzer, Michael. 1984. "Liberalism and the Art of Separation." *Political Theory* 12, no. 3: 315–330.

Wang, Haidong, Katherine R. Paulson, Spencer A. Pease, Stefanie Watson, Haley Comfort, Peng Zheng, et al. 2022. "Estimating Excess Mortality Due to the COVID-19 Pandemic." *The Lancet* 399: 1513–1536.

Weber, Max. 1976 [1922]. *Wirtschaft und Gesellschaft*. Mohr: Tübingen.

Weiler, Joseph. 1991. "The Transformation of Europe." *Yale Law Journal* 100: 2403–2483.

Weiler, Joseph. 1994. "A Quiet Revolution: The European Court and its Interlocutors." *Comparative Political Studies* 26, no. 4: 510–534.

Weiss, Volker. 2017. *Die autoritäre Revolte: Die Neue Rechte und der Untergang des Abendlandes*. Stuttgart: Klett-Cotta.

Weiss, Volker. 2018. "Rechte Identitätspolitik." In *Die sortierte Gesellschaft: Zur Kritik der Identitätspolitik*, edited by Johannes Richardt, 80–90. Frankfurt am Main: Novo Argumente Verlag.

Weyland, Kurt. 1996. "Populism and Neoliberalism in Latin America: Unexpected Affinities." *Studies in Comparative International Development* 31: 3–31.

White, Jonathan. 2013. "Emergency Europe." *Political Studies* 63: 300–318.

Whittle, Stephen, and Lewis Turner. 2007. "'Sex Changes'? Paradigm Shift in 'Sex' and 'Gender' Following the Gender Recognition Act?" *Social Research Outline* 12, no. 1: 75–89.

Whyte, Jessica. 2019. *The Morals of the Market: Human Rights and the Rise of Neoliberalism*. London: Verso.

Wilderson, Frank B. 2016. "Afro-Pessimism and the End of Redemption." *HumanitiesFutures*. https://humanitiesfutures.org/papers/afro-pessimism-end-redemption/.

Wilensky, Harold. 1975. *The Welfare State and Equality*. Berkeley: University of California Press.

Wilkinson, Michael. 2021. *Authoritarian Liberalism and the Transformation of Modern Europe*. Oxford: Oxford University Press.

Williamson, Oliver. 1996. *The Mechanisms of Governance*. New York: Oxford University Press.

Wimmer, Andreas. 2015. "Race-Centrism: A Critique and a Research Agenda." *Ethnic and Racial Studies* 38, no. 13: 2186–2205.

Winner, Langdon. 1980. "Do Artifacts Have Politics?" *Daedalus* 109, 1: 121–136.

Wolf, Martin. 2023. *The Crisis of Democratic Capitalism*. New York: Penguin.

Wolin, Sheldon. 1996. "The Liberal/Democratic Divide: On Rawls's *Political Liberalism*." *Political Theory* 24, no. 1: 97–119.

Wolinetz, Steven, and Andrej Zaslove. 2018. "The Impact of Populist Parties on Party Systems." In *Absorbing the Blow: Populist Parties and their Impact on Parties and Party Systems*, edited by A. Zaslove and S. Wolinetz, 3–24. Colchester: ECPR Press.

Wood, Peter W. 2021. "Critical Witchcraft Theory." *American Greatness*, July 23.

Woolhouse, Mark. 2022. *The Year the World Went Mad*. Muir of Ord (Scotland): Sandstone Press.

World Health Organization (WHO). 2019. *Non-Pharmaceutical Public Health Measures for Mitigating the Risk and Impact of Epidemic and Pandemic Influenza*. Geneva: WHO.

Yglesias, Matthew. 2019. "The Great Awokening." *Vox*, April 1.

Yoffe, Emily. 2017. "The Uncomfortable Truth About Campus Rape Policy." *The Atlantic*, September 6.

Yoffe, Emily. 2018. "Reining in the Excesses of Title IX." *The Atlantic*, September 4.

Young, Iris Marion. 1990. *Justice and the Politics of Difference*. Princeton, NJ: Princeton University Press.

Young, Michael. 1958. *The Rise of the Meritocracy, 1870–2033: An Essay on Education and Equality*. London: Thames and Hudson.

Zaitchik, Alexander. 2021. "How Bill Gates Impeded Global Access to Covid Vaccines." *The New Republic*, April 12.

Zaloom, Caitlin. 2019. *Indebted: How Families Make College Work at Any Cost*. Princeton, NJ: Princeton University Press.

Ziblatt, Daniel. 2017. *Conservative Parties and the Birth of Democracy*. New York: Cambridge University Press.

Zielonka, Jan. 2020. "The Politics of Pandemics." *Global Perspectives* 1, no. 1: 16702.

Zizek, Slavoj. 1997. "Multiculturalism, or, the Cultural Logic of Multinational Capitalism." *New Left Review* 225: 28–51.

Zizek, Slavoj. 2020. *Pandemic! COVID-19 Shakes the World*. New York: OR Books.

Zuboff, Shoshana. 2015. "Big Other: Surveillance Capitalism and the Prospects of an Information Civilization." *Journal of Information Technology* 30: 75–84.

Zuboff, Shoshana. 2019. *The Age of Surveillance Capitalism*. New York: Public Affairs.

Zwan, Natascha van der. 2014. "Making Sense of Financialization." *Socio-Economic Review* 12: 99–129.

Index

For the benefit of digital users, indexed terms that span two pages (e.g., 52–53) may, on occasion, appear on only one of those pages.

Accetti, C., 86–89
Adam, I., 210
AfD (Alternative für Deutschland), 150–152, 157, 280–281, 320 n.3, 321 n.12, 330 n.128, 333 n.37. *See also* radical right parties
Agamben, G., 272–275
al-Gharbi, M., 211
Alexander, M., 199–202
Alla, F., 305–306
Amable, B., 127
America, *see* United States
Amlinger, C., 279–281
Anderson, E., 42
Anderson, P., 52, 95, 311
Andreessen, M. (Netscape founder), 304
Antidiscrimination, *see also* neoliberal multiculturalism
  in Europe, 136–137
  and multiculturalism, 135
  in United States, 135–136
Antiracism, 10–11, 199–221. *See also* identity left
  as academy-based and language-focused, 215–217
  Black Lives Matter (BLM), 195, 202–203, 207, 216–217, 220, 221–222
  and Black Power compared, 202–206
  corporate support for, 217–219
  Critical Race Theory (CRT), 132–133, 197, 203–204, 210–211, 214, 217–218
  "equity" in, 206
  "institutional racism", 203, 205–206, 212–215
  intersectionality, 191–192, 220, 222
  liberalism opposed by, 210
  neoliberal formatting of, 219–221
  "New Jim Crow" (M.Alexander), 199–202
  from "oppression" to "marginalization" (Torpey), 206
  postmodernist epistemology, 206–211

1619 Project, 204
  "race-centrism" (Wimmer), 212–214
  religion analogy, 215
  transracialism tabooed by, 243–244
Arendt, H., 14–15, 300
Aristotle, 162–163
Arnault, B. (French billionaire), 294
Ashley, F., 235–236
Authoritarianism, 4–5, 9–12, 59–68. *See also* neoliberalism
  authoritarian liberalism, 59–68
  European Union and, 139–144
  Hayek on, 43–44, 63–64
  Linz on, 62–63
  post-democracy and, 62–65
  punitive turn (of neoliberalism), 65–67
  and technopopulism, 87–88
  tension with governance, 107
  as third phase of neoliberalism, 136–144
Avineri, S., 247

Baldwin, P., 249, 252–253, 285–286
Bank of England, 82–83
Bannon, S., 256–257
Bartels, L., 151, 161–162
Bartolini, S., 61–62, 144
Becker, G., 50–51, 116
Beckert, J., 146
Beckett, S., 158
Bell, D. (Daniel), 18, 81
Bell, D. (Derrick), 197, 203–204
Bell, K. (British transwoman), 237
Benioff, M., 295
Benjamin, W., 309
Benoist, A., 42, 175, 176–177, 195–196
Berle, A., 70–71
Berlin, I., 15, 26–27, 183
Berman, S., 166–167, 188
Bezos, J., 294
Bickerton, C., 84–89, 97
Biden, J., 236

376 INDEX

Biebricher, T., 64
Big Pharma, 236, 283, 284, 286–287, 294
Big State, 11–12, 303, 311
Big Tech, 118, 251–252, 294–296, 303,
    306–307. *See also* GAFAM
Birx, D. (U.S. medical official), 290
Black Lives Matter (BLM), 195, 202–203, 207,
    216–217, 220, 221–222. *See also*
    antiracism
Blair, T., 74, 85, 102–103, 114, 115–118, 121,
    123
Blauner, R., 202–203, 206
Blockchain technology, 306–307
Blyth, M., 143–144
Bobbio, N., 24–25
Bodin, J., 26–27
Bolsonaro, J., 275
Boltanski, L., 218–219
Bonilla-Silva, E., 208, 212–216
Bonoli, G., 122–123
Bork, R., 299–300
Bourdieu, P., 30, 166
Bourla, A. (Pfizer chief), 282–284, 290, 294
Bratton, B., 274–275
Braunstein, J.F., 207–208, 241, 242–243
Bretton Woods financial regime
    (1944-1971), 108
Brexit, 86, 150–151, 167–168, 171
Britain, *see also* Brexit
    Conservatives *versus* Labour (1950s), 17
    COVID deaths projected, 265
    COVID management, 315 n.22
    education costs rising, 163, 317 n.54
    education expansion
        (post-secondary), 167–168
    Falkland Islands war ("Operation
        Corporate"), 64–65
    fighting inflation (1990s), 82–83
    Gender Recognition Act (GRA) (2004), 226
    home ownership rising, 112
    Keir Starmer on transwomen, 237–238
    "new liberalism", 18–19
    New Public Management (NPM) in, 71
    Poor Law Reform Act (1834), 24
    public opinion on COVID
        measures, 279–280
    Speenhamland welfarism (early 19th
        century), 24
    Swine-flu deaths, 261, 264–265
    temporary migrants excluded from social
        benefits, 178
    Tony Blair about, 85

transwomen in prison, 228–229
    as "truly global", 150–151
    unhappy about Europe, 150
    welfare-to-workfare, 121
Brown, W.
    on Foucault, 50, 79–80
    on governance, 28–29
    on Hayek, 46, 48–49
    on identity left, 8, 196–197
    on neoliberalism, 2, 6, 49–50
    on populist right, 8, 189
Brubaker, R., 197–198, 222, 249, 300, 301
Bruff, I., 137, 139
Buchanan, J., 64
Bude, H., 272
Bugariç, B., 182
Burke, E., 17, 41, 45–46
Bush, G. (Jr.)., 64–65, 164–165
Butler, J., 222–224, 226, 309–310

Callison, W., 6, 279–280
Campbell, B., 195
Canovan, M., 149–150
Caporaso, J., 97–98
Caramani, D., 158
Carmichael, S., 203–205
Cartel party theory (Katz and Mair), 6, 63, 157
Carter, J., 164–165
Case, A. 167
CEPI ("global partnership" for vaccine
    development), 283–284
Chamayou, G., 70–71
Cheney, R. ("Dick"), 64–65
Chiapello, E., 218–219
Chinese health code, 305–306. *See also*
    COVID-19 pandemic
Chinese social credit system, 251–252, 297,
    306
Christi, R., 59–60
Cinque Stelle (Italian populist party), 86. *See
    also* technopopulism
Citizen's income, 1
Citizenship
    conditional, 195, 305–306
    as consumption, 73–75
    cybernetic, 306
    earned, 306
    of European Union, 98–100, 139–140
    "global corporate" (B.Gates), 258
    in Gulf States, 67–68
    liberal, 1–2
    and nationhood, 101–102

INDEX 377

neoliberal, 1, 31, 67–68
return of during COVID (M.Wolf), 247
social rights, 1, 37, 115–116, 193–194
Cleavage structures, 153–156
Clinton, B., 37, 66, 75, 102–103, 113–118, 121, 124–125, 134–135, 211
Clinton, H., 220–221
Clyburn, J. (U.S. Congressman), 220–221
Coates, T.-N., 211
Coleman, J., 39–40
Collier, P., 157–158
Collier, S., 2–3
Collins, F. (U.S. public health official), 262–263
Colloque Lippmann (1937), 31–33
Combahee River Collective, 191–192
Condorcet, N., 47
Conservatism, 16–17, 19
Hayek on, 45–47
liberalism and, 17
"Merchant Right" (Piketty), 125
neoliberalism and, 114, 116
white identity politics and, 242
Constant, B., 15–17, 20, 22–23, 59–60, 65
Constitutionalism, 4–5, 10, 59. *See also* liberalism, neoliberalism
and European Union, 89–100
in Federalist Papers, 22–23
and liberal democracy, 26–27
market rules locked in by, 4–5
and minority protection, 108
opposed by populism, 158–159, 187
"post-sovereign" (Habermas), 144
among Spanish *liberales* (19th century), 22–23
Cooper, M., 55–56, 116
COVID-19 pandemic, 2, 11–12, 22, 34, 65, 87–89, 107, 224–225
Agamben's critique of COVID management, 272–275
biosecurity and crisis simulations, 256–258
campaign against the non-vaccinated, 290–293
China as lockdown pioneer, 266–269
doxa, 252–293
end-of-neoliberalism claimed due to state management of, 247–248, 308
Europe adopting lockdown, 269–271
Gates as vaccine promoter, 258–259, 284–285
Great Barrington Declaration (GBD), 261–263

and inequality increased, 294–295, 309
leftists in, 275–279, 309–310
lockdown, 261–282
mass vaccination, 282–293
Mill's harm principle and, 268–269, 292
neoliberal causes of, 248–249
neoliberal management of, 249–251
neoliberal order impacted by, 251, 293–311
non-pharmaceutical interventions (NPI): from rejected to endorsed, 263–264
"normal" social science and, 252–255
opposition to Covid restrictions, 279–281
public support for Covid restrictions, 278–279, 293
right to life *versus* freedom rights (legal debate), 275–279
scientific expertise in, 264–266, 272
therapeutic alternatives to vaccines repressed, 285–290
vaccine development as public-private partnership, 282–285
world governance in, 256–261
World Health Organization (WHO) in predecessor pandemic (2009), 260–261
Crenshaw, K., 206–208
Critical Race Theory (CRT), 132–133, 197, 203–204, 210–211, 214, 217–218. *See also* antiracism
Crouch, C., 1–2, 62–63, 71, 74, 107, 112–113, 152–153, 295–296, 320 n.8
Culpepper, P., 299–300
Cummings, D., 279
Cuomo, A., 247–248

Darling, A., 115–116
Dataist state (Fourcade and Gordon), 301. *See also* neoliberal state
Davidson, N., 138–139
Davies, W., 143, 146
De Beauvoir, S., 222
De Filippi, P., 306
De Maistre, J., 190–191
Dean, M., 77
Deaton, A., 167
Deleuze, G., 297–298, 307
Delgado, R., 208, 210
DeLong, B., 146
Delors, J., 95
Democracy. *See also* liberal democracy, post-democracy
crisis of (populist), 161–162
crisis of (Trilateral Commission), 81–82

INDEX

Democracy (*Continued*)
 liberal, 26, 57–58, 158–159, 277
 Madison on, 22–23
 radical, 58–59
 Schumpeter on, 27–28
 social, 36–37, 39–40, 110, 113–117, 196
Derrida, J., 207–208
Desai, S. (American vascular
  surgeon), 286–287
Descartes, R., 47
Dewey, J., 14, 18, 34–35
Diamanti, I., 88
DiAngelo, R., 208–209, 212–213, 215–216
Digitalization, 11–12, 251–252, 293–308. *See
  also* neoliberalism
 Big Tech as winner of COVID
  pandemic, 294–296
 code as new form of rule, 297–298
 consumer complicity in, 300–301
 and "cybernetic citizenship", 306
 cyberspace utopia, 296
 digital dystopia, 303–304
 digital identity, 305–308
 digital platforms, 296–301
 freedom imperilled by, 299–300, 307–308
 neoliberalism enforced by, 301
 privatizing public functions, 297
 "untact society" enabled by, 302–304
Diversity, 129–134. *See also* neoliberal
  multiculturalism
 Bakke case (U.S. Supreme Court), 129–131
 corporate support for, 131–134
 in EU ("United in Diversity"), 129
 in Europe, 134
 in United States, 131–134
Dodo's dictum (Alice in Wonderland), 41
Donzelot, J., 77
Doublethink (Orwell), 272–273, 275, 291–292,
  309, *see also* COVID-19 pandemic
Douhat, R., 218–219
Downs, A., 73–74
Draghi, M., 84–85, 143–144, 292, 305–306
Drosten, C. (German virologist), 288–289

Elbe, L. (early 20th century Danish
  transwoman), 225–226
Elephant Curve (Milanovic), 57, 164
Eley, J.H., 108
En Marche (French political party), 86–89
Engels, F., 218–219
Engler, S., 253
Esmark, A., 80–81

Esping-Andersen, G., 119–121
EU Digital Covid Certificate, 291–292,
  305–306, *see also* COVID-19 pandemic
EU Digital Identity Wallet, 307, *see also*
  digitalization
Eucken, W., 63–64
European Court of Justice (ECJ), 92–100. *See
  also* European Union
European Exchange Rate Mechanism
  (ERM), 82–83
"European Saints" (Adenauer, Schuman,
  Spaak, de Gasperi) (Milward), 91–92
European Union (EU), 4–5, 9–10, 59, 71–72,
  84–85, 108, 113, 118, 123, 129, 136–137,
  139–146, 179–180, 186, 234, 248–249,
  283–284, 287–288, 303, 305–307
 as airport, not city (Somek), 100
 "authoritarian liberalism" (Wilkinson)
  in, 4–5, 143
 Cassis de Dijon case (ECJ 1979), 95–96
 citizenship of, 98–100
 Cologne School, 97
 and constitutionalism, 89–100
 Dano case (ECJ 2014), 98–99
 democratic deficit in, 94, 108
 direct effect and implied powers (legal
  doctrines), 92–94
 as federation, 89–100
 Financial Crisis (2008) in, 139–144
 Grzelczyk case (ECJ 2001), 98–99
 Hayek's blueprint of, 90–91
 individualism in, 100
 "integration by law", 92–93
 intergovernmentalism approach, 93–94
 Lisbon Strategy (2000), 118–120, 127
 Luxembourg Accord (1965), 93–94
 Maastricht Treaty (1992), 84–85, 139–140
 "member states" (Bickerton) in, 84, 97, 136
 mobility in, 99–100
 "multi-level governance" approach (Hooghe
  and Marx), 94
 mutual recognition (legal doctrine), 95–97
 negative *versus* positive integration
  (Scharpf), 95–98
 neofunctionalism approach, 94
 as neoliberal polity, 89–100
 Open Method of Coordination
  (OMC), 71–72
 political origins of, 91–92
 preliminary rulings (legal doctrine), 93
 Single European Act (SEA) (1985), 94
 "Social Europe" (Delors), 95

Viking and *Laval* cases (ECJ 2005), 96–97
Event 201 (pandemic simulation, 2019), 256–258. *See also* COVID-19 pandemic

Fassin, D., 268–269, 310
Fauci, A. (U.S. public health official), 262–263, 288
Fausto-Sterling, A., 231
Fazi, T., 254–255, 266, 268–269, 278–279, 286–287
Federation, 4–5, 9–10. *See also* neoliberalism
  and European Union, 89–100
  and Geneva School of Globalists, 59
  Hayek on, 90–92, 97–98, 140–141
Ferguson, N. (Neil), 261, 264–267, 269–270. *See also* COVID-19 pandemic
Ferguson, N. (Niall), 268
Financial Crisis (2008), 10, 113, 137–139, 143, 145–146, 180–181, 247, 251, 278–279, 283
Financialization (of capitalism), 112–113, 283
Flaherty, T., 167
Fleck, Z., 185
Floyd, G., 133–134, 216–217
Ford, R., 167–168
Fordist mass production, 74, 299
Forman, J., 201–202
Fortuyn, P., 152
Foucault, M.
  on biopolitics, 2, 50, 79, 223
  democratic deficit in work of, 79–80
  on government, 76–77
  on governmentality, 76–80
  on liberalism, 9, 76–79
  on neoliberalism, 2–3, 9, 31, 42, 50–52, 79, 138
  on postmodern condition, 207–208
  on sovereignty, 143
Fourcade, M., 301
France
  Nouvelle Droite (New Right), 7, 42, 175–177, 195–196
  Revolution (1789), 39–40, 151–152, 190–191, 273–274
Frankfurt School (Critical Theory), 82–83, 209–210
Fraser, N., 7, 10, 123–124, 194
  "progressive neoliberalism", 10, 124–125
  "recognition" *versus* "redistribution", 7, 206
Fredrickson, G., 213–214
Freeden, M., 56–57

Friedman, M., 30, 32, 33–34, 126–127, 132–133, 152
Friedrich, C., 59–60
Frost, R., 14–15
Fukuyama, F., 57–58, 172, 195–196, 216–217
Functional differentiation, 3, 13, 19–20, 29, 72
  neoliberalism as weakening of, 49–51

GAFAM (Google, Apple, Facebook, Amazon, Microsoft), 295–297. *See also* Big Tech
Galbraith, J.K., 73–74, 81
Garland, D., 66
Garza, A. (BLM leader), 220
Gates, B., 81, 247–248, 255, 257–260, 270, 272–273, 283, 284–285, 294
Gates Foundation, 256, 258, 283–284
Gellner, E., 149, 172
Germany, *see also* AfD
  in EU, 140–142
  Hartz IV social policy, 99–100
  Querdenker (pandemic lockdown opponents), 279–281
  Schuldenbremse (debt brake), 142–143
  soziale Marktwirtschaft, 32, 96–97
  Weimar Republic, 4
Gerstle, G., 5–6, 110, 113–114, 144–145
Geuss, R., 14–15, 20, 22–25, 30
Ghebreyesus, T. (WHO chief), 259, 262, 267–268
Giddens, A. 113–120
Gig economy, 297
Gitlin, T., 215–216
Globalization, 2, 57, 118, 124, 155, 251. *See also* hyperglobalization
  and cultural cleavage, 154, 174, 187–189
  and economic cleavage, 72–73, 187–188
  losers and winners, 153–156, 164, 167, 169–171, 188–189
  and neoliberalism, 57, 111–112, 151
  right-wing backlash against, 174
  "shocks" (Rodrik), 173
Goldberg, Z., 217–218
Goldthorpe, J., 81–82
Goodman, P., 36
Gordon, J., 301
Governance, 4, 9–10, 68–80. *See also* neoliberal state, neoliberalism
  and citizenship as consumption, 73–75
  corporate origin of, 69–71
  and democracy, 68–69
  global, 11–12, 31
  and "governmentality" (Foucault), 76–80

380 INDEX

Governance (*Continued*)
  as minimal state, 69
  as network, 72–73
  as normative concept, 71–72
  as "socio-cybernetic system" (Rhodes), 72
  state as loser ("hollowing out", Rhodes), 73
Governmentality (Foucault), 76–80. *See also* governance
Gramsci, A., 195–196
Gray, J., 197, 247
Great Barrington Declaration (GBD) (2020), 261–263. *See also* COVID-19 pandemic
Green, T., 254–255, 266, 268–269, 278–279, 286–287
Grewal, D.S., 72–73
Guerini, S. (Macronist), 270–271
Guiraudon, V., 136
Gupta, V., 240
Gyurcsány, F. (former Socialist Hungarian Prime Minister), 181–182

Habermas, J., 81–83, 116–117, 144, 275–277–278–279
Habsburg Empire, 90–91
Hacker, J., 110–111
Hägel, P., 258
Haidt, J., 217, 234–235
Hall, S., 152
Hamilton, C., 203–205
Hannah-Jones, N., 204–205, 218
Hans, T. (German political official), 291–292
Harcourt, B., 65–66
Hayek, F. 4–5, 9–10, 17, 25, 30, 31–34. *See also* liberalism, neoliberalism
  on authoritarianism, 63–64
  on British *versus* French liberal traditions, 30, 46–47
  in and on Chile under Pinochet, 44, 63–64
  on conservatism (opposed), 114
  as conservative liberal, 45–46
  on democracy, 43–46, 61
  on formal equality, 37–38
  on freedom, 34–37, 47
  on inequality, 36
  on "interstate federation" (1939), 90–92, 97–98
  on *isonomia* (rule of law), 37–38
  on knowledge (as limited), 40, 52, 101, 157
  and liberalism (traditional), 59
  on markets, 35–36, 41, 42
  on meritocracy (opposed), 41, 101
  in Mont Pèlerin Society, 49–50
  and moral traditionalism, 46–49
  on nationalism (opposed), 124
  as neoliberal master thinker, 51–52
  on nomocratic (spontaneous) *versus* teleocratic (planned) order, 39–40, 45
  and Schmitt, 45, 59–61
  on self-responsibility, 36–37
  "social" and "society" attacked by, 48, 194
  on social justice (opposed), 39–42
  on socialism (opposed), 35–37, 40, 124
  on technocracy (opposed), 80
  on totalitarianism (opposed), 43–44
Hayton, D. (British transwoman editorialist and activist), 237–238
Heller, H., 4, 45, 68
Hindess, B., 76–77
Hirschman, A., 222
Hobbes, T., 1–2, 14–15, 17–18, 21, 26–27, 128
Hobhouse, L., 18–19, 23–24
Hobsbawm, E., 59, 114, 190–191
Höpner M., 96–98
Holmes, S.
  on antiliberal tradition, 190–191, 193
  on crisis of liberalism, 56–57, 150
  on liberal democracy, 26–27
  on liberalism and functional differentiation, 29
Hollande, F., 87–88
Hooghe, L., 94–95, 155–156
Hopkin, J., 187–188
Horton, R. (editor of *Lancet* medical journal), 286–287
Humboldt, W., 20, 24, 34
Hume, D., 46–47
Hyperglobalization (Rodrik), 96–97. *See also* globalization

Identity left
  as academy-based, 191–192, 215–217
  antiracism, 199–221
  antiracism and transgender compared, 242–243
  civil-rights and antidiscrimination laws as basis of, 192–193
  corporate support for ("woke capital"), 217–219
  givenness *versus* choice, 198, 243–244
  "loss of futurity" (Brown), 196–197, 243
  neoliberal context of, 193–194, 196–198
  postmodernist epistemology, 206–211, 222–223

public-private distinction undermined by, 8, 193–194
and "social justice", 242
transgender, 221–241
victim posture, 192, 195, 196, 208
Identity politics. *See also* identity left, populism
after class politics, 146, 190–191, 204
left-right spiral, 7, 197–198
left-wing, 7, 192
neoliberal context of, 8, 110–111, 144–146, 194, 197
right-wing (populism), 7, 149
as threat to liberalism, 193–194, 241, 244
victim posture, 192, 195, 196, 208
IGLYO (international LGBT youth and student organization), 233–234. *See also* transgender
Ignazi, P., 7
Illiberal democracy, 156–162
Illiberal state, 8, 156, 179–180, 183–184
Illiberalism, 10–12, 20, 152, 156, 157–159, 161–162, 177, 179–180, 183–186, 192–193, 209–210, 239. *See also* illiberal democracy, illiberal state
Inglehart, R., 153, 188–189
International Monetary Fund (IMF), 71–72, 108, 142
Ionescu, G., 149
Islam, 152, 176–177

Jasanoff, S., 192
John Snow Memorandum (JSM) (2020), 263, *see also* COVID-19 pandemic
Johns Hopkins Center for Health Security (JHCHS), 256, 263–264
Johnson, B., 86, 279
Jones, C., 67–68
Joyce, H., 224–226

Kafka, F., 309–310
Kahan, A., 15
Kahn, A. (French medical scientist), 268–269
Kant, I., 15, 184
Katz, R., 6, 63, 157
Kendi, I.X., 197, 206, 214–215, 218, 240. *See also* antiracism
Keynesianism, 33, 81–82, 111
"privatized" (Crouch), 112–113
Klein, N., 6, 64–65, 107, 247–248
Klinenberg, E., 293–294
Kohl, H., 97
Koschorke, A., 192–194

Kraemer, K., 249
Krastev, I., 56–57, 150
Kriesi, H., 154–156, 161–162, 167, 188
Kukathas, C., 128
Kurer, T., 170–171
Kymlicka, W., 127–128

Lakoff, A., 266
Latour, B., 309–310
Lenin, V.I., 298
Lepsius, O., 275–276
Lessig, L., 297–298
Levitsky, S., 161–162
Levy, J., 123
Lewis, J. (U.S. Congressman), 220–221
LGBT movement, 8, 220–221, 225–226, 232, 233–234, 237–238. *See also* transgender
Liberal democracy, 10, 26–28, 55, 57–59, 139–140, 157–159, 161, 194–195, 242, 277
Liberal state, 26, 29, 93, 178, 184, 254–255
Liberales (Spanish political party, 1810-1811), 14–15, 22–23
Liberalism
as "art of separation" (Walzer), 3, 13, 28–30, 78
and autonomy/individualism (Geuss Quartet), 22
crisis of (2016), 150–151
and democracy, 26–28, 59
economic, 31–32, 50, 57
and equality, 23–25
and freedom (Geuss Quartet), 21
historical (economic *and* political), 24–25
and limiting discretionary power (rule of law) (Geuss Quartet), 22–23
"negative liberty" (Berlin), 15, 21, 26–27
Physiocrats (French), 65–66
political, 20, 210
as political ordering (*versus* philosophical) principle, 9, 13, 14–16
"positive liberty" (Berlin), 15, 26–27, 30, 183
public-private distinction in, 19, 29
and toleration (Geuss Quartet), 21
Lindblom, C., 42
Lindsay, J., 207–208, 242
Linz, J., 62–63
Lippmann, W., 32
Lipset, S.M., 153–154, 162–163, 185
Littman, L., 234–236
Locke, J., 14–15, 17–18, 21
Lord Cecil, R. (late 19th to mid-20th century British politician), 45–46

382 INDEX

Loveman, M., 214
Lowi, T., 73
Luhmann, N., 29, 72
Lukes, S., 160
Lukianoff, G., 217, 234–235
Lyotard, J.F., 207–208

Maastricht Treaty (1992) (EU), 84–85,
    139–140. See also European Union
Macbeth (Shakespeare), 61–62
MacKinnon, C., 239
Macron, E., 87–89, 100–101, 266, 270–271,
    280–281, 291–292
Madison, J., 34, 45–46
    Federalist Letter No.10, 22–23
Maine, H.S., 1–2, 46–47
Mair, P., 6, 63, 86, 157
Mallet, T., 303
Manfredi, Z., 6
Manin, B., 63
Mann, M., 2, 111
Manning, B., 195
Manow, P., 280–281
Marcuse, H., 209–210
Markovits, D., 103–105, 127, 165
Marks, G., 94–95, 155–156
Marshall, T.H., 1, 36–37, 119, 121, 312 n.2
Marx, K., 16–18, 24, 41, 218–219
    on liberalism, 19–20
    on public-private distinction, 19–20
Mau, S., 106, 112–113
Mazzucato, M., 259, 262, 267–268
McGoey, L., 258
McWhorter, J., 215
Means, G., 70–71
Mehra, M. (Harvard professor of
    medicine), 286–287
Ménendez, A., 98
Meritocracy, 5, 9–10, 41, 100–106. See also
    neoliberalism
    antidiscrimination and, 127, 134–135, 138
    class and, 103–104, 106
    "educationism", 106
    Hayek on, 101–102
    inequality and, 104–106, 165
    Macron and, 100–101
    as neoliberal legitimacy, 5, 108–109, 127,
        134–135
    popular acceptance of, 105–106
    "rhetoric of rising" (Sandel), 102–103
    Third Way left and, 102–103, 117, 125
    as variant of capitalism (Milanovic), 103

Young (1958) on, 101–102, 104–105
Merkel, A., 88, 142–143, 268
Meyer, J., 138
Middle classes
    complicity in rise of neoliberalism, 111–113
    decline of, 57, 87–88, 162–172
    new (educated), 74, 124–125, 168, 235–236
    old, 177
    struggle within (old versus new), 196
    as vision of classless society, 156, 162–163
Middle East (Gulf States), 67–68
Mijs, J., 105–106
Milanovic, B., 57, 103
Mill, J.S.
    on British rule in India, 17
    epistemology, 13
    harm principle, 34, 292
    on liberalism, 14–15, 18, 20, 24, 26–27, 34,
        45–46, 59, 209–210
    on society as non-contractual, 1
Miller, D., 101–102, 242
Miller, P., 76, 301
Milward, A., 91–92
Mirowski, P., 35–36, 45–46, 50, 51–52, 138,
    221–222
Mises., L., 31–32
Mitsotakis, K. (Greek Prime
    Minister), 292–293
Möllers, C., 20, 24
Moisï, D., 269
Monson, J., 73–74
Mont Pèlerin Society, 32–34, 49–52. See also
    Hayek, neoliberalism
Morozov, E., 299–301
Morris, L., 99–100
Mounk, Y., 37, 55–56, 126, 159
Moyn, S., 125–126
Mucchielli, L., 254–255, 282
Mudde, C., 149–150, 157–158, 172, 175
Müller, Jan-Werner, 26–27, 159
Münch, R., 247–249, 291
Multiculturalism, 113–114, 123–124. See also
    neoliberal multiculturalism
    and antidiscrimination, 134–136
    "deschooled" (Kymlicka), 128
    and diversity, 129–134
    and human rights, 125–126
    liberal (Kymlicka), 127–128
    neoliberal, 110, 113, 136–144
Murray, C., 232
Murswiek, D., 276
Myrdal, G., 203

INDEX 383

Nachtwey, O., 279–281
Nassehi, A., 268
Neoliberal multiculturalism, 10, 110, 123–136, 138, 145–146, 241
  as antidiscrimination, 134–136
  as diversity, 129–134
Neoliberal state, 66, 68, 78–79, 301
Neoliberalism
  as absolutizing freedom, 34–37
  and antidiscrimination, 126–127, 134–136
  "authoritarian liberalism", 4–5, 45, 59–62, 247–248
  Bourdieu on, 30
  Chicago Law and Economics School, 50–51, 65–66, 299–300
  constitutionalism in, 89–100
  democracy feared by, 43–46
  federation in, 89–100
  and formal equality (rule of law), 37–38
  functional differentiations weakened by, 49–51
  Geneva School (Globalists), 59, 89, 125–126
  governance in, 68–80
  in Gulf States, 67–68
  as "market fundamentalism" (Block and Somers), 3–4, 31, 51, 114
  meritocracy in, 100–106
  narrow *versus* broad understandings, 2–3, 119
  New Public Management (NPM), 71, 74, 75, 82–83
  "no such thing (as society)" (Thatcher), 33–34, 36–37, 39, 55–56, 225–226, 274–275
  Ordoliberalism, 4, 32, 50–51, 63–64, 78–79
  as polemical concept, 2, 13
  as political creed, 31–34
  public-private distinction blurred, 3, 8, 75, 193–194, 259, 295–296, 300–301
  public-private partnerships, 11–12, 73, 250–252, 256, 258–259, 284
  punitive turn of, 65–67
  as responsibilization, 36–37, 48, 56–57, 102–103, 115–118, 126, 179, 300–301
  and shareholder values, 70–71, 112–113
  social justice rejected by, 39–42
  social policies, 36–37, 66, 99–100, 116, 119–123
  and stakeholder ideology, 4, 69
  status to contract, 1–2
  technocracy in, 80–89

TINA (There is no alternative), 2, 55, 56–57, 196–197
"trickle down" economics, 36, 81–82, 164–165
New Public Management (NPM), 71, 74, 75, 82–83. *See also* governance, neoliberal state, neoliberalism
Nietzsche, F.
  aristocratic freedom, 21, 36
Nisbet, R., 16–17
Non-pharmaceutical interventions (NPI), 263–264. *See also* COVID-19 pandemic
Norris, P., 188–189
Nullmeier, F., 275
Nunn, S. (U.S. Senator), 256–257
Nuremberg Code (of medical ethics) (1947), 290. *See also* COVID-19 pandemic
Nussbaum, M., 223

Oakeshott, M., 17
Obama, B., 102–103, 116, 117, 139, 211, 229–230, 298
OECD (countries), 163–164, 254, 266, 302–303
Oesch, D., 152–153, 169–170
Offe, C., 277–278
Olsen, E., 98
Omi, M., 204
Orbán, V., 154, 157–158
Ordoliberalism, 4, 32, 50–51, 63–64, 78–79. *See also* neoliberalism
Orenstein, M., 182
Orgad, L., 306

Page, L., 294
Paine, T., 16–17
Pap, A., 186
Pappas, T., 157–158
Parsons, T., 46–47, 134–135
Pfaller, R., 193, 196
Philanthropy (private foundations), 215–216, 258–259, 282, 284
Philippot, F., 280–281
Phillips Curve, 33
Pierson, P., 110–111
Piketty, T., 125, 165, 168–169
Pinochet, A., 44–46, 64–65, 111
Plato, 209–210
Plessner, H., 28–29
Pluckrose, H., 207–208, 242

INDEX

Pöhl, K.O. (former president of German Bundesbank), 140–141

Polanyi, K., 3–4, 119

Political, *see also* political order, political rupture

  Hobbes's understanding of (Bartolini), 61–62

  Rousseau's understanding of, 15

  Schmitt's understanding of, 25, 28–29

Political order, 3–6

Political rupture, 6–8

Popper, K., 17, 32

Populism, *see also* radical right parties, technopopulism

  in *annus miserabilis* (2016) (Brexit and Trump), 150

  as anti-immigrant, 10

  Cinque Stelle (Italy), 86

  class and occupational basis of, 169–172

  and cleavage structures, 153–156

  constitutionalism opposed by, 158–159

  cultural concerns in (as dominant), 10, 155, 172, 188

  as "direct representation" (Urbinati), 159–160

  economic causes of, 156

  economic *versus* cultural explanations of, 10, 172–174, 176, 187–188

  and education (low level), 167–169

  as expression of or threat to democracy, 10, 107–108, 149–150, 156

  in Hungary, 179–186

  as illiberal democracy, 157–162

  left *versus* right, 149–150

  and middle-class decline, 162–165

  and nationalism (ethnopluralism), 157–162

  and neoliberalism, 151–152

  as opposition to technocracy, 85

  pluralism opposed by, 158

  as polemical concept, 15

  political economy concerns in (as marginal), 10, 152–153, 172

  respectable version of (P.Mair), 86

  as strategy, 149

  as style, 149

  technopopulism (Bickerton and Accetti), 85–89, 107–108, 278–279

  as "thin-centered ideology" (Mudde), 149

  victim posture, 192, 195, 196

  and welfare chauvinism, 154

Posner, R., 50–51, 116

Post-democracy (Crouch), 62–65, 88, 107, 157. *See also* authoritarianism, democracy, neoliberalism

Post-Fordist consumption model (Streeck), 74. *See also* citizenship

Powell, L. (U.S. Supreme Court judge), 110–111, 130, 131

Prasad, M., 111–112

Przeworski, A., 159, 161–164

Queer Theory, 222–223. *See also* transgender

Querdenker (lateral thinkers) (German oppositionists to pandemic restrictions), 279–281. *See also* COVID-19 pandemic

Quesnay, F., 65–66

Radical right parties, 161–162. *See also* populism

  AfD (Germany), 150–152, 157, 280–281, 320 n.3, 321 n.12, 330 n.128, 333 n.37

  Fidesz (Hungary), 161, 179–180

  FÖP (Austria), 151–152

  Front National (France), 151–152, 172–173, 175, 280–281

  People's Party (Denmark), 172–173

  PiS (Poland), 181

  PVV (Netherlands), 178

  Republican Party (as American equivalent of), 175

  social-structural basis of (class and occupations), 169–172

  TAN (Traditional, Authoritarian, Nationalist), 156

  and welfare chauvinism, 177–179

Raoult, D. (French virologist), 285–287. *See also* COVID-19 pandemic

Rathenau, W. (German foreign minister, Weimar Republic), 70

Rawls, John, 9, 14–15, 18–19, 22, 25, 38, 58. *See also* liberal democracy, liberalism

Reagan, R., 37, 55–56, 65, 66, 111, 113–114, 116, 121, 132–133, 146, 199–200

Rechtsstaat (rule of law), 22–23, 63. *See also* Hayek, liberal state, neoliberal state

Reckwitz, A., 8, 124–125

Reed, A., 198–199, 219–220

Reed, T., 220

Reijers, W., 306

Rennwald, L., 169–170

Rhodes, R.A.W., 69–73

Rodgers, D., 242–243

INDEX 385

Rodrik, D., 96, 172–174
Röpke, W., 31–32, 63–64
Rogowski, R., 167
Rokkan, S., 153–154, 162–163
Rome Treaty (European Economic
    Community) (1957), 92–93. See also
    European Union
Romney, M., 211
Roosevelt, F., 31–32
Rose, N., 76, 301
Ross, A., 242
Rousseau, J.J., 15, 25, 47
Rüstow, A., 31–32, 63–64
Rufo, C., 192, 210–211

Savage, M., 166
Schäfer, A., 96–98
Schäuble, W. (former German Minister of
    Finance), 142
Schama, S., 287, 303–304
Scharpf, F., 95–97, 99–100
Scheuerman, W., 61
Schmidt, E., 247–248
Schmitt, C., 14–15
    "Adolph Hitler's crown jurist" (Hayek), 45
    and "authoritarian liberalism" (Heller), 45,
        59–60
    on democracy, 25, 27–28
    "dominium" versus "imperium", 89–90
    "extraordinary German student of politics"
        (Hayek), 61
    on liberalism, 25, 28–29
    on the political, 25, 28–29
    on sovereignty, 45
    in and on Weimar Republic, 60–61
Schreyer, P., 256–257
Schröder, G., 103, 117–118, 141
Schuck, P., 129
Schüll, N.D., 299–300
Schumpeter, J.
    on class, 104–105
    on democracy, 27–28
    on socialism, 17–18
Schwab, K. (WEF chief), 303
Sennett, R., 193–194
Sharing economy, 297
Sharpton, A. (U.S. Congressman), 220
Shklar, J., 26, 58
Silicon Valley, 81, 124–125, 299
Simmel, G., 249
Single European Act (SEA) (1985), 84–85, 94,
    95, 97. See also European Union

Slobodian, Q., 30–32, 89–90, 279–280
Smith, A., 17, 27, 42, 52
Sobolewska, M., 167–168
Social Darwinism, 36–37. See also Hayek,
    neoliberalism
Social Democracy, 36–37, 39–40, 110,
    113–117, 196
Social investment (social policy), 119–123. See
    also Third Way left
Social policies (neoliberal), 36–37, 66, 99–100,
    116, 119–123. See also neoliberalism
Socialism, 20, 32, 175, 190–191
    "death of" (after 1989), 116–117
    Hayek on, 35–37, 40, 91, 124
    and liberalism, 17–20
    and populism, 149
    Oscar Wilde on, 15–17
Somek, A., 100, 136–137
Soros, G., 182
Spanish Flu (1918-1919), 261, 263
Starmer, K., 237–238
Starr, P., 28, 30
Stefancic, J., 208, 210
Stern, F., 192–193
Stichweh, R., 293–294
Stiegler, B., 269, 305–306
Stieglitz, J., 166
Stock, K., 231–235, 238
Stoker, G., 68
Streeck, W., 4, 55, 74, 110–111, 143–144, 273
    on "state people" versus "market people", 7,
        141
Sullivan, A., 242
Summers, L., 103
Surveillance capitalism (Zuboff), 299–301. See
    also digitalization
Szetela, A., 220

Taguieff, P.A., 205–206, 214
Tajfel, H., 291
Tallien, J.M., 190–191
Tarrow, S., 97–98
Technocracy, 4, 9–10, 59, 80–89. See also
    neoliberal state, neoliberalism
    as allied with bureaucracy, 80–81
    as allied with democracy, 80–81
    and depoliticization, 82–85
    and governance, 107–108
    origins of, 4, 80
    and populism, 85–89
    as solutionism (Tech), 81

386 INDEX

Technopopulism (Bickerton and
Accetti), 85–89, 107–108, 278–279. *See
also* populism, technocracy
Thatcher, M., 33–34, 39, 55–56, 76, 82–83,
111, 114, 119, 121, 152, 194, 196–197
Thelen, K., 299–300
Therborn, G., 251
Thierse, W., 241
Third Way left, 5–6, 10, 48, 55–58, 66, 74,
102–103, 110, 113–119, 145, 151–154,
169, 174, 190. *See also* neoliberalism
and antidiscrimination, 134–136
and diversity, 129–134
neoliberal multiculturalism, 123–136
Schröder-Blair Paper (1999), 117–118
social investment (welfare policy), 119–123
Thomas, W.I. (theorem), 214
Tocqueville, A., 20–24, 34–35, 45–46, 59, 100
Tooze, A., 139, 268, 273–274, 309
Topol, E. (American cardiologist), 288
Torpey, J., 197, 204–206, 215–216
Toshkov, D., 253
Transgender, 10–11, 198–199, 221–241. *See
also* identity left
civil rights bureaucracy in support of
(United States), 239–240
corporate support for, 240–241
in the culture wars (United States), 236
gender dysphoria (social causes), 234–236
gender identity, 223–225
"hyper-individualism" of, 222
intersectionality in, 222
legal recognition of, 225–228
as "neoliberal personhood"
(Mirowski), 221–222
postmodernist epistemology (Queer
Theory), 222–223
social conventions challenged by, 237–241
versus transrace, 198, 243–244
transwomen as site of conflict, 228–233
trans-youth and the problem of
transiting, 233–237
Trickle down economics, 36, 81–82, 164–165.
See also neoliberalism
Trilateral Commission (1975) ("Crisis of
Democracy"), 81–82
Trump, D., 150–151, 159, 161, 167, 168, 171,
174, 182, 188–189, 202, 211, 217–219, 231,
256–257, 267–268, 274–275, 297
Tuvel, R., 243–244

UNESCO, 198

Unger, R., 58
United Kingdom, *see* Britain
United States
Bathroom Law (HB-2) (North Carolina,
2016), 219
Christian Right, 48
culture wars, 7, 113–114, 210–211, 236
Glass Steagall Act (1999), 118
Gore Report (1993), 75
Great Depression (1929), 31–32
liberalism in, 22–23
New Deal, 31–33
North American Free Trade Agreement
(NAFTA) (1993), 118
"Peace of Palo Alto", 219
Personal Responsibility and Work
Opportunity Reconciliation Act
(PRWORA) (1996), 37, 115–116
Revolutionary War (1776), 204
"Screen New Deal" (Klein), 247–248
Stop the Wrongs to Our Kids and Employees
(W.O.K.E.) Act (Florida, 2022), 210–211
"Treaty of Detroit", 70, 219
U.S. Federal Reserve Bank, 139
U.S. Supreme Court
1st Amendment cases, 49
Bakke case (1978), 129–131
Brown v. Board of Education case
(1954), 203–204
McCleskey v. Kemp case (1987), 203–204
SOGI laws (overruled), 49
Untact society (South Korea), 302–303. *See
also* COVID-19 pandemic
Urbinati, N., 159–160

Van Dyk, S., 191
Varian, H. (former Google chief
economist), 298
Varieties of Capitalism (Hall and
Soskice), 96–97
Varoufakis, Y., 142
Veblen, T., 73–74
Vibert, F., 83–84
Vico, G. (Italian philosopher), 46

Wacquant, L., 66
Walzer, M., 3, 13, 18–19, 28, 29
Weber, M., 39–40, 213–214
Weiler J., 92–94
Whittle, S. (British transman, lawyer, and
activist), 226, 229
Wilders, G., 178

INDEX   387

Wilensky, H., 115–116
Wilkinson, M., 139–140, 143, 144
Wimmer, A., 212–213
Winant, H., 204
Wittig, M., 231
Wodarg, W., 261
Wolf, M., 247
Wolin, S., 58
Wood, P., 215
World Bank, 71–72, 306–307
World Economic Forum (WEF), 31, 166, 256, 258, 259, 306–308
World Health Organization (WHO), 11–12, 250, 252–253, 256, 258–268, 282–283, 285–288, 309
World Trade Organization (WTO), 4–5, 96, 118

Wuhan Institute of Virology, 248–249

Xi, J. (Chinese leader), 267–268

Yglesias, M., 216
Yogyakarta Principles (2007 and 2017) (international transgender rights document), 238. *See also* transgender
Young, I.M., 193–194
Young, M., 101–102, 104–105

Zaks, T. (chief medical officer of Moderna pharmaceutics), 289–290
Ziblatt, D., 161, 174
Zielonka, J., 249–250
Zizek, S., 125, 274–275, 309, 310
Zuboff, S., 299–301
Zuckerberg, M., 80–81, 294, 297